MW00973919

Culture and Economic Action

NEW THINKING IN POLITICAL ECONOMY

Series Editor: Peter J. Boettke, *George Mason University, USA*

New Thinking in Political Economy aims to encourage scholarship in the intersection of the disciplines of politics, philosophy and economics. It has the ambitious purpose of reinvigorating political economy as a progressive force for understanding social and economic change.

The series is an important forum for the publication of new work analysing the social world from a multidisciplinary perspective. With increased specialization (and professionalization) within universities, interdisciplinary work has become increasingly uncommon. Indeed, during the 20th century, the process of disciplinary specialization reduced the intersection between economics, philosophy and politics and impoverished our understanding of society. Modern economics in particular has become increasingly mathematical and largely ignores the role of institutions and the contribution of moral philosophy and politics.

New Thinking in Political Economy will stimulate new work that combines technical knowledge provided by the 'dismal science' and the wisdom gleaned from the serious study of the 'worldly philosophy'. The series will reinvigorate our understanding of the social world by encouraging a multidisciplinary approach to the challenges confronting society in the new century.

Titles in the series include:

Culture and Economic Action

Edited by

Laura E. Grube

Mercatus Center Dissertation Fellow, George Mason University and Visiting Instructor, Economics Department, Beloit College, USA

Virgil Henry Storr

Senior Research Fellow and Director, Graduate Student Programs, Mercatus Center and Research Associate Professor of Economics, George Mason University, USA

NEW THINKING IN POLITICAL ECONOMY

Cheltenham, UK • Northampton, MA, USA

© Laura E. Grube and Virgil Henry Storr 2015

All rights reserved. No part of this publication may be reproduced, stored in a retrieval system or transmitted in any form or by any means, electronic, mechanical or photocopying, recording, or otherwise without the prior permission of the publisher.

Published by
Edward Elgar Publishing Limited
The Lypiatts
15 Lansdown Road
Cheltenham
Glos GL50 2JA
UK

Edward Elgar Publishing, Inc.
William Pratt House
9 Dewey Court
Northampton
Massachusetts 01060
USA

A catalogue record for this book
is available from the British Library

Library of Congress Control Number: 2015933354

This book is available electronically in the **Elgar**online
Economics subject collection
DOI 10.4337/9780857931733

Printed on elemental chlorine free (ECF)
recycled paper containing 30% Post-Consumer Waste

ISBN 978 0 85793 172 6 (cased)
ISBN 978 0 85793 173 3 (eBook)

Typeset by Servis Filmsetting Ltd, Stockport, Cheshire
Printed and bound in the USA

Contents

Contributors

Paul Dragos Aligica, Senior Research Fellow at the F.A. Hayek Program for Advanced Study in Philosophy, Politics, and Economics at the Mercatus Center at George Mason University.

Peter J. Boettke, BB&T Professor for the Study of Capitalism at George Mason University, Vice President for Research, and Director of the F.A. Hayek Program for Advanced Study in Philosophy, Politics, and Economics at the Mercatus Center at George Mason University.

Emily Chamlee-Wright, Provost and Dean of the College, Washington College.

Bridget Colon, Economist with the US government.

Christopher J. Coyne, F.A. Harper Professor of Economics at George Mason University and Associate Director of the F.A. Hayek Program for Advanced Study in Philosophy, Politics, and Economics at the Mercatus Center at George Mason University.

Laura E. Grube, Mercatus Center Dissertation Fellow at George Mason University and Visiting Instructor, Department of Economics at Beloit College.

Arielle John, Assistant Professor, Department of Economics at Beloit College.

Ryan Langrill, Evaluator at the Idaho Legislature Office of Performance Evaluations.

Don Lavoie, formerly the David H. and Charles G. Koch Chair of Economics at the School of Public Policy at George Mason University.

Peter T. Leeson, Duncan Black Professor of Economics and Law at George Mason University.

Aura Matei, Researcher, The Center for Institutional Analysis and Development in Eleutheria, Bucharest.

Kyle W. O'Donnell, H.B. Earhart Fellow, Department of Economics at New York University and Mercatus Center Dissertation Fellow at George Mason University.

Petrik Runst, Senior Researcher at the Institute for Small Business Economics at the University of Göttingen.

Solomon Stein, Research Fellow at the F.A. Hayek Program for Advanced Study in Philosophy, Politics and Economics at the Mercatus Center at George Mason University.

Virgil Henry Storr, Senior Research Fellow, Director of Graduate Student Programs at the Mercatus Center at George Mason University, and Research Associate Professor of Economics in the Department of Economics at George Mason University.

1. Introduction

Laura E. Grube and Virgil Henry Storr

Culture shapes economic behavior and colors economic outcomes. Although we may choose to avoid explicitly discussing culture within the social sciences, it will be implicit in our assumptions.[1] The question, then, becomes how to incorporate culture into economic analysis. Some economists have conceived of culture as a tool or a resource as they have attempted to operationalize a difficult concept. Others have discussed culture as if it were a set of blinders, closing off some opportunities and focusing attention on others. Still others have treated culture as a lens through which we view the world, or perhaps colored glasses that establish a certain hue to our vision.

In order to understand how culture shapes economic behavior, we might ask how culture influences a person's expectations in the market as well as in what may be considered non-market settings. Do they believe that their peers and colleagues are trustworthy? Do they imagine that hard work is rewarded? Do they think that their family is likely to provide emotional and/or financial support? Economic outcomes and economic institutions are intimately tied to our answers to these questions. And the answers to these questions are in part shaped by culture. Moreover, when we discuss challenging topics such as economic development, we can benefit from paying attention to how culture has influenced economic activity in that context. Culture, for instance, plays a role in how markets are organized, whether we rely on small firms or large firms, and whether those firms are vertically or horizontally integrated. Culture plays a role in which opportunities are pursued and which opportunities are overlooked.

Until recently, culture had generally been understudied within economics. Thus culture remains an area that needs further exploration. To many economists, culture is simply a vague concept that is difficult to separate from other variables which impact human behavior. Others avoid topics that might require engagement with or the importation of ideas from other disciplines. The avoidance is closely intertwined with the way that economics has been traditionally defined and, relatedly, beliefs about what constitutes the appropriate methods for exploring economic subject matter. Moreover, there are economists who deny culture has any real value, emphasizing that relative prices can explain why we select some decisions over others (Stigler and Becker 1977).

In an effort to make culture more concrete, economists have conceived of culture as a form of capital, treating it like a set of tools or a resource that certain groups possess or other groups do not possess. Although there may be reasons to argue that aspects of culture may not be easily understood by analogy to capital (Storr 2008), the culture as capital approach is arguably the most popular. Efforts to identify and quantify culture have relied on survey data, trying to pinpoint several survey questions that can act as proxies for culture.[2]

Still, some economists have chosen another approach. Austrian school economists have contributed a great deal to our understanding of the relationship between culture and economic action.[3] Austrian economics is a science of human beings that is primarily concerned with making sense of meaningful human action. Austrian economists, because they view economics as a science of human beings and a science of meaning, are particularly well suited to inject cultural considerations into economic analysis.

Austrian economists have argued that in order to understand an individual's behavior it is important to look to the meanings that individuals attach to their actions. As Mises explains ([1963] 1966: p. 26), 'We cannot approach our subject if we disregard the meaning which acting man attaches to the situation, in other words, the given state of affairs, and to his behavior with regard to this situation.' Similarly, Hayek has said that meaning is at the center of understanding human action. As Hayek writes (1952: p. 44), 'so far as human actions are concerned . . . things are what the acting people think they are . . . [and] unless we can understand what the acting people mean by their actions any attempt to explain them . . . is bound to fail.'

Arguably, a focus on culture, which can color and shape meanings, is a natural outgrowth of the Austrian emphasis on meaning. Not surprisingly, Austrian economists have written a great deal about the relationship between culture and economic action. Some of those explorations are reproduced in the chapters that follow alongside original research that attempts to expand or apply Austrian insights about how culture shapes economic activity.

THIS VOLUME

This volume brings together recent contributions within Austrian economics on the relationship between culture and economic action. Part I offers more theoretical contributions. Several of these chapters have been published elsewhere. Rather than arrange the chapters chronologically, we assemble them into a conversation. For example, Lavoie's critique of Kirzner's theory of entrepreneurship for apparently closing the door to cultural considerations follows a chapter that was written after the Lavoie piece but offers a broad perspective on why economists should study culture. Still, there is unavoidably some overlap between the chapters, as the authors are attempting to cover similar territory. Part I concludes with Storr's discussion of a Weberian approach to cultural economy. Storr's theoretical contribution and application to the Bahamas serve as a bridge to Part II.

In Part II, we bring together new and previously published applied works that explore how culture impacts economic action in specific contexts. The chapters explore a diversity of contexts and move from post-disaster New Orleans, to Eastern Europe, to the African continent, to a space that operates outside of traditional geographic locations. The methods employed are also quite diverse. Several studies make use of in-depth interviews, while others find common narratives in literature. Together, the applied chapters present a rich collection that aids in our understanding of the relationship between culture and economic action.

Part I begins with Storr's argument for why economists ought to study culture. In Chapter 2, 'Economists should study culture,' Storr argues that, although there are good reasons why economists tend to avoid incorporating culture into the analysis, ultimately they can ignore but cannot avoid culture. The only choice they face is between employing culture implicitly and employing it explicitly.

The next two chapters engage Kirzner's theory of entrepreneurship and the market process. In Chapter 3, 'The discovery and interpretation of profit opportunities: culture and the Kirznerian entrepreneur,' Lavoie critiques Kirzner's theory of entrepreneurship and argues that culture is a neglected and yet critical aspect of a theory of entrepreneurship. Chapter 4, 'The determinants of entrepreneurial alertness and the characteristics of successful entrepreneurs,' by Storr and John, defends Kirzner's theory against claims that it is too simplistic, arguing that by isolating the role of alertness Kirzner is able to locate the essence of entrepreneurship and explain how the market process tends toward equilibrium. The authors then frame their project as *extending* Kirzner's theory of entrepreneurship to develop a theory that incorporates how culture is the missing piece to understanding how some individuals are alert to an opportunity while others are not.

In Chapter 5, 'Markets as an extension of culture,' Chamlee-Wright explores the relationship between markets and culture. According to

Chamlee-Wright, many of the existing market theories do not help us to understand culture and how culture affects economic action. According to Chamlee-Wright, Austrian economics holds the key to cultural economics. In Chapter 6, 'Institutional stickiness and the New Development Economics,' Boettke, Coyne and Leeson outline a framework for exploring the relationship between *mētis* (culture) and institutions. They argue that institutions are more likely to *stick* the more closely they are compatible with *mētis*. The theory of institutional stickiness is utilized in several of the applied chapters in the volume.

Next, Lavoie and Chamlee-Wright ask 'How does culture influence economic development?' in their chapter of the same title (Chapter 7). Lavoie and Chamlee-Wright criticize attempts to identify particular cultural traits that support economic development and perform 'checklist ethnographies' to diagnose cultural deficiencies. Instead, the authors argue that in-depth case studies can help to uncover and improve our understanding of entrepreneurship across various contexts.

Chapter 8, 'Context matters: the importance of time and place in economic narratives,' by Storr, follows Lavoie and Chamlee-Wright's chapter. Storr recommends a 'Weber–Austrian approach' to studying culture and economic action. He also responds to Lavoie and Chamlee-Wright's notion of cultural comparative advantage (Chapter 7) and recommends adopting an alternative metaphor, 'culture as a constitution.' In Chapter 9, 'A critical appraisal of the concept of cultural capital,' Storr more thoroughly argues against the idea of 'culture as capital,' which he suggests must underlie any conception of cultural comparative advantage.

In a new contribution, 'Culture as a constitution' (Chapter 10), John develops Storr's claim in Chapter 8 that culture can be thought of as a constitution. John skillfully decodes 'culture as a constitution' and, in doing so, brings forth ways in which culture enables exchange among individuals with diverse preferences and plans. She engages examples of two countries—the Bahamas and Trinidad and Tobago—to show how a concrete and 'thin' concept of culture as a constitution may frame 'thick' cultural narratives.

The final chapter in Part I, Chapter 11, is Storr's 'Weber's spirit of capitalism and the Bahamas' Junkanoo ethic.' As Storr explains, despite the controversy surrounding Weber's Protestant ethic the book remains a model for performing culturally aware economic analysis. Utilizing Weber's approach, Storr examines the history of the Bahamas and the particular history of slavery on the island, the stories that contribute to the country's culture (including its folklore), and how different metaphors may help us to understand business in the Bahamas.

Part II of the volume begins with Chapter 12, an applied chapter by

Chamlee-Wright entitled 'Pastor response in post-Katrina New Orleans: navigating the cultural economic landscape.' Chamlee-Wright engages her 'cultural economy' framework, which recognizes that economic, political and social entrepreneurs are situated within a particular cultural context, see the world and identify opportunities through a culturally defined lens and draw upon cultural narratives to make sense of the world and carve out strategies of effective action (Chamlee-Wright 2006).

In Chapter 13, 'National cultures, economic action and the homogeneity problem: insights from the case of Romania,' Aligica and Matei focus on the theoretical and methodological problems of cultural nationalism, referring to the view as the 'homogeneity-central tendency' perspective, and posit an alternative view, the 'heterogeneity-variance' perspective. Relying on the European Social Survey and other statistics and using Romania as an example, the authors illustrate that there is an array of factors that would support a heterogeneity-variance perspective. In the Romanian case, some of these are differences in ethnicity, language, religion, the various minority groups, regional attributes, and the characteristics of urban and rural populations. Although the homogeneity-central tendency perspective has its place, they conclude, considerations of culture would gain further explanatory and descriptive power by deconstructing aggregate variables to examine the diversity beneath.

Runst explores differences in attitudes towards market economies, comparing attitudes in East Germany with attitudes in West Germany in Chapter 14, 'Between community and society: political attitudes in transition countries.' Using Tönnies's ([1887] 1957) distinction between community (*Gemeinschaft*) and society (*Gesellschaft*), Runst argues that the prolonged absence of a market economy in East Germany led to attitudes that resemble and are conducive to small-group norms. Runst performs in-depth interviews with individuals from former East and West Germany to examine why these differences in attitude exist.

Storr and Colon argue in Chapter 15, 'Subalternity and entrepreneurship: tales of marginalized but enterprising characters, oppressive settings and haunting plots,' that understanding entrepreneurship in any context requires attention to prevailing cultural beliefs and both formal and informal institutions that affect economic behavior. Understanding entrepreneurship within subaltern or marginalized groups, they argue, is no different even if accessing their beliefs and institutions may be more difficult. Using fiction from the former Soviet bloc and literature from anglophone Africa and the British Caribbean, Storr and Colon access these cultural beliefs and institutions by examining stories or tales of entrepreneurship.

In Chapter 16, 'Indigenous African institutions and economic development,' Chamlee-Wright discusses the role of female entrepreneurs, or street hawkers, in Accra, Ghana. Chamlee-Wright astutely locates a number of factors that play a role in female entrepreneurship in Ghana, including the role of gender in trading relations as well as how small-group repeated interactions generate knowledge of a trader's character and trustworthiness.

Grube examines the persistence of traditional leadership and communal land in South Africa in Chapter 17, 'The role of culture in the persistence of traditional leadership: evidence from KwaZulu Natal, South Africa.' Although the existing South African constitution was adopted in 1996 with further legislative reform in the years following, many communities are still organized under traditional leadership and/or traditional councils. Similarly, communal land tenure continues in many rural areas. Vested interests and lack of political competition provide some clues as to why these institutions persist. Relying on interview data from KwaZulu Natal Province (South Africa) as well as secondary sources, Grube argues that culture is also an important piece to the puzzle.

Langrill and Storr similarly incorporate ideas of social identity in Chapter 18, 'Network closure, group identity and attitudes toward merchants.' Langrill and Storr explore social identity and group status investments amongst merchants in Edo and Osaka, Japan, during the Tokugawa period. Differences in the closure exhibited by merchant networks in Edo and Osaka, the authors argue, can help to explain differences in social identities as well as in intra-group status investments amongst merchants in the two cities.

O'Donnell's contribution, Chapter 19, discusses, 'The cultural and political economy of drug prohibition.' Prior to prohibition, O'Donnell points out, many drug users were middle-class housewives, lawyers and doctors. In this setting, drug users could more easily share information about drug use and establish norms for how to use drugs more safely. After prohibition, moderate users responded to the increasing cost of drug use (for example, fines and incarceration) and exited the market. The effect is today's association of drug users as 'hard-core users' and the emergence of the culture associated with hard-core drug use.

Finally, in Chapter 20, 'Cultural and institutional co-determination: the case of legitimacy in exchange in Diablo II,' Stein considers the relationship between institutions and culture and argues that the explanation for why a certain culture develops in a particular area may be causally linked to the institutional forms chosen before the distinctive elements of that culture emerge. Stein investigates this hypothesis by studying the in-game behavior of players of Diablo II, a multi-player online game. Stein finds that the initial institutional choice of different communities led to the development of different cultures regarding certain kinds of in-game behavior.

NOTES

1. Storr elaborates on this in Chapter 2.
2. See, for instance, the World Values Survey and questions related to trust.
3. Hereafter, we refer to simply as 'Austrian economists' or 'Austrian economics.'

REFERENCES

Chamlee-Wright, Emily (2006), 'The Development of a Cultural Economy: Foundational Questions and Future Direction,' in Jack High (ed.), *Humane Economics: Essays in Honor of Don Lavoie*, Cheltenham, UK and Northampton, MA, USA: Edward Elgar Publishing, pp. 181–98.

Hayek, F.A. (1952), *The Counter-Revolution of Science*, Indianapolis, IN: Liberty Press.

Mises, Ludwig von ([1963] 1966), *Human Action: A Treatise on Economics*, 3rd rev. ed., San Francisco: Fox & Wilkes.

Stigler, G. and G. Becker (1977), 'De Gustibus Non Est Disputandum,' *American Economic Review*, **67**, 76–90.

Storr, Virgil Henry (2008), 'Should We Continue to Describe Culture as Capital? An Austrian Approach,' *Kultura Współczesna*, **55**(1).

Tönnies, Ferdinand ([1887] 1957), *Community and Society: Gemeinschaft and Gesellschaft*, Charles P. Loomis (trans. and ed.), East Lansing: Michigan State University Press.

PART I

Theorizing the relationship between culture
and economic activity

2. Economists should study culture*

Virgil Henry Storr

2.1 INTRODUCTION

The truism is apt: context matters. Consider, for instance, how we understand the meaning of a sentence. Of course, the meanings of the individual words in the sentence matter a great deal. The meanings of the sentences that immediately precede and follow it as well as the broader conversation of which it is a part also matter, as does the speaker and her tone, her dialogical partners, her relationships to her dialogical partners, and the location in which she is speaking. Is she being serious or sarcastic? Is she issuing a command or making a plea or voicing a complaint? When Henry II of England, for instance, asked aloud if someone would 'rid him' of 'this meddlesome priest'—his close friend and Archbishop of Canterbury Thomas Becket—we understand both that he likely meant it as a lament and also why his subjects assumed it was a royal edict and carried out Becket's assassination.

It is simply not enough to know the words in a sentence if we wish to understand its meaning. We have to know something about its context. As Gadamer (1994: p. 44) explains,

> when we want to understand sentences that have been handed down to us, we engage in historical reflections, from which it is determined just where and how these sentences are said, what their actual motivational background is and therewith what their actual meaning is. When we want to represent a sentence as such to ourselves we must, therefore, represent its historical horizon.

The same is true for understanding the actions of others. Recall Ryle's (2009) now famous insight that we cannot figure out the meaning of an action without some knowledge of the context and the actor's motivations. A twitch is an involuntary, reflexive opening and closing of an eye that has no intended recipient and no special meaning. A wink, on the other hand, looks identical to a twitch, but, unlike a twitch, a wink is done intentionally as a communicative act and is meant as a signal or to convey some sly meaning; it has an intended recipient and is meant to convey a particular message. The external physical changes to an individual's body that occur when he/she winks or blinks do not tell us anything about the meaning of those movements. Did the wind just blow an irritant into Ruthie's left eye? Or are Ruthie and Tara best friends who are about to play a practical joke on another? Or is Ruthie's gesture not aimed at Tara at all, but at the cute boy who is staring at her from across the room? How, Ryle asks, can we distinguish between a wink (a conspiratorial gesture between compatriots) and an eye twitch (an involuntary response to an irritant) without knowing anything else about its context? Of course, we cannot. As Geertz (1973: p. 6) explains, 'the two movements are, as movements, identical; from an I-am-a-camera, "phenomenalistic" observation of them alone, one could not tell which was twitch and which was wink, or indeed whether both or either was twitch or wink.' We simply cannot tell the difference between a meaningful action and a reflex without knowing something more about the incident than that someone's left eye closed and opened rapidly. We would need to know a lot more about the scene in order to conclude whether it was a twitch or not. 'Yet the difference, however unphotographable, between a twitch and a wink,' as Geertz (ibid.) reminds us, 'is vast; as anyone unfortunate enough to have had the first taken for the second knows.' We cannot distinguish Ruthie's wink from a simple twitch and cannot determine what her wink, if it is a wink, is meant to signal unless we know a great deal about her situation and the circumstances surrounding the act. As Schütz (1967: p. 27) explains, 'questions of subjective meaning . . . cannot be answered by merely watching someone's behavior.' Instead, 'we first observe the bodily behavior and then place it within a larger context of meaning' (ibid.).[1]

Although economists have always been comfortable examining context in the form of constraints (in other words, the limited resources or rules prohibiting certain activities), they have been less eager to look to context in the form of culture and cultural systems. Economic anthropologists and economic sociologists, however, have not been so reticent about studying the impact of culture on economic behavior.

Economic anthropologists have focused on how culture affects preferences as well as economic practices and performance. For economic anthropologists, culture is something that shapes economic behavior. As Henrich (2002: p. 255) summarizes, for 'most economic anthropologists . . . "culture" may provide individuals with certain preferences, perspectives, context-specific heuristic rules.' Similarly, Bird-David (1990: p. 190) has argued that cultures organize their economic activities and relationships on the basis of 'primary metaphors' that 'not only offer [a] means of "seeing" the world but also govern everyday functioning [of individuals] down to the most mundane details.'[2] And, as Wilk and Cliggett

(2007: p. 143) explain, for economic anthropologists who focus on culture, 'understanding economic behavior depends on mapping the symbolic and social order that underlies it, gives people the values they pursue, and constrains the strategies they follow.'[3]

Most efforts by economic anthropologists to study the relationship between culture and economic phenomena highlight the folk models that individuals employ as they engage in economic activity. Bird-David (1990), for instance, has contrasted the Nayaka, a South Indian hunter-gatherer people, with neighboring communities in order to show how patterns of economic distribution and property relations vary widely depending on the 'primary metaphors' or 'metaphorical models' of the people in question.[4] Because the Nayaka consider the forest as a parent and each other as siblings, she explains, the Nayaka economy is one based on familial giving. As Bird-David (ibid.: p. 191) writes,

> Nayaka give to each other, request from each other, expect to get what they ask for, and feel obliged to give what they are asked for. They do not give resources to each other in a calculated, foresighted fashion, with a view to receiving something in return, nor do they make claims for debts.

Furthermore, since the forest as parent provides 'unconditionally' to its children, the Nayaka believe that land cannot be owned by anyone.

Browne (2004: p. 10) has, similarly, explained how the creole culture that emerged in Martinique as a result of over 400 years of uninterrupted French control pushes Martiniquais 'to make undeclared money in ways that earn them social status as well as income.' Martiniquais, she asserts, prefer to work for themselves. Martiniquais, Browne (ibid.: p. 11) explains, also aspire to be thought of as *débrouillards* (in other words, as willing to pursue economic success in ways that 'may extend beyond what is legal,' though not beyond what is moral) and as not only gifted, intelligent and resourceful but also 'economically cunning and successful in unorthodox ways.' According to Browne, both aspirations (in other words, personal autonomy and to be perceived as cunning) make sense given Martinique's creole culture and can be traced to people's experiences during slavery and colonialism.

Economic sociologists have also attempted to demonstrate how culture shapes economic life. As Swedberg (2003: p. 218) suggests, economic sociologists have recognized that, 'for a full understanding of economic phenomena, it is not only necessary to pay attention to their political and legal dimension, but also to the role that is played by culture.' Similarly, as Zukin and DiMaggio (1990: p. 17) explain, for economic sociologists, culture sets limits to economic rationality: it proscribes or limits market exchange in sacred objects and relations (for example, human beings, body organs, physical intimacy) or between ritually classified groups . . . Culture provides scripts for applying different strategies to different classes of exchange. Finally, norms and constitutive understandings regulate market exchange, causing persons to behave with institutionalized and culturally specific definitions of integrity even when they could get away with cheating.

In addition to being embedded in systems of social relations as well as in a political/legal institutional matrix, for economic sociologists, economic behavior is, thus, also culturally embedded (DiMaggio 1979). Moreover, as Levin (2008: p. 114) describes, the 'new sociology of markets incorporates culture into analyses of economic action by treating culture as something that constitutes markets or else affects their operation.' For sociologists, then, culture is either something that affects how markets are developed or something that affects how markets work.[5]

Most efforts by economic sociologists to study the economic impact of culture treat it as constitutive of markets or as constraining markets. Nee (1998), for instance, stresses the role of informal constraints—norms and networks—in shaping social interactions within organizations. He has argued that, where informal constraints match the formal rules, the costs of monitoring and enforcement are low and organizational performance is high. Similarly, Zelizer (1978) has explored how culturally prescribed prohibitions against establishing monetary equivalents for certain objects and relationships can limit exchange and how cultural shifts can legitimize enterprises that had previously been proscribed.[6] The life insurance industry in the United States, Zelizer (ibid.: p. 597) explains, was not successful when it first emerged, because there was, at the time, a 'cultural aversion' to treating death as a commercial or monetary event. As Zelizer (ibid.: p. 598) writes, 'particularly, although not exclusively, during the first half of the nineteenth century, life insurance was felt to be sacrilegious because its ultimate function was to compensate the loss of a father or husband with a check to his widow or orphans.' By the second half of the nineteenth century, however, life insurance had come to be seen as a secular ritual parallel to the religious ritual of the funeral that helped the bereaved to overcome the sadness of losing a loved one. Having life insurance also came to characterize what it meant to 'die a good death' and a way to promote (economic) immortality. 'As an efficient mechanism to ensure the economic provision of dependents,' Zelizer (ibid.: p. 603) states, 'life insurance gradually came to be counted among the duties of a good and responsible father.' And 'theological concern with personal immortality was replaced in the nineteenth century by a growing concern with posterity and the social forms of immortality.' The change in cultural attitudes toward life insurance allowed the industry to thrive. Culture, then, determines what does and what does not count as a legitimate commodity. All successful commodities have to be culturally or at least sub-culturally sanctioned.

These accounts by economic anthropologists and sociologists of how culture affects economic behavior and outcomes can certainly be reconciled with economic accounts. Still, there are several reasons why economists should not be altogether pleased with a division of labor where economists focus exclusively on institutions and incentives and leave the study of the relationship between culture and economics to others. First, focusing exclusively on institutions and incentives and excluding culture is not actually a possibility. Of course, culture, which acts as a lens through which economic actors make sense of the world and their options in it, has not been and need not be at the fore of any economic analysis. But, if culture really is a source of meanings, if it really does play a key role in shaping choices and preferences, then culture necessarily enters into every economic analysis.

Second, there is something dissatisfying, at least from the perspective of an economist, with the efforts of economic anthropologists and economic sociologists to examine the relationship between culture and markets. Economic anthropologists sometimes make arguments that, for an economist, are simply too relativistic. Consider, for instance, Gudeman's (1986) claim that non-Westerners filter their economic decisions through 'local economic models' that bear little resemblance to the economic models deployed by Westerners. Modern Western economic behavior, for him, is simply different than economic behavior in non-Western, primitive or exotic cultures. An economist, however, would insist that, even if preferences and the makeup of utility functions differ across contexts, economic actors across all contexts are in some respects quite similar (for example, they prefer more of what they value to less, and so on). Additionally, rather than agreeing with Bird-David (1992a: p.30) that the hunter-gatherers that she is describing 'care about going on forays just as they do about the value of their products,' an economist would likely insist that, if it is true that these hunter-gatherers occasionally walk through the forest with no hope of collecting something of value, we should consider the forays themselves as a good that they desire. Similarly, economic sociologists sometimes make arguments that, for an economist, focus too heavily on how culture shapes economic activity to the exclusion of how culture is shaped by economic activity. For instance, while Zelizer (1978) is certainly correct that the 'cultural aversion' to treating death as a commercial event had to be overcome before the life insurance industry could thrive, she arguably understates the role that the life insurance industry played in bringing about the requisite cultural shift.

Third, and perhaps most importantly, absent a focus on how culture affects economic activity, economists can only offer (woefully) incomplete explanations of cross-cultural variations in economic behavior. Admittedly, some economists are beginning to recognize that they should not leave the study of the culture of markets to the economic anthropologists and the economic sociologists.[7] But, with a few exceptions, economists have little interest in studying how culture affects economic behavior. This chapter explores why economists should study culture.

2.2 WITH A FEW EXCEPTIONS, ECONOMISTS HAVE LITTLE INTEREST IN STUDYING THE EFFECTS OF CULTURE

If you pressed an economist to explain why he/she was not all that interested in culture, he/she would likely offer one or more of the following reasons: (a) culture may be important but it is a hazy concept, which it is difficult to define and isolate; (b) culture may be important but anthropologists and sociologists (in other words, non-economists) should focus on it; and (c) culture is not that important, as it is not cultural shifts and their effect on preferences but price differences and price changes that explain economic behavior (*de gustibus non est disputandum*).[8] Each of these reasons, I believe, is understandable and widely held by economists but, ultimately, as I shall argue toward the end of the chapter, invalid. Let us, however, take each in turn.

2.2.1 Because Economists Believe That Culture Is a Hazy Concept

One justification that an economist might offer for ignoring cultural considerations in economic analysis is that culture is simply too vague a concept. Culture is difficult to define and almost impossible to separate from other factors that condition human behavior. Thus, measuring culture presents a challenge for economists. In this view, economists simply cannot meaningfully talk about culture, whether they would want to or not. As Casson and Godley (2000: p. 2) write, 'culture is a potentially nebulous concept. Many economists deny culture any place in their theories on the grounds that the concept is so imprecise.' Similarly, as Fukuyama (2001: p. 3132) explains, economists are reluctant to study culture because 'cultural factors are, methodologically, very difficult to measure and to disentangle from other kinds of variables.'[9] Likewise, as Guiso et al. (2006: p. 23) explain, until recently, economists have been reluctant to rely on culture as a possible determinant of economic phenomena. Much of this reluctance stems from the very notion of culture: it is so broad and the channels through which it can enter economic discourse so ubiquitous (and vague) that it is difficult to design testable, refutable hypotheses.

Indeed, that culture is arguably a part of every potential factor that affects economic behavior means that it is problematic to treat it as a separate causal factor.

The recent increase in the number of economists who are exploring the role of culture suggests that they have found strategies for isolating and measuring cultural factors (ibid.). Even those economists who have attempted to examine how culture affects the economic aspects of behavior, however, have pointed to the challenges of incorporating culture into economic analysis. According to Tabellini (2008: p. 259), for instance, culture is an 'ambiguous' term that has at least two different meanings within economics. As Tabellini (ibid.) explains,

> the most common meaning of culture [within economics] is that it refers to the social conventions and individual beliefs that sustain Nash equilibria as focal points in repeated social interactions or when there are multiple equilibria . . . An alternative interpretation is that culture refers to more primitive objects, such as individual values and preferences.

Although 'the two interpretations are not mutually exclusive' and 'beliefs and values could interact in systematic fashions,' Tabellini (ibid.) argues that the two are distinct. Notice, as Tabellini (ibid.: p. 260) points out, that beliefs and values change at different rates, beliefs being less persistent than values. Ultimately, Tabellini (ibid.) settles on the prevalence of certain individual values and codes of good conduct, specifically codes of conduct that suggest either limited or generalized morality as being the aspect of culture that is relevant for explaining differences in economic performance. And he concludes that the diffusion of generalized morality is positively associated with economic development.

Importantly, the measures of the diffusion of generalized morality that Tabellini (ibid.: p. 262) employs are, by his own admission, 'imperfect indicators.' In his study, he constructed two variables from the World Values Survey, one measuring generalized trust toward others and the second measuring tolerance and respect for others (ibid.: p. 261). As Tabellini (ibid.: p. 262) confesses,

> not only are they measured with error, but their interpretation is also somewhat ambiguous . . . besides measuring individual values, these variables might also

capture social conventions or beliefs about others. Even interpreting them as values, their specific meaning in terms of the distinction between generalized vs. limited morality is only one of the possible interpretations.

Tabellini has, thus, focused on the diffusion of generalized morality as the important aspect of culture that explains economic outcomes and has attempted to construct measures that indicate the levels of generalized morality in various countries but concedes that he cannot be confident that his measures really do capture levels of generalized morality, nor can he be confident that they are not capturing some other aspect of culture that may, thus, be more or as important for economic development. Moreover, as Tabellini (2010: p. 711) confesses, 'culture' in his work 'is still largely a black box.' His goal is to establish that aspects of culture can shape economic outcomes, not to explain how culture does shape economic outcomes. Because Tabellini finds culture difficult to isolate and measure, he also finds that establishing the relationship between culture and economic outcomes is a challenge and explaining the relationship between culture and economic outcomes is even more difficult.

Of course, this difficulty of isolating and measuring culture as well as explaining how culture affects economic outcomes is not peculiar to Tabellini's specific approach.[10] If true, the supposedly nebulous nature of culture would present a challenge for any economist who attempted to advance a cultural explanation of economic phenomena and might explain some economists' reluctance to emphasize the role of culture. Indeed, the incorporation of culture into economics, they must feel, presents challenges at both the theoretical and the empirical levels. Even if they wished to incorporate culture into their analysis, because they believe that culture is so difficult to define, isolate and quantify, it would make sense for them to doubt that they can successfully do so. That incorporating culture into economics presents certain (perceived) theoretical and empirical challenges might explain why economists are reluctant to focus on culture but is ultimately separable from the question of whether or not economists should pay attention to culture.

2.2.2   Because Economists Believe That Cultural Considerations Are Outside the Domain of Economics

A second justification that an economist might offer for ignoring culture is that cultural considerations remain outside the domain of economics even if examining the role of culture may be important to understanding economic phenomena. Unlike anthropology, sociology and the other social sciences, which ought to be and are deeply concerned about the role of culture, economics, in this view, is only interested in a particular aspect of human behavior (in other words, rational decision-making subject to preferences). Tastes and their origins, thus, ought to be considered data to the economist. The role of the economist qua economist in explaining differences in behavior ends when differences in tastes come into question. Culture, in this view, both can and should be kept out of economic analysis.

Robbins's ([1932] 1945: p. 16) assertion that economics is 'the science which studies human behavior as a relationship between ends and scarce means which have alternative uses' is consistent with and could very well be the source of this view.[11] Rather than seeing economics as being principally concerned with particular activities such as exchange, consumption and production or with particular phenomena such as the accumulation of material wealth or with behavior that occurs within a particular domain such as market behavior, Robbins (ibid.) sees economics as being chiefly concerned with a particular aspect of all activities (in other words, 'the disposal of scarce means'). As Robbins (ibid.) explains, the economist

> is interested in the way different degrees of scarcity of different goods give rise to different ratios of valuation between them, and he is interested in the way in which changes in conditions of scarcity, whether coming from changes in ends or changes in means—from the demand side or the supply side—affect these ratios.

Since all human behavior involves the use of scarce goods and services that could have been employed elsewhere, all human behavior can be said to have an economic aspect, and so aspects of every human action fall within the domain of economics. As Robbins (ibid.: p. 17) writes, 'it follows from this, therefore, that in so far as it presents this aspect, any kind of human behavior falls within the scope of economic generalizations . . . There are no limitations on economic science save this.'

It follows from this definition of economics as being concerned with a particular aspect of all human behavior that economists qua economists should not be concerned with the origins, nature or ethical status of the various ends that individuals pursue. As Robbins (ibid.: p. 24) writes, 'economics is entirely neutral between ends . . . in so far as the achievement of any end is dependent on scarce means, it is germane to the preoccupations of the economist. Economics is not concerned with ends as such.' It would, thus, not matter to an economist whether the goal is to accumulate treasures on earth or in heaven, and it would not matter to an economist whether the goal is profane or sacred; the economist would only be concerned with how the scarcity of means limits the attainment of desired ends. And, since time is necessarily scarce, all goals that require an investment of time are of interest to economists. Time, for instance, cannot simultaneously be spent in active efforts to accumulate wealth and in quiet meditation, so there is a necessary trade-off between material and spiritual riches. In this case, the economist would be concerned with how the scarcity of time results in this trade-off, not with the ends being traded off. For an economist, then, ends are to be the starting point of an inquiry into how the satisfaction of various competing ends is affected by the scarcity of means.

It also follows from this definition of economics as being concerned with the disposal of scarce means that economists qua economists should not be concerned with the various ways that particular means can be used or the context in which the disposal of scarce means occurs. The 'technical arts of production' and 'the social environment' are, for Robbins, outside the scope of economics. As Robbins (ibid.: p. 33) explains, these 'are simply to be grouped among the given factors influencing the relative scarcity of different economic goods.' Consider the writing of books. The tools used to produce books (for example, the editorial services, the word processing technology, the printing presses) can be used for various other purposes. Moreover, the social status of books has changed over time as literacy levels, the availability of other sources of entertainment and information, the availability of other mechanisms for transmitting the written word, and the esteem given to publishers and authors have changed. The technical aspects of the production of books and the social setting in which book production occurs, however, would not be relevant to economists. Instead, economists are to be concerned with how the existence of particular techniques for producing books, which can also be used to produce other goods, and with how the social factors affecting the production of books influence the adaptations that book manufacturers make to any changes in the valuation of books by consumers.

For an economist, then, that particular means are capable of satisfying various ends and that the disposal of means occurs within particular social environments would be the *starting point* of an economic inquiry.

Economics, according to Robbins, should primarily be concerned with the linking of available scarce means to the satisfaction of particular ends. As Robbins (ibid.: p. 36) asserts, 'it is one of the characteristics of the world as we find it that our ends are various and that most of the scarce means at our disposal are capable of alternative application.' In this view, the reason and process through which particular ends come to be desired and the reason and process through which particular means come to be viewed as appropriate for the satisfaction of particular wants are, thus, beyond the scope of economics. The domain of economics, Robbins (ibid.: p. 38) argues, is essentially a series of relationships—relationships between ends conceived as the possible objectives of conduct, on the one hand, and the technical and social environment on the other. Ends as such do not form part of this subject-matter nor does the technical and social environment. It is the relationships between these things and not the things in themselves which are important for the economist.

The cultural aspect of human behavior and the economic aspect of human behavior are, thus, conceptually separate and practically separable. Jackson (2009) has pointed to Robbins's narrowing of the field of economics as being responsible for the removal of cultural considerations from economics. As Jackson (ibid.: p. 89) writes,

> By the mid-twentieth century, the Robbins definition of economics as the scientific study of scarcity and resource allocation had narrowed the scope as a discipline . . . The severing of economics from culture was now institutionalized . . . culture is not an active issue, since considering it would take them outside the domain of economics.[12]

Similarly, Beugelsdijk and Maseland (2011) have described the disappearance of culture from economics as being linked to this conception of economics as a subject principally concerned with the economic aspects of human behavior. As Beugelsdijk and Maseland (ibid.: p. 47) explain, 'the distinction between cultural factors and economic phenomena was a first step in the removal of context from economics. The second step was the redefinition of non-orthodox economists as not really economists.' Veblen, Beugelsdijk and Maseland (ibid.) argue, was described as doing something other than economic theory because he challenged the removal of culture, psychology and institutions from economics. Beugelsdijk and Maseland (ibid.), similarly, explain that Weber came to be viewed as a sociologist because he was interested in behavior that could not be fully explained using marginal utility.

In this view, culture is conceived of as 'a pattern of meanings' that conditions the desirability of particular ends, and perceptions of the appropriateness of particular means to the satisfaction of those ends would be of only indirect relevance to economists. The effect that particular cultural characteristics (in other words, specific tastes and preferences) had on the disposal of scarce means, however, would be relevant. Arguably, Parsons's (1935: p. 666) complaint that, 'in the theoretical sense, there has been . . . too much sociology (as well as biology, psychology, and so on) in economics and too much economics in sociology' is consistent with the notion advanced by Robbins that the various social sciences ought to concern themselves with different aspects of human behavior. Like

Parsons, Robbins would undoubtedly agree that economists should be interested in the disposal of scarce means and leave the concern over the other aspects of human behavior (in other words, the cultural, psychological and sociological aspects) to the other disciplines.

A potential modification of this view is that, while cultural considerations have no place in economic theory (for example, in Kirzner's theory of entrepreneurship), because of the important role that culture plays in shaping human behavior, discussing culture might be permissible and even necessary in the applied branches of economics such as economic history.[13] As Kirzner (1994: p. 329) has suggested, the observation that culture influences the economic aspects of human behavior should matter in the application of economic theory but not in the formulation of economic theory. As Kirzner (ibid.) argues, 'it does not follow that, for the purposes *within economic theory* for which the entrepreneurial role has been introduced, it is necessary to go beyond the bare propensity of being alert.' It is not necessary to consider culture *within economic theory*. However, 'in applying economic theory,' Kirzner (ibid.) explains, 'one immediately looks for the cultural, historical, and social detail . . . through which the economic processes make themselves manifest.' According to Kirzner, to the extent that understanding some particular real world phenomena requires that we pay attention to culture then the economic theory employed to describe it would necessarily be incomplete. But, 'to suggest that the "incompleteness" of such pure theory is in any way an inadequacy,' Kirzner (ibid.) explains, 'would be an unfortunate misunderstanding of what theory is all about.' Admittedly, recent efforts to discuss the relationship between culture and economic behavior have primarily been within applied economics.[14] They have not (with a few exceptions) attempted to advance economic theory. In fact, rather than incorporating culture into economic theory, economists are beginning to theorize about the economic aspects of culture (see, for instance, Bisin and Verdier 2000, 2001, 2011).

2.2.3   Because Economists Believe It Is All about Prices and Price Changes[15]

A third justification for eschewing cultural considerations in economic analysis is that much of what is frequently explained or explained away by reference to culture can be explained using economic theory. There are, goes this argument, non-economic aspects of human behavior, but the economic aspects of human behavior and so the scope for economics are much larger than is frequently supposed.[16]

In this view, tastes need not be treated as data by economists or as explainable only by referencing non-economic factors. Instead, tastes can be examined using economic theory. According to Stigler and Becker (1977), saying that people behave differently because they have different tastes is too simplistic and is ultimately unsatisfactory. Recourse to cultural considerations, they contend, offers little analytically. 'No significant behavior,' Stigler and Becker (ibid.: p. 87) argue,

> has been illuminated by assumptions of differences in tastes. Instead, they, along with assumptions of unstable tastes, have been a convenient crutch to lean on when the analysis has bogged down. They give the appearance of considered judgment, yet really have only been ad hoc arguments that disguise analytical failures.

Rather than assuming that differences in tastes are pronounced or that tastes are unstable, Stigler and Becker (ibid.: p. 89) assert that tastes are remarkably stable over time and do not differ importantly among individuals. Consequently, 'all changes in behavior,' Stigler and Becker (ibid.: p. 89) argue, 'are explained by changes in prices and incomes, precisely the variables that organize and give power to economic analysis.' Consider, for instance, the apparent change in tastes for certain addictive goods that occurs as we spend increasing amounts of time consuming them. Over time, we appear to acquire a greater taste for certain kinds of music, foods and friends as well as for drinking certain beverages and smoking certain substances. Stigler and Becker (ibid.: p. 78) argue, however, that this apparent change in tastes is really a change in the (non-monetary) price of consuming these goods. As we consume these goods, they assert, we build 'consumption capital' that actually lowers the costs of consuming them in the future. Thus, it actually becomes cheaper to consume those addictive goods than their alternatives. With types of music it is that over time one additional minute spent listening to the type of music that an individual has built up consumption capital in becomes increasingly more enjoyable relative to one minute spent listening to other types of music, *ceteris paribus*. The type of music that the individual has consumption capital in, thus, becomes relatively cheaper. Doing useful economics, according to Stigler and Becker (ibid.: p. 89), requires that 'one searches, often long and frustratingly, for the subtle forms that prices and incomes take in explaining differences among men and periods.'

Stigler and Becker (ibid.: p. 81) directly challenge the analytical efficacy of referencing custom and tradition in order to explain why and under what conditions behavior will sometimes remain stable in the face of changing conditions. According to Stigler and Becker (ibid.: p. 82), people continue to behave traditionally in the face of changing circumstances when behaving in step with tradition is cheaper than breaking with tradition. Customs and traditions, they explain, 'result from investments of time and other resources in the accumulation of knowledge about the environment, and of skill with which to cope with it.' Customs and traditions, for them, act as a form of capital.[17] Since decision-making involves our searching for relevant information about the environment as well as analyzing and making use of that information, customs and traditions, they argue, can lower the cost of decision-making. 'The costs of searching for information and of applying the information to a new situation,' Stigler and Becker (ibid.) write, 'are such that habit is often a more efficient way to deal with moderate or temporary changes in the environment than would be a full, apparently utility-maximizing decision.' When a temporary change in the environment occurs, it often does not make sense to abandon traditions or to invest in the acquisition of different types of knowledge about the environment or different recipes for negotiating it. When a permanent change in the environment occurs, those who are relatively young—those individuals who have a greater incentive to disinvest from capital attuned to the old environment and to develop capital relevant to the new environment than to retain and act consistently with customs and traditions—will tend to adopt new modes of behavior. In this view, people maintain certain modes of behavior over generations not because they are under the sway of particular customs and traditions but because it is often prohibitively expensive to learn to do things differently. Economic theory can, they argue, explain behavior that is consistent with habits as well as deviations from habitual behavior.

If Stigler and Becker (ibid.) are correct, it would, thus, not be necessary to reference culture or other non-economic factors in order to explain unstable behavior where environments are stable or to explain stable behavior in the face of changing environments. Price and income shifts rather than cultural shifts or cultural constancy would explain human behavior. Arguably, this view explains Stigler's (1984) advocacy of economic imperialism (in other words, the belief that economics can explain ostensibly non-economic phenomena even though the reverse is not true). Moreover, Hirshleifer's (1985) claim that there is 'only one social science' is also consistent with this view. 'It is ultimately impossible,' Hirshleifer (ibid.: p. 53) writes,

> to carve off a distinct territory for economics, bordering upon but separated from other social disciplines. Economics interpenetrates them all, and is reciprocally penetrated by them ... What gives economics its imperialist invasive power is that our analytical categories—scarcity, cost, preferences, opportunities, and so on—are truly universal in applicability ... Economics really does constitute the universal grammar of social science.

Economics is, thus, (almost) all that we need to use in order to understand human behavior, if by economics we mean the study of rational decision-making in a world where ends are plenty and resources are necessarily scarce.

In this view, it is simply unclear what culture would add to the economist's analytical apparatus. Consider, for instance, Acemoglu and Robinson's (2010) discussion of why African societies are so poor. Rejecting cultural explanations of African development that point to cultural disincentives to entrepreneurship because 'we have little systematic evidence of such ideas,' and there is much evidence that there is dynamic entrepreneurship in Africa, Acemoglu and Robinson (ibid.) advance an institutional argument. 'The current poverty of African societies,' Acemoglu and Robinson (ibid.: p. 45) argue, 'is explained by the nature of their institutions, not their geography or cultures.' Absent secure property rights, markets cannot thrive and economic growth will not occur. Policies that undermine private property, control prices and restrict profits stifle market exchange and retard wealth creation. Where the institution of private property is tenuous, they argue, underdevelopment necessarily follows. According to Acemoglu and Robinson (ibid.: p. 22), 'the main reasons that African nations are poor today is that their citizens have very bad interlocking economic and political incentives. Property rights are insecure and very inefficiently organized, markets do not function well, states are weak and political systems do not provide public goods.' Institutions and not culture, they conclude, play the key role.

If economists are going to reference culture, it would thus follow from this view, they should not treat it as an independent factor that impacts economic behavior. Instead, culture can and should be understood using the tools of economics. Bisin and Verdier (2001), for instance, argue that cultural attitudes are endogenously determined.[18] For them, 'preferences of children are acquired through an adaptation and imitation process which depends on their parents' socialization actions, and on the cultural and social environment in which children live' (ibid.: p. 299). In their analysis, parents are rational, paternalistic agents who wish to produce children who share their preferences (because they believe it is in their children's own interest). Parents, thus, determine which cultural traits to transmit to their children and how much to invest in socialization. Because the socialization of children within the family and children's cultural adaptation from society are substitutes, families who belong to cultural minorities will socialize their children more intensely than families who are a part of the majority, since members of majority groups can rely on the transmission of cultural traits by the society at large. As a result, Bisin and Verdier (ibid.: p. 300) explain, 'there exists a heterogeneous distribution of preferences in the population, which is globally stable.'

This way of justifying the exclusion of culture as an independent factor from economic analysis (in other words, economics explains culture but culture does not explain economic behavior) is notably different from the view that the other social sciences (for example, anthropology, political science, sociology, and so on) have unique and important contributions to make to our understanding of human behavior that are simply outside the purview of economics. In this view, economics or rather rational choice theorizing is the only valid approach to understanding social phenomena.

2.3 BUT ECONOMICS IS A SCIENCE OF MEANING AND SO ECONOMISTS SHOULD LOOK AT THE ROLE OF CULTURE

Friedman (1953) has argued that economics ought to be a predictive science.[19] As Friedman (ibid.: p. 4) writes,

> its task is to provide a system of generalizations that can be used to make correct predictions about the consequences of any change in circumstances. Its performance is to be judged by the precision, scope, and conformity with experience of the predictions it yields. In short, positive economics is, or can be, an 'objective' science, in precisely the same sense as any of the physical sciences.

The goal, then, is not to understand economic behavior but to predict economic behavior. The concern is how individuals will respond to this or that stimulus not why they respond as they do to some particular stimulus. Thus the realism of assumptions is beside the point. As Friedman (ibid.: p. 14) writes, 'truly important and significant hypotheses will be found to have "assumptions" that are wildly inaccurate descriptive representations of reality, and, in general, the more significant the theory, the more unrealistic the assumptions (in this sense)?'

If economics is a predictive science, then whether or not to include culture in an analysis would simply be an empirical question. It will depend on its predictive power. If economics, however, is an interpretive science, then the case for including culture becomes quite strong. There are, in fact, good reasons to believe that economics is and ought to be an interpretive science.

Arguably, the essential data of all of the social sciences including economics are subjective in character. The facts of social sciences are the meanings that individuals attach to their actions and their environments. As Knight (1990: p. 226) argues, 'we can learn about human phenomena, in the significant sense of knowledge, chiefly by studying, and practicing, communication with other minds.' Similarly, as Mises (1949: p. 26) argues, 'we cannot approach our subject if we disregard the meaning which acting man attaches to [his] situation.' And 'the task of the [social sciences] is the comprehension of the meaning and relevance of human action' (ibid.: p. 51). Likewise, as Hayek (1979: p. 53) argues, 'unless we can understand what . . . people mean by their actions any attempt to explain them . . . is bound to fail.' Also,

> the facts of the social sciences are merely opinions, views held by the people whose actions we study. They differ from the facts of the physical sciences in being beliefs or opinions held by particular people, beliefs which as such are our data, irrespective of whether they are true or false. (Hayek 1942: p. 279)

And 'in the social sciences the things are what people think they are' (Hayek 1943: p. 3). In order to explain social phenomena, the social sciences must be concerned with what people think and believe, their assessments and valuations, the importance they place on particular relationships vis-à-vis others, and the way they see the world and their place within it.

The opinions and beliefs that guide the actions of the individuals under study simply cannot be ignored, even if those beliefs are wrong, or irrational, or based on superstition rather than reason. The interactions between two individuals, for instance, are explainable only in terms of what they believe about the nature of their relationship (Hayek 1948: p. 60). If Latoya believes that Keisha is her blood relative, whether Latoya is in fact mistaken or not is irrelevant to any explanation of Latoya's behavior toward Keisha. Similarly, if Latoya and Keisha were in fact blood relatives but neither of them knew it, a valid explanation of Latoya's behavior toward Keisha or Keisha's toward Latoya could not be based on their genetic connection to one another. The same is true, of course, for efforts to explain religious rituals. It is not the social scientists' 'objective' assessments of the efficacy of prayer but individuals' 'subjective' perceptions of the power of prayer that explain why some people pray and others do not. Reference to what people think and believe is necessary in order to explain why people accept certain metal discs as money and not others, why they eat certain animals and plants and not others, and why they ingest certain chemical concoctions when they are sick and not others. Like all the other social sciences, then, economics is a science that must be preoccupied with meanings.

What, though, does it mean to be a science of meaning? Schütz's (1967) efforts are quite helpful in this regard. To say that a person's experience has meaning, that it is a meaningful lived experience, Schütz (ibid.: p. 41) informs, is to say that acting man has reflected upon it and isolated it 'from the abundance of experiences coexisting with it, preceding it, and following it' and, in so doing, has constituted it as meaningful.[20] As Schütz (ibid.: p. 71) explains, 'the reflective glance signals out an elapsed

lived experience and constitutes it as meaningful.' And, in constituting an
item as meaningful, the item is 'selected out' and 'rendered discrete by a
reflexive act' (ibid.: p. 19). Meaning then, in a generic sense, is a certain
way of regarding an item or experience. '*Meaning*,' as Schütz (ibid.: p. 42)
points out, '*is a certain way of directing one's gaze at an item of one's own
experience.*'

It becomes clear at this point that 'meaningfulness,' contrary to Weber's
view, is not a useful criterion for distinguishing between mere behavior
and action (what Weber called 'meaningful behavior').[21] In fact, Weber's
hope to separate out meaningful behavior (as rational, purposive action)
from purely emotional behavior and traditional/habitual behavior completely breaks down when we think of meaning as a way of seeing an
item.[22] 'It is useless to say that what distinguishes action from behavior,'
Schütz (ibid.: p. 19) writes, 'is that the former is subjectively meaningful
and the latter meaningless. On the contrary, each is meaningful in its own
way.' All of my experiences can be selected out and distinguished from
other experiences and so constituted as meaningful, be they 'purposive'
in Weber's sense or merely 'automatic' reactions to stimuli. In fact, even
my involuntary responses to stimuli (for example, coughing, sneezing,
choking, and so on) can be isolated and made meaningful. As Schütz
(ibid.) states, 'when I look closely, I find that none of my experiences is
entirely devoid of meaning.'[23]

What, then, is the difference between action and mere behavior? Can we
draw any meaningful distinctions between them? In which way are actions
meaningful? According to Schütz (ibid.: p. 61), '*action is the execution of a
projected act*,' and '*the meaning of any action is its corresponding projected
act*.' A person acting rationally first chooses a goal or an end. He/she then
imagines a completed act and that projection becomes the thing that he/
she tries to bring about through action. Consider, for example, Michaela
wanting to get out of bed to go into the living room. 'What is visible to the
mind,' Schütz (ibid.: p. 60) explains, 'is the completed act, not the ongoing
process that constitutes it.' She does not count her steps before beginning
to head to the living room nor does she, at least at this initial stage, think
of the obstacles she will encounter along the way (in other words, she does
not see the doors she will have to open, the furniture she will have to walk
around, and so on). Instead, what she projects (at first) is 'herself in the
living room.' Next, she identifies the means that are necessary to achieve
the desired ends and, perhaps, projects those as intermediate goals. This
process, Schütz (ibid.: p. 61) explains, is a recognition of 'a certain causal
regularity' between the means available to her and her particular goal. To
continue with our example, Michaela is able to conceive of a plan that
gets her from her bed to the living room because she is aware (through

experience in this case) that lifting herself from her bed, walking toward the bedroom door, opening said door and walking through it will get her from the bed to the living room. An action and the sub-actions that contribute to bringing about a particular act, as Schütz (ibid.: p. 63) concludes, 'are meaningless apart from the project that defines it.'

Although the 'projected act' can be fairly thought of as 'the meaning of an action,' reference to the projected act only gives us the 'in-order-to motive' of the action.[24] As Schütz (ibid.: p. 89) explains,

> if, therefore, I give as the motive of my action that it is in-order-to-such-and-such, what I really mean is the following: The action itself is only a means within the meaning-context of the project, within which the completed act is pictured as something to be brought to fulfillment by my action. Therefore, when asked about my motive, I always answer in terms of 'in-order-to' if the completed act is still in the future.

But the term 'motive' can mean more than 'the orientation of the action to a future event' (ibid.: p. 87). It can also mean 'its relation to a past lived experience' (ibid.). Stating that a murderer committed murder for money is an 'in-order-to' statement. Stating that a murderer committed murder because he grew up under difficult circumstances is an altogether different kind of statement. Although we are inclined, Schütz (ibid.: p. 91) explains, to call this second statement an 'explanation of the deed,' it is ultimately only a statement that 'certain past experiences of the murderer have created a disposition on the part of the murderer to achieve his goals by violence rather than by honest labor.' The so-called 'explanation of the deed' speaks to the 'genuine because-motive' of the action.

Determining the 'genuine because-motive' of an action, as Schütz (ibid.: p. 95) points out, is a backward looking effort.[25] As Schütz (ibid.: p. 93) explains, 'the formulation of a genuine why-question is generally possible only after the motivated experience has occurred and when one looks back on it as something whole and complete in itself.' Moreover, the motivating experience must certainly be past at the time that a genuine because-statement is made. A future event cannot be the genuine because-motive of a past event. As Schütz (ibid.) notes, 'the meaning-context of the true because-motive is thus always an explanation after the event.' Suppose, for instance, we say that the murderer killed his victim because his victim was going to kill him at some later date. Notice that the in-order-to motive behind the murderer's killing was to prevent his own demise in the future, and that the because-motive is not really his impending doom but his past perception of the possibility of his future death. It is his prior realization of the threat to his life and not his future death that motivated him to kill.

Identifying how meaning is constituted, however, does not tell us anything about its content nor does it tell us anything about how, if at all, we can gain access to the in-order-to motives let alone the genuine because-motives of others. There is, according to Schütz, no method available to us which we can follow in hopes of gaining access to the actual intended meanings of others, the in-order-to and genuine because-motives of an actor as the actor understands them. As Schütz (ibid.: p. 218) explains, 'it is one thing to interpret one's own experience and quite another to interpret the experiences of someone else.' We have 'direct' access to our own experiences. We have access only to the external signs, products and indications of each other's lived experiences. In order to interpret the experiences of someone else, we have to begin with these signs and trace them back to their (possible) subjective meanings.[26] This process of tracing signs back to subjective meanings of the actor is not without its challenges. There is not a one-to-one mapping between signs and meanings. Instead, 'the subjective meaning that the interpreter *does* grasp is at best an approximation to the . . . [individual's] intended meaning, but never that meaning itself, for one's knowledge of another person's perspective is always necessarily limited' (ibid.: p. 129). Although our knowledge of another person's perspective is limited, interpretation is nonetheless possible, because everyone's actions belong to an 'intersubjective world common to us all' (ibid.: p. 218).

The task of a science of meaning that aims at exploring the actions of others must attempt to explicate the interpretive schemes that actors employ to understand their own acts and the stock of knowledge from which they draw the subjective meanings of their actions.

Schütz has stressed the importance of the 'social stock of knowledge' in providing individuals with 'interpretive schemes,' 'relevance systems,' 'skills,' 'useful knowledge' and 'recipes.'[27] As Schütz and Luckmann (1973: p. 100) explain, 'each situation [that individuals encounter and experience in the everyday life-world] is defined and mastered with the help of the stock of knowledge.' An individual's 'subjective stock of knowledge' contains everything that he has 'learned' over the course of his life: how to walk, talk, read, ride a bicycle, drive a car, relate to his friends and colleagues, program a computer, or reason like an economist; what his capabilities are and his limitations; what is appropriate and inappropriate in a variety of circumstances; what is typically relevant and what is usually irrelevant in various situations; which phenomena he should view as common and which uncommon; his own life history; the stories he was told as a child; what he gained through interacting with his fellows; and the customs and folklore of his community. When an event occurs or he is confronted with a (novel or not so novel) state of affairs, he draws on his subjective stock of knowledge as he defines his circumstances and decides his path.

Although some of an individual's subjective stock of knowledge was developed as a result of his own experiences in the life-world, much of it was derived from the social stock of knowledge. As Schütz and Luckmann (1973: p.254) explain, 'when the individual enters into a situation, he brings with him a biographically modeled, and to a large extent socially derived, stock of knowledge.' And 'the subjective stock of knowledge consists only in part of "independent" results of experience and explication. It is predominantly derived from elements of the social stock of knowledge' (ibid.: p.262).

All social knowledge, Schütz and Luckmann (ibid.: p.262) point out, is the result of the 'subjective acquisition of knowledge' that occurs through experience in the life-world. The social stock of knowledge, however, contains both 'more' than the sum of each individual's subjective stock and 'less' than each individual's subjective stock. It contains 'more' in the sense that no person in any community is in possession of all of that community's social stock of knowledge; there is a social distribution of knowledge (ibid.: p.264). It contains 'less' in the sense that the individual's subjective stock of knowledge contains elements that were acquired during novel or unique experiences and so do not make their way into the social stock of knowledge (ibid.).

Arguably, it is possible to think of the social stock of knowledge as culture.[28] Recall, culture is fairly thought of as a collection of meanings that we received from our predecessors. Again, as Geertz (1973: p.89) writes, 'it denotes an historically transmitted pattern of meanings ... a system of inherited conceptions ... by means of which men communicate, perpetuate, and develop their knowledge about and attitudes toward life.' Like Schütz's 'social stock of knowledge,' cultural systems have both moral and cognitive aspects that shape our decisions regarding good and bad ways of thinking about and behaving in the world.

As a science of meaning, then, economics must highlight the role of the social stock of knowledge (in other words, it must be concerned with culture if economists are to understand the in-order-to and genuine because-motives of actors). This is true at a theoretical level, where the economist should (when appropriate) point out how culture can affect economic behavior. This is also true at an empirical level, where the economist should (when appropriate) point out how specific cultures have affected the economic behavior of certain individuals and groups and led to certain economic outcomes. Rather than ignoring, or explaining away, or leaving to others the study of the relationship between culture and economic behavior, economists should pay attention to how culture will affect the actors in their models and how culture does affect the actors that they study. Economics is and should be recognized as a cultural science.

2.4   AND THE MARKET ORDER IS A CULTURAL PHENOMENON

The market is typically conceptualized as an area where buyers and sellers exchange goods and services. It could refer to a particular geographic location or marketplace where a variety of goods and services are exchanged (for example, the local shopping plaza). Or it can be conceived of as the sphere where buyers and sellers trade a particular good (for example, the market for tennis shoes).

Conceived of in one or both of these ways, the market ought to be of interest to economists. It should be a central category within economics. After all, price theory and its constituents (in other words, consumer and producer theory) are efforts to tease out the implications of rational choice in a market setting. They are ultimately efforts to elucidate market behavior. Consumers and producers are market figures. Competition and exchange are activities that take place within and lead to the emergence of markets. Much of economic theory is, therefore, concerned with market phenomena.

Ironically, the market has not been a central concern for economists. This peculiarity has not gone unnoticed by economists. For instance, as North (1977: p.710) observes, 'it is a peculiar fact that the literature on economics ... contains so little discussion of the central institution that underlies neo-classical economics—the market.' Similarly, as Coase (1988: p.7) remarks, 'although economists claim to study the working of the market ... in the modern textbook, the analysis deals with the determination of market prices, but discussion of the market itself has entirely disappeared.' And, as Stigler (1967: p.291) observes, 'economic theory is concerned with markets much more than with factories or kitchens. It is, therefore, a source of embarrassment that so little attention has been paid to the theory of markets.' Non-economists have also noticed this peculiarity. As Lie (1997: p.342), for instance, has argued, 'the market is [allegedly] a central category of economics ... It is then curious that the market receives virtually no extended discussion in most works of economic theory or history ... The market, it turns out, is the hollow core at the heart of economics.' Similarly, as Swedberg (1994: p.257) observes, 'astonishingly little work has been done' on the market within economic thought.

The market, thus, occupies a strange position within economics

(Storr 2008). It is in a sense ever-present. It is the site where much of the activity that interests economists takes place. But it is more often than not in the background of the analysis.[29] As I have argued elsewhere, 'in economics, we often portray markets as sterile spaces lacking either souls or sounds. We talk about transactions and prices and profits but seldom mention people (except when we refer to the faceless profit maximizing suppliers and hedonistic utility maximizing demanders)' (ibid.: p. 141). Bringing the market to the forefront of economic analysis would require recognizing it as a social structure in its own right where both competition and exchange occur that is supported by a variety of norms and more formal institutions which enable it to function. In the real world, 'markets . . . are vibrant, colorful social spaces' (ibid.).

It is probably uncontroversial to suggest that real world markets are cultural phenomena. The differences between the New York Stock Exchange, the Mall of America in Minnesota, the Makola Market in Ghana and Amazon.com are obvious to anyone familiar with them. Of course, in many respects, the actors in these markets are very similar to each other. Buyers in all of these markets are hoping to pay as little as possible. Sellers in all of these markets are hoping to earn a profit. All participants are trying to advance their subjectively perceived interests as best they are able given their constraints. But there are also key differences. Haggling, for instance, does not generally occur in the American mall or when buying from an e-commerce website (except for resellers and auction sites) but is acceptable and expected in an African bazaar and is even essential to the functioning of a stock exchange. Similarly, the nature of the relationships between trading partners in different markets can vary considerably. If electronic commerce offers the possibility for largely anonymous exchange, trading partners in stock exchanges and bazaars tend to have more intimate relationships. Additionally, what would constitute a fair deal can differ across markets.

Consider, for instance, Geertz's (1963) discussion of the differences between the culture of markets in Modjokuto and Tabanan, two towns in Indonesia. As Geertz (ibid.: p. 122) describes, 'Modjokuto's entrepreneurs emerge directly from a bazaar economy in which individualistic, everyman-for-himself activity is carried almost to an extreme in contrast to the lineage-like organization of the relatively solidary and corporate ruling family from which Tabanan's new men come.' While the Modjokuto peddlers are ego-focused, Tabanan traders are group-focused. Tabanan markets are high trust environments. Because deception is rampant in Modjokuto's bazaar economy, however, Modjukutans develop shrewd bargaining skills in order to overcome the low level of trust that overlies economic activity. Not surprisingly, the more successful merchants in

Modjokuto are the pious Muslims, who embrace more systematic, stable and efficient business behaviors and are able to set themselves apart from the more opportunistic peddlers in the bazaar.

Modjokuto and Tabanan's different entrepreneurial cultures have shaped the types of transactions that occur as well as the nature and size of the enterprises that exist in each town. 'Almost all Modjokuto's modern enterprises,' Geertz (ibid.) explains, 'are individual or immediate concerns, and capital must be raised either through personal savings or (increasingly) through government loans . . . In Modjokuto even partnerships . . . are almost non-existent.' In Tabanan, however, partnerships and large cooperatives are fairly typical, and modern enterprises are able to raise capital from villagers to support large-scale collective efforts. Unlike the cultural tradition of the Modjokutans, Geertz (ibid.) explains, 'the cultural tradition from which [Tabananers] draw provides ready-made forms for collective activity.' One Tabananer cultural tradition that has proven especially useful in this regard is the seka group. According to Geertz (ibid.: p. 84), village life in Tabanan is best described as a series of overlapping seka groups which are organized to serve some specific political, social or economic function. Tabananers can belong to as many as a dozen of these groups. The existence of these seka groups, Geertz (ibid.) offers, explains why economic activities in Tabanan tend to be strongly collective.

It is quite clear how employing culture might improve economists' understanding of (actual, existing, real world) markets. Economists' understanding of the (conceptual) market, however, would also improve by treating it as a cultural phenomenon. The concepts that economists employ to explain market interactions are all culturally constructed. Culture (partly) determines who can buy and sell, when a deal between them is properly consummated, which items buyers and sellers can trade, and what counts as an acceptable unit of exchange. Moreover, culture (partly) determines why entrepreneurs notice some opportunities and not others as well as why they choose to pursue certain paths to exploit the opportunities that they and not others notice. Since culture plays a significant role in determining who can legitimately engage in market transactions, what constitutes an acceptable exchange, which items and services can be traded and what counts as money, it would seem to make sense for economists to concern themselves with how culture affects economic behavior.

2.5 BESIDES, THE CHOICE IS REALLY BETWEEN EMPLOYING CULTURE IMPLICITLY AND EMPLOYING IT EXPLICITLY

Ignoring culture may be possible, but avoiding culture is impossible. While it is not inaccurate to assert, as many economists do, that relative price shifts, or differences in the size of expected profits, or differences in the institutional framework can explain all of the meaningful differences in economic behavior and outcomes, it is not accurate to assert that prices, profits and property can explain any of the meaningful differences in economic behavior and outcomes without (at least implicitly) employing culture.[30]

The choice before economists is not between employing culture and not employing culture. Instead, it is a choice between implicitly and explicitly employing culture. Changes in relative prices do explain why individuals might begin to use a particular good more sparingly that they once used wastefully (Hayek 1948). Differences in the size of expected profits do explain why entrepreneurs pursue some opportunities and not others (Kirzner 1973). Differences in the rules governing property do explain why individuals in some contexts engage in productive entrepreneurship and individuals in other contexts engage in destructive entrepreneurship (Baumol 1990). But what meaning should be attached to price changes, when a difference between revenues and expenses in fact signifies a large enough profit to make pursuing an opportunity attractive, and what constitutes an appropriate disposition of property are (partly) determined by culture.

The meanings attributed to price changes are culturally constructed. Recall that the price system, as Hayek (1948: p. 87) explains, can be thought of

> as a kind of machinery for registering change, or a system of telecommunications which enables individual producers to watch merely the movement of a few pointers, as an engineer might watch the hands of a few dials, in order to adjust their activities to changes of which they may never know more than is reflected in the price movement.

The 'marvel' of the market, as Hayek (ibid.) asserts, is that with very little information thousands of people respond appropriately to a change in the relative scarcity of a product without anyone issuing a directive. But, notice, price changes have to be interpreted. The meaning of a price shift is not unambiguous. A price increase could reflect a permanent or temporary change in the scarcity of a good. An individual's response will undoubtedly differ depending on whether or not she decides that the shift is temporary.[31] Of course, she could invest in obtaining additional information about the underlying cost of the price shift and will certainly do so as long as the expected returns from investing in additional information are greater than the cost of acquiring additional information. Correctly weighing expected benefits against expected costs of searching for additional information, however, requires that she not only correctly assesses the value of the information sought and the cost of searching but that she accurately assigns a probability to her finding the desired information. Our assessments of value and our assignments of probabilities come from our stocks of knowledge, parts of which are derived from the social stock of knowledge. Assuming that the meaning of the price change is unambiguous, or that she will be neither overly pessimistic nor overly optimistic in assessing the costs and benefits of acquiring additional information or estimating the likelihood that her search will be successful, then, is to assume that she possesses an appropriate cultural frame.[32]

The meanings attributed to profit opportunities are similarly culturally constructed. Recall that 'the entrepreneurial element in the economic behavior of market participants,' as Kirzner (1973: pp. 15–16) writes, 'consists . . . in their alertness to previously unnoticed changes in circumstances which may make it possible to get far more in exchange for whatever they have to offer than was hitherto possible.' Entrepreneurship, Kirzner (ibid.) explains, consists in recognizing opportunities to buy low and sell high. But, again, the entrepreneur does not uncover unambiguous opportunities. Entrepreneurship requires interpretation. Assuming that profit opportunities are like dollar bills lying on the beach waiting to be picked up, as Kirzner (ibid.) has, might make the act of interpretation a trivial one but does not eliminate the need for interpretation. A piece of paper lying on the ground could be a dollar bill that can be exchanged for valuable items or it could be a worthless piece of paper. Whether an entrepreneur will bend down to pick up the piece of paper or not will depend on whether she believes that the paper represents a dollar bill or a worthless scrap. It will also depend on whether or not she believes that she can successfully pick up the paper without exerting more effort than the piece of paper is worth. And it will depend on whether or not she believes that the piece of paper is hers for the taking. It may, in fact, belong to someone whom she does not yet notice. Again, her assessments will be influenced by her stock of knowledge, part of which is derived from her social stock of knowledge. And, again, assuming her assessments will be correct is to assume that she possesses an appropriate cultural frame.[33]

That culture has to be (implicitly or explicitly) employed when pointing to differences in the rules of the game (in other words, the institutional matrix) as an explanation for differences in economic outcomes is perhaps easier and is certainly less controversial than arguing that prices and profit opportunities are culturally constructed. Recall that, as Baumol (1990: pp. 898–9) writes, 'the exercise of entrepreneurship can sometimes be unproductive or even destructive, and that whether it takes one of these directions or one that is more benign depends heavily on the structure of payoffs in the economy—the rules of the game.' The rules of the game, however, both emerge from a society's cultural system and are interpreted through a cultural lens. As North (2005: p. 49) explains, 'the institutional structure reflects the accumulated beliefs of the society over time. And change in the institutional framework is usually an incremental process reflecting the constraints that the past imposes on the present and the future.' Also, as North (ibid.) continues, 'there is an intimate relationship between belief systems and the institutional framework.' Cultural systems composed of belief and value systems are thus the source of society's pay-off structure. To say that the rules of the game in one society encourage productive entrepreneurship and that the institutional matrix in another encourages unproductive or even destructive entrepreneurship is to make a statement about those societies' cultures.

Economists, simply, cannot avoid making assumptions about the relationship between culture and economic behavior. If the aim of economics is prediction, then, not specifying and not defending the cultural assumptions embedded in a particular economic analysis might not matter all that much. As Greif (1994) and others have shown, however, there is reason to believe that including cultural factors in our models could improve their predictive power. If the aim is to explain and understand economic behavior, then, leaving our assumptions about culture implicit (and so unspecified and undefended) necessarily impoverishes our analysis.

2.6 CONCLUSION

The classical economists were aware of the important role that culture plays in shaping economic behavior and discussed the role of culture, particularly in the form of belief systems, customs and habits, in their analysis. For instance, Mill (1848: II. IV. 3) observes in a chapter on competition and custom that

it is only in the great centres of business that retail transactions have been chiefly, or even much, determined, by competition. Elsewhere it rather acts,

> when it acts at all, as an occasional disturbing influence; the habitual regulator
> is custom, modified from time to time by notions existing in the minds of pur-
> chasers and sellers, of some kind of equity or justice.

Similarly, as Say (1803: I. XXI. I) observes when discussing the nature
of money, 'custom . . . and not the mandate of authority, designates the
specific product that shall pass exclusively as money, whether crown
pieces or any other commodity whatever.' Likewise, Smith (1776: I. I.
II) observes that 'the difference between the most dissimilar characters,
between a philosopher and a common street porter, for example, seems to
arise not so much from nature, as from habit, custom, and education,' and
Smith (ibid.: I. I. IX) also discusses how custom can make certain kinds of
employment fashionable and other kinds unattractive.

Early in the twentieth century, however, most economists stopped
talking about culture. As economics became more formal, culture began
to seem too vague a concept to incorporate into economic analysis. As the
other social sciences developed, culture was seen as the province of these
other disciplines; economists could leave the analysis of culture's role to
the anthropologists and the sociologists. As economics began to be seen
as the grammar of the social sciences, it seemed as if cultural differences
should be explained using the tools of economics rather than treated as
an independent factor. Although these three reasons for the removal of
culture from economics push in the same direction, they are not all consistent with one another. Stressing that there is an economic aspect of all
human action (as Robbins does), for instance, does not imply that the economic aspect of all human behavior is the only important aspect of human
behavior (as Stigler and Becker do). Similarly, claiming that culture is too
nebulous a concept to be incorporated into economics undermines the
claim that culture can be explained using economic analysis.

But if economics is to be viewed as a science of meaning then it must
pay attention to culture. There are, of course, better and worse ways to
incorporate culture into economics. In Chapters 4 and 5 of *Understanding
the Culture of Markets* (Storr 2013), I recommend an approach to studying the culture of markets and suggest why the benefits of adopting this
approach are likely to outweigh the costs. Culture need not be seen as a
nebulous concept nor need it be seen as the domain of other disciplines.
Economists can still be imperialists if they wish, but that implies that they
should engage in export (in other words, utilize rational choice theorizing
to explore subjects outside the traditional domain of economics) as well
as import (in other words, they should benefit from the methods and substantive efforts of social scientists from other disciplines).

NOTES

* This chapter previously appeared in Virgil Henry Storr, *Understanding the Culture of Markets* (Routledge, 2013). It is reprinted here with minor edits with the permission of the publisher.

1. Schütz (1967) points to naming as a way of contextualizing another's behavior. Calling an eye twitch a wink, for instance, places it within what Schütz calls an 'objective context of meaning.'

2. 'Primary metaphors' are concepts that some groups of people use to make sense of their environment and, so, to guide their actions. They are, thus, also concepts that social scientists can sometimes use to make sense of the economic actions and arrangements of various peoples.

3. See Wilk and Cliggett (2007) for a review and critique of the efforts of anthropologists to discuss how culture affects economic life. 'The problem with cultural economics,' they argue (ibid.: p. 142),

   > is that once you make rationality relative and culturally embedded, you only have two choices in evaluating or analyzing people in other cultures. The easiest course is to portray some groups as more rational than others, with all the chauvinism such a judgment implies . . . The second is to relativize *all* rationality and conclude that *no* culture is more rational than another and that scientific, objective knowledge about other cultures is therefore impossible.

   In Chapters 3 and 4 of *Understanding the Culture of Markets* (Storr 2013), I engage a handful of these studies to demonstrate the efficacy of enlisting culture in order to explain economic phenomena and propose a third direction for cultural economics that avoids chauvinism but does not embrace relativism.

4. See also Bird-David (1992b) for her use of 'primary metaphors' to explain economic practices in other contexts.

5. See Levin (2008) for a review and critique of these efforts. Although economic sociologists have been somewhat reluctant to discuss the role of culture (Zelizer 1988), at least since Parsons, however, sociologists have recognized the importance of culture. As Parsons (1937: p. 764) explained,

   > the relations of culture systems to action are highly complex. Here it is necessary to state only that they may, on the one hand, be considered as products of processes of action; on the other, as conditioning elements of further action, as for instance is true of scientific and other 'ideas.' The sciences of action can no more avoid concern with them than they can with 'physical' facts. But the logical relation is essentially the same. They constitute unproblematical data, knowledge of which is essential to the solution of concrete problems.

6. See Zelizer (2010) for a collection of her work on how culture shapes the economy.

7. In Chapter 3 of *Understanding the Culture of Markets* (Storr 2013), I review and critique some of these efforts.

8. Jones (1995, 2006) has described these latter two reasons as 'cultural nullity.' As Jones (2006: p. 5) explains,

   > strictly speaking, [cultural nullity] can take more than one form and is often adopted unconsciously. One version is vague about whether cultures really exist but assumes that, even if they do, they are so marginal to economic concerns that they may be safely ignored. Another version accepts that cultures do exist but hypothesizes that they are creatures of the economy, able to adjust so painlessly to changing incentives that in this case, too, they may be ignored . . . the professional culture of economists

prevents most of them from seeing that culture matters at all. The topic has been left to other disciplines.

Ironically, although he is critical of this position, Jones ends up adopting a form of cultural nullity. He concludes, for instance, that culture is not particularly important. 'In many instances,' he (ibid.: p. 259) writes, 'the effects are likely to be small and will wash out over time.' And, cultural explanations may still be valid but we should 'not expect too much' (ibid.: p. 260). Billig (2000: p. 784) has similarly observed that

> the great majority of economists will go on completely ignoring culture or invoking it without actually incorporating it into their analyses. For them culture represents the unimportant, irrational, messy noise that we must hold constant if we ever hope to get on with formal analysis.

Alternatively, Harrison (2006: pp. 11, 13) has argued that 'the thesis of culture matters makes a lot of economists uncomfortable ... The reluctance of many economists to confront culture reflects in part the difficulty of quantifying cultural factors and identifying clear patterns of cause and effect.' Although I recommend qualitative approaches to studying the relationship between culture and economic behavior in Chapter 5 of *Understanding the Culture of Markets* (Storr 2013), I believe that more fundamental barriers to the inclusion of cultural considerations into economics are at work.

Although very different in tone, Jackson's (2009) discussion of why economists avoid cultural explanations is more closely aligned with the reasons that I identify. Jackson (ibid.: p. 187) has argued that

> economics has followed core doctrines that exclude cultural thought. This cultural vacuum was a by-product of the desire to imitate natural sciences, rather than a deliberate disavowal of culture. Most economists were busy with increasingly specialized research and felt no need to ponder the doubts raised by cultural critics— cultural thought was nullified by being ignored. Economics has not been nakedly anti-cultural, but the gist of its theories and methods has been to debar culture.

Jackson (ibid.: p. 202) points to three barriers to incorporating culture into economics: neoclassical theory, disciplinary boundaries and quantitative techniques. According to Jackson (ibid.: pp. 202–03),

> [1] Neoclassical theory is ahistorical, claims universal relevance, plays down institutions ... an economics built on these principles will never accommodate culture properly and epitomizes the mechanistic thinking that cultural critics have abhorred ... [2] The economics discipline, as presently constituted, regards cultural methods as non-economic and irrelevant. In a climate of extreme specialization, cultural arguments are beyond the purview of economics ... [3] A third barrier to cultural thought in economics has been the mathematization of the subject.

Jackson believes that these barriers are likely to prove stubborn in the face of any effort to employ cultural considerations in economics. While I agree that disciplinary boundaries do pose a challenge to introducing cultural considerations into economics and I recommend that economists interested in the role of culture embrace qualitative methods, I do not believe that the approach that I advance is necessarily inconsistent with neoclassical economics if by neoclassical economics Jackson simply means rational choice theory. The three reasons that I argue explain why economists have little interest in culture are, thus, similar but are not identical to Jackson's 'three barriers.'

Lavoie (1994: pp. 52–5) has also argued that universalism, formalism, quantitativism and causalism have kept economics from dealing with culture. In Chapter 3 of *Understanding the Culture of Markets* (Storr 2013), I discuss how some of these philosophical presuppositions of modern economic theory have (unfortunately) influenced many of the efforts to incorporate culture into economics, but I do not believe that they explain why most economists ignore culture.

9. Critiquing cultural explanations of economic development in Asia, Fukuyama (2001: p. 3132) goes on to argue that

> Asian underdevelopment could be explained not just by culture, but also by political conditions, poor economic policy, weak institutions, global economic conditions, and a host of other factors. Those promoting culturalist interpretations usually had no empirically convincing way of demonstrating that cultural factors were indeed as important as they claimed.

10. As I discuss and critique in Chapter 3 of *Understanding the Culture of Markets* (Storr 2013), a number of the studies that explore how culture impacts economic behavior and outcomes rely on measures constructed from the type of survey that Tabellini utilizes.

11. This conception of economics as being concerned with certain aspects of human behavior, which Robbins describes as an *analytical* conception, is a break from the *classificatory* conception of economics that the classical economists embraced which considered certain kinds of behavior as being the subject matter of economics. For instance, Marshall (1890: p. 14) has described economics as the 'study of men as they live and move and think in the ordinary business of life. But it concerns itself chiefly with those motives which affect, most powerfully and most steadily, man's conduct in the business part of his life.' Economics, for the classical economists, was about human beings interacting in the business sphere. Notice, then, that Robbins's argument is quite different than the one offered by Marshall (ibid.). Marshall (ibid.: p. 20), instead, argued that

> the side of life with which economics is specially concerned is that in which man's conduct is most deliberate, and in which he most often reckons up the advantages and disadvantages of any particular action before he enters on it. And further it is that side of his life in which, when he does follow habit and custom, and proceeds for the moment without calculation, the habits and customs themselves are most nearly sure to have arisen from a close and careful watching of the advantages and disadvantages of different courses of conduct. There will not in general have been any formal reckoning up of two sides of a balance-sheet: but men going home from their day's work, or in their social meetings, will have said to one another, 'It did not answer to do this, it would have been better to do that,' and so on. What makes one course answer better than another, will not necessarily be a selfish gain, nor any material gain; and it will often have been argued that 'though this or that plan saved a little trouble or a little money, yet it was not fair to others,' and 'it made one look mean,' or 'it made one feel mean.' It is true that when a habit or a custom, which has grown up under one set of conditions, influences action under other conditions, there is so far no exact relation between the effort and the end which is attained by it. In backward countries there are still many habits and customs similar to those that lead a beaver in confinement to build himself a dam; they are full of suggestiveness to the historian, and must be reckoned with by the legislator. But in business matters in the modern world such habits quickly die away.

Additionally, Marshall (ibid.: IV. VII. 3) argues that

> the causes which control the accumulation of wealth differ widely in different countries and different ages. They are not quite the same among any two races, and perhaps not even among any two social classes in the same race. They depend much on social and religious sanctions; and it is remarkable how, when the binding force of custom has been in any degree loosened, differences of personal character will cause neighbours brought up under like conditions to differ from one another more

widely and more frequently in their habits of extravagance or thrift than in almost any other respect.

Unlike Robbins, then, Marshall did not seem to think that there was an economic aspect to all human behavior. Instead, for Marshall, there were spheres of life where individuals acted economically (in other words, weighed costs and benefits) and spheres where they did not act economically. Economists did not need to pay attention to culture, because the effects of culture were limited in the economic spheres of life.

12. Although I agree that this is what took place, Robbins's definition of economics because it is concerned with the relationship between the social environment and the economic aspect of behavior need not have been seen as ruling out any mention of culture within economics. It could, for instance, have been read as allowing for and even necessitating the study of the relationship between culture and economics.

13. In fact, I have advanced that very argument elsewhere (see Storr and John, this volume, Chapter 4).

14. See, for instance, Knack and Keefer (1997), Glaeser et al. (2000), Tabellini (2008) and Jackson (2009) for a handful of efforts to elucidate the connection between various aspects of culture and economic outcomes. Kreps (1990) and Greif (1994) did, of course, attempt theoretical advances vis-à-vis the role of culture.

15. Or, perhaps, changes in institutions which result in price changes.

16. This is a counter to the behaviorist move that, arguably, attempts to shrink the scope of pure economic theory.

17. I challenge this way of conceiving of culture (in other words, as a form of capital) in Chapter 3 of *Understanding the Culture of Markets* (Storr 2013).

18. See also Bisin and Verdier (2000, 2011) and Bisin et al. (2004, 2009).

19. Friedman (1953), of course, is not without his critics. See Boland (1979) for a summary of the criticisms of Friedman's methodology and a response to those criticisms. See also Hayek's (1964) argument that pattern predictions are sometimes all that are possible.

20. That the meaning of a lived experience can be different depending on when and from what vantage point it is viewed is perhaps the clearest indication that meaning has to do with reflection. As Schütz (1967: p. 74) writes,

> the meaning of a lived experience is different depending on *the moment from which* the Ego is observing it . . . its meaning is different depending upon the *temporal distance* from which it is remembered and looked back upon. Likewise, the reflective glance will penetrate more or less deeply into lived experience depending on its point of view.

21. Recall that Weber has argued that 'in [the category] "action" is included all human behavior when and in so far as the acting individual attaches a subjective meaning to it' (cited in Schütz 1967: p. 15).

22. Mises (2003: pp. 88–92) has alternatively challenged Weber's categories of action on the grounds that all human action is purposeful, even habitual action which can seem automatic.

23. And, Schütz (1967: p. 19) explains,

> there is one fact which shows that most of my actions do have meaning. This is the fact that, when I isolate them from the flux of experience and consider them attentively, I then do find them to be meaningful in the sense that I am able to find in them an underlying meaning.

24. See Weigert (1975) for a critical exposition of Schütz's theory of motivation.

25. Characterizing 'genuine because-statements' as referring necessarily to past projects motivated by events that are even further past has huge implications for any delineation of the scope and aim of social science. Recall that Mises drew a sharp distinction

between praxeology (theoretical social science) and history (applied social science). In Mises's (1949: p. 51) view, praxeology employs conceptual cognition and aims at explaining 'what is necessary [and universal] in human action.' History, on the other hand, aims at understanding specific historical events. Recast in Schützian language, providing genuine because-statements is, thus, the province of historical sciences. Praxeology is an interpretive frame that can, at best, reveal what Schütz called 'pseudo-because-motives.'

26. Schütz calls this tracing back a move from the objective meaning to the subjective. As he (1967: p. 217) writes,

> it is only when I begin to grasp the other person's point of view as such, or, in our terminology, only when I make the leap from the objective to the subjective context of meaning, that I am entitled to say that I understand him ... Now, we have already seen that all knowledge of the subjective experiences of others must be obtained signitively ... we can start out from the external sign itself and, regarding it as a product, trace it back to the original actions and subjective experiences of its inventor or user. This is how, within the world of signs, the transition is made from the objective to the subjective context of meaning.

I should note that 'objective meaning,' for Schütz (ibid.: pp. 31, 33), can be defined both negatively (in other words, the meaning of an act that's different than the actor's intended meaning) and positively (in other words, the meaning of a sign or the product of an act that is intelligible in its own right). See Storr (2010) for a discussion of Schütz's views on objectivity.

27. I should note that the book where this concept is developed was completed after Schütz's death by his co-author and former student Thomas Luckmann. As Schütz's biographer Barber (2004: p. 220) describes,

> On the basis of Schütz's manuscripts (in the form of notebooks) Thomas Luckmann brought The Structure of the Life-World to its final form ... Luckmann ... altered Schütz's plans, expanding a section on typifications in the third chapter on the subjective stock of knowledge [and] producing an entirely new chapter, the fourth, on knowledge and society.

The arguments presented in these sections, however, draw heavily on Schütz's work in this area and fit neatly into his body of work. See Schütz (1967: pp. 78–83) for Schütz's own writings on the stock of knowledge.

28. Admittedly, the social stock of knowledge does not map neatly into culture. There are, indeed, times when the social stock of knowledge appears to be more akin to institutions as 'points of orientation' than culture as 'patterns of meaning.' Schütz did not, however, seem to have this distinction in mind, and he ascribed both functions to the 'social stock of knowledge.'

29. As Lie (1997) describes, 'the neoclassical market is shorn of social relations, institutions, or technology and is devoid of elementary sociological concerns such as power, norms, and networks.' Arguably, there are good reasons why economists pay such scant attention to the market. As Coase (1988: p. 7) explains,

> this [absence of the market in economic theory] is less strange than it seems. Markets are institutions that exist to facilitate exchange, that is, they exist in order to reduce the cost of carrying out exchange transactions. In an economic theory which assumes that transaction costs are nonexistent, markets have no function to perform.

30. As I explain in Chapter 5 of *Understanding the Culture of Markets* (Storr 2013), this does not imply an acceptance of radical cultural relativism. It is instead an acknowledgement

that, though rationality is universal, the culturally specific ways of interpreting those
circumstances that influence our choices are not universal.

31. I have left aside issues such as whether or not the price change constitutes a significant
     enough change to warrant notice, which is more obviously culturally conditioned.
32. The problem, of course, does not go away if we allow her to make errors but assume
     that on average the group of individuals to which she belongs will interpret the price
     change correctly or that the group will not make systematic errors in making their
     assessments. We can argue that systematic errors are not a problem, because the market
     corrects errors. But, we should remember, the market corrects errors by offering feed-
     back to market actors (in other words, profits when people behave as they should and
     losses when individuals make errors). That feedback also has to be interpreted. And to
     assume that those feedback mechanisms will be correctly interpreted is to assume that
     for the most part group members possess the appropriate cultural frame. The point here
     is not that assuming that group members by and large possess the appropriate cultural
     frame is an unreasonable assumption. Group members would soon die off if their cul-
     tural frames allowed for systematic errors across a wide range of activities. The point
     here is simply that assuming that group members by and large possess the appropriate
     cultural frame is a necessary assumption of this theoretical position.
33. Lavoie (this volume, Chapter 3) has, similarly, argued that 'Entrepreneurship neces-
     sarily takes place within culture, it is utterly shaped by culture, and it fundamentally
     consists in interpreting and influencing culture. Consequently, the social scientist can
     understand it only if he is willing to immerse himself in the cultural context in which the
     entrepreneurial process occurs.'
     Additionally, as Lavoie and Chamlee-Wright (this volume, Chapter 7) write,

> one of the main things that directs the entrepreneur's vision is culture.
> Entrepreneurial decision-making is not some sort of pure calculation but a complex
> reading of the polysemic dialogue of the market. It is necessarily embedded within
> a cultural context . . . culture provides a framework of meaning that allows entre-
> preneurs to make sense of all the various, often conflicting pieces of information
> [they have available to them]. Culture gives shape to the interpretive process that is
> entrepreneurship.

REFERENCES

Acemoglu, D. and J. Robinson (2010), 'Why Is Africa Poor?,' *Economic History of
     Developing Regions*, **25**(1), 21–50.
Barber, M. (2004), *The Participating Citizen: A Biography of Alfred Schütz*,
     Albany, NY: SUNY Press.
Baumol, W. (1990), 'Entrepreneurship: Productive, Unproductive, and
     Destructive,' *Journal of Political Economy*, **98**(5) part 1, 893–921.
Beugelsdijk, S. and R. Maseland (2011), *Culture in Economics: History,
     Methodological Reflections, and Contemporary Applications*, Cambridge:
     Cambridge University Press.
Billig, M. (2000), 'Institutions and Culture: Neo-Weberian Economic
     Anthropology,' *Journal of Economic Issues*, **34**, 771–88.
Bird-David, N. (1990), 'The Giving Environment: Another Perspective on the
     Economic System of Gatherer-Hunters,' *Current Anthropology*, **31**(2), 189–96.
Bird-David, N. (1992a), 'Beyond "The Affluent Society": A Culturalist
     Reformulation, and Discussion,' *Current Anthropology*, **33**, 25–34.
Bird-David, N. (1992b), 'Beyond "The Hunting and Gathering Mode of

Subsistence": Culture-Sensitive Observations on the Nayaka and Other Modern Hunter-Gatherers,' *Man*, **27**, 19–44.

Bisin, A. and T. Verdier (2000), 'A Model of Cultural Transmission, Voting and Political Ideology,' *European Journal of Political Economy*, **16**, 5–29.

Bisin, A. and T. Verdier (2001), 'The Economics of Cultural Transmission and the Dynamics of Preferences,' *Journal of Economic Theory*, **2**, 298–319.

Bisin, A. and T. Verdier (2011), 'The Economics of Cultural Transmission and Socialization,' in J. Benhabib, A. Bisin and M. Jackson (eds.), *Handbook of Social Economics*, Amsterdam: North-Holland, pp. 340–416.

Bisin, A., G. Topa and T. Verdier (2004), 'Cooperation as a Transmitted Trait,' *Rationality and Society*, **16**, 477–507.

Bisin, A., G. Topa and T. Verdier (2009), 'Cultural Transmission, Socialization, and the Population Dynamics of Multiple-State Traits Distributions,' *International Journal of Economic Theory*, **5**, 139–54.

Boland, L. (1979), 'A Critique of Friedman's Critics,' *Journal of Economic Literature*, **27**, 503–22.

Browne, K. (2004), *Creole Economics: Cunning under the French Flag*, Austin: University of Texas Press.

Casson, M. and A. Godley (eds.) (2000), *Cultural Factors in Economic Growth*, New York: Springer.

Coase, R. (1988), *The Firm, the Market, and the Law*, Chicago: University of Chicago Press.

DiMaggio, P. (1979), 'Review Essay: On Pierre Bourdieu,' *American Journal of Sociology*, **84**(6), 1460–74.

Friedman, M. (1953), *Essays in Positive Economics*, Chicago: University of Chicago Press.

Fukuyama, F. (2001), 'Culture and Economic Development: Cultural Concerns,' in N.J. Smelser and P. Baltes (eds.), *International Encyclopedia of the Social and Behavioral Sciences*, Oxford: Pergamon, pp. 3130–34.

Gadamer, H. (1994), 'What Is Truth?,' in B. Wachterhauser (ed.), *Hermeneutics and Truth*, Evanston, IL: Northwestern University Press, pp. 33–46.

Geertz, C. (1963), *Peddlers and Princes: Social Development and Economic Growth in Two Indonesian Towns*, Princeton, NJ: Princeton University Press.

Geertz, C. (1973), *The Interpretation of Cultures: Selected Essays*, New York: Basic Books.

Glaeser, E., D. Laibson, J. Scheinkman and C. Soutter (2000), 'Measuring Trust,' *Quarterly Journal of Economics*, **115**, 811–46.

Greif, A. (1994), 'Cultural Beliefs and the Organization of Society: A Historical and Theoretical Reflection on Collectivist and Individualist Societies,' *Journal of Political Economy*, **102**(5), 912–50.

Gudeman, S. (1986), *Economics as Culture: Models and Metaphors of Livelihood*, London: Routledge.

Guiso, L., P. Sapienza and L. Zingales (2006), 'Does Culture Affect Economic Outcomes?,' *Journal of Economic Perspectives*, **20**(2), 23–48.

Harrison, L. (2006), *The Central Liberal Truth: How Politics Can Change a Culture and Save It from Itself*, New York: Oxford University Press.

Hayek, F.A. (1942), 'Scientism and the Study of Society,' *Economica*, **9**(35), 267–91.

Hayek, F.A. (1943), *The Road to Serfdom*, Chicago: University of Chicago Press.

Hayek, F.A. (1948), *Individualism and Economic Order*, Chicago: University of Chicago Press.

Hayek, F.A. (1964), 'The Theory of Complex Phenomena,' in M.A. Bunge (ed.), *The Critical Approach to Science and Philosophy: Essays in Honor of Karl R. Popper*, New York: Free Press of Glencoe.

Hayek, F.A. (1979), *The Counter-Revolution of Science: Studies on the Abuse of Reason*, Indianapolis, IN: Liberty Fund.

Henrich, J. (2002), 'Decision-Making, Cultural Transmission and Adaptation in Economic Anthropology,' in J. Ensminger (ed.), *Theory in Economic Anthropology*, Walnut Creek, CA: Altamira Press, pp. 251–89.

Hirshleifer, J. (1985), 'The Expanding Domain of Economics,' *American Economic Review*, **75**(6), 53–68.

Jackson, W. (2009), *Economics, Culture and Social Theory*, Cheltenham, UK and Northampton, MA, USA: Edward Elgar Publishing.

Jones, E. (1995), 'Culture and Its Relationship to Economic Change,' *Journal of Institutional and Theoretical Economics*, **151**(2), 269–85.

Jones, E. (2006), *Cultures Merging: A Historical and Economic Critique of Culture*, Princeton, NJ: Princeton University Press.

Kirzner, I. (1973), *Competition and Entrepreneurship*, Chicago: University of Chicago Press.

Kirzner, I. (1994), 'Book Review: Brigitte Berger (editor), *The Culture of Entrepreneurship*,' *Advances in Austrian Economics*, **1**, 327–30.

Knack, S. and P. Keefer (1997), 'Does Social Capital Have an Economic Payoff? A Cross-Country Investigation,' *Quarterly Journal of Economics*, **112**(4), 1251–88.

Knight, F. (1990), *The Caribbean: The Genesis of a Fragmented Nationalism*, New York: Oxford University Press.

Kreps, D. (1990), 'Corporate Culture and Economic Theory,' in J. Alt and K. Shepsle (eds.), *Perspectives on Positive Political Economy*, Cambridge: Cambridge University Press, pp. 90–143.

Lavoie, D. (1994), 'Cultural Studies and the Conditions for Entrepreneurship,' in W. Boxx and G.M. Quinlivan (eds.), *The Cultural Context of Economics and Politics*, Lanham, MD: University Press of America, pp. 51–70.

Levin, P. (2008), 'Culture and Markets: How Economic Sociology Conceptualizes Culture,' *Annals of the American Academy of Political and Social Science*, **619**, 114–29.

Lie, J. (1997), 'Sociology of Markets,' *Annual Review of Sociology*, **23**, 341–60.

Marshall, A. (1890), *Principles of Economics*, London: Macmillan.

Mill, J.S. (1848), *Principles of Political Economy with Some of Their Applications to Social Philosophy*, London: Longmans, Green.

Mises, L. von (1949), *Human Action: A Treatise on Economics*, Auburn, AL: Ludwig von Mises Institute.

Mises, L. von (2003), *Epistemological Problems of Economics*, Auburn, AL: Ludwig von Mises Institute.

Nee, V. (1998), 'Norms and Networks in Economic and Organizational Performance,' *American Economic Review*, **88**(2), 85–9.

North, D. (1977), 'Markets and Other Allocation Systems in History: The Challenge of Karl Polanyi,' *Journal of European Economic History*, **6**, 703–16.

North, D. (2005), *Understanding the Process of Economic Change*, Princeton, NJ: Princeton University Press.

Parsons, T. (1935), 'Sociological Elements in Economic Thought,' *Quarterly Journal of Economics*, **49**(3), 414–53.

Parsons, T. (1937), *The Structure of Social Action*, Columbus, OH: McGraw-Hill.

Robbins, L. ([1932] 1945), *An Essay on the Nature and Significance of Economic Science*, London: Macmillan.

Ryle, G. (2009), 'The Thinking of Thoughts: What Is "Le Penseur" Doing?,' in *Collected Essays 1929–1968: Collected Papers*, Vol. 2, New York: Routledge.

Say, J.B. (1803), *A Treatise on Political Economy*, Philadelphia, PA: Lippincott, Grambo.

Schütz, A. (1967), *The Phenomenology of the Social World*, Evanston, IL: Northwestern University Press.

Schütz, A. and T. Luckmann (1973), *The Structures of the Life-World*, Evanston, IL: Northwestern University Press.

Smith, A. (1776), *An Inquiry into the Nature and Causes of the Wealth of Nations*, London: Methuen.

Stigler, G. (1967), 'Imperfections in the Capital Market,' *Journal of Political Economy*, **75**(3), 287–92.

Stigler, G. (1984), 'Economics: The Imperial Science?,' *Scandinavian Journal of Economics*, **86**(3), 301–13.

Stigler, G. and G. Becker (1977), 'De Gustibus Non Est Disputandum,' *American Economic Review*, **67**(2), 76–90.

Storr, Virgil Henry (2008), 'The Market as a Social Space: On the Meaningful Extra-Economic Conversations That Can Occur in Markets,' *Review of Austrian Economics*, **21**(2–3), 135–50.

Storr, Virgil Henry (2010), 'The Social Construction of the Market,' *Society*, **47**(3), 200–206.

Storr, Virgil Henry (2013), *Understanding the Culture of Markets*, New York: Routledge.

Swedberg, R. (1994), 'Markets as Social Structures,' in N. Smelser and R. Swedberg (eds.), *The Handbook of Economic Sociology*, Princeton, NJ: Princeton University Press, pp. 255–82.

Swedberg, R. (2003), *Principles of Economic Sociology*, Princeton, NJ: Princeton University Press.

Tabellini, G. (2008), 'Presidential Address: Institutions and Culture,' *Journal of the European Economic Association*, **6**(2–3), 255–94.

Tabellini, G. (2010), 'Culture and Institutions: Economic Development in the Regions of Europe,' *Journal of the European Economic Association*, **8**(4), 677–716.

Weigert, A. (1975), 'Alfred Schütz on a Theory of Motivation,' *Pacific Sociological Review*, **18**(1), 83–102.

Wilk, R. and L. Cliggett (2007), *Economies and Cultures*, Boulder, CO: Westview Press.

Zelizer, V.A. (1978), 'Human Values and the Market: The Case of Life Insurance and Death in 19th-Century America,' *American Journal of Sociology*, **84**(3), 591–610.

Zelizer, V.A. (1988), 'From Baby Farms to Baby M,' *Society*, **25**(3), 23–8.

Zelizer, V.A. (2010), *Economic Lives: How Culture Shapes the Economy*, Princeton, NJ: Princeton University Press.

Zukin, S. and P. DiMaggio (1990), *Structures of Capital: The Social Organization of the Economy*, Cambridge: Cambridge University Press.

3. The discovery and interpretation of profit opportunities: culture and the Kirznerian entrepreneur*

Don Lavoie

It is beginning to be evident that the vast literature on growth and development conceals a yawning gap. This void refers to an understanding of the role of the entrepreneur in economic development, both at the theoretical level and at the level of past and prospective economic history . . .
In the literature dealing more narrowly with growth models, this hiatus is almost complete and is hardly surprising in view of its predominant concern with macroeconomic relationships. In contrast, the literature dealing with development proper gives some attention to entrepreneurship, although little effort has been devoted to formulating a clear theoretical understanding of the entrepreneurial role. (Israel Kirzner, *Perception, Opportunity, and Profit*, 1979)

3.1 INTRODUCTION

There is an increasing recognition that to understand economic development we need an adequate theory of entrepreneurship. The entrepreneur is the driving force of economic change, bringing innovation, creativity, and coordination to the economy. Centrally planned economies are widely thought to have failed, at least in part, because they left little scope for the entrepreneurial process. In the field of economic development, attention is shifting from attempts to engineer economic improvements from the top down to attempts to design institutions that enable entrepreneurship to flourish and produce development from the bottom up. A theory of entrepreneurship should help us identify the conditions—economic, political, legal, and cultural—that enhance decentralized developmental processes.[1]

Social scientists in general, and economists in particular, often refer to entrepreneurship in a manner that suggests that culture has little to do with it. Indeed, mainstream social science has, with the notable exception of anthropology, largely ignored culture not only as it might pertain to entrepreneurship but also as it might pertain to any other aspect of society. Political scientists, sociologists, and economists typically depict the social process as a causal mechanism, rather than as a means of establishing meaningful human discourse and understanding.[2] The methodological task of the social scientist is understood to be discerning regularities in objective patterns of change but not coming to terms with what these changes mean to human agents or how this meaning contributes to the causes of change. Social scientists see culture in general as a matter for the humanities, not for the social sciences.

To the extent that social scientific research on entrepreneurship takes culture into account at all, such research usually seeks only to identify those cultural groups whose individual members have greater than average entrepreneurial traits. Entrepreneurship is in this case being treated as a psychological attribute of individual people. It is the distribution of individual psychological traits within populations categorized by culture, rather than features of the culture as a whole, that is being examined. We all know, for example, that the overseas Chinese are very entrepreneurial, but we do not seem to know much about *why* they are. To be sure, even finding such culturally specific patterns is an important contribution, because the patterns may suggest possibilities for answering the 'why' question. The social sciences, however, do not appear to be making much progress on that crucial explanatory front. In the social sciences, culture is little more than an aggregative classification for grouping individuals, not a substantive theoretical notion in its own right (Lavoie and Chamlee-Wright, this volume, Chapter 7; Aligica and Matei, this volume, Chapter 13).

For the purposes of this chapter, culture is to be understood broadly as the complex of meanings that allows us to comprehend human action; it is the background context that renders purposeful action intelligible. Culture is the language in which past events are interpreted, future circumstances are anticipated, and plans of action are formulated. Although not a language in the sense of a static set of words and grammatical rules, culture is a discourse. This view has been most eloquently articulated in Hans-Georg Gadamer's philosophy of hermeneutics. Language, in this view, is a continually evolving conversation, an open-ended communicative process (Gadamer [1960] 1989). As such it is a complex phenomenon in its own right, which, if it is to be taken seriously, requires explicit theoretical attention by the social scientist.[3]

Unfortunately, the scholars in the humanities who seem to have taken culture more seriously have had little to say about its processual nature. One reason the cultural side of entrepreneurship has been neglected is that anthropologists, who have examined culture more thoroughly than anyone else, have generally restricted themselves to statics rather than dynamics. Researchers have concentrated on getting a snapshot of a cultural pattern already in place, rather than understanding the circumstances that bring about change. Neither the ways culture shapes developments in economic, political, or social institutions, not the ways those institutions influence culture, nor the ways culture reshapes itself, leading to different cultural patterns in the future, have been as well researched as the various cultural 'stills' have been. In other words, the study of the relationship between culture and entrepreneurship demands working with both meaning and economic change, whereas, the way disciplinary divisions have evolved, few researchers are capable of handling both categories together.[4]

Perhaps more than other social scientists, economists have failed to leave room for meaning and have not done well with change either. Even though some economists claim to study causal change, their methodological approach tends to neglect the radical change generally thought to be involved in entrepreneurship. Change usually appears in economists' models only as deterministic tendencies toward a fixed equilibrium, like the movements of a clockwork mechanism, not as a truly creative process. Thus economists usually explain entrepreneurial action as maximizing an objective function according to given constraints. To act entrepreneurially is simply to take advantage of concrete profit opportunities neglected by others. Success is a matter of who takes the initiative, of who is alert and exploits the gains that are 'out there' to be found in the objective situation. Profit opportunities are conceived as quantitative facts that are strictly dictated by the measurable discrepancy between costs and revenues. Culture, in this view, merely shapes what kinds of goods the society happens to prefer, the subjective meaning that goods have to people, not the objective economic circumstances and causal processes with which economic science is concerned. Culture is seen to pertain to the underlying conditions that precede the economic process that entrepreneurship propels, not to the process itself.

This chapter clarifies some aspects of the entrepreneurial process and argues that culture has everything to do with it. Entrepreneurship necessarily takes place within culture, it is utterly shaped by culture, and it fundamentally consists in interpreting and influencing culture. Consequently, the social scientist can understand it only if he is willing to immerse himself in the cultural context in which the entrepreneurial process occurs.

The purpose here is not to develop a whole theory of entrepreneurship as a cultural process, but to sketch some of the main elements such a theory would need.[5] Two properties of entrepreneurship that need to be accounted for better are connoted by the notions of 'discovery' and 'interpretation.' Discovery suggests an element of radical change, a surprising find, an unanticipated break with past patterns. In discussions of economic development, entrepreneurship entails a capacity to introduce new products, new production methods, new marketing strategies—in general, things not already contained in the previous situation. Entrepreneurship should include genuine novelty and creativity and should not be rendered as a mechanical search for pre-existing profit opportunities.

Interpretation suggests the point that the profit opportunities entrepreneurs discover are not a matter of objective observations of quantities, but a matter of perspectival interpretation, a discerning of the intersubjective meaning of a qualitative situation. Profits are not measured; they are 'read.' Entrepreneurship, I argue, is primarily a cultural process. The seeing of profit opportunities is a matter of cultural interpretation. And, like any other interpretation, this reading of profit opportunities necessarily takes place within a larger context of meaning, against a background of discursive practices, a culture. That is to say, entrepreneurship is the achievement not so much of the isolated maverick who finds objective profits others overlooked as of the culturally embedded participant who picks up the gist of a conversation.

The words 'discovery' and 'interpretation' also have connotations that pull in opposite, undesirable directions, which I would like to try to avoid partly by taking them together. To some people 'discovery' suggests that the thing to be discovered is already there before the discovery process begins, that the process merely 'uncovers' something latent in the objective circumstances. And, to many, 'interpretation' suggests an arbitrariness, as in the phrase 'That is just a matter of interpretation.' I believe that proper theory of entrepreneurship needs to steer between the rigid objectivism of seeing all change as latent in previous circumstances and the flaccid relativism of seeing change as utterly arbitrary. The objectivistic extreme, toward which most mainstream economics tends, reduces change to mere mechanistic dynamics. The relativistic extreme, toward which some leading critics of mainstream economics are thought to tend, seems to make change unintelligible. What is needed is a theory of entrepreneurial change that makes it intelligible without reducing it to a predetermined mechanism.

One school of economics, the so-called market-process or Austrian school, has partially overcome these difficulties. Its critique of mainstream economics can serve as a useful point of departure for my own discussion. The work of Ludwig von Mises, Friedrich A. Hayek, and others provides a promising alternative to mainstream economics for both aspects of entrepreneurship the mainstream has neglected. In von Mises's insistence on the principle he calls 'subjectivism,' meaning is made central to economic theorizing.[6] In Hayek's notion of 'spontaneous order' the idea of radical change is incorporated into a theory of nondeterministic evolutionary processes, and in his latest book he applies this spontaneous order approach to culture (Hayek 1988). Here, I believe, are the building blocks for a substantive theory of the cultural dimension of entrepreneurship.

Of all the contributors to the market-process school, Israel Kirzner has undoubtedly had the most to say about the nature of entrepreneurship. His work elaborates on the interpretive aspect of von Mises as well as the discovery aspect of Hayek and is especially helpful in connecting them together. Although I believe his work is the best in economics on the subject, I argue that as it stands it does not adequately account for culture.

3.2   MAXIMIZING AND THE KIRZNERIAN CRITIQUE

A market consisting exclusively of economizing, maximizing individuals does not generate the market process we seek to understand. For the market process to emerge, we require in addition an element which is itself not comprehensible within the narrow conceptual limits of economizing behavior. This element in the market . . . is best identified as entrepreneurship. (Kirzner, 1963b)

Building on the strengths of his mentors, von Mises and Hayek, Kirzner expands on the implications of their economics for entrepreneurial processes. Under the influence of von Mises's methodological principle of subjectivism, Kirzner's theory emphasizes the importance of the interpretive perspective of the human actor. Action is meaningful only in relation to the purposes, plans, and expectations of the actor. The actor's objective circumstances are not important in themselves, but the specific opportunities and constraints he perceives are. Action, Kirzner says, is not a direct confrontation with objective reality itself but always takes place within an interpretive framework.[7]

Under the influence of Hayek's work on spontaneous order, Kirzner's theory stresses entrepreneurial competition as a discovery procedure, not a predetermined mechanism. The competitive process works through a continuous, multidirectional, and rivalrous tugging and pulling of separate minds and actions, thereby generating an overall order greater than can be comprehended by its participating individuals. In this sense, the process is recognized to be a radically social one, fundamentally dependent on the free interplay of the individuals but not reducible to them. The function of such competition is to disclose information that cannot be obtained in any other way (Hayek 1948; Lavoie 1985b).[8]

Kirzner locates the difficulty mainstream economics faces in its fundamental notion of individual choice as a matter of 'maximizing.' The favorite theoretical device of economists is the idea of the maximization of a given goal subject to given constraints. Scarce means are described as being deliberately deployed to yield a maximum in regard to predetermined ends.

Mainstream economics typically deploys the maximizing idea on two levels, the individual choice level, where what is maximized is called utility, and the market level, where what is maximized is wealth. For the individual, his preferences, objective opportunities, and constraints are taken as the inputs, and the analysis focuses on the individual's choice as a solution to this maximization problem (this is sometimes called the economics of Robinson Crusoe). Economists contend that this mental experiment provides a general theory of human action, which can serve as a basis for looking at the specific properties of action within market contexts. Human action in general can be interpreted as attempts by individuals to exchange one state of affairs for another, whether they are making exchanges with nature or with one another. The innovative aspect of action can then be theoretically isolated as individual entrepreneurship. 'Psychic profit' is the name economists give to the perceived gain the entrepreneur reaps when he exploits an opportunity.

Such individual mental experiments of Robinson Crusoe economics are then combined into a 'market experiment,' where the hypothetical choices of the various individuals are the inputs and an equilibrium solution, a pattern of mutually compatible choices, is taken as the output.[9] Parallel to psychic profit on the individual level is money profit on the market level. In this way the analysis focuses in turn on the way preferences interact with objective circumstances to yield individual choices and then on the way these choices interact with one another to yield a social outcome.[10]

Kirzner's theory also proceeds on these two levels, so that he identifies what he calls Crusoe entrepreneurship as an aspect of individual choice that eludes the maximizing framework, and what he calls market entrepreneurship as an aspect of social situations that eludes equilibrium analysis. The difficulty at the individual level, Kirzner argues, is not with the maximizing notion itself but with the crucial questions it begs when it takes goals and constraints as given. Human action encompasses more than the mechanical performance of maximization exercises within given choice frameworks; there is also the process by which actors develop those frameworks. Likewise, the problem with treating the interplay of choices in the marketplace as an attempt to find an equilibrium solution involving complete mutual coordination is not, Kirzner says, a problem with the equilibrium concept itself. The difficulty is that equilibrium analysis leaves out the process by which a degree of mutual coordination is achieved. Mainstream economics, according to Kirzner, is not so much wrong as simply incomplete, and on both the individual and the market levels it needs to add a theory of entrepreneurship (1979: pp. 154–81).[11]

Economists' fondness for maximizing and equilibrium leads them to try to subsume entrepreneurship under these concepts. When Crusoe, for example, makes the entrepreneurial discovery of how to use vine to produce a fishnet, mainstream economics treats it as a deliberate allocation of his scarce attention to the discovery of hitherto unknown production processes. In a broader social context, the arbitrage entrepreneur who discovers an opportunity to buy low in one market and sell high in another is treated as allocating his entrepreneurial attention to this discovery. Entrepreneurship, then, is a scarce resource like any other, which needs to be deployed economically.

Kirzner argues that the attempt to treat entrepreneurship just like any other scarce resource is a mistake. He suggests the idea of 'alertness' to new opportunities as something that cannot be subsumed within a given maximizing problem. To treat the discovery of an arbitrage opportunity as itself a maximizing problem presupposes that the opportunity was already within the entrepreneur's choice framework, in which case it was not in need of discovery in the first place. As Kirzner puts it, entrepreneurial alertness 'is not an ingredient to be deployed in decision-making; it is rather something in which the decision itself is embedded and without which it would be unthinkable.' He goes on to say:

> If an entrepreneur's discovery of a lucrative arbitrage opportunity galvanizes him into immediate action to capture the perceived gain, it will not do to describe the situation as one in which the entrepreneur has 'decided' to use his alertness to capture this gain. He has not 'deployed' his hunch for a specific purpose; rather, his hunch has propelled him to make his entrepreneurial purchase and sale. The entrepreneur never sees his hunches as potential inputs about which he must decide whether they are to be used. (1985: pp. 21–2)

Thus Kirzner argues that there is something primordial about entrepreneurial discovery, something that involves the creation of a choice framework, so that it cannot be treated as itself a consequence of maximizing within that framework. Important policy implications follow from the primordial nature of entrepreneurial discovery. If discovery is not simply a scarce resource that can be rationally allocated to predefined goals, then policies designed to enhance entrepreneurship need to recognize that fact. As Kirzner has pointed out, discovery cannot be centrally engineered; it can only be cultivated by setting in place conditions in which the decentralized, entrepreneurial process can be expected to flourish.[12]

The approach to discovery Kirzner defends explicitly strives to steer between the two hazards I referred to above as objectivism and relativism. Kirzner takes T.W. Schultz, the famous development economist, as an example of the extreme that makes the entrepreneur's action purely responsive to prior circumstances, leaving no room for true novelty. He takes G.L.S. Shackle, the great critic of mainstream economics, as an example of the other extreme, which makes the entrepreneur's action purely initiatory, leaving no room for any intelligible systematic connectedness with the previous circumstances:

> The one view sees the entrepreneur as responding systematically and frictionlessly to the conditions of the market, with pure entrepreneurial profit the smoothly corresponding reward that these market conditions require and make possible. From this perspective entrepreneurship is 'called forth' systematically, if not quite predictably, by these market conditions . . . The second view sees entrepreneurship not as *responding to* external market conditions, but as independently and spontaneously *injecting* new elements *into* those conditions, in a manner totally unpredictable from and wholly undetermined by existing circumstances. (Kirzner 1985: pp. 8–9)

The hazards have, I believe, been appropriately identified by Kirzner here, even if we may not completely agree with his interpretations of Schultz and Shackle. Navigating between the hazards is particularly difficult because of the prevailing notions in economics about causal explanation. To many economists, explanations that are not fully mechanistic are necessarily unintelligible (Klamer 1983).[13] Indeed, in the next section I suggest that Kirzner's theory has not completely avoided these hazards. The general approach to intelligible causation arising from the modern market-process school does, I think, offer a way to avoid these hazards by making room for what I have called the discovery and interpretation aspects of entrepreneurship.

To me, the greatest strength of Kirzner's contribution lies not only in making room for discovery and interpretation, but in linking them together. According to mainstream economics, individual choice takes place within a given interpretation of opportunities and constraints. Discovery for Kirzner necessitates the transcending of the prior interpretive framework and the emergence of a new one. Thus, Crusoe interprets his world in a fundamentally different way after he discovers the possibility of producing fishnet out of vine. Where before he had seen vine only as an obstacle, as something to avoid getting tangled up in, he now sees it as an opportunity to make psychic profits. As phenomenological philosophers put the point, we do not see an objective thing; we always see something *as* a certain kind of thing. The vine seen as an obstacle is a radically different kind of thing from the vine seen as a possible fishnet. 'Seeing,' then, is itself interpreting.

Similarly, in the social context the arbitrageur interprets the world in a fundamentally different way after he has discovered the price discrepancy others had overlooked. The alert arbitrageur sees prices others consider of no particular interest as an opportunity to make money profits. According to Kirzner's subjectivist approach, then, human action has to be understood as something that is interpreted from a particular perspective. Discovery amounts to a shift in such perspectives, a fundamental change in the way the opportunities and constraints are seen.

3.3   LIMITATIONS OF KIRZNER'S THEORY OF THE ENTREPRENEUR

> Although maximizing is . . . a part of market process theory, it is not the fundamental notion. Human action is. Human action is partly guided by maximizing, but it is also guided by other mental processes. Alertness, creativity, and judgment also influence what we do. The primary importance of action to economic theory is that it sets in motion a market process. (High 1982)

If Kirzner benefits from the strengths of his teachers, von Mises and Hayek, he has also inherited some of their apparent shortcomings. Although Hayek's contribution points toward a nonmechanistic rendering of discovery processes, most of his work in economics ties the process to the notion of equilibrium, which appears to keep it within a mechanistic framework.[14] Whereas mainstream economics is pre-occupied with states of equilibrium, Hayek sometimes seems to be only drawing attention to the systematic tendencies by which equilibrium is achieved. As Hayek's own later work on spontaneous order shows, though, this equilibration approach fundamentally depends on a strict distinction between the data, usually said to be tastes and resources, and the entrepreneurial process, which systematically pushes the economy toward the equilibrium. Changes in the data, which are thought to exhibit no systematic patterns, are disequilibrating, in the sense that they redefine the equilibrium toward which the economy tends. Only in his more recent work—and primarily in the context of law and culture as spontaneous orders, rather than in the context of economic questions—has Hayek decisively moved beyond the equilibrium style of thinking. This more recent work understands spontaneous orders as open-ended and genuinely creative evolutionary processes, rather than mechanisms that focus on a predetermined end state (Hayek 1973, 1976, 1979, 1988).[15]

Kirzner has not been willing to follow some of Hayek's extensions of spontaneous order theory to nonmarket phenomena, clinging to Hayek's earlier position that entrepreneurship is a strictly equilibrating process. Discovery, for Kirzner, brings about a systematic tendency toward an equilibrium, even though long before that equilibrium is reached the data are bound to change, impelling the market away from that equilibrium. Even when talking specifically about grasping future opportunities, Kirzner insists on treating them as equilibrating, as in some sense finding their way toward a pre-existing equilibrium. Although this is an attempt to deal with radical change, talking about grasping opportunities that are already 'out there' obscures the genuinely creative element of entrepreneurship. Despite his warning that Schultz's approach reduces entrepreneurial action to a purely responsive role, Kirzner's theory also seems to treat the entrepreneur's action as something 'called forth' by prior circumstances. Entrepreneurship appears to be a passive reaction to the equilibrium dictated by the data. A number of critics have charged that Kirzner's theory falls into the very problem he has identified in mainstream economics, ultimately leaving no room for genuine novelty, for truly creative change.[16] Although von Mises's economics leans more toward an interpretive orientation than can be found in mainstream economics, von Mises was not willing or able to go all the way to a fully interpretive approach. Kirzner too seems unwilling to commit himself fully to an interpretive economics. Part of the difficulty, I believe, is their use of the Robinson Crusoe starting point, an issue to which I will return briefly at the conclusion. Much of the problem with Kirzner's theory of the entrepreneur, however, stems from his unfortunate selection of illustrative examples, which seriously distorts his rendering of the interpretive dimension. Although the subjectivism Kirzner inherits from von Mises is perhaps reconcilable with a fully interpretive orientation to entrepreneurship, the examples consistently undercut his argument.

The example par excellence of Kirzner's theory is the pure arbitrageur who simply notices a profit opportunity. By making this special case stand for entrepreneurship in general, Kirzner makes alertness the 'essence' of entrepreneurial action. The theory has come under criticism by other market-process economists on the grounds that alertness in itself is insufficient to cover all the aspects of entrepreneurship that maximizing leaves out. As Jack High (1982) argues, creativity and judgment are also involved in entrepreneurship. I would add only that a crucial component of judgment and creativity is interpretation. The arbitrageur immediately 'sees' the chance to buy low and sell high. The case is misleading in that the interpretation is trivial and has already taken place. Kirzner likens the arbitrageur's discovery of profit to finding a 20-dollar bill on the beach. This example reinforces the impression of profit that one gets from mainstream economics, that it is an objective 'find' that does not require interpretation. Most acts of entrepreneurship are not like an isolated individual finding things on beaches; they require efforts of the creative imagination, skillful judgments of future cost and revenue possibilities, and an ability to read the significance of complex social situations.

   The Kirznerian entrepreneur 'sees' psychic or money profits—he notices them—but he does not seem to have to read them. He uncovers unambiguous opportunities to improve his situation that others have simply failed to notice, as if fixed collections of things called profits were lying around and certain individuals were just more alert than others in finding them. Being more alert seems to be simply a matter of opening one's eyes to see what is right there under one's nose. I would argue that if entrepreneurship is like vision, though, it is like human vision, which does not see merely patches of color but meaningful things. Like visual perception, it involves focusing on an object *as* a certain sort of thing, seeing it against a background. The profit opportunities the entrepreneur discovers are not directly copied off reality in itself; they are interpreted from a point of view.

   Kirzner insists that, in spite of economists' propensity to assign every choice a cost, the discovery of profit opportunities is 'costless.' He stresses the primordial nature of entrepreneurship by pointing out that an entrepreneur does not *deliberately* set aside a known alternative when he notices a new opportunity. Ex ante, of course, there is no alternative being purposely set aside in the act of noticing something, but surely ex post there will be things that remain unnoticed because attention was directed one way rather than another. Kirzner sometimes seems to be denying even this second, ex-post sense of cost to alertness, making entrepreneurship appear more mysterious than it needs to be. Alertness seems to be some kind of general-purpose attentiveness that is 'switched on or off,' as Kirzner likes to say, or at best is a unidimensional quantity, such that there can be more or less of it, and more is always better. The only opportunity cost of not opening one's eyes, after all, is leaving them closed. The only 'opportunity' forgone by opening one's eyes is seeing nothing at all.

   I do not see why alertness has to appear to be an exception to the economist's principle that costs accrue to any action, that there are necessarily opportunities forgone. Being alert in any one respect implies that one is not being alert in some other respects. Asking one question is passing over the asking of an infinite number of others. The suggestion that alertness has a directedness about it indicates that it is a matter not so much of seeing what is under one's nose as it is of looking or listening for certain kinds of things. This systematic directedness of the discovery process makes some potential opportunities more likely to be found by certain sorts of alertness. In principle, it is conceivable within Kirzner's approach that someone could be perfectly alert—could see 'all the opportunities there are'—even though Kirzner does not believe anybody actually achieves this degree of alertness. Since the very act of paying attention to one aspect of reality inherently involves removing attention from other aspects, however, it makes no sense, even in principle, for someone to be alert to everything. Alertness is multidimensional. It is misleading to treat it like an on/off switch or to say there is simply more or less of it. There are qualitatively diverse ways of being alert.

While Kirzner shows that entrepreneurship involves the displacement of an old framework by a new one, he confines this change to the situation where something under one's nose that was previously ignored gets noticed. In the trivial examples Kirzner uses, profit opportunities are implicitly treated as atomistic—that is, finding a new opportunity need not have any effect on the entrepreneur's understanding of the old opportunities he had already found. But a shift of interpretive framework can bring about a more fundamental change than simply adding to a stock of things that have been noticed.

An interpretive framework can change in a far more profound manner: all the old opportunities will suddenly look different, indeed may no longer be considered opportunities at all, when a new one is found. And of course the circumstances one has been alert to in the past help determine the kinds of situations one will be apt to notice in the future. That is, profit opportunities are not independent atoms but connected parts of a whole perspective on the world. And the perspective is in turn an evolving part of a continuing cultural tradition, constantly being reappropriated to new situations.

The way Kirzner renders the idea of alertness leaves inexplicable the systematic process by which one means/ends framework gets replaced by another. It appears to be an arbitrary matter why some things get noticed before others. In this respect his theory comes dangerously close to the hazard he associates with Shackle, cutting change off from any systematic connection to its history. Taking culture more seriously would allow Kirzner's theory to make the process by which perspectives change more intelligible.

Profit opportunities are not so much like road signs to which we assign an automatic meaning as they are like difficult texts in need of a sustained effort of interpretation. Entrepreneurship is not only a matter of opening one's eyes, of switching on one's attentiveness; it requires directing one's gaze.[17] When an entrepreneur sees things others have overlooked, it is not just that he opened his eyes while they had theirs closed. He is reading selected aspects of a complex situation others have not read. And this raises the question of what gives a predirectedness to the entrepreneur's vision, of why he is apt to read some things and not others. I submit that the answer to this question is culture.

3.4 CRUSOE ECONOMICS, CARTESIAN PHILOSOPHY AND HERMENEUTICS

In learning the language, the child absorbs a way of thinking and of express-ing his thoughts that is predetermined by language, and so he receives a stamp that he can scarcely remove from his life. The language opens up the way for a person exchanging thoughts with all those who use it; he can influence them and receive influence from them. (Mises [1919] 1983)

It is less accurate to suppose that thinking man creates and controls his cultural evolution than it is to say that culture, and evolution, created his reason . . . So far as scientific explanation is concerned, it was not what we know as mind that developed civilization, let alone directed its evolution, but rather mind and civilization which developed or evolved concurrently. What we call mind is not something that the individual is born with, as he is born with his brain, or some-thing that the brain produces, but something that his genetic equipment . . . helps him acquire, as he grows up, from his family and adult fellows by absorb-ing the results of a tradition that is not genetically transmitted . . . Shaped by the environment in which individuals grow up, mind in turn conditions the preservation, development, richness, and variety of traditions on which indi-viduals draw. By being transmitted largely through families, mind preserves a multiplicity of concurrent streams into which each new comer to the commu-nity can delve. It may well be asked whether an individual who did not have the opportunity to tap such a cultural tradition could be said even to have a mind. (Hayek 1988)

I suggest that the reason why the economic theory of entrepreneurship—even when at its best as in the contributions of Kirzner—has not gotten very far in elucidating the cultural dimension is traceable to its Crusoe economics orientation. Economics has based itself more than it realizes on the case of Robinson Crusoe, a fictional, isolated individual confronting the natural world, and has essentially 'added in' Friday, to try to make the analysis into social theory.[18] Choice in general, and thus entrepreneurial choice in particular, is first studied on what is thought to be the more basic Crusoe level and only then complicated by the introduction of other choosing individuals. This analytical procedure has, I believe, led to a failure to grasp fully the radically social element of the human mind and thus of choice.

Questioning the foundational role of Robinson Crusoe is no minor quibble with contemporary economics. Economic theorizing, both in its mainstream and in its market-process variations, usually considers microeconomics the basis of the rest of economics and treats the choice situation of the isolated individual as the basis of microeconomics. The cherished principle economists call 'methodological individualism' is in question here.[19] If this principle claims only that the social whole has no purposes but is a complex resulting from the choices of its participating individuals, then the principle is unobjectionable. To most economists, however, methodological individualism seems to mean more than that. It is generally interpreted as demanding an analytical privileging of the study of the individual over the study of society. It seems to insist that Crusoe, the theoretical construct of an isolated individual, must come first to serve as the foundation of the analysis of markets. As Kirzner put it at the beginning of his book on price theory, 'Society consists of individual human beings' (1963a).[20] We need to make sense of the single individual's actions before we can make sense of the way such actions interact in society. The isolated individual becomes the analytical framework for studying human action in general, of which action in regard to market institutions is then taken as a special case.

When the analysis starts from Crusoe, a special difficulty seems to face the agent when other agents are introduced, since now what he needs to know about includes not only external and observable facts of the natural world but also the contents of the other agents' minds. In the theory of entrepreneurship this presents itself as the problem of how the entrepreneur can come to 'read the minds' of his potential customers, whether they are consumers or producers, and provide what they will want. It is one thing for Crusoe to see a new use for vine, where he has to anticipate only his own wants, but it is a substantially more difficult thing for him to figure out what Friday will want. Something seems highly mysterious, from this perspective, about the entrepreneur's ability to look into the contents of other minds.

This procedure of starting with the individual mind, which is presumed to be a self-contained, unproblematic entity, and then moving on to address the problem of 'Other Minds' has been the mainstream approach in philosophy ever since Descartes. It has come under powerful criticism by a number of contemporary philosophical schools, from which economics could learn a great deal.[21] Among the most interesting critics of Cartesian philosophy is Hans-Georg Gadamer, who shows that the mind is already social before it is rational and thus that a whole variety of special difficulties with the analysis of interpersonal communication prove to be pseudo-problems. The individual agent, Gadamer argues, is already operating within a linguistic process even when he is confronting nature. He is already, as it were, reading other people's minds when he thinks about uses of vine or when he thinks about anything whatsoever. Human beings should have no special difficulty reading the minds of others, since our linguistic practices are tapping into a shared culture all the time.

As the epigraphs by von Mises and Hayek suggest, the market-process school has at least partially glimpsed the main thrust of this critique of Cartesian thinking. The fact that the mind thinks in language, which it acquires in the process of enculturation, makes 'the mind' a profoundly social entity. Although Kirzner is right when he declares that society consists of individual human beings, it is also true that individuals consist of society. They are not isolated, self-contained things but interdependent parts of an integral process of cultural dynamics. All understanding of the natural world is already social understanding, embedded in and meaningful only in relation to culture. The methodological priority given to the rational choice of individual minds implicitly treats them as if they could exist in isolated, cultureless, languageless brains.

The peculiarly cultureless 'agent' of Crusoe economics is an odd construction to use as a basis for human action in general. Choice theory is constructed as if it does not matter whether the mind operates with a social language or not. The Crusoes of economics, unlike the character from Defoe's novel, need know nothing of language. They simply apply means to ends. All the minds we have experience with, though, can conceive of means and ends only through their language, that is, through their ability to tap into the cultural process. If economics aspires to be about human action as we know it, it should take language and cultural transmission seriously. As von Mises put it, we need to 'consider what immense significance language has for thinking and for the expression of thought, for social relations, and for all activities of life' ([1919] 1983: p. 13).

Economists may say in their own defense that economic analysis only begins with this strange, cultureless, Crusoe character and that it then moves on to the theory of markets, where it specifically takes up the mutual influences of individuals on one another. But where one starts can have important influences on the way one moves on. Not enough seems to change when the analysis moves from the individual experiment to the market experiment. The market seems to be populated with many Crusoes, each devoid of culture and communicating with one another only by price 'signals.'

The entrepreneur is typically pictured as a loner bucking the crowd, a maverick who sees things differently from everybody else. This view contains an element of truth, of course, in that the entrepreneur comes upon a new reading of his situation that may be qualitatively different from the readings others have been able to make. But his ability to read new things into a situation is not primarily due to his separateness from others but, indeed, to his higher degree of sensitivity to what others are looking for. The really successful entrepreneurs we know are not unusually separate from others; on the contrary, they are especially well plugged into the culture. What gives them the ability to sense what their customers will want is not some kind of mysterious alertness that gets 'switched on' but their capacity to read the conversations of mankind. They can pick up the sense of where their fellows in the culture stand, what values they adhere to, what purposes they pursue, what they consider beautiful, and what they deem profane.

Different entrepreneurial acts are the readings of, and contributions to, different conversations. The successful supplier of consumer goods listens to the discourse of the consuming public, senses what they will be likely to find attractive and what they will not, and is thereby more persuasive in getting them to try new products. The successful venture capitalist listens to the concerns of the banking community and thereby enhances his ability to persuade the loan officer to make an investment. The successful supplier of innovative industrial inputs listens to the technological conversations of his potential customers, exploits his skill in anticipating their specific requirements, and thereby gains an ability to persuade them to explore hitherto ignored technological possibilities. The successful employer listens to the discourse of existing and potential employees and tries to shape an attractive work environment that will persuade new workers to come and old ones to stay. What makes entrepreneurs successful is their ability to join conversational processes and nudge them in new directions.

Conversational processes about production and consumption plans existed in human societies before the evolution of market processes and provided the foundation on which primordial elements of markets began to evolve. The process by which direct exchange evolved out of reciprocal gift giving and by which money evolved out of exchange must have been a discursive process. Advanced market institutions such as contract law, the price system, accounting conventions, banking methods, and so forth are emergent properties of the process of cultural evolution. A modern market is still a discursive process, but now one in which the participants are able to use not only spoken and written words but also prices, advertising, stock markets, and other media of communication.

Perhaps, then, a better starting point than Crusoe from which to proceed to the analysis of markets would be the premarket communicative process of language and cultural transmission. Rather than consider the interactions of individuals in a market context as fundamentally analogous to Crusoe's isolated actions, we might consider market forms of interaction as fundamentally analogous to linguistic interaction. In particular, Gadamer's theory of language might be a promising place to start. Gadamer's challenging argument—that it is not so much we who speak language as language that speaks us—underscores the point that the process by which we comprehend our world takes place on the social level. If we appreciate the way language constitutes the basis of all understanding, it seems clear that the communicative processes involved in market institutions are emergent extensions of the linguistic process. What existed historically before the emergence of markets was not Robinson Crusoe but processes of cultural evolution in which interacting human beings participated. Markets can be viewed as offshoots of, and complements to, the process of cultural dynamics.[22]

Gadamer's work on the way tradition is 'appropriated' is, I believe, an approach to cultural change that can steer between the hazards Kirzner warns against. It makes change intelligible as something that grows out of history; yet it permits radical, nonmechanistic change. I think the theory of entrepreneurship could more fully account for the discovery and interpretation aspects of economic change if it were built on the hermeneutical theory of language and culture.

NOTES

*   This chapter previously appeared in Brigitte Berger (ed.), *The Culture of Entrepreneurship* (Institute for Contemporary Studies, 1991). It is reprinted here (with minor edits) with the permission of the publisher.

      I would like to thank Arjo Klamer for steering my thoughts in this direction and the participants in the 'Culture of Entrepreneurship' conference and Karen Vaughn for helpful comments on an earlier draft.

1.   I am deliberately confining the idea of entrepreneurship to the creative actions that contribute to economic development in market contexts and will not address entrepreneurial actions in government contexts.

2.   In most of the social sciences, however, there are encouraging signs that culture is being taken more seriously, for example in the studies on political culture, and in the management literature's attention to corporate culture. Yet mainstream social science still treats human society as if it were a cultureless mechanism, and economics remains almost completely oblivious to cultural aspects of economic institutions and processes.

3.   This chapter proceeds using a still-incomplete theory, which I would call an 'interpretive' approach to economics. It has been influenced not only by the classic works of the market-process school of economists and by my teachers in that school, Israel Kirzner and Ludwig Lachmann, but also by a school of contemporary philosophy, hermeneutics, especially the work of Gadamer. See Gadamer ([1960] 1989). This study is part of a larger effort to clarify how economics could be strengthened by an infusion of hermeneutics. I have started to spell out the implications I believe hermeneutics has for economics in other related studies; see Lavoie (1986a, 1987, 1990b, 1990c).

4.   The exception that proves the rule is a new journal called *Cultural Dynamics*, which is aimed specifically at addressing this problem. See especially the journal's opening editorial by Pinxten et al. (1988).

5.   This chapter does not attempt to offer a full-blown theory of the entrepreneurial process, or of the role of culture in that process. It focuses on the more deliberate aspects of entrepreneurship, while a fuller theory would also have to deal with unintended consequences. Moreover, it emphasizes only what happens when entrepreneurs *notice* opportunities, while a fuller theory would also have to deal with the exploitation of those opportunities. Klamer's work, for example, on the ability of entrepreneurs to form coalitions and persuade others to follow them illuminates this practical side. See Klamer (1989). This chapter does not take up the questions of the differential strengths and weaknesses of cultures in their degree of 'entrepreneurialness.' Some cultures, no

doubt, encourage entrepreneurship more effectively than others. My question here is, I think, a more fundamental one: How does any entrepreneurial act depend on a cultural context?

6. I will argue, however, that the Austrian school's overly individualistic way of thinking about subjective meaning limits its ability to grapple with culture.

7. Von Mises's main methodological contributions are contained in von Mises ([1949] 1966, 1969, [1933] 1981).

8. Hayek's exposition of the theory of spontaneous order can be found in many of Hayek's works. See, for example, Hayek (1948, 1955, 1967, 1978). My own interpretation of Hayek's argument appears in Lavoie (1985b).

9. A classic exposition of the standard methodology of individual and market mental experiments can be found in Patinkin (1965: pp. 11–12).

10. Economists are so fond of the maximizing and equilibrium ideas that they sometimes carry their application beyond economics to cases many noneconomists would consider absurd. Describing a parent's expenditures on a child's education as a form of capital investment, a matter of deploying resources toward the maximization of the present value of the child's future income stream, may not be a particularly helpful contribution to the sociology of the family. And describing a pattern of balance in special interest politics as an equilibrium may not be the best way to interpret political processes. But, whether the economists' uses of the concept of maximizing and its partner concept of equilibrium are always appropriate, they certainly have aided enormously in the clarification of many problems in economics.

11. In an essay entitled 'Alertness, Luck, and Entrepreneurial Profit,' Kirzner elaborates on what he finds to be a 'remarkable parallelism' between the entrepreneurial role on the strictly individual level and the market entrepreneur, identifying 12 propositions that pertain to each. See Kirzner (1979: pp. 154–81).

12. For the distinction between control, in the sense of social engineering, and cultivation, in the sense of legitimate policy making, see Hayek (1955: p. 19).

13. See for example the comments by Robert Lucas and others in Arjo Klamer's revealing book *Conversations with Economists: New Classical Economists and Opponents Speak Out on the Current Controversy in Macroeconomics* (1983).

14. In Hayek's work on business cycle theory, for example, all systematic market forces are said to be equilibrating, with the exception of trade cycles themselves, which is why he thought they deserved special treatment.

15. See, especially, Hayek (1973, 1976, 1979, 1988).

16. For critiques of the 'equilibration approach,' see Fehl (1986) and High (1986). For elaborations of an alternative approach to spontaneous order analysis that is not equilibrium-bound, see Boettke et al. (1986) and Horwitz (1989).

17. And of course, beyond reading opportunities, entrepreneurship involves the ability to act on them and to persuade others to join in such action. Here I am following Kirzner in focusing on the more intellectual side of the entrepreneurial process, but neither he nor I intend to underestimate the extent to which the process is a practical one. For an elaboration of the practical aspects, see Klamer (1989).

18. Even Defoe's famous character was first a social participant and only later shipwrecked. All his actions were clearly stamped with his English cultural background. But the theoretical Crusoes of economic theorizing are treated as if they are devoid of culture altogether. They have goals and deploy means to achieve them, but they are not beneficiaries of, or participants in, a larger cultural process.

19. In my view the Austrian school's version of methodological individualism is far less guilty of the difficulties I am identifying than mainstream economics is. I do believe, however, that even Austrian economics has depended too much on the imaginary construction of a Crusoe world and has accordingly failed to address the cultural dimension as much as it should.

20. Kirzner (1963a); Mises ([1919] 1983).

21. The version of contemporary philosophy whose critique of Cartesian thinking I find

the most compelling is that of philosophical hermeneutics, but one could find similar challenges in the work of the later Wittgenstein and others.
22. I have tried to develop this point about the similarities between language and market processes in Lavoie (1985a, 1986b, 1987, 1990a, 1990c). A more extensive elaboration of the analogy between language and markets is provided in Horwitz (1989).

REFERENCES

Boettke, P., S. Horwitz and D. Prychitko (1986), 'Beyond Equilibrium Economics: Reflections on the Uniqueness of the Austrian Tradition,' *Market Process*, **4**(2), 6–9, 20–25.
Fehl, Ulrich (1986), 'Spontaneous Order and the Subjectivity of Expectations: A Contribution to the Lachmann–O'Driscoll Problem,' in Israel Kirzner (ed.), *Subjectivism, Intelligibility and Economic Understanding: Essays in Honor of Ludwig M. Lachmann on His Eightieth Birthday*, New York: NYU Press, pp. 72–86.
Gadamer, Hans-Georg ([1960] 1989), *Truth and Method*, 2nd rev. ed., New York: Crossroad.
Hayek, F.A. (1948), *Individualism and Economic Order*, Chicago: University of Chicago Press.
Hayek, F.A. (1955), *The Counter-Revolution of Science*, London: Free Press.
Hayek, F.A. (1967), *Studies in Philosophy, Politics, and Economics*, Chicago: University of Chicago Press.
Hayek, F.A. (1973), *Law, Legislation, and Liberty*, Vol. 1: *Rules and Order*, Chicago: University of Chicago Press.
Hayek, F.A. (1976), *Law, Legislation, and Liberty*, Vol. 2: *The Mirage of Social Justice*, Chicago: University of Chicago Press.
Hayek, F.A. (1978), 'Competition as a Discovery Procedure,' in *New Studies in Philosophy, Politics, Economics and the History of Ideas*, Chicago: University of Chicago Press.
Hayek, F.A. (1979), *Law, Legislation, and Liberty*, Vol. 3: *The Political Order of a Free People*, Chicago: University of Chicago Press.
Hayek, F.A. (1988), *The Fatal Conceit: The Errors of Socialism*, Chicago: University of Chicago Press.
High, Jack (1982), 'Alertness and Judgment: Comment on Kirzner,' in Israel M. Kirzner (ed.), *Method, Process and Austrian Economics: Essays in Honor of Ludwig von Mises*, Lexington, MA: D.C. Heath, pp. 161–8.
High, Jack (1986), 'Equilibration and Disequilibration in the Market Process,' in Israel Kirzner (ed.), *Subjectivism, Intelligibility and Economic Understanding: Essays in Honor of Ludwig M. Lachmann on His Eightieth Birthday*, New York: NYU Press, pp. 111–21.
Horwitz, S. (1989), 'The Private Basis of Monetary Order: An Evolutionary Approach to Money and the Market Process,' Ph.D. dissertation, George Mason University, Fairfax, VA.
Kirzner, Israel M. (1963a), *Market Theory and the Price System*, Princeton, NJ: D. Van Nostrand.
Kirzner, Israel M. (1963b), *Competition and Entrepreneurship*, Chicago, University of Chicago Press.

Kirzner, Israel (1979), *Perception, Opportunity, and Profit: Studies in the Theory of Entrepreneurship*, Chicago: University of Chicago Press.

Kirzner, Israel (1985), *Discovery and the Capitalist Process*, Chicago: University of Chicago Press.

Klamer, Arjo (1983), *Conversations with Economists: New Classical Economists and Opponents Speak Out on the Current Controversy in Macroeconomics*, Totowa, NJ: Rowman & Allenheld.

Klamer, Arjo (1989), unpublished manuscript on entrepreneurship and rhetoric presented at the Austrian Economic Colloquium, Center for the Study of Market Processes, George Mason University, Fairfax, VA, Spring.

Lavoie, Don (1985a), *National Economic Planning: What Is Left?*, Cambridge, MA: Ballinger.

Lavoie, Don (1985b), *Rivalry and Central Planning: The Socialist Calculation Debate Reconsidered*, New York: Cambridge University Press.

Lavoie, Don (1986a), 'Euclideanism versus Hermeneutics: A Reinterpretation of Misesian Apriorism,' in Israel Kirzner (ed.), *Subjectivism, Intelligibility, and Economic Understanding: Essays in Honor of Ludwig M. Lachmann on His Eightieth Birthday*, New York: NYU Press, pp. 192–209.

Lavoie, Don (1986b), 'The Market as a Procedure for Discovery and Conveyance of Inarticulate Knowledge,' *Comparative Economic Studies*, **28** (Spring), 1–19.

Lavoie, Don (1987), 'The Accounting of Interpretations and the Interpretation of Accounts: The Communicative Function of "The Language of Business,"' *Accounting, Organizations and Society*, **12**, 579–604.

Lavoie, Don (1990a) 'Computation, Incentives, and Discovery: The Cognitive Function of Markets in Market-Socialism,' *Annals of the American Academy of Political and Social Science*, **507**, 72–9.

Lavoie, Don (1990b), 'Hermeneutics, Subjectivity, and the Lester/Machlup Debate: Toward a More Anthropological Approach to Empirical Economics,' in Warren Samuels (ed.), *Economics as Discourse*, Boston, MA: Kluwer Academic Publishing, pp. 167–87.

Lavoie, Don (1990c) 'Understanding Differently: Hermeneutics and the Spontaneous Order of Communicative Processes,' *History of Political Economy*, Annual Supplement to **22**, 359–77.

Mises, Ludwig von ([1949] 1966), *Human Action*, Chicago: Henry Regnery Company.

Mises, Ludwig von (1969), *Theory and History: An Interpretation of Social and Economic Evolution*, New Rochelle, NY: Arlington House.

Mises, Ludwig von ([1933] 1981), *Epistemological Problems of Economics*, George Reisman (trans.), New York: NYU Press.

Mises, Ludwig von ([1919] 1983), *Nation, State, and Economy*, New York: NYU Press.

Patinkin, Don (1965), *Money, Interest, and Prices: An Integration of Monetary and Value Theory*, New York: Harper & Row.

Pinxten, R., E. Balu, D. Soberon, D. Verboven and K. Snoeck (1988), 'Cultural Dynamics: A Vision and a Perspective,' *Cultural Dynamics*, **1**(1), 1–28.

4. The determinants of entrepreneurial alertness and the characteristics of successful entrepreneurs*

Virgil Henry Storr and Arielle John

4.1 INTRODUCTION

Israel Kirzner has made considerable contributions to our understanding of capital theory (Kirzner 1966), the nature and meaning of the market process (Kirzner 1992), the problems with theories of distributive justice (Kirzner 1989) and the history of economic thought, particularly the history of the Austrian school (Kirzner 1960). Most importantly, however, Kirzner (1973, 1979) has made key contributions to our understanding of the critical role that entrepreneurship plays in markets. For Kirzner, understanding the role of the entrepreneur is essential to understanding how errors get corrected in the market and understanding the role of alertness is essential to understanding how it is that entrepreneurs come to identify these errors. As he explains, in a world where knowledge is necessarily dispersed and individuals are necessarily ignorant of all changes that occur in markets, alert entrepreneurs discover profit opportunities (in other words, opportunities to buy at a low price and sell at a high price) and, thus, drive the market process toward equilibrium.

Kirzner's insights on entrepreneurship have been widely celebrated and have had considerable influence in economics, public policy and entrepreneurship studies. Although Kirzner's work on entrepreneurship has been widely celebrated, it has been criticized on several fronts. Specifically, his theory of entrepreneurship has been criticized for abstracting from the psychological characteristics of real world entrepreneurs and the determinants of alertness. High (1982, 1990), for instance, has criticized Kirzner for abstracting from the uncertainty that necessarily surrounds real world entrepreneurship and so neglecting the critical role played by judgment in entrepreneurial activity in practice.[1] Additionally, Lavoie (1994) has criticized Kirzner for abstracting from the cultural dimension of entrepreneurship and so neglecting the critical role played by interpretation in real world entrepreneurship.

These criticisms, we contend, are unfair and misunderstand Kirzner's project. In order to identify the essence of entrepreneurship, he purposely abstracted from the circumstances that condition entrepreneurship in the real world (including both the psychological and the cultural determinants of successful entrepreneurial activity in practice). Kirzner separates the ignorance that plagues market participants from the uncertainty that necessarily conditions all human action in the world. Rather than being a shortcoming of Kirzner's theory, Kirzner's abstraction allows him to identify and elucidate the entrepreneurial element in economic behavior. As Kirzner (1973: pp. 15–16) writes, 'the entrepreneurial element in the economic behavior of market participants consists in their alertness to previously unnoticed changes in circumstances which may make it possible to get far more in exchange for whatever they have to offer than was hitherto possible.' Similarly, by assuming an environment where opportunities are readily identifiable rather than focusing on the challenges that real world entrepreneurs face in identifying profit opportunities (in other words, his focus on arbitrage), he was able to isolate the role that entrepreneurship plays in the market process. As Kirzner writes, an analytical world without alert entrepreneurs 'completely lacks the power to explain how prices, quantities and qualities of inputs and outputs are systematically changed during the market process' (ibid.: p. 42) and so cannot explain how the market equilibrates (ibid.: p. 73).

Rather than closing off inquiry, we contend, his theory of entrepreneurship makes a fruitful analysis of the psychological characteristics of entrepreneurs and the determinants of alertness possible. As we problematize the environment in which Kirzner's entrepreneur operates by complicating the simple theoretical model with a single period and a single good that he employed, we are better able to explain how entrepreneurs are likely to behave and to isolate which traits entrepreneurs must possess if they are to be successful in different environments. Consider how with the aid of Kirzner's theory we might discuss the impact of culture on entrepreneurship. We might, for instance, expect that culture will direct an entrepreneur's gaze as well as her ability to recognize certain opportunities as in fact opportunities. We might also expect entrepreneurs with different traits to be more successful or less successful at identifying and deciding between different opportunities in different contexts. Entrepreneurs with different cultural backgrounds will likely be alert to different sorts of opportunities and so will see and fail to see different opportunities.

Admittedly, Kirzner has at times objected to extending his analysis in this way and insisted that such a discussion requires moving beyond his theory of entrepreneurship. Kirzner (1979: p. 8), for instance, has remarked that 'we do not clearly understand how entrepreneurs get their superior foresight. We cannot explain how some men discover what is around the corner before others do.' And

> my own work has nothing to say about the secrets of successful entrepreneurship. My work has explored, not the nature of the talents needed for entrepreneurial success, not any guidelines to be followed by would-be successful entrepreneurs, but, instead, the nature of the market process set in motion by the entrepreneurial decisions (both successful and unsuccessful ones!). (Kirzner 2009: p. 145)

Still, Gaglio (1997), Venkataraman (1997), Shane and Venkataraman (2000), Gaglio and Katz (2001), Shane (2003) and others have relied on Kirzner's theory of entrepreneurship and specifically his emphasis on alertness in their explorations of the process and dynamics of opportunity identification. And Kirzner has acknowledged that the determinants of entrepreneurial alertness are not entirely mysterious (see, for instance, Kirzner and Sautet 2006: p. 17).

This chapter has a dual purpose. First, we wish to defend Kirzner against the criticism that his theory of entrepreneurship is too simplistic. Although he does not discuss the role of judgment or interpretation, his simple model, because it isolates the role of alertness, actually helps us to identify how interpretation and judgment enter into the entrepreneurial process. Second, we wish to explore how a discussion of the determinants of entrepreneurial alertness (and in particular the role of culture in entrepreneurship) might proceed. By extending Kirzner's theory of entrepreneurship, it is possible to discuss how culture affects entrepreneurship theoretically and to explain real word differences in entrepreneurship across cultures. Section 4.2, thus, summarizes Kirzner's theory of entrepreneurship. Section 4.3, then, explains some of the most trenchant critiques of Kirzner's theory of entrepreneurship and attempts to defend his theory of entrepreneurship against these critiques. Next, section 4.4 extends Kirzner's theory to explore the determinants of entrepreneurial alertness and the characteristics of successful entrepreneurs. Special emphasis will be placed on how culture might affect an entrepreneur's alertness to and her ability to see and evaluate particular opportunities. Section 4.5, then, offers concluding remarks.

4.2 KIRZNER'S THEORY OF ENTREPRENEURSHIP AND THE CRITICAL ROLE OF ALERTNESS

For Kirzner, the entrepreneur is at center stage in the market process and, so, the process of economic development. As Kirzner (1997a: p. 31) summarizes, 'the success which capitalist market economies display is the result of a powerful tendency for less efficient, less imaginative courses of action, to be replaced by newly discovered, superior ways of serving consumers— by producing better goods and/or by taking advantage of hitherto unknown, but available, sources of resource supply.' Entrepreneurs in the market, Kirzner explains, notice and exploit opportunities to earn profits by replacing 'less efficient, less imaginative courses of action' with 'superior ways of serving consumers.' For Kirzner, the entrepreneur also plays a key role in micro-economic theory. Ironically, though most economists will employ the entrepreneur in classroom discussions of how the market moves from disequilibrium to equilibrium, 'standard theory has not been able to explain how markets systematically gravitate towards the equilibrium states (relevant to the given conditions of those markets)' (Kirzner 2009: p. 4). Introducing the entrepreneur and outlining her role in 'driving the process of equilibrium' is critical to understanding the market as a dynamic process. Kirzner's theory of entrepreneurship, thus, makes an important contribution to standard price theory and our understanding of real world markets. This section will outline the basic elements of Kirzner's theory of entrepreneurship.

In an effort to understand the nature of the market process and to tease out the essential role that the entrepreneur performs, Kirzner (ibid.: p. 4) begins his theorizing in the '*simplest* Marshallian demand–supply context,' that is, a single period world with a single commodity and no scope for uncertainty. The only assumption that typically accompanies this framework that Kirzner relaxes is the perfect knowledge assumption. In a world of perfect knowledge, individuals do not really make decisions about how to succeed but instead calculate optimum strategies on the basis of given data. Deciding is merely a matter of deciding to exchange something that is less preferred or valued for something that is more preferred or valued. The result of this 'decision' is implied in and perfectly determined by the decision-maker's situation. 'If each individual knows with certainty what to expect,' as Kirzner (1973: p. 37) explains, 'his plans can be completely explained in terms of economizing, of optimal allocation, and of maximizing—in other words, his plans can be shown to be in principle implicit in the data which constitutes his knowledge of all the present and future circumstances relevant to his situation.' In such a world, there is no possibility of the same good selling for different prices in the market. Any apparent price discrepancies that did exist would necessarily be explained by differences in transaction costs, like differences in transportation costs between the space where the good was produced and the two points-of-sale. Thus, in a world of perfect competition, there is no possibility of earning pure profits (that is, profits apart from normal rates of return on investments) and so there is simply nothing for the entrepreneur as seeker of pure profit to do.

In Kirzner's view of the world, however, knowledge is imperfect and imperfectible. And it is the very imperfection of knowledge that allows the entrepreneur to have a function and market process to take place. Because knowledge is imperfect, Kirzner (1973: p. 37 footnote 4) points out, there is the possibility of the same good selling for different prices in the market and, thus, the possibility for arbitrage. As an example, in a world of imperfect knowledge, Store A may be selling a particular Brand X shoe for $50.00 while Store B sells the same Brand X shoe for $100.00 with neither the storeowners nor their customers being aware of the price discrepancy. In such a market, it would be possible for some individual to buy shoes from Store A and sell them to customers of Store B at a profit.

These arbitrage opportunities exist because, where knowledge is imperfect, buyers and sellers can make errors of over-optimism which lead to frustrated plans and errors of over-pessimism which lead to unexploited opportunities. Because of their ignorance and 'errors made in the course of market exchanges,' Kirzner (1999: p. 6) explains, market participants can be led:

> (i) over-optimistically to insist on receiving prices that are 'too high' (to enable them to sell all that they would like to sell at those prices) [or on paying prices that are 'too low' (to enable them to buy all that they would like to buy at those prices)]; or (ii) over-pessimistically to enter into transactions that turn out to be less than optimal in the light of the true market conditions as they in fact reveal themselves (for example, a buyer discovers that he has paid a price higher than that being charged elsewhere in the market; a seller discovers that he has accepted a price lower than that which has been paid elsewhere in the market).[2]

The over-optimistic seller is unable to sell her wares. Similarly, the over-optimistic buyer is unable to find the goods she desires at the price she is willing to pay. On the other hand, the over-pessimistic buyer or seller has left money on the table. She could have made more or saved more than she did on the transaction.

According to Kirzner, individuals qua entrepreneurs are alert to these arbitrage opportunities (that result from errors of over-pessimism and over-optimism), and it is their alertness to these opportunities that explains the tendency of entrepreneurs to equilibrate the market. As

Kirzner (2000: p. 16) explains, 'each market is characterized by opportunities for pure entrepreneurial profit. These opportunities are created by earlier entrepreneurial errors which have resulted in shortages, surplus, misallocated resources. The daring, alert entrepreneur discovers these earlier errors, buys where prices are "too low" and sells where prices are "too high."' If these errors or opportunities are to be discovered, individuals must be vigilant and embody a 'natural alertness' to such errors (ibid.: p. 18). As he (ibid.: p. 23) writes, alertness is a key factor: 'discovery is attributable, at least in significant degree, to the entrepreneurial alertness of the discoverer.'

This alertness, it is important to point out, is quite different from possessing superior knowledge. It is true that the entrepreneur knows something that his fellow market participants do not know. He knows, for instance, that there is an opportunity to buy Brand X shoe from Store A and sell it at a higher price to the customers of Store B. But it is not that he possesses superior knowledge that he can take advantage of—he is not at all like the doctor who possesses superior knowledge of medicine than lay individuals that he can take advantage of—but it is that the entrepreneur notices the opportunity when others who might have noticed it did not that explains the essence of entrepreneurship.[3]

It is also important to point out that deliberately searching for profit opportunities is altogether different than an entrepreneur being alert to and so discovering profit opportunities. An individual will only decide to engage in a deliberate search for knowledge if the costs of search are less than the expected returns from search. In order to calculate the costs and benefits of a deliberate search, an individual must possess some degree of knowledge about the landscape and the likelihood of finding what he hopes to find. That knowledge of the landscape and the likelihood of finding what he is looking for must necessarily be given to him in advance of his search. Consequently, any so-called 'search for profitable opportunities' necessarily follows the discovery of an opportunity to potentially benefit from a particular kind of search.[4]

For Kirzner, then, entrepreneurship is an equilibrating force that consists of (and is reducible to) an alertness to arbitrage opportunities which are readily discernible and that only exist because of widespread ignorance in the market. Admittedly, this view of the market process is quite simplistic. In the real world (in other words, where there are multiple periods and multiple commodities), market participants are not simply prone to commit errors because of their ignorance but are also necessarily uncertain as to the best course of action available to them (in other words, there is scope for creativity and judgment). Furthermore, they are not able to unambiguously make sense of their circumstances and their options (in other words, there is scope for interpretation). However, in working with this simple model, Kirzner is able to isolate the essence of entrepreneurship. He is able to demonstrate that if the market is to move toward equilibrium (in other words, the elimination of errors of over-optimism and over-pessimism) it must not only be composed of agents who can economize (in other words, Robbinsian maximizers) but must also contain agents who are alert to profit opportunities (in other words, pure entrepreneurs). As will be argued in the next section, those criticisms of Kirzner's project that argue he focuses too exclusively on alertness and disregards the creativity, judgment and interpretation that are necessarily a part of entrepreneurship in the world are somewhat unfair. He should not be faulted for not discussing the determinants of entrepreneurial alertness and the psychological characteristics of successful entrepreneurs, particularly, since (as we hope to show in section 4.4) his theory of entrepreneurship actually makes a fruitful analysis of the determinants of alertness and the psychological characteristics of successful entrepreneurs possible.

4.3 IGNORING JUDGMENT AND INTERPRETATION WHEN DISCUSSING THE ESSENCE OF ENTREPRENEURSHIP

As noted above, Kirzner's theory of entrepreneurship has been criticized for abstracting from the psychological characteristics of real world entrepreneurs and the determinants of alertness. Kirzner's theory of entrepreneurship, it is suggested, overemphasizes the role played by alertness and ignores the critical role played by judgment and interpretation. Arguably, the most compelling critiques along these lines were articulated by High (1982, 1990) and Lavoie (1994). High (1982, 1990), for instance, criticized Kirzner for stressing ignorance rather than uncertainty and, as a result, neglecting the critical role played by judgment in entrepreneurial activity in practice. Additionally, Lavoie (1994) has criticized Kirzner for describing profit opportunities as if they were readily identifiable (for example, $20 bills on the sidewalk) and so minimizing the critical role played by interpretation in real world entrepreneurship (also see Lavoie, this volume, Chapter 3).[5] Kirzner (1994, 1999, 2009) has offered direct and indirect defenses against both charges. Ironically, while his indirect defense against the charge that he too quickly disregards uncertainty and judgment is quite effective,[6] his direct defense against the charge that he leaves no scope for the interpretive element of entrepreneurship (though accurate) deserves to be augmented. This section will, thus, focus on Lavoie's critique of Kirzner's theory of entrepreneurship.

Lavoie (1994) argues that Kirzner's theory of entrepreneurship does not take into account the interpretive dimension that is a part of all human action including entrepreneurship. For Kirzner, Lavoie (ibid.: pp. 43–4) correctly explains, the entrepreneur is an individual who notices a hitherto undiscovered opportunity for pure arbitrage. These opportunities, though only spotted by the alert entrepreneur, are unambiguous. The same Brand X shoe is being sold at different prices in the market. There is a clear opportunity to buy the shoe at a relatively low price from Store A and sell it at a relatively high price to the customers of Store B. Kirzner has at times likened the profit opportunity to be discovered by the entrepreneur to a 20-dollar bill lying on the beach, waiting to be snatched up. That picking up the 20-dollar bill would be beneficial is entirely obvious. Once the entrepreneur notices the 20-dollar bill as a 20-dollar bill, there is nothing left to do other than pick it up.

As Lavoie (ibid.: p. 43) explains, however, individuals do not experience the world unambiguously. We must attach meaning to our environment and to the opportunities in front of us before we can choose between the courses of action available to us. Interpretation necessarily precedes all human action. The problem with the '20-dollar bill' example is that it trivializes the interpretive element that is a necessary part of entrepreneurship. Recognizing that this piece of paper lying on the beach with colored ink stenciled across it is in fact a 20-dollar bill does require an act of interpretation. However, the interpretative act involved here is quite straightforward for almost everyone who comes across the bill. The profit opportunities that the real world entrepreneur must discover if the market is to tend toward social coordination, then, are not really like 20-dollar bills lying on the beach. The interpretive act involved in real world discoveries is much more complex. As Lavoie (this volume, Chapter 3: p. 57) states, 'Most acts of entrepreneurship are not like an isolated individual finding things on beaches; they require efforts of the creative imagination, skillful judgments of future cost and revenue possibilities, and an ability to read the significance of complex social situations.'

Lavoie contends that, for Kirzner, the entrepreneur is like the person who has sight in a world where blindness and sight are predetermined. Thus there is no real choice in the matter. The blind simply never get to see. Those with sight need only open their eyes to see. And, so, many individuals just do not see profit opportunities that might be right in front of their faces, because they are not alert to them. The person with 'sight,' however, notices yet to be discovered opportunities that others might have noticed had they only been alert to them. Lavoie (ibid.: p. 58) contends that, for Kirzner, 'Being more alert seems to be simply a matter of opening one's eyes to see what is right there under one's nose.'

Kirzner's view of alertness, Lavoie (ibid.: pp. 56–9) complains, is too simplistic and says far too little about why certain individuals are alert to certain opportunities and about why some profit opportunities are discovered and others are not. As Lavoie (ibid.: p. 58) explains, 'if entrepreneurship is like vision ... it is like human vision, which does not see merely patches of color but meaningful things.' That is, when we open our eyes and look around, we attach meanings to what we see. And, thus, different individuals see the same phenomena in different ways. Consider, for instance, what Jack and Jill notice from their shared vantage point at the top of the hill. As Jack looks round, he might see a large tree, their black minivan and a crowd of ten children. Jill, however, from the same plateau, looking at the same objects, might see a large, dying sequoia, their black walnut colored Toyota Sienna, and ten neighborhood teenagers walking home from high school. Jack and Jill essentially see the same things but interpret what they see in different ways. Similarly, Lavoie maintains, this difference in perception and interpretation is crucial in explaining why some individuals are able to notice opportunities that others have been unable to see. As he (this volume, Chapter 3: p. 58) maintains, 'The profit opportunities the entrepreneur discovers are not directly copied off reality in itself; they are interpreted from a point of view.' That Jill might see an opportunity to provide transportation services for the neighborhood teenagers to and from school while Jack does not see this opportunity makes sense given the different meanings they attach to this situation.

If we are to understand entrepreneurship we must understand why certain individuals are alert to certain opportunities and not others. Understanding entrepreneurship, it would thus seem, must involve a discussion of the role of not only alertness but interpretation as well. Lavoie (ibid.: p. 59) worries that, in failing to emphasize the interpretive dimension of entrepreneurship, Kirzner's theory leaves too much of the entrepreneurial process unexplained. As Lavoie (ibid.) complains, in Kirzner's theory, 'It appears to be an arbitrary matter why some things get noticed before others.' Statements by Kirzner that entrepreneurs are alert to what it is in their interest to be alert to do not satisfactorily elucidate the determinants of entrepreneurial alertness or the characteristics possessed by successful entrepreneurs. As Lavoie (ibid.) suggests,

> Profit opportunities are not so much like road signs to which we assign an automatic meaning as they are like difficult texts in need of a sustained effort of interpretation. Entrepreneurship is not only a matter of opening one's eyes, of switching on one's attentiveness; it requires directing one's gaze. When an entrepreneur sees things others have overlooked, it is not just that he opened his eyes while they had theirs closed. He is reading selected aspects of a complex situation others have not read.

For Lavoie, recognizing that alertness is not merely about 'opening one's eyes' but about 'directing one's gaze' raises the question about 'what gives a predirectedness to the entrepreneur's vision, of why he is apt to read some things and not others' (ibid.: p. 59). The answer that Lavoie poses has to do with culture. In failing to address the interpretive dimension of entrepreneurship, then, Kirzner's theory of entrepreneurship is, according to Lavoie, unable to discuss the cultural dimension of entrepreneurship.

For Lavoie, culture is a lens through which individuals see and make sense of the world. Stated another way, it is a source of their interpretations; it is the fount from which they derive meanings. As such, it is akin to the 'social stock of knowledge' that Schütz ([1932] 1967) explained individuals employed when they were attaching because-of and in-order-to motives to their actions and the actions of others. According to Lavoie, Kirzner's theory of entrepreneurship does not acknowledge the role of culture in entrepreneurial discovery and so ignores a key factor that affects entrepreneurs. But, as Lavoie (this volume, Chapter 3: pp. 62–3) explains, the entrepreneur's

> ability to read new things into a situation is not primarily due to his separateness from others but, indeed, to his higher degree of sensitivity to what others are looking for. The really successful entrepreneurs we know are not unusually separate from others; on the contrary, they are especially well plugged into the culture. What gives them the ability to sense what their customers will want is not some kind of mysterious alertness that gets 'switched on' but their capacity to read the conversations of mankind. They can pick up the sense of where their fellows in the culture stand, what values they adhere to, what purposes they pursue, what they consider beautiful, and what they deem profane.

Successful suppliers are able to figure out what their consumers will like, are able to tweak their product to better suit their customers' preferences, and are able to present those products in the manner that they sense will appeal to their customers, all because they are 'especially well plugged into the culture.' This entire process is interpretive, and interpretation necessarily occurs through a cultural lens. Being immersed in a culture thus allows the entrepreneur to make accurate interpretations. For Lavoie (ibid.: pp. 60–64), then, a more complete theory of entrepreneurship must begin with a hermeneutical theory which stresses cultural transmission and the interpretive dimension that is a part of all human decision-making.

Kirzner (1994: p. 329) has conceded that Lavoie is likely correct when he stresses the interpretative dimension of entrepreneurship and how culture impacts entrepreneurial alertness. But, Kirzner argues, Lavoie's insights ought only to affect the application of economic theory not the content of economic theory. 'It does follow,' Kirzner (ibid.) argues, 'that for the purposes *within economic theory* for which the entrepreneurial role has been introduced, it is necessary to go beyond the bare propensity of being alert. In *applying* economic theory, one immediately looks for the cultural, historical, and social detail through which the economic processes make themselves manifest.' Kirzner believes that Lavoie has confused economic theory with economic history. Paying attention to culture does not add to an understanding of the 'systematic market forces.' The market is driven toward equilibrium because of the existence of entrepreneurs who are alert to yet to be discovered profit opportunities. This is true regardless of the cultural context. 'To suggest that the "incompleteness" of such pure theory is in any way an inadequacy,' Kirzner (ibid.) explains, 'would be an unfortunate misunderstanding of what theory is all about.' Kirzner is, of course, correct that theory necessarily abstracts from cultural and institutional detail and that understanding the theory must precede any effort to understand actual entrepreneurs within a particular context. As Kirzner (ibid.) explains, 'it is only when one has grasped the pure entre- preneurial character of market processes that one can begin to enrich one's understanding of the real world by drawing attention to cultural and institutional detail.'

It is our contention, however, that, while it is unfair to criticize Kirzner's theory of entrepreneurship for not accounting for culture, it is also pos- sible for a theory of entrepreneurship to elucidate the interpretive dimen- sion of entrepreneurial activity and the role for culture in directing the gaze of entrepreneurs. Though incompleteness is not a fair criticism of theory, it is possible to extend theories in an effort to make them more complete. Rather than seeing Lavoie's criticisms of Kirzner as critiques, we believe that it may be more appropriate to view them as suggestions for how Kirzner's theory of entrepreneurship may be fruitfully amended. It is simply not true that Kirzner's theory of entrepreneurship, because it is silent on the role of interpretation and culture, 'leaves no room for culture.' Instead, we contend, his theory of entrepreneurship makes a fruitful analysis of the psychological characteristics of entrepreneurs and the determinants of alertness possible. Indeed, as Storr (this volume, Chapter 8: p. 192) argues, 'if Kirzner's theory of entrepreneurship was not amenable to discussions of culture then Lavoie would have had to discard it.' Lavoie, however, did not abandon Kirzner's framework but set out to build upon it. The next section extends Kirzner's theory to explore the determinants of entrepreneurial alertness and the characteristics of suc- cessful entrepreneurs. Ironically, Kirzner's own efforts in this regard have not been all that successful.

4.4 A KIRZNERIAN THEORY OF THE CULTURE OF ENTREPRENEURSHIP

In discussing the consequences of extending his model to discuss a multi-period, multi-commodity market process where not only ignorance but uncertainty is endemic, Kirzner contends that the entrepreneur would not only have to be alert but possess the psychological characteristics that Schumpeter attributes to the entrepreneur.[7] 'To see things in [my] way,' Kirzner (2009: p. 9) has written, 'did not (as the critics have somehow understood) mean that I was in any way denying the elements of boldness, creativity, and innovativeness which, in the real world, certainly do characterize entrepreneurial activity.' And Kirzner (1997b: p. 12) has conceded that,

> once we permit the multi-period character of real world entrepreneurial behavior to be explicitly considered, the relevance of the active aggressive characteristics of Schumpeter's entrepreneurs becomes understandable and important. Entrepreneurial alertness, in this essentially uncertain, open-ended, multi-period world must unavoidably express itself in the qualities of boldness, self-confidence, creativity and innovative ability.

This concession of Kirzner, however, concedes both too much and too little. He concedes too much because he seeks to add to the realm of theory attitudes and propensities that we have no reason to believe would characterize all entrepreneurs in all contexts. For instance, one might imagine that the successful entrepreneurs in some contexts are not the bold ones, but the unassuming ones who are alert to the profit opportunities that might come from marketing the familiar and making only minimal changes to what is already popular. Similarly, the copycat rather than the innovator might prove to be more successful in some contexts. Thus boldness and creativity may sometimes actually obscure rather than enhance an entrepreneur's ability to notice hitherto undiscovered profit opportunities. Kirzner concedes too little, on the other hand, because he does not admit that, once the market environment utilized in the model becomes more complex, the scope for interpretation grows larger and it becomes necessary to employ something like culture to explain why some opportunities get noticed and others do not.

A discussion of the determinants of entrepreneurial alertness and the characteristics of successful entrepreneurs, we suggest, would result in a Kirznerian theory of the culture of entrepreneurship. A Kirznerian theory of the culture of entrepreneurship would not try to single out characteristics that may or may not describe actual entrepreneurs. Instead, such a theory would focus on how cultural and psychological factors affect the opportunities that entrepreneurs perceive. It would also have to give some hint as to what cultural factors scholars wanting to understand entrepreneurship in some particular context should look for when they seek to apply their theory of entrepreneurship.

A Kirznerian theory of the culture of entrepreneurship, we contend, would proceed as follows: (a) entrepreneurs alert to profit opportunities are the driving force in the market process and explain the tendency toward equilibrium in the market; (b) these opportunities exist to all market participants because there is widespread ignorance (and uncertainty) in the market; (c) these opportunities are not readily identifiable as opportunities but must be interpreted as such; (d) differences in stocks of knowledge (both individualized and social/cultural) explain why different individuals are alert to certain opportunities and not others; (e) applied efforts to make sense of real world entrepreneurship must pay attention to the differences in stocks of knowledge that might explain the differences in interpretative frameworks across contexts. Kirzner (Kirzner and Sautet 2006: p. 17) has largely endorsed this way of moving forward. 'Culture,' he explains, 'can shape what an individual perceives as opportunities and thus what he overlooks, as entrepreneurship is always embedded in a cultural context . . . culture for the most part has to do with orientation (affecting where an entrepreneur may direct his gaze) and results in entrepreneurship looking differently across contexts.'

To illustrate how a Kirznerian theory of the culture of entrepreneurship might help us explain real world entrepreneurship, we turn to two examples from our own research into entrepreneurship in the Bahamas and in Trinidad and Tobago. Storr (2004) gives an account of the economic history of the Bahamas, in order to explain the particular flavor of enterprise there. In Storr's narrative, there are two 'ideal types' of entrepreneurs. The first is the 'master pirate,' who is alert, like the Kirznerian entrepreneur. However, because of the importance of piracy in the Bahamas' past, she is alert to profiteering opportunities (ibid.: p. 10). The master pirate Bahamian entrepreneur is therefore a 'trickster,' who is known for her cunning, has a 'narrow radius of trust' (ibid.: p. 106), and is rather impatient with a high discount rate. The other ideal type is the 'enterprising slave' type, who, because of Bahamians' previous experiences with slavery, has come to understand the value of hard work even when obstacles are evident. The enterprising slave is alert to profit opportunities in the regular sense. Both the piratical and the enterprising entrepreneurial types are evident in Bahamian culture, sometimes even within the same individual (ibid.: p. 106). Storr explains how the culture has evolved so that entrepreneurship in the Bahamas is explainable and fairly predictable using those two metaphors.

While Storr's narrative elucidates the cultural dimension of entrepreneurship in the Bahamas, we never lose sight of that Kirznerian entrepreneurial process at work. To illustrate the point, we refer to the cultural legacy of the master pirate type of entrepreneur. Remember that the master pirate is always alert to opportunities for profiteering. The way the master pirate's culturally inherited behaviors manifest themselves in individual business activity is often through the 'nepotism and predominance of small, hierarchically organized family firms' (ibid.: p.107), the relatively low national savings rates, and the underinvestment in capital-intensive industries that are all typical of the Bahamian entrepreneur. As Storr (ibid.: p.108) describes, 'the master pirate is on the lookout for the quickest route to prosperity,' which explains why Bahamians 'tend to invest in restaurants, salons, clothing stores, and other retail or service oriented companies and not in large-scale manufacturing or commercial agriculture.' Thus, the master pirate's alertness to alternative business types seems to be switched off, whereas she appears to be hyper-alert to opportunities for quick and easy bounty in the form of rent seeking and political profits. The Kirznerian discovery process is still at work, in that the master pirate is alert to arbitrage opportunities. However, the spheres of business activity to which she is alert are to a large extent determined by her historical experiences with piracy, her culture.

Similarly, the narrative of the enterprising slave also involves the Kirznerian discovery process. 'The peculiarity of Bahamian slavery,' Storr (ibid.: p.99) contends, 'and the presence of a large population of free and materially well-to-do blacks in the Bahamas gave birth to the *enterprising slave* (an equally prominent figure in the economic story of the Bahamas).' During slavery, blacks were assigned to task groups where they were made responsible for particular chores (ibid.: p.89). Additionally, they were allowed to work on their own plots of land when official work was completed for the day. As a last point, slaves in the Bahamas did not work on tropical staple crops, and, faced with so much free time, the farmers allowed slaves to seek paid work on their own when their slaves had the time. Storr argues that these experiences with slavery explain, at least in part, the attitudes of the present Bahamian entrepreneur, who displays ingenuity and a 'strong work ethic' (ibid.: p.109). Furthermore, Storr (ibid.: pp.110–11) claims that this spirit of 'resourcefulness' and hard work in the face of difficulty is the reason why the Bahamian entrepreneur, 'whether he is a "peanut boy" or a straw vendor or a shopkeeper or a restaurateur,' is a capable, creative creature. Like the master pirate, the enterprising slave is an entrepreneur in the Kirznerian sense, in that she is alert to a different set of opportunities for profit. She notices the errors made by other entrepreneurs, and, seeing hungry tourists waiting near docks and parking lots, she exploits those opportunities by setting up shop there.

Colonialism has, likewise, left a particular legacy in Trinidad and Tobago that colors entrepreneurial alertness in that context. John and Storr (2010) have detailed the peculiar arrangement of entrepreneurship in Trinidad by race/ethnicity—the distinct ethnic groups exhibit distinct entrepreneurial patterns. John and Storr's empirical study of the labor force revealed that those Trinidadians of African descent have the lowest self-employment rate of the four ethnic groups in Trinidad, at 16.1 percent. This number is below the average self-employment rate for the entire sample, which is 19.7 percent. In fact, Trinidadians of African descent are the only ethnic group to perform below average. One-fifth of mixed persons in the sample are self-employed, and therefore their rate is average. Indians (now considered the new business class) have an internal group self-employment rate of 22.7 percent, which ranks second only to the Chinese, Syrian–Lebanese and white Trinidadians, who outperform all the other groups substantially. If a person in Trinidad is of Chinese, Syrian–Lebanese or European ancestry, he/she is 35.5 percent likely to be self-employed, which makes him/her at least twice as likely as an African person to be self-employed (ibid.).

What explains these patterns in Trinidad? As with Storr's work on the Bahamas, culture and history have a lot to contribute to the explanation. Because of colonialism, whites have traditionally been the owners of big businesses, and this minority ethnic group retained control over the most important sectors of the economy (ibid.). Over generations, this control has been passed down, and the children who inherit their ancestors' companies tend to remain in the same business. Crichlow (1998) adds that the whites were able to consolidate their dominant position in business in the 1960s and 1970s because the elites benefited most from post-independence industrialization programs created by the government. In general, then, members of different ethnic groups in Trinidad, because of their different experiences during and after colonialism, are alert to different kinds of opportunities. The Syrian–Lebanese control over the garment industry in Port of Spain, for instance, provides evidence of this. Ryan and Barclay (1992) claim that the advantages that the other ethnic groups had over blacks were 'those resources they possess which have proven critical to their entrepreneurial success,' resources that were both 'cultural and ethnic' (ibid.: p.143). Indians, Chinese and Syrian–Lebanese learned the virtues of hard work, thrift and planning for the future from their ancestors, who saved greatly in preparation for their return to their homelands (ibid.: p.145). Those three groups, like whites, also formed business associations to support their race's success in business. Bridget Brereton, in her book *Race Relations in Colonial Trinidad 1870–1900* (1979: p. 36), also mentions that, among the white elite, 'a high value was placed on family connections' and French Creoles routinely inbred and intermarried to keep economic networks and kinship tight. These cultural patterns map somewhat neatly to present-day Trinidad and Tobago, where Indians, Chinese, Syrian–Lebanese and whites have relatively high internal group self-employment rates.

A combination of practices that occurred during and after slavery appears to determine African Trinidadians' low entrepreneurship rates in comparison. In the early 1900s, the planter class took deliberate steps to raise taxes and make land acquisition difficult for blacks (Ryan and Barclay 1992: p. 4), blacks depended on volatile crop prices for their success yet spent their incomes 'lavishly' (ibid.: p. 8), and blacks tended to borrow too much credit from white planters, who ended up seizing blacks assets when the blacks could not repay (ibid.: p. 9). Blacks also frequently migrated to urban areas in search of jobs and schools, thus forfeiting their lands to Indians, who preferred to work in rural areas (ibid.: p. 11). Furthermore, in contrast to whites and Indians, blacks never saw themselves as transients in Trinidad's history—they always regarded themselves as Trinidadians and hence focused instead on 'education rather than business as a vehicle for social mobility' (Brereton 1979: p. 146). Brereton (ibid.: p. 85) argues that Afro-Trinidadians were more likely to seek status by investing in education, as opposed to entrepreneurship, because 'school represented the main chance of mobility for the sons of the black and coloured lower class and lower middle class.' Black parents discouraged their children from becoming businessmen, choosing instead to instill academic values so that their children could grow up and secure status from 'good' jobs, particularly in the public service. Contemporary findings indicate a preponderance of blacks in the public sector and a low rate of self-employment for the group.

The Trinidad and Tobago case study shows that, while Africans have a different 'taste' for entrepreneurship than other ethnic groups, and this taste is a cultural legacy, this is tantamount to saying that blacks in Trinidad are more likely to have their alertness to commercial entrepreneurial opportunities switched off. Stated another way, while some ethnic groups (say Trinidadians of African descent) are likely to be alert to opportunities for political and bureaucratic entrepreneurship, members of other groups appear to be more acutely alert to particular opportunities for commercial entrepreneurship. Blacks are less likely to discover these opportunities, because they are generally looking elsewhere to improve their standard of living. In contrast, the other ethnic groups have their alertness switched on. They see arbitrage opportunities in economic markets, while blacks have a propensity to notice opportunities in politics (John and Storr 2010).

The examples of the Bahamas and Trinidad and Tobago are presented here in order to show that the Kirznerian theory of the culture of entrepreneurship can actually be quite useful in helping us explain cultural differences in entrepreneurship. Indeed, while all decisions are made within a cultural context, as Lavoie pointed out, the process of entrepreneurial discovery that occurs because of the fundamental ignorance and radical uncertainty in the world can still be identified.

4.5 CONCLUSION

If entrepreneurship is the driving force of capitalism and hence economic growth and development, then economists should engage in the project of understanding how that force works. Israel Kirzner has made significant strides in advancing a theory of entrepreneurship. While the theory is not without its limitations, it has proved useful and is a point of departure for theories that attempt to incorporate culture in the decision-making process of entrepreneurs. Those who would object to Kirzner's theory based on its simplicity must recall that certain indelible tenets in economics such as 'People are rational' and 'Demand curves slope downward' also involve basic observations about human action. Without such foundational statements of theory, economics as a social science would be constrained. While critics are correct in pointing out that a discussion of culture is largely absent in Kirzner's earlier work, this is not to say that Kirzner's project is not useful in helping to explain how entrepreneurship differs across culture. On the contrary, the concepts of alertness and discovery can and arguably should be conjured even when highlighting at a theoretical level how culture impacts entrepreneurship and at an applied level when discussing the specific cultural aspects of entrepreneurship in some context. An opportunity, as Kirzner pointed out, can exist to the discoverer only when she notices it. In order to notice it, she must be alert to it. Culture will largely explain why she is alert to certain activities and not to others.

NOTES

*   This chapter previously appeared in Emily Chamlee-Wright (ed.), *Annual Proceedings of the Wealth and Well-Being of Nations*, Vol. 2 (Beloit College Press, 2011). It is reprinted here (with minor edits) with the permission of the publisher.

1. Foss and Klein (2010) have criticized Kirzner along similar lines. Foss and Klein's critique, though borrowing a lot from High, is much more extensive.
2. Stated another way,

> a state of market disequilibrium is characterized by widespread ignorance. Market participants are unaware of the real opportunities for beneficial exchange which are available to them in the market. The result of this state of ignorance is that countless opportunities are passed up. For each product, as well as for each resource, opportunities for mutually beneficial exchange among potential buyers and sellers are missed. The potential sellers are unaware that sufficiently eager buyers are waiting, who might make it worth their while to sell. Potential buyers are unaware that sufficiently eager sellers are waiting, who might make it attractive for them to buy. Resources are being used to produce products which consumers value less urgently, because producers (and potential producers) are not aware that these resources can produce more urgently needed products. Products are being produced with resources badly needed for other products because producers are not aware that alternative, less critically needed resources can be used to achieve the same results. (Kirzner 1973: p. 69)

3. As Kirzner (1973: p. 67) states, though

> the element of knowledge is tied to the possibility of winning pure profits, the elusive notion of entrepreneurship is, as we have seen, not encapsulated in the mere possession of greater knowledge and market opportunities. The aspect of knowledge which is crucially relevant is not so much the substantive knowledge of market data as *alertness, the 'knowledge' of where to find market data.*

> Furthermore, (1979: p. 8), 'entrepreneurial knowledge is a rarefied, abstract type of knowledge—the knowledge of where to obtain information (or other resources) and how to deploy it.'

4. As Kirzner (1985: p. 22) states,

> If an entrepreneur's discovery of a lucrative arbitrage opportunity galvanizes him into immediate action to capture the perceived gain, it will not do to describe the situation as one in which the entrepreneur has decided to use his alertness to capture this gain. He has not 'deployed' his hunch for a specific purpose; rather his hunch has propelled him to make his entrepreneurial purchase and sale. The entrepreneur never sees his hunches as potential inputs about which he must decide whether they are to be used.

5. Baker et al. (2005: p. 495) issue a similar critique of Kirzner's ignoring cultural context and argue that 'people perceive opportunities through a cultural or institutional lens' and that 'individuals are influenced by social circumstance and express a broad range of idiosyncratic motives as they enact entrepreneurial opportunities. By drawing attention to—rather than holding constant—differences in human motivations and national contexts, we base the CDEE framework on the view that entrepreneurial opportunities—and not just their discovery—are inescapably subjective and context dependent.'
6. See, for instance, Kirzner's (2000: pp. 247–8) discussion of why he did not stress creativity:

> In recognizing how, (in order to act entrepreneurially in the uncertain context of time-consuming producing possibilities) the entrepreneur will need to display qualities of boldness and creativity. There was no intention (and no real need) to see these qualities as essential to the pure entrepreneurial role, as that role enters into our analysis and understanding of the market process. In acknowledging that, for Mises, the uncertainty within which the entrepreneur operates is an essential defining condition

for the situations in which scope for entrepreneurship exists, there was no intention (and no need) to see boldness and creativity as anything more than the psychological qualities needed in order for the entrepreneur to effectively recognize, in peering into the future, those pure price differentials in which prospective entrepreneurial profits are to be won.

Kirzner continues (ibid.: p. 247) to say that,

while psychological and personal qualities of boldness, creativity and self-confidence will doubtless be helpful or even necessary in order for a person to 'see' such price-differentials in the open-ended, uncertain world in which we live (with 'seeing' defined as necessarily implying the grasping of the opportunity one has seen), the analytical essence of the pure entrepreneurial role is itself independent of these specific qualities.

The same logic would apply to the critique that he did not stress the superior judgment that entrepreneurs would have to possess.

7. See Schumpeter (1960) for his discussion of the attributes of the entrepreneur.

REFERENCES

Baker, Ted, Eric Gedajlovic and Michael Lubatkin (2005), 'A Framework for Comparing Entrepreneurship Processes across Nations,' *Journal of International Business Studies*, **36**(5), 492–504.

Brereton, Bridget (1979), *Race Relations in Colonial Trinidad 1870–1900*, Cambridge: Cambridge University Press.

Crichlow, Michaeline (1998), 'Reconfiguring the Informal Economy Divide: State, Capitalism, and Struggle in Trinidad and Tobago,' *Latin American Perspectives*, **25**, 62–83.

Foss, Nicolai J. and Peter G. Klein (2010), 'Alertness, Action, and the Antecedents of Entrepreneurship,' *Journal of Private Enterprise*, **25**(2), 145–64.

Gaglio, C.M. (1997), 'Opportunity Identification: Review, Critique, and Suggested Research Directions,' in J.A. Katz and R.H. Brockhaus (eds.), *Advances in Entrepreneurship, Firm Emergence and Growth*, Greenwich, CT: JAI Press, pp. 139–202.

Gaglio, C.M. and J.A. Katz (2001), 'The Psychological Basis of Opportunity Identification: Entrepreneurial Alertness,' *Journal of Small Business Economics*, **3**(4), 70–79.

High, Jack (1982), 'Alertness and Judgment: Comment on Kirzner,' in I.M. Kirzner (ed.), *Method, Process and Austrian Economics: Essays in Honor of Ludwig von Mises*, New York: Lexington Books, pp. 161–8.

High, Jack (1990), *Maximizing, Action, and Market Adjustment: An Inquiry into the Theory of Economic Disequilibrium*, Munich: Philosophia.

John, Arielle and Virgil Henry Storr (2010), 'Entrepreneurs in Context: The Case of Trinidad and Tobago,' working paper.

Kirzner, Israel M. (1960), *The Economic Point of View*, New York: Van Nostrand.

Kirzner, Israel M. (1966), *An Essay on Capital*, New York: A.M. Kelley.

Kirzner, Israel M. (1973), *Competition and Entrepreneurship*, Chicago: University of Chicago Press.

Kirzner, Israel M. (1979), *Perception, Opportunity, and Profit: Studies in the Theory of Entrepreneurship*, Chicago: University of Chicago Press.
Kirzner, Israel M. (1985), *Discovery and the Capitalist Process*, Chicago: University of Chicago Press.
Kirzner, Israel M. (1989), *Discovery, Capitalism, and Distributive Justice*, Oxford: Basil Blackwell.
Kirzner, Israel M. (1992), *The Meaning of Market Process: Essays in the Development of Modern Austrian Economics*, London: Routledge.
Kirzner, Israel M. (1994), 'Entrepreneurship,' in P. Boettke (ed.), *The Elgar Companion to Austrian Economics*, Aldershot, UK and Brookfield, VT, USA: Edward Elgar Publishing, pp. 103–10.
Kirzner, Israel M. (1997a) *How Markets Work: Disequilibrium, Entrepreneurship and Discovery*, Hobart Paper No. 133, London: Institute of Economic Affairs.
Kirzner, Israel M. (1997b), 'Entrepreneurial Discovery and the Competitive Market Process: An Austrian Approach,' *Journal of Economic Literature*, **35**(1), 60–85.
Kirzner, Israel M. (1999), 'Creativity and/or Alertness: A Reconsideration of the Schumpeterian Entrepreneur,' *Review of Austrian Economics*, **11**, 5–17.
Kirzner, Israel M. (2000), *The Driving Force of the Market: Essays in Austrian Economics*, London: Routledge.
Kirzner, Israel M. (2009), 'The Alert and Creative Entrepreneur: A Clarification,' *Small Business Economics*, **32**, 145–52.
Kirzner, Israel M. and Frederic Sautet (2006), *The Nature and Role of Entrepreneurship in Markets*, Mercatus Policy Series, Policy Primer No. 4, Arlington, VA: Mercatus Center, George Mason University.
Lavoie, Don (1994), 'Cultural Studies and the Conditions for Entrepreneurship,' in T.W. Boxx and G.M. Quinlivan (eds.), *The Cultural Context of Economics and Politics*, Lanham, MD: University Press of America, pp. 51–69.
Ryan, Selwyn and Lou Anne Barclay (1992), *Sharks and Sardines: Blacks in Business in Trinidad and Tobago*, St. Augustine, Trinidad and Tobago: University of the West Indies.
Schumpeter, Joseph A. (1960), *The Theory of Economic Development*, New York: Oxford University Press.
Schütz, Alfred ([1932] 1967), *The Phenomenology of the Social World*, Evanston, IL: Northwestern University Press.
Shane, Scott (2003), *A General Theory of Entrepreneurship: The Individual–Opportunity Nexus*, Cheltenham, UK and Northampton, MA, USA: Edward Elgar Publishing.
Shane, Scott and S. Venkataraman (2000), 'The Promise of Entrepreneurship as a Field of Research,' *Academy of Management Review*, **25**(1), 217–26.
Storr, Virgil Henry (2004), *Enterprising Slaves and Master Pirates: Understanding Economic Life in the Bahamas*, New York: Peter Lang.
Venkataraman, S. (1997), 'The Distinctive Domain of Entrepreneurship Research,' in J.A. Katz and R.H. Brockhaus (eds.), *Advances in Entrepreneurship, Firm Emergence and Growth*, Greenwich, CT: JAI Press, pp. 119–38.

5. Markets as an extension of culture*
Emily Chamlee-Wright

5.1 INTRODUCTION

A walk through central Accra, the capital city of Ghana, is almost a religious experience for an economist. Ghanaian marketplaces are the site of intense and vigorous bargaining. Although it is officially illegal to trade outside the market area designated by the city council, the streets teem with hawkers selling produce and fish from their head trays. What strikes the economist most is the precision and efficiency of these small transactions. The sidewalks are scarcely passable, as market women perch four deep on either side. Their voices rise and fall in laughter and conversation, while they briefly pause to catch the attention of potential customers. The camaraderie and good nature of the market should not deceive the observer into seeing the marketplace only as a point of social contact, however. While it undoubtedly fills this role as well, a keen alertness to the smallest of profit opportunities is always at work. In southern Ghana and many cities of West Africa, this is the work of women. Some young men dot the marketplace selling frozen yogurt or second-hand clothing, yet the majority of goods are marketed by women and girls (Lawson 1971; Pellow 1977; Clark 1994).

A striking pattern which emerges is the hierarchical nature of goods sold and the conditions under which women and girls trade. Girls sell water from jugs atop their heads to bus commuters, parched from the dusty hot car-park. Girls and young women hawk baked goods or traditional foods that their mothers or aunts have prepared. Women of various ages sell fish and produce either from head trays or seated on the sidewalks. The most comfortable conditions are those within the established market stalls. Here is where one will find more expensive items such as imported cloth for sale, as well as staple foods, canned goods, jewelry, and a few services such as sewing.[1] While the conditions here are cooler and cleaner, access requires financial capital many market women do not have—limited access to capital being the most frequently cited problem microenterprise entrepreneurs face throughout the developing world (Squire 1981; Lycette and White 1989; Kurwijila and Due 1991; Steel and Webster 1991; Levy 1993; United Nations 1995).

In the first four decades of research on developing countries, the role of women in the market system was all but ignored by mainstream economists. The male bias of the profession in the early years of the economic development discipline, along with Western notions of women's role in economic activity, contributed to this oversight. The main mechanism for the oversight was the miscategorization of female market activity as a variant of domestic labor (Smith 1978). The habit of not counting domestic labor as real economic activity still pervades the discipline and is itself problematic (Waring 1988; Anker 1994; Goldschmidt-Clermont 1994). This mistake is compounded, however, when the public nature of female work is systematically ignored. Indeed, much of the indigenous African market is driven by women, in part as a means to fulfilling their domestic responsibilities. According to the United Nations Development Fund for Women, female labor and entrepreneurship account for 80 percent of all the food produced, processed, and marketed in sub-Saharan Africa. This may even be too conservative an estimate, given the hidden character of women's work in Muslim areas (Hill 1969; Schildkrout 1982). The tragedy is not just that women have been slighted by not receiving due recognition for their role in economic growth. The real tragedy lies in the fact that, since women were ignored, the indigenous economy was also overlooked for its role in economic development.

More recent research has significantly improved our understanding of the importance of informal market trading to economic development. For various reasons—including the questionable legal status of firms in the informal economy, the desire to avoid revealing income levels to government officials, and the ease with which entrepreneurs both enter and leave the informal market—measuring the size of the informal sector presents many practical problems. But recent attempts to establish a more accurate accounting of the informal sector relate to the significant role indigenous markets play around the world. In their extensive survey of the informal sector in Peru, for example, Hernando De Soto (1989: p.61) and the Instituto Libertad y Democracia found that 85 percent of market trading in Lima was attributed to the informal sector. The International Labour Organization (ILO) estimates that 61 percent of the urban labor force in sub-Saharan Africa are employed in the informal sector (ILO 1990). Thus, if for no other reason, the role indigenous markets play in employment, production, and distribution necessitates that they capture the attention of development theorists and policy makers.

Much of the literature concentrates upon the limitations indigenous markets face, particularly their inability to take advantage of economies of scale. Yet the small and medium-sized enterprises characteristic of the informal sector also have particular advantages in production and marketing. Relative to large-scale industry, microenterprises within the informal sector can often take advantage of low-cost labor, can more easily fill niche markets, and have the potential to be more flexible in responding to changing market conditions (Sandesara 1991). With the advent of structural adjustment programs designed to reduce the size of the bureaucratic sector, indigenous markets often represent the best hope of avoiding widespread unemployment and deepening poverty; but this also means that those who already operate within the indigenous economy will face even greater competition (Steel and Takagi 1985; Parker et al. 1995).

It is clear that development analysts must now take informal or indigenous markets seriously in their search for solutions to continued economic stagnation. What is less clear, however, is what tools to employ in our attempt to better understand the potential and limitations of indigenous markets: to understand the contributions made by and the constraints faced by indigenous entrepreneurs. Further, finding such tools is essential if we expect to make wise policy recommendations.

As we study indigenous markets up close, we find that standard economic models pass over much of the context-specific detail of market and other social processes. Rules which govern credit acquisition and capital accumulation, for instance, differ dramatically from one cultural context to another. (See, for example, Timberg and Aiyar (1984) for India; Shanmugan (1991) for Malaysia; Hiebert (1993) for Vietnam; and Little (1965) for West Africa.)

Corporate practices which support economic success in one cultural context, such as the Japanese use of Confucian symbolism, ceremony, and training, often meet with failure in another (Clegg and Redding 1990), as they do not fit the new cultural context (Lavoie and Chamlee-Wright, working paper). Government institutions often meet with different records of success depending on the cultural and historical context, as Putnam et al. (1983; Putnam 1993) found in their studies of Italian regional governance. Patterns of economic development once assumed to be universal are now recognized as contingent and dependent upon cultural and historical influences. Trade among the Kenyan pastoralists known as the Orma, for example, became widespread as a result of the conversion to Islam, as it provided a common institutional structure by which to engage in long-distance and inter-temporal exchange (Ensminger 1992). Standard neoclassical economics cannot adequately address such issues, as it has no way of incorporating the role of culture in the market process. This chapter is an attempt to integrate cultural analysis within our economic methodology so that we might be in a position to better understand the nature of economic development itself, and to have a better guide in our search for sound economic policy.

The term 'culture,' as it is used here, is not simply meant as an independent force imposing itself on social institutions and individual behavior. Rather, culture is intimately connected to social institutions and individual behavior. Culture is better characterized as a context rather than an independent force. Culture is not just a list of rules constraining behavior that would otherwise maximize profit or utility. Culture is the context in which meaning is negotiated and renegotiated. Social institutions depend upon this framework of meaning, as it provides legitimation to institutional rules. Police and court systems would be incapable of enforcing property rights and contracts, for instance, if most members of a society did not accept the legitimacy of the institutional rules. Such acceptance comes not from social contracts devised in the abstract, but through an evolutionary process within the culture of a community.

Not only does culture provide the 'glue' which enables social institutions to stick, but it is the context in which individuals make sense of the world around them. Objects and actions have no inherent meaning in and of themselves. Individuals must interpret their meaning within a particular language community, at a particular point in history, in reference to a complex of meanings that have already been read out of previous experience. Culture provides the interpretive framework that allows us to understand objects as symbols, actions as part of an overall plan, or interaction as social relationship. The world is never experienced directly. It must be interpreted through the lens of culture. Thus, understanding complex social interaction—the sort which is most interesting to economists, anthropologists, and other social scientists—will require us to address the cultural context in which it takes place.

Introducing aspects of culture is not novel to economics, yet a full appreciation has not yet been realized. Economists usually recognize only two functions of culture within the economy—determining preferences and constraining optimizing behavior. The first approach, or what we might call 'Culture as Preferences,' is the most dismissive. Since economic analysis generally takes preferences as given, the forces which shape those preferences tend to be of little interest. This position assumes that, once preferences are formed, they play a neutral role in the market process. Yet, if cultural influences promote distrust for one's fellows as the basis for wise business practices, we can expect that the costs of acquiring credit are higher in this case than in cultures where trust is the initial response. The Grameen Bank in Bangladesh has used the trust and shared sense of mutual obligation present among women in that culture to generate a 98 percent loan recovery rate from their practice of group-lending

(Wahid 1994). The capacity of some ethnic groups, such as within Jewish, Chinese, and Indian cultures, to resettle across vast distances while maintaining tight bonds of kinship, nationality, and identity have enabled them to establish successful global economic networks (Kotkin 1992). Cultural and economic processes do not neatly separate out from one another. Such 'preferences' for caution, trust, and ethnic identity are not neutral. Rather, the specific cultural context shapes and directs individual economic choices and the market process.

The second approach, or what we might call 'Culture as Constraints,' concedes a slightly more active role to culture, as it recognizes the non-neutral role customary rules, which evolve out of the cultural context, might play in constraining optimizing behavior. For example, Akerlof (1980) describes how individuals may adhere to social customs over time, even if it is economically disadvantageous, if there is a corresponding cost in lost reputation for non-compliance. Thus, the social custom of a 'fair' (but above market clearing) wage may result in unemployment and the inefficient allocation of resources. Within development literature, customary practices or value systems are blamed for discouraging the efficient allocation of resources (Lewis 1955; McClelland 1961). Traditional allegiance to the family farm rather than expansion into alternative trade, for example, is blamed for stifling economic development.

Yet this approach fails to recognize the *enabling* role culture plays in economic processes. By selecting out only those aspects of culture which inhibit allocative efficiency, we set culture up as a counter-rational force: as if, without culture, market exchange would be a smooth, frictionless process. Yet, in accepting this account of the world, we forget that, in a world without culture, property rights, legal custom, and language would not emerge. We have to ask ourselves how smooth and frictionless exchange would be without the benefit of such institutions. Further, culture is the context of shared meaning that enables the entrepreneur to make sense of the economic environment. Neoclassical literature tends to treat economically efficient or 'correct' decisions as separable from the cultural context. However, in the abstract, efficiency means only that certain criteria are well balanced against other criteria. Just what those criteria are has to be interpreted. Other than at the most abstract level, any meaningful notion of efficiency will be, at least in part, culturally defined. Wise or efficient decisions will be so only with reference to a particular context—including the cultural context. Thus, rather than a counter-rational force which inhibits efficient decision-making, culture provides the framework within which to interpret the best course of action.

Economic anthropologists have a much longer history than economists in attempting to bridge the gaps between culture and economic theory (see, for example, Malinowski [1922] 1961). By the late 1950s, economic anthropologists were beginning to accept the principles of neoclassical economics as their theoretical guide in what were then called 'primitive societies.' For the time, this was a significant move, as it suggested that all peoples—whether European or African, colonialist or native—shared the universal quality of rationality. If all individuals were essentially the same in this respect, then neoclassical tools and concepts ought to be equally applicable around the globe. Many within anthropology saw this as a radical advance, as it provided a theoretical framework within which to model and understand non-Western cultures. Similarly, such a move represented a crowning achievement for neoclassical theory, as it could generate explanations for social and economic behavior across the globe.

But the match which seemed to be made in heaven was not to survive. By the 1950s and into the 1960s, neoclassical economics faced serious challenges as to its universal applicability. Many economic anthropologists argued that a theoretical paradigm which grew out of an advanced industrialized context would ultimately distort rather than explain the realities of pre-industrial societies. Cultural anthropologists also rejected neoclassical theory as incapable of addressing the differences among cultures with regard to economic decisions and institutions. Most anthropologists accepted the validity of neoclassical theory when applied within a Western industrialized context. But, for their own areas of interest, most were willing to leave the principles of economic theory behind.

The debate over the role neoclassical theory can play in pre-industrialized contexts dominated the economic anthropology literature of the 1960s. The 'formalists' were those who argued in favor of the universal applicability of neoclassical theory, even in pre-industrial societies. The 'substantivists' were those who saw this as an empty enterprise, given the industrialized context out of which neoclassical economics had emerged. The formalist–substantivist debate has been detailed elsewhere (LeClair and Schneider 1968). The point behind revisiting the debate here is to identify the subtler shortcomings of neoclassical theory which were missed by both sides. This new perspective of the debate will open the way for an alternative route by which the connections between culture and economy can be investigated, yet perhaps this time with greater success.

The 'new institutionalist economics' represents an important advance in this direction, as it attempts to ground neoclassical analysis within specific institutional contexts—a dimension of the market process essentially missed within standard theory. We will move a step beyond this by investigating the cultural context which gives rise to social institutions, on the one hand, and shapes the perspective with which entrepreneurs carve out opportunities for profit, on the other. In order to make this next step, Austrian economics offers an alternative to the institutionless, cultureless neoclassical paradigm. In particular, the interpretive tradition within Austrian economics and cultural anthropology makes it possible to address the role culture plays in shaping entrepreneurship and the social institutions necessary for economic development. Such an approach may convince social scientists outside of economics to consider once again the value of economic theory in their own investigations. Further, cultural analysis will allow economists to address questions that are systematically pushed aside by neoclassical theory, but which are fundamental to the development process.

5.2 ECONOMIC THEORY AND ECONOMIC ANTHROPOLOGY

Considered by many to be the father of economic anthropology, Bronislaw Malinowski was among the first to investigate the social context of economic activity. His ethnographic studies of the Trobriand Islands ([1922] 1961) detailed the complex rituals of indigenous exchange practices, and explored the functions of magic in instilling hope and confidence before setting out upon trade expeditions. The talent Malinowski possessed as an ethnographer, however, did not save him from drawing some erroneous conclusions.

Malinowski ([1922] 1961) rejected the notion that Trobriand Islanders were motivated by self-interest. In fact, he held economic theory in disdain and characterized the 'primitive economic man' concept in mocking tones. In his account of the Trobriand Islanders' yam harvest, Malinowski argues that, rather than self-interest, the prestige behind the title *tokwaba-gula* or 'good gardener' was the primary motivation.

> The most important point about this is, however, that all, or almost all of the fruits of his work, and certainly any surplus he can achieve by extra effort, goes not to the man himself, but to his relatives-in-law . . . [I]t may be said that about three quarters of a man's crop go partly as tribute to the chief, partly as his due to his sister's (or mother's) husband and family.
>
> But although he thus derives practically no personal benefit in the utilitarian sense from his harvest, the gardener receives much praise and renown from its size and quality, and that in a direct and circumstantial manner. For all the crops, after being harvested, are displayed for some time afterwards in the gardens, piled up in neat, conical heaps under small shelters made of yam vine. Each man's harvest is thus exhibited for criticism in his own plot, and parties of natives walk about from garden to garden, admiring, comparing, and praising the best results. (Malinowski [1922] 1961, reprinted in LeClair and Schneider 1968: p. 20)

The contradictions within these paragraphs appear evident to any student of modern economic theory. Malinowski missed the point that economic ends do not necessarily have to involve monetary or material ends, and that all wants, whether monetary, material, or social, are part of the fundamental economic problem if scarce means must be employed to satisfy them. The gardeners Malinowski described use scarce means (land, labor, time, seed, equipment, and so on) to achieve the ends of prestige and social obligation. Rather than denying the self-interested rationality of the Trobriand Islanders, Malinowski's own account serves to demonstrate the keen efficiency they display in the pursuit of the ends they found most important.[2] Yet, as apparent as these mistakes seem today, others followed Malinowski's disdain for economic theory. 'By following Malinowski, anthropologists were systematically and uncritically cutting themselves from the one body of theory which sought to illuminate economic phenomena' (LeClair and Schneider 1968: p. 5).

Within the period of a single year, however, three anthropologists independently offered devastating critiques of Malinowski. D.M. Goodfellow (1939), Melville Herskovits ([1940] 1952), and later Raymond Firth (1951) made use of rational choice theories in their studies of economic phenomena in South Africa, West Africa, and Polynesia, respectively. To varying degrees, all three followed a Robbinsian approach to the nature of the economic problem. The universal nature of economics, according to Robbins (1932), does not lie in a universal pursuit of material wealth. The universal nature of the economic problem lies in the fact that human wants are virtually boundless, while the means to satisfy these wants are relatively scarce.

Firth, Goodfellow, and Herskovits recognized that economic differences are generated by different cultural influences. Gifts in religious ceremonies and dietary restrictions will influence demand for specific goods, for example. Similarly, production may be shaped by beliefs and traditions which do not necessarily serve to maximize output or profit. Herskovits ([1940] 1952) cites, for example, Dolmatoff's account of the Kogi Indians in the Sierra Nevada. According to Dolmatoff, the Indians abstain from cultivating productive terrace land for supernatural reasons. Lastly, the ends which individuals find worthwhile will be determined in part by the cultural context. All three argued, however, that this does not change the fundamental economic problem. Though they agreed that cross-cultural implications of the universal phenomenon known as 'economizing' exist, they argued that economic theory is valid in all settings. Firth described the Muslim 'preference' for risk sharing and profit in providing capital over the charging of interest, but he argued that the Muslim is no less rational than the Western entrepreneur. Here, what is demonstrated is not a lack of self-interest, but rather 'a positive desire for conformity to moral and religious ideals' (Firth 1951: pp. 152–3). Thus, they argued, neoclassical maximization models are universally valid, even though what is being maximized will differ according to the social context. Whether the end is to maximize profit, social status, or security, the process can be modeled with the calculus of optimization.

Of the three, Goodfellow was the most ardent supporter of the neoclassical paradigm. He relied heavily upon the Robinson Crusoe construct of economic theory to make his point.

> It has been shown that Robinson Crusoe has something more than a strictly methodological significance; that an individual in his position would indeed feel the pressure of needs upon resources, would in fact make choice between the applications of his various resources, would encounter varying returns and would have to choose between present and future and between work and leisure. Wicksteed . . . has shown how the greater part of the apparatus of economic theory may be evolved without going outside a single household. This being so, it would be surprising if modern economic theory failed to apply to the peoples known as primitive. (Goodfellow 1939: p. 6)

The value of the Crusoian or single household construct is that it demonstrates the all-pervasive reality of scarcity—an important point which, as it turns out, was missed by many within economic anthropology. Yet, another lesson which is often taken away from such constructs is the notion that economic processes operate independently of the social and cultural context. Further, this notion implies that any differences which do persist from one society to another are simply benign differences in preference.

From the start, Crusoian economics assumes that cultural or institutional differences are irrelevant. As Goodfellow argued,

> [T]he phenomena of social science are nothing if not universal. The groups, the behavior, the fundamental social relationships such as those of kinsmen, and neighbors, are qualitatively the same the world over. Wherever we look at Mankind we see motives of accumulation, of competitive display, of obligations towards kinfolk, of religious organization and political activity; these, and such, make up the body of fact with which social science must deal. The fundamental differences between 'civilized' and 'savage' . . . have now been so effectively exploded that we need not here waste space upon them. (Goodfellow 1939: p. 14)

It should not come as a surprise that many cultural anthropologists objected to the use of economic constructs which effectively assumed culture and the rest of their subject matter into the background. Many economists have also objected to Crusoian economics on the grounds that it cannot address the extended economic order which is generated among millions of disparate human beings. The elements of the extended order, including the price system, financial markets, and international trade, are facilitated by social institutions such as law, property, and monetary systems. As these and other social institutions do not arise out of an acultural context, an acultural model will not adequately serve in their study.

Both Firth and Herskovits were somewhat critical of Crusoian economics. Yet, without a clear alternative, neoclassical economic theory was better than no economic theory.

> One of the principles of early economic theory was to regard the individual as the point from which all development of theoretical principles must begin. We have come to realize that the individual never exists alone; that a society, as it has been put, is more than an aggregate of Robinson Crusoes; and that social interaction in terms of cultural tradition dictates reconsideration of the earlier starting point. The process of economizing, we recognize, is essentially based on the broader organization of society. Yet, the individual cannot be left out of the picture, for all forms of social behavior, in the final analysis, must be referred to as the behavior of individual members of a given society in specific situations. (Herskovits [1940] 1952: pp. 6–7)

Thus, even the neoclassical economic anthropologists were somewhat aware of the paradigm's shortcomings. However, the mistakes which were made in the absence of any economic theory were reason enough to defend it.

The late 1950s gave rise to the 'substantivist' school of thought as a counter-attack upon the formalist or neoclassical paradigm within anthropology. But, rather than moving the debate forward by exposing the acultural nature of the neoclassical paradigm, the debate continued to revolve around the basic issue of scarcity. This retrenchment unfortunately drew attention away from the substantivists' point that economic processes in pre-industrial societies are embedded within a complex cultural context. The implications of this point for neoclassical economics were never fully considered, and thus alternatives to acultural economics were never explored.

Economic historian Karl Polanyi (1957) argued that societies are 'integrated' in one of three ways: through the market mechanism, through reciprocal relationships such as kinship, or through redistribution via a central authority. Polanyi and his associates argued that neoclassical economics is applicable only if the primary form of integration is the market. Polanyi argued further that market integration is a relatively isolated and recent phenomenon. Thus, neoclassical economic theory, he argued, is applicable only to the modern Western context from which it arose. In

Trade and Market in the Early Empires, Polanyi et al. (1957) were primarily arguing against the use of modern economic concepts in historical contexts, but economic anthropologists such as George Dalton (1961) and Marshall Sahlins (1960, 1972, 1976) were quick to employ similar arguments in non-Western contexts.

Polanyi suggested two meanings of 'economic':

> The substantive meaning of economic derives from man's dependence for his living upon nature and his fellows. It refers to the interchange with his natural and social environment, in so far as this results in supplying him with the means of material want satisfaction.
> The formal meaning of economic derives from the logical character of the means–ends relationship, as apparent in such words as 'economical' or 'economizing.' It refers to a definite situation of choice, namely that between the different uses of means induced by an insufficiency of those means. If we call the rules governing the choice of means the logic of rational action, then we may denote this variant of logic, with an improvised term, as formal economics. (Polanyi 1957: p. 243)

Formal economics, then, refers to technical efficiency between means and ends—the logic of rational action. Whether or not an economy is faced with scarcity, Polanyi argued, is an empirical question. This is where he saw the flaw of formal economics—in its application to areas in which scarcity induced choice is not significant, such as in tribal societies. Polanyi stated that only in market societies will scarcity be present. Thus, only the substantive meaning of 'economic' matters to empirical investigations of pre-industrial society.

In response to Polanyi, two points need to be made here. First, most societies exhibit all three forms of integration to one degree or another. Markets do not control the distribution of all resources in advanced Western society. Accelerated tax rates, charitable organizations, and family obligations speak to the redistributive and reciprocal forms of integration operating in this context. Nor are soviet-type systems merely redistributive. Market coordination, in the form of black markets, second economies, and shadow economies, often determines the flow of resources in such contexts (Katsenelinboigen 1977; Grossman 1982). Second, even if redistribution or reciprocity dominates in any particular context, scarcity is still a determining factor in choice. Even the heaviest of welfare states faces scarcity. The difference is the allocation mechanism, not the presence or absence of scarcity. The very fact that an allocation mechanism is necessary suggests that scarcity is present. The benevolent king must still decide who gets what and how much.

Essentially, the substantivist school emptied economic theory of its core concept: choice. Polanyi argued that substantive economics does not necessarily entail choice, nor does it imply insufficiency of means:

> [M]an's livelihood may or may not involve the necessity of choice and, if choice there be, it need not be induced by the limiting effect of a 'scarcity' of the means; indeed, some of the most important physical and social conditions of livelihood such as the availability of air and water or a loving mother's devotion to her infant are not, as a rule, so limiting. (Polanyi 1957: pp. 243–4)

Polanyi's own examples defeat his point, however. It is exactly the usual abundance of air and, in some circumstances, water that places their acquisition outside of the economic problem. Further, scarcity persists in many things other than material resources. The example of a mother's love is an excellent case in point. The sentiment that love knows no bounds is pleasant, but any mother of two knows that she is unable to offer the second infant the same amount of attention that she was able to offer the first. Even if love is boundless, a mother's time and energy certainly are not. Scarcity necessitates choice, as one course of action must be given up in pursuit of another. In short, any definition of 'economic' which does not have both the elements of scarcity and choice is meaningless. It is precisely at the point at which scarcity is not a factor that the situation is outside of the fundamental economic problem.

In line with Polanyi, Dalton (1961) argued that scarcity is socially, not physically, defined. Dalton challenged the formalist assertion that wants are unlimited. He argued that market organization compels the individual to seek self-gain. Outside of a market context, he asserted, individuals would not be compelled to increase their material wants, so the issue of scarcity is not relevant. Similarly, Sahlins (1968, 1972) argued that, by restricting wants, hunter-gatherer societies could enjoy relative affluence, characterized by high consumption of leisure time, even in the absence of material abundance.

An important point was being made in this literature: which criteria are associated with self-interest, which activities, goods, or services provide satisfaction, and what material circumstances constitute 'affluence' are all culturally defined. As Sahlins (1976) later argued, in order to understand non-Western societies it is necessary to understand the natives' own cultural constructions as the starting point of analysis. Such constructions will indeed have real effects on the relative scarcity of some things, as scarcity of any particular resource must be defined in relation to the demand for that resource. A society which has no use or desire for chickens will not experience a scarcity of chickens, no matter how many or how few exist in close proximity. Yet, even though culture helps to define the relative scarcity of resources in the particular case, no society is immune from the basic circumstance of scarcity in the general sense. Even for an ascetic people whose material wants have been fully satiated, limited time and energy must always be allocated to competing ends. Time spent preparing meals is time that cannot be spent in prayer, for example. Or, in response to Sahlins (1968, 1976), even people of affluence must decide how to spend their perhaps abundant, but still limited, leisure time. What Dalton and Sahlins could have argued is that commodity fetishism is not a universal phenomenon. But this does not mean that only some societies are subject to the constraints of scarcity.

In short, the substantivists made many of the same mistakes Malinowski made years earlier, and the formalists were quick to recognize them (Burling 1962; Cook 1966). Such corrections were necessary, but the retrenchment of the debate into the basic issue of scarcity continued to divert attention away from the very real shortcomings of neoclassical economics. Sahlins's (1963) work on the role of kinship in economic relations, for instance, demonstrated the failure of maximization models to characterize adequately economic decisions which were embedded within the social context. The substantivists argued that, in pre-industrial societies, all economic decisions were made within a complex web of social institutions and customary rules. For this reason, applying maximization techniques in pre-industrialized contexts emptied the analysis of any substantive content. While neoclassical economics was on solid ground in its defense of the fundamental economic problem, the limitations of the theory to characterize complex decision-making outside of the acultural model presented a more challenging critique—a critique that was never fully addressed.

Perhaps one of the reasons this part of the substantivist challenge was not addressed directly in the debate was that the substantivists did not take their challenge far enough. The substantivists emphasized the cultural specificity of neoclassical economics as its major shortcoming. But the Western origin of neoclassical economics is not the source of its limitations. The reason why many economic anthropologists find neoclassical constructs at odds with their work is that it represents an acultural model of the economic process. The substantivists did not recognize the radical potential of their own critique. Not only are pre-industrial economies embedded within a complex cultural context, but so too are advanced capitalist economies. Neoclassicism is just as ill suited to address the cultural context of Western markets as it is ill suited to address the cultural context of West African markets.

The formalist–substantivist debate was never fully resolved. As Plattner (1989: p. 14) suggests, economic anthropologists 'did not stop doing empirical research but stopped arguing about how to go about doing it.'

Neoclassical economics did not provide a satisfying theory for social scientists interested in economics and culture, yet the substantivist position did not offer a better alternative. Thus, rather than pushing the debate further, most simply left the discussion.

By the 1970s, the vacuum left in the wake of neoclassical theory was quickly filled with Marxist and neo-Marxist theories attempting to explain economic phenomena in the developing world. The so-called 'new economic anthropology' redirected the discussion away from the formalist–substantivist debate towards economic development issues. Marxism, in part through the influence of the 'new French school' of economic anthropology, was reintroduced into the discipline (Althusser 1969; Godelier 1972; Meillassoux 1972, 1976; Terray 1972, 1974; Dupre and Rey 1973). Marxist economic anthropology sought to shift the focus from transactions (either ceremonial or market transactions) to production and the class relations which emerge out of the particular mode of production.

Marxist economic anthropologists rejected the formalist reliance upon neoclassical theory, but they were equally critical of the substantivists for arguing that industrialized and pre-industrial societies were fundamentally different. The Marxist critique of capitalism was taken for granted. The point of the new economic anthropology was to explain how the developing world fit into a generalized Marxist paradigm. As developing countries became defined in terms of world capitalist domination, Marxian concepts of class, class dominance, and exploitation in the mode of production were applied across the globe. Marxist theory also had a significant influence in economic anthropology through the 'dependency school' of the 1970s. Underdevelopment, it was argued, was not the outcome of internal deficiencies, but a direct consequence of Western growth and affluence, and/or neocolonialism (Frank 1969; Cockcroft et al. 1972; Kahn 1978). In either case, economic anthropology essentially had become applied Marxism in the context of underdeveloped countries. As Godelier argues,

> [I]t is the concept of the mode of production which constitutes the primary concept of economic anthropology. The task of the latter is to determine the types of mode of production which exist in the societies it studies and which transform themselves through articulation with, and under the domination of, the capitalist world economy. (Godelier 1972: p. 195)

In describing the new economic anthropology of the 1970s, among which he counts himself a contributor, Seddon says it best.

> For the 'new economic anthropology' is neither 'economic' in the usual limited sense, nor is it 'anthropology.' It is rather a branch of historical materialism predominantly but not exclusively concerned with the dynamic and structure

of pre-capitalist social formations and the conditions of their transformation. (Seddon 1978: pp. 62–3)

The crucial issue here is that, as economic anthropology became increasingly dominated by the influence of Marxism, the questions regarding the interplay of culture and economic processes or, more importantly, the embeddedness of economic processes within culture, which were never adequately addressed within the formalist–substantivist debate, were completely subverted. No sacred cows were spared in this pursuit. For instance, Marxist anthropologists sought to de-throne the central role of kinship held within anthropology. Of far greater importance to the Marxist is the control of the means of production.

> Classical Marxism has a definite conception of the necessary structure of society. A society is conceived as a social formation, an articulated structure of three interdependent levels, dominated by the structure of a particular mode of production consisting of an economic, a political-legal, and a cultural level. The levels are thought to be related in such a way that the first (in other words, economic) always plays a primary role, that of determination in the last instance. (Cutler et al. 1977: p. 174)

The mode of production is central to Marxist social theory, as it is the engine which drives all other social phenomena. 'The key questions are: what is produced, by what social groups? How are the groups organized and by whom? What is the purpose of production (for example, use or exchange)?' (Frankenberg 1967, quoted in Clammer 1978: p. 7). The concept of 'class relations' took the place of any cultural theory. The attempt to overthrow kinship as a key component within economic anthropological analysis was only one celebrated example. Within the Marxist paradigm, the mode of production drives and takes precedence over social relations, custom, kinship, religion, and ideology—all of which were central to cultural analysis. What ground cultural theory had lost in the formalist–substantivist debate in the 1960s was reinforced by the resurgence of Marxian economic anthropology in the 1970s.

5.3 BEYOND ACULTURAL ECONOMICS: NEW INSTITUTIONAL ECONOMICS

To the broader field of anthropology, the lack of attention paid to culture among formalist and Marxist economic anthropologists was not a tremendous loss, given that cultural anthropology was still a thriving sub-discipline within the field. More significantly, the opportunity to introduce cultural analysis into economics was not pursued. Certainly, many would argue that this was no great tragedy—that the acultural nature of neoclassical economics is an asset. After all, exogenous policy shifts such as price controls, import quotas, and restricted government licensing generate systematically similar results, no matter what the cultural context. Indeed, cultural analysis is not necessary for all questions an economist might ask, and in this respect the neoclassical paradigm often serves us well.

Yet advances such as those made by the 'new institutionalist' school of economics have revealed some important limitations of neoclassical economic theory. Following on the insights presented by Ronald Coase (1957, 1960), new institutional economics argues that neoclassical conclusions will rarely hold in the real world, as positive transaction costs are almost always present (Wallis and North 1986). Wherever transaction costs exist, institutions become relevant as individuals seek out ways to minimize the costs associated with exchange. Establishing enforceable contracts, for instance, reduces moral hazard problems associated with long-distance and inter-temporal exchange. New institutional economics has effectively argued that the social institutions neoclassicism assumes into the background of analysis, such as contract and dispute resolution procedures (North 1987, 1990), property rights (Alchian and Demsetz 1973), and the role of the state (Bates 1981), are the key to understanding economic history and development. The division of labor and the expansion of trade depend upon institutions which reduce transaction costs associated with production and market exchange. As an economic historian, North (1994) identifies another important limitation of neoclassical theory in that it has no time dimension—no way of understanding how institutions and economic performance change. This emphasis has allowed new institutional economics to influence development economics (Nabli and Nugent 1989; North 1989, 1995; Harris et al. 1995) and, to a lesser extent, anthropology (Ensminger 1991, 1992).

In order to understand economic development in any particular context, the economist must investigate entrepreneurship and the social institutions that mediate the development process. The smooth functioning of the market relies on enforceable contracts, a method of resolving disputes, financial safety nets, and an environment conducive for entrepreneurship: advantages which all arise from the cultural context. Institutional analysis at its best is that which provides rich historical and cultural detail of this process. Yet it is precisely in this regard that neoclassical economics exhibits its limitations, because it has no way of addressing complex, institutionally defined, culturally informed choice within the market.

North recognizes the pivotal role culture has in supplying informal enforcement mechanisms (North 1990) and in generating the path-dependent nature of institutional change (North 1994). For institutions to work, they must be supported by cultural norms that reduce the costs associated with formal enforcement mechanisms. Contractual obligation, private property rights, and the justice system cannot function in a society without a commonly held notion of what a contract actually is, what can and cannot legitimately be bought and sold, and what constitutes fairness. The market process depends on the underlying culture, as it provides the source of legitimation for the social institutions crucial to a successful economy. Further, the renegotiation of institutional rules will take place within the given cultural context, so the past will always exert its influence upon the present and future institutional context.

Nowhere is North clearer about the significance of culture than in his discussion of culturally defined 'mental models.' In his work with Arthur Denzau, North argues that

> [i]deas matter; and the way ideas are communicated among people is crucial to theories that will enable us to deal with strong uncertainty problems at the individual level. For most of the interesting issues in political and economic markets, uncertainty, not risk, characterizes choice-making. Under conditions of uncertainty, individuals' interpretation of their environment will reflect their learning. Individuals with common cultural backgrounds and experiences will share reasonably convergent mental models, ideologies, and institutions; and individuals with different learning experiences (both cultural and environmental) will have different theories (models, ideologies) to interpret their environment ... [I]n order to understand decision-making under such conditions of uncertainty we must understand the relationship of the mental models that individuals construct to make sense out of the world around them, the ideologies that evolve from such constructions, and the institutions that develop in a society to order interpersonal relationships. (Denzau and North 1994: pp. 3–4)

While the role culture plays in shaping institutions and entrepreneurial perspective is recognized, it is far from the central focus of the new institutional economics. In this sense, the present project can be seen as complementary to the work of North and others interested in the role institutions play in markets. The present project turns our focus not only to the fact that markets are embedded within a particular institutional context, but to the *cultural* embeddedness of markets as well.

In another sense, however, this project represents an alternative approach to that taken by the new institutionalists, in that North and others have continued to adhere to a 'relaxed' version of the neoclassical paradigm, rather than abandon it for one that might directly address the crucial questions they raise. Even within the 'relaxed' version of the neoclassical paradigm, institutions are still characterized as separable from the cultural context from which they evolve. Alchian and Demsetz (1973), for instance, merely see culture as a less than desirable substitute for property rights. If, for example, a community fails to establish private property rights, it would then have to rely on cultural indoctrination to alleviate the tendency to shirk and free-ride off others' efforts. Thus, Alchian and Demsetz argue that a system of values and behavioral norms will compensate (though imperfectly) where property rights fail to emerge.

By characterizing the possible solutions as *either* coordination through private property rights *or* cultural indoctrination, Alchian and Demsetz imply that culturally informed systems such as values or informal rules of behavior are not at work in the formation of private property rights. The point is not that values are at work in one situation and not the other but, rather, that different value systems are at work in each. A strongly held ethic of 'earn respect and honor through sharing' may work to ration resources in a setting of communal rights. But an equally strong ethic such as 'respect the fruits of your neighbors' labor as their own' is just as necessary for the private property setting. These ethics are part of the cultural framework which gives rise to and supports effective rules of property. Without this framework, rules of property—private or otherwise—have no source of legitimation and are therefore not sustainable. Stein (1995), for example, argues that socialist policies in parts of Eastern Europe and Africa have eroded the cultural sources of legitimation for private property, explaining the often disappointing results of privatization efforts. To be complete, investigations seeking to understand the success or failure of social institutions to generate economic growth must make reference to the particular cultural context in which the institution emerged (or was imposed). Private property rights can be expected to generate economic development only if the community at large accepts such arrangements as legitimate (also see Boettke et al., this volume, Chapter 6; Grube, this volume, Chapter 17).

Similarly, contractual arrangements which involve credit, partnership, or supply agreements will expand markets, but only if a reliable system of conflict resolution is in place. Entrepreneurs are not likely to offer resources and supplies on credit if they have no recourse in the case of default. Thus, economic progress cannot emerge in a world of rational maximizers without guarantees of property and justice. Yet accepted attitudes towards the sanctity of private property, shared notions about whom to trust, what constitutes justice, or appropriate behavior in trading relationships do not surface out of thin air. They evolve out of a specific cultural context. Tribal and religious traditions, for example, may provide the justification for what is fair, or how land is divided and passed from one generation to the next. Kinship structure may determine the individual's financial obligation to the community and vice versa. In short, markets are an extension of culture because it is culture that shapes the rules necessary for a market to function.

By trying to add culture into what is essentially an acultural model, the new institutional economics often suffers from the same shortcomings as standard neoclassical economics. North and others explicitly reject the narrow view of mechanistic rationality inherent within neoclassical constructs, charging that 'such version[s] of the rational actor model have simply led us astray. The actors frequently must act on incomplete information and process the information that they do receive through mental constructs that can result in persistently inefficient paths' (North 1990: p. 8). Yet, as we see here, North sets up the neoclassical world of zero transaction costs as the only context in which 'correct' or perfectly efficient decisions can be made, because it is only within this context that we do not have to deal with the distorting effects of the cultural lens. Rather than culture being seen as the context in which contentious interpretations of the world are worked out, culture is seen mainly as distorting an otherwise clear and objective reality.

Though the time dimension that new institutional economics adds is a critical improvement to standard theory, this still retains a mechanistic and narrowly rationalistic approach to institutional change. For example, in her study of institutional change among the Orma of Kenya, Ensminger characterizes institutional choice as follows:

> In all cases, institutions impose costs (social, political, or economic) on certain forms of behavior, and therefore those who wish to engage in such proscribed behavior have an incentive to change the institutional structure. Furthermore, individuals try to structure institutions toward their own ends ... by committing resources to bring about change to the institutional environment. (Ensminger 1992: p. 19)

To be sure, it is important to recognize that in certain contexts, particularly political contexts, those who are in a position to concentrate benefits upon themselves by changing formal institutional rules, while dispersing the costs to an uninformed and/or unorganized public, may very well seek to do so (Olson 1965, 1982). But to view all institutional change as if it is the outcome of cost–benefit calculus is misleading, in that it suggests that institutions emerge out of a cultural vacuum. Ensminger (1992: 167) later addresses the role of ideology in institutional change, but again the role takes on an instrumental quality. She argues that the Orma recognized that by converting to Islam they seized an opportunity to reduce transaction costs and reap the economic benefits. It may indeed be the case that some such 'calculus' was going on inside the heads of the converted. As Berger and Luckmann (1966) note, the construction of social reality is rarely a disinterested enterprise. Yet, in this accounting of institutional change, culture *qua* ideology is treated as another argument in the objective function, as if any society could make a similar choice. In this objectified view of institutional choice, no account is taken of the cultural symmetries between indigenous and Islamic belief structures that allowed for the acceptance of both the 'letter' of Islamic practice and the 'spirit' of its teachings. In other words, why did Islam, with all the economic benefits it conveyed, 'fit' the indigenous cultural context? While ethnographies such as Ensminger's represent critical contributions to the literature on institutions and development, they are still limited by the neoclassical framework.

5.4 BEYOND ACULTURAL ECONOMICS: THE AUSTRIAN SCHOOL OF ECONOMICS

The best way to move beyond acultural characterizations of choice is to abandon the neoclassical model altogether. It is here that we turn to the Austrian school of economics. The Austrian economics literature reaches back to contributions made by Carl Menger in the marginalist revolution of the 1870s. Along with William Stanley Jevons and Leon Walras, Menger changed the course of economic inquiry. The marginalist revolution marks a pivotal point in the history of economic thought, as it replaced the objectivistic labor theory of value with the subjective marginal theory of value. The implications of this transition are far reaching. For instance, Marx's descriptions of exploitation under capitalism and the eventual transformation into socialism are crucially dependent upon the debunked labor theory of value. Such implications are explored in detail elsewhere (Kolakowski 1978). For our purposes here, the significance of the subjectivist turn rests with the recognition that the value or meaning of objects presented in the physical world must be interpreted by the human subject. Human beings impute value to goods and services in accordance with their perception of how such goods and services will satisfy their wants. Further, the value attached to any particular unit of the good or service will depend upon the context in which the human decision-maker finds herself. If the item in question is in relative abundance, human beings will in general attach a lower level of value to the last unit than if the item is relatively scarce. The valuation of raw materials and other inputs works in much the same way, except that in this case the value human beings attach to such 'goods of a higher order' depend upon the value consumers attach to the final goods and services the inputs help to produce.

Jevons, Walras, and Menger came to essentially these same conclusions, yet, as other scholars followed, different elements of the marginalist revolution were emphasized. Those following Jevons and Walras further mathematized economic theory in models which emphasized equilibrium solutions, while those who followed in the Mengerian tradition—what came to be known as the Austrian school of economics—continued to emphasize and expand upon the subjective or interpretive aspects of the marginalist revolution. Following in Menger's footsteps, Ludwig von Mises ([1922] 1932, [1949] 1966, [1933] 1981) sought to expose what he saw as the weakness of economic theory which narrowly defined choice as the outcome of maximization of a particular goal within a given set of means and ends (Robbins 1932). Mises argued that such an approach rendered choice a mere mechanical computation and missed the interpretive dimension of human decision-making. A broader conception of *human action*, as opposed to the narrow Robbinsian notion of economizing, would not only allow us to recognize the computational aspect of choice within a given framework of means and ends, but also allow us to recognize the novelty and creativity at work when the individual proactively altered that framework, For Mises, this sort of reinterpretation of the available data was the essence of entrepreneurship. Entrepreneurial perception—that which allows for the creation of a new means/ends framework—lies outside of the mechanical depiction of choice as optimal resource allocation.

Building upon the Misesian conception of human action, Israel Kirzner (1973, 1979) advanced the Austrian theory of entrepreneurship as an alternative to standard neoclassical portrayals of the market. Kirzner's critique of neoclassical theory centers on the model's inability to account for entrepreneurship—a critical challenge considering that the entrepreneur is the driving force behind the learning process of the market, and ultimately behind economic development itself. Standard economics emphasizes not the process by which market coordination takes place, but rather the end state equilibrium in which all resources are said to be efficiently allocated. If equilibrium solutions are the central focus of economic inquiry, one must pay considerable attention to identifying and describing the limited conditions under which such results might emerge. In particular, one must assume that all economic actors possess the relevant information for making perfectly efficient decisions. Only then will equilibrium be guaranteed within the theoretical construct. Yet it is precisely at this point that we fail to understand the market as a process. With all the information readily available to economic actors, individuals immediately jump to the new point of perfect allocation. F.A. Hayek ([1946] 1948) recognized the irony that, within this so-called 'competitive solution,' there is in fact no behavior we would actually call competitive—no advertising, and no product innovation or differentiation. Further, Kirzner recognized that, in such an economy, no entrepreneurship need exist, as the equilibrium solution is always obvious. Once the equilibrium solution is achieved, competition—in the sense of seeking to provide customers with more attractive options—ceases to be a meaningful concept, as no more adjustment is needed or even possible.[3]

Yet, here on the ground, human beings live in a world of fundamental ignorance. It is only within this context of ignorance, in which human action is shrouded by uncertainty, that entrepreneurship exists. In the absence of full information, individuals cannot immediately adjust their plans so that they perfectly dovetail with the plans of other market participants. Producers in search of the highest possible returns in one market may not know of consumers in another market willing to pay more. Such ignorance leads to a lack of coordination on the one hand, and profit opportunities on the other. Some people will be alert to the opportunities that exist, buying in the first market, selling in the second, and facilitating an overall trend towards increased coordination. For Kirzner, the quintessential characteristic of entrepreneurship is this alertness.

Kirzner (1980: 24) argues that entrepreneurial alertness is not a resource to be deployed in the course of maximizing profits or some other goal. When one is alert to an opportunity, one has discovered something previously unrecognized. To characterize entrepreneurial alertness as Robbinsian optimization within given means and ends is to suggest that the profit opportunity was already within the means/ends framework, and in no need of being discovered. The alertness which allows some to discover arbitrage opportunities before others is extra-economic, as it lies outside of the optimization problem. The significance of this is that, if we are to understand the market process, we must move beyond the standard account of economic decision-making which depicts choice as isolated, mechanistic calculations. By seeking out profit opportunities missed by others, Kirzner argues, the entrepreneur moves the market from a position of relative discoordination to one in which plans and expectations are more coordinated. Standard neoclassical economics cannot account for entrepreneurship because it assumes away uncertainty within the market. If all market participants have perfect information, no profit opportunities are left to be exploited, and thus no entrepreneurship and no competitive process need exist. The point is not simply that the assumption of perfect information is unrealistic. Rather, the assumption of perfect information assumes away the very thing that sets the market clearing forces into motion.

Also essential to Kirzner's representation of entrepreneurship is the discovery aspect of the market process. Following Mises ([1949] 1966, [1933] 1981), Hayek (1948, 1967, 1978), and other Austrian theorists, Kirzner recognizes not only the allocative role markets play, but also the role they play in enabling market participants to discover the proper course of action.

> [O]nce we become sensitive to the decision-makers' alertness to new possibly worthwhile ends and newly available means, it may be possible to explain the pattern of change in an individual's decisions as the outcome of a learning process generated by the unfolding experience of the decisions themselves. An analysis confined to allocative explanations must fail entirely to perceive such continuity in any sequence of decisions, since each decision is comprehended purely in terms of its own relevant ends–means framework. With purely allocative explanations, no earlier decision can be used to explain later decisions on the basis of learning . . . We must recognize what I have called the entrepreneurial element in order to perceive that the changing patterns of ends–means held relevant to successive decisions are the possible understandable outcome of a process of experience in which the decision-maker's alertness to relevant new information has generated a continuously changing sequence of decisions. (Kirzner 1973: pp. 36–7)

Human action can only be understood within the context of an individual's overall plan or set of plans, not as isolated moments of optimization. In the course of working out those plans—through action and imagination— the individual learns and adjusts his or her plans, constantly reinterpreting the data. It is here that Kirzner makes his principal contribution: the linking of the Misesian concept of human action, one which reaches far beyond a narrow allocational role of economic choice, to the discovery process inherently tied to entrepreneurship (Lavoie, this volume, Chapter 3).

Though Kirzner's contributions represent some of the best work on entrepreneurship, they are still in need of modification if we are to take culture into account. Kirzner largely ignores the role of culture in entrepreneurship. Lavoie (this volume, Chapter 3) argues that, because Kirzner still holds to the equilibrium construct set out by neoclassical theory, he has failed to see the cultural implications of his own argument. Though Kirzner shifts the emphasis away from equilibrium solutions, he maintains that the role of the entrepreneur is an equilibrating one. If exogenous shifts were to cease, entrepreneurial activity would result in an equilibrium solution. Kirzner is quick to point out that such an end state will never occur, as change is inevitable, but the tendency of the market process and entrepreneurial discovery is towards a pre-existing equilibrium. While on the one hand Kirzner characterizes entrepreneurship as a creative process and the source of genuine novelty, on the other hand Kirzner holds to an objectivistic view of entrepreneurial opportunities.

'Alertness' as the quintessential aspect of entrepreneurship has drawn criticism. Rather than an equilibrating force, entrepreneurship might very well be the simultaneously creative and destructive force inherent in Schumpeter's view of entrepreneurship. For Schumpeter, economic development is more about disrupting the status quo than bringing the economy closer to an equilibrium position.

> Development in our sense is a distinct phenomenon, entirely foreign to what may be observed in the circular flow or in the tendency towards equilibrium. It is spontaneous and discontinuous change in the channels of the flow, disturbance of the equilibrium, which forever alters and displaces the equilibrium state previously existing. (Schumpeter [1934] 1983: p. 124)

Further, High (1982) argues that entrepreneurship also involves judgment and a capacity to envision new possibilities. McCloskey (1994; McCloskey and Klamer 1994) argues that persuasion, and not simply alertness, is crucial to entrepreneurship. For an entrepreneurial venture ever to get off the ground, the entrepreneur must persuade investors that his or her ideas are profitable ones, and consumers that the new product or service is a desirable one. Lavoie adds that interpretation is also an essential aspect of entrepreneurship, arguing that mere alertness to arbitrage opportunities, of buying low and selling high, is

> misleading in that the interpretation is trivial and has already taken place. Kirzner likens the arbitrageur's discovery of profit to finding a 20-dollar bill on the beach. [Kirzner's] example reinforces the impression of profit that one gets from mainstream economics, that it is an objective 'find' that does not require interpretation. Most acts of entrepreneurship are not like an isolated individual finding things on beaches; they require efforts of the creative imagination, skillful judgments of future cost and revenue possibilities, and an ability to read the significance of complex social situations. (Lavoie, this volume, Chapter 3: p. 57)

How the entrepreneur teases out the meaning of all the bits of information available to him or her is a complex interpretive process largely shaped by culture. Economic inquiry within the Austrian school centers on human action, whether it be entrepreneurship, investment, or the acquisition of credit. An acultural depiction of these and other actions assumes away their very substance. An entrepreneur's decision to offer a new product or service is not an objectively defined course of action. The entrepreneur is not simply following an algorithm. Rather, he or she must interpret the meaning of the information available. As Lavoie suggests, entrepreneurial decisions are less calculus and more akin to a close 'reading' of profit opportunities from a complex social context.

Entrepreneurial activity and the discovery process which follows from it are of course carried out by real human beings operating within a specific context, not the cultureless and institutionless *homoeconomicus* of neoclassicism. Nor are entrepreneurial decisions a mechanical uncovering of something already in existence, as Kirzner's alertness seems to suggest, but rather a creative process—a series of judgments—which results when the individual entrepreneur brings his or her own interpretive framework to bear upon the situation as it is presented.

An established Ghanaian cloth trader named Beatrice who wished to expand her business provides an apt illustration. By supplying newcomers in the market with cloth, Beatrice could take advantage of the discounted wholesale price she was able to secure after years of high-volume trading. As new entrants are usually young and cash poor, she would have to provide the cloth on credit. Beatrice then had to make a judgment as to whether this truly represented a profit opportunity or not. She lamented, 'The new market women will sometimes run away—back to their village. If they go, there goes my profit.' When asked how she determined to whom she would extend credit, Beatrice replied, 'You can tell by the way they look, if she is neat, if she has people. If she has friends in the market, I will talk to them to see.'

In order to acquire credit, an entrepreneur must establish his or her creditworthiness according to the rules operating in that community. The key indicator for this trader was the network of local connections, both of family and of friends, the newcomer could demonstrate. In turn, the trader has to judge whether she can trust the word of those who vouch for the newcomer—whether they feel responsible for the welfare of the young entrepreneur or their own reputations. In other cultures, the judgments governing the assessment of creditworthiness may be quite different. Kinship status may be the dominant factor elsewhere, a documented credit history in still another.

Good entrepreneurial decisions are not simply a matter of noticing a price discrepancy, as we might conclude from Kirzner's depiction of the entrepreneur as arbitrageur. As Richard Ebeling explains,

> A seller finds himself with unsold inventory of a product in excess of desired levels at a particular price. But what exactly is the market telling him at that price? That he needs to relocate his store? That he has failed to advertise the existence or availability of the product sufficiently? That the price is 'right' but the quality or characteristics of the product is 'wrong'? What the price has conveyed is information that *something* is wrong, that the seller's plans and expectations are inconsistent with those of others. It has not unambiguously told him in which direction the error lies. The price's information, in other words, needs *interpretation as to its meaning* concerning the preferences and plans of others. (Ebeling 1986: p. 45)

Prices are not marching orders which entrepreneurs blindly and mechanically follow. Opportunities for profit are forged through an interpretive process which is dependent upon the cultural framework. Good entrepreneurial decisions require that judgments be made about trustworthiness, risk, potential demand, reliability of supply lines, and countless other factors. Each of these elements will at least in part be tied to the specific cultural context. Culture provides the framework within which entrepreneurs not only notice but also creatively piece together profit opportunities from the world around them.

What is called for is an economic paradigm which accounts for this interpretive process. Kirzner's concept of alertness is helpful here, but is in need of modification. Rather than a view of alertness as a monitoring device that is either 'switched on' or 'switched off,' entrepreneurship is more like *directed* alertness. Even the most astute entrepreneur is never fully alert—capable of noticing all profit opportunities. Rather, an individual entrepreneur will be alert to certain kinds of opportunities. An urban money lender in Accra (called a *susu*-man) will be alert to a certain sort of profit opportunity, as his focus is directed towards particular aspects of the market process, while the focus of a fish retailer will be directed elsewhere. The difference in what two entrepreneurs see—the differences in how they creatively piece together profit opportunities—may be generated by their different positions within the market, their unique life histories, their gender, or their obligations to family. In summary,

> Profit opportunities are not so much like road signs to which we assign an automatic meaning as they are like difficult texts in need of a sustained effort of interpretation. Entrepreneurship is not only a matter of opening one's eyes, of switching on one's attentiveness; it requires directing one's gaze. When an entrepreneur sees things others have overlooked, it is not just that he opened his eyes while they had theirs closed. He is reading selected aspects of a complex situation others have not read. And this raises the question of what gives a predirectedness to the entrepreneur's vision, of why he is apt to read some things and not others. I submit that the answer to this question is culture. (Lavoie, this volume, Chapter 3: p. 59)

This is the point to which Austrian economics brings us with respect to the question of culture and the market process. Austrian contributions to entrepreneurship and the economic methodology of radical subjectivism have carved out a space within which we might now introduce cultural analysis as a part of understanding market processes.

5.5   BUILDING UPON TWO INTERPRETIVE TRADITIONS

In building a 'cultural economics,' we bring together two interpretive traditions—one economic, the other anthropological. The most vocal proponent of an interpretive economics was Ludwig Lachmann (1971, 1976, 1978; see also Lavoie 1986; Ebeling 1986). Lachmann extended the notion of subjectivism to all perception and action within the market process. Both Austrian and neoclassical economics are subjective in the sense that values are determined by the wants and desires of market participants. Yet Austrian economics, as influenced by Lachmann, is *radically* subjective in that strategies for profit, perception of information, and the construction of individual plans are also subjectively determined. Prices and other market signals are meaningful only inside a particular context in which human beings are interpreting their significance.

The main voice in the call for an interpretive anthropology belongs to Clifford Geertz. The role of the social scientist, Geertz (1973) argues, is to sort out the 'structures of significance' among those who hold them—to render that which is at first unintelligible to the outsider intelligible. Borrowing from Gilbert Ryle, Geertz provides an example of two boys, both rapidly moving their eyelid. For one, the movement is an involuntary twitch, for the other a conscious wink. The two movements look the same, yet

> the difference, however unphotographable, between a twitch and a wink is vast: as anyone unfortunate enough to have had the first taken for the second knows. The winker is communicating, and indeed communicating in a quite precise and special way: 1) deliberately, 2) to someone in particular, 3) to impart a particular message, 4) according to a socially established code, and 5) without cognizance of the rest of the company. As Ryle points out, the winker has done two things, contracted his eyelids and winked, while the twitcher has done only one, contracted his eyelids. Contracting your eyelids on purpose when there exists a public code in which so doing counts as a conspiratorial signal is winking. That's all there is to it: a speck of behavior, a fleck of culture, and—*voila!*—a gesture. (Geertz 1973: p. 6)

More recent work in anthropology has developed a culturalist method of economic analysis which also applies an interpretive approach. By studying the primary metaphors at work within a particular culture, the social scientist comes to understand the subjects' perspectives (Gudeman 1986; Bird-David 1990, 1992). In her study of modern hunter-gatherer societies, Bird-David argues that '[t]he primary metaphor of "sharing" is thus a concept with which we can make sense of hunter-gatherers' economic arrangements and moreover, a metaphorical concept by which *they* make sense of their environment, one that guides their action within it' (1992: p. 31). Much of the apparently wasteful behavior exhibited by modern hunter-gatherer societies makes sense within their own interpretive context. This alone says nothing as to whether a particular primary metaphor leads to economic stability or volatility, capital accumulation, or subsistence production. Yet it may provide a means of understanding the subjects' cultural perspective which renders the economic environment meaningful for them, and thereby guides action.[4] This is not to suggest that pre-industrial societies operate in the 'false' world of metaphors, while industrialized society experiences the 'real' world directly. Similar to what Denzau and North (1994) describe as 'mental models,' metaphor is just as essential to the modern entrepreneur in order to make sense of his or her world. Money, for instance, depends upon the power of myth. The monetary system works only because people believe that account balances and currency represent value. The world is never experienced directly. It is always interpreted through the cultural lens.[5]

As Geertz argues, the value of an interpretive anthropological investigation is determined by whether it can solve a piece of the mystery: 'whether it sorts winks from twitches.'

> The claim to attention of an ethnographic account does not rest on its author's ability to capture primitive facts in faraway places and carry them home like a mask or a carving, but on the degree to which he is able to clarify what goes on in such places, to reduce the puzzlement—What manner of men are these?—to which unfamiliar acts emerging out of unknown backgrounds naturally give rise. (Geertz 1973: p. 16)

What might be lost in such an enterprise is the neatness and exactitude abstract and acultural theory so often affords. But what is gained is understanding.

5.6 CONCLUSION

The formalist–substantivist debate never definitively answered the question of whether economic theory was applicable to the non-Western developing world. On the one hand, neoclassical theory seemed inadequate given the sorts of questions being asked. The cultural foundations and the endogenous nature of economic development have little if any place within the neoclassical paradigm. Yet, to many, economic theory seemed too important to abandon altogether, even considering its shortcomings. With no apparent resolution and no clear alternative, the debate faded into the background of economic anthropology.

The Austrian school of economics has the potential to provide an alternative. Austrian methodology provides the link by which we can incorporate cultural analysis into economic investigations. The radical subjectivism posed by the Austrian school embraces the fact that markets are inhabited with creative interpreting beings, not atomistic reactive agents. Culture and interpretive perspective never emerge as relevant concepts in the neoclassical paradigm, as atomistic agents have no culture; indeed, they have no perspective. With the exception of Friedrich Hayek's work on the role culture plays in facilitating the extended order, cultural analysis has not yet played a principal role in the body of Austrian economic thought. Yet its position of radical subjectivism meant that it was only a matter of time before Austrians turned to the cultural framework that shapes the subjective perspective that defines Austrian economics.

NOTES

* This chapter previously appeared in Emily Chamlee-Wright, *The Cultural Foundations of Economic Development: Urban Female Entrepreneurship in Ghana* (Routledge, 1997). It is reprinted here (with minor edits) with the permission of the publisher.
1. For a detailed description of the wholesale markets in Kumasi, see Clark (1994).
2. Note also that Malinowski's explanation implies that Western economic agents do not display this sort of behavior, but rather are narrow maximizers of material wealth. The difference between the Trobriand Islander and the American who proudly tends his own garden only to give the produce away to neighbors and co-workers is a difference in degree, not in kind.
3. O'Driscoll and Rizzo (1996) argue further that neoclassical search theories which purport to demonstrate how economic agents acquire knowledge over time still fail to explain the process of market discovery, as what is to be discovered in such models is already determined within the starting assumptions of the model.
4. In Chapter 3 of *The Cultural Foundations of Economic Development: Urban Female Entrepreneurship in Ghana* (Chamlee-Wright 1997), suggestions for further research on what may be primary metaphors operating for Ghanaian market women are offered, but conclusions cannot be drawn here, as the present author does not possess the linguistic expertise required for such analysis.
5. For comparative anthropological work on production, see Halperin (1988). Halperin employs an evolutionary approach to demonstrate how the systematic differences in divisions of labor across gender and age, and political structure affect production methods over time.

REFERENCES

Akerlof, G.A. (1980), 'The Theory of Social Custom, of Which Unemployment May Be One Consequence,' *Quarterly Journal of Economics*, **94**(4), 749–75.
Alchian, Armen and Harold Demsetz (1973), 'The Property Rights Paradigm,' *Journal of Economic History*, **55**(1), 17–25.

Althusser, L. (1969), *For Marx*, Harmondsworth, UK: Penguin Books.

Anker, Richard (1994), 'Measuring Women's Participation in the African Labor Force,' in A. Adepoju and C. Oppong (eds.), *Gender, Work and Population in Sub-Saharan Africa*, London: James Currey, pp. 64–75.

Bates, Robert H. (1981), *Markets and States in Tropical Africa*, Berkeley: University of California Press.

Berger, Peter L. and Thomas Luckmann (1966), *The Social Construction of Reality: A Treatise in the Sociology of Knowledge*, New York: Doubleday.

Bird-David, Nurit (1990), 'The Giving Environment: Another Perspective on the Economic Systems of Gatherer-Hunters,' *Current Anthropology*, 31(2), 189–96.

Bird-David, Nurit (1992), 'Beyond "The Affluent Society": A Culturalist Reformulation' [and comments and reply], *Current Anthropology*, 33 (February), 25–34.

Burling, Robbins (1962), 'Maximization Theories and the Study of Economic Anthropology,' *American Anthropologist*, 64, 802–21.

Chamlee-Wright, Emily (1997), *The Cultural Foundations of Economic Development: Urban Female Entrepreneurship in Ghana*, Abingdon, UK: Routledge.

Clammer, John (ed.) (1978), *The New Economic Anthropology*, New York: St. Martin's Press.

Clark, Gracia (1994), *Onions Are My Husband: Survival and Accumulation by West African Market Women*, Chicago: University of Chicago Press.

Clegg, Stewart and S. Gordon Redding (eds.) (1990), *Capitalism in Contrasting Cultures*, New York: Walter de Gruyter.

Coase, Ronald H. (1957), 'The Nature of the Firm,' *Economica*, 4(3), 386–405.

Coase, Ronald H. (1960), 'The Problem of Social Cost,' *Journal of Law and Economics*, 3, 1–44.

Cockcroft, James D., A.G. Frank and D.L. Johnson (1972), *Dependence and Underdevelopment: Latin America's Political Economy*, Garden City, NY: Doubleday.

Cook, Scott (1966), 'The Obsolete Anti-Market Mentality: A Critique of the Substantive Approach to Economic Anthropology,' *American Anthropologist*, 68, 323–45.

Cutler, A., B. Hindess, P. Hirst and A. Hussain (1977), *Marx's Capital and Capitalism Today*, New York: Routledge & Kegan Paul.

Dalton, George (1961), 'Economic Theory and Primitive Society,' *American Anthropologist*, 63, 1–25.

Denzau, Arthur and Douglass C. North (1994), 'Shared Mental Models: Ideologies and Institutions,' *Kyklos*, 47(1), 3–31.

De Soto, Hernando (1989), *The Other Path: The Invisible Revolution in the Third World*, New York: Harper & Row.

Dupre, G. and P. Rey (1973), 'Reflections on the Pertinence of a Theory of the History of Exchange,' *Economy and Society*, 2(2), 131–63.

Ebeling, Richard (1986), 'Toward a Hermeneutical Economics: Expectations, Prices, and the Role of Interpretation in a Theory of the Market Process,' in I. Kirzner (ed.), *Subjectivism, Intelligibility and Economic Understanding: Essays in Honor of Ludwig M. Lachmann on His Eightieth Birthday*, New York: New York University Press, pp. 39–55.

Ensminger, Jean (1991), 'The Political Economy of Changing Property Rights: Dismantling a Pastoral Commons,' *American Ethnologist*, 18(4), 683–99.

Ensminger, Jean (1992), *Making a Market: The Institutional Transformation of an African Society*, Cambridge: Cambridge University Press.

Firth, Raymond (1951), *Elements of Social Organization*, London: C.A. Watts & Co.

Frank, Andre Gunder (1969), *Capitalism and Underdevelopment in Latin America: Historical Studies of Chile and Brazil*, New York: Monthly Review Press.

Frankenberg, R. (1967), 'Economic Anthropology: One Anthropologist's View,' in R. Firth (ed.), *Themes in Economic Anthropology*, London: Tavistock Publications, pp. 47–90.

Geertz, Clifford (1973), 'Thick Description: Towards an Interpretive Theory of Culture,' *The Interpretation of Cultures: Selected Essays*, New York: Basic Books, pp. 3–30.

Godelier, M. (1972), *Rationality and Irrationality in Economics*, London: New Left Books.

Goldschmidt-Clermont, Luisella (1994), 'Assessing Women's Economic Contributions in Domestic and Related Activities,' in A. Adepoju and C. Oppong (eds.), *Gender, Work and Population in Sub-Saharan Africa*, London: James Currey, pp. 76–87.

Goodfellow, D.M. (1939), *Principles of Economic Sociology*, London: Routledge & Kegan Paul.

Grossman, Gregory (1982), 'The Shadow Economy in the Socialist Sector of the USSR,' in *The CMEA Five-Year Plans (1981–1985) in a New Perspective: Planned and Non-Planned Economies*, NATO: Economics and Information Directories, pp. 99–115.

Gudeman, Stephen (1986), *Economics as Culture: Models and Metaphors of Livelihood*, London: Routledge.

Halperin, Rhoda (1988), *Economies across Cultures: Towards a Comparative Science of the Economy*, New York: St. Martin's Press.

Harris, J., J. Hunter and C.M. Lewis (eds.) (1995), *The New Institutional Economics and Third World Development*, London: Routledge.

Hayek, F.A. ([1946] 1948), 'The Meaning of Competition,' in *Individualism and Economic Order*, Chicago: University of Chicago Press, pp. 92–106.

Hayek, F.A. (1948), *Individualism and Economic Order*, Chicago: University of Chicago Press.

Hayek, F.A. (1967), *Studies in Philosophy, Politics and Economics*, Chicago: University of Chicago Press.

Hayek, F.A. (1978), 'Competition as a Discovery Procedure,' in *New Studies in Philosophy, Politics, and Economics*, Chicago: University of Chicago Press, pp. 57–68.

Herskovits, Melville J. ([1940] 1952), *Economic Anthropology*, New York: Alfred A. Knopf.

Hiebert, Murray (1993), 'Chain Lending: Informal Credit Fills Void Left by Vietnam's Banks,' *Far Eastern Economic Review*, March 4.

High, Jack (1982), 'Alertness and Judgment: Comment on Kirzner,' in I. Kirzner (ed.), *Method, Process, and Austrian Economics*, Lexington, MA: Lexington Books, pp. 161–8.

Hill, Polly (1969), 'Hidden Trade in Hausaland,' *Man*, **4**, 392–409.

ILO (International Labour Organization) (1990), *African Employment Report*, Addis Ababa: ILO.

Kahn, Joel (1978), 'Marxist Anthropology and Peasant Economics: A Study of the

Social Structure of Underdevelopment,' in J. Clammer (ed.), *The New Economic Anthropology*, London: Macmillan, pp. 110–37.

Katsenelinboigen, A. (1977), 'Coloured Markets in the Soviet Union,' *Soviet Studies*, **29**(1), 62–85.

Kirzner, Israel (1973), *Competition and Entrepreneurship*, Chicago: University of Chicago Press.

Kirzner, Israel (1979), *Perception, Opportunity and Profit: Studies in the Theory of Entrepreneurship*, Chicago: University of Chicago Press.

Kirzner, I.M. (1980), 'The Primacy of Entrepreneurial Discovery,' in Institute of Economic Affairs, *The Prime Mover of Progress: The Entrepreneur in Capitalism and Socialism*, Papers on the Role of the Entrepreneur, London: Institute of Economic Affairs, pp. 3–28.

Kolakowski, Leszek (1978), *Main Currents of Marxism*, Vol. I: *The Founders*, New York: Oxford University Press.

Kotkin, Joel (1992), *Tribes: How Race, Religion, and Identity Determine Success in the New Global Economy*, New York: Random House.

Kurwijila, R. and J.M. Due (1991), 'Credit for Women's Income Generation: A Tanzanian Case Study,' *Canadian Journal of African Studies*, **25**(1), 90–103.

Lachmann, Ludwig M. (1971), *The Legacy of Max Weber*, Berkeley, CA: Glendessary Press.

Lachmann, Ludwig M. (1976), 'From Mises to Shackle: An Essay on Austrian Economics and the Kaleidic Society,' *Journal of Economic Literature*, **14**, 54–62.

Lachmann, Ludwig M. (1978), *Capital and Its Structure*, Kansas City, MO: Sheed, Andrews and McMeel.

Lavoie, Donald C. (1986), 'Euclideanism vs. Hermeneutics: A Reinterpretation of Misesian Apriorism,' in I. Kirzner (ed.), *Subjectivism, Intelligibility and Economic Understanding: Essays in Honor of Ludwig M. Lachmann on His Eightieth Birthday*, New York: New York University Press, pp. 192–210.

Lavoie, Donald C. and Emily Chamlee-Wright (working paper), 'Culture and the Spirit of Enterprise,' Cato Institute, Washington, DC.

Lawson, Rowena M. (1971), 'The Supply Response of Retail Trading Services to Urban Population Growth in Ghana,' in C. Meillassoux (ed.), *The Development of Indigenous Trade and Markets in West Africa*, London: Oxford University Press, pp. 377–98.

LeClair, Edward and Harold Schneider (1968), *Economic Anthropology: Readings in Theory and Analysis*, New York: Holt, Rinehart and Winston.

Levy, B. (1993), 'Obstacles in Developing Indigenous Small and Medium Enterprises: An Empirical Assessment,' *World Bank Economic Review*, **7**(1), 65–83.

Lewis, W.A. (1955), *The Theory of Economic Growth*, London: Allen & Unwin.

Little, Kenneth (1965), *West African Urbanization: A Study of Voluntary Associations in Social Change*, Cambridge: Cambridge University Press.

Lycette, Margaret and K. White (1989), 'Improving Women's Access to Credit in Latin America and the Caribbean: Policy and Project Recommendations,' in M. Berger and M. Buvinic (eds.), *Women's Ventures: Assistance to the Informal Sector in Latin America*, West Hartford, CT: Kumarian Press, pp. 19–44.

Malinkowski, Bronislaw ([1922] 1961), *Argonauts of the Western Pacific*, New York: Dutton & Co.

McClelland, D.C. (1961), *The Achieving Society*, Princeton, NJ: D. Van Nostrand.

McCloskey, D. (1994), *Knowledge and Persuasion in Economics*, Cambridge: Cambridge University Press.

McCloskey, D. and Arjo Klamer (1994), 'One Quarter of GDP is Persuasion,' Keynote Address for the Southern Economic Association.

Meillassoux, Claude (1972), 'From Reproduction to Production: A Marxist Approach to Economic Anthropology,' *Economy and Society*, **1**(1), 93–105.

Meillassoux, Claude (1976), 'The Social Organization of the Peasantry,' in D. Seddon (ed.), *Relations and Production: Marxist Approaches to Economic Anthropology*, London: Frank Cass, pp. 159–70.

Mises, Ludwig von ([1922] 1932), *Socialism*, Indianapolis, IN: Liberty Press.

Mises, Ludwig von ([1949] 1966), *Human Action*, New Haven, CT: Yale University Press.

Mises, Ludwig von ([1933] 1981), *Epistemological Problems of Economics*, G. Reisman (trans.), New York: New York University Press.

Nabli, Mustapha K. and Jeffrey B. Nugent (1989), 'The New Institutional Economics and Its Applicability to Development,' *World Development*, **17**(9), 1333–47.

North, Douglass C. (1987), 'Institutions, Transactions Costs, and Economic Growth,' *Economic Inquiry*, **25** (July), 419–28.

North, Douglass C. (1989), 'Institutions and Economic Growth: An Historical Introduction,' *World Development*, **17**(9), 1319–32.

North, Douglass C. (1990), *Institutions, Institutional Change, and Economic Performance*, Cambridge: Cambridge University Press.

North, Douglass C. (1994), 'Economic Performance through Time,' *American Economic Review*, **84**(3), 359–67.

North, Douglass C. (1995), 'The New Institutional Economics and Third World Development,' in J. Harris, J. Hunter and C.M. Lewis (eds.), *The New Institutional Economics and Third World Development*, London: Routledge, pp. 17–26.

O'Driscoll, Gerald and Mario Rizzo (1996), *The Economics of Time and Ignorance*, rev. ed., London: Routledge.

Olson, Mancur (1965), *The Logic of Collective Action*, Cambridge, MA: Harvard University Press.

Olson, Mancur (1982), *The Rise and Decline of Nations: Economic Growth, Stagflation, and Social Rigidities*, New Haven, CT: Yale University Press.

Parker, Ronald L., Randall Riopelle and William F. Steel (1995), *Small Enterprises Adjusting to Liberalization in Five African Countries*, World Bank Discussion Papers: African Technical Department Series No. 271, Washington, DC: International Bank for Reconstruction and Development.

Pellow, Deborah (1977), *Women in Accra: Options for Autonomy*, Algonac, MI: Reference Publications.

Plattner, Stuart (ed.) (1989), *Economic Anthropology*, Stanford, CA: Stanford University Press.

Polanyi, Karl (1957), 'The Economy as Instituted Process,' in Karl Polanyi, C.W. Arensberg and H.W. Pearson (eds.), *Trade and Market in the Early Empires*, New York: Free Press, pp. 243–70.

Polanyi, Karl, C.W. Arensberg and H.W. Pearson (eds.) (1957), *Trade and Market in the Early Empires*, New York: Free Press.

Putnam, Robert D. (1993), *Making Democracy Work: Civic Traditions in Modern Italy*, Princeton, NJ: Princeton University Press.

Putnam, Robert D., R. Leonardi, R. Nanetti and F. Pavoncello (1983), 'Explaining

Institutional Success: The Case of Italian Regional Government,' *American Political Science Review*, **77**, 53–74.

Robbins, Lionel (1932), 'The Subject Matter of Economics,' in *An Essay on the Nature and Significance of Economic Science*, London: Macmillan; New York: St. Martin's Press, pp. 1–22.

Sahlins, M. (1960), 'Political Power and the Economy in Primitive Society,' in G.E. Dole and R.L. Carneiro (eds.), *Essays in the Science of Culture*, New York: Crowell, pp. 390–415.

Sahlins, M. (1963), 'On the Sociology of Primitive Exchange,' in M. Banton (ed.), *The Relevance of Models for Social Anthropology*, London: Tavistock Publications, pp. 139–236.

Sahlins, M. (1968), 'Notes on the Original Affluent Society,' in R.B. Lee and I. De Vore (eds.), *Man the Hunter*, Chicago: Aldine, pp. 85–9.

Sahlins, M. (1972), 'The Original Affluent Society,' in *Stone Age Economics*, London: Tavistock, pp. 1–39.

Sahlins, M. (1976), *Culture and Practical Reason*, Chicago: University of Chicago Press.

Sandesara, J.C. (1991), 'Small-Scale Industrialization: The Indian Experience,' in H. Thomas, F. Uribe Echevarria and H. Romijn (eds.), *Small-Scale Production*, London: IT Publications.

Schildkrout, Enid (1982), 'Dependence and Autonomy: The Economic Activities of Secluded Hausa Women in Kano,' in E. Bay (ed.), *Women and Work in Africa*, Boulder, CO: Westview, pp. 55–81.

Schumpeter, Joseph ([1934] 1983), *The Theory of Economic Development*, New Brunswick, NJ: Transaction Books.

Seddon, David (1978), 'Economic Anthropology or Political Economy? (II): Approaches to the Analysis of Pre-Capitalist Formations in the Maghreb,' in J. Clammer (ed.), *The New Economic Anthropology*, New York: St. Martin's Press, pp. 61–109.

Shanmugan, Bala (1991), 'Socio-Economic Development through the Informal Credit Market,' *Modern Asian Studies*, **25**(2), 209–25.

Smith, Paul (1978), 'Domestic Labor and Marx's Theory of Value,' in A. Kuhn and A. Wolpe (eds.), *Feminism and Materialism*, London: Routledge & Kegan Paul, pp. 198–219.

Squire, L. (1981), *Employment Policy in Developing Countries: A Survey of Issues and Evidence*, Oxford: Oxford University Press.

Steel, William and Yasuoki Takagi (1985), 'Small Enterprise Development and the Employment–Output Trade-Off,' *Oxford Economic Papers*, **35**, 423–46.

Steel, William F. and Leila M. Webster (1991), *Small Enterprises under Adjustment in Ghana*, World Bank Technical Paper No. 138, Industry and Finance Series, Washington, DC: World Bank.

Stein, Howard (1995), 'Institutional Theories and Structural Adjustment in Africa,' in J. Harris, J. Hunter and C.M. Lewis (eds.), *The New Institutional Economics and Third World Development*, London: Routledge, pp. 109–32.

Terray, E. (1972), *Marxism and Political Societies*, New York: Monthly Review Press.

Terray, E. (1974), 'Long Distance Exchange and the Information of the State: The Case of the Abron Kingdom of Gyaman,' *Economy and Society*, **3**(1), 315–45.

Timberg, Thomas A. and C.V. Aiyar (1984), 'Informal Credit Markets in India,' *Economic Development and Cultural Change*, **33** (October), 43–59.

United Nations (1995), 'Issues Concerning SMEs' Access to Finance,' in United Nations Conference on Trade and Development, 2nd Session, July 3.

Wahid, Abu N.M. (1994), 'The Grameen Bank and Poverty Alleviation in Bangladesh: Theory, Evidence and Limitations,' *American Journal of Economics and Sociology*, **53**(1), 1–15.

Wallis, Tina and Douglass C. North (1986), 'Measuring the Transaction Sector in the American Economy, 1870–1970,' in S.L. Engerman and R.E. Gallman (eds.), *Long-Term Factors in American Economic Growth*, Chicago: University of Chicago Press, pp. 95–164.

Waring, Marilyn (1988), *If Women Counted: A New Feminist Economics*, San Francisco: Harper & Row.

6. Institutional stickiness and the New Development Economics*

Peter J. Boettke, Christopher J. Coyne and Peter T. Leeson

> Teeth-gritting humility, patience, curiosity and independent thinking are called for in learning how superior foreign technology works and how it can be improved. Without these conditions the technical assistance 'does not take.' The cut flowers wither and die because they have no roots. (Paul Streeten, *Thinking about Development*, 1995: pp. 11–12)

6.1 INTRODUCTION

First introduced by North (1990), the notion of institutional 'path dependence' has received increasing attention among those interested in the connection between institutions and economic growth (see, for instance, Buchanan and Yoon 1994; Pierson 2000a, 2000b). Path dependence emphasizes the increasing returns to institutions, which tend to 'lock in' particular institutional arrangements that have emerged in various places for unique historical reasons.

Locked-in institutional arrangements may be suboptimal in the sense that, given today's information, agents would be better off if they moved to some other arrangement. In such cases, it is typically argued that, in order to put agents on a new and improved institutional path, some outside entity, like the development community, is required to provide the exogenous 'shock' necessary to break society out of the suboptimal scenario. This belief has presently led development economists to emphasize the role of exogenous institutions in determining economic growth. Current analyses of economic development thus concern themselves with finding the 'right' institutional mix to promote progress in various countries.

However, the success of these efforts has been spotty at best. For instance, most underdeveloped countries in sub-Saharan Africa and many post-socialist transitioning nations continue to struggle despite development-community attempts to exogenously introduce institutional change. We argue that this failure stems at least partly from the fact that the concept of path dependence as it has been applied to institutions to date tells us only that 'history matters' in the development of institutions. It does not, however, tell us *how* history matters. Research that considers culture suffers from a similar problem. While this work performs an important function in pointing out that 'culture matters,' it does virtually nothing in terms of telling us analytically or empirically how culture matters (see, for instance, Buchanan 1992; Boettke 2001b; Pejovich 2003).

We aim to provide the missing 'how' in these closely related streams of research. We contend that institutional 'stickiness'—the ability or inability of new institutional arrangements to take hold where they are transplanted—is central to understanding how history matters for institutions. Furthermore, it is central to understanding how the relationship between history and institutions matters for development economics.

We provide a framework for understanding stickiness based on the regression theorem.[1] The regression theorem maintains that the stickiness, and therefore likely success, of any proposed institutional change is a function of that institution's status in relationship to indigenous agents in the previous time period. This framework for analyzing institutional stickiness is at the core of what we call the New Development Economics.

The New Development Economics builds directly on the voluminous body of research that examines the emergence, operation, and effectiveness of spontaneously ordered institutional arrangements. The idea that these institutions tend to be efficient and most effective in promoting the ends of indigenous agents is not original to us. On the contrary, Hayek (1960, 1973, 1991) was among the first to emphasize these aspects of spontaneously emergent institutions, in particular law. Following him, a number of others, including Posner (1973), Benson (1989), La Porta et al. (1998), Glaeser and Shleifer (2002), and Djankov et al. (2003), have examined the comparative properties of endogenously emergent common law systems versus exogenously created civil law systems, and in several cases their relationship to economic development, and have empirically confirmed Hayek's insights. Others, such as Hay and Shleifer (1998), Nenova and Harford (2004), and Leeson (2006, 2007a, 2007b), have pointed to the effectiveness of spontaneously emergent institutions for the provision of 'public goods,' including property rights protection, normally thought of as being capably provided only by the state. Still others have noted the effectiveness of monetary institutions when they emerge as spontaneous orders, and contrasted this with the relative ineffectiveness of such institutions when they are created in a 'top-down' fashion by government (see, for instance, Menger [1871] 1994; Selgin 1994; Selgin and White 1994). Important work by Elinor Ostrom (1990, 2000) and James Scott (1998) also has highlighted the importance and success of endogenously emergent institutional solutions to a range of coordination problems, as well as the potential for unintended, undesirable outcomes when political authorities artificially construct institutional solutions to these problems.

These important strands of research have tended to contrast two kinds of opposing institutional emergence: those that emerge entirely spontaneously (what in our framework we call 'indigenously introduced endogenous institutions'), and those that are constructed and imposed by 'outsiders' (what in our framework we call 'foreign-introduced exogenous institutions'). In addition to these opposing ends of the institutional spectrum, this chapter introduces a third class of institutions—those that are indigenously introduced but exogenous in nature. In introducing this third class of institutions and considering its 'stickiness' properties alongside those institutions that fall on either side of it, we hope to illuminate what characteristics give institutions their stickiness and, in doing so, to provide a framework for investigating proposed institutional reforms in the context of economic development.

Finally, this chapter should also be seen as building on existing work in comparative institutional analysis. In addition to North (1990, 2005), Aoki (2001) emphasizes the importance of informal complementary institutions that allow formal institutions to function in the desired manner. Similarly, Platteau (2000) notes the importance of norms and complementary institutions for the operation of formal institutions such as the legal system.

The remainder of this chapter is organized as follows. Section 6.2 provides an institutional taxonomy for the purposes of analyzing the stickiness properties of various types of institutional arrangements. Section 6.3 presents the regression theorem and uses it to analyze the stickiness properties of institutional types. Based on this insight, this section also explores what our analytical findings suggest for the development community. In section 6.4, we examine our framework in light of cases of postwar reconstruction and transition efforts in former communist countries. To illuminate the regression theorem and its implications for economic development, we consider successful reconstruction in Germany and Japan and unsuccessful reform in Bosnia. We then consider cases of successful (Poland) and failed (Russia) transition efforts. In section 6.5, we conclude.

6.2   A TAXONOMY OF INSTITUTIONS

We can broadly conceive of institutions as belonging to one of three separate categories: foreign-introduced exogenous (FEX) institutions, indigenously introduced exogenous (IEX) institutions, and indigenously introduced endogenous (IEN) institutions. The foreign or indigenous component in each of these categories is fairly self-explanatory: institutions designed chiefly by outsiders are foreign-introduced, while those designed chiefly by insiders are indigenously introduced. Of course, this breakdown significantly oversimplifies institutional origin. Nearly any institutional arrangement can be found to exhibit influence from outsiders at some point in time. Thus, institutions are never purely foreign- or indigenously introduced. Nevertheless, we can broadly view institutions as being primarily the creation of foreign or indigenous forces in most instances, and it is in this spirit that we propose the distinction.

The exogenous/endogenous component of institutional origin requires additional explanation. Exogenous institutions are constructed and imposed from above. These are the creations of governments or other formal authorities like the IMF, USAID, or the World Bank. Note that these can be created indigenously by national governments or by outsiders when they are foreign-introduced. In contrast, endogenous institutions emerge spontaneously as the result of individuals' actions, but are not formally designed. Thus, by their nature, endogenous institutions are indigenously introduced.

Concretely, FEX institutions are those we typically associate with development-community policy. For instance, a legal system change introduced by the development community in a reforming nation would constitute a FEX institution. Although the decision regarding such a change ultimately lies in the hands of the indigenous government, the policy change is chiefly the creation of outsiders, and the institutional change is constructed.

IEX institutions are those we associate with the internal policies created by national governments. For example, federalism in the United States is an IEX institution. Federalism represents a state-constructed institution designed by Americans. Similarly, the British Parliament constitutes an IEX institution. It is a designed institution of British construction.

Finally, IEN institutions are those we associate primarily with spontaneous orders. These embody the local norms, customs, and practices that have evolved informally over time in specific places. Language, for instance, is an IEN institution.

Of course, these institutional categories are purely conceptual. Furthermore, they are not rigid, as presented above. The same institutions may fall into different categories in different places; perhaps even more importantly, the same institution may fall into different categories at different times in the same place. Consider, for instance, the institution of money. Before the advent of central banking, money constituted an IEN institution in much of nineteenth-century Europe (Rothbard 1990; White 1995). However, in the twentieth century, money creation was monopolized by national governments in most places in the world. Thus, in the twentieth century, money in Europe would be classified as an IEX institution.

6.3 THE REGRESSION THEOREM: A FRAMEWORK FOR ANALYZING INSTITUTIONAL STICKINESS

It is widely agreed that the underlying institutional framework of an economy influences its ability to progress (see, for instance, North 1990; Scully 1992; Kasper and Streit 1999; Platteau 2000). More specifically, there is a broad consensus within the development community that the market institutions of private property, rule of law, and liberal trade—so-called growth-inducing institutions—are required for successful development.[2] However, while generally identifying growth-enhancing institutions is an important step in creating prosperity, questions remain about how to operationalize these answers to economic growth.

In this regard, perhaps the most important question we must consider is: Are these institutions transportable? Mixed empirical evidence heightens the significance of this question. On the one hand, recent attempts at imposing these institutions in developing nations abroad have met mostly with failure (Easterly 2001, 2006). On the other hand, not all institutional impositions have failed (Coyne 2007).

For instance, for reasons explored in section 6.4, postwar economic reconstruction in Japan and Germany proved relatively successful. When we are talking about transporting institutions, we are necessarily talking about FEX institutions. Whether we are dealing with the introduction of development-community-devised policy in post-socialist transition nations or the imposition of new politico-economic orders in war-torn Europe, we are dealing with FEX institutions. The question thus emerges: What are the stickiness properties of FEX institutions, and how are they related to the stickiness properties of IEX and IEN institutions?

6.3.1 Indigenously Introduced Endogenous (IEN) Institutions

To answer this question, we begin by analyzing the properties of IEN institutions. This serves as an appropriate starting point for our analysis because, as we discuss below, IEN institutions necessarily precede effective FEX and IEX institutions historically. As spontaneous orders, IEN institutions have their roots in the behavior of individual agents pursuing their own ends (see, for instance, Menger [1871] 1994; Hayek 1996). To the extent that agents' ends are at least partially dependent upon social interaction, various obstacles to this pursuit emerge along the way. For instance, agents desiring exchange who lack a coincidence of wants find this problematic for executing desired transactions.

IEN institutions can be thought of as endogenously emergent solutions to such obstacles confronting socially interacting agents (Hayek 1996). For instance, in the example above, agents resort to indirect exchange to overcome the lack of coincidence of wants in a barter economy. At first the medium of exchange employed between two traders for this purpose is a peculiarity. Only over time do agents find certain media of exchange more useful for facilitating exchange than other media, and only over time do more and more traders find it useful to resort to indirect exchange. At some point, particular media of exchange desired for their properties in enabling trade become so widespread that they take on the status of an institution. This is the spontaneous evolution of money (see, for instance, Mises 1949; Menger [1871] 1994; Selgin and White 1994).

Several things are worth noting about the process by which IEN institutions, like money, surface. First, they emerge endogenously. The institution is not constructed by some entity like government, exogenous to the market process. Second, the institution's endogenous emergence is necessarily indigenously introduced. As we have noted, precisely for these two reasons, we call these institutions IEN institutions.

The features that make an institution an IEN institution are of particular importance in analyzing its stickiness properties. First, the endogenous emergence of the institution points to its desirability as seen from indigenous inhabitants' point of view. IEN institutions are informal in the sense that they are not compelled and are flexible to the changing preferences of the individuals they assist. Thus their persistence tends to indicate their preferredness to other informal arrangements that might supplant them (Hayek 1991).

Second, both features of IEN institutions suggest that these institutions are firmly grounded in the practices, customs, values, and beliefs of indigenous people. In other words, both the indigenous introduction of an IEN institution and its endogenous emergence strongly suggest an IEN institution's foundation in *mētis*.

A concept passed down from the ancient Greeks, *mētis* is characterized by local knowledge resulting from practical experience.[3] It includes skills, culture, norms, and conventions, which are shaped by the experiences of the individual. This concept applies to interactions both between people (for example, interpreting the gestures and actions of others) and with the physical environment (for example, learning to ride a bike). The components of *mētis* cannot be written down neatly as a systematic set of instructions. Instead, knowledge regarding *mētis* is gained only through experience and practice.

In terms of a concrete example, think of *mētis* as the set of informal practices and expectations that allow ethnic groups to construct successful trade networks. For instance, the diamond trade in New York City is dominated by orthodox Jews who use a set of signals, cues, and bonding mechanisms to lower the transaction costs of trading. The diamond trade would not function as smoothly if random traders were placed in the same setting. This difference can be ascribed to *mētis*. Because it is based in the accepted, understood, and habituated mentalities and practices of indigenous peoples, the presence or absence of *mētis* explains the stickiness of various types of institutions. In fact, *mētis* can be thought of as the glue that gives institutions their stickiness.

IEN institutions ensure their foundation in *mētis* for two reasons. First, the fact that they emerge endogenously in an informal, unconstructed fashion means that they emerge directly from *mētis*. Similarly, their indigenous introduction means that they are in harmony with local conditions, attitudes, and practices. This fact is closely related to Frey's (1997) important work on the 'intrinsic motivations' of individuals, which suggests that spontaneously emergent institutions effectively reflect and in fact grow out of the preferences of local actors. In this sense, IEN institutions are institutionalized *mētis*. As such, IEN institutions tend to be the stickiest institutions of all.

Stephen Innes's (1995) study of the economic culture of Puritan New England provides an excellent example of the stickiness of IEN institutions based on their strong foundation in *mētis*. According to Innes, the social ecology of Puritanism led to the success of the Massachusetts Bay Colony in the seventeenth century. A mutated cultural mix of British culture with Puritan ideology among the settlers combined to free the economy of restraints and place moral sanction on private property and the work ethic.

The settlers' fierce devotion to God in this case led to a social commitment to engage with the world and to prosper. This underlying customary belief system that constituted part of Puritanical *mētis* was reinforced by market-based IEN institutions within the Puritan commonwealth, which promoted economic growth and development. Much of America's modern private property order is based upon Puritanical *mētis*. Indeed, precisely because of this foundation in *mētis*, the institution of private property in the United States is extremely sticky, as evidenced by its persistence over centuries.

Private international commercial law provides another example of a highly sticky IEN institution rooted in *mētis*. This law constitutes an outgrowth of the *lex mercatoria*, an informal system of customary law rooted in international commercial norms that evolved spontaneously from the desires of individuals to engage in cross-culture exchange in eleventh- and twelfth-century Europe (Benson 1989; Leeson 2006). The contractual arrangements and procedures for dispute settlement that emerged endogenously as flexible solutions to obstacles confronting international traders under the *lex mercatoria* strongly reflected the evolved practices, norms, and customs of the traders, rooting these IEN institutions of international exchange in *mētis*. These institutions have exhibited tremendous stickiness and, while continually evolving, remain the institutions that govern most international commerce in the modern world (see, for instance, Berman 1983; Benson 1989; Volckart and Mangels 1999).

6.3.2 Indigenously Introduced Exogenous (IEX) Institutions

We have seen how *mētis* acts as the glue that gives institutions their stickiness. Furthermore, we have seen why IEN institutions, with their close relationship to *mētis*, tend to be the stickiest institutions. But what about FEX and IEX institutions? Where do they fall in terms of stickiness?

As our analysis suggests, the further an institution falls from *mētis*, the less sticky it will be. IEX institutions are indigenous, but are exogenously introduced. This means that, while some formal authority is responsible for creating the institution, this formal authority is not foreign. Because IEX institutions are exogenously imposed, the tendency for them to be as closely connected to *mētis* as IEN institutions is missing. The fact that formal authorities lack intimate knowledge of *mētis* creates a greater likelihood for incongruities between the imposed institution and the underlying *mētis*.

Consider, for example, J. Stephen Lansing's (1991) study of the Balinese water temples. The water temples scattered across Bali were places of worship of various gods, but they also managed the irrigation schedule for farmers throughout Bali. In the 1960s and 1970s, the International Rice Research Institute sought to eradicate the backward native practices of rice production throughout Asia. This was known as the 'Green Revolution.'

Indigenous methods of rice production would be replaced with a variety of rice that required the use of fertilizers and pesticides. In Bali, the government introduced an agricultural policy in conformity with the Green Revolution, which promoted continuous cropping of the new rice. Rice farmers were encouraged to plant rice without taking account of the traditional irrigation schedule dictated by the water temples. The immediate effect was a boost in rice production, but the policy soon resulted in a water shortage and a severe outbreak of rice pests and diseases. In short, the IEX institution created by the Balinese not only failed to have its desired effect but actually made matters worse. In this way, because IEX institutions are exogenously imposed, they often fail to conform to underlying *mētis*.

However, given that the authority creating an IEX institution is familiar to some degree with local practices, attitudes, and so forth—that is, it may itself be part of a larger local *mētis*—it stands to reason that the authority is able to craft institutions in such a way as to be relatively consistent with these factors. In this way, some relationship between IEX institutions and *mētis* remains intact. The dual components of IEX institutions thus pull them in two opposing directions relative to *mētis*. On the one hand, the fact that they are indigenously introduced pulls them closer to *mētis*. On the other hand, the fact that they are created by formal authorities that tend to be somewhat remote from actors pulls them away from *mētis*. So, while less sticky than IEN institutions, IEX institutions retain some stickiness.

As we note above, many formerly IEN institutions, such as law and money, have become IEX institutions as governments have grown and taken control over them. Precisely because these IEX institutions have their roots in IEN institutions closely connected to *mētis*, they have proved quite sticky despite their changed institutional status. Much of the American legal code, for instance, essentially codifies preexisting informal common law arrangements. Similarly, with money, the US dollar is historically connected to the thaler (pronounced 'tholler')—a unit of silver currency from the days of privately minted commodity money in fifteenth-century Europe (Rothbard 1990). These examples illustrate successful IEX institutional impositions.

As the Balinese example points out, however, these successes do not mean that all IEX institutions are always sufficiently sticky. Their relative lack of stickiness compared to IEN institutions does place some parameters on what successful IEX institutions can look like. For instance, if the US government decided that ashtrays should circulate tomorrow as the new legally mandated medium of exchange, this institutional change would not stick. People would simply refuse to use ashtrays for this purpose or would resort to a black market in currency, where dollars or gold would circulate as the de facto medium of exchange. The notion of ashtrays as money strongly conflicts with American *mētis*. Thus the glue needed to make this new institution stick would be absent. In this way, the necessity of having some IEN institution to act as a *mētis*-based core for IEX institutions constrains what IEX institutions are possible.

When it comes to IEX institutions, there are again two countervailing forces at work. Local authorities have better knowledge than foreign authorities about existing focal points that serve to coordinate the local population's activities. Pulling in the other direction, however, is the fact that institutional change in this case occurs exogenously, and so may not fully respect existing nodes of orientation.

6.3.3   Foreign-Introduced Exogenous (FEX) Institutions

Following our logic, FEX institutions tend to be the least sticky of all. On the one hand, unlike IEN and IEX institutions, FEX institutions are foreign-introduced. This means that the distance between the process of institutional design and the location of hoped institutional 'take-hold' is considerable. Foreign institutional designers are less equipped to tailor institutions in such a way that they do not conflict with indigenous *mētis* because of this increased physical and social distance, which tends to make designers less aware of the local conditions where they desire to transplant institutions. Compounding this increased distance, FEX institutions are exogenous. So, like IEX institutions, they are less connected to *mētis* because formal authorities that tend to be more remote from parochial environments create them.

Both of these features tend to make FEX institutions lack the stickiness for them to be effective. Consider, for instance, Robert Blewett's (1995) study of the pastoral policy of the Maasai in Kenya. Precolonization, the Maasai followed a practice of communal ownership governed by tacit norms of restricted access. This practice evolved as a method to reduce the transaction costs associated with the collective action necessary for cooperation, including pastoral coordination and environmental risk management.

British colonial rule, however, substituted explicit contracts for the tacit norms governing land usage in practice. Explicit contracts did not codify an existing IEX or IEN institution, but instead were created in direct conflict with existing underlying *mētis* about land usage. As a result, the complex IEN institutional land structure of the Maasai was disrupted, and the long-term viability of the common land was destroyed. According to Blewett, this destruction undermined the existing Maasai social structure that enabled cooperative agriculture and created a situation of rampant conflict among formerly cooperative agents that manifested itself in the form of rent-seeking activities.[4]

Since, concretely, FEX institutions are those created by the development community for transplant in reforming countries, their tendency to lack stickiness is a severe problem indeed. This suggests that, even if the development community can correctly identify what institutions are required for growth in general terms, it cannot transplant these institutions where they do not exist as a means of promoting development. Attempts to do so are unlikely to work, because host countries reject FEX institutions, which lack the glue required to stick.

This is certainly not to say that host countries always reject FEX institutions. FEX institutions can successfully take hold, and have done so in some cases, where they are transplanted. As we discuss below, Japan and Germany's post-World War II reconstruction provides a case in point. However, the relative lack of FEX institution stickiness places significant constraints on what successful FEX institutions can look like.

In the same way that successful IEX institutions are connected to IEN institutions, successful FEX institutions are connected to IEX institutions. In other words, because FEX institutions that embody formerly IEX institutions are closer to *mētis*, they are more likely to stick than FEX institutions that do not embody formerly IEX institutions. For instance, while attempts at imposing private property orders among stateless tribes in sub-Saharan Africa are unlikely to work, creating constitutional provisions in post-World War II Germany that embody some elements of pre-Nazi Germany's constitution have a greater chance of working. Likewise, the use of preexisting institutions by the occupiers in the post-World War II reconstruction of Japan was a major reason for the stickiness of FEX institutions.

In short, the connection to *mētis* weakens as we move from IEN to FEX institutions. Thus, stickiness falls as we move in this direction as well. Figure 6.1 illustrates this relationship graphically.

Because successful IEX institutions form the basis for effective FEX institutions and successful IEX institutions must embody IEN institutions, indirectly IEN institutions constrain the form of FEX institutions as well. In circumscribing what shape FEX and IEX institutions may take, IEN institutions point to an important result for development economics. Successful institutional changes in developing parts of the world

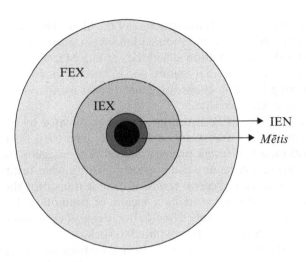

Figure 6.1   Institutional stickiness

must have IEN institutions at their core.[5] We place this claim at the center of the New Development Economics. To determine if any particular development-community proposal for institutional change meets this criterion, we suggest the following test: If the proposed change cannot be traced back to an IEN institution, it should not be attempted.

We call the claim that successful institutional changes must be ultimately traceable to IEN institutions the regression theorem. The regression theorem states that the stickiness, S, of any given institution, I, in time t is a function of that institution's stickiness in time $t - 1$. The stickiness of this institution in $t - 1$ is in turn a function of its stickiness in $t - 2$, and so on. In other words, $S_t^I = S_t^I(S_{t-1}^I)$, where $S_{t-1}^I = S_{t-1}^I(S_{t-2}^I)$, and, generally, $S_{t-n}^I = S_{t-n}^I(S_{t-(n+1)}^I)$.

This chain, however, does not infinitely regress. This is because the stickiness of an institution at the time of its emergence an arbitrarily large number of periods ago, N, is determined by its status vis-à-vis agents when it first emerges as an institution in $t - N$. That is, in $t - N$, the stickiness of institution I depends upon whether it is an IEN, IEX, or FEX institution. So, $S_{t-N}^I = S_{t-N}^I(I^{IEN}, I^{IEX}, I^{FEX})$, where $S^{I^{IEN}} > S^{I^{IEX}} > S^{I^{FEX}}$ in accordance with our analysis from above. In this way, the regression theorem grounds the stickiness of institutions today in their past stickiness, which is ultimately a function of how closely they are connected to *mētis*.

It is important to note that, in our framework, institutional stickiness is *not* equivalent to institutional 'goodness.' Although Hayek (1960,

1991) and others have highlighted a tendency for efficient institutions to evolve when they do so endogenously, it is not the case that every endogenously created institution in all circumstances is efficient or conducive to economic development. Thus, that a particular institution is traceable back to an IEN institution does not itself establish that it is conducive to economic growth. In fact, many IEN institutions are themselves growth inhibitors. For instance, if the embedded local custom in Tanzania has a taboo on private ownership, Tanzania will have difficulty progressing. The regression theorem points out only that, if the institution of private property is imposed on Tanzania, it will have trouble sticking and will probably not produce the desired effects. In this sense, we should understand the traceability of a proposed institutional change to an IEN institution under the regression theorem as providing insight regarding the limitations of development-community activity, rather than as establishing evidence of having met the institutional requirements that progress demands.

It is equally important to point out that not all FEX institutions that exhibit sufficient stickiness to take hold where they are imposed promote growth. For instance, in many parts of Stalinist Eastern Europe, FEX institutions imposed by force stuck, but harmed economic progress. The fact that a particular FEX institution sticks speaks only to the fact that an IEX institution (and indirectly IEN institution rooted in *mētis*) is at its core. The core IEX or IEN institution it is built around may be 'bad' in the sense that it is an obstacle to development. Stickiness is therefore a necessary though not sufficient institutional attribute for creating economic growth.

6.4 HISTORICAL EXAMPLES

Historically, we find empirical support for the framework outlined above. We first focus on cases of postwar reconstruction in which new political and economic orders are imposed upon a populace. We look at what are considered relatively successful reconstructions—post-World War II Japan and West Germany. Next, we look briefly at Bosnia as a case in which reconstruction efforts have been unsuccessful owing to the failure of FEX institutions to dovetail with *mētis*. We then turn to cases of transition economies, where we consider successful (Poland) and failed (Russia) transition efforts within the framework developed above.

6.4.1   Successful Reconstruction in Japan and West Germany: Dovetailing *Mētis* with FEX Institutions

Japan and West Germany are usually considered instances of successful reconstruction, meaning the development of a self-sustaining democracy. In both cases, there was an occupation by external military forces and a democratic political order was imposed in a short period of time.

Americans—notably General Douglas MacArthur, the Supreme Commander of the Allied Powers for the Occupation and Control of Japan (SCAP)—played a key role in rebuilding Japan. MacArthur produced an English-language draft of the new Japanese constitution in ten days. After eight months of negotiations in which minor changes were made, Japanese politicians presented the constitution, in Japanese, to the populace as their own innovation. Following the reconstruction period (1945 through the early 1950s), Japan experienced a period of high growth, lasting through about 1990.

We can attribute the success of Japan's reconstruction to the fact that a significant portion of the Japanese *mētis* remained intact in the postwar period. For centuries, Japanese culture has been geared toward large-scale organizations and a positive view of trade and market exchange (Fukuyama 1996: pp. 161–70). Such a culture aligns well with the incentives of a liberal political and economic structure. In the reconstruction process, while *mētis* indeed changed, the key aspects of the commercial heritage remained intact. The practical knowledge that allowed people to coordinate in the prewar period allowed for similar results in the postwar period.

Moreover, the translation of the imposed constitution from English to Japanese shows the potential value of ambiguity. While the native Japanese did not play a large role in drafting the new constitution, they did play a role in translating it into Japanese. The English and the Japanese versions differ, because in many cases the two languages do not have equivalent terminology (Inoue 1991). While the Japanese adopted a constitution affirming their commitment to Western democratic institutions, much of the language expresses pre-World War II traditional Japanese social and political values. In other words, the FEX institutions created under the constitution retained key elements of traditional Japanese *mētis* and in this sense embodied preexisting IEX and IEN institutional arrangements. Finally, US occupiers relied on existing IEX and IEN institutions, such as the emperor and the Diet, to implement policy changes. The use of these established and accepted solutions facilitated the acceptance of FEX institutions.

The fact that *mētis* remained intact played an important role in postwar

Germany as well. Given that German governments at the local level had a strong tradition of self-government, a 1944 *US Civil Affairs Guide* indicated that local politics was to be the springboard for political reform throughout Germany (Boehling 1996: p. 156). Writing on British plans to democratize Germany, Marshall notes: 'It was recognized, however, that beneath the nationalist and aggressive policies perpetuated by German central governments, there had existed a healthy democratic tradition at the local level' (1989: p. 191).

Allied advisors, many of whom were experts in German history, recommended retaining particular indigenous traditions. The reconstruction process, for instance, included some native Germans. The military governments in the US zone appointed Germans in villages, towns, and cities to assist in the implementation of Allied policies. In the choice of native Germans for these positions, emphasis was placed on past administrative experience and the perceived ability to cooperate with military authority rather than on pro-democracy/anti-Nazi leanings (Boehling 1996: p. 271). As a result, at least part of the German *mētis* was incorporated into the political rebuilding process, which in turn supported the stickiness of FEX institutions in the reconstructed political order.

In sum, while there was widespread physical destruction in both Japan and Germany, the preexisting endowment of *mētis* remained largely intact. As Eva Bellin notes, despite the physical damage, 'Japan and Germany retained the human, organizational, and social capital (that is, skilled workers, skilled managers, and social networks)' (2004–05: p. 596). The endowment of *mētis* included the complementary institutions required to allow externally reconstructed formal institutions to sustain and operate in the desired manner.

6.4.2 Unsuccessful Reconstruction in Bosnia: Conflict between *Mētis* and FEX Institutions

Bosnia is a case in which postwar reconstruction has failed to develop self-sustaining institutions that facilitate economic development. The three and a half years of internal ethnic conflict in Bosnia ended with the signing of the Dayton Peace Agreement (DPA) in 1995 and then the arrival of international peacekeepers. It is critical to note that, while there was no occupying force present to 'impose' order in Bosnia, the DPA was reached 'only after the United States and other key participants exerted substantial pressure on the . . . parties' (Kreimer et al. 2000: p. 25). In other words, the DPA did not arise through indigenous desires to achieve peace, but from outside pressures coupled with the presence of peacekeepers.

Despite obtaining some semblance of peace, the DPA has failed to put

Bosnia on a path of sustainable development. Indeed, it is far from clear
that a sustainable order would exist if troops and peacekeepers were to
withdraw. The fact that the FEX institutional-based peace treaty was not
aligned with the underlying *mētis* of the parties involved, coupled with the
stipulations of the DPA regarding the political order, is to blame for the
reconstruction's failure.

The DPA implemented a single state, but it also created a multilayered
political structure consisting of multiple entities with often conflicting
interests. For instance, the two entities created by the DPA, the Federation
of Bosnia and Herzegovina and Republika Srpska, share some common
institutions in the form of a General Council of Ministers. Further, the
tripartite presidency consists of one Bosnian, one Bosnian Croat, and one
Bosnian Serb, who rotate power every eight months. These common FEX
political institutions oversee a range of policy issues including foreign relations, monetary and fiscal policy, and other social policies and regulations.

However, it is important to note that the existence of additional sover-
eign institutions below these common FEX institutions has created an
ongoing conflict of interests. For instance, each entity has a separate
constitution, president, vice-president, and political system. Further, the
Office of High Representative (OHR) has overriding authority implementing the peace process. The composition of the OHR, a FEX institution, is nominated by the Peace Implementation Council, which consists
of 55 countries and organizations involved in the peace process, approved
by the UN Security Council. The complicated structure of the Bosnian
government along with the outside influence of the OHR creates a clash
between the newly created FEX institutions and underlying *mētis*. The
very structure of the government allows for a continued conflict of interests at virtually all levels. The existence of multiple constitutions has
allowed different entities to pursue different and often conflicting ends.

The reconstruction of Bosnia illustrates another problem: the FEX
democratic process was rushed before the political order aligned with
underlying *mētis*. The timing of elections was set at the signing of the DPA
and stated that elections should take place no later than nine months after
the signing. The rushed elections prevented the development of grassroots
support for democracy, and existing nationalist parties thus had a distinct
advantage.

It may be argued that the reason efforts in Bosnia and elsewhere (such
as Haiti, Afghanistan, and Kosovo) have failed is because of a lack of
international aid and manpower. However, a consideration of international funding and military presence across reconstruction efforts demonstrates that this is not the case. If one looks at the per capita assistance
during the first two years after the end of conflict, it is clear that relatively

high levels of external assistance do not guarantee success. Bosnia received approximately $1400 per person, while Kosovo received slightly over $800 per resident, Germany approximately $300, Haiti approximately $200, and Japan and Afghanistan approximately $100 per resident (Dobbins et al. 2003: p. 158).[6] Bosnia, Kosovo, Haiti, and Afghanistan must all be considered unsuccessful if our benchmark is a self-sustaining democracy.

Likewise, the number of soldiers per thousand inhabitants of each country at the conclusion of conflict does not guarantee success.[7] Initial deployment was relatively high in Germany (approximately 100 soldiers per 1000 inhabitants), Bosnia (18.6 soldiers per 1000 inhabitants), and Kosovo (20 soldiers per 1000 inhabitants). However, initial force levels were relatively low in Japan (5 soldiers per 1000 inhabitants), Haiti (3.5 soldiers per 1000 inhabitants), and Afghanistan (2 soldiers per 1000 inhabitants) (Dobbins et al. 2003: pp. 149–51). Again, we observe successes and failures in the case of both relatively high and relatively low military presence. Clearly, aid and military presence cannot, by themselves, explain successful reconstruction. It is our contention that *mētis* is one of the key factors that allows for the achievement of such successes. If underlying *mētis* does not dovetail with the institutions being imposed, these institutions will fail to stick regardless of the level of aid or military presence provided.

6.4.3 The Transitions of Poland and Russia: Contrasting Cases of *Mētis's* Relationship to Institutional Reform

As with reconstruction efforts, transition involves the shifting of institutions. Whether these institutions stick and have the desired effects depends upon the degree to which they dovetail with the *mētis* of politicians and the populace. This fact is evident in the privatization efforts in both Poland and Russia. We must note upfront that both Poland's and Russia's transitions are vast topics and we do not pretend to cover all of their nuances or angles. Nonetheless, we seek to provide some basic insights in the context of the framework developed above.

Poland's transition must be considered a relative success compared to that of other countries in similar situations. From 1992 to 2000, its GDP grew at an average of 5 percent to 6 percent a year. Russia's economic performance in the transition period stands in clear and dramatic contrast to Poland's. In the aftermath of transition efforts, Russia's GDP fell by 40 percent from 1991 to 1998, with a 5 percent decline in 1998. Moreover, Poland has not been plagued by the extensive corruption, crony capitalism, or theft of state property that characterize Russia (Goldman 2003:

p. 200). Both countries were communist and began undertaking reforms at the same time. Why do we observe this dramatic difference?

By looking closely at the pre- and postwar *mētis* in both countries, it is clear that Poland had the underlying *mētis* to support privatization efforts while Russia did not. Considering Poland first, its transition to the market was facilitated by the fact that a small but legitimate number of private firms had been tolerated throughout the communist reign. Although it is clear that these private firms were not a dominant part of Poland's economy during the communist period, they did serve to develop a *mētis* of 'how to get things done' in the context of private business interactions. Following the collapse of communism and the subsequent privatization efforts, it was easier for both the populace and politicians to build on that underlying *mētis* and accept private business on a much grander scale.

Even before the collapse of communism, Poland passed the 1988 Law on Economic Activity, which granted every Polish citizen the right to engage in private business. During 1990–95, about two million new businesses were registered, with an additional one million registered over the next five years (Goldman 2003: pp. 200–201). A survey of the richest 100 businessmen in Poland concluded that most Polish citizens built their fortunes via startups. As we will see below, this stands in stark contrast to Russia, where most of the oligarchs became wealthy by taking over control of state assets. It must also be noted that close to 80 percent of the farms in Poland were not collectivized. While this does not mean that they operated efficiently, it does mean that they developed a unique *mētis* based on private ownership that served to facilitate privatization efforts.

We have already noted Russia's poor economic performance in the post-communist period. As with Poland, a brief consideration of the pre- and post-communist *mētis* in Russia adds insight into Russia's failure. In 1992, those in charge of reform—Yegor Gaider and Anatoly Chubais—along with economic and legal advisors from both the United States and Russia formulated a bold plan for privatization, and reformers moved immediately to privatize up to 70 percent of state enterprises. These privatization efforts failed, largely because after 70 years of communism the social, political, and economic climate was not ready for privatization (Goldman 2003: p. 76). In other words, the underlying *mētis* necessary to support the privatization efforts was lacking and had no roots in the pre-transition period. The reformers recognized this but proceeded nonetheless. As Shleifer and Vishny (who were part of the reform team) wrote, '[t]he architects of Russian privatization were aware of the dangers of poor enforcement of property rights' but assumed they would come into existence after privatization (1998: p. 11). As a result, privatization efforts failed to stick as expected.

In Poland, even under communist rule, some private business was allowed. There was nothing, however, comparable in the Soviet Union. The pre-transition *mētis* allowing for the smooth post-communist shift to privatization that existed in Poland was missing in Russia. The result was widespread corruption, crony capitalism, and the prevalence of organized crime. Reform efforts failed to be effectively supported by both politicians and the populace—the *mētis* that acts as the glue to give institutional changes their stickiness was absent.

It is also important to note that, as in the case of Bosnia, the inability of designed institutional changes to stick in Russia was not the result of insufficient aid. Between 1991 and 1999, Russia received over $90 billion in assistance from the international community. In today's dollars, this sum is roughly equivalent to the $13.3 billion provided by the United States between 1948 and 1951 to Europe for postwar reconstruction (Boettke 1999). While Russia's transition has been relatively unsuccessful, postwar reconstruction efforts proved largely effective. Foreign aid thus cannot explain institutional stickiness. Something else, which we identify as the degree of congruity between proposed institutional changes and existing *mētis*, must be at work.

The cases of Poland and Russia offer key insights into why some transition countries have performed relatively better as compared to others. In the case of Poland, where the underlying pre-transition *mētis* dovetailed with reform efforts, the institutions stuck and were successful. In Russia, where an underlying *mētis* supporting privatization did not exist, these reforms failed to have the desired impact.

As we have seen here, the only way such a regime can be effective is if enough politicians and the populace coordinate around and support the regime change. In other words, an underlying *mētis* must exist to support such a system. Before concluding, we must reiterate that *mētis* is not a static concept. It is possible for a new and unique *mētis* to develop over time. Therefore, it must be realized that it is at least possible for economies trapped in underdevelopment to eventually change paths. But, until that new *mētis* is in place, reformers must realize that efforts to impose institutions, whether from within or from without, are likely to fail.

6.5   CONCLUSION

Our analysis has significant implications for economic development. First, recognition of the importance of IEN institutions in creating sustainable development suggests that current programs aimed at affecting reform exogenously are unlikely to work. IEN institutions emerge endogenously as spontaneous orders to overcome obstacles that otherwise stand in the way of individuals' ability to interact for mutual gain. Institutions that are imposed exogenously do not have the social memory grounded in *mētis* that gives IEN institutions their credibility and workability among local agents. In ignoring this fact, the development community overestimates its ability to promote growth and underestimates the role of internally driven change in creating prosperity.

Furthermore, by using stickiness to explain how history matters for institutional development, our analysis suggests an important corollary result for development economics. Though theoretically exogenous force is needed to jolt agents out of suboptimal institutional arrangements, such force has low voltage precisely because it is exogenous. In other words, despite the fact that exogenously introduced change provides a conceptual way out of locked-in, inferior institutional arrangements, realistically its power to alter institutional paths is severely limited.

Our application of the regression theorem to institutions provides a means of analyzing ex ante the potential success or failure of various institutions that the development community is considering introducing in varying developing nations. As our examination of West Germany and Japan's post-World War II reconstruction histories illustrates, if the institution being considered is traceable back to an IEN institution (or an IEX institution that is itself traceable to an IEN institution) its chances of success are significantly increased. On the other hand, as the cases of Bosnia and Russia suggest, if this is not the case, institutional changes are unlikely to stick despite development-community efforts to the contrary. Thus, while it may be an overstatement to say that the only path to progress is an indigenous one, it does not seem an exaggeration to say that any path to progress with a reasonable probability of success must ultimately be rooted in indigenous institutional order.

This is an important insight given the post-September 11 focus of Western policy on spreading liberal democratic institutions to the Middle East. Timur Kuran (2004) has analyzed several evolutionary 'bottlenecks' that have contributed to the persistence of economic underdevelopment in the Middle East region. These bottlenecks have prevented the indigenous development of the complementary institutions necessary for the operation of formal Western institutions. The framework developed here can contribute to understanding how these bottlenecks may prevent the ability of external actors to implement Western-style institutions in this region.

Finally, our framework offers a potentially fruitful avenue for future research. We have sketched the key features of the New Development Economics, which uses the insights of the regression theorem to emphasize the critical role that indigenous institutions and institutional stickiness play in promoting or inhibiting economic growth. In addition to use of the regression theorem to evaluate current proposals for exogenous institutional reform in the developing world, an important first step in building the New Development Economics approach might examine historical cases in this light as a means of giving us a better idea about how indigenous and endogenously emergent institutions influence the process of reform.

NOTES

* This chapter previously appeared in the *American Journal of Economics and Sociology*, Vol. **67**, No. 2 (April 2008). It is reprinted here (with minor edits) with the permission of the publisher.

    We thank the Editor and an anonymous referee for helpful comments and suggestions. The financial support of the Earhart Foundation, the Oloffson Weaver Fellowship, the Mercatus Center, and the Kendrick Fund is also gratefully acknowledged.
1. The idea of the regression theorem comes from Mises ([1912] 1980), who created the concept to explain why grounding the purchasing power of money in marginal utility theory did not lead to an infinite regress, as some before him had maintained. See also Selgin (1994) on assuring the acceptance of fiat currency.
2. This is not meant to be an exhaustive list of the ingredients necessary for economic growth. It is simply intended to highlight that there is some agreement on the general, underlying institutions required for development. For example, there is significant empirical evidence that the socialist model of planned industrialization does not work (see Boettke 1990, 1993, 1994, 2001a, 2001b). Furthermore, there is evidence that market economies grounded in a rule of law that protects private property and freedom of contract demonstrate robust progress (see, for example, Scully 1992; Gwartney et al. 1996, 1998, 1999; Gwartney and Lawson 2003; O'Driscoll et al. 2003).
3. The anthropologist James Scott (1998) has recently attempted to revive the concept of *mētis*.
4. For more on how colonial-created institutions inconsistent with indigenous, informal institutions created havoc in Africa, see Leeson (2005).
5. As noted above, our argument here is closely related to that of Frey (1997), who emphasizes the need to build institutions that respect the intrinsic motivations of agents.
6. Assistance per capita is in 2001 US dollars.
7. The figure for Germany represents the level of US troops at the end of the war as a proportion of the population in the US sector. Note also that the troop presence was the highest in each case at the conclusion of conflict and declined thereafter.

REFERENCES

Aoki, Masahikao (2001), *Toward a Comparative Institutional Analysis*, Cambridge, MA: MIT Press.

Bellin, Eva (2004–05), 'The Iraqi Intervention and Democracy in Comparative Historical Perspective,' *Political Science Quarterly*, **119**(4), 595–608.

Benson, Bruce (1989), 'The Spontaneous Evolution of Commercial Law,' *Southern Economic Journal*, **55**(3), 644–61.

Berman, Harold (1983), *Law and Revolution: The Formation of the Western Legal Tradition*, Cambridge, MA: Harvard University Press.

Blewett, Robert A. (1995), 'Property Rights as a Cause of the Tragedy of the Commons: Institutional Change and the Pastoral Maasai of Kenya,' *Eastern Economic Journal*, **21**(4), 477–90.

Boehling, Rebecca (1996), *A Question of Priorities: Democratic Reform and Economic Recovery in Postwar Germany*, Providence, RI: Berghahn Books.

Boettke, Peter J. (1990), *The Political Economy of Soviet Socialism: The Formative Years, 1918–1928*, Boston, MA: Kluwer Academic Publishers.

Boettke, Peter J. (1993), *Why Perestroika Failed: The Politics and Economics of Socialist Transformation*, New York: Routledge.

Boettke, Peter J. (ed.) (1994), *The Collapse of Developmental Planning*, New York: New York University Press.

Boettke, Peter J. (1999), 'The Russian Crisis: Perils and Prospects for Post-Soviet Transition,' *American Journal of Economics and Sociology*, **59**(3), 371–84.

Boettke, Peter J. (2001a), 'The Political Infrastructure of Economics Development,' in *Calculation and Coordination: Essays on Socialism and Transitional Political Economy*, New York: Routledge, pp. 234–47.

Boettke, Peter J. (2001b), 'Why Culture Matters: Economics, Politics, and the Imprint of History,' in *Calculation and Coordination: Essays on Socialism and Transitional Political Economy*, New York: Routledge, pp. 248–65.

Buchanan, James M. (1992), *Post-Socialist Political Economy: Selected Essays*, Aldershot, UK and Brookfield, VT, USA: Edward Elgar Publishing.

Buchanan, James and Yong Yoon (1994), *The Return of Increasing Returns*, Ann Arbor: University of Michigan Press.

Coyne, Christopher (2007), *After War: The Political Economy of Postwar Reconstruction*, Stanford, CA: Stanford University Press.

Djankov, Simeon, Rafael La Porta, Florencio Lopez-de-Silanes and Andrei Shleifer (2003), 'Courts,' *Quarterly Journal of Economics*, **118**(2), 495–517.

Dobbins, James, John G. McGinn, Keith Crane, G. Jones Seth, Rollie Lal, Andrew Rathmall, Rachel Swanger and Anga Timilsina (eds.) (2003), *America's Role in Nation-Building: From Germany to Iraq*, Santa Monica, CA: RAND.

Easterly, William (2001), *The Elusive Quest for Growth: Economists' Adventures and Misadventures in the Tropics*, Cambridge, MA: MIT Press.

Easterly, William (2006), *The White Man's Burden: Why the West's Efforts to Aid the Rest Have Done So Much Ill and So Little Good*, New York: Penguin Press.

Frey, Bruno S. (1997), *Not Just for the Money: An Economic Theory of Personal Motivation*, Cheltenham, UK and Lyme, NH, USA: Edward Elgar Publishing.

Fukuyama, Francis (1996), *Trust*, New York: Simon & Schuster.

Glaeser, Edward and Andrei Shleifer (2002), 'Legal Origins,' *Quarterly Journal of Economics*, **117**(4), 1195–1229.

Goldman, Marshall I. (2003), *The Privatization of Russia: Russian Reform Goes Awry*, New York: Routledge.

Gwartney, James D. and Robert Lawson (2003), *Economic Freedom of the World: 2003 Annual Report*, Vancouver: Fraser Institute.

Gwartney, James D., Robert Lawson and Walter Block (1996), *Economic Freedom of the World: 1975–1995*, Vancouver: Fraser Institute.

Gwartney, James D., Randall Holcombe and Robert Lawson (1998), 'The Scope of Government and the Wealth of Nations,' *Cato Journal*, **18**, 163–90.

Gwartney, James D., Randall Holcombe and Robert Lawson (1999), 'Economic

Freedom and the Environment for Economic Growth,' *Journal of Institutional and Theoretical Economics*, **155**, 643–63.

Hay, Jonathan and Andrei Shleifer (1998), 'Private Enforcement of Public Laws: A Theory of Legal Reform,' *American Economic Review*, **88**(2), 398–403.

Hayek, F.A. (1960), *The Constitution of Liberty*, Chicago: University of Chicago Press.

Hayek, F.A. (1973), *Law, Legislation, and Liberty*, Vol. 1, Chicago: University of Chicago Press.

Hayek, F.A. (1991), *The Fatal Conceit*, Chicago: University of Chicago Press.

Hayek, F.A. (1996), *Individualism and Economic Order*, Chicago: University of Chicago Press.

Innes, Stephen (1995), *Creating the Commonwealth: The Economic Culture of Puritan New England*, New York: Norton.

Inoue, Kyoko (1991), *MacArthur's Japanese Constitution: A Linguistic and Cultural Study of Its Making*, Chicago: University of Chicago Press.

Kasper, Wolfgang and Manfred E. Streit (1999), *Institutional Economics: Social Order and Public Policy*, Cheltenham, UK and Northampton, MA, USA: Edward Elgar Publishing.

Kreimer, Alcira, Robert Muscat, Ann Elwan and Margaret Arnold (2000), *Bosnia and Herzegovina: Post-Conflict Reconstruction*, Washington, DC: World Bank.

Kuran, Timur (2004), 'Why the Middle East Is Historically Underdeveloped: Historical Mechanisms of Institutional Stagnation,' *Journal of Economic Perspectives*, **18**(3), 71–90.

Lansing, J. Stephen (1991), *Priests and Programmers: Technologies of Power in the Engineered Landscape of Bali*, Princeton, NJ: Princeton University Press.

La Porta, Rafael, Florencio Lopez-de-Silanes, Andrei Shleifer and Robert Vishny (1998), 'Law and Finance,' *Journal of Political Economy*, **106**(6), 1113–55.

Leeson, Peter T. (2005), 'Endogenizing Fractionalization,' *Journal of Institutional Economics*, **1**(1), 75–98.

Leeson, Peter T. (2006), 'Cooperation and Conflict: Evidence on Self-Enforcing Arrangements and Heterogeneous Groups,' *American Journal of Economics and Sociology*, **65**(4), 891–907.

Leeson, Peter T. (2007a), 'Efficient Anarchy,' *Public Choice*, **130**(1–2), 41–53.

Leeson, Peter T. (2007b), 'Trading with Bandits,' *Journal of Law and Economics*, **50**(2), 303–21.

Marshall, Barbara (1989), 'British Democratisation Policy in Germany,' in Ian D. Turner (ed.), *Reconstruction in Postwar Germany*, Oxford: Berg Publishers, pp. 189–214.

Menger, Carl ([1871] 1994), *Principles of Economics*, Grove City, PA: Libertarian Press.

Mises, Ludwig von (1949), *Human Action: A Treatise on Economics*, New Haven, CT: Yale University Press.

Mises, Ludwig von ([1912] 1980), *The Theory of Money and Credit*, Indianapolis, IN: Liberty Fund.

Nenova, Tatiana and Tim Harford (2004), *Anarchy and Invention*, Public Policy for the Private Sector Note No. 280, Washington, DC: World Bank.

North, Douglass C. (1990), *Institutions, Institutional Change, and Economic Performance*, Cambridge: Cambridge University Press.

North, Douglass C. (2005), *Understanding the Process of Economic Change*, Princeton, NJ: Princeton University Press.

O'Driscoll, Gerald P., Edwin J. Feulner and Mary Anastasia O'Grady (2003), *Index of Economic Freedom*, New York: Heritage Foundation and Dow Jones & Company.

Ostrom, Elinor (1990), *Governing the Commons: The Evolution of Institutions for Collective Action*, New York: Cambridge University Press.

Ostrom, Elinor (2000), 'Collective Action and the Evolution of Social Norms,' *Journal of Economic Perspectives*, **14**(3), 137–58.

Pejovich, Svetozar (2003), 'Understanding the Transaction Costs of Transition: It's the Culture, Stupid,' *Review of Austrian Economics*, **16**(4), 347–61.

Pierson, Paul (2000a), 'The Limits of Design: Explaining Institutional Origins and Change,' *Governance*, **13**(4), 475–99.

Pierson, Paul (2000b), 'Returns, Path Dependence and the Study of Politics,' *American Political Science Review*, **94**(2), 251–67.

Platteau, Jean-Philippe (2000), *Institutions, Social Norms, and Economic Development*, Amsterdam: Harwood Academic Publishers.

Posner, Richard (1973), *The Economic Analysis of Law*, Boston, MA: Little, Brown.

Rothbard, Murray (1990), *What Has Government Done to Our Money?*, Auburn, AL: Ludwig von Mises Institute.

Scott, James C. (1998), *Seeing Like a State*, New Haven, CT: Yale University Press.

Scully, Gerald W. (1992), *Constitutional Environments and Economic Growth*, Princeton, NJ: Princeton University Press.

Selgin, George (1994), 'On Ensuring the Acceptability of a New Fiat Currency,' *Journal of Money, Credit and Banking*, **26**, 808–26.

Selgin, George and Lawrence White (1994), 'How Would the Invisible Hand Handle Money?,' *Journal of Economic Literature*, **52**(4), 1718–49.

Shleifer, Andrei and Robert Vishny (1998), *The Grabbing Hand: Government Pathologies and Cures*, Cambridge, MA: Harvard University Press.

Streeten, Paul (1995), *Thinking about Development*, New York: Cambridge University Press.

Volckart, Oliver and Antje Mangels (1999), 'Are the Roots of the Modern *Lex Mercatoria* Really Medieval?,' *Southern Economic Journal*, **65**(3), 427–50.

White, Lawrence (1995), *Free Banking in Britain: Theory, Experience and Debate 1800–1845*, London: Institute of Economic Affairs.

7. How does culture influence economic development?*

Don Lavoie and Emily Chamlee-Wright

A culture is an aggregate of divergent and contradictory pictures, and each picture is true. (Hidetoshi Kato, cited in Kotkin 1992: p. 10)

Agrarian reform, economic reform, financial reform, constitutional reform? Certainly Brazil needs reforms and achievements of all kinds—railways and highways, hydroelectric energy . . . but what is really needed is a reform within the Brazilian mind. Don't have any illusions: without a reform within the mind . . . that makes us shape within ourselves, not only intellectually but . . . above all emotionally, a radical shift of concepts and attitudes about life, Brazil, and the universe . . . we shall continue to be what we are: a country that progresses but does not ennoble itself, a country without a message for the world, a disorganized collectivity that lacks moral initiative and public spirit . . . that permanently awaits miracle workers or caudillos to solve the problems that only spiritually, morally, and organically integrated communities can really resolve. (Clodomir Vianna Moog, *Bandeirantes e Pioneiros*, 1964: p. 198, cited in Harrison 1992: p. 50)

7.1 INTRODUCTION

Why are some societies better able to use their natural endowments of resources? Why do some readily embrace growth-friendly institutions and others resist them? We will claim that one of the most important elements in economic development is something that sounds thoroughly subjective: the culture. If there is a spirit of enterprise, a set of stories or images in the culture that celebrate some form of entrepreneurial creativity, then economic prosperity is more likely. If you want to get a sense of whether a community is apt to grow wealthier, we are suggesting you find out what stories they tell, what myths they believe, what heroes they admire and what metaphors they use. Economic development is, at its heart, a cultural process.

How does a 'culture'—in the anthropologist's sense of a context, a shared set of attitudes and values which constitutes what people find meaningful and significant in life—influence economic performance? This is the kind of question that Max Weber ([1924] 1968) investigated in his masterful two volume work *Economy and Society*, and that Hernando de Soto (1988) explored in his study of the informal sector in Peru. It is what, under an unmistakably Weberian influence, Peter Berger and his colleagues at the Institute for the Study of Economic Culture have been investigating at length in regard to Asian, Latin American and African development (see Martin 1990; Redding 1990; B. Berger 1991). We cannot undertake such detailed ethnographic work here, but what we would like to do is clarify a bit how best to pose this question.

Cultural conservatives discuss culture in terms of identifying, and perhaps reinforcing, the hegemony of a unitary 'national culture,' say, American Values. We want to encourage a different approach. Ethnographic research that is sensitive to the subtle difficulties of under-standing, such as is found in the cultural studies literature, can flesh out the details of the economists' own theories. One example is the issue of entrepreneurship. Economists have been asking the question in the abstract: What is the 'essence' of entrepreneurship? In fact some very useful understanding of some fundamental aspects of entrepreneurship has come from the work of Joseph Schumpeter, Ludwig von Mises, Israel Kirzner and others. But it might be argued that the theoretical develop-ment of the notion of entrepreneurship has reached something of an impasse. Perhaps a more useful direction for research to take in order to develop such theories further is that of examining the specific local cultural contexts of actual entrepreneurial activity. Here one finds some interesting differences, for example, between the contexts of American, Japanese and Chinese entrepreneurship, which we will examine later in this chapter.

7.2   WHICH CULTURE PROSPERS? COMPARATIVE CULTURAL ADVANTAGE

Development economists such as P.T. Bauer (1954, 1957, 1971, 1984) and new institutional economists such as Douglass North (1989, 1990, 1994) have made significant strides in moving economics away from the institution-less world of mainstream economics. Their contributions have centered around identifying institutional structures conducive to lower transactions costs, the expansion of trade, and improved economic per-formance. The next step, we think, is to understand the cultural processes which support the institutions so crucial to economic performance. Such a pursuit is not at odds with the work of Bauer or North. Both scholars have recognized the significance of culture within the market process. Bauer (1954) recognized the customary dimension of informal markets in his study of West African trade. Douglass North, in his work with Arthur Denzau, argues that

> [i]deas matter; and the way ideas are communicated among people is crucial to theories that will enable us to deal with strong uncertainty problems at the individual level. For most of the interesting issues in political and economic markets, uncertainty, not risk, characterizes choice-making. Under conditions of uncertainty, individuals' interpretation of their environment will reflect their learning. Individuals with common cultural backgrounds and experiences will share reasonably convergent mental models, ideologies, and institutions; and individuals with different learning experiences (both cultural and environmental) will have different theories (models, ideologies) to interpret their environment ... [I]n order to understand decision making under such conditions of uncertainty we must understand the relationship of the mental models that individuals construct to make sense out of the world around them, the ideologies that evolve from such constructions, and the institutions that develop in a society to order interpersonal relationships. (Denzau and North 1994: pp. 3–4)

Though hinted at here and there, the study of the cultural foundations of institutions and economic performance is not yet a well-developed line of inquiry within the new institutionalist school, and is utterly invisible to most of the economics profession. Much more work is needed if we are to understand the cultural processes which underlie institutions and market processes.

The way not to ask the question about the relationship between culture and economic prosperity is to score different 'national cultures' against a set of universal cultural strengths to see which one wins, that is, which one best promotes economic development. Such 'cultural nationalism' begs important questions about what economic prosperity really means in different cultural contexts, and equates culture with some sort of (probably mythical) averaged-out, prevailing, national consciousness. Neither the notion of a single, homogeneous national culture, nor that of a universal list of cultural strengths, nor even that of a single objective definition of economic prosperity, will stand up to close scrutiny.

7.2.1 The Meaning of Economic Development

Our first task is to clarify what we mean by 'economic development.' Many of the scholars who are drawn to cultural studies and economics share a serious concern about poverty in the world, so one might expect that they would be talking with one another about how culture might shape development. But the communicative challenges are so great here that it is difficult even to begin the discussion, for example to even agree about what 'economic development' is, much less on whether in some sense culture is relevant to it. Economists refer unreflectively to economic growth or development as if these words stood for obvious and uncontested objective things, but the study of culture makes one alert to the radical diversity of human meanings and practices, and thus to the fact that 'prosperity' can mean radically different things to different people. We need to take seriously the culture's own notions of what prosperity or 'wealth' is, realizing that for some it may mean more leisure time, for others more technological gadgets, for some cleaner air, for others a better sense of community, for some more cars, and for others cheaper bread. Indeed, for any individual person it must mean a whole set of such things in a complex pattern, dozens of criteria with widely different weights assigned to each.

Yet we think there is overall pragmatic agreement about roughly what we mean by 'improvements in the economy's performance,' and few of us would have any trouble deciding between the Democratic Republic of Congo's (DRC) or Hong Kong's economic performance over the past couple of decades. Controversies exist over what to do to try to respond to *poverty* problems, and over how best to improve the economy's ability to generate *wealth*, but there is strong agreement that we can, for practical purposes, tell the difference, and that the one is bad and the other good.

For our purposes we would like to characterize the economic development process as a discovery procedure, as a process in which the coordinating capacity of the market improves, leading to an increase in the complexity of the structure of production of goods and services, which in turn improves the living standards of most of the participants. We contend that the economy's wealth-generation process, its ability, roughly speaking, to produce more output of valued goods and services, for the same level of input of labor and other scarce resources, is real, and is really important. Even after duly considering all the difficulties of aggregation, we need to acknowledge that there is some meaning to the everyday observation that our ability to afford more of whatever it is we want varies with different locations and times, and changes for the better in certain reasonably identifiable circumstances. For the purposes of this study we would like to take as given the notion that we can often tell whether an economy is prospering or declining, and that research in economic development can contribute something by elucidating conditions that would be conducive to a prosperity-generation process.

Aggregate statistics, such as per capita gross domestic product (GDP) levels and growth rates, are useful tools for comparing economic conditions across countries and time. We cannot silence the sincere complaints of the Romanians about the poor performance of their economy with hair-splitting about the imprecision of GDP measurements or the diversity of human tastes. Their poor are not, in general, simply choosing to consume more leisure time; they are desperately struggling for an adequate material standard of living. We are not interested here in debates about whether an estimate of the DRC's per capita GDP growth from 1980 to 1994 at negative 3.7 percent and an estimate of Hong Kong's for the same period at positive 5 percent (Gwartney et al. 1996: p. xxiii) are precisely accurate, but we have no doubt that such numbers tell us something. Such statistics give us at least a rough sense of whether the country is 'prospering' or not, and in the extreme cases it is obvious enough from anecdotal evidence whether an economy is doing very well or very badly.

GDP statistics are not enough. By themselves they beg the question of what counts as 'prosperity.' The 'basic needs' literature within development economics has already criticized the use of growth statistics as a proxy for development (Ghosh 1984). Basic needs theorists argue that true development has more to do with the average person's access to clean water, health care, balanced nutrition, and education than to the aggregate level of GDP. Further, many development theorists have pointed out that per capita growth rates often obscure the picture of development, when the overwhelming bulk of resources are held in the hands of an elite few.

Moreover, while avoiding poverty and achieving some degree of material wealth is in itself a rather uncontroversial shared goal, there is no reason it should become an all-embracing goal of public policy. We do not embrace the 'wealth fetishism' one finds in some of the economic development literature, the notion that whatever increases material living standards is good. Economic development policy agendas have been frequently used, for example, to justify the violation of fundamental democratic freedoms. In our own view public policy should not be directed at targeting some sort of growth level for the whole society, but should be primarily concerned with protecting the civil and economic freedom of individual citizens. As the television advertisement puts it, there is no law that says you need to contribute every day to the gross national product. It is their own business if the citizens of Ruritania decide to live for today, or go back to nature, or do other things that reduce reported national incomes.

The subjectivist approach to economics, which is at the center of this study, helps us to identify additional problems with the use of growth statistics as a proxy for development. First, the actual makeup of GDP is just as important as the rate at which GDP is rising (or falling). For example, the sales of locks, bars, guns and other anti-theft devices count towards a growing GDP. But the growth of such industries may be indicative of general social decay in which theft and violent crime are on the rise. Depending upon the content of GDP, its growth may or may not indicate a better overall quality of life.

Secondly, aggregate growth statistics often do not capture the structural health of the economy. If half of GDP is the result of political choices, rather than the free and voluntary market choices of individuals, then a growing GDP does not necessarily indicate a healthier economy. Aggregate statistics may serve a useful purpose, but they can never tell a complete story.

Roughly, though, we know 'economic development' when we see it. We can tell, for example, without claiming to measure such things precisely, that at the beginning of the twenty-first century there is severe poverty throughout most of the society in Romania, and relative wealth in Canada. In principle, it could conceivably be that what people want is ascetic serenity, purity of the soul, and a simple life, so that increasing the economy's capacity to generate wealth is considered a bad thing, or at least irrelevant to their subjective meaning of 'wealth.' But when you see people starving you can pretty much tell that food is high enough on their priority list, and that the problem is that they simply cannot afford enough of it.

What most people around the world have tended to want in practice is increases in wealth that can be translated into more leisure time, better working conditions on the job, or more or better consumption of goods and services. There is nothing sacred about what people currently want, and there is nothing wrong with any of us as individuals trying to change people's minds about what we think they ought to want. But at the same time we need to respect the empirical fact that most people today tend to want something that can be roughly called material wealth. Experience suggests that there are certain developmental processes, which some countries have undergone to a greater extent than others, by which people come to better afford more of whatever it is they want. We think that we have a good enough understanding of economic development processes to be able to explain fairly well why Romanians have less of this thing called wealth than Canadians, and to identify in broad terms what sorts of things Romanians could do to improve their economy's performance.

So let us agree for the moment that having more rather than fewer goods and services available for consumption, or better wages or working conditions, or more leisure time, or let us just call it having a 'higher standard of living,' is an essential piece of what we mean by the relative economic success of a country. Yet increases in output are more the effect of the development process, rather than its essence. For the purposes of this study we mean by the 'development process' one in which human society is able to grow in complexity, because the coordinating capacity of the market has grown (Hayek 1988: pp. 38–47). As social institutions such as property rights, contract law and conventional rules of business evolve, the division of knowledge and labor potentially becomes extended. The development of credit and financial markets, for example, represents the growth of a certain kind of specialized knowledge. Lenders and investors become increasingly knowledgeable of and responsive to the conditions that affect the overall stability of the market. The development of this specialized knowledge allows for greater complexity in terms of the kinds of projects that can be pursued across time and distance. It becomes increasingly commonplace that producers and consumers of the same goods have no awareness of the other's identity. This is not to suggest that face-to-face interaction becomes unimportant in a developing market. Rather, the point is that individuals increasingly make use of and benefit from the specialized knowledge others possess. Greater productivity and material wealth are then the result of this process.

Like any definition of economic development, the one offered here is informed by a particular disciplinary and cultural perspective. It is important to acknowledge that the values implied in our characterization of economic progress may not be universally shared. An Amish community, for instance, may place a higher value on master craftsmanship than the benefits associated with the division of labor and knowledge. Yet any characterization of the development process will inevitably run into limitations of this kind. If we are to take the subjectivist approach seriously, we must recognize that 'progress' will be a culturally defined concept. But we think that the characterization of economic development as a process by which rules and institutions are able to coordinate increasingly complex productive arrangements is a reasonable and helpful starting point.

7.2.2 Cultural Nationalism

Culture, as Max Weber understood a century ago, and as the cultural studies literature shows today, is a rich set of diverse and complexly interwoven strands and conflicting tendencies. For cultural nationalism 'our culture' (mainstream, middle-class, American, and so on) is pitted against 'theirs.' If there is one thing cultural studies scholarship has demonstrated decisively it is that any nation (and especially the United States) is not really a unitary culture, but a system of interacting cultures (see Aligica and Matei, this volume, Chapter 13). For example, Republican American values represent only some of the many strands that the diverse culture of North American society contains. One thing the contemporary world does not need is more rhetoric to inflame the already overheated notions of 'national culture' that pit us against them.

The cultural nationalist way of talking about culture is often little more than a weapon with which cultural conservatives can beat various ethnic groups and other subcultures they do not tolerate into submission. When, for example, William J. Bennett and Lawrence E. Harrison address issues of culture, they are primarily trying to promulgate their own conservative American values, not trying genuinely to understand the specific strengths and weaknesses that each cultural system contains.

In his *Index of Leading Cultural Indicators* (1994: pp. 8–9) William J. Bennett, former drug czar and Secretary of Education, tries to gauge the extent to which our culture has undergone 'social decomposition.' Now we can admit that some of what he means by social decomposition does in fact represent an erosion of values that are conducive to economic prosperity. When family structures grow fragile, when the value of the work ethic is undermined, and when respect for property and law is lost, the society's capacity for economic prosperity is correspondingly weakened. But Bennett seems to mean by decomposition the extent to which values stray from the particular form of prosperity-enhancing values that represent what he considers the good old-fashioned, Anglo-American, middle-class culture that he likes. Uncomfortable with a culture that places higher value than he would on 'things like self-expression, individualism, self-realization, and personal choice,' he uses his research on culture to assert the superiority of middle-class American culture over that of all deviations from it. Such attempts to homogenize American culture into a single, national consciousness can only aggravate the anxieties America's diverse cultures already have about one another.

Or take a book that actually presents itself as arising from the Weberian tradition, Lawrence E. Harrison's *Who Prospers? How Cultural Values Shape Economic and Political Success* (1992). Harrison is interesting here in that he represents neither of the scholarly disciplines we have critically surveyed in *Culture and Enterprise* (Lavoie and Chamlee-Wright 2000), cultural studies and economics, and so lacks the defects and the strengths of both disciplines. His book does not suffer from the systemic misdirection both economics and cultural studies have often had, in presuming that markets are objective forces, external to human meaning, but tries to treat cultural values and market performance together. Yet it also lacks the strengths that economics can supply in terms of a more solid understanding of the way markets work, and that cultural studies could supply in terms of a better appreciation of the nature of culture.

Although Harrison's work, like that of Bennett, makes a number of insightful observations about many of the kinds of cultural values that are conducive to economic development, his analysis is severely crippled by a tendency to homogenize the societies whose cultures he is studying. This tendency to try to undertake large-scale comparisons of grossly aggregated cultural groupings can be overcome by drawing from the strengths of the fields of economics (for example, its notion of comparative advantage) and cultural studies (for example, its notion of fragmentation). The upshot of the critique of economics and cultural studies should not be that we abandon these fields, but that we deploy what is good in each to correct for the deficiencies of the other.

7.2.3 Value: Conducive to Economic Development

In his introductory chapter Harrison (1992: pp. 16–19) draws from an Argentine journalist, Mariano Grondona, who laid out a binary opposition between 'development-prone' and 'development-resistant' cultures, and identified some 20 factors that one could look for to determine whether any given culture is growth-friendly or not. It may be worth quoting from Harrison's paraphrasing of Grondona's thesis, not only because there is an element of truth here, but also to suggest how misleading this way of setting up the issue can be. Here are the dozen factors Harrison lists:

- *Religion* explains and justifies success in a development-prone culture. In a development-resistant culture, religion relieves or explains suffering.
- *Wealth* is *created* as the product of human initiative and effort in the favorable culture. Wealth is the natural or physical resources that *exist* in the resistant culture, and life is a struggle to acquire (or redistribute) it.
- *Competition* is viewed in a progress-prone culture as a positive force that promotes excellence and enriches the society. The resistant culture discourages competition as a form of aggression that threatens the stability and solidarity of the society, in part because it nurtures envy.
- *Economic justice* demands saving and investment for the benefit of future generations in the progressive culture. In the resistant culture, economic justice demands equitable distribution to the current generation.
- *Labor* is a moral, social duty and a central form of self-expression and satisfaction in a favorable culture. In a resistant culture it is a burden, a necessary evil; real pleasure and satisfaction are attainable only outside the workplace.
- *Heresy*, or dissent, is crucial to progress, reform and the search for truth in the favorable culture, which encourages innovation. The heretic is a criminal who threatens stability and solidarity in the resistant culture.
- *Education* nurtures inquisitiveness and creativity in a favorable culture. In a resistant, traditional culture, it transmits orthodoxy.

- *Pragmatism, rationalism, empiricism and utilitarianism* are central values in a favorable culture, and threats to stability, solidarity and continuity in a resistant culture. Tradition, emotion and chance substitute for rationality, with stagnating consequences.
- *Time focus* is the manipulable future in the favorable culture. The resistant culture focuses on the past, and the concept of future is one of destiny, reflecting a fatalistic world view.
- *The world* is a setting for action and achievement in a favorable culture; one approaches it with optimism. In the resistant culture, the world is controlled by irresistible forces; one approaches it with pessimism, if not fear.
- *Life* is 'something I will do' in the favorable culture. In the resistant culture life is 'something that happens to me.'
- *Optimism* is nurtured in the favorable culture. In the resistant culture, survival is the goal and pessimism the mood.

There are some truths in this list, though they are perhaps somewhat obvious ones. When people put a high value on creativity or savings, powerful economic rewards can result. Certain growth-friendly attitudes, such as considering work a duty or even a form of self-expression as opposed to a burden, are likely to make the individuals who have them more inclined to attain economic prosperity than the opposite attitude. Attitudes toward wealth that are less oriented toward envy of what others have, and more toward creating wealth for oneself, will be conducive to economic development. Willingness to invest in the future promotes the accumulation of wealth.

Yet all of these categories, including the idea of 'wealth' itself, cry out for clarification and interpretation. The last four factors for growth-friendliness, for example, basically say that it is better to be optimistic than fatalistic. Yet what exactly is a culture's approach to fatalism or optimism? There is a certain fatalism in the Calvinism Weber thought he had found behind Western economic development, and a different one in the Confucianism many find behind East Asian prosperity. There could be optimism in cultures that value leisure so highly that they exhaust their society's accumulated capital. Is deep respect for the past necessarily a weakness of a culture—a hindrance to economic prosperity? Perhaps yes, in a culture where respecting the past means that new agricultural techniques are never explored. In another context, however, respecting the past may carve out a place of honor for those who preserve history and tradition. In such a circumstance, the productive potential of the elderly may be more readily recognizable, for instance, as caretakers of young children. The point is that, outside of any context, we cannot know if any particular item on Harrison's check-list will inhibit or enable prosperity.

Cultural nationalism asks the wrong question. The research mode here should not be to formulate a binary categorization of a culture—Is it opti-mistic or not?—but to qualitatively examine specific cultural advantages on their own terms. Within every society are competing definitions of economic prosperity, and each has a heterogeneous array of conflicting cultural tendencies that resist aggregation. The question is posed as if the issue were to compare different countries in terms of their dominant cul-tural values, when we would argue that the real question is which among the various values found in different national cultures (sometimes, it is worth stressing, in competition with other values) are the ones whose cul-tivation would lead to what people would agree is economic prosperity. Ultimately it seems to us that Harrison and other cultural conservatives ask important questions about the relationship between values and eco-nomic success, questions that desperately need asking, but pose them so poorly that we end up learning little from the asking.

7.2.4 Checklist Ethnography

Harrison's list of good values amounts to a rather lame set of homilies, and his summaries of thousand-year-old cultures in three paragraphs are breathtakingly simplistic. What we have is really only a skeleton of an account of the role of culture in economic performance. We learn little about even the bare bone truths that are contained in Harrison's writings, because he does not do anything with them. In trying to survey so many diverse national cultures, this kind of research fails to engage with any par-ticular culture at the level of detail cultural phenomena demand. It merely articulates the issue in a single, abstract sentence—Are they pro-savings or not?—and then attempts to go through the checklist, in effect keeping score on a dozen diverse cultures to see how many come out on the 'resist-ant' or the 'favorable' side.

Aside from fueling resentment among different cultures, nothing much follows from scoring better in such contests. Without saying more about what policy implications follow, keeping score on national cultures in this manner does little but offend the cultures that come out losers. Even if it did make sense to 'score' a whole nation's culture on some sort of universal growth-friendliness scale, and even if one country's score were higher in all measurable dimensions, what, from the point of view of economic development, would follow from this? Sometimes cultural nationalism underlies the discussions of whether we might import cultural values from societies that, so to speak, score well. Can Americans benefit from embracing Japanese management practices, or Chinese educational customs, in order to mimic their success? We return to this question in the next section.

Some cultural conservatives including Harrison want to use such assessments of national cultures as a basis of immigration policy. Should we allow more Vietnamese immigrants rather than Mexicans because they score higher on our index of leading cultural indicators? To the extent that national income statistics can measure such things, it might look as though our GDP has benefited more from the per capita economic contribution of one group than another. But so what? What kind of politics is it that excludes people from our borders on this kind of basis? What kind of politics identifies human beings by the address they happen to come from, and calculates how wealthy this group would make us, in order to decide whether they have the right to come and live here or not? Is this not the very worst sort of 'wealth fetishism' that compromises fundamental civil liberties against the idol of some measure of national income? When whole cultures are assessed in this checklist fashion, and when individual members of cultural groups are evaluated not on their individual merits but on their group's presumed score, one can see the dangers of this approach.

This is what comes from a social scientific theory that is too thin to do the job. Cultural nationalism resorts to categorizing and counting things, when it should spend some effort on understanding what it is counting. It is a mistake to try to understand the cultural elements of a society by first characterizing the overall growth-friendliness of 'The Culture as a Whole,' that is, treating the nation as the unit of analysis, and 'its' culture as a national trait that one can rank as more or less growth-friendly in comparison to those of other nations. Indeed the nation-state is both too big and too small a unit of analysis. As shown in Joel Kotkin's (1992) work on *Tribes*, by which he means cultural networks that transcend national boundaries, a culture can be larger or smaller than any particular nation-state. The main point is that the nation-state is not the appropriate unit.

We are not trying to answer the question of which national cultures are most conducive to economic prosperity—whether, say, German culture, as a whole, is more or less likely to generate economic prosperity than American culture, as a whole. This approach obscures the heterogeneity of each culture, reducing cultural studies to a crude sort of Values Nationalism, and ends up unhelpfully comparing apples and oranges. Nor are we arguing a position of cultural relativism, however, by which all cultures are uncritically accepted as being no more or less conducive to prosperity than any other. Relativism also obscures the inherent heterogeneity within and among cultures. How can social scientists account for cultural differences if we are banned from making any pronouncements about the effects of those differences? The position we are taking here is that each culture carries with it advantages particular to its own context, which might serve to advance economic development. Yet those advantages will vary according to time and place. Thus, the question we need to ask is: Which elements of American culture (or of this or that particular subculture of American society) constitute its 'comparative cultural advantages,' and which (probably different) elements of German culture constitute *its* advantages?

7.2.5   Comparative Cultural Advantage

Each society has cultural advantages which will support varying aspects of market coordination to varying degrees. As Peter Berger suggests, 'Two countries with a comparative advantage in two different products can trade the products to their mutual benefit. Perhaps cultural factors operate in the same manner' (P. Berger and Hsiao 1988: p. 11). Each society has within its grasp a unique repertoire of 'cultural resources.' Nature endows some societies with rich oil deposits and others with fertile soil. As in the case of these natural resources, culture provides some societies with a kinship network conducive to building complex credit markets and other societies with a strong work ethic. Just as markets will develop differently according to their specific natural resources, they will also develop differently according to their cultural resources. As Douglass North (1990: p. 44) recognized, culture establishes a path dependence in the evolution of institutions and economic development itself. For instance, capital accumulation takes place in starkly different ways depending on whether it is within West Africa, Japan, the United States or an overseas Chinese community, because the cultures which support such institutions differ dramatically.

The typical entrepreneur in the Chinese context is the sole proprietor, whereas the typical entrepreneur within Japanese culture is the team player. Young women are brought up to be entrepreneurs in West Africa, quite unlike the Western norm which encourages the male entrepreneur. Weber argues that the culture of Protestantism inspires the hard work and asceticism necessary for economic growth. Many argue that certain interpretations of Confucianism are the cultural inspiration for Asian economic progress.

To the extent that some institutional policies succeed in promoting economic growth and prosperity in one society, there may be important limitations on the wider applicability of those same policies in other contexts, as Cornell and Kalt (1995) found in their comparative study of Native

American economic development. The same constitutional structure was imposed upon both the Apache and the Sioux in the 1930s by the Indian Reservations Act, yet the records of economic performance are dramatically different. Cornell and Kalt argue that the social and economic success of the Apache is due largely to the fact that the indigenous governance structure among the Apache closely matched the constitution that was imposed upon them. Yet indigenous governance among the Sioux is far more decentralized than the constitutional order imposed by the Indian Reservations Act. This lack of symmetry has been a major contributing factor in the economic stagnation and social decay that have taken place within Sioux communities. While a highly centralized constitutional order works in one cultural context, it falters in another. Similarly, the success a set of policies might enjoy in one context may not have the supporting cultural resources needed to allow the new policies to take hold.

As essential as they are, free trade and private property rights are no guarantee of economic progress. They may be necessary conditions, but are not sufficient to guarantee prosperity. The culture must be one which in general supports commerce and entrepreneurship, but once again the particular manner in which the spirit of enterprise can be encouraged will be culturally specific. Western child-rearing techniques which reinforce the value of self-reliance may tend to foster bold entrepreneurial behavior in adulthood. Kinship structure among many African tribes provides the networks through which business people can acquire training and start-up capital. Confucian philosophy, which values long-term planning over short-sighted results, may in part account for the high savings rates in some Asian societies. Different societies can emphasize varying aspects of markets by drawing upon their unique comparative cultural advantage.

Ever since David Ricardo's clear articulation of the Law of Comparative Advantage it has been understood by economists that the logic applies to relative advantages, and not merely absolute advantages. If a doctor is better than a receptionist at both serving as a receptionist and performing heart surgery, it does not follow that the doctor should fire the receptionist and try to do both jobs. Even if it were the case that producers in Japan were better at producing in each and every industry than producers in Bolivia, all would still benefit from specializing in those production activities in which they had *relative* strengths. The issue is not 'inter-country' comparison, but 'within-country' comparison. It is not whether some kind of aggregated conglomerate of the whole country's values is better than that of another country, but whether the relative cultural strength within a country is, say, its work ethic or its propensity to save, its trust networks or its attitude toward creativity.

This exposes cultural nationalism as rather misleading. Even if the checklist could be done well, and even if a culture were judged to have 'worse values' across the whole checklist, it is difficult to see what would follow from this. From a comparative advantage perspective, a culture *must* have a relative cultural advantage, no matter how poorly it scores in absolute checklists. The interesting question in regard to comparative advantage is which of a society's cultural strengths are those that can help it promote its own development, as this culture understands what development means. The issue in economic comparative advantage is not which country, say Mexico or the US, is better in more things, but which of each culture's strengths are those most suitable for *it* to focus on. Mexicans are not playing a sporting match against the US; they are engaging in mutually beneficial trade. Mexicans should not care about keeping score; they should work on identifying which elements of their culture are the most promising for them to cultivate in order to achieve what they would consider to be prosperity.

The economists' understanding of comparative advantage is a marvelously general notion, as applicable to cultural as it is to material resources, but, like much of economics, it is also crying for some flesh on the bone. What cultural studies could provide here is the specific details of any particular culture's comparative advantages, from which we might gain insights into its likely paths toward economic prosperity. It could help us in the always difficult job of appreciating the differences in another culture, and avoiding the ever-present tendency we have of presuming that our own culture's manner of doing things is the only possible way they can get done. It could help us to accomplish a better reading of the world's cultures, and to find in them possibilities by which their economies can attain emergent patterns of performance which their own participants would call prosperous. It could add to the *general* understanding economists have of the institutional circumstances that conduce to prosperity a *specific* appreciation for the nuances of a particular culture that constitute its own way to foster an enterprising spirit.

Take the reforming soviet-type economies as a case in point. First of all the institutional policies of traditional soviet-type systems are clearly crucial explanatory factors in assessing their poor performance. The main difference between, say, South and North Korea, or between the Western and the Eastern parts of Germany, or between Hong Kong or Taiwan and mainland China, stems from the failed pattern of institutional policies of soviet-type economies. But still, the way communism worked historically in Korea or Germany or China has been shaped in fundamental ways by the specific cultures in these societies, and the particular paths they will need to take in the future to build working market economies will depend on culture. Indeed, it could be argued that especially now, in the aftermath of the collapse of orthodox communism, the question of economic culture is crucial. So long as we faced stark policy choices in terms of communism versus capitalism, the divergent institutional patterns of these systems could dominate over the issue of culture, but now, when nearly the whole world is trying to make market systems work better, the cultural underpinnings of economic institutions have gained a new importance.

If only the universal characteristics of markets were relevant in assessing the prospects for a successful reform process, then we would expect that the removal of restrictive laws banning trade in formerly soviet economies would automatically inspire a flood of entrepreneurial activity. The inefficiencies of the former system would quickly be swept away. In some cases there has not been enough privatization of property to lead economists to have expected much economic improvement anyway, but in many Eastern European countries the institutional changes have been rather substantial and it would seem should have yielded more significant results. Without taking cultural factors into account, we are unable to explain why the reforms have not inspired a swift return to market coordination and a rapid charge towards prosperity. Only when we take notice of the cultural shifts which took place during the soviet experiment can we understand the difficulties facing economic recovery today. For example, within the soviet-type economy, affluence was broadly recognized as a sign of being politically advantaged within a totalitarian system, so naturally the wealthy do not tend to inspire much trust. The derogatory term 'New Russians' is applied equally to those who have earned their wealth through legitimate business ventures as it is to those who have used mafioso tactics. Transforming this attitude will be crucial if the business community is to achieve legitimacy in the eyes of ex-soviet citizens.

Further, these recommendations must be appropriate to the specific context. We may point to the East Asian dragons as the shining examples of what a high savings rate can do for an economy, but this may be inappropriate to the former soviet situation. Appeals to these citizens to increase the national savings rate fell upon deaf ears. Or, more precisely, the appeals cannot be heard over the sound of the television sets, stereos, dishwashers and countless other items so long denied to the average soviet citizen. Rather than generalizing a model from a specific context in the East Asian experience, we ought to be identifying the potential sources of growth within the former soviet context. For example, entrepreneurial talent was often exhibited in dealings within the black market. Even more often, meeting one's goals meant traversing mountains of bureaucracy, and coordinating complex deals of favor swapping. Such skills are sometimes translated into organized crime, but they may also be translated into certain forms of commerce. Perhaps the ex-soviet skill at deal making and power brokering can make for market niches in negotiating with foreign business groups. Successful entrepreneurs will be those who identify, either consciously or tacitly, the particular cultural resources the economies possess to foster new opportunities. Successful policy will, in part, depend upon whether the cultural resources are available to support the given policy.

7.3   FOR EXAMPLE, DIFFERENT KINDS OF ENTREPRENEURSHIP

Identifying the comparative cultural advantages of a society involves the kind of intimate familiarity with the culture that ethnography can achieve. This means we may need to forsake the grand account that sums up all the world's cultures in a single book, but it may bring us to some useful specifics about how market and cultural processes actually work.

For the purposes of this study, culture is a society's collection of meanings which emerges through social interaction, and which allows the individual to interpret her own circumstances. This interpretive process results in patterns of behavior across individuals that we call cultural structures. We will be arguing that important cultural structures underlie each of the institutional and policy factors driving economic development which economists properly emphasize, so that a better grasp of a particular culture would greatly enhance our understanding of its economic processes.

7.3.1   Entrepreneurship in Its Context

The kind of theoretical reconciliation between individualist and communalist anthropologies that Albrecht Wellmer (1991) proposed (as discussed in Chapter 3 of *Culture and Enterprise* (Lavoie and Chamlee-Wright 2000)) has its counterpart in the empirical diversity of the communal or individual tendencies one finds across cultures. He says that the individualists had a point about negative freedoms. A protected domain of individual rights, including property rights, civil liberties, religious freedom and so forth, is *necessary* to a free and democratic society, as argue the individualists.

But it is *not sufficient*, as argue communalists. It is not enough merely for each person to enjoy a protected sphere of liberty. A free democratic society requires a public space, a forum of public discourse about our common concerns, mutual rights and responsibilities, whether it takes the form of the agora of Greek democracy, or the traditional New England town meeting, or some sort of hypertextual discourse over the Internet, or some other forum. Moreover, one might add, markets and business organizations require their own public spaces, and are, for most human societies, key elements of communal life. For markets to work it is not enough that individuals are protected from attack by one another; there needs to be a shared culture of respect for certain contractual and property rights, and some sort of forum—such as a common law court system—at which to deliberate about just what our rights are, to adjudicate among parties in conflict, and to articulate common principles and standards of conduct.

The variety of the mix between individualism and communalism that one finds in different cultures—from highly individualistic market exchange to communal structures on a rich variety of corporate, caste, kinship or other bases—is rather wide. But there is no purely atomistic individualist culture; nor is there a purely communal society. No matter how 'individualistic' a maverick American entrepreneur may appear to observers from other cultures, none is an island. There are always credit, customer/supplier, and information sharing networks that link entrepreneurs into regularized patterns of exchange. In short, all production is team production, and thus, by its very nature, production is social. On the other hand, no matter how communally focused some cultures may appear to us, one can usually find underneath a fundamental, perhaps even somewhat principled, respect for the autonomy of individuals. Working societies find their own balance—just how independent, or how interconnected in various dependent networks, entrepreneurs are—that works in their context (see Landa 1991).

Consider, for example, the relative success of direct selling organizations, such as Amway and Mary Kay Cosmetics, in three distinct settings: the United States, Taiwan and Japan. Such organizations are based on two key principles: individualism and community. Success is gained primarily through individual initiative, but this is supported with community recognition of individual effort. This support is sometimes in the form of ritual through award ceremonies, is sometimes tangible in the awarding of company vehicles, and is always structural, as the hierarchical commission schedule encourages peer monitoring.

Nicole Biggart (1990) argues that the reasons for the success of direct selling organizations differ from one culture to another. The emphasis on individual effort fits in well with the American work ethic, but the emphasis on community has been a particular draw for American women. Often inexperienced in business and suffering from a lack of confidence in commerce, many American women find the direct selling organizations a nurturing (rather than invasive) environment in which to seek personal as well as financial growth. Taiwanese direct selling organizations excel in the recruitment of family members to join the organization while at the same time advancing their own status in the hierarchy. Given American attitudes against nepotism, this has not been a significant part of US experience. Taiwanese direct selling organizations allow the entrepreneur to operate more like a sole proprietor than working for a more traditional business. This aspect of the direct selling organization tends to be emphasized far less in Japan, where loyalty to the corporation is stressed. Each society draws upon a different set of cultural tools to make the most of this particular form of direct marketing.

Similar cultural patterns conducive to economic growth may emerge from vastly different sources. For example, while Weber's Calvinist ethic of hard work came from the doctrine of predestination, the ethic of hard work among the industrious class of Quakers in the eighteenth and nineteenth centuries emerged from their conviction that salvation occurred through the good works done here on earth.

The spirit of enterprise comes in many different flavors. Each culture creates a unique entrepreneurial pattern; each culture articulates its own genre of stories in which economic leaders achieve wealth-generating success within the specific institutional and customary contours of the society in which they live. Appreciating the rich diversity of these narratives requires many of the skills that the discipline of cultural studies fosters. For example, different societies establish different rules for acquiring credit and different routes for entree into the business world. (See Kotkin 1992 for an analysis of how some ethnic groups have established international networks which capitalize on culturally specific characteristics.)

Consider the distinct cases of the Japanese and the overseas Chinese entrepreneur. In either case, the entrepreneur performs the vital functions of innovation and coordination within the market. Yet, in each case, the ideal type or quintessential entrepreneur will be described as having quite different qualities. This is because the role of the entrepreneur in each society originates from fundamentally different sources. The typical entrepreneur will reflect the specific cultural context out of which he or she emerges. The process of acquiring credit, accumulating capital and getting started in business will also reflect this specific context. The primary source of capital may be the extended family, trade organizations or formal banking institutions. The rules which operate under each set of circumstances will support some kinds of entrepreneurship, while inhibiting others. Thus the framework within which this ideal typical entrepreneur must operate will set out both opportunities and limits.

In Western and Chinese cultures we often think of entrepreneurs as mavericks, yet the standard account of Japanese business culture is centered around team and group identity. The ideal typical Japanese entrepreneur fits into an already existing structure of authority and power. Within the firm, corporate unity is held in high regard, while individual identity is subordinated to that of the corporation. Employment within the corporation can even supersede kinship connections in terms of loyalty and priority. Though the ideal of life-long employment within the company has come under tremendous pressure over the past decade, tight bonds of firm loyalty are still characteristic of Japanese corporate culture. Firms converge into higher and higher levels of vertical and horizontal integration. Through mergers and layers upon layers of subcontracting agreements, firms assemble themselves into large corporate groups, referred to as 'enterprise group capitalism.' Once firms begin the process of aligning themselves into corporate groups, other competing firms must follow suit or perish (Tam 1990). The result is a remarkable stability both within the firm and among firms.

Though the thesis has been criticized, many have argued that this model for industrial organization has emerged as a result of Confucian ethics. As described by Herman Kahn as early as 1979, the Confucian tradition of Chun-tzu, or the principal concern for duty and propriety, is responsible for the work ethic found in Japanese society (Kahn 1979). It is argued that out of this philosophical system emerged a strong ethic towards a stringent meritocracy, but one within the context of an exacting hierarchy. Thus, there is a balance being struck between individual achievement and the eventual subordination of the purposes of the individual to the larger goal of the collective.

Others have challenged this thesis on the role of the Confucian ethic. Murakami (1986) argues that the Confucian ethos is not the primary cultural force at play, but rather that the Samurai military organization has had the greatest influence on corporate culture in Japan. The subordination of kinship ties to corporate ties relates to the functional role of membership within the military organization (Clegg et al. 1990). Placement within the hierarchy of the corporation is not primarily a consequence of class, but on the contrary there is the opportunity for upward (as well as downward) mobility within the same firm. Murakami suggests that this is the modern manifestation of cultural structures adopted within the Samurai era where not one's class but one's function within the hierarchy was what defined status. This functional role of membership had the advantage of inspiring individual effort in hopes of upward mobility, but this was mobility within the confines of a stable authority. In much the same way, the modern Japanese firm inspires individual effort and peer competitiveness, but within the framework of the corporation, which offers a level of authority that transcends individual ambition in relative importance.

Japanese training practices involve not only the technical expertise needed to accomplish the job, but the socialization of the employee into the corporate culture as well. Training is highly firm specific. Positions within one company are not usually seen as stepping stones to other firms or industries. The hope (if not expectation) on the part of both the employer and the employee is a career-long commitment. This has a moral dimension, much like the life-long commitment people may have to their family. The effect has been a lack of mobility across the market for most Japanese workers. They tend not to seek employment with competitors, nor are they likely to be sought. The high degree of job security one has does not mean that status within the hierarchy is guaranteed, however, again allowing for innovation as the result of individual effort and ambition, but at the same time subordinating the goals of the individual employee to that of the corporate authority. This appeal to authority stems from traditional beliefs concerning the family. Munkata (1988) argues that corporate employees identify with the corporation, as individuals once identified with the family or village community. Munkata (1988: p. 174) observes:

> In industrial enterprises, the role of managers is important for integrating the organizations, which is done by the enterprise as a culturally meaningful system to newly 'adopted' employees. The managers usually set up well-prepared in-house educational programs, some of which include intensive training in foreign languages or even in the practice of contemplation in Zen temples.

7.3.2 Culture versus Rationality?

Stewart Clegg et al. (1990) challenge theses such as these which place culture at the forefront of analysis when explaining Japanese economic growth. They argue that culture is not the source of Japanese success. Rather, the success has come from performance measures such as quality control and segmentary work practices where corporate firms train their employees in such a manner that their skills will be firm specific, and therefore of little use to a competing firm. Clegg et al. contend that these measures are not the product of post-Confucian or Samurai military culture, but rather simply savvy corporate management at work. To the extent that these practices have any cultural component (such as morning ceremonies or group exercise), they argue that it is the calculated choice of management to use these symbols of culture. Traditional symbolism and ceremonies, they argue, are mere 'decorative additions' and have no real consequence. Thus the adoption of these rules of conduct, and the use of traditional rules of authority and hierarchy are the result of an attempt to maximize profits, not a reflection of deep-seated cultural responses. To reinforce this argument, Clegg et al. cite P. Berger and Luckmann

(1966), who caution that 'the social construction of reality should never be regarded as a disinterested affair.' In short, they argue that culture has little to do with Japanese growth. Profit motive is the only explanation needed.

The essential problem with this argument is that it understands cultural influences to be a counter-rational force; it says that if one is under the influence of culture one must not be 'acting rationally.' Further, it misunderstands economic decisions to be 'purely' calculating and atomistic, that is, having nothing at all to do with culture. On the first point, clearly an individual does not wholly choose his culture as he would choose an item in the grocery store. The individual inherits a language community, values and ethics. On the other hand, this does not mean that cultural influences lie outside of rationality. While we do not choose the cultural influences which shape our perspective, we have it within our grasp to challenge inherited cultural norms. While an individual cannot wholly transform his cultural perspective, he can choose to broaden it, to amend it and, perhaps most important to the discussion at hand, to *use it*. Berger and Luckmann's counsel was aimed directly to this point.

Not only should we not completely divorce culture from rationality, but we make a similar mistake if we see decisions concerning profit, the epitome of rational choice, as lying outside the influence of culture. All profit-making decisions take place within a specific cultural context. What constitutes a wise economic decision will depend upon the cultural context in which it is made. Entrepreneurship is not calculation. Wise entrepreneurial decisions do not come algorithmically. As Lavoie has argued elsewhere, entrepreneurship is an interpretive process, requiring that the interpretation come from a specific perspective.

> Profit opportunities are not so much like road signs to which we assign an automatic meaning as they are like difficult texts in need of a sustained effort of interpretation. Entrepreneurship is not only a matter of opening one's eyes, of switching on one's attentiveness; it requires directing one's gaze. When an entrepreneur sees things others have overlooked, it is not just that he opened his eyes while they had theirs closed. He is reading selected aspects of a complex situation others have not read. And this raises the question of what gives a pre-directedness to the entrepreneur's vision, of why he is apt to read some things and not others. (Lavoie, this volume, Chapter 3: p. 59)

We think that one of the main things that directs the entrepreneur's vision is culture. Entrepreneurial decision-making is not some sort of pure calculation but a complex reading of the polysemic dialogue of the market. It is necessarily embedded within a cultural context. In most cases, however, exactly how culture shapes entrepreneurial perspective is not a process that can be explicitly specified. Entrepreneurs may not be aware of how their own focus is directed by the cultural context in which they operate. In fact, it is usually when the cultural context is unfamiliar that entrepreneurs are likely to pay closer attention to it. Learning how to 'read' any particular cultural context—learning to discern profit opportunities, for example—is a process which makes use of tacit or inarticulate knowledge. Friedrich Hayek made this point about economic knowledge. Certainly, any entrepreneurial decision will employ explicit data such as the prices of inputs and demographic statistics. But Hayek pointed out that entrepreneurs also make use of inarticulate knowledge, perhaps derived from the experience of many years within a particular industry, which enables them to make sense of all the many bits of information available to them. Similarly, one might be able to explicitly define a list of cultural rules one wishes to employ in securing greater productivity, such as in the case of the Japanese managers. But 'cultural knowledge' is not just a list of rules one holds inside one's head. Rather, culture provides a framework of meaning that allows entrepreneurs to make sense of all the various, often conflicting pieces of information: Culture gives shape to the interpretive process that is entrepreneurship.

It may indeed be the case that Japanese managers are making a conscious choice to use traditional rules of authority and hierarchy when training their employees. The possibility that they are, however, does not undermine the thesis that the cultural influences at play in society are important in explaining economic performance. In this case, the crucial question is not what is motivating the manager but, rather, why does this particular strategy work?

7.3.3 Cultural Fit

As a way of making the argument that cultural symbolism, ceremony, and training techniques are mere window dressing, Clegg et al. point to the fact that, in many of the overseas Japanese firms, in Singapore for example, management has chosen to drop these elements of Japanese culture. In other countries such as the US, where the practices were not abandoned, 'Difficulties [were] experienced ... Personnel and labor management, often cited as the cultural locus of the organizational expression of "Post-Confucianism", [were] in fact, the weak points of Japanese management overseas' (Clegg et al. 1990: p. 46). American employees often find morning exercise rituals to be paternalistic and presentations designed to instill a 'team-spiritedness' to be forced camaraderie.

Yet, rather than proving the 'culture as window dressing' thesis, this speaks directly to the importance such cultural influences play in the economic sphere. If the elements of Japanese culture used in management were simply window dressing, then there should have been no differences when they were transported abroad. The fact that they were a weak point in overseas management suggests that these practices 'fit' in one context, but not in another. We should not be surprised by the fact that practices which seem paternalistic and invasive (in one context) will lead to lower productivity. Yet this also suggests that these same practices might yield positive results if they reflect and accommodate the particular cultural context elsewhere.

Again, consider the differences among the Japanese emphasis upon hierarchy and the Chinese emphasis on sole proprietorship. One would normally expect that strong traditions of mutual trust would be a necessary condition for the effective development of markets. (See, for example, Fukuyama 1995.) As Tam points out, there is something to be explained here. The overseas Chinese economic success flies in the face of much conventional wisdom. Relating the Hong Kong experience, Tam (1990: p. 153) reports:

> widespread disloyalty and lack of commitment of employees to companies, pervasive neglect of human resource development within companies, extremely limited trust and openness between employers and employees, constant disintegration of firms into units of atomistic size, thereby sacrificing the economies of scale. And yet despite these anomalies Hong Kong has a highly effective work force, an abundant supply of first class entrepreneurs and businessmen, constant renewal of firms and gigantic industrial power.

Similar accounts could be given for South Korea, Taiwan and Singapore, as well as the many immigrant Chinese communities in the United States, the UK and Canada (see Sowell 1983: pp. 21–49; Kotkin 1992: pp. 165–200). To the extent that overseas Chinese workers stay within the same firm, it tends to be a family business. Firms owned by non-relatives tend to split apart rapidly. The Chinese firm is seen as belonging to the family. Thus, hiring kin into the business is seen as a virtue, not nepotism (Acton 1990). As is the custom with family property, the firm is often divided among family members equally, leading to an inherent decentralization even when the firm is owned by a single family (Tam 1990). While one may enter the business world by working for another firm, only family can expect to advance in the hierarchy, as there exists a pervasive lack of trust for anyone except close relations. Success is seen as ownership: making the jump from employee to employer. Since the chance for a non-relative to achieve ownership of a firm for which he works is virtually nil, the employee eventually leaves the firm, ultimately in pursuit of sole proprietorship.

Given the common experiences of success, the differences among Japanese and overseas Chinese firms are staggering. Whereas Japanese firms foster a life-long sense of stability among workers, Chinese workers are beset with a pervading insecurity. However, both contexts manage to generate a remarkable work ethic.

> The Japanese work hard for their family, as which they see the firm . . . In a secure context the Japanese employee has learned to depend on the company. In an insecure context the Chinese employee has learned to be self-reliant. In many ways the Chinese are motivated to work in the company but not for the company. (Tam 1990: p. 177)

Thus while interfirm mobility is highly unlikely in the Japanese context, it is the rule within the overseas Chinese context. The ideal typical Chinese entrepreneur is one who learns by doing. Even with the direct links between kinship and business, most entrepreneurs do not go through an extended apprenticeship. They build their skills through practice, rather than indoctrination.

Alongside the deeply rooted Chinese respect for family is a maverick individualist spirit. The question arises as to why this has emerged as a pervasive influence in the overseas Chinese communities, yet not Japanese society. One reason might be the particular political climate. In Hong Kong, for example, the decades leading up to the return of the province to China may have inspired a single-minded pursuit towards market prosperity (Fong 1988). While this has no doubt had an influence on the operative time horizon among Hong Kong's entrepreneurs, and the energy with which many have pursued their fortune, a similar explanation is lacking for Singapore, Taiwan and South Korea. Another possible explanation for the unique form of East Asian individualism is the influence that Buddhism and folk religions or Shamanism have had. As P. Berger and Hsiao (1988: p. 8) suggest:

> It is possible to make the argument that, as Buddhism crossed the Tibetan plateau and the great Himalayan passes, it underwent a profound transformation, changing from what was perhaps the most world-denying religion in human history to an emphatically world-affirming one . . . [Thus, it was in] East Asia that salvation was located consistently in this world.

They go on to say that ultimately it was neither Confucianism nor Buddhism which gave rise to the 'in-this-worldliness' but rather the more deeply rooted, highly pragmatic folk religions.

The important point to be made here is that the model for entrepreneurship which operates within the overseas Chinese setting works because it emerges out of that specific context. The Japanese model for the entrepreneur and the firm works because the cultural context supports this ideal. The pessimistic view of this situation would be that, since there is no generalizable model for economic development, there is little hope for African, Latin American or reforming soviet-type countries. Given the cultural specificity of the successful experiences of East Asian countries, there is little chance of mimicking that performance.

The optimistic view, on the other hand, is that, with an appreciation for the role culture plays in economic processes, we are in a far better position to identify appropriate courses of action. This does not mean that we should attempt to import cultural systems. Forcing African school children to read Confucius in hopes of creating an Asian work ethic will be about as successful as requiring middle-aged American factory workers to do morning group calisthenics. What is possible, however, is to identify what cultural advantages are at work within a particular society so as to tap into their potential.

7.3.4 Cultural Studies and Public Policy

And then there is the question of 'So what?' Say we establish that culture is important in gauging potential economic performance, is there anything we can do about culture? Is it possible to change culture for the better, such that we manage to promote whatever we mean by economic progress? Some discussions of culture and the economy suggest that the more powerful an influence culture is found to be, the less hope there is for us to develop policy measures that can improve the economy. If the economic success of East Asian societies is due simply to judicious trade, fiscal and monetary policies, then these policies are likely to foster similar results no matter what the context. Yet, if the economic success of East Asian societies is due to Confucian philosophy and Chinese social institutions, habits and customs, then our chances of detecting a generalized model to be transported elsewhere are dim.

Many developing countries (as well as many Western countries) seek to mimic the economic performance experienced by East Asian countries such as South Korea, Taiwan, Hong Kong, Singapore and Japan. If the 'Asian miracle' is due to growth-friendly institutions and policies, it is argued, then we can embrace such institutions and policies here, but if it is due to 'Asian values' then there is nothing we can do. We can try to mimic tax policy but we cannot wholly transport cultural value systems from one place to another. P. Berger and Hsiao (1988: p. 9) offer two possibilities.

> The answer to the question will hinge to a considerable degree on the role one will eventually ascribe to cultural factors in the economic performance of the region. Broadly speaking, two hypotheses are possible here, one 'culturalist,' the other 'institutionalist' . . . If the 'institutionalists' are right, there is indeed a model to be exported; if the 'culturalists' are right, one must be skeptical of such exportability.

What their argument may lead many economists to conclude, though it certainly is not the conclusion they intended to draw from their analysis, is that, since the only actionable part of the causal complex influencing economic development is its institutional part, culture, however powerful its influence, can be ignored.

The study of hundreds of years of experience has shown rather conclusively that no matter what the cultural advantages held by a particular society are, without the policies of free trade, a reliable legal framework, a stable monetary system and a functioning system of private property rights, economic success is highly unlikely if not impossible (see Baechler 1975; Rosenberg and Birdzell 1986). In examining the reasons for success in Hong Kong and Singapore, Pang Eng Fong (1988) finds that economic growth was the result of free trade, low tax rates and minimal levels of state intervention. But we still need to ask what cultural influences are at play in fostering such an institutional setting? Was there, for example, a significant impact on Hong Kong's culture from its years of British colonial rule? Policies are enacted from a specific cultural context. Underlying politics is what is sometimes called the political culture. Thus, even in recognizing the universal importance of certain institutional factors, we are still drawn back to the issue of culture. To be sure, comparative economic studies between North and South Korea, or East and West Germany, in which the cultural contexts are initially similar, also bear out the significance institutional structure plays in economic success, but this does not render the issue of culture irrelevant. As post-communist countries seek to enact reforms, for example, we see that the institutions necessary for economic progress are often met with marked social resistance. In the course of totalitarian rule, cultural norms conducive to the market order are apt to erode and public policy will have to contend with cultural dimensions of reform.

The role of culture in fostering a vigorous economy goes beyond the momentous function of establishing the social institutions upon which markets rely. The way Berger frames the problem is misleading both because he deploys the language of culture as a factor and because, as he is fond of saying, he does not accept the Ancient Curse theory of culture. Granted, it would be absurd to suppose that one could 'pass a law' that American values should be 'more Confucian' or some such, but this is not to say that the cultural domain is not actionable.

Many institutional maladies are resistant to the top-down, Pass-a-Law mentality, and can be overcome only by a gradual change in attitudes and practices, but this does not mean there is nothing we can do about them. Knowing what elements of a culture contribute to its economic prosperity is important, even if it cannot be directly translated into a bill in the Senate or a constitutional amendment. Many of us spend a good deal of our lives in a different sort of 'policy activity,' and perhaps it is this kind of policy work that is more likely to lead to lasting change. We attempt to pass along to our co-workers, our friends, our neighbors and our children the values we take to be conducive to the good life. Some of us spend hours in classrooms, clubs, temples, mosques or churches conveying values to our students or audiences or congregations, whether we explicitly admit that we are doing so or not. Some of us write articles, letters to the editor, e-mails or books, in which this or that value of our culture is encouraged or discouraged. Coaches of Little League teams and Girl Scout troop leaders who impart a work ethic, a pride in accomplishments, self-esteem and an ability to work with others are perhaps more important policy makers in the end than legislators are.

Robert Putnam (1993) refers to the norms and networks of civil society that emerge from such activity as 'social capital.' Social capital contributes to economic prosperity by lowering transactions and transformation costs. In a study of regional governance in Italy, Putnam et al. (1983) found that successful economic performance was correlated with high levels of social capital. Putnam (1993: p. 37) observes that

> [t]hese communities did not become civic simply because they were rich. The historical record strongly suggests precisely the opposite: They have become rich because they were civic. The social capital embodied in norms and net-works of civic engagement seems to be a precondition for economic develop-ment, as well as for effective government. Development economists take note: Civics matters.

The former President of the Czech Republic, Vaclav Havel (1992: pp. 14–15), certainly recognized that civic culture matters.

> I consider it immensely important that we concern ourselves with culture not just as one among many human activities, but in the broadest sense—the 'culture of everything,' the general level of public manners. By that I mean chiefly the kind of relations that exist among people, between the powerful and the weak, the healthy and the sick, the young and the elderly, adults and

children, business people and customers, men and women, teachers and students, officers and soldiers, policemen and citizens, and so on ... [H]owever important it may be to get our economy back on its feet, it is far from being the only task facing us. It is no less important to do everything possible to improve the general cultural level of everyday life ... I would go even farther, and say that, in many respects, improving the civility of everyday life can accelerate economic development.

Policy analysts and policy makers usually take only institutional factors, not cultural factors, into consideration when developing economic policy. The reasons for this most likely lie in one of two perspectives: they think either that culture is of little or no consequence or that, while it is possible to dictate institutional policy measures, it is impossible to dictate culture. To the first point, we have already offered a detailed response, that indeed cultural processes play a crucial role in defining the economic course a society will take. To the second point, we recognize the questionableness of asking government to dictate cultural values. Most economic analysts do not see it as their role to 'preach' a certain set of moral or ethical values, even if by following the prescribed values society would have a better chance of enriching itself.

But we must recognize that in endorsing institutional policies, by necessity, we endorse cultural values as well. Consider the cultural shift being endorsed by proposing a 'Work to Welfare' reform, or the abandonment of tax-financed transfer payments altogether. Think of the cultural changes we are recommending when we tell reforming soviet-type systems that they need to establish private ownership and allow free trade. Thus, in advocating one or another institutional policy, we are also advocating a specific set of cultural values which go along with that policy. To suggest that policy makers ought to stay out of the business of cultivating values is to misunderstand the nature of values. Public policy cannot help but be value laden.

The hesitation to advocate cultural values as a deliberate political policy is understandable. Such preaching conjures up images of social engineering, or ethnocentric chauvinism of the kind Lawrence Harrison exhibits. If a kind of policy activism in regard to culture is possible, it needs to be tempered with a profound sense of respect for existing cultural beliefs. In the age of rationalist constructivism, of aspirations to engineer society's values, we have seen attempts to indict entire systems of social institutions as illegitimate, as Marxism and fascism did in taking to task the 'bourgeois institutions' of family, private ownership and religion. The intricate interrelationships among cultural values and economic institutions should remind us that any attempt to make wholesale changes to culture puts us in danger of losing the valued functions these institutions perform.

The greatest social, political and economic progress has come not from rebuilding social institutions from the ground up, but from evolving incremental changes to our values and practices from within the existing social structure. Change generally occurs gradually and on the margin, where individual norms are questioned and challenged one at a time, still from within the cultural framework, and with the preponderance of the evolved social institutions firmly intact.

Not only are efforts at social engineering or sweeping criticisms of whole cultures repugnant, but it is ludicrous to suppose that anybody has the ability to act on these attitudes, to successfully engineer values from on high, or to change a whole society's values. Clearly, the political apparatus can have a major effect on the prevailing culture, but it is an entirely different question as to whether a political apparatus can engineer a culture so as to bring about positive results. The ability to influence and the ability to control are radically different prospects. Surely we do not want politicians (or academics for that matter) trying to dictate what our culture should be.

There is a broader notion of 'politics' or of 'public policy' that takes neither to mean only how we try to get government to behave. In much of the cultural studies literature the site of politics has shifted, so that we are concerned instead with how we interact with one another in the politics of everyday life, in all our forms of community. What we are suggesting is that the question of culture needs to come into the forefront of public discussion: to include not only academics, but business people, media, parents, even politicians. The point is to recognize that culture plays an important role in both our social and our economic lives. By identifying the developmentally relevant cultural resources that are operative within different contexts, we will be in a far better position to make policy recommendations for not only developing and reforming economies, but our own as well.

After all, it is always possible for some members of society to influence their culture profoundly. Historically the most influential avenue for the shaping of values has been through 'popular culture,' the stories, poetry, theatre and so forth by which fundamental values are imparted. A novel by a Russian revolutionary energized Lenin and led to the Bolshevik experiment, with all its attendant horrors. In our time, movies and television shape the attitudes of millions of citizens in ways that may be seen to be development-resistant or development-promoting.

NOTE

* This chapter previously appeared in Don Lavoie and Emily Chamlee-Wright, *Culture and Enterprise* (Routledge, 2000). It is reprinted here (with minor edits) with the permission of the publisher.

REFERENCES

Acton, Thomas A. (1990), 'Ethnicity and Religion in the Development of Family Capitalism: Seui-Seung-Yahn Immigrants from Hong Kong to Scotland,' in S.R. Clegg, S.G. Redding and M. Cartner (eds.), *Capitalism in Contrasting Cultures*, New York: Walter de Gruyter, pp. 391–408.

Baechler, Jean (1975), *The Origins of Capitalism*, Oxford: Basil Blackwell.

Bauer, P.T. (1954), *West African Trade: A Study of Competition, Oligopoly, and Monopoly in a Changing Economy*, Cambridge: Cambridge University Press.

Bauer, P.T. (1957), *The Economics of Underdeveloped Countries*, Chicago: University of Chicago Press.

Bauer, P.T. (1971), *Dissent on Development*, Cambridge, MA: Harvard University Press.

Bauer, P.T. (1984), *Reality and Rhetoric: Studies in the Economics of Development*, London: Weidenfeld & Nicolson.

Bennett, William J. (1994), *The Index of Leading Cultural Indicators: Facts and Figures on the State of American Society*, New York: Simon & Schuster.

Berger, Brigitte (ed.) (1991), *The Culture of Entrepreneurship*, San Francisco: Institute for Contemporary Studies.

Berger, Peter L. and Hsin-Huang Michael Hsiao (eds.) (1988), *In Search of an East Asian Development Model*, New Brunswick, NJ: Transaction Books.

Berger, Peter L. and Thomas Luckmann (1966), *The Social Construction of Reality: A Treatise in the Sociology of Knowledge*, New York: Doubleday.

Biggart, Nicole Woolsey (1990), 'Charismatic Capitalism: Direct Selling Organizations in the USA and Asia,' in S.R. Clegg, S.G. Redding and M. Cartner (eds.), *Capitalism in Contrasting Cultures*, New York: Walter de Gruyter, pp. 409–28.

Clegg, Stewart R., S. Gordon Redding and Monica Cartner (eds.) (1990), *Capitalism in Contrasting Cultures*, New York: Walter de Gruyter.

Cornell, Stephen and Joseph Kalt (1995), 'Constitutional Rule among the Sioux and Apache,' *Economic Inquiry*, **333**, 402–26.

Denzau, Arthur and Douglass C. North (1994), 'Shared Mental Models: Ideologies and Institutions,' *Kyklos*, **47**, 3–30.

Fong, Pang Eng (1988), 'The Distinctive Features of Two City-States' Development: Hong Kong and Singapore,' in Peter L. Berger and Hsin-Huang Michael Hsiao (eds.), *In Search of an East Asian Development Model*, New Brunswick, NJ: Transaction Books, pp. 220–38.

Fukuyama, Francis (1995), *Trust: The Social Virtues and the Creation of Prosperity*, New York: Free Press.

Ghosh, P.K. (1984), *Third World Development: A Basic Needs Approach*, Westport, CT: Greenwood Press.

Gwartney, James, Robert Lawson and Walter Block (1996), *Economic Freedom of the World, 1975–1995*, Vancouver: Frasier Institute.

Harrison, Lawrence E. (1992), *Who Prospers? How Cultural Values Shape Economic and Political Success*, New York: Basic Books.

Havel, Vaclav (1992), *Summer Meditations*, Paul Wilson (trans.), New York: Alfred A. Knopf.

Hayek, F.A. (1988), *The Fatal Conceit: The Errors of Socialism*, London: Routledge.

Kahn, H. (1979), *World Economic Development: 1979 and Beyond*, London: Croom Helm.

Kotkin, Joel (1992), *Tribes: How Race, Religion, and Identity Determine Success in the New Global Economy*, New York: Random House.

Landa, Janet (1991), 'Culture and Entrepreneurship in Less-Developed Countries: Ethnic Trading Networks as Economic Organizations,' in B. Berger (ed.), *The Culture of Entrepreneurship*, San Francisco: Institute for Contemporary Studies Press, pp. 53–72.

Lavoie, D. and E. Chamlee-Wright (2000), *Culture and Enterprise*, New York: Routledge.

Martin, David (1990), *Tongues of Fire*, Oxford: Basil Blackwell.

Moog, Clodomir Vianna (1964), *Bandeirantes e Pioneiros*, Rio de Janeiro: Editora Civilizacao Brasileira.

Munkata, Iwao (1988), 'The Distinctive Features of Japanese Development: Basic Cultural Patterns and Politico-Economic Processes,' in Peter L. Berger and Hsin-Huang Michael Hsiao (eds.), *In Search of an East Asian Development Model*, New Brunswick, NJ: Transaction Books, pp. 155–78.

Murakami, Y. (1986), 'Technology in Transition: Two Perspectives on Industrial Policy,' in H. Patrick and L. Meissner (eds.), *Japan's High Technology Industries: Lessons and Limitation of Industrial Policy*, Seattle: University of Washington Press, pp. 211–41.

North, Douglass C. (1989), 'Institutions and Economic Growth: An Historical Introduction,' *World Development*, **179**, 1319–32.

North, Douglass C. (1990), *Institutions, Institutional Change, and Economic Performance*, Cambridge: Cambridge University Press.

North, Douglass C. (1994), 'Economic Performance through Time,' *American Economic Review*, **843**, 359–68.

Putnam, Robert D. (1993), 'The Prosperous Community: Social Capital and Public Life,' *American Prospect*, **13** (Spring), 35–41.

Putnam, Robert D., R. Leonardi, R. Nanetti and F. Pavancello (1983), 'Explaining Institutional Success: The Case of Italian Regional Government,' *American Political Science Review*, **77**, 55–74.

Redding, S. Gordon (1990), *The Spirit of Chinese Capitalism*, New York: Walter de Gruyter.

Rosenberg, Nathan and L.E. Birdzell, Jr. (1986), *How the West Grew Rich: The Economic Transformation of the Industrial World*, New York: Basic Books.

Soto, Hernando de (1988), *The Other Path*, New York: Harper & Row.

Sowell, Thomas (1983), *The Economics and Politics of Race: An International Perspective*, New York: William Morrow.

Tam, Simon (1990), 'Centrifugal versus Centripetal Growth Processes: Contrasting Ideal Types for Conceptualizing the Developmental Patterns of Chinese and

Japanese Firms,' in S.R. Clegg, S.G. Gordon and M. Cartner (eds.), *Capitalism in Contrasting Cultures*, New York: Walter de Gruyter, pp. 153–83.

Weber, Max ([1924] 1968), *Economy and Society*, Guenther Roth and Claus Wittich (eds.), originally published as *Wirtschaft und Gesellschaft: Grundriss der verstehenden Soziologie*, 4th ed., Tübingen: Mohr, 1956, Berkeley: University of California Press.

Wellmer, Albrecht (1991), 'Models of Freedom in the Modern World,' in Michael Kelly (ed.), *Hermeneutics and Critical Theory in Ethics and Politics*, Cambridge, MA: MIT Press, pp. 227–52.

8. Context matters: the importance of time and place in economic narratives*

Virgil Henry Storr

8.1 INTRODUCTION

How do we come to understand the thoughts, words and deeds of others? Why, for instance, do we think of Romeo and Juliet as 'star-crossed lovers'? Why are they seen as tragic figures and not, say, as foolish romantics? Why, for instance, aren't we disturbed by Hamlet's madness or surprised by Macbeth's fear of Macduff? Why do we believe Richard when he offers his kingdom for a horse? The answers to all of these queries, I think, is that we can understand others (be they characters in a Shakespearean play, historical figures or our contemporaries) because we can appreciate their historical and cultural circumstances. That is, we can understand the actions of others (we can understand their life stories) because we can appreciate their prejudices and constraints; we can appreciate the effect that the past (in other words, prior events in the plot) might have had on their proclivities and opportunity sets; we can appreciate the time and place in which they live and act.

Indeed, context matters. Knowing their circumstances, for instance, it would be difficult to view Romeo and Juliet as anything but star-crossed. An 'ancient grudge' divides their 'two households, [though] both [are] alike in dignity' and so the consequences of their falling in love with each other were bound to be dire. That they had to marry in secret, that Romeo would kill Tybalt, Juliet's cousin, less than a day after that secret marriage, that Juliet would rather fake her death than tell her parents of her marriage all makes sense given the 'ancient grudge' that separated the families of Romeo and Juliet. Their double suicide saddens but does not 'surprise' us. Similarly, we understand the stories of Richard III, Macbeth and Hamlet because we understand the time and place in which they are set; we understand the characters' historical and cultural contexts.

Understanding the actions of others requires the same sort of appreciation for time and place, for setting, for context, that understanding a Shakespearean plot requires. A science like economics, predicated on understanding the meanings that individuals associate with their actions and primarily concerned with telling stories, must therefore be preoccupied with context. Individuals are not atomistic creatures but are, instead, social characters. They 'do not behave or decide to behave as atoms outside a social context' (Granovetter 1985: p. 487). Rather, they are members of families, of clubs, of bowling leagues, of churches and of communities; they are employers or employees; they are citizens of countries with particular ethnicities. They are not, however, social automata. Individuals do not 'adhere slavishly to a script written for them by the particular intersection of social categories that they happen to occupy' (ibid.: p. 487). They do not 'follow customs, habits or norms automatically and unconditionally' (ibid.: p. 483). Romeo, for instance, still falls in love with Juliet although he is a Montague and she is a Capulet.

Unfortunately, many in the human sciences have fallen prey to the pitfalls of positing either an *over-* or *under-socialized* view of the individual and so have failed to recognize that an individual's behavior may be '*affected* by, *influenced* by, even *directed* by social structures and relations but [is] not determined by them' (Boettke and Storr 2002, italics in original). Max Weber and the Austrian school (headed by Mises and Hayek), however, have proposed an *interpretive social science*, a *social economics*, that avoids both the *over-* and the *under-socialized* misconceptions of the individual (ibid.). This interpretive science, I contend, is the appropriate vehicle for the study of economic culture (particularly, and we shall see why later, the culture of entrepreneurship) and so, in this chapter, I intend to push at the boundaries of Weber and the Austrians' *social economics* to see if it is up to this task.

8.2 THE WEBER–AUSTRIAN APPROACH: THE CASE FOR THE TRI-EMBEDDED ACTOR

For Weber, 'social economics deals with those phenomena that are scarce, that are necessary to satisfy ideal and material interests, and that can only be provided through planning, struggle, and in cooperation with other people' (Swedberg 1998: p. 192). Thus 'it draws on elements from both historical and theoretical economics' (ibid.). 'The range of social-economics,' according to Weber, 'is [thus] almost overwhelming' (Weber [1949] 1997: p. 66), covering the study of (a) *economic*, (b) *economically relevant* and (c) *economically conditioned* phenomena and institutions.

The first of these categories refers to 'events and constellations of norms, institutions, and so on, the economic aspect of which constitutes their primary cultural significance for us' (ibid.: p. 64). Customs like satisfying open accounts within 30 days, institutions like money and credit, and organizations like banks and the stock exchange, that is, phenomena which interest us primarily because of their economic significance, thus fall within this category. As we can see, unlike mainstream economics, Weber's interpretive science was at its core an institutional economics. Weber knew full well that *institutions matter* and believed that *looking at institutions is critical* even when considering purely economic phenomena. Thus the institution-less, a-contextual *homoeconomicus* never played a role in Weber's *social economics*. That Weber extended the range of his science beyond the study of economic phenomena in the strictest sense, however, only served to deepen the chasm between the economic agent of Weber's thought and his cousin in the mainstream.

Weber was concerned not only with pure economic phenomena but also with 'all the activities and situations constituting an historically given culture [that] affect the formation of the material wants, the mode of their satisfaction, the integration of interest-groups and the types of power which they exercise' (ibid.: p. 66). Phenomena like religious sentiments, political beliefs and aesthetic considerations, as Weber points out, do not primarily interest us because of their 'economic significance,' but they are *economically relevant*; they have 'consequences which are of interest from the economic point of view' (ibid.: p. 64). These phenomena, though not economic in the strict sense, affect the nature of economic life and/or the course of economic development.

Although much of Weber's work in applied *Sozialökonomik* focused on *economically relevant phenomena*, he was aware that the relationship between economic and other social phenomena is not so one-sided and that another category of economic phenomena exists. The third category of his social economics, thus, concerns *economically conditioned phenomena*, that is, 'non-economic phenomena that are directly influenced by economic phenomena' (Swedberg 1998: p. 193). Recognizing that material considerations affect everything from the composition of the law to the structure of the family to the aesthetic values that exist in a given context, I should note, is not a unique insight of Weber. Marx, you may remember, argued that the superstructure (in other words, the organization of the state and the socio-political mores that prevail in a society) has its foundation in the base (in other words, the organization of the means of production in that society). Thus 'any particular set of economic relations determines the existence of specific forms of state and social consciousness' (Larrain 1983: p. 45). While not embracing the totality of Marx's historical materialist claims, Weber's schema does intend to capture (albeit in a weaker form) this aspect of Marx's thought. Public choice and new institutionalist arguments that economic considerations and incentives impact constitutional, legislative and regulatory decision-making would also be included in this category of Weber's schema.

In an article entitled 'Post Classical Political Economy: Polity, Society and Economy in Weber, Mises and Hayek,' Boettke and Storr (2002) tease out the intellectual links between Weber's *Sozialökonomik* and the Austrian school of economics (led by Mises and Hayek). As Boettke and Storr (ibid.: p. 173) assert, 'Weber and the Austrians have a deep and symbiotic relationship; they share many of the same intellectual forebears and a commitment to the same methodological approach.' Weber, Mises and Hayek were all a part of the same research program.[1]

Boettke and Storr (ibid.: p. 168) enlist the imagery of 'three circles of potentially different sizes, representing the society, the polity and the economy respectively' in order to describe the unique character of the Weber–Austrian approach. If we were to arrange these circles into a configuration that would reflect Marx's materialist arguments, Boettke and Storr (ibid.) assert, we would have to place the circles representing the society and the polity within the economy circle. Although Marx is correct in asserting that economic factors affect the society and the polity, as Boettke and Storr (ibid.) argue, 'there is nothing logically inconsistent with imagining an [alternate] configuration.' The economy, for instance, could be placed within the polity and the society; economic activity could be viewed as always occurring in a context of 'concrete ongoing social relations.' According to Boettke and Storr (ibid.), this configuration, with the circle representing the economy located within the polity and society circles, is precisely the configuration that Granovetter had in mind when he developed his embeddedness arguments.[2] In an article that Swedberg (1998: p. 268) described as a key article in the 'new sociology of economic life,' Granovetter (1985), like Weber and the Austrians, calls attention to the social context in which individuals live and act. Unlike Weber and the Austrians, however, Granovetter does not seem to recognize that some social relations may be economically conditioned.

Indeed, the essential idea of the Weber–Austrian approach is that the individual is embedded in the polity, the economy and the society. Rather than privileging Marx's or Granovetter's configuration, Weber (and the Austrians) 'suggests a third way of conceiving the relationship between the society, the economy and the polity' (Boettke and Storr 2002). As Boettke and Storr (ibid., emphasis added) argue,

> Whereas the embeddedness argument suggests that we place the economy within the society and Marx's materialist arguments suggest the opposite,

Weber's insistence that we consider both economically relevant and economically conditioned phenomena suggests that we view the economy, the society
and the polity as three overlapping circles. The society, the polity and the
economy are elevated, if you will, to the same level of prominence and *dual, and
treble notions of embeddedness are conceived of and utilized.*

Stated another way, Weber and the Austrians, by focusing on *economically
relevant* and *economically conditioned phenomena*, have moved beyond
both the single embeddedness of Granovetter and the historical materialism of Marx, and have instead proposed a *treble embedded* individual. As
Weber asserts, 'the boundary lines of "economic" phenomena are vague
and not easily defined' (Weber [1949] 1997: p. 65) and, as a result, discussing economic activity without acknowledging its political and economic
aspects, without discussing the 'social mores and political and legal institutions' which affect and influence it, becomes nearly impossible in his
schema. Similarly, discussing social or political activity becomes nearly
impossible without discussing its economic aspects.

According to Boettke and Storr (2002), Weber and the Austrians were
able to move beyond the problems of Marxian materialism and the incompleteness of Granovetter's 'single' embeddedness arguments by embracing
verstehen. Weber and the Austrians are chiefly concerned with the meanings that individuals attach to their actions and to their circumstances,
that is, the meanings they attach to the geographic, economic, social and
historical places where they act and to the times in which they live. 'Social
phenomena, social structures, social relationships and social actions are
unintelligible [for Weber and the Austrians] without considering how
actors subjectively perceive them' (ibid.).

Their commitment to *verstehen* thus leads them to situate the actor
within a *context of ongoing social meanings*, and to conceive of her as
both an influencer of the *context of meanings* in which she is located and
as being influenced by that context (ibid.). As Boettke and Storr (ibid.)
asserted, the Weber–Austrian approach 'neither proceeds with disembod-
ied actors, unaffected by the social institutions within which their actions
are embedded, nor with social structures and relations dissociated from
the web of meanings that give them life.' What distinguishes economic
phenomena from social and political phenomena, in Weber, Mises and
Hayek, is, therefore, 'only the meaning[s] that actors attach to them and
the context within which actions are attributed meaning[s]' (ibid.). Boettke
and Storr position the Weber–Austrian approach as an *economics of
meaning*. Where these meanings come from and how some phenomena
come to be viewed as political and others as economic or social are questions that Boettke and Storr leave unresolved. In that article our task
was principally to show the parallels in Weber, Mises and Hayek and to

argue that they were able to articulate a rich conception of embeddedness because of their commitment to *verstehen*. Although my co-author and I identified a *treble embeddedness* argument in Weber, Mises and Hayek, we stopped short of articulating the full implications of their *verstehen* commitment: a commitment to meaning *ipso facto* moves the study of culture to the fore of the analysis. In fact, we may have confused/conflated society with culture in that project.[3]

8.3   CULTURE: MEANING UNDERNEATH THE SOCIAL, THE ECONOMIC AND THE POLITICAL

Society, as such, is not the same thing as culture. Culture is, in fact, a much broader concept. It is the background against which all (political, social and economic) activity takes place. It is, as Lavoie and Chamlee-Wright (2000: p.14) assert, 'an *aspect* of virtually any causal factor one might identify, not a separate causal factor of its own. It is the background that provides the linguistic framework with which we understand the world around us.' It is, therefore, my conjecture that a focus on the meanings that actors associate with their actions and contexts, a focus required by a commitment to the method of *verstehen*, means that we must focus on culture. This elevation of culture to the fore of our economic, political and social analyses will, I contend, improve our understanding of, amongst other things, the nature of entrepreneurship (Lavoie 1994, this volume, Chapter 3), the meaning of prices (Ebeling 1990), the problems of transition (Boettke 2001) and development (Chamlee-Wright 1997, 2002; Boettke 2001; Storr 2002; Storr and Colon, this volume, Chapter 15) and the institutional organization of the economy (Geertz 1963; Gudeman 1986; Bird-David 1990, 1992b).

Bird-David (1990, 1992a, 1992b), for instance, in articulating an interpretive approach to economic anthropology, has argued that cultures organize their (economic) activities and relationships on the basis of what she calls 'primary metaphors.' These metaphors, also called local economic models (see Gudeman 1986), 'not only offer [a] means of "seeing" the world but also govern everyday functioning [of the individuals who hold them] down to the most mundane details' (Bird-David 1990: p.190). As such, they offer us a way of understanding economic life in contexts that are even *radically dissimilar* to the environments with which we are familiar. Amongst the Nayaka, a society of gatherer-hunters in Southern India, for instance, the forest is viewed as a parent; that is, the 'forest as a parent' is the primary metaphor.[4] As Bird-David (1990: p.190) explains, the Nayaka 'look on the forest as they do on a mother or a father. For them, it is not something "out there" that responds mechanically or passively but like a parent; it provides food unconditionally to its children.'[5]

A number of Nayaka practices begin to make sense when we recognize that the Nayaka believe that the *forest is as a parent*. For instance, their views on land ownership, their practice of distributing the spoils of the hunt based on need instead of concerning themselves with who actually killed or captured the animals, and perhaps even the reason why they do not cultivate the land like many of the communities that live near them (the neighboring Bette and the Mullu Kurumbas, for example, are both agrarian communities) can be explained by reference to the primary metaphor that prevails in that context. As might be expected between siblings (in other words, children of the father forest), the

> Nayaka give to each other, request from each other, expect to get what they ask for, and feel obliged to give what they are asked for. They do not give resources to each other in a calculated, foresighted fashion, with a view to receiving something in return, nor do they make claims for debts. (Bird-David 1990: p. 191)

Similarly, the primary metaphor of the 'forest as parent' can be used to explain the Nayaka view of land ownership. The Nayaka are quite familiar with notions of shared ownership. To be sure, the obligation to share which dominates that context suggests an acceptance that objects can be legitimately owned or at least possessed. Although they seem to accept that objects can be owned, however, they do not believe that land can be owned; they believe in private property but not in real estate. Remember, the Nayaka view each other as siblings, children of the forest. They 'believe that the forest as parent gives wild resources to all Nayaka, that is, that all Nayaka are born with rights of direct personal access to land and unearned resources' (Bird-David 1990: p. 192).

Bird-David (1992a) has found similar patterns of economic organization and similar belief systems operating amongst the Batek of Malaysia and the Mbuti of Zaire. Like the Nayaka, the Batek and the Mbuti are hunter-gatherer societies with immediate-return systems. While the primary metaphor at work amongst the Nayaka was the *forest as parent*, the primary metaphor amongst the Batek and the Mbuti is one of *sharing*. 'Through their close interaction with the environment they have come to perceive it, and act with it,' according to Bird-David (1992a: p. 31), 'as with a friend, a relative, a parent who shares resources with them.' These hunter-gatherers, thus, behave as if resources are not scarce but in abundance; 'they enjoy and exhaust what they have obtained, however much it is, and persist in their demands for shares, irrespective of what they already have' (ibid.).

That cultural characteristics and metaphors can and do influence the pattern of economic organization across contexts has also been suggested by Lipset's (1990) comparison of values and institutions in the United States and Canada. Canadian businessmen, Lipset (1990: p. 120) points out, are often described as being 'less aggressive, less innovative, [and] less risk-taking than their American counterparts.' These differences in entrepreneurial cultures seem to have stemmed from more general differences in the national identities of these two neighbors. Americans are harder working and more concerned with material success, while Canadians are more cautious and more concerned with their quality of life, or so the stereotypes go. Public opinion polls (cited by Lipset), however, seem to confirm these stereotypes. In Gallup and market research polls taken in the late 1970s and early 1980s, Canadians appeared to be more reluctant to try new products and less likely to invest in research and development than their American cousins. Similarly, Canadians tended to pursue more conservative investment strategies than American investors.

Not surprisingly then, as a result of these cultural differences, that is, these differences in national cultural identities, the Canadian economy has come to be organized quite differently from the US economy. 'The Canadian economy,' according to Lipset (1990: p. 130), is 'organized more like the economies of Europe than that of the United States.' There is 'a much greater concentration of ownership and control among Canadian corporations than American firms' (Lipset 1990: p. 129). Business networks in Canada are more closely tied (are more dense) than they are in the United States, and Canadian firms have a greater proportion of directors in common than firms south of the border.[6] The anti-elitist, anti-big-business sentiments that color business practices in the United States and have been institutionalized into that nation's regulatory environment are not as prevalent in the Canadian context. And in Canada even the weak anti-trust legislation that exists is rarely enforced. Lipset's study thus suggests that differences in cultural identities, even the necessarily subtle differences that exist between peoples living in close proximity to one another, can have a dramatic effect on the way economies come to be organized and regulated and on the business practices that evolve across contexts.

Similarly, Geertz's (1963) investigation of social development and economic change in Modjokuto and Tabanan, two towns in Indonesia, bears out the contention defended again here (and suggested also by Bird-David's and Lipset's work) that context matters.[7] Geertz's groundbreaking study *Peddlers and Princes* (1963) compared economic life in Modjokuto, in eastern central Java, and Tabanan, in southwest Bali. Modjokuto is a small Javanese sea port where 'the market forms the hub of a far-flung and intensely active trade network through which a fabulous variety of goods flow and from which probably a majority of the town population in one way or another draws its living' (Geertz 1963: p. 8). In Indonesia, generally, and Java, in particular, Modjokuto was unique in this respect. The 'trader class' was more numerous in Modjokuto than it was in other Javanese towns of comparable size and the 'civil service corps' much smaller. What accounts for these differences? Why has Modjokuto evolved as a town of peddlers when other Javanese towns have not?

According to Geertz, most Javanese towns of Modjokuto's size were regency capitals, while Modjokuto was just a district capital. The cadre of public servants, of the political and cultural elite, that were attracted to and that came to dominate the social landscape elsewhere in Java were, therefore, not as numerous in Modjokuto. This meant that 'the impact upon the town as a whole of the etiquette and the art-centered, heavily Hinduized, court-oriented style of life affected by these aristocrats turned bureaucrats was rather less intense than elsewhere and the domination of their somewhat over-civilized "high society" less stupefying' (Geertz 1963: p. 12). In Modjokuto, peddlers, stunted in other Javanese towns, thrived in a cultural landscape more conducive (or rather less hostile) to trade and barter.

The relative absence of an aristocracy, however, was not the only reason that there was a thriving bazaar in Modjokuto. In the late nineteenth and the early twentieth centuries Modjokuto had a booming economy. The textile, tobacco, sugar and rice industries were all expanding rapidly, and by 1930 'the urbanization of Modjokuto had been greatly advanced, and the town had become a thriving center of trade' (Geertz 1963: p. 10). But in the 1930s the plantation economy collapsed and a large number of peasants who hitherto had worked as seasonal laborers on the plantations 'flooded' the market as 'small-scale' traders. Successive declines in the economy led, according to Geertz (1963: p. 11), to 'an intensification rather than a slowing down of economic activity' and continued 'the overall trend toward the conversion of the bulk of Modjokuto's citizens into small-scale businessmen.'[8]

The bustling Modjokuto stands in sharp contrast to Tabanan, a Balinese court town, where it was not 'the bazaar but the palace which has stamped its character upon the town, not the Islamized trader but the Hinduized aristocrat who has been its distinctive figure' (Geertz 1963: p. 18). The population in Tabanan is less dense than it is in Modjokuto (in other words, Tabanan is less urbanized), and its citizens are much less market-oriented. Tabanan is a largely agrarian society where most peasants are able to support themselves through their subsistence activities. Capital-intensive agricultural activities, agricultural wage labor, the renting of rice fields for money and the buying/selling of foodstuffs on the open market, all quite common in Modjokuto, are relatively rare in Tabanan.

Geertz suggests several reasons why Tabanan has had a different development path than Modjokuto. One reason is that the nobility have always been and, indeed, continue to be central to life in Tabanan. Another is that village life in Tabanan is organized into what 'is perhaps best seen as a set of the overlapping and intersecting corporate associations the Balinese call *seka*' (Geertz 1963: p. 84). These *seka* or social groups are each organized to serve some particular political, economic or social function, and the Balinese, each of whom belong to between three and a dozen *seka*, are quite loyal to these groups. Consequently, economic activities in Tabanan tend to be strongly collective; cooperatives and even partnerships, quite rare in other parts of Indonesia, are quite common there.

Like Bird-David and Lipset's studies, Geertz's investigation suggests that there is a certain path dependence to economic development, that business practices and entrepreneurial attitudes may differ widely across contexts, and that the pattern of economic organization that emerges in a particular context is shaped by that community's particular economic history and culture. The disparate histories/cultures of Modjokuto and Tabanan, for instance, have led to economic life being dominated by peddlers in one community and princes in the other.

These moves to offer cultural explanations of social economic phenomena are quite compatible with the *interpretive social science*, the *social economics*, proposed by Weber and developed by Austrian scholars. As argued before, Weber and the Austrians, at least implicitly, appreciate the importance of culture and insist on recognizing, as Mises does, that

> Inheritance and environment direct a man's actions. They suggest to him both the ends and the means. He lives not simply as man *in abstracto*; he lives as a son of his family, his people, and his age; as a citizen of his country; as a member of a definite social group; as a practitioner of a certain vocation; as a follower of definite religious, metaphysical, philosophical, and political ideas; as a partisan in many feuds and controversies. He does not himself create his ideas and standards of value; he borrows them from other people. His ideology is what his environment enjoins upon him. (Mises [1934] 1963: p. 46)

Although Mises does not mention the word 'culture,' it is clear that 'inheritance' and 'environment,' as Mises employs them, and 'culture,' as I mean it here, are synonymous. As North (1994: p. 364) argues, culture embodies 'the cumulative experience of past generations.'[9] Man, for Mises, is, therefore, a *cultural creature*; he does not live *in abstracto*. Indeed, culture directs (but does not determine) his actions and acts as the prism through which he views his problem situation; it 'suggests to him both means and ends.'

Acknowledging that culture plays a critical role in directing a man's actions, however, does not (by itself) give us any insight into how we might construct a *cultural economics*. Nor does it suggest how we should incorporate cultural considerations into our analysis or which parts of our science can benefit most from a dose of cultural awareness. There seems to be at least an implicit agreement amongst the proponents of a more culturally attuned economics, however, that the study of entrepreneurship is the area of our science that can benefit most (or most readily) by an engagement with culture. Remember, Geertz's *Peddlers and Princes* (1963) was primarily a study of the way entrepreneurship differed across contexts. Similarly, Berger's (1991a) *The Cultures of Entrepreneurship*, sponsored by the Institute for the Study of Economic Culture, made a significant contribution to both the study of entrepreneurship and the development of a culturally attuned economics (see particularly Lavoie's (1991) and Berger's (1991b) contribution to that volume). Even in Harrison's two volumes *Underdevelopment is a State of Mind* (1985) and *Who Prospers* (1992), where he tends to scapegoat rather than incorporate culture, the focus is primarily on how culture impedes or impairs entrepreneurs.

8.4 ENTREPRENEURS IN CONTEXT: CREATING A CULTURAL ECONOMICS

The entrepreneur is at the heart of market processes, at the heart of economic development and, increasingly, at the heart of development theory. Our recognition of these 'facts' owes much to Israel Kirzner. Kirzner, building on Mises's contention that 'entrepreneurial perception . . . lies outside of the mechanical depiction of choice as optimal resource allocation' (Chamlee-Wright, this volume, Chapter 5: p. 108), that is, outside of the rational choice framework employed by neo-classical economists, constructs a theory of entrepreneurship that emphasizes the creative and novel character of entrepreneurial efforts. Admittedly, if human beings lived in a world where actors had perfect knowledge, that is, where all possible means were already identified and all possible ends were already conceived, then Kirzner's emphasis on the extra-optimizing efforts by economic agents would be unnecessary.[10]

But human beings live in a world of radical uncertainty and fundamental ignorance (Hayek 1948, 1955; Mises [1934] 1963; Kirzner 1973, 1979). Knowledge is not perfect nor is it perfectible. Thus there are always means that have not hitherto been identified and ends that have not hitherto been conceived. For instance, buyers in a given locality are often unaware that a good that they desire is available in a neighboring area. Similarly, sellers are often unable to locate their prospective buyers. It is in these 'spheres of ignorance' that Kirzner's entrepreneur operates and is effective.[11]

So long as there is ignorance, Kirzner argues, there will be arbitrage opportunities and individuals who are *alert* to them. Stated another way, so long as there are opportunities to buy low in one market and sell high in another, there will be actors who will recognize that opportunity. For Kirzner, an unfocused but nonetheless purposeful 'generalized intentness upon noticing the useful opportunities that may be present within one's field of vision' (Kirzner 1994: p.107), that is, an alertness to unexploited opportunities for profit, is, therefore, his entrepreneur's chief characteristic. Although this way of conceiving entrepreneurial activity, as the discovery of new ends and means, and the designation of alertness as the essential trait of entrepreneurs, teaches us quite a bit about the essence of entrepreneurship, it is not without its problems and, as such, it is not without its critics. Don Lavoie, for instance, while maintaining that Kirzner's work is 'the best in economics on the subject,' has produced several forceful critiques of Kirzner's theory of entrepreneurship (see particularly Lavoie 1994, this volume, Chapter 3; and Lavoie and Chamlee-Wright 2000).

For Lavoie (1994: p.58), the principal weakness of Kirzner's theory is that it 'has not gotten very far in elucidating the cultural dimension' of entrepreneurship. The Kirznerian entrepreneur is ultimately acultural. It is not so much that Kirzner contends that culture does not matter but rather that he (at least in writing) has refused to acknowledge that it does and so has not grappled with the consequences of imbuing his entrepreneur with culture. Lavoie offers several reasons why Kirzner has been unable to concede (or possibly recognize) that 'entrepreneurship necessarily takes place within culture, [that] it is utterly shaped by culture, and [that] it fundamentally consists in interpreting and influencing culture' (Lavoie, this volume, Chapter 3: p.50).

One reason for this inadequacy, according to Lavoie, is that Kirzner trivializes the role of interpretation in the discovery process. Remember, for Kirzner (1979: p.148), *entrepreneurial alertness* 'consists in the ability to notice without search opportunities that have been hitherto overlooked.' Discovering profit opportunities, Kirzner suggests, is like serendipitously finding money on a beach. Indeed, for Kirzner, alertness is a flash of 'superior foresight,' a discovery of 'what is around the corner before others do' (ibid.: p.8). But, as Lavoie (this volume, Chapter 3: p.58) points out, 'most acts of entrepreneurship are not like an isolated individual finding things on beaches; they require efforts of the creative imagination, skillful judgments of future cost and revenue possibilities, and an ability to read the significance of complex social situations.'[12]

The entrepreneur does not merely 'notice' profits, and being alert is not simply 'a matter of opening one's eyes to see what is right there under one's nose' (ibid.: p. 58). It is not simply a matter of seeing 'unambiguous' things that are out there just waiting to be grasped. As Lavoie (ibid.) argues, 'if entrepreneurship is like vision . . . it is like human vision, which does not see merely patches of color but meaningful things.' Ours is a world of plants, and animals, and furniture, and buildings, and automobiles and not simply a world of greens, and grays, and blacks. To be sure, when looking out of our windows we do 'see' that there is a red object next to a brown object both sitting below a canopy of blue specked with white; patches of color are not beyond our detection. But we are also able to recognize those patches as a car, a townhouse and a cloudy sky (with their attending meanings) and to differentiate one from the other.[13] Entrepreneurship, 'like visual perception . . . involves focusing on an object *as* a certain sort of thing' (ibid.: p. 58).

And, as suggested earlier, an entrepreneur interprets what he sees from a particular cultural perceptive. The entrepreneur has a particular 'point of view,' and the seeing of profit opportunities is not a matter of 'objective observation' (as Kirzner implies) but is rather 'a discerning of the intersubjective meaning of a qualitative situation' (ibid.: p. 51); it is, as Lavoie (ibid.) contends, 'a matter of cultural interpretation.' Entrepreneurs 'read' profit opportunities, and this reading takes place within culture. Stated another way, 'entrepreneurship is the achievement not so much of the isolated maverick who finds objective profits others overlooked as of the culturally embedded participant who picks up the gist of a conversation' (ibid.).

While I agree with Lavoie's contention that recognizing the cultural dimension of entrepreneurship is critical to our being able to understand entrepreneurship and with his contention that this dimension is largely absent in Kirzner's work, I disagree with his assertion that in the end Kirzner's theory 'leaves no room for culture' (Lavoie 1994: p. 58). Kirzner has not, so to speak, closed the door to culture. In fact, many of his statements argue for just the opposite. Kirzner, for instance, was aware that different contexts produced (qualitatively) different kinds of entrepreneurs. He knew full well that there is a difference between an entrepreneur operating in the market and a bureaucrat (see Kirzner 1979: p. 11).[14] That the entrepreneur living in Soviet Russia behaved differently, faced different incentives, than the entrepreneur living in America was not lost on Kirzner (see, for instance, ibid.: pp. 11–12). Although Kirzner (ibid.: p. 8) confessed that he did not 'clearly understand how entrepreneurs get their flashes of superior insight,' he was aware that context mattered. Indeed, if Kirzner's theory of entrepreneurship was not amenable to discussions of culture then Lavoie would have had to discard it. Rather than abandoning

Kirzner's work, however, Lavoie (1994, this volume, Chapter 3; Lavoie and Chamlee-Wright 2000), has proposed several correctives (one more fruitful than the other).

8.5 THE LIMITS OF COMPARATIVE CULTURAL ADVANTAGE AND CONSIDERING CULTURE AS CAPITAL[15]

One way of constructing a cultural economics might be to extend standard economic concepts so that they address cultural matters. Lavoie and Chamlee-Wright (this volume, Chapter 7), for instance, have proposed that we treat aspects of culture in the same way that we do natural resources and that we employ terms like *cultural capital* and *comparative cultural advantage* when considering how culture affects economic behavior. According to Lavoie and Chamlee-Wright (ibid.: p. 159),

> Each society has within its grasp a unique repertoire of 'cultural resources.' Nature endows some societies with rich oil deposits and others with fertile soil. As in the case of these natural resources, culture provides some societies with a kinship network conducive to building complex credit markets and other societies with a strong work ethic. Just as markets will develop differently according to their specific natural resources, they will also develop differently according to their cultural resources.

Stated another way, each society has a distinct set of cultural assets (and liabilities) available to its entrepreneurs.

Throsby (2001: p. 44) has pursued a similar line of inquiry, suggesting that the concept of cultural capital represents cultural phenomena in a way that 'captures their essential characteristics in a manner comprehensible within both an economic and a broadly cultural discourse.' Cultural capital can thus be seen as bridging the gap between economics on one side and cultural studies and anthropology on the other. And, by treating cultural phenomena (beliefs, customs, practices, languages, values, and so on) as 'intangible assets in the possession of the group to which they refer,' we can, according to Throsby (ibid.: p. 45), understand the 'economic value' of cultural resources.

Of course, we can point out several parallels between cultural capital (as defined by Throsby) and natural capital (as employed by ecological/ environmental economists). Nature, goes the argument, has given us an endowment of arable land, and deposits of oil and minerals, and agreeable climates, and, similarly, we've been endowed by our ancestors with certain cultural resources (a strong work ethic in one context, a wide radius of trust in another). There is also an analogy that can be drawn between 'the function of natural ecosystems in supporting and maintaining the "natural balance" and the function of what might be referred to as "cultural ecosystems" in supporting and maintaining the cultural life and vitality of human civilization' (ibid.: p. 51).

Rather than making me more comfortable with the concept of cultural capital, however, these similarities have made me more uneasy. In fact, it's the parallels that can be drawn between natural and cultural phenomena that expose the problems inherent in that whole approach. To be sure, there is something about a 'cultural ecosystem' that makes it possible for us to think of it in the same way that we might think of a computer, or an automobile, or a machine; (if functioning) it can improve our productivity. But there is so much that distinguishes cultural phenomena from capital assets. Cultural phenomena are certainly less tradable than traditional capital assets and probably cannot be traded at all (although it is possible to buy/sell cultural artifacts and symbols, it is quite another thing to purchase cultural sensibilities and values). Similarly, even though one might contend that cultural assets, like traditional capital assets, have varying degrees of specificity (language, for instance, can support many more activities than, say, an affinity for the color red), it would be extremely difficult and likely impossible to replace a society's current stock of 'cultural capital' for a more appropriate/desirable stock.[16] And, perhaps the most telling, cultural capital does not involve a deliberate sacrifice of present income for future benefits.[17]

Gadamer's (1979) discussion of language also proves relevant here. As Gadamer (ibid.: p. 62) asserts, 'language is by no means simply an instrument, a tool. For it is in the nature of the tool that we master its use, which is to say we take it in hand and lay it aside when it has done its service.' But, as Gadamer contends, something else is going on when we pluck a set of words from our vocabulary, use them to express this or that thought, and let them return, if you will, to our store of possible words and expressions. Indeed, as Gadamer (ibid.) points out,

> Such an analogy is false because we never find ourselves as consciousness over against the world and, as it were, grasp after a tool of understanding in a wordless condition. Rather, in all our knowledge of ourselves and in all knowledge of the world, we are always already encompassed by the language that is our own.

The same can be said of culture. We are never able to simply take it off, to set it aside, to be completely free from its affect and influence. I am not suggesting here that we are slaves to our cultural heritages, but as stated before we do not live *in abstracto*. Viewing culture as merely a resource or a tool is, therefore, deeply unsatisfactory.

To my mind, *culture is much more like a constitution than it is like capital.* Remember, constitutions define the formal rules which govern a society. As Hayek (1960: p.178) describes, a constitution assigns 'specific powers to different authorities,' while limiting 'their powers not only in regard to the subjects or the aims to be pursued but also with regard to the methods to be employed.' A constitution, thus, defines the rules of the games (for the referees and the players, the authorities and individual citizens) and, consequently, both imposes constraints and defines and delimits the set of opportunities that an individual can legitimately exploit. It, therefore, directs an individual away from certain types of activities and towards others, with constitutional rules serving as points of orientation.[18] Culture operates in the same way. Even Throsby (2001: p.9) recognizes that 'economic agents live, breathe and make decisions within a cultural environment' and that 'this environment has some influence on shaping their preferences and regulating their behavior.' Thus one wonders if cultural capital is in fact capital at all and whether the concept of cultural comparative advantage can be meaningfully pursued once we recognize that culture cannot satisfactorily be thought of as a resource.

With Ricardo's careful articulation of the law of comparative advantage, we realized that what was important when considering the benefits of trade was not absolute advantages but relative ones. If a director of information technology, for instance, is better at both project management and software development than a particular programmer working for him, it is not necessarily true that he should fire that programmer and perform both functions. Even with the difference in skill levels, the department is probably better off if the manager manages and the programmer programs; they should both specialize in their relative strengths. There are gains to be had from specialization.

For Lavoie and Chamlee-Wright (this volume, Chapter 7: p.161), 'the economists' understanding of comparative advantage is a marvelously general notion, as applicable to cultural as it is to material resources.' At issue, however, is not

> 'inter-country' comparison, but 'within-country' comparison. It is not whether some kind of aggregated conglomerate of the whole country's values is better than that of another country, but whether the relative cultural strength within a country is, say, its work ethic or its propensity to save, its trust networks or its attitude toward creativity. (ibid.: p.160)

Entrepreneurs should, therefore, 'work on identifying which elements of their culture are the most promising for them to cultivate in order to achieve what they would consider to be prosperity' (ibid.).

Although on the surface Lavoie and Chamlee-Wright's discussion of

comparative cultural advantages seems compelling, ultimately notions
of comparative cultural advantage (and cultural capital) miss the point.
Rather than revealing, as Lavoie and Chamlee-Wright (this volume,
Chapter 7: p. 161) suggest, 'the specific details of any particular culture's
comparative advantages,' studies of culture offer (and are best situated to
offer) us insight into how institutions (necessary for development) might
be adapted to fit particular cultural milieus and how different 'patterns of
entrepreneurship' have been impacted by culture. Cultures simply cannot
be readily catalogued in terms of their absolute or relative *strengths* and
weaknesses. Remember, we cannot satisfactorily talk in terms of cultural
resources.

The problem with the concept of cultural comparative advantage is not
that it is 'wrong' but that it is misleading and terribly inadequate. Lavoie
and Chamlee-Wright want to take a concept that has its place within discussions of international trade and use it to make the point that no culture
is growth resistant and that all cultures can find ways (possibly quite distinct ways) to grow. While agreeing completely with that sentiment, I have
to object strenuously to the path that they have traveled to get us there.
It simply does not deal with culture as I (or they themselves) understand
it. They have, however, proposed another (more promising) method of
constructing a cultural economics.

8.6   PROMOTERS, PEDDLERS AND PIRATES

As Lavoie and Chamlee-Wright (this volume, Chapter 7: p. 165) have also
noted, the 'spirit of enterprise comes in many different flavors.' Although
the entrepreneur plays the vital roles of innovation and coordination
within all markets, the ideal-typical entrepreneur may differ considerably
across time and place. Context does matter. And, because entrepreneurs
from different cultures operate on the basis of different primary metaphors and possess different models of entrepreneurial success, the 'quintessential entrepreneur will be described as having quite different qualities'
in different contexts (ibid.).

The Japanese entrepreneur, for instance, typically operates his firm
as a father would his family or a coach/team-captain would his team.[19]
Corporate unity is stressed, and employees are expected to subordinate
their individual identities to the team. Compare this with the 'entrepreneurial pattern' that emerges in more individualistic cultures, where entrepreneurs are typically thought of as cowboys or mavericks. Correspondingly,
the British entrepreneur at the time of the industrial revolution and the
contemporary Jamaican haggler, while sharing many similarities (a *spirit*

of enterprise infects both characters), also differ from each other in many respects. The haggler, for example, is less likely to expect that her activities will be translated into real material success, and her opportunities and avenues for attaining capital and credit will also differ.[20]

'Each culture,' Lavoie and Chamlee-Wright (ibid.) point out, 'creates a unique entrepreneurial pattern; each culture articulates its own genre of stories in which economic leaders achieve wealth-generating success within the specific institutional and customary contours of the society in which they live.' It is not that entrepreneurs exploit their society's cultural advantages or utilize its cultural strengths, as Lavoie and Chamlee-Wright sometimes seem to be suggesting, but instead that they correctly 'read' and 'interpret' the opportunities to profit and the avenues to economic success particular to their context. Culture, as Chamlee-Wright (this volume, Chapter 5: p. 113) has reminded us, 'provides the framework within which entrepreneurs not only notice but also creatively piece together profit opportunities from the world around them.' And, as I have cited before, 'The seeing of profit opportunities is a matter of cultural interpretation' (Lavoie, this volume, Chapter 3: p. 51). What Lavoie and Chamlee-Wright (this volume, Chapter 7) recommend, therefore, is that we pay attention to, that we *appreciate*, 'the rich diversity of these narratives' if we intend to understand entrepreneurship within its context. How do we do this? How do we contextualize the entrepreneur? How do we give the cultural muscles and flesh that they are calling for to the skeleton of the entrepreneur developed by Kirzner and others? Both separately and together Lavoie and Chamlee-Wright have given us several well-developed hints as to the path they suggest (Lavoie 1994, this volume, Chapter 3; Chamlee-Wright 1997; Lavoie and Chamlee-Wright 2000).

What they propose is (ultimately) that we shift our focus from the entrepreneurial function and, instead, pay attention to the entrepreneur, that we, as they put it, find out which stories are told in her community, the myths that are widely shared and believed by her fellows, the heroes that are admired and the metaphors that are used in her context (Lavoie and Chamlee-Wright 2000: p. 52). We should, as they have suggested, focus on the ideal-typical, the quintessential entrepreneurs in particular cultures; the Ghanaian market woman and the Harare market woman that Chamlee-Wright (1997, 2002) has so adroitly described in her applied work are both classic examples of this method.

I should note at this stage that Lavoie and Chamlee-Wright's proposal that we focus on the entrepreneurial form in addition to looking at the essential nature of the entrepreneurial function is not unique to them. Mises ([1934] 1963: p. 254), for instance, just over a half century before Lavoie and Chamlee-Wright, conceded that economics (particularly its descriptive and historical branches) cannot do without the entrepreneur as both an ideal type and an economic category. The entrepreneurs of pure economic theory, he notes, 'are not living men as one meets them in the reality of life and history. [Rather,] they are the embodiment of distinct functions in the market operations' (ibid.: p. 253). But, Mises asserted later on, there is another way in which economics 'always did and still does' use the term, that is, to designate an ideal type. Economics 'calls entrepreneurs those who are especially eager to profit from adjusting production to the expected changes in conditions, those who have more initiative, more venturesomeness, and a quicker eye than the crowd, the pushing and promoting pioneers of economic improvement' (ibid.: p. 255).

Mises (ibid.) recommended that we call this *entrepreneur qua ideal type* a promoter (to avoid confusion) and argued that

> Economics cannot do without the promoter concept. For it refers to a datum that is a general characteristic of human nature, that is present in all market transactions and marks them profoundly. This is the fact that various individuals do not react to a change in conditions with the same quickness and in the same way. The inequality of men, which is due to differences both in their inborn qualities and in the vicissitudes of their lives, manifests itself in this way.

Promoters are an essential part of the market process, and 'how they play that part' is subsequently of interest to economists. Presumably, as with other men, the ends they desire and the means they employ are suggested to them by their cultures. As Mises (ibid.: p. 46) asserts, 'inheritance and environment directs a man's actions . . . [and] he lives as a man of his people.'

Lavoie and Chamlee-Wright's program is thus entirely consistent with the program proposed by Mises (again almost a half century before), and their recommendation that we pay attention to *entrepreneurs qua ideal types* (particularly if we're engaged in descriptive economics or economic history) should be seen as part of Mises's (and Weber's) project. The peddlers that Geertz found in Modjokuto and described in *Peddlers and Princes* (1963) are, therefore, representative of the embedded entrepreneur that Lavoie and Chamlee-Wright have proposed we look at.

Remember, 'Modjokuto from its beginning has had a bazaar economy' peopled with a large number of 'highly competitive commodity traders who relate to one another mainly by means of an incredible volume of *ad hoc* acts of exchange' (ibid.: p. 29). Geertz describes these peddlers in graphic detail. They are determined, innovative and driven characters who are opportunistic, perhaps to their detriment. The Modjokuto peddler is an 'entrepreneur without an enterprise' who is not interested in reducing his cost of doing business but is instead focused on 'petty speculation' (ibid.). He does not or, as Geertz asserts, is unable to 'search out and create new sources of profit.' Instead, he merely grasps 'occasions for gain as they fitfully and, from his point of view, spontaneously arise' (ibid.). As discussed earlier, the history of Modjokuto and the peculiar structure (at least for Java) of the Modjokuto township (for instance, the absence of a significant landed gentry) have given rise to this particular entrepreneurial culture and have created the Modjokuto peddler.

Another character that I contend is consistent with Lavoie and Chamlee-Wright's embedded entrepreneur is the Bahamian *master pirate*. The most successful industries in the Bahamas' economic story have been pirate-like in character. Whether they were pirates, or ship-wreckers, or blockade runners, or rum smugglers, or drug dealers, or even off-shore bankers, many of the entrepreneurs who appear in the Bahamian economic narrative were engaged in activities that were morally dubious at best. The Bahamas' economic past, I contend, has given rise to an entrepreneur who is alert to opportunities to profiteer rather than profit. In *Enterprising Slaves and Master Pirates* (2004), I attempt to describe and develop this ideal type of the *master pirate* as well as the ideal type of the *enterprising slave*, the other figure that I contend is an important part of the economic story of the Bahamas.

NOTES

* This chapter previously appeared as Chapter 2 in *Enterprising Slaves and Master Pirates: Understanding Economic Life in the Bahamas* (Peter Lang, 2004). It is reprinted here with minor edits with the permission of the publisher.
1. As Lachmann (1977: p. 94) asserts, 'In reading [Mises's *Human Action* ([1934] 1963)] we must never forget that it is the work of Max Weber that is being carried on here.'
2. It should be noted, however, that the polity, the state, was largely absent from Granovetter's arguments.
3. Weber, however, did at least hint at the importance of cultural studies in his social economics. 'The quality of an event as a "social-economic" event,' he contends, 'is not something which it possesses "objectively." It is rather conditioned by the orientation of our interest of understanding, as it arises from the specific cultural significance which we attribute to the particular event in a given case.' (Weber [1949] 1997: p. 64)
4. This study, similarly, can be read as arguing that, in the Bahamas, two competing metaphors of entrepreneurship—*business as piracy* and *business as enterprise*—are at work. In *Enterprising Slaves and Master Pirates* (Storr 2004), Chapters 3 (piracy) and 4 (enterprise) trace the evolution of those two metaphors and Chapter 5 traces the way these metaphors affect contemporary business practices. The arguments of this project, thus, closely parallel Bird-David's work on the Nayaka.
5. As Gudeman (2001: p. 34) describes,

> Around the world, many constructions of the commons [the natural environment] and its connection to people are found. But in countless instances, the base [that is, the underlying economic reality] of a group is modeled as part of community itself,

not as a separate, mechanically driven object, as in the Newtonian construct of capital. Such cultural models do not distinguish between the human and nonhuman constituents of community, or between people and material; the social, spiritual, and material sustenance of the community are one.

6. As Lipset (1990: p. 129) reports,

    a 1984 study by the Ontario Securities Commission reports that four-fifths of the companies on the Toronto Stock Exchange's 300 Index are controlled by seven families. Crossnational data reveal that Canada's 32 wealthiest families plus five conglomerates 'control about one-third of the country's non-financial assets . . . By comparison, in the U.S. the 100 largest firms, few of which are controlled by individuals, own one-third of the non-financial assets.' Only 15 percent of the 500 companies on the American Standard and Poor's stock index have a large stock-holder; in Canada, at least one-quarter of the stock in 93 percent of the country's largest publicly-held corporations 'is held by a family or conglomerate.' While the United States has literally thousands of small banks, Canada's five largest chartered banks almost totally dominate the industry in their country, holding 80 percent of all deposits; another five have an additional 10 percent.

7. As Geertz (2000: p. 65) remarked, the principal objection to the claim that *culture does not matter*

    is not that it rejects an it's-all-how-you-look-at-it approach to knowledge or a when-in-Rome approach to morality, but that it imagines that they can only be defeated by placing morality beyond culture and knowledge beyond both. This, speaking of things which must needs be so, is no longer possible. If we wanted home truths, we should have stayed at home.

    Like Geertz, I simply believe that context makes a difference.

8. As I described in *Enterprising Slaves and Master Pirates*, the decline of the plantation economy in the Bahamas had a similar effect on economic activities in that context. The death of the cotton plantations meant the birth of the *enterprising slave* (Storr 2004).

9. As North (1994: p. 364) remarked, 'The current learning of any generation takes place within the context of the perceptions derived from collective learning. Learning then is an incremental process filtered by the culture of a society.'

10. High (1990) summarizes quite succinctly the implications of assuming omniscient actors, as is done by mainstream economists. As High (ibid.: p. 51) suggests, when 'the set of possible alternatives from which [a maximizer] chooses is assumed to be comprehensive,' then 'his attempt to achieve the most desirable of these opportunities always succeeds.' There would be no need for entrepreneurship in that context.

11. It is important to note that these 'spheres of ignorance' are at the same time evidence that the economy is in disequilibrium and that there are opportunities to capture profits (see High 1990). The former point is an important one but, since it is not necessary for me to pursue this claim for this current effort, it will not be developed here. Instead, I will turn my attention to the latter point regarding the opportunities for entrepreneurial profits given our fundamental ignorance, and focus on their role in entrepreneurial efforts. See Kirzner (1973) for a discussion of the equilibrating nature of the entrepreneur. See Lavoie (this volume, Chapter 3) and Schumpeter ([1934] 1983) for an alternate view.

12. As High (1990: p. 54) argued, 'uncertainty introduces a mental operation into choice that is absent from maximizing subject to known constraints. A person who does not know all the various influences that will determine an outcome, or who does not know the strength of the various influences, must exercise judgment.' Pointing out that 'alertness is also important in uncertain situations,' High (ibid.) argues that,

by being alert to the various influences that will determine an outcome, one can improve one's judgment. Similarly, by being alert to information that indicates how strong the various influences will be, a person can make better judgments. Obviously, those in the market who are able to judge uncertain situations better than others will profit.

13. As Gadamer (1979: p. 71) remarks, 'in general, we are not at all ready to hear things in their own being'; instead 'they are [first] subjected to man's calculus.' Hayek has made a similar point. As he (1948: p. 63) suggests,

> If we consider for a moment the simplest kinds of actions where this problem arises, it becomes, of course, rapidly obvious that, in discussing what we regard as other people's conscious actions, we invariably interpret their action on the analogy of our own mind: that is, that we group their actions, and the objects of their actions, into classes or categories which we know solely from the knowledge of our own mind. We assume that the idea of a purpose or a tool, a weapon or food, is common to them with us, just as we assume that they can see the difference between different colors or shapes as well as we. We thus always supplement what we actually see of another person's action by projecting into that person a system of classification of objects which we know, not from observing other people, but because it is in terms of these classes that we think ourselves. If, for example, we watch a person cross a square full of traffic, dodging some cars and pausing to let others pass, we know (or we believe we know) much more than we actually perceive with our eyes. This would be equally true if we saw a man behave in a physical environment quite unlike anything we have ever seen before. If I see for the first time a big boulder or an avalanche coming down the side of a mountain toward a man and see him run for his life, I know the meaning of this action because I know what I would or might have done in similar circumstances.

14. Indeed, Kirzner would likely have agreed with Coppin and High's (1999: p. 12) assertion that 'the bureaucratic entrepreneur is no less a force of American life than the business entrepreneur.' As Coppin and High (1999: p. 11) suggest,

> Enterprising bureaucrats have changed American social life. They have influenced the food we eat, the clothes we wear, the environment we work in, the schools our children attend, the terms we trade on, and our political process. They have built huge organizations with budgets that run into the hundreds of millions of dollars and with control over land, labor, and capital that rival the resources of successful business leaders.

While entrepreneurs in a market context generally seek to maximize their profits, they argue, 'bureaucratic entrepreneurs are appointed government officials who exercise creativity, alertness, judgment, and persuasion in attempting to increase their control over scarce [public] resources.' (Coppin and High 1999: p. 13)

15. Also see Storr (this volume, Chapter 9).
16. This is not to say that cultures are immutable. To be sure, cultural beliefs, practices, values, ideals, symbols, meanings and so on (though not in flux) are constantly evolving and adapting. New artifacts are continually being produced that are beyond replicas of existing artifacts. New 'texts' are continually being written. Although cultural systems are changeable, however, they are not fungible. Even the so-called 'Cultural Revolution' in China (and its attending violence)—which (arguably) aimed at destroying traditional Chinese culture and replacing it with Maoism—really only succeeded at destroying Chinese cultural artifacts. Similarly, though francophone colonialism was a brutal attempt at cultural imperialism, it failed to transform the Algerians or the Vietnamese into little Frenchmen.

17. See Arrow (2000) for a similar critique of social capital.
18. As Lachmann (1977: p. 62) says of institutions,

> there also are certain superindividual schemes of thought, namely, *institutions*, to which the schemes of thought of the first order, the plans, must be oriented, and which serve therefore, to some extent, the coordination of individual plans. They constitute, we may say, 'interpersonal orientation tables,' schemes of thought of the second order.

19. See Trompenaars and Hampden-Turner (1998).
20. And, as Baumol (1990: p. 894) suggests, although

> entrepreneurs are always with us and always play *some* substantial role ... there are a variety of roles among which the entrepreneur's efforts can be reallocated, and some of those roles do not follow the constructive and innovative script that is conventionally attributed to that person ... How the entrepreneur acts at a given time and place depends heavily on the rules of the game—the reward structure in the economy—that happen to prevail.

Those rules, I should add, are necessarily filtered through each entrepreneur's cultural lens.

REFERENCES

Arrow, Kenneth J. (2000), 'Observations on Social Capital,' in P. Dasgupta and I. Serageldin (eds.), *Social Capital: A Multifaceted Perspective*, Washington, DC: World Bank, pp. 3–5.

Baumol, William J. (1990), 'Entrepreneurship: Productive, Unproductive, and Destructive,' *Accounting, Organizations and Society*, **12**, 579–604.

Berger, Brigitte (ed.) (1991a), *The Culture of Entrepreneurship*, San Francisco: Institute for Contemporary Studies Press.

Berger, Brigitte (1991b), 'The Culture of Modern Entrepreneurship,' in B. Berger (ed.), *The Culture of Entrepreneurship*, San Francisco: Institute for Contemporary Studies Press, pp. 13–32.

Bird-David, Nurit (1990), 'The Giving Environment: Another Perspective on the Economic System of Gatherer-Hunters,' *Current Anthropology*, **31**, 189–96.

Bird-David, Nurit (1992a), 'Beyond "The Affluent Society": A Culturalist Reformation' and Discussion, *Current Anthropology*, **33**, 25–34.

Bird-David, Nurit (1992b), 'Beyond "The Hunting and Gathering Mode of Subsistence": Culture-Sensitive Observations on the Nayaka and Other Modern Hunter-Gatherers,' *Man*, **27**, 19–44.

Boettke, Peter J. (2001), 'Why Culture Matters: Economics, Politics, and the Imprint of History,' in Peter Boettke (ed.), *Calculation and Coordination*, New York: Routledge, pp. 248–65.

Boettke, Peter J. and Virgil H. Storr (2002), 'Post Classical Political Economy: Polity, Society and Economy in Weber, Mises and Hayek,' *American Journal of Economics and Sociology*, **61**(1), 161–91.

Chamlee-Wright, Emily (1997), *The Cultural Foundations of Economic Development: Urban Female Entrepreneurship in Ghana*, New York: Routledge.

Chamlee-Wright, Emily (2002), 'Savings and Accumulation Strategies of Urban

Market Women in Harare, Zimbabwe,' *Economic Development and Cultural Change*, **50**(4), 979–1005.

Coppin, Clayton A. and Jack High (1999), *The Politics of Purity: Harvey Washington Wiley and the Origins of Federal Food Policy*, Ann Arbor: University of Michigan Press.

Ebeling, Richard M. (1990), 'What Is a Price? Explanation and Understanding (with Apologies to Paul Ricoeur),' in D. Lavoie (ed.), *Economics and Hermeneutics*, London: Routledge, pp. 174–91.

Gadamer, Hans-Georg (1979), *Philosophical Hermeneutics*, Berkeley: University of California Press.

Geertz, Clifford (1963), *Peddlers and Princes: Social Development and Economic Growth in Two Indonesian Towns*, Princeton, NJ: Princeton University Press.

Geertz, Clifford (2000), *Available Light: Anthropological Reflections on Philosophical Topics*, Princeton, NJ: Princeton University Press.

Granovetter, Mark (1985), 'Economic Action and Social Structure: The Problem of Embeddedness,' *American Journal of Sociology*, **91**, 481–510.

Gudeman, Stephen (1986), *Economics as Culture: Models and Metaphors of Livelihood*, London: Routledge.

Gudeman, Stephen (2001), *The Anthropology of Economy: Community, Market, and Culture*, Oxford: Blackwell.

Harrison, Lawrence E. (1985), *Underdevelopment Is a State of Mind: The Latin American Case*, New York: Madison Books.

Harrison, Lawrence E. (1992), *Who Prospers: How Cultural Values Shape Economic and Political Success*, New York: Basic Books.

Hayek, F.A. (1948), *Individualism and Economic Order*, Chicago: University of Chicago Press.

Hayek, Friedrich A. (1955), 'Degrees of Explanation,' *British Journal for the Philosophy of Science*, **6**(23), 209–25.

Hayek, Friedrich A. (1960), *The Constitution of Liberty*, Chicago: University of Chicago Press.

High, Jack (1990), *Maximizing, Action, and Market Adjustment: An Inquiry into the Theory of Economic Disequilibrium*, Munich: Philosophia.

Kirzner, Israel M. (1973), *Competition and Entrepreneurship*, Chicago: University of Chicago Press.

Kirzner, Israel M. (1979), *Perception, Opportunity, and Profit: Studies in the Theory of Entrepreneurship*, Chicago: University of Chicago Press.

Kirzner, Israel M. (1994), 'Entrepreneurship,' in Peter Boettke (ed.), *The Elgar Companion to Austrian Economics*, Aldershot, UK and Brookfield, VT, USA: Edward Elgar Publishing, pp. 103–10.

Lachmann, Ludwig M. (1977), *Capital, Expectations, and the Market Process: Essays on the Theory of the Market Economy*, Kansas City, MO: Sheed, Andrews and McMeel.

Larrain, Jorge (1983), *Marxism and Ideology*, London: Macmillan.

Lavoie, Don (1991), 'The Discovery and Interpretation of Profit Opportunities: Culture and the Kirznerian Entrepreneur,' in B. Berger (ed.), *The Culture of Entrepreneurship*, San Francisco: Institute for Contemporary Studies Press, pp. 33–51.

Lavoie, Don (1994), 'Cultural Studies and the Conditions for Entrepreneurship,' in T.W. Boxx and G.M. Quinlivan (eds.), *The Cultural Context of Economics and Politics*, Lanham, MD: University Press of America.

Lavoie, Don and Emily Chamlee-Wright (2000), *Culture and Enterprise*, New York: Routledge.

Lipset, Seymour Martin (1990), *Continental Divide: The Values and Institutions of the United States and Canada*, New York: Routledge.

Mises, Ludwig von ([1934] 1963), *Human Action: A Treatise on Economics*, 3rd rev. ed., San Francisco: Fox & Wilkes.

North, Douglass C. (1994), 'Economic Performance through Time,' *American Economic Review*, **84**(3), 359–68.

Schumpeter, Joseph A. ([1934] 1983), *The Theory of Economic Development*, New Brunswick, NJ: Transaction Publishers.

Storr, Virgil Henry (2002), 'All We've Learnt: Colonial Teachings and Caribbean Underdevelopment,' *Journal des Economistes et des Etudes Humaines*, **12**(4), 589–615.

Storr, Virgil Henry (2004), *Enterprising Slaves and Master Pirates: Understanding Economic Life in the Bahamas*, New York: Peter Lang.

Swedberg, Richard (1998), *Max Weber and the Idea of Economic Sociology*, Princeton, NJ: Princeton University Press.

Throsby, David (2001), *Economics and Culture*, Cambridge: Cambridge University Press.

Trompenaars, Fons and Charles Hampden-Turner (1998), *Riding the Waves of Culture: Understanding Cultural Diversity in Global Business*, New York: McGraw-Hill.

Weber, Max ([1949] 1997), *Methodology of the Social Sciences*, Glencoe, IL: Free Press.

9. A critical appraisal of the concept of cultural capital

Virgil Henry Storr

9.1 INTRODUCTION

Some of our excursions into other disciplines have been quite profitable. Public Choice's application of economic methods to the study of political behavior, for instance, was a significant contribution to the field of political science. Its insistence that all individuals, even bureaucrats and politicians, rationally seek to maximize their self-interest has improved (amongst other things) our understanding of why bureaucracies grow, why interest groups are effective and why voters are typically uninformed (rational ignorance) and are sometimes irrational (rational irrationality). In the latter half of his influential *An Economic Theory of Democracy* (1957), Downs explained that given the tiny probability that any individual's vote will affect the election it is not in the interest of the rational voter to become informed about his political beliefs. Similarly, Caplan (2001) pointed out that the personal cost of maintaining irrational political and religious beliefs is virtually nonexistent and, thus, it makes sense that irrational views are commonplace in these areas.

Other forays, however heralded by my fellow economists, have not been so successful. In some spheres where we have journeyed, the language of economics (though sometimes illuminating) seems out of place and, at times, can sound a little crass. Think of the economics of the family. Indeed, even many economists are uncomfortable with thinking about the family as simply a specialized small firm, with thinking about children, love and companionship as 'products' of the family firm, with thinking about marriage vows as a contract establishing a business-like relationship. Certainly economic laws are at play here as they are everywhere. But, although thanks to Becker we can now all describe the workings of a family using economic concepts, we married folk tend to think that there is more to it.[1]

The concept of cultural capital is the result of an exchange between sociology, cultural studies and capital theory. The term has become quite popular in some fields since Bourdieu first employed it. Following Bourdieu, sociologists have used the term to explain why academic achievement differs across communities and classes. Others have used it in a more generic sense to discuss the value of different kinds of cultural endowments. Recent issues of *Cultural Trends* and the *British Journal of Sociology* have been devoted to exploring how the concept of cultural capital relates to cultural policy and social inequality.[2] As Savage and Bennett (2005: p. 1) state,

> Over the past thirty years, the concept of cultural capital has emerged as an important means of stimulating interdisciplinary debate about the ways in which cultural processes are implicated in the reproduction, generation, and contestation of social division. This special issue brings together papers which explore how the concept can be applied across a range of social and cultural practices, encompassing contributions from sociology, history, cultural studies, media studies, and feminist scholarship, while also ranging over a broad range of cultural practices including the culture industries, the book trade, and museums.

Much of this work has been fruitful. Unfortunately, much of this work has also been hampered by confusion surrounding the concept of cultural capital. This chapter is an attempt to highlight some of the conceptual and empirical challenges that social scientists encounter when we attempt to make fruitful use of the term. Before proceeding, however, it is useful to clearly define the concept of cultural capital.

9.2 WHAT IS CULTURAL CAPITAL, REALLY?

The term 'cultural capital' has at least two competing (albeit similar) uses, one in sociology (following Bourdieu) and another in economics (where Throsby has presented the clearest articulation). In his groundbreaking article 'The Forms of Capital' ([1983] 2002: p. 280), the French sociologist Pierre Bourdieu sought to reintroduce 'capital in all its forms' in order 'to account for the structure and functioning of the social world.' Anybody dissatisfied with the way that economics deals with matters of culture will find the motivation behind Bourdieu's project appealing. He (ibid.: p. 281) is absolutely right, for instance, when he complains that, 'by reducing the universe of exchanges to mercantile exchange, which is objectively and subjectively oriented toward the maximization of profit, in other words, (economically) *self-interested*, [economic theory] has implicitly defined the other forms of exchange as noneconomic, and therefore *disinterested* and outside the scope of economics.

Certainly since Weber, but even before, economists have been aware not only that human beings are goal oriented but that they act on the basis of traditions, emotions and substantive values as well (Weber [1921] 1978). Similarly, we should have recognized by now that non-economic events and phenomena are often economically conditioned; there are several occurrences that are not economic in the pure sense but are nonetheless affected by economics. Economists, however, have been reluctant to talk about the ways that the economy, or the advent of industrial capitalism, or the so-called Great Depression, or the stagflation of the 1970s or, to cite a contemporary example, the advent of globalization has affected society. And, similarly, economic theory has focused almost exclusively on 'practices that have narrowly economic interest as their principle and only with goods that are directly and immediately convertible into money' (Bourdieu [1983] 2002: p. 281). As Bourdieu's effort suggests, and as I have stated elsewhere, a narrowly defined economics cedes many of the interesting and important questions to others (Storr 2004).

It is unclear, however, if introducing or reintroducing 'capital in all its forms,' particularly the concept of cultural capital, is the right way to proceed. Cultural capital, originally conceived of by Bourdieu as a way of explaining why academic achievement differs across classes and class fractions, describes the benefits that individuals can gain because they are members of particular families, clubs, classes or societies. Academic success or failure, he asserts, has less to do with natural aptitudes and monetary investments in education and much more to do with investments of cultural capital; 'scholastic yield from educational action depends on the cultural capital previously invested by the family' (Bourdieu [1983] 2002: p. 282).[3] For Bourdieu, cultural capital acts as an endowment of views, attitudes and dispositions that (like other forms of capital) increases our effectiveness as we pursue our goals. Our cultural capital helps us to identify and exploit opportunities.

According to Bourdieu (ibid.: p. 282), cultural capital in the *embodied state*, 'in the form of what is called culture, cultivation, *Bildung*,' is its fundamental form.[4] In the *embodied state* it is 'external wealth converted into an integral part of the person, into a habitus' (ibid.: p. 283). It makes sense that Bourdieu would seek to link his notion of cultural capital with his understanding of the habitus. The habitus, in Bourdieu's (1977: p. 76) thought, 'is a socially constituted system of cognitive and motivation structures.' It is 'the product of history' which 'produces individual and collective practices' (ibid.: p. 82). Bourdieu (ibid.: p. 82) has also described the habitus as a 'system of dispositions' that is the root cause of whatever 'continuity and regularity' we are able to 'discern in the social world.' The habitus is 'a past [that] survives in the present and tends to perpetuate itself in the future by making itself present in the practices structured according to its principles' (ibid.: p. 82).

We get our initial endowment of cultural capital by virtue of our belonging to a particular class, and we grow it through efforts at self-improvement.

> The work of acquisition is work on oneself (self-improvement), an effort that presupposes a personal cost (*on paie de sa personne*, as we say in French), an investment, above all of time, but also of that socially constituted form of libido, *libido sciendi*, with all the privation, renunciation, and sacrifice that it may entail. (Bourdieu [1983] 2002: p. 283)

'The accumulation of cultural capital in the *embodied* state,' Bourdieu (ibid.: p. 283) suggests, 'presupposes a process of embodiment, incorporation, which, insofar as it implies a labor of inculcation and assimilation, costs time, time which must be invested personally by the investor.' You are not born knowing how to pick out the salad fork, what side of the street to walk on when walking with a lady, how to choose the appropriate wine for a particular dish, when to wear white or how to be a pleasant dinner guest. These are lessons that you learn over time and that can be used to capture symbolic and material profits; possessing cultural capital sets you apart from others. 'Any given cultural competence (for example, being able to read in a world of illiterates) derives a scarcity value from its position in the distribution of cultural capital and yields profits of distinction for its owner' (ibid.: p. 283).

Cultural capital in the embodied state, then, is fairly viewed as a set of skills, a group of assumptions about the world and a system of dispositions as to how to behave in the world that we employ as members of particular classes and class fractions to help us to further our ends, to capture symbolic and material profits. And Bourdieu's overall project is fairly described as an attempt to construct an economics that can explain the structures that we observe in the social world by extending economic concepts like capital to non-economic aspects of social life (Wilk 1996: p. 144).

Throsby's project *Economics and Culture* (2001) has a similar ambition; he hopes to bridge 'the gap between economics and culture' (ibid.: p. 44). Cultural capital, Throsby argues, 'can provide a common basis [for both disciplines] from which the analysis of both economic and cultural aspects of cultural goods, services, behaviour and other phenomena can proceed' (ibid.: p. 44). He (ibid.: p. 44) asserts that the notion of cultural capital is a way of 'representing cultural phenomena that captures their essential characteristics in a manner comprehensible within both an economic and a broadly cultural discourse.' It is 'a means of representing both tangible and intangible manifestations of culture' (ibid.: p. 15). Cultural capital treats both cultural products and phenomena 'as long-lasting stores of value and providers of benefits for individuals and groups' (ibid.: p. 44). Thus Throsby, like Bourdieu, who spoke of both embodied and objectified capital, is able to capture cultural products like paintings, music and buildings, as well as cultural phenomena like beliefs, customs, practices and language with this schema. Throsby (ibid.: p. 44) believes that the notion of cultural capital gives economists a way to talk about culture without having to step too far outside our familiar terrain and gives cultural theorists a way to talk about the cultural and economic value that flows from cultural assets.

Throsby (ibid.: p. 46) defines cultural capital as 'an asset which embodies, stores or provides cultural value in addition to whatever economic value it may possess.' Because cultural value is what distinguishes cultural capital from other kinds of capital, understanding his definition of cultural value is critical to understanding his notion of cultural capital. While primarily economic values are embodied in and flow from physical capital (plants and machines), human capital (embodiment of skills) and natural capital (resources provided by nature), cultural values live in and flow from cultural capital. By cultural value, he simply means the worth, importance or usefulness of a cultural asset or phenomenon that is not captured by traditional definitions of economic value and that cannot readily be converted into an economic price or even measured. Throsby (ibid.: p. 29) has in mind here sources of value that flow from the aesthetic, spiritual, social, historical and symbolic qualities of cultural objects and processes. Though distinct, cultural and economic values are certainly related to one another, and Throsby recognizes that assets can have both cultural and economic worth. As he (ibid.: p. 47) suggests, the cultural content of tangible assets tends to 'augment' its economic value and, although intangible cultural capital has no economic value per se, 'it is the flows of services to which these stocks [of intangible cultural capital] give rise which yield both the cultural and the economic value of assets.'

Throsby (ibid.: p. 51) draws several parallels between his understanding of cultural capital and the concept of natural capital (as employed by ecological/environmental economists); 'the definition of cultural capital has much in common with the definition of natural capital.' Both natural capital and cultural capital are thought of as free gifts 'inherited from the past . . . provided to us as an endowment,' by nature, in one case, and by our ancestors, in another. Just as nature has given us large deposits of minerals, forests full of lumber and oceans full of seafood, our ancestors have left us a cache of cultural assets (buildings, original artwork, respect for the rule of law, a strong work ethic, and so on). And, according to Throsby (ibid.: p. 51), 'a similarity can be seen between the function of natural ecosystems in supporting and maintaining the "natural balance" and the function of what might be referred to as "cultural ecosystems" in support- ing and maintaining the cultural life and vitality of human civilization.'

An ecosystem not only describes the biotic environment where organ- isms live but the interrelationships between different entities in a particular system and their relationships with their physical space. Healthy ecosys- tems are valuable because they provide a wide variety of services including climate stabilization, food control, mitigation of droughts and floods, the purification of water and air and the maintenance of arable soil, in short because they provide the services necessary for life. The 'cultural ecosys- tem' (value systems, language, beliefs, customs and practices), Throsby suggests, operates in the same way: girding social institutions and provid- ing a context where human society can thrive. There is a set of cultural resources in the Bahamas (perhaps the Junkanoo work ethic that thrives there or the religiosity of Bahamians), to use an example that I'm familiar with, that are as vital to (living a prosperous) life in that country as the sun, sand and sea that Bahamians have traditionally claimed as their chief resources (Storr, this volume, Chapter 11).

9.2.1   Recent Uses of Cultural Capital

Although both Bourdieu's formulation and Throsby's borrow liberally from economic theory, 'cultural capital' remains a term that is chiefly (though not exclusively) employed by non-economists. Education sociolo- gists, in particular, have embraced the term and used it extensively in their efforts to explain how social group origin impacts educational success. What follows is a sampling of the recent literature on cultural capital. The intention is not to create an exhaustive survey but to highlight and appraise some of the different ways the term has been used in the various fields.[5]

Silva (2005: p. 99), for instance, believes that 'an investigation of cultural capital as applied to the home and family remains a worthwhile enterprise' even though there are several 'shortcomings of the Bourdieusian analyses of contemporary gender and family dynamics.' Silva focuses on a prob- lematic fissure in Bourdieu's work. On the one hand, Bourdieu stresses that the social dispositions (in other words, tastes, traits, values and practices) that ensure academic success and reproduce social positioning are transmitted to the child by the family. In fact, Bourdieu ([1983] 2002: p. 284) stresses that

> the initial accumulation of cultural capital, the precondition for the fast, easy accumulation of every kind of useful cultural capital, starts at the outset,

without delay, without wasted time, only for the offspring of families endowed with strong cultural capital; in this case, the accumulation period covers the whole period of socialization.

On the other hand, Bourdieu fails to recognize the central role of mothers and homemakers in ensuring 'the transmission of particular values of cultural capital, which cannot be guaranteed otherwise' (Silva 2005: p. 84). Instead, Bourdieu defines 'social and cultural origins . . . as deriving from the father' (ibid.). Silva finds this especially problematic given 'recent transformations in home family living, which are part of the process of a destabilized gender' (ibid.: p. 98). As she (ibid.: p. 97) reminds us,

Contemporary families are constituted by second marriages; married women working is 'natural'; households of gays and lesbians can be described as 'families' . . .; multi-racial/multi-cultural/multi-lingual households have increased in numbers; husband, wife and children have different surnames; non-standard ways of acquiring children proliferate; the proportion of lone-mother households has grown enormously; and increased mobility is found through the life course creating tensions with the givens of parental class and one's 'natural' socialization.

These transformations make Bourdieu's contention that the father plays the prime role in the transmission of social dispositions and so social status difficult to sustain.

Still, Silva (ibid.: p. 99) insists, 'the concept of cultural capital . . . brings to the fore the importance of personal areas and inherited social dispositions where women, children, and homes have significant roles, and where the roles of men are currently shifting.' Unfortunately, Silva never explains how or why the concept of cultural capital is helpful in the kind of project that she endorses. Silva is urging us to focus on how social dispositions are inherited and the transformation in gender roles that continues to affect that process. A focus on cultural capital might actually hamper our efforts by encouraging us to privilege in our analysis those differences in social disposition that have to do with differences in academic attainment and social status. In this way, the concept of cultural capital actually constrains rather than promotes new areas of investigation. The changing family dynamics that Silva points to, for instance, are no longer intrinsically interesting but are interesting to us only if, as she proposes, they 'offer greater [or lesser] resources for enhancing cultural capital than the traditional nuclear family' (ibid.: p. 100).

While Silva (ibid.) wants to employ Bourdieu's concept of cultural capital to discuss gender dynamics, Gunn (2005) wants to use cultural capital to discuss middle-class identity in nineteenth- and twentieth-century England. For Gunn (ibid.: p. 54), culture broadly conceived and cultural capital 'as its social and historical embodiment' are 'closely linked in Bourdieu's work.' Consequently, Gunn relies on the concept to tease out the various mechanisms through which class-specific cultural characteristics, practices and goods are inherited and acquired. One example that he focuses on is 'the role of the extended family in the transmission of cultural capital across generations' (ibid.: p. 56). According to Gunn, the system of inheritance in nineteenth- and twentieth-century England ensured that the benefits of privilege were shared throughout the whole 'clan' and not just within the nuclear family. The English upper middle class were able to use family connections (extended clan connections) to gain entrance into exclusive schools as well as placement in exclusive firms and the upper levels of the civil service. 'Cultural capital,' Gunn (ibid.) explains, 'was an essential part of the family legacy, whether in the "objectivated" state of cultural goods, the transmission of houses, books and antique furniture, or in the "institutionalized" state represented by the expectation of high educational qualifications.'

Gunn (ibid.: p. 60) also emphasized 'the "incorporated" dimension of cultural capital' where a particular set of manners, style of dress and way of speaking and standing were evidence of a particular social position and requisite for gaining access into certain spheres. Consequently, in the Victorian period,

> an upright (though 'natural') posture, precise (though not excessive) attention to dress, control of emotions and desires (though a 'proper' show of grief), were all urged through training in etiquette, and minute attention was directed to details of behaviour since these were seen to distinguish the gentleman from the upstart, the lady from the prostitute. Although the codes of gentility became less exacting in the twentieth century, they remained difficult for newcomers to imitate, thus maintaining boundaries between old and new wealth while providing a model which all sections of the middle classes might recognize and aspire to.

Gunn believed that much of the English middle class's cultural capital is transmitted in 'incorporated' or 'bodily' forms which make class differences appear as natural differences and, as such, they have been difficult to transcend until perhaps quite recently.

According to Gunn (ibid.: p. 62), Bourdieu's concept of cultural capital reminds us that class is not just an economic and political category but a cultural category as well. Although Gunn is quite right that employing cultural capital forces us to focus on the cultural forms of particular classes, he does not explain why using cultural capital is essential or even particularly useful in this kind of study. It is simply not true, as Gunn (ibid.) asserts, that historians interested in the English middle class would not have paid attention to class-specific cultural representations without Bourdieu. See, for example, Davidoff and Hall's *Family Fortunes: Men and Women of the English Middle Class, 1780–1850* (1987), perhaps the gold standard in British middle-class studies. Davidoff and Hall are able to discuss English middle-class attitudes, beliefs and practices without using Bourdieu to orient their effort and while making only scant use of the term 'cultural capital' (there are only two casual appearances of the term in the 500-plus page book).

Additionally, in Gunn's (2005) work, as in others that have sought to engage the concept in a similar manner, 'cultural capital' (perhaps necessarily) becomes a very fluid term. There seems to be a great deal of overlap between cultural capital and other forms of capital like social capital and human capital; at times Gunn seems to be describing social relations as cultural capital (ibid.: p. 57) and at other times using the term to refer to practical skills (ibid.: p. 62). If, as Gunn appears to suggest at times, all cultural phenomena are cultural capital then it is difficult to determine what if anything it adds to our discourse.

Reay's (2004) study reviews the different conceptions of cultural capital that have been employed in the field of education research (where the term originated) and, using recent data on school choice and parental involvement, examines the relationship between cultural capital (broadly conceived) and academic achievement. That there is a positive correlation between parental involvement and academic success has been widely established. That working-class parents are less effective when dealing with teachers than middle-class parents is, according to Reay (ibid.: p. 77), a point that can readily be seen by focusing on cultural capital. As she writes,

> Many of the middle-class parents had themselves done very well at school and this educational success translated into self-confidence and a sense of entitlement in relation to parental involvement. As a consequence, the middle-class mothers were far more adept at getting their viewpoint across in dialogue with teachers when there were any disagreements or tensions between home and school, displaying certainty, self-assurance and an ability to counter opposing viewpoints, all aspects of cultural capital. In contrast, the working-class mothers were much more hesitant and apologetic and far more likely to disqualify and, at times, contradict themselves when talking to teachers. (Ibid.)

Differences in levels of cultural capital (in terms of knowledge about schooling and confidence in a school setting) between working-class and middle-class parents mean that they have different abilities to intervene effectively on behalf of their children. Thus differences in academic attainment are (again) related to differences in cultural capital. Similarly, Reay (ibid.: p. 79) explains, because they lack the sense of entitlement (an aspect of cultural capital) that their middle-class counterparts feel, working-class families have not taken full advantage of the school choice policies that are now *en vogue*.

'The new educational marketplace and the policies underpinning it,' Reay (ibid.: p. 83) explains, 'are allowing the growing middle classes to either re-establish their historic educational advantages or newly achieved status positions.' Reay, thus, worries about whether current educational policies, which emphasize school choice and parental involvement, entrench rather than dissolve social divisions because of differences in cultural capital. In the end, her account of educational inequalities is, as Bennett and Savage (2004: p. 12) claim, both 'sensitive and subtle.' Arguably, she was able to avoid many of the pitfalls that hamper other efforts because her use of the concept of cultural capital is closest to the way that Bourdieu employed it.

Although Reay is able to get at cultural capital only through indirect measures and so a number of empirical difficulties with profitably employing the term still abound, it is understandable why it is conceptually appealing to talk about the relationship between class and academic achievement in this way. The concept, as we shall see, becomes problematic only when we attempt to introduce it into spheres for which it is ill suited. In my view, conceiving of culture writ large or social dispositions writ large as forms of capital is misguided. This becomes quite clear when we consider the efforts by economists to treat culture as a resource in the way suggested by Throsby (2001).

This way of thinking about culture—treating it as a resource, as if it were capital like land, oil or the environment—is at the root of Berger and Hsiao's (1988) concept of 'cultural comparative advantage.' As Lavoie and Chamlee-Wright (this volume, Chapter 7: p. 159) explain,

> Each society has within its grasp a unique repertoire of 'cultural resources.' Nature endows some societies with rich oil deposits and others with fertile soil. As in the case of these natural resources, culture provides some societies with a kinship network conducive to building complex credit markets and other societies with a strong work ethic. Just as markets will develop differently according to their specific natural resources, they will also develop differently according to their cultural resources.

'From a comparative advantage perspective,' Lavoie and Chamlee-Wright (ibid.: p. 161) point out, 'a culture *must* have a relative cultural advantage,' since it is 'within-country' comparisons which matter.

Indeed, with Ricardo's careful articulation of the law of comparative advantage, we realized that the logic of comparative advantage applies to relative not absolute differences; what was important when considering the benefits of trade was whether you could produce a particular good or service more cheaply than you could produce another good and not whether or not you could produce it more cheaply in absolute terms than your trading partner. If a director of information technology, for instance, is better at both project management and software development than a particular programmer working for him, it is not necessarily true that he should fire that programmer and perform both functions. Even with the difference in skill levels, the department is probably better off if the manager manages and the programmer programs; they should both specialize in their relative strengths. There are gains to be had from specialization. The same is true when we are talking about countries. And, according to Lavoie and Chamlee-Wright, the same is true when we are discussing cultures. Societies should, thus, 'work on identifying which elements of their culture are the most promising for them to cultivate in order to achieve what they would consider to be prosperity' (ibid.: p. 161).

Although there is something appealing about this way of talking about culture, particularly for us economists, I remain very uncomfortable with the notions of cultural capital and comparative cultural advantage. To be sure, there is something to the notion that each culture has strengths that can help it to progress. It is possible to think of culture as a resource. But culture, for me, is much more than just resources that we use and then put away. The real problem, then, with the concept of cultural capital or cultural comparative advantage, as I have stated elsewhere, is not that it is 'wrong' per se but that it is misleading and terribly inadequate (Storr, this volume, Chapter 8: p. 196).

So I contend that Bourdieu's concept of cultural capital gets into trouble when it moves in the direction of Throsby's conception. As Bennett and Savage (2004: p. 10) warn, 'if it is not to be distorted beyond all recognition, the concept of cultural capital offers meaningful purchase only . . . [when it is] concerned with the ways in which different kinds of cultural knowledge and skill gets translated into particular kinds of economic advantage (and vice versa).' Admittedly, Bourdieu (when he links cultural capital to habitus) is sometimes as guilty as many of his followers in attempting to extend the concept of cultural capital beyond its natural borders. To see why these attempts are problematic, it is necessary to unpack what exactly we mean by both culture and capital.

9.3 THE PROBLEM WITH TREATING CULTURE AS CAPITAL

Capital has traditionally been thought of in physical terms: as the existing stock of assets that can be used to produce other goods. It, thus, includes everything from plant and equipment (fixed capital, which tends to be quite durable) to stockpiles of raw materials and semi-finished goods (circulating capital, which is generally exhausted during the production process). More important though than its physical qualities is capital's role in production and the deliberate sacrifice of present income for expected future benefits (in other words, investment) that is necessarily involved in its accumulation. Although 'culture' is a somewhat ambiguous term, used to describe high art, good manners, certain attitudes and so on, in its broadest sense the term describes the 'webs of significance' in which man is suspended and which 'he himself has spun' (Geertz 1973: p. 5). 'As interworked systems of construable signs,' Geertz (ibid.: p. 14) explains, 'culture is not a power, something to which social events, behaviors, institutions, or processes can be causally attributed; it is a context, something within which they can be intelligibly—that is, thickly—described.' Culture is an environment, a backdrop where certain events are intelligible, understandable and possible, while others are not. To talk about culture (in this sense) as if it were analogous to capital reveals a misunderstanding of both concepts.

9.3.1 Notions of Cultural Capital Misunderstand Capital Theory and Capital's Essential Characteristics

Accumulating capital necessarily involves the deliberate sacrifice of current benefits for the possibility of future income. As Mises (1949: p. 260) taught us a long time ago,

> At the outset of every step forward on the road to a more plentiful existence is saving—the provisioning of products that makes it possible to prolong the average period of time elapsing between the beginning of the production process and its turning out of a product ready for use and consumption. The products accumulated for this purpose are either intermediary stages in the technological process, in other words, tools and half-finished products, or goods ready for consumption that make it possible for man to substitute, without suffering want during the waiting period, a more time-absorbing process for another absorbing a shorter time. These goods are called capital goods. Thus, saving and the resulting accumulation of capital goods are at the beginning of every attempt to improve the material conditions of man; they are the foundation of human civilization. Without saving and capital accumulation there could not be any striving toward non-material ends.

Culture, however, cannot be 'acquired' through prudence or thrift.

To be sure, individuals can invest in the production of 'cultural goods' like paintings or the acquisition of some so-called 'cultural skills' like a second language (in other words, cultural objects which take time to produce and do yield income streams in the future). But so many aspects of culture, let alone entire cultural systems, cannot be acquired by deliberate investment.[6] Neither the tourist, nor the actor, nor the anthropologist can, for instance, ever become authentically Bahamian. They can certainly describe, or mimic, or even understand Bahamians, but time spent visiting the Bahamas, watching Bahamians or studying Bahamian folklore, attitudes and practices does not convey Bahamianness. Similarly, time spent by Bahamians abroad does not strip them of their Bahamianness. Perhaps their accents may become less pronounced or even undetectable, but at heart they remain *true-true Bahamians*, as the colloquialism goes.

Arrow's (2000) observations about 'social capital' are certainly relevant here. Social capital has been used to describe social networks and to make the point that elements like trust relations and social clubs can promote economic progress. For Arrow (ibid.: p. 4),

> the term 'capital' implies three aspects: (a) extension in time; (b) deliberate sacrifice of future benefit; and (c) alienability . . . The aspect defined as (a) above may hold in part; we speak of building a reputation or a trust relation. But these are not like physical investment; a little trust has not much use. But it is especially (b) that fails.

Social networks, Arrow points out, are not typically entered into with the hopes of any future material payoff. And, as Arrow (ibid.: p. 3) asserts, 'the motives for interaction are not economic. People may get jobs through networks of friendship or acquaintance, but they do not, in many cases, join the networks for that purpose.' Similarly, we may gain access to credit or a loyal clientele because we are members of this fraternity or that congregation, but usually that's not why we pledge a fraternity or attend a church service. Joining a social club or a religious organization cannot, fairly, be characterized as an investment; there are usually more immediate, more proximate, non-economic benefits that we derive from our involvement (for example, enjoying the fellowship with others).

Additionally, many aspects of social capital are acquired without our deciding to acquire them. Learning our first language and being born into a particular family, caste or ethnicity does not involve any deliberate act on our part and, moreover, neither learning to speak nor being born can meaningfully be said to involve sacrifice (Sobel 2002: p. 144). Arguably, the same is true about culture (even more true, if I can be permitted to use that phrase).

Culture, because it so clearly fails the deliberate sacrifice test, is obviously not capital as it is conceived of by Arrow and other neo-classical economists. But there are other ways of conceiving of capital, ways that do not emphasize the physical aspects of capital, and ways that do not focus primarily on capital represented as physical things. Although many of the Austrian definitions of capital, for instance, also highlight its material or physical character,[7] they differ from traditional definitions because they also stress the knowledge aspects of capital. It is, therefore, possible that an Austrian conception of capital may lend itself more readily as an analogy to culture because of this emphasis on knowledge. Indeed, Chamlee-Wright (2008), for instance, was able to 'repair' the concept of social capital by making a similar move. As Baetjer (1998: p. 10) explains, the Austrian view

> is more radical than simply that capital goods have knowledge in them. It is rather that capital goods *are knowledge*, knowledge in the peculiar state of being embodied in such a form that it is ready-to-hand for use in production. The knowledge aspect of capital goods is the fundamental aspect. Any physical aspect is incidental.

Baetjer uses the example of the hammer to elaborate the point. 'A hammer,' he explains,

> is physical wood (the handle) and minerals (the head). But a piece of oak and a chunk of iron do not make a hammer. The hammer is those raw materials plus all the knowledge required to shape the oak into a handle, to transform the iron ore into a steel head, to shape it and fit it, and so on . . . Even with a tool as bluntly physical as a hammer, the knowledge component is of overwhelming importance. (Ibid.: p. 10)

Although culture has been described as a kind of knowledge—knowledge about how to respond to certain situations, how to interpret the actions of others, and so on—even Austrians who stress the knowledge aspects of capital conceive of capital as a resource; capital is 'knowledge in the peculiar state of being embodied in such a form that it is *ready-to-hand for use in production*.'[8] It is unclear, however, if culture is appropriately thought of as merely a thing that we use.

9.3.2 Notions of Cultural Capital Misunderstand Culture and Its Significance

By capital we generally mean tools or resources that are employed in production. As Ricardo (1821: Chapter 5) has taught us, 'Capital is that part of the wealth of a country which is employed in production, and consists of food, clothing, tools, raw materials, machinery, and so on, necessary to give effect to labour.' And, as Lachmann (1978: p. 53) explained,

> All capital goods are, directly and indirectly, instruments of production. Not all of them are man-made (for example, mineral resources are not) but all of them are man-used. It is indeed characteristic of such 'natural' capital resources that but for the existence of man-made capital designed to be employed in conjunction with them, they would not even be economic goods. The theory of capital is thus primarily a theory of the material instruments of production.

While capital describes tools or resources that are used in production, can culture be meaningfully thought of as a tool or resource? Is culture something that capitalists 'employ' for one purpose or another? Is it just an instrument of production? Clearly, it is not.

It is true, however, that entrepreneurs rely on culture to 'discover' profit opportunities. Indeed, Lavoie (this volume, Chapter 3: p. 51, emphasis added) has made the point as eloquently as anyone that

> the profit opportunities entrepreneurs discover are not a matter of objective observations of quantities, but a matter of perspectival interpretation, a discerning of the intersubjective meaning of a qualitative situation. Profits are not measured; they are 'read.' *Entrepreneurship . . . is primarily a cultural process. The seeing of profit opportunities is a matter of cultural interpretation.* And, like any other interpretation, this reading of profit opportunities necessarily takes place within a larger context of meaning, against a background of discursive practices, a culture. That is to say, entrepreneurship is the achievement not so much of the isolated maverick who finds objective profits others overlooked as of the culturally embedded participant who picks up the gist of a conversation.

But an entrepreneur picking up the gist of a conversation because she is embedded in a particular culture is not the same thing as her using culture to read profit opportunities. Her reliance on culture, as Lavoie understood, is entirely different than, say, the carpenter's reliance on hammers and nails to build tables and chairs. Culture is not something that entrepreneurs use for this or that and then put away when it's no longer needed. Rather, we lug around much of our cultural baggage unaware that we are even carrying it. And it comes into play entirely against or, more accurately, outside of our will.

Gadamer's ([1966] 1976) discussion of language also proves relevant here. As Gadamer (ibid.: p. 62) asserts, 'language is by no means simply an instrument, a tool. For it is in the nature of the tool that we master its use, which is to say we take it in hand and lay it aside when it has done its service.' But, as Gadamer contends, something different is going on when we choose a word or set of words from our store of possible words and expressions, use them to convey some sentiment and then let them return to our cache, our vocabulary, ready-to-hand for use another day. Indeed, as Gadamer (ibid.) points out,

> Such an analogy is false because we never find ourselves as consciousness over against the world and, as it were, grasp after a tool of understanding in a word-less condition. Rather, in all our knowledge of ourselves and in all knowledge of the world, we are always already encompassed by the language that is our own.

The same can be said of culture. We are never able to simply take it off, to set it aside, to be completely free from its affect and influence. I am not suggesting here that we are slaves to our cultural heritages, but we do not live *in abstracto*. Neither an under- nor an over-socialized conception of man will do (Boettke and Storr 2002).

9.3.3 And So We Should Stop Using the Term 'Cultural Capital' to Describe Cultural Systems

The term 'cultural capital' remains for me something that is woefully inadequate and misleading when used to describe cultural systems or social dispositions or habitus. Capital is no more than a tool 'ready-to-hand for use in production.' Whether we emphasize its physical properties or its knowledge aspects, things and thoughts become capital only when entrepreneurs put them to use. Culture, on the other hand, is not merely a tool that we invest in to yield future value. Instead, culture is a context, a backdrop against which economic (and all other) activity takes place. The analogy to capital, in my view, does not serve us as well as its champions might have thought. It does not really help us 'to account for the structure and functioning of the social world' as Bourdieu hoped. Nor does it give us a way of 'representing cultural phenomena that captures their essential characteristics in a manner comprehensible within both an economic and a broadly cultural discourse' as Throsby imagined it could. Rather, cultural capital does a disservice to the concepts of both capital and culture.

Along those lines, a fair question for Throsby is why is an automobile or a typewriter any less an expression of our cultural identity than our artwork or architecture? Why, for instance, is the bazaar less a center for culture than the museum or the cathedral? Under Throsby's articulation of cultural capital, if it is to remain a meaningful category at all, there has to be a difference between the typewriter and the painting. Recall that cultural capital yields cultural value and perhaps economic value as well (if it is tangible goods), while other forms of capital yield only economic value; that's how we distinguish them (Throsby 2001: p. 45). Although Throsby (ibid.: p. 31) argues that economic value does not encompass cultural value, he does not (and cannot) make the case for the reverse. It is difficult to imagine any capital asset that does not give rise to cultural value (as he defines it), and so it is difficult to imagine any capital that isn't always also cultural capital. In the same way that the hoe, the whip and the cotton gin are deeply significant symbols of the Antebellum South, the cellular phone, the internet and the automobile are amongst the important symbols of modern America; they are all sources (to one degree or another) of aesthetic, social and historical value.

Similarly, a fair question to put to Bourdieu is how is it that he is able to conceive of culture as both a habitus, a deeply embedded set of assumptions that we may or may not be aware of, and a set of skills that we use to further our ends? These proposals are mutually exclusive. As Bourdieu (1977: p. 18) describes, 'agents are possessed by their habitus more than they possess it . . . it acts within them as an organizing principle of their actions.' The habitus acts as a '*modus operandi* of which he is not the producer and has no conscious mastery' (ibid.: p. 79). It is not something that we master. Instead, it masters us. 'As an acquired system of generative schemes objectively adjusted to the particular conditions of which it is constituted, the habitus engenders all the thoughts, all the perceptions, and all the actions consistent with those conditions, and no others' (ibid.: p. 95). Cultural capital does not even capture culture or habitus as Bourdieu understands it, let alone the semiotic view of culture that is advanced here.[9]

'Cultural capital' thus reveals itself to be a deeply troublesome term when we attempt to use it to discuss cultural phenomena broadly conceived. It is an analogy that, in my view, obscures as much as it reveals. To be sure, it reminds us that culture is at work in many areas where we might have forgotten to look for it. But it implies that there are areas of economic life that are not impacted by culture. Similarly, by describing culture as capital we treat it as a resource (something we use to accomplish our ends) rather than as a context where goals are shaped and pursued. Treating culture as a resource also encourages us to try to score cultures, to catalogue their absolute or relative strengths and weaknesses, to employ phrases like 'more cultural capital' and to talk about 'the size of cultural capital.' Indeed, this is exactly what Bourdieu ([1983] 2002: p. 284) and Throsby (2001) seem to be advocating at times. This kind of checklist ethnography, however, has been roundly discredited (see Lavoie and Chamlee-Wright, this volume, Chapter 7; Storr, this volume, Chapter 11).

9.4   CONCLUSION

Shockley (2005: p. 2) has argued that 'Bourdieu's conception of cultural capital stands at the crossroads of sociology and economics . . . gesturing to both academic disciplines.' His recommendation is that 'Bourdieuan cultural capital should move *upwards*, which is to say, Bourdieu's micro-level, economistic conception of cultural capital needs to link to Throsby's macro-level, economic conception' (ibid.: p. 20). This, in my view, moves Bourdieuan cultural capital in the wrong direction.

First, both culture and capital are poorly served by broadly conceived notions of cultural capital. Culture is not simply a tool that entrepreneurs use to attain this or that end and then put away once it is no longer needed. 'It denotes an historically transmitted pattern of meanings embodied in symbols, a system of inherited conceptions expressed in symbolic forms by means of which men communicate, perpetuate, and develop their knowledge about and attitudes toward life' (Geertz 1973: p. 89). Culture, then, is not merely an instrument in the entrepreneur's toolkit but is, instead, the arena where she decides which tools are available to her and how she will use them. Similarly, capital is just a tool: a tool that need not be man-made but is always man-used. Notions of cultural capital that try to extend upwards to encompass broader notions of culture, thus, in my view obscure the broader role that culture plays in directing economic life.

NOTES

1. See, for example, the volumes written on the sociology of the family. Newman's *Sociology of Families* (2002) provides a good overview.
2. See *Cultural Trends*, 13(2) (2004) and *British Journal of Sociology*, 56(1) (2005).
3. Usually,

> measurement[s] of the yield from scholastic investment takes account only of monetary investments and profits, or those directly convertible into money, such as the costs of schooling and the cash equivalent of time devoted to study; they are unable to explain the different proportions of their resources which different agents or different social classes allocate to economic investment and cultural investment because they fail to take systematic account of the structure of the differential chances of profit which the various markets offer these agents or classes as a function of the volume and the composition of their assets. (Bourdieu [1983] 2002: p. 282)

4. Cultural capital can also exist in the *objectified* state as cultural artifacts (like books and paintings) and in the *institutionalized* state as in the case of educational qualifications.
5. See Kingston (2001) for a more comprehensive critical appraisal of the term.
6. As Bourdieu ([1983] 2002: p. 283) has admitted, 'Cultural capital can be acquired, to a varying extent, depending on the period, the society, and the social class, in the absence of any deliberate inculcation, and therefore quite unconsciously.'

7. Recall that Lachmann (1978: p. 11) has described capital as 'the (heterogeneous) *stock of material resources*.'
8. As Lachmann (1978: p. xv) argued,

> The generic concept of capital without which economists cannot do their work has no measurable counterpart among material objects; it reflects the entrepreneurial appraisal of such objects. Beer barrels and blast furnaces, harbour installations and hotel-room furniture are capital not by virtue of their physical properties but by virtue of their economic functions. Something is capital because the market, the consensus of entrepreneurial minds, regards it as capable of yielding income.

Capital is capital because entrepreneurs believe that it can be used to generate income.
9. As Wilk (1996: p. 144) complained, Bourdieu 'ends up promising much more than he delivers, because his economics remains so vague and imprecise.'

REFERENCES

Arrow, Kenneth J. (2000), 'Observations on Social Capital,' in P. Dasgupta and I. Serageldin (eds.), *Social Capital: A Multifaceted Perspective*, Washington, DC: World Bank, pp. 3–5.

Baetjer, Howard, Jr. (1998), *Software as Capital: An Economic Perspective on Software Engineering*, Los Alamitos, CA: IEEE Computer Society.

Bennett, Tony and Mike Savage (2004), 'Introduction: Cultural Capital and Cultural Policy,' *Cultural Trends*, 13(2), 7–14.

Berger, Peter L. and Hsin-Huang Michael Hsiao (1988), *In Search of an East Asian Development Model*, New Brunswick, NJ: Transaction Books.

Boettke, Peter J. and Virgil H. Storr (2002), 'Post Classical Political Economy: Polity, Society and Economy in Weber, Mises and Hayek,' *American Journal of Economics and Sociology*, 61(1), 161–91.

Bourdieu, Pierre (1977), *Outline of a Theory of Practice*, Cambridge Studies in Social and Cultural Anthropology, Cambridge: Cambridge University Press.

Bourdieu, Pierre ([1983] 2002), 'The Forms of Capital,' in Nicole Woolsey Biggart (ed.), *Readings in Economic Sociology*, Malden, MA: Blackwell Publishers, pp. 81–93.

Caplan, Bryan (2001), 'Rational Ignorance versus Rational Irrationality,' *Kyklos*, 54(1), 3–26.

Chamlee-Wright, Emily (2008), 'The Structure of Social Capital: An Austrian Perspective on Its Nature and Development,' *Review of Political Economy*, 20(1), 41–58.

Davidoff, Leonore and Catherine Hall (1987), *Family Fortunes: Men and Women of the English Middle Class, 1780–1850*, Chicago: University of Chicago Press.

Downs, Anthony (1957), *An Economic Theory of Democracy*, New York: Harper.

Gadamer, Hans-Georg ([1966] 1976), *Philosophical Hermeneutics*, Berkeley: University of California Press.

Geertz, Clifford (1973), *The Interpretation of Cultures: Selected Essays*, New York: Basic Books.

Gunn, Simon (2005), 'Translating Bourdieu: Cultural Capital and the English Middle Class in Historical Perspective,' *British Journal of Sociology*, 56(1), 49–64.

Kingston, Paul W. (2001), 'The Unfulfilled Promise of Cultural Capital Theory,' *Sociology of Education*, **74**, 89–99.

Lachmann, Ludwig M. (1978), *Capital and Its Structure*, Kansas City, MO: Sheed, Andrews and McMeel.

Mises, Ludwig von (1949), *Human Action: A Treatise on Economics*, New Haven, CT: Yale University Press.

Newman, David M. (2002), *Sociology of Families*, Thousand Oaks, CA: Pine Forge Press.

Reay, Diane (2004), 'Education and Cultural Capital: The Implications of Changing Trends in Education Policies,' *Cultural Trends*, **13**(2), 73–86.

Ricardo, David (1821), *The Principles of Political Economy and Taxation*, London: J.M. Dent & Sons.

Savage, Mike and Tony Bennett (2005), 'Editors' Introduction: Cultural Capital and Social Inequality,' *British Journal of Sociology*, **56**(1), 1–12.

Shockley, Gordon (2005), 'Whither Bourdieuan Cultural Capital? At the Crossroads of Sociology and Economics,' 37th World Congress of the International Institute of Sociology, Stockholm, Sweden.

Silva, Elizabeth B. (2005), 'Gender, Home and Family in Cultural Capital Theory,' *British Journal of Sociology*, **56**(1), 83–103.

Sobel, Joel (2002), 'Can We Trust Social Capital?,' *Journal of Economic Literature*, **XL**, 139–54.

Storr, Virgil (2004), 'Can a Focus on Culture Be Justified without Relying on Hermeneutics?,' working paper.

Throsby, David (2001), *Economics and Culture*, Cambridge: Cambridge University Press.

Weber, Max ([1921] 1978), *Economy and Society: An Outline of Interpretive Sociology*, two volumes, Berkeley: University of California Press.

Wilk, Richard R. (1996), *Economies and Cultures: Foundations of Economic Anthropology*, Boulder, CO: Westview Press.

10. Culture as a constitution

Arielle John

10.1 INTRODUCTION

Many of the concepts economists use to explain why some countries are rich and others are poor—concepts like institutions, legal origins, ethnic fractionalization, and geography—do not have controversial definitions. The concept of 'culture,' however, means different things to different economists. Achieving consensus on the meaning of culture may improve our understanding of how it influences economic activity, in the same way that a shared understanding of institutions, for example, allows for advances in institutionalist economic theory. If consensus is not possible, making available to economists a strategy for modeling the effect of culture on economic activity that captures how culture shapes, determines and colors economic action could be a useful advance in cultural economy.

Economists, I argue, should consider modeling culture as a constitution. Why is it useful to model culture as a *constitution* to explain culture's impact on economic activity? I argue that, just as a constitution frames interactions between government and citizens, culture provides people with a shared framework of meaning in which to make their economic decisions. People with different cultural constitutions will ascribe different meanings to their experiences. As a result of culture, then, they make different decisions.

Why culture? The 'institutions matter' thesis is arguably now a leading explanation of economic development. People are unable to prosper without guaranteed freedoms in private property, business, finance, and trade. Yet institutional explanations of development leave some open questions that cultural explanations might answer. For example, why do certain institutions of economic freedom malfunction when introduced in specific contexts, despite being effective in others? Some argue that culture determines whether an imposed institution will 'stick' in a country or not (Boettke et al., this volume, Chapter 6).

Furthermore, institutions can apply uniformly to all citizens of a country, yet we may still observe unequal performance across groups of people living there (Aligica and Matei, this volume, Chapter 13; Runst, this volume, Chapter 14). Why would we observe groups of people, ostensibly facing the same institutional and even monetary constraints, making different patterns of market decisions? Why would some groups prosper under the prevailing institutions, while others do not? Economists observe that, ceteris paribus, culture induces a specific response to an incentive. Thus people of different cultures may react differently to the same incentives. Much as personality differences can sometimes wholly explain the difference in life outcomes of two people who otherwise face the same objective constraints, culture therefore seems to explain a great deal of the disparate performance of individuals in social groups, holding institutions constant.

I propose that we think about culture as a constitution in order to overcome two problems that affect the existing conceptions of culture. First, those economists who already identify the impact of culture as something to be explained often are looking for substantively different theoretical explanations of this impact. Economists agree that institutions work by providing constraints. We then dutifully search for and identify the actions and interactions incentivized by these constraints. But we have no comparable consensus of the general way in which culture works.

For example, Greif (1994) shows that people in 'individualist' cultures trust, communicate with, and depend on each other less than people in 'collectivist' cultures. Thus, the individualists require formal institutions to keep interactions honest. Such institutions 'support anonymous exchange' and therefore 'facilitate economic development' (ibid.: p.943). On the other hand, Harper (2003) theorizes that people in individualist cultures value being unique, assertive, ambitious, and creative. Furthermore, they are more likely to want to change their environment as opposed to themselves. Individualist entrepreneurship is therefore more self-centered, while people in collectivist cultures partake in group-centered entrepreneurship.

Both Greif and Harper define culture as something that can make people 'individualist' or 'collectivist.' However, one story focuses on how culture influences the development of a particular institutional climate that can be more or less favorable to economic development; the other story focuses on how culture represents a psychological orientation that manifests itself in a particular style of entrepreneurship. In the first story, institutions are formed and henceforth do all of the work. The individual's conception of herself and her agency drives the second story. Perhaps these approaches to the impact of culture can be unified. Presently, however, they offer disparate theoretical notions of how culture affects economic activity.

The second problem concerns the way economists define culture. Not all economists who examine culture define it outright. More importantly, however, the principal features of culture disappear in these definitions and analogies.

Dissatisfied with the prevailing concepts of culture, Storr (this volume, Chapter 8: p. 195) proposes a novel one: 'To my mind, *culture is much more like a constitution*,' since a constitution 'directs an individual away from certain types of activities and towards others, with constitutional rules serving as points of orientation.' Accordingly, for any individual, 'culture directs (but does not determine) his actions and acts as the prism through which he views his problem situation' (ibid.: p. 189). This is a reasonable analogy, but Storr does not give us the details. To demonstrate the strength of the analogy, one must demonstrate the number and relevance of similarities between both concepts. My proximate goals are therefore twofold. I first demonstrate that both culture and constitutions (1) emerge as spontaneous orders, (2) constrain and thus enable certain actions in order to generate predictable behavior and encourage cooperation within groups, and (3) bind decision-making in an 'intermediate' way, making them rigid, but not static. Secondly, I use examples of two countries—the Bahamas and Trinidad and Tobago—to show how a concrete and 'thin' concept of culture as a constitution may adequately frame cultural and cross-cultural narratives that are 'thick' in description.

I believe that elaborating on Storr's analogy raises understanding in cases where Austrian economics typically is not applied. Storr (2004) constructs a narrative that improves our picture of economic life in the Bahamas. Similar to the Bahamas in history, geography, and even political structure (both nations follow the Westminster system), Trinidad and Tobago presents a distinct underdevelopment puzzle that one also may address through cultural narrative. The grand problem is to thickly describe why people who we do not know make the choices that they make.[1] If the analogy of culture as a constitution permits some understanding of economic outcomes in the Bahamas and in Trinidad and Tobago, we justify its use.

Section 10.2 summarizes the research program in cultural economics. In section 10.3, I list and defend the similarities between culture and constitutions, first offering definitions of each concept. Before concluding, I use examples of the Bahamas and Trinidad and Tobago to demonstrate that the analogy helps us understand how culture affects economic outcomes.

10.2 CULTURAL ECONOMICS

Economists have fairly recently engaged in the study of culture—a research program central to the work of anthropologists, sociologists, historians, geographers, and cultural studies scholars. In a chapter entitled 'The Revival of Cultural Explanation,' Jones (2006: pp. 3–30) argues that development economist Peter Bauer's arguments most directly influenced the 'intellectual *volte face* of the 1990s'—the reintroduction of culture to economic analysis. Cultural economics looks at the relationship between culture and economic outcomes.

Both mainstream and heterodox economists study culture. Jackson (2009: p. 195) explains that economic sociologists like Mark Granovetter and Richard Swedberg, influenced by Durkheim and Weber, maintain an academic perspective that is harmonious with culture. Economic sociologists aim to 'analyse the elements of a capitalist economy—markets, firms, workers/consumers, government, property rights and so forth—from the viewpoint of sociological theory,' and, for them, 'among the key ideas has been embeddedness, such that markets and other institutions are embedded in social structures and cannot be separated from them.'[2]

Austrian economists embrace the goals of economic sociology.[3] Austrians, however, emphatically deny that to study culture involves abandoning the pure logic of choice. Lavoie and Chamlee-Wright (2000: pp. 38–9) address this point, arguing that:

> If there is a core of universal, abstract theory that economists like to claim is valid across the whole range of human societies, this core does not try to claim much that anybody would find controversial. That demand curves slope downward may be something that economists tend to feel very strongly about, but properly understood, it is not something non-economists need to consider as an ethnocentric bias that is open to challenge. It does not imply that what is demanded will be material things rather than spiritual values, or that businesses will necessarily do what they think will bring money profits. It comes down to saying that whatever people want, they want it at less cost in terms of other things they want. *By itself* economic theory is empty of any empirical punch. And yet it is a profoundly useful framework when it is *not* left by itself, that is, when it is put to work on interpreting real historical and cultural phenomena in all their richly diverse detail.

Thus, to say that Jack's context colors his choices is perfectly consistent with the statement that Jack acts rationally. The contextual explanation only adds body to the story of why Jack acts the way he does. To say that he is acting rationally is simply not enough. Lavoie and Chamlee-Wright insist that 'this whole contrast between rational self-interest and culture is misconceived' (ibid.: p. 42), since:

> All rational deliberation takes place within cultural parameters. What serves as an incentive for somebody depends on what the person wants. What seems rational depends on the prevailing culture's understanding of things. Culture is

not another factor to be considered in addition to rational incentives, it is the underlying meaning of the specific content of any rational choice.

It is easy to forget, when we belong to a similar culture, that other people do not simply live in different environments, but perceive the world differently. We can, however, reconcile the notion that relative price changes affect behavior with the awareness that prices, costs, and benefits are strictly a matter of interpretation. Our plans and purposes stem from the meanings we attribute to things, and this meaning we derive from our culture. As Storr (this volume, Chapter 2: p. 35) explains,

> While it is not inaccurate to assert, as many economists do, that relative price shifts, or differences in the size of expected profits, or differences in the institutional framework can explain *all* of the meaningful differences in economic behavior and outcomes, it is not accurate to assert that prices, profits and property can explain *any* of the meaningful differences in economic behavior and outcomes without (at least implicitly) employing culture.
>
> The choice before economists is not between employing culture and not employing culture. Instead, it is a choice between implicitly and explicitly employing culture.

Since Austrians understand that interpretation of the world is culturally contingent, Austrian economics provides a decent starting point for the study of culture's impact on economic activity.

Moreover, Austrian economics subscribes to the core precepts of methodological individualism and methodological subjectivism. And contemporary Austrians profit from the legacy of scholars like Mises, Hayek, and Buchanan. These intellectual benefactors have equipped Austrian economists with insights relating to the spontaneous emergence of social orders as well as the evolutionary nature of the rules and customs that direct our behavior. These scholars focus on the impact of time and place—that is, of context—and enlighten us about the fundamental constraints on our cognition.

Finally, compared to mainstream economists, Austrians do not bother with isolating the impact of culture, as they do not perceive it as an instrument or separate causal factor on its own.[4] Nor is Austrian economics so much concerned with generating testable hypotheses about culture as it is with thick ethnographic descriptions.[5] The Austrian economic sociology appears more conducive to the study of culture than other research programs in or outside of economics.

But are the Austrians getting it right? While the Austrians have overcome most of the major objections to cultural economics (see Jones 2006 for a discussion of these objections), many of their discussions about how culture affects decision-making appear fraught with problems.

Lavoie and Chamlee-Wright (this volume, Chapter 7: p. 159), for instance, utilize concepts like cultural resources and cultural capital.[6] Capital is seen as a set of endowments of resources, natural or manmade, that give persons, firms, or countries an edge in the production of one thing or another. Different cultures do seem to have different resources and different levels of human capital. However, capital conveys a sense of something that can be straightforwardly acquired, stocked, replaced, traded, restricted, denied, and even chosen. It is unclear that this applies to culture, especially since people are born into a cultural environment that is not of their choosing. Moreover, persons rarely purposely seek to accumulate culture.

Furthermore, the concept of comparative cultural advantage, which Lavoie and Chamlee-Wright (ibid.: p. 161) claim a culture '*must* have . . . no matter how poorly it scores in absolute checklists,' also appears reasonable. However, as Storr (this volume, Chapter 8: p. 196) explains, the idea of comparative cultural advantages also frustrates, because 'Cultures simply cannot be readily catalogued in terms of their absolute or relative *strengths* and *weaknesses*,' since, as stated before, 'we cannot satisfactorily talk in terms of cultural resources.' In sum, the major critiques of Austrian concepts of culture are: (1) imperfect correspondence with the concept of culture (as understood by anthropologists); and (2) loss of the essential criteria that encompass culture.

If we are going to attempt to find an analog in economics that is close to culture, there is good reason to adopt the one that is superior to the others. As Geertz (1973) puts it, 'Eclecticism is self-defeating not because there is only one direction in which it is useful to move, but because there are so many: it is necessary to choose.' Homing in on the contextual feature of culture, Storr (this volume, Chapter 8, p. 195) asserts:

> To my mind, *culture is much more like a constitution* . . . Remember, constitutions define the formal rules which govern a society. As Hayek (1960: p. 178) describes, a constitution assigns 'specific powers to different authorities,' while limiting 'their powers not only in regard to the subjects or the aims to be pursued but also with regard to the methods to be employed.' A constitution, thus, defines the rules of the games (for the referees and the players, the authorities and individual citizens) and, consequently, both imposes constraints and defines and delimits the set of opportunities that an individual can legitimately exploit. It, therefore, directs an individual away from certain types of activities and towards others, with constitutional rules serving as points of orientation. Culture operates in the same way.

Storr's book entitled *Enterprising Slaves and Master Pirates: Understanding Economic Life in the Bahamas* (2004) offers an analytical narrative that introduces and implicitly operationalizes the constitution notion in the above paragraph, but does not defend the 'constitution' analogy. I wish to expand Storr's concept to show why his analogy of culture as a constitution is appropriate or, at least, more appropriate than other concepts. Even if the concept of culture as constitution is imperfect, it more closely resembles what culture is by showing how it actually works. Although I did not discuss in detail the shortcomings of the alternative concepts, I intend for these shortcomings to be illuminated as I elaborate on the constitution analogy.

10.3 WHY IS CULTURE LIKE A CONSTITUTION?

The task of comparing culture to a constitution demands an adequate definition of both.

Culture is a context that enables a person to ascribe meaning to every aspect of his existence. Clifford Geertz (1973: p.89) defines culture as 'an historically transmitted pattern of meanings . . . a system of inherited conceptions . . . by means of which men communicate, perpetuate, and develop their knowledge about and attitudes toward life.' People ascribe meaning to every aspect of their environment, and these meanings transmit through generations in patterns. A culture is thus a pattern of meaning. Culture operates by systematically matching a people's ethos— 'the tone, character, and quality of their life, its moral and aesthetic style and mood'—to their worldview—'the picture they have of the way things in sheer actuality are, their most comprehensive ideas of order.' Cultural systems operate at many levels, including, for example, the national, ethnic, religious, ideological, musical, and academic level. Common references we make to 'French culture,' 'Arabic culture,' or 'hip-hop culture' testify to this aspect of cultural systems.

Brennan and Buchanan (1980: p. 5) define a constitution in fundamental terms as 'the set of rules, or social institutions, within which individuals operate and interact with one another.'[7] Brennan and Buchanan (ibid.) use the analogy of a game to explain what a constitution is: 'A game is described by its rules—its constitution. These rules establish the *framework* within which the playing of the game proceeds; they set boundaries on what activities are legitimate, as well as describing the objects of the same and how to determine who wins' (emphasis added). Brennan and Buchanan's definition clearly overlaps with Storr's description of a constitution as a set of rules that shape behavior. Likewise, Hayek (1960: p.178) defines the term 'constitution' with a political inflection:

A constitution which in such manner is to limit government must contain what in effect are substantive rules, besides provisions regulating the derivation of authority. It must lay down general principles which are to govern the acts of the appointed legislature. The idea of a constitution, therefore, involves not only the idea of hierarchy of authority or power but also that of a hierarchy of rules or laws, where those possessing a higher degree of generality and proceeding from a superior authority control the contents of the more specific laws that are passed by a delegated authority.

Hayek thus views a constitution as a structure of rules defining and delimiting the functions of a political entity. Within that structure, some rules are more general. Those types of rules determine the tone of the lesser, more specific rules.

Constitutions exist in different forms—codified, uncodified, formal (written), and unwritten. Typically, governmental constitutions consist of codified rules. That is, one single document contains the constitution of a nation. Constitutions also exist at different levels.[8] Despite differences in form, all constitutions constrain the actions of the central authority in order to enable a range of actions by the governed.

How are the two concepts similar? For some (Pejovich 2008), both constitutions and culture are essentially types of institutions.[9] But, even if we concede that culture represents the informal rules of the game (which I am not inclined to do), we still do not know which specific institutions culture is more or less like. The concept of culture is also too intricate—even esoteric—to treat too generally.[10] Therefore, saying culture is like any another institution limits us from saying all that we can about it.

Constitutions and cultures demonstrate the following similarities:

1. They are shared by multiple people, and hence represent public, collective phenomena.
2. They bind participants' decision-making but only generally. Indeed, they both place limits on acceptable decisions but just enough to allow for a wide range of possible actions by any person impacted by that constitution or culture.
3. They serve to transmit meaning. They prompt negative feelings in a person when that person's actions are interpreted to be out of bounds by others. They prompt positive feelings and positive feedback when that person's actions are interpreted to be within bounds.
4. They facilitate consistent and predictable interaction among different, separate individuals. They make life intelligible and navigable, and allow for interdependence among people.
5. They simultaneously act as markers or signals to outsiders, which becomes useful to these outsiders who might wish to interact with those people governed by the culture or constitution.

6. They represent a system, framework, order, or constellation of decision-making rules. Constitutions and cultures are simply not reducible to their component/constituent parts. They are not reducible to laws or rights (for constitutions) or meanings and conception (for cultures). Cultures and constitutions are not simply aggregates of these parts in the same way a building is not simply a pile of steel and wood. Instead, like a building, cultures and constitutions are very particular arrangements of their constituent parts, which stand in a particular relationship to one another. Cultures and constitutions represent internally consistent patterns of meanings and laws. Without this consistency, this structure, they are useless in their function of making life navigable.
7. Neither cultures nor constitutions are intentionally designed by any particular user. They are emergent and open to changes.
8. Neither is consciously consulted in decision-making, but they are nevertheless adopted and obeyed. They operate in the background of a person's life, structuring every decision the person might make. Since people have consciousness, they can still choose to act counter-culturally/counter-constitutionally. But robust cultures and constitution have mechanisms for dealing with disobedience.

Some of the above are worth further discussion. A constitution is a shared decision-making framework that emerges to facilitate sustained interaction and interdependence in the public sphere. Constitutions emerge to address problems that naturally arise between people who are motivated to interact with one another because their desires and values differ. When a shared framework for making decisions is adopted, public life becomes much more predictable for every person involved. For example, without constitutional limits on what presidents could do, citizens would be vulnerable to the vagaries of different presidential personalities. Constitutions mitigate much of the uncertainty inherent in dealing with other people. Thus, they emerge as a way to make public life navigable. Ideally, a constitution promotes cooperation and coordination among very different people.

Buchanan and Tullock ([1962] 1999: p. 4) clearly explain the importance of interpersonal differences for the development of constitutions:

> In a genuine sense, economic theory is also a theory of collective choice, and, as such, provides us with an explanation of how separate individual interests are reconciled through the mechanism of trade or exchange. Indeed, when individual interests are assumed to be identical, the main body of economic theory vanishes. If all men were equal in interest and in endowment, natural or artificial, there would be no organized economic activity to explain. Each

man would be a Crusoe. Economic theory thus explains why men co-operate through trade: They do because they are different.

In keeping with Buchanan's understanding of the purpose of constitutions, I want to emphasize two facts about human nature that drive the emergence of constitutions: (1) that people are separate and different from one another, and (2) that they have a natural propensity to exchange. Trade in the market happens because we are not alike. Buchanan reminds us that political exchange happens for the same reason. Political constitutions develop to promote exchange in an environment where people have different ideals regarding government and are highly motivated to prevent opportunism. Such constitutions will or can emerge where these people recognize the benefits of cooperating and desire to make some decisions collectively. Thus they develop a framework for collective decision-making, but only because they quickly realize they are separate and different.

Since my goal is to argue that cultures should be conceptualized like constitutions, I must again emphasize that people are naturally different and separate persons. Without these differences and this separateness, there would be no need for culture. Everyone would simply act the same, being of exactly the same mind. People would not need to pass down a system of shared meanings in such a world. They would naturally share total understanding of each other's actions and of the world. Interaction uncertainty would be nil.

In insisting that culture arises because people are different, I subtly depart from existing economic conceptions of culture. Culture, according to some economists, is best understood as a collection, a set, or an aggregation of values and attitudes prevalent among a population of people. But consider that, within the same culture, 50 percent of people may call beef a good, while 50 percent call beef a bad. Should we argue that those people actually represent two different cultures? To give another example, across cultures, two people may both enjoy eating beef. Should we claim that they actually belong to the same culture?

The answer to both questions can safely be no. We can respect people's own designations of cultural belonging once we realize that values can and will differ among people within a culture. Culture cannot be expressed as the array of all values in a population, which necessarily differ from person to person. The reason culture is like a constitution is because culture represents a shared *pattern* of meanings against which the actions of others can be interpreted. In the first culture, you might eat beef and I might not. But, as long as you and I both understand what the other is doing, why, and the meaning of the other's actions, we share a culture. This is how culture systematically facilitates interaction. People rely on culture precisely because they are separate individuals with multiple and conflicting aims and purposes. They require a mechanism to help them interpret each other's actions or else the resulting confusion would be crippling.

Constitutions are also not reducible to individual laws or legislations, and cannot be properly understood as an array of individual laws or legislations. As an analogy, a language is more than a collection of words or sounds. Many languages have the same words in them, spelling-wise. Sometimes the words have similar meanings, but many times they do not. The use of individual words or sounds, however, is a separate matter from the *system or framework*. The entire framework of rules within the language that allows a group of people to use it together is the defining characteristic of the language. And note that the language originates and evolves for the same reason as the constitution and culture: to facilitate interaction among *different* individuals.

Like constitutions, cultures provide general parameters or bounds but do not command what should happen. Culture is only a framework for interpreting or judging and, thus, responding to anything that could happen. Many laws are possible under a single constitution. Similarly, many customs and practices (some even competing with one another) are possible within a single culture. Moreover, different individuals living under the same constitution and from the same culture can act differently.

Additionally, constitutions include meta-rules for governance, which work in the background so we can economize on information. The constitution is the background against which every possible legislation is interpreted; it is the background against which every public action is deemed lawful or unlawful. In this way, it gives meaning to actions. Consider, for instance, the effect of a change in a particular law. If say an increase in the minimum wage leads to greater unemployment, the unemployment was triggered by the legislation change. But it was only possible to change the legislation because the constitution allowed it to change. This is how constitutions are not necessarily a separate causal factor but are the backdrop against which all other causal factors are interpreted and enabled.

Further, a constitution applies to a whole group for all activities generally. It is not just one rule or one set of rules that applies to some specific activity. It is a pattern of rules. This is why it is inaccurate to describe a constitution as a list or set of rules. A constitution cannot be defined by its individual parts, just as a culture cannot be defined by individual values.

Finally, constitutions represent an emergent spontaneous order. It is important to note here that I am not referring to the formal documents that are ratified and printed but the constitution as understood and internalized by citizens. Although it might make sense to describe the formal constitution as designed, the constitution as experienced emerges out of the actions and interpretations of countless legislators, judges, and citizens. Similarly, cultures are not designed but emerge out of the practices of cultural members.

10.4   EXAMPLES FROM THE BAHAMAS AND TRINIDAD

Storr (2004) gives an account of the economic history of the Bahamas, in order to explain the particular culture of entrepreneurship there. In Storr's narrative, there are two 'ideal types' of entrepreneurs. The first is the 'master pirate,' who is alert, but she is alert to *profiteering* opportunities (ibid.: p. 10) because of the Bahamas' experiences with piracy. According to Storr (ibid.: p. 106), the master pirate Bahamian entrepreneur is a 'trickster,' who is known for her cunning, has a 'narrow radius of trust,' and is rather impatient with a high discount rate. The other ideal type that Storr highlights is the 'enterprising slave,' who, because of Bahamians' previous experiences with slavery, has come to understand the value of hard work even when obstacles are evident. Both the piratical and the enterprising entrepreneurial types are evident in Bahamian culture. Storr explains how the culture has evolved so that entrepreneurship in the Bahamas is influenced by two distinct constitutions or, rather, a single cultural constitution that supports and encourages two very different kinds of entrepreneurship.

Master pirates may be said to be supported by the Bahamas' cultural constitution. Rum-smuggling and other forms of piracy were active from the seventeenth to the twentieth century in the Bahamas. Given that 'viable alternatives to piratical enterprises' were lacking (ibid.: p. 53), Bahamians learned over successive generations to be particularly alert to piratical opportunities. Comparing history to the present, Storr finds that the archetypal master pirate remains alert to opportunities for profiteering. Hence, her behavior is constrained by this aspect of her culture. Her culturally inherited behaviors manifest themselves in individual business through the 'nepotism and predominance of small, hierarchically organized family firms' (ibid.: p. 107), the relatively low national savings rates, and the underinvestment in capital-intensive industries that are all typical of the Bahamian entrepreneur. These are the entrepreneurial opportunities that she notices—other opportunities do not readily fall within her gaze, as her 'constitution' does not readily permit them. As Storr (ibid.: p. 108) describes, 'the master pirate is on the lookout for the quickest route to prosperity,' which explains why Bahamians 'tend to invest in restaurants, salons, clothing stores, and other retail or service oriented companies and not in large-scale manufacturing or commercial agriculture.' Thus, the master pirate's alertness to alternative business types seems to be switched off. The spheres of business activity that she is alert to have generally emerged from her historical experiences with piracy—her culture—and those general principles in her constitution that point her toward piratical activities.

Similarly, the narrative of the enterprising slaves shows that the Bahamas' cultural constitution also supports an entirely different kind of entrepreneurship. 'The peculiarity of Bahamian slavery,' Storr (ibid.: p. 99) contends, 'and the presence of a large population of free and materially well-to-do blacks in the Bahamas gave birth to the *enterprising slave* (an equally prominent figure in the economic story of the Bahamas).' During slavery, blacks were assigned to task groups where they were made responsible for particular chores (ibid.: p. 89). Additionally, they were allowed to work on their own plots of land when official work was completed for the day. As a last point, slaves in the Bahamas did not work on cash crops that could grow consistently in the colony, and so slave owners allowed slaves to grow their own crops and to participate in weekend markets. Storr argues that these experiences with slavery explain, at least in part, the attitudes adopted by the present Bahamian entrepreneur, who displays ingenuity and a 'strong work ethic' (ibid.: p. 109). Furthermore, Storr (ibid.: pp. 110–11) claims that this spirit of 'resourcefulness' and hard work in the face of difficulty is the reason why the Bahamian entrepreneur, 'whether he is a "peanut boy" or a straw vendor or a shopkeeper or a restaurateur, is a capable, creative creature.'

As with many ex-colonies in the Caribbean, history provided Trinidad and Tobago with a society of many ethnicities, whose distinct original cultures have by now fused into something manifestly 'Trinidadian.' In John and Storr (2013), we show, using the 2008 Continuous Sample Survey of Population sample, that the different ethnic groups exhibit distinct economic patterns. Africans have the lowest self-employment rate (16.7 percent), a rate which is not comparable to that of Indians or mixed persons, and especially not to Chinese, Syrians–Lebanese, and whites, the CSW group (35.5 percent). The CSW group has the highest self-employment rate. Furthermore, while Indians, Africans, and mixed persons have roughly the same distribution of educational attainment, the majority of Chinese, Syrians–Lebanese, and whites are university graduates/foreign educated or have attained secondary school completion. On the basis of monthly income, we see that, once again, Africans, Indians, and mixed persons have similar relatively normal distributions. CSW, on the other hand, are over-represented at high levels of income.

Chinese, Syrians–Lebanese and whites almost appear then to be living in a different country than the other ethnic groups given these patterns. Substantial differences exist between African and Indian economic performance too, particularly with the emergence of a new business class of Indian entrepreneurs. How does culture account for these differences? Selwyn Ryan and Lou Anne Barclay's book entitled *Sharks and Sardines: Blacks in Business in Trinidad and Tobago* (1992) tells a story about Afro-Trinidadians (and other ethnic groups) attempting to become entrepreneurs after independence in 1962. Ryan and Barclay's book is littered with possible explanations for the relatively poor performance of blacks by 1992. In the early 1900s, the planter class took deliberate steps to raise taxes and make land acquisition difficult for blacks (ibid.: p. 4), blacks depended on volatile crop prices for their success yet spent their incomes 'lavishly' (ibid.: p. 8), and blacks tended to borrow too much credit from white planters, who ended up seizing blacks assets when the blacks could not repay (ibid.: p. 9). Blacks also frequently migrated to urban areas in search of jobs and schools, thus forfeiting their lands to Indians, who preferred to work in rural areas (ibid.: p. 11).

Many of these behavioral patterns persisted amongst Afro-Trinidadians over time. Ryan and Barclay's (1992) survey (conducted in 1991) found that blacks continued to exhibit low educational attainment and run smaller size firms, with limited family involvement in their businesses and a decreased propensity to employ professional consultants to assist them (ibid.: p. 18). Black females preferred sole proprietorship (ibid.: p. 27), their parents were not supportive, and these women were inclined to pursue self-employment only out of economic hardship (ibid.: p. 115). One black businessman surveyed suggested that, since blacks had always been provided for as slaves, they did not develop ethics of struggle and survival like Indians (ibid.: p. 65). On the other hand, the bankers surveyed claimed that blacks especially exhibited irresponsibility and 'immorality' with their debt, and that the need to signal style and status was more important to the black culture than frugality (ibid.: p. 77). Bankers also claimed that blacks cared little about legal incorporation, management training, auditing, and getting insurance (ibid.: p. 78). All of this implies that blacks exhibited culturally derived patterns of economic and social behavior.

In terms of other ethnic groups, Ryan and Barclay claim that Indians, Chinese, and Syrians–Lebanese learned the virtues of hard work, thrift, and planning for the future from their ancestors, who saved greatly in preparation for the return to their homelands (ibid.: p. 145). Those three groups, like whites, also formed business associations to support their ethnic group's success in business. Brereton, in her book *Race Relations in Colonial Trinidad 1879–1900* (1979: p. 36), also mentioned that, among the white elite, 'a high value was placed on family connections,' and French

Creoles routinely inbred and intermarried to keep economic networks and kinship tight. The whites' cultural frame prevented them for the most part from marrying outside their group, but enabled them to stick closely together, and cultural transmission within the group was very powerful.

In contrast, blacks never saw themselves as transients—in their world-view, they always regarded themselves as Trinidadians and hence focused instead on 'education rather than business as a vehicle for social mobility' (Ryan and Barclay 1992: p. 146). Black parents discouraged their children from becoming businessmen, choosing instead to instill academic values so that their children could grow up and secure status from 'good' jobs, particularly in the public service. Brereton (1979: p. 85) also argues that Afro-Trinidadians were more likely to seek status by investing in education, not entrepreneurship—'school represented the main chance of mobility for the sons of black and coloured lower class and lower middle class' (ibid.: p. 85). Investing in school featured predominantly in the African cultural frame, which directed their behavior towards business activities.

As mentioned in the literature, Chinese, Syrian–Lebanese, and white Trinidadians established strong ties and kinship and fostered associations to help each other. Many of them are now successful entrepreneurs. These groups have developed different cultural constitutions that point them away from certain actions (public sector jobs) but encourage and enable them to follow others (business). This would explain why these groups economically outperform Africans, whose families tended not to support their business endeavors. The persistence of these patterns demonstrated by Ryan and Barclay (1992) and by my recent work implies the emergence and evolution of sub-cultures in Trinidad with particular cultural constitutions after independence in 1962.

10.5 CONCLUSION

The curious aspect of the 'culture matters' research program is that it removes from but, at the same time, adds to the frustration of those members of the economics profession who are inclined to offer development-enhancing strategies for economies. In the mainstream, some economists perceive culture as a roadblock or dismiss it as an obfuscating notion. Others focus on foreign aid or exporting institutions that have been successful in Western cultures to try to help countries formulate the right policy and institutional mixes in order to quicken their economic development. However, culture indirectly but fundamentally shapes economic outcomes to a large extent, and therefore to assume that much can be done in the way of implanting institutions, injecting financial capital, and increasing foreign direct investment and foreign aid is often misguided and disastrous, when these top-down impositions do not conform to underlying institutions or rules (Boettke 2001; Ostrom 2005).

In Austrian economics, the cultural economics research program attempts to document how the cultural systems and rules of the game for heterogeneous groups of people have originated and evolved, and how that evolution has taken place in response to changing physical, political, and economic conditions. Yet the Austrian formulation has some missing pieces, particularly in their current discussion over whether culture should be treated as capital or if it can be reduced to the rules of the game or a set of mental models.

We may reasonably think of culture as a constitution, since both emerge spontaneously, constrain behavior to generate predictable outcomes, and are rigid, but not static. Storr's conception is relatively novel but also still applicable in the real world. The constitution analogy gives us an opportunity to frame cultural economic analysis in a way that is perhaps more profitable than is currently being undertaken.

NOTES

1. Boettke (2001: p.11), on the ideal cultural theory, says: 'We need universal theory to understand, but we need uniqueness to whet our desire to understand *the other*. We are enough alike to learn from one another, but we are also different enough so as to have something to learn.'
2. Although Jackson (2009: p.194) submits that 'the best prospects lie with heterodoxy,' because the work of heterodox economists is 'historically specific, interpretive, and glad to have culture as a core concept' (ibid.: pp.200–201), he laments that heterodox economists 'proceed with their own research agendas and specialized literatures,' while 'the same ideas are expressed in different conceptual language, which leads to overlap and misunderstandings. Pluralism of ideas and methods is valuable, but duplicating terminology hinders the heterodox cause and reduces its ability to present coherent alternatives to orthodoxy.' Finding an adequate and agreed upon conception of culture plagues even the economic sociologists.
3. For an Austrian critique of sociological approaches, see Boettke and Storr (2002).
4. Geertz (1973: p.14) also rejects the concept of culture as an independent causal factor, insisting: 'Culture is not a power, something to which social events, behaviors, institutions, or processes can be causally attributed; it is a context . . . within which they can intelligibly . . . be described.' Lavoie and Chamlee-Wright (2000: p.8) also quote Mark Jacobs, saying: 'We now tend to view culture as a context rather than a force; a "tool kit" of habits, skills, and styles from which people construct strategies of action in everyday life, rather than a set of ultimate values.'
5. Guiso et al. (2006: p.23), for example, in full agreement with Avner Greif, remark, 'Without testable hypotheses, however, there is no role for culture in economics except perhaps as a selection mechanism among multiple equilibria.' Their article entitled 'Does Culture Affect Economic Outcomes?' proceeds by employing both religion and ethnicity as instrumental variables for culture. By the exclusion restriction, culture and economic development may affect each other, but, since religion and ethnicity do not

directly affect economic development, they isolate the impact of culture on development without worrying about reverse causality.

6. See Storr (2013: pp.49–54) for a critique of treating culture as capital.
7. Various definitions of the word 'constitution' include the terms 'rules,' 'laws,' 'conventions,' and 'principles.' For example, the *Political Dictionary* defines a constitution as 'the set of fundamental rules governing the politics of a nation or a subnational body.' 'In political theory,' the *Philosophy Dictionary* says, a constitution contains 'the written or unwritten laws or conventions that govern the powers and limits of political authority in the state.' Finally, the *Columbia Encyclopedia* defines a constitution as the 'fundamental principles of government in a nation, either implied in its laws, institutions, and customs, or embodied in one fundamental document or in several.'
8. Only in New Zealand, Israel, and the United Kingdom do uncodified governmental constitutions exist; one cannot pinpoint the constitution of the United Kingdom in a single document, since that constitution exists as a set of laws, statutes, and judicial decisions written down in various documents. As an example of level differences, Massachusetts has a state constitution, and the articles of incorporation of any firm function as a constitution.
9. 'Formal rules,' Pejovich (2008: p.11) remarks, 'are constitutions, statutes, common laws and other governmental regulations,' while institutionalized informal rules include 'traditions, customs, moral values, religious beliefs and all the other norms of behavior that . . . are transmitted from one generation to another via oral interpretation . . . Informal rules are also called culture, the old ethos.' Pejovich implicitly grants the correspondence between constitutions and culture *qua* meta-institutions. But no one readily compares cultures with constitutions *per se*.
10. Jackson (2009: p.15) agrees: 'The various meanings of culture testify to its subtlety and depth. Social sciences have complex, protean subject matter, and social or cultural theory should be correspondingly rich. As long as the meanings of culture do not get out of hand, its plurality can be beneficial and dissuade us from simplistic theorising.' Here, Jackson is referring to plurality in defining culture, not theorizing about it.

REFERENCES

Boettke, Peter J. (2001), 'Why Culture Matters,' in Peter J. Boettke (ed.), *Calculation and Coordination: Essays on Socialism and Transitional Political Economy*, London: Routledge, pp.248–65.

Boettke, Peter J. and Virgil Henry Storr (2002), 'Post-Classical Political Economy: Polity, Society and Economy in Weber, Mises and Hayek,' *American Journal of Economics and Sociology*, **61**(1), 161–91.

Brennan, Geoffrey and James M. Buchanan (1980), *The Power to Tax: Analytical Foundations of a Fiscal Constitution*, Indianapolis, IN: Liberty Fund.

Brereton, Bridget (1979), *Race Relations in Colonial Trinidad 1879–1900*, Cambridge: Cambridge University Press.

Buchanan, James M. and Gordon Tullock ([1962] 1999), *The Calculus of Consent: Logical Foundations of Constitutional Democracy*, Indianapolis, IN: Liberty Fund.

Geertz, Clifford (1973), *The Interpretation of Cultures*, New York: Basic Books.

Greif, Avner (1994), 'Cultural Beliefs and the Organization of Society: A Historical and Theoretical Reflection on Collectivist and Individualist Societies,' *Journal of Political Economy*, **102**(5), 912–50.

Guiso, Luigi, Paola Sapienza and Luigi Zingales (2006), 'Does Culture Affect Economic Outcomes?,' *Journal of Economic Perspectives*, **20**(2), 23–48.

Harper, David A. (2003), *Foundations of Entrepreneurship and Economic Development*, New York: Routledge.

Hayek, Friedrich A. (1960), *The Constitution of Liberty*, Chicago: University of Chicago Press.

Jackson, William A. (2009), *Economics, Culture and Social Theory*, Cheltenham, UK and Northampton, MA, USA: Edward Elgar Publishing.

John, Arielle and Virgil Henry Storr (2013), 'Ethnicity and Self-Employment in Trinidad and Tobago: An Empirical Assessment,' *International Journal of Entrepreneurship and Small Business*, **18**(2), 173–93.

Jones, Eric L. (2006), *Cultures Merging*, Princeton, NJ: Princeton University Press.

Lavoie, Don and Emily Chamlee-Wright (2000), *Culture and Enterprise*, New York: Routledge.

Ostrom, Elinor (2005), *Understanding Institutional Diversity*, Princeton, NJ: Princeton University Press.

Pejovich, Svetozar (2008), *Law, Informal Rules and Economic Performance: The Case for Common Law*, Cheltenham, UK and Northampton, MA, USA: Edward Elgar Publishing.

Ryan, Selwyn and Lou Anne Barclay (1992), *Sharks and Sardines: Blacks in Business in Trinidad and Tobago*, St. Augustine, Trinidad and Tobago: University of the West Indies.

Storr, Virgil Henry (2004), *Enterprising Slaves and Master Pirates: Understanding Economic Life in the Bahamas*, New York: Peter Lang.

Storr, Virgil Henry (2013), *Understanding the Culture of Markets*, New York: Routledge.

11. Weber's spirit of capitalism and the Bahamas' Junkanoo ethic*

Virgil Henry Storr

11.1 INTRODUCTION

There is a growing consensus among economists that culture impacts economic behavior. There isn't, however, a consensus about how we might create a culturally aware economics. There are at least two competing views, both claiming intellectual links to Max Weber. One camp insists that the focus should be on the ways in which culture promotes or impedes economic progress and political democratization in various contexts. They believe in the efficacy of thin descriptions of culture, checklist ethnographies and cultural scapegoating. For them, cultural factors operate as independent variables and, consequently, cultures can be 'scored' on the degree to which they have value systems that are favorable or resistant to economic development.

Lavoie and Chamlee-Wright (2000: p. 24) argue against 'the mechanistic forms of explanation' that the *checklist ethnographers* advocate and instead insist that the focus should be on 'the specific ways in which cultural meanings shape institutions and practices of societies' (also see Lavoie and Chamlee-Wright, this volume, Chapter 7). As they explain, 'the problem with only looking at culture as a specific causal factor is that it underestimates the pervasiveness of culture in all social causes' (Lavoie and Chamlee-Wright 2000: p. 23). They suggest that culture forms the backdrop against which all social activity takes place and is 'an aspect of every causal factor one might identify, not a separate causal factor of its own' (ibid.: p. 14). They, therefore, recommend that we 'engage in interpretive ethnographic inquiry . . . construct coherent historical narratives . . . mine archives for historical clues . . . interview the participants to economic processes . . . [and] grapple with ethical ambiguities of business decisions' rather than simply cataloguing cultural factors (ibid.: p. 24).

Both camps, however, cannot claim that their approach is the intellectual offspring of Weber's theory. Did Weber think of culture as a separate causal factor or as an aspect of all causal factors (like Lavoie and

Chamlee-Wright)? Did he prefer checklist ethnography or coherent histor-ical narratives? Did he seek to scapegoat culture or to understand cultural phenomena?[1] When we focus on the broad thrust of Weber's work, the answers are obvious. Indeed, Weber and Lavoie and Chamlee-Wright's projects are quite similar.

Weber, for instance, (like Lavoie and Chamlee-Wright) was commit-ted to *verstehen* and recognized that understanding the actions of an individual requires that we not only focus on the subjective meanings that she attaches to her acts but also place her acts 'in an intelligible and more inclusive context of meaning' (Weber 1947: p.95). 'Thus for science which is concerned with the subjective meaning of action,' Weber (ibid.) recognized, 'explanation requires a grasp of the complex of meaning in which an actual course of understandable action thus interpreted belongs.' For Weber, the 'complex of meaning' (read culture) in which all actions take place was not a separate causal factor but an aspect of all explainable events.

Similarly, Weber (like Lavoie and Chamlee-Wright) had a broad view of what counts for economic analysis. Weber emphasized that there were three categories of economic phenomena: (1) pure 'economic' phenomena, (2) 'economically relevant' phenomena, and (3) 'economically condi-tioned' phenomena. 'A phenomenon is "economic,"' Weber (1949: p.65) explains, 'only insofar as and *only* as long as our *interest* is exclusively focused on its constitutive significance in the material struggle for exist-ence.' Thus this category includes economic events like real estate acquisi-tions, wage payments and stock purchases, institutions like banks and the stock market 'which were *deliberately* created or used for economic ends' and constellations of norms, like the five day, forty hour work week, 'the economic aspect of which constitutes their primary cultural significance for us' (ibid.: p.64).[2]

The second category, 'economically relevant' phenomena, includes events and institutions 'which do not interest us, or at least do not pri-marily interest us with respect to their economic significance but which, however, under certain circumstances do acquire significance in this regard because they have consequences which are of interest from the economic point of view' (ibid.). 'Economically relevant' phenomena are occurrences which *affect* economic activity. Cultural phenomena like religious beliefs and family structures which impact economic events and motives fall within this category.

The final category, 'economically conditioned' phenomena, includes those occurrences that are '*not* "economic" in our sense' but which are *affected by* economic factors. Weber suggested that culture not only influences but is also influenced by economic factors; the base (factors of production) can also affect the superstructure (political beliefs and social phenomena), to borrow Marx's terminology.

In all fairness, however, the checklist ethnographers do not usually address themselves to Weber's *social economics* but instead they specifically address his *Protestant ethic*. They often, for instance, make positive references to Weber's ([1930] 1992) *The Protestant Ethic and the Spirit of Capitalism* without mentioning the controversy surrounding that particular book.[3] And they frequently describe themselves as the 'intellectual heirs' of the Max Weber who linked the rise of capitalism to Protestantism, not to, say, the Max Weber who wrote *Economy and Society* ([1921] 1978). Do they have a case?

Putting the claims of the *cultural scapegoaters* aside, Lavoie and Chamlee-Wright's interpretive approach to questions of culture and economy is much more consistent with not only the broad thrust of Weber's social economics but his effort in *The Protestant Ethic* as well.[4] *The Protestant Ethic* is not an enterprise in checklist ethnography. Instead, it is an earnest effort to consider the cultural significance of the *economic spirit* that Weber believed animated Western capitalism and the religious ethos that Weber held responsible for creating that spirit. Thus Weber (even in *The Protestant Ethic*) and Lavoie and Chamlee-Wright (in *Culture and Enterprise*) both deal with 'the specific ways in which cultural meanings shape institutions and practices of societies' (Lavoie and Chamlee-Wright 2000: p. 24).

Consequently, *The Protestant Ethic and the Spirit of Capitalism* (in spite of the controversy surrounding that book) can be held up as *a model for doing culturally aware economic analysis*, of the sort that Lavoie and Chamlee-Wright promote.[5] Although critics often ignore this nuance in Weber's thought, Weber knew full well that the 'spirit of capitalism' can come in many different flavors. As Weber ([1930] 1992: p. 48) concedes, 'it is by no means necessary to understand by the spirit of capitalism only what it will come to mean to *us* for the purposes of our analysis.' The Protestant ethic which, according to Weber, contributed to economic development in the West is only one of a variety of economic spirits that can be identified and studied. This becomes evident when we apply Weber's conception of the 'spirit of capitalism' to other contexts. For instance, consider the Bahamas, a context that has had economic success but whose enterprising spirit cannot be said to come from anything like the Protestant ethos that inspired economic progress in Europe. Indeed, the difference between the Bahamas and Europe, we shall see, is the difference between the colonized and the colonizer, between the periphery and the center, between the sons and daughters of capital and the progeny of capitalists. But, first, Weber's basic contentions in *The Protestant Ethic* should be considered.

11.2   REANIMATING THE SPIRIT OF CAPITALISM

The Protestant Ethic is typically (and somewhat crudely) understood as Weber's attempt to demonstrate how Protestantism (particularly Calvinism) *caused* modern capitalism. Weber, however, never had a deterministic view of the relationship between religion and economic activity. He, similarly, understood that religion and all other cultural phenomena could be both *economically relevant* and *economically conditioned*. Individuals, for Weber, were neither *over-socialized* nor *under-socialized*; they were 'not assumed to maximize within an institutionless vacuum, nor are they assumed to be merely puppets of structural force beyond their control' (Boettke and Storr 2002: p. 176).

Weber made at least four distinct claims in *The Protestant Ethic* that should be of interest to the student of culture and economy, none so boorish as what he's often accused of attempting to demonstrate in that controversial book. Weber, for instance, has taught us (amongst other things) that:

- capitalism and the spirit of capitalism both come in different flavors;
- the *spirit of modern capitalism* in the West can be described as a *worldly asceticism*;
- the particular ethos of modern capitalism and the attitudes toward work that emerge from Protestantism (particularly Puritanism) are (in many respects) identical; and
- the spirit of modern capitalism found a consistent ethical basis in Protestantism.

Weber argued that there are *capitalisms* and not just one brand of capitalism, and that each kind of capitalism is animated by a particular spirit, a particular ethos.[6] He understood that 'one may . . . rationalize life from fundamentally different basic points of view and in very different directions' (Weber [1930] 1992: p. 78). The version of capitalism that he discussed in *The Protestant Ethic* was meant as just one example; 'for all its fame, *The Protestant Ethic* is a fragment' (Giddens 1992: p. 14). As Weber ([1930] 1992: p. 48) conceded,

> The concept spirit of capitalism is here used in this specific sense, it is the spirit of modern capitalism. For that we are here dealing only with Western European and American capitalism . . . Capitalism existed in China, India, Babylon, in the classic world, and in the Middle Ages. But in all these cases, as we shall see, this particular ethos was lacking.

These different capitalisms had spirits that were quite different than the spirit that existed in modern Western capitalistic contexts. Weber went on to demonstrate this in his much longer and much more detailed studies of *The Religion of India* (1958) and *The Religion of China* (1964), which were 'intended as analyses of divergent modes of the rationalisation of culture, and as attempts to trace out the significance of such divergencies for socio-economic development' (Giddens 1992: p. 14).[7]

Others have made similar claims. Bird-David (1990), for instance, has argued that different societies organize their economic lives on the basis of different 'primary metaphors.' These metaphors impact how an individual in this or that context views her activities, her economic relationships and her environment. Similarly, North (1994: p. 362) recognized that 'ideas, ideologies, myths, dogmas, and prejudices matter,' and that economic life can differ significantly from context to context depending on the economic models at play there.

Modern capitalism in Western Europe and America, Weber ([1930] 1992: p. 53) asserted, was animated by a spirit of capitalism which combined the penchant for 'earning more and more money . . . with the strict avoidance of all spontaneous enjoyment of life.' Under the sway of this worldly asceticism, Weber (ibid.) states, 'Man is dominated by the making of money, by acquisition as the ultimate purpose of his life. Economic acquisition is no longer subordinated to man as the means for the satisfaction of his material needs.' This ethic, however, is 'completely devoid of any eudemonistic, not to say hedonistic, admixture' (ibid.). According to Weber, this 'peculiarly calculating sort of profit-seeking' (ibid.: p. 55), this 'attitude which seeks profit rationally and systematically' (ibid.: p. 64), transformed the accumulation of capital into a virtue.

Weber contrasted the spirit of capitalism that he found in the West with the spirit of *traditionalism* that he said it had to contend with and eventually overcome.[8] The quest for more and more money 'as a definite standard of life claiming ethical sanction,' that is, the rationalization of business practices (using capital, profit and loss accounting, and so on), was what distinguished the modern capitalistic enterprise and the spirit of modern capitalism from their predecessors. Traditionally, a man simply wished 'to live as he was accustomed to live and to earn as much as necessary for that purpose' (ibid.: p. 60). Moreover, 'in ancient times and in the Middle Ages,' Weber (ibid.: p. 56) explains, the acquisitive instinct, rather than earning social sanction let alone being regarded as a virtue (as it is now), 'would have been proscribed as the lowest sort of avarice and as an attitude entirely lacking in self-respect.'[9]

Weber claimed this new ethos which elevated work to the status of an ethical calling was (in many respects) identical to the attitude toward work that emerged out of Protestantism (particularly Puritanism); 'the essential elements of . . . the spirit of capitalism are the same as . . . the content of the Puritan worldly asceticism' (ibid.: p. 180). Calvin stressed that natural man is in a state of total depravity and can do nothing to change his condition. Some men, those who were called, however, were 'predestined unto life.' The elect have been transformed and, unlike 'those who are foreordained to everlasting death,' the saints are reoriented toward what is good. Weber argued that this doctrine created a serious challenge for Calvin's followers: 'The question, Am I one of the elect? must sooner or later have arisen for every believer' (ibid.: p. 110).[10] Puritan pastors, thus, taught two strategies for dealing with this difficulty. One held that it was the obligation of all believers to assume that they are among the elect. The other (of relevance to us) recommended 'intense worldly activity . . . as the most suitable means. It and it alone disperses religious doubts and gives the certainty of grace' (ibid.: p. 112).

For the saints, then, work—'hard, continuous bodily or mental labor'—became an ethical duty; 'Not leisure and enjoyment, but only activity serves to increase the glory of God, according to the definite manifestations of His will' (ibid.: p. 157). The 'systematic organization of labor and capital,' the division of labor, profit and loss accounting, the rationalization of economic life, in short the salient characteristics of the modern capitalistic enterprise, thus, achieve moral force. Similarly, the productive investment of capital is encouraged, while the consumption of luxuries is discouraged. The Puritans believe, Weber (ibid.: p. 160) explained, that

> for everyone without exception God's Providence has prepared a calling, which he should profess and in which he should labour. And this calling is not, as it was for the Lutheran, a fate to which he must submit and which he must make the best of, but God's commandment to the individual to work for the divine glory.

Weber saw much more than a causal link between the Puritan ethic and the spirit of capitalism; 'one of the fundamental elements of the *spirit of modern capitalism*, and not only of that but of all modern culture: rational conduct on the basis of the idea of calling, was born . . . from the spirit of Christian asceticism' (ibid.: p. 180).

According to Weber (ibid.: p. 170), 'it was in the ethic of ascetic Protestantism that [the spirit of capitalism] first found a consistent ethical foundation.' This had huge implications, in his view, for the development of modern capitalism. As he (ibid.: p. 172) explained,

> the religious valuation of restless, continuous, systematic work in a worldly calling, as the highest means to asceticism, and at the same time the surest and most evident proof of rebirth and genuine faith, must have been the most

powerful conceivable lever for the expansion of that attitude toward life which
we have . . . called the spirit of capitalism.

Although the religious foundations of this worldly asceticism have
withered away, when it was alive 'it did its part in building the tremendous
cosmos of the modern economic order' (ibid.: p. 181).[11]

To recap, Weber made (at least) four important claims in *The Protestant
Ethic*: (1) each kind of capitalism has a matching ethic that gives it life-
force, (2) a worldly asceticism animates capitalism in the West, (3) this
ethic is the same as the Protestant ethic, and (4) the Protestant ethic gave
birth to the spirit of modern capitalism. Although these claims are related
and appear more tightly woven together in *The Protestant Ethic* than in
this chapter, they are not wholly dependent on one another. They do not
operate as the legs of a stool or the pillars of a building. Indeed, only one
of Weber's claims in *The Protestant Ethic* is foundational: his notion that
in each context there is an economic spirit that impacts economic life. The
others can be removed without tipping over the stool or destroying the
temple.

Thus, Weber could have gotten the theology completely wrong, for
no Puritan ethic need exist to support his claim that something like the
worldly asceticism he identified is present in modern capitalist economies.
And the link that he tries to establish between the spirit of capitalism and
what he described as the Protestant ethic can, similarly, be seen as a useful
explanatory/expository move, even if nothing like that ethos could be
found in Protestantism. Indeed, using analogies to describe aspects of economic life is a common rhetorical device, and the market, for instance, has
variously been described as an auction, a social contract, a beauty contest
and a conversation.[12] Note, however, that, even if the images employed
in those analogies are unlike the real phenomena they are said to portray,
we can still benefit from the effort; the market may still be like what
the author (perhaps erroneously) calls a conversation even if real-world
conversations are nothing like the author's exposition.[13] In emphasizing
(even if mistakenly) those aspects of Protestantism that Weber thought
of as economically relevant, he taught us quite a bit about the spirit of
capitalism.

Likewise, it is possible to maintain that a spirit like the one that
Weber described both animated modern capitalism and flowed from
Protestantism without accepting that one gave birth to the other, or that
the relationship was in the direction that Weber implied. As Weber (ibid.:
p. 170) conceded, 'so many aspects of capitalism [extend] back into the
Middle Ages.' The Protestant ethic and the spirit of capitalism may, in
fact, be twin children of the same father; the same historical circumstances

may have given rise to both attitudes. Both the spirit of capitalism and the Protestant ethic could have a basis in, say, nationalism (see Greenfeld 2001) or ethnicity (see Chow 2002) or in some shared historical experience like slavery, colonialism or communist rule (see Storr and Colon, this volume, Chapter 15). Similarly, Protestantism might also have been economically conditioned. Again, as Weber ([1930] 1992: p. 183) confessed at the end of *The Protestant Ethic*, it is also 'necessary to investigate how Protestant Asceticism was in turn influenced in its development and its character by the totality of social conditions, especially economic.' Weber saw *The Protestant Ethic* as only a first step; it was meant to serve as a 'preparation' for a larger sociological work. He understood that the relationship between the Protestant ethic and the spirit of capitalism was never as strong or as one-sided as he had implied in that monograph.

Also, even if Weber misidentified the spirit of modern capitalism and no worldly asceticism can be found in modern capitalistic contexts, it is still possible to maintain that many different kinds of capitalism exist and that each is animated by a particular spirit. That I walk into the cathedral, look up at the roof, and mistake the decorative posts for support beams does not mean that there is not a ceiling overhead or that there is not something holding it up. Recall that, for Weber, the spirit of modern capitalism was just a particular rationalization of economic life. He realized, however, that 'one may . . . rationalize life from fundamentally different basic points of view and in very different directions' (ibid.: p. 78) and that 'it is by no means necessary to understand by the spirit of capitalism only what it will come to mean to *us* for the purposes of our analysis' (ibid.: p. 48).

Understanding the relationships between Weber's claims in *The Protestant Ethic and the Spirit of Capitalism* in this way allows us to view the many negative critiques of his work and the almost 100 years of controversy surrounding that book in their proper perspective. Tawney ([1937] 1953), for instance, has correctly called into question what he saw as Weber's central claim, specifically that Protestantism created the spirit of modern capitalism. As Tawney (cited in Greenfeld 2001: p. 18) stated,

> The 'capitalistic spirit' is as old as history, and was not, as has sometimes been said, the offspring of Puritanism . . . At first sight, no contrast could be more violent than that between the iron collectivism . . . the remorseless and violent rigours practiced in Calvin's Geneva and preached elsewhere . . . by his disciples, and the impatient rejection of all traditional restrictions on economic enterprise which was the temper of the English business world after the Civil War.

It is more likely, Tawney argued, that the Protestant ethic was economically conditioned. As Greenfeld (2001: p. 19) explains, 'To Tawney, it was economics that gave rise to 'the Protestant ethic,' picking out and cultivating one of several currents in the doctrine, and selecting, or in effect constructing, an appropriate ideology for economic development.'

Additionally, Marshall (1982: p. 67) has complained that

> Weber offers little or no independent evidence concerning the motives and worldview of either modern or medieval businessmen and labourers. His evidence concerning the former, apart from the 'provisional description' offered by Franklin's advice, is drawn exclusively from Protestant teaching. This, of course, suggests a . . . tautology whereby the Protestant ethic and the spirit of modern capitalism are defined in terms of each other.

Hamilton (1996) has levied a similar charge against Weber. According to Hamilton (ibid.: p. 60), Weber provided 'no serious evidence' for many of his claims about Calvinism, the doctrine of predestination and the duty to engage in 'intense worldly activity' that resulted from that doctrine. Weber should, therefore, signal his conclusions, in Hamilton's (ibid.: p. 63) opinion, 'as hypothetical options rather than confirmed findings.'

Similarly, there is some evidence that Weber got his theology wrong, that the theologians whom Weber employed were not representative of the broader thrust of Puritanism, that Weber presented a biased interpretation of Protestantism where he culled only those principles and themes that supported his thesis, and that Weber exaggerated the differences between Puritanism and other Protestant faiths and between Protestantism and Catholicism.[14] Stuijvenberg (cited in Hamilton 1996: p. 74), for instance, concluded after a review of Dutch Calvinist writings that 'There never was this theological hinge around which everything turns in Weber's thesis. On this point the theological base which Weber lays under his thesis has never existed.' Similarly, MacKinnon (1988) has argued that Weber exaggerated Calvinism's uniqueness; the Calvinist generally was not any more oriented to these worldly concerns than his Lutheran or Catholic counterparts. 'The Calvinist,' MacKinnon (ibid.: p. 170) states,

> was a semi-Pelagian tool of the divine will. Yet as God operates through man in the performance of good works, he also assists in the discernment of true saving faith . . . this coupling transports the ultimate value away from the mundane: the Reformed layman was both an other-worldly instrument and vessel of the Almighty. Hence Calvinism is not unique in its this-worldliness as Weber would have us believe. Accordingly its prevalence in England did not promote capitalist accumulation by directing the ultimate value to seek success in an ordinary calling, though it may have done so in other ways. Conversely, the continental dominance of Catholicism and Lutheranism did not retard capitalistic development in the way that Weber claims but, again, may have done so by other means.

If MacKinnon is correct and Calvinism retained the other-worldly focus of its counterparts (instead of encouraging an 'intense worldly activity'), then it would be impossible to maintain that either a specifically 'Protestant' ethic exists or that Protestantism had anything to do with the capitalistic spirit.

Admittedly, Weber's (so-called) central thesis—that the Protestant ethic gave rise to the spirit of modern capitalism—has been seriously damaged by these critiques. Notice, however, that, although Weber's assertions about the strength and the direction of the link between the Protestant ethic and the spirit of modern capitalism and between Protestantism and modern capitalism have been seriously challenged, his contention that capitalism comes in a variety of flavors and his claims about the importance of the capitalistic spirit to economic progress have escaped these critiques unscathed. Similarly, although Marshall was right that Weber did not prove his case, even Marshall conceded this is not the same thing as saying that Weber was wrong. A spirit like the one Weber called the Protestant ethic might very well exist.

Additionally, many of Weber's critics misunderstood his project at a fundamental level. To condemn him for failing to do what he did not set out to do and never believed that he accomplished is to implicitly distort his effort. Weber understood that *The Protestant Ethic* was a preliminary 'sketch' and, as such, was incomplete in many respects; he was only attempting to 'trace the fact and the direction of [the Protestant ethic's] influence . . . [on our economic] motives in one, though a very important point' (Weber [1930] 1992: p. 183). Weber knew that he was a long way from providing the kind of quantitative empirical evidence that Hamilton and Marshall have demanded.[15] What is more, Weber did not share Hamilton and Marshall's view of what counts as 'empirical' evidence and what would constitute proof.[16]

The critiques against Weber are not, then, devastating to his whole schema, as some have claimed. A large amount has survived, much of it quite useful for any discussion of culture and economy. Though Weber may have gone down the wrong path (the Protestant ethic may not have given birth to the spirit of modern capitalism), the way that he drove still exists as a model for conducting culturally aware economic analysis. His method is exactly what one would have to do if one wanted to get at the spirit that animates capitalism in a particular context: (a) identify and describe the particular spirit of capitalism and (b) sketch out its probable historical and cultural roots. This requires a degree of historical and cultural sophistication; checklists, crude ethnographies, and surface, thin descriptions will not work. It is informative that Weber began his view of the impact of religion where many of the crude cultural economists end—with an apparent link between some cultural phenomena and economic development. Thick descriptions, of the sort that Weber offered, are required. The best way to see the contribution that Weber made to the way we should see culture and economy is to employ his approach elsewhere. In the next section, Weber's theory will help identify the spirit that animates economic life in the Bahamas.

11.3   BAHAMAS' ECONOMIC SPIRIT[17]

I have argued elsewhere that two primary metaphors, two distinct capitalist spirits, color economic life in the Bahamas. One, call it a *spirit of rabby-ism*, promotes piracy over enterprise, celebrating 'the trickster (that is, the person who gets something for nothing) while ridiculing the hard worker' (Storr 2004: p. 56; see also Storr 2009). The essential elements of this spirit can be gleaned from even a cursory read of Bahamian folklore. Indeed, the Bahamas is a country that once had a vibrant storytelling tradition, and the preeminent figure in that orature was B' Rabbi, 'the archetypal hero-trickster character' (Kulii and Kulii 2001: p. 46; see also Glinton 1993). Often pitted against his friend and foil, the dimwitted B' Bouki, B' Rabbi has cunning, quick thinking and an ability to manipulate and deceive—in short, his wiles and his wits—as his chief assets, operating as both defensive and offensive weapons. As Glinton (1993: p. 59) describes, employing the kind of vivid imagery characteristic of Bahamian folktales,

> Nowhere else on earth could you ever find a pair like Bouki and Rabbi. The two friends resembled each other as little as a barracuda resembles a turbot. Rabbi was so sharp, he could teach a wasp a better way to sting. He could smell the odours from a pot and tell whether the cook had added goat peppers. Being a thief, Bouki's friend could look at a field of ripened corn and estimate to the last grain how much he could steal without getting caught. Bouki was different. On a good day, one and one could be three or four or, on a bad day, as many as sixteen.

This difference in cunning, as demonstrated in one B' Bouki and B' Rabbi tale after another, meant that B' Rabbi always got the better of his friend and, while Bouki 'could hardly find food for his family,' Rabbi's household 'looked plump and prosperous' (Turner 1998: p. 52). Not surprisingly then, B' Rabbi's cunning wins him a great deal of admiration, and his figure emerges out of the Bahamian tradition of *talking ol' story* as a model for 'entrepreneurship' in the Bahamas.

There is, however, another spirit of capitalism—a competing set of attitudes and proclivities which animates economic affairs in the Bahamas. A definite spirit of enterprise, which I call the Bahamas' Junkanoo ethic, also colors economic life in that nation of islands. As Glinton-Meicholas (1994: p. 64, emphasis added) explains, 'Bahamians have *an extraordinary yen and flair* for entrepreneurship and all the necessary optimism.' Much of the Bahamas' economic success has been based on the strength of tourism, its leading industry, and the 'yen and flair' of so many Bahamian entrepreneurs are oriented towards earning dollars from the 4 million tourists who pass through that country annually.[18] The porters in the airports or at the cruise ship docks, the neatly dressed taxicab drivers often wearing brightly colored neckties, the fruit vendors along the roadside, the straw market vendors who shower you with *hi, darlings* and *come here, sweeties* as you pass by their stalls, the hagglers who litter some of the beaches and offer to braid hair 'a dollar a plait' or to rent you jet skis or scooters are all in the business of chasing tourist dollars. Many are quite successful.[19] Although 'there was no going home for straw vendors' (Knowles 1998: p. 16) as one market woman put it, 'there are many [Bahamian professionals and parliamentarians] whose school and college fees were paid for by the hard work of their straw vending parents' (ibid.: p. 43). Similarly, the neatly dressed taxicab drivers who chauffeur tourists about the islands are 'among the most aggressively enterprising ... Bahamians' (Craton and Saunders 1998: p. 204) and—when willing to work 12 or 13 hours a day, six or seven days a week (as many of them do)—can earn middle-class incomes. Consequently, Bahamians, while celebrating B' Rabbi's penchant for getting something for nothing, have also come to appreciate that success is possible through hard work, even in the face of obstacles. What explains this enterprising spirit? What are some of its characteristics and how did it evolve? Which aspects of Bahamian culture promote and reinforce this spirit of capitalism? The spirit of enterprise that colors economic life in the Bahamas is very much like the ethos evident during the semi-annual Junkanoo festival.

Thousands of Bahamians and their visitors dance through downtown Nassau in the early morning hours of Boxing Day and New Year's Day dressed in colorful costumes made of crepe paper and cardboard, shaking cowbells, blowing whistles, bugles or (more recently) brass instruments, or beating out rhythms reminiscent of African rhythms on large drums made by stretching goat skin over metal barrels. Thousands more come to watch.[20] Junkanoo, however, is more than just a popular semi-annual cultural event. It is *the quintessential Bahamian cultural experience* and *is the essence of what it means to be a Bahamian*. Indeed, it has variously been described as the heartbeat, the pulse, the spirit and the soul of the Bahamian people. Craton and Saunders (ibid.: p. 488), for instance, have called Junkanoo 'the essential expression of Bahamian identity,' and

Ferguson (2000: p. 2) affirms that 'Junkanoo is tightly plaited into the Bahamian psyche.'

Consider, also, Ferguson's (ibid.: p. 30) moving description of the excitement that Junkanooers feel in the days leading up to a Junkanoo parade. As she reports,

> It was like coming home again after a long absence. And everyone coming through the door said the same thing: 'I come to get me!' They meant that they had come to get their costumes.
>
> 'I come to get me.' I felt a tinge stir in my chest. With those words, the door to our heritage had slowly opened again, and our forefathers were reaching out across the centuries, bequeathing a proud and indomitable heritage through the power of Junkanoo. There was in those of us called to carry on the tradition, the subconscious realization that Junkanoo was the place to keep our souls. The real 'me' would emerge in our costumes, the colours of our character, the design of our personalities, the pattern of our tastes, our pride, and our signature . . . in our costumes, we would feel complete.
>
> Within this crude, unfinished building [the Junkanoo 'shack' where the costumes are constructed] was the bridge to the past, confirmation of the proud story heard at my grandparents' knees. This ancient ritual that we had begun again was a gift from our ancestors, an annual renewal of self . . . we would now reverse the trend of History and joyously proclaim the triumph of the Bahamian spirit: parade it in the intricate steps of the dance, thunder it from the pounding of our drums, shout it in the sound of our cowbells.

So what kind of ethic evolves and what sort of habits and attitudes are developed during the preparation for the semi-annual celebrations? What are some of the beliefs embedded in that ritual? What does Junkanoo teach Bahamians about themselves and their abilities? Who is the 'me' that Ferguson and the other revelers came to get?

Certainly, the most important lesson that Bahamians learn from Junkanoo is *that success and hard work are inextricably linked.* Parades are not only about pretty costumes and powerful music. They are also highly contested competitions between as many as a dozen Junkanoo groups. The larger groups begin preparing for the next set of parades almost as soon as the results of the New Year's Day parade are announced. There are costumes to design and build. The cowbellers, the drummers and the choreographed dancers have to practice their music and their dance routines. By mid-year, when preparations are in full swing, Junkanooers are spending hours upon hours at the parks (where they hold practice) and in the shacks (the warehouses where Junkanoo costumes are built and housed). As Wood (1995: p. 19) reports, 'each year from June to the close of the New Year's Day parade Junkanooers direct their energies fully toward the production of costumes and music for the parade.' And, as Glinton-Meicholas (1994: p. 103) states, 'bands of men and women expend

astonishing energy and artistry, from about midyear to the last moments
of Christmas Day, designing and constructing costumes and huge, mobile
sculptures of cardboard and wire, all covered with finely fringed, brightly
coloured crepe paper.' Revelers know full well that their success in a given
parade has as much to do with the time they spend in the shacks back in
June as it has to do with their performances on Bay Street (downtown
Nassau) in December and January.[21]

Additionally, Junkanoo *recasts the relationship that Bahamians have
with the fruits of their labor.* Marx (1994: p. 59), you may recall, has
complained that, under capitalism, 'the object which labor produces, its
product, stands opposed to it as an *alien thing*, as a *power independent* of
the producer.' This objectification of labor's product, this estrangement
of workers from the things that they produce, has resulted, Marx asserts,
in laborers being alienated from the sensuous external world about them,
the act of production, themselves and other laborers. Junkanoo, however,
transforms the relationships that Bahamians have with the fruits of their
labor and teaches them that economic relationships are not necessarily alienating. Although Junkanoo is big business in the Bahamas (a lot
of money changes hands during the year-long preparation for the two
parades), none of the products of Junkanoo are alien to Junkanooers.
Rather than alienating Bahamians, Junkanoo, instead, brings them closer
to themselves and each other. The Junkanoo costume is a symbolic
expression of Bahamianness, and the Junkanoo beat is the heartbeat of
the Bahamian people; neither confronts Bahamians as 'hostile' or 'alien'
externalized objects. Recall that, when people come to pick up their completed costumes (that they, in some instances, have spent months building), they remark that they have 'come to get me' and that they believe that
'the real "me" would emerge in our costumes, the colours of our character,
the design of our personalities, the pattern of our tastes, our pride, and our
signature' (Ferguson 2000: p. 30).

Similarly, Junkanoo dissolves what Marx thought of as the 'inevitable'
class divisions, the 'necessary' separation that results under capitalism
between the rich and the poor, the entrepreneur and the wage earner,
the owners of capital and the exploited workers. According to Marx and
Engels (1998: p. 80), 'Society as a whole is more and more splitting up into
two great hostile camps, into two great classes directly facing each other—
bourgeoisie and proletariat.' In the shacks, however, the store owner is
often putting the final touches on her costume inches away from the sales
clerk who is finishing his. In the park, the doctor may be taking orders
from his band major, who by day works as a janitor. On Bay Street, the
main commercial thoroughfare in Nassau, the members of the so-called
bourgeoisie and the proletariat are dancing and beating their drums and

blowing their whistles and shaking their cowbells right next to each other. As Glinton-Meicholas (1994: p. 103) states, 'in this society, Junkanoo is the great leveler, where . . . the rich make merry with the poor, the magistrate dances with the felon he may later prosecute, and members of the Government make brief accord with parliamentarians in opposition.'[22]

Another significant lesson that Bahamians learn from Junkanoo is to trust in their own creativity. Junkanoo costumes have become large, elaborate, colorful creations where everything from insects, to fish and wildlife, to natural phenomena, to national and international figures, to world events have been constructed out of a combination of cardboard, metal wire, plastic and wood and are 'fringed' with strips of varied colored crepe paper 'pasted' in complex patterns like a kaleidoscope. Although aspects of Junkanoo are reminiscent of Trinidadian Carnival, Jamaican Jonkonnu and Belizean John Canoe celebrations, Junkanoo grew out of the Bahamas' particular cultural milieu. The Junkanoo artists, designers, engineers, builders and decorators are almost all Bahamian, and the sound of Junkanoo is unlike anything else. To be sure, the beat of Junkanoo has African roots. The eclectic mix of drums, cowbells, whistles, horns and brass instruments, however, is uniquely Bahamian.

The Junkanoo ethic, thus, describes a set of beliefs about work, success, class and creativity which are embedded in and find their clearest expression in Junkanoo. This ethic is very much like the Protestant ethic that Weber contends contributed to economic development in Europe (Storr 2004: p. 97): that is, with one major exception. Recall that Weber ([1930] 1992: p. 71) described the modern capitalist entrepreneur as someone who 'avoids ostentation and unnecessary expenditure, as well as conscious enjoyment of his power, and is embarrassed by the outward signs of the social recognition which he receives. His manner of life is . . . distinguished by a certain ascetic tendency.' There is nothing either ascetic or austere about Junkanoo or the ethos that accompanies it. There is an aspect of Junkanoo and, indeed, of Bahamian identity that is all about flashiness. Junkanooers delight in decorating their already elaborate costumes with feathers, and glitter, and pieces of colored glass and even battery powered Christmas tree lights. Similarly, Bahamians are not (to put it politely) a modest people. 'In this country,' as Glinton-Meicholas (1998: p. 40) states, 'you are not considered upwardly mobile unless you are demonstrably, visibly and even vulgarly so.' Bahamians do, however, believe that success through hard work is possible even in the face of obstacles. And, as mentioned earlier, this ethic is very much like the spirit of enterprise that informs economic life in the Bahamas.

Indeed, the lessons that arise during Junkanoo about the importance of creativity, the possibility of success through hard work, and the

fluidity of class divisions also color business life in the Bahamas. The 99¢
breakfast industry that emerged in the mid-1990s is a classic example. As
Glinton-Meicholas (ibid.: pp. 102–03) describes,

> In about 1996 or 1997, an enterprising Bahamian went one better in the usual
> mobile Bahamian restaurant theme. He or she had a miniscule clapboard
> cottage built on wheeled base. Transporting this structure daily to a vacant lot
> near a busy intersection, the owner opened shop advertising a 99¢ breakfast to
> instant success.
>
> Before you could say 'Kukamakai!' wave a magic wand or twinkle an eye, the
> 99¢ venture was imitated all over town, either in the form of other picturesque
> mobile restaurants or reflected in a new price-structure in existing and non-
> mobile take-away restaurants. The sign '99¢ breakfast' thus fastened unbreak-
> able tentacles on the psyche of Bahamians and became a symbol of the late
> 1990s.

Clearly evident in this account are the ingenuity and hard work that
often fuel Bahamian entrepreneurship: the small, colorfully decorated,
low cost, mobile structures that reminded (even successful) Bahamians of
the homes their grandparents would have lived in on the family islands or
in the poorer neighborhoods in Nassau; the simple pricing structure that
tapped into the Bahamian penchant for getting something for nothing;
and the subtle but significant variant on the familiar mobile Bahamian res-
taurant theme. Also, Bahamians of all walks, stripes and economic classes
frequented these mobile restaurants. Mixing here as they frequently do in
the Junkanoo shacks, the successful lawyer and the less wealthy gardener
both regularly queued up to buy corn beef and grits, tuna and grits, or
sardines and grits for just under a dollar.

That the Junkanoo ethic would be so similar to the spirit of enterprise
that exists in the Bahamas makes sense, since both evolved out of the same
unique cultural milieu. In the Bahamas, hundreds of thousands of blacks
lived and died as slaves. They lived under the constant threat and sting
of the whip. Their movements were severely circumscribed. Their ankles
and wrists were bound by cold, metal shackles. Slavery in the Bahamas,
however, was different than slavery in the other West Indian colonies.

While most countries in the West Indies were plantation hinterlands,
the plantation economy never really developed in the Bahamas. The 'thin,
scattered, and easily exhausted' soil in the Bahamas was never able to
sustain the production of sugar, the major commercial crop in the rest of
the West Indies during the slavery era (Craton and Saunders 1992: p. 196).
And, though cotton was tried and thrived in the Bahamas for a time, as
Johnson (1996: p. 28) notes, 'the commercial industry barely survived the
eighteenth century.' Bahamian slaves 'benefited' from this failure.

A common feature of slavery in the West Indies was to give slaves 'use rights' to a portion of the plantation to grow rations and to give them time in the evenings and on the weekends to tend to these provision plots. They were also allowed to sell whatever surplus crops they produced in weekend markets. The precipitate collapse of the cotton industry in the Bahamas, however, meant that 'Bahamian slaves ended up with a great deal of time to devote to their subsistence and market activities. And, as a result, they were able to both improve their standard of living and develop the skills and practices necessary to maintain a market economy' (Storr 2004: p. 88). Stated another way, a key factor in the development of the spirit of capitalism which thrives in the Bahamas is the opportunity that Bahamians had even during slavery to engage in entrepreneurial activities, to grow their own crops and to sell them in the market.

The Bahamian slave's experience with the *practice of self-hire* also contributed to the peculiarity of the system of slavery in the Bahamas and, undoubtedly, the spirit of capitalism which still thrives. Slave owners in the Bahamas, faced with the difficulty of keeping their slaves occupied, simply 'allowed their slaves to seek their own employment in return for a sum, mutually agreed upon, that was paid to them at regular intervals. By that arrangement, labor services that were due to the slave owners were commuted into cash payments' (Johnson 1996: p. 34). This was a mutually beneficial arrangement. The slave owners were able to get some kind of return for their investment, which was a difficult undertaking in the Bahamas. The slaves were able to achieve an unprecedented degree of freedom and economic success. As Johnson (ibid.: p. 36) informs, 'by the late 1790s, slaves on self-hire controlled important areas of the urban economy.' And, 'In 1799, for example, [there were complaints] that slave middlemen were monopolizing the supply of fruits, ground provisions, and vegetables in Nassau and forcing up prices' (ibid.). The practice of self-hire should, thus, be credited not only with easing the transition of blacks in the Bahamas from slavery to freedom (see Johnson 1996) but 'with laying the foundation for an economic system altogether different than the plantation economics found throughout the West Indies' (Storr 2004: p. 93). Through the self-hire system, Bahamian blacks gained valuable experiences negotiating wages and marketing their skills (in other words, manning a service economy) even when they were slaves.

It is easy to see how the spirit of enterprise which lives in the Bahamas, as well as Junkanoo and the Junkanoo ethic, could have emerged out of this particular history. Indeed, one of the most important formative features in the development of Junkanoo, as Craton and Saunders (1998: p. 488) argue, was 'the absence of a prolonged and intensive plantation economy and the consequent opportunities for the black majority to sustain and develop their own traditions.' Junkanoo, like the Bahamas' spirit of enterprise, has African roots and evolved out of the peculiar experiences of African slaves in the Bahamas. 'It grew out of the celebrations of enslaved people in the eighteenth and nineteenth centuries, when they had three days off at Christmas, and were relatively free during that period to pursue their own entertainment' (Wood 1995: p. 3). Originally, these events included slaves dressing up in costumes and parodying their white slave masters, safely ensconced behind masks. After emancipation, however, these festivals developed into the organized competitions that we see today, with large groups of revelers dancing down Bay Street to the sound of cowbells and goat skin drums in the costumes that they have spent almost a year designing and building. 'The uniqueness of the Bahamas' system of slavery should,' as I state elsewhere, 'be credited with cementing the belief that *enterprise could lead to economic success* into the Bahamian consciousness. And, with creating a festival (the semi-annual Junkanoo celebrations) and culture (the Junkanoo ethos) where hard work and creativity are celebrated' (Storr 2004: p. 93).

11.4 RETHINKING THE STUDY OF CULTURE AND ENTERPRISE

To return now to the question that we asked at the outset: does the approach advocated by Weber in his theoretical writings on social economics and modeled in his *The Protestant Ethic* suggest that we should be pursuing the thin descriptions of culture advocated by some of the more nuanced reading of culture and its impact on economic life advocated by others?

Ryle's (2009) discussion of *thick and thin descriptions* is quite instructive here. Ryle asks us to imagine two boys rapidly blinking their right eyes, one twitching involuntarily and the other winking at a co-conspirator.

> The two movements are, as movements, identical; from an I-am-a-camera, 'phenomenalistic' observation of them alone, one could not tell which was twitch and which was wink, or indeed whether both or either was twitch or wink. Yet the difference, however unphotographable, between a twitch and a wink is vast; as anyone unfortunate enough to have had the first taken for the second knows. (Geertz 1973: p. 6)

The wink has an intended recipient and is meant to convey a particular message. The twitch, on the other hand, has no intended recipient and no special meaning. Although a thin description does not distinguish between winks and twitches, a thick description reveals these differences; events are like 'piled-up structures of inference and implication' of which only the bottom layer is catered for by the thinnest descriptions (ibid.: p. 7).

Similarly, economic life in two contexts may seem quite similar. Both may be populated with businesses which are open during standard business hours, have plum locations, employ a handful of employees and have systems in place for controlling inventories, tracking sales and measuring profits. Both, however, need not be run by entrepreneurs who are influenced by the same ethic. Only by undertaking a *thick read* of both contexts can the differences between them be understood. A thick description of Junkanoo and the ethic that it inspires, for instance, teaches us a great deal about an important cultural phenomenon in the Bahamas and, because it evolved out of the same cultural context and is so similar to the spirit of capitalism that thrives there, it also teaches us a great deal about the attitudes that inform Bahamian entrepreneurs.

Economists, then, are faced with a choice. They can perform checklist ethnographies. They can ignore culture or at worst they can use culture as a scapegoat. They can give in to their methodological prejudices which make thin descriptions more comfortable. Or they can embrace a rich view of culture and act accordingly. They can believe, 'with Max Weber, that man is an animal suspended in webs of significance he himself has spun, [and they can] take culture to be those webs, and the analysis of it to be therefore not an experimental science in search of law but an interpretive one in search of meaning' (Geertz 1973: p. 5). Economists can use *The Protestant Ethic*, in spite of its flaws, as a model for telling culturally informed economic narratives.

NOTES

*   This chapter previously appeared in *Review of Austrian Economics*, Vol. **19**, No. 4 (2006). It is reprinted here (with minor edits) with the permission of the publisher.

   I would like to thank the participants of the 'Economic Development in Latin America and the Caribbean' panel as well as Nicola Virgill, Amy Shillady and an anonymous referee for helpful comments on earlier versions of this chapter. The standard disclaimer applies.
1.   The answers to these questions are important. If Weber's schema does not support the checklist ethnographers' project then (a) they cannot legitimately claim Weber as a forebear and (b) Weber's work would stand as another powerful (if implicit) indictment of their efforts.
2.   Note that, at its core, Weber's social economics was an institutional economics. He never asserted that people were *acontextual*.
3.   Even though several of Weber's arguments in that book have been savagely criticized, most notably by Samuelsson (1964), Viner (1978), Marshall (1982) and Hamilton (1996).
4.   This is true even though Lavoie and Chamlee-Wright (2000) make only one passing reference to *The Protestant Ethic*. They do, however, remind us there that

Similar cultural patterns conducive to economic growth may emerge from vastly different sources. For example, while Weber's Calvinist ethic of hard work came from the doctrine of predestination, the ethic of hard work among the industrious class of Quakers in the eighteenth and nineteenth centuries emerged from their conviction that salvation occurred through the good works done here on earth. (Ibid.: p. 69)

5. This echoes Berger (1991: p. 19), who has argued that, 'Among the various explanations of the rise of the modern world, that undertaken by Max Weber in his brilliant *The Protestant Ethic and the Spirit of Capitalism* may serve as the best available foil for a first attempt to identify the constitutive elements of the culture of modern entrepreneurship.'

6. Although the relationship between a particular kind of capitalism and the spirit that is said to animate it is 'not one of necessary interdependence,' it is more than just coincidental. As Weber ([1930] 1992: p. 64) explains (using the example of modern capitalism), 'the capitalistic form of an enterprise and the spirit in which it is run generally stand in some sort of adequate relationship to each other.' There can, of course, be modern capitalist enterprises with traditional characters and vice versa. But linking a particular ethos to a particular brand of capitalist enterprise is justified when 'that attitude of mind has on the one hand found its most suitable expression in [that type of] capitalistic enterprise, while on the other the enterprise has derived its most suitable motive force from the spirit of capitalism' (ibid.).

7. Note however that, although 'social action needs to be built on an ethical foundation,' the spirits that 'give motive force' to the various capitalisms need not be linked to religion; it is not necessary that they have a continued relationship with the religious views which gave them life, nor is it necessary, for that matter, that they have a basis in any religion (Greenfeld 2001: p. 16). As Weber also recognized, even in his epoch what he characterized as the Protestant ethic was losing its religious connections. 'Any relationship between religious beliefs and conduct is generally absent,' Weber ([1930] 1992: p. 70) confessed, 'and where any exists, at least in [the Germany of his day], it tends to be of the negative sort. The people filled with the spirit of capitalism to-day tend to be indifferent, if not hostile, to the Church.'

8. According to Weber ([1930] 1992: p. 56), 'The spirit of capitalism . . . had to light its way to supremacy against a whole world of hostile forces.'

9. As Weber ([1930] 1992: p. 56) asserts, 'It is, in fact, still regularly thus looked upon by all those social groups which are least involved in or adapted to modern capitalistic conditions.' It is not, however, the case that 'acquisitiveness' was unique to the modern capitalist epoch. Nor is it that the modern capitalist entrepreneur is any greedier than a Batswana trader or a merchant in ancient Greece. Indeed, not only is greed universal, but 'the universal reign of absolute unscrupulousness in the pursuit of selfish interests by the making of money has been a specific characteristic of precisely those countries whose bourgeois-capitalistic development, measured by Occidental standards, has remained backward' (ibid.: p. 57).

10. Calvin himself did not have this problem and did not think that it should be one:

He felt himself to be a chosen agent of the Lord, and was certain of his own salvation. Accordingly, to the question of how the individual can be certain of his own election, he has at bottom only the answer that we should be content with the knowledge that God has chosen and depend further only on that implicit trust in Christ which is the result of true faith. (Weber [1930] 1992: p. 110)

11. Influenced by this worldly asceticism, the successful entrepreneur is

filled with the conviction that Providence had shown him the road to profit not without particular intention. He walked it for the greater glory of God, whose blessing was unequivocally revealed in the multiplication of his profit and possessions. Above all, he could measure his worth not only before men but also before God by success in his occupation, as long as it was realized through legal means. (Weber [1921] 1978: p. 1124)

12. See McCloskey (1985) on the use of analogies as a rhetorical move in economics.
13. This is perhaps worth further consideration. If I contend that the market is like an open ended conversation where speech partners do not talk off of a script but instead engage in a play of questions and answers, and that consequently the conversation that ensues is not the result of either participant's intentions, then markets, for instance, could still be spontaneous orders—the result of human actions but not human design—even if all conversations in practice are really scripted dialogues. To be sure, the metaphor loses its rhetorical force, but the trip was not wasted; we do still learn something about markets.
14. This is not an uncontested point. Marshall (1982) has suggested that there is reason to believe that Weber got the theology right.
15. As Weber ([1930] 1992: p. 182) concluded in *The Protestant Ethic*,

> this brings us to the World of judgments of value and of faith, with which this purely historical discussion need not be burdened. The next task would be rather to show the significance of ascetic rationalism, which has only been touched in the foregoing sketch, for the content of practical social ethics, thus for the types of social organization and the functions of social groups from the conventicler to the State. Then its relations to humanistic rationalism, its ideals of life and cultural influence; further to the development of philosophical and scientific empiricism, to technical development and to spiritual ideals would have to be analysed. Then its historical development from the mediaeval beginnings of worldly asceticism to its dissolution into pure utilitarianism would have to be traced out through all the areas of ascetic religion. Only then could the quantitative cultural significance of ascetic Protestantism in its relation to the other plastic elements of modern culture be estimated.

16. Although Hamilton (1996: p. 60) conceded that Weber's 'conclusions—which are simultaneously comparative, historical, and social psychological—are, for all practical purposes, beyond the reach of historical and social scientific method,' he nonetheless criticized Weber for not supporting his conclusions.
17. This section is an expansion of an argument that I introduced in *Enterprising Slaves and Master Pirates* (2004).
18. Thanks to tourism, the Bahamas is the richest country in the West Indies. In the Bahamas, GDP per capita (in constant 1995 US dollars) was just under $14 000 in 2000. In Antigua, the next richest, GDP per capita was $8876 (World Bank, 2002 World Development Indicators).
19. Even though it is sometimes difficult in the Bahamas to gain access to capital and credit for business ventures.
20. They also come to dance. 'Junkanoo is a phenomenon,' as Wood (1995: p. 34) states, 'that demands the full involvement of those who are either witnessing or participating in the event.' As Wood (ibid.: p. 49) continues,

> In the case of Junkanoo . . . the spectators of the parade co-perform by dancing, chanting and shouting, and thus enter the inner flux of the music while also 'execut[ing] activities gearing into the outer world and this occurring in spatialized outer time' (Schütz 1964: p. 175). The nature of the Junkanoo event is such that spectators share emotionally, verbally and kinesically in the performance.

21. As a corollary to this, Junkanoo *teaches Bahamians to value competition*. They recognize that the costumes are more beautiful, the music is more intense and the camaraderie between group members is more pronounced because, in addition to whatever else it is, Junkanoo is also a 'battleground.'
22. This is certainly true of Junkanoo in the post-Independence, post-Majority Rule era. Before that time, however, Junkanoo was not an arena where class divisions melted but

was instead an opportunity for the oppressed majority population to gain a temporary, if only symbolic, victory in their struggle to overcome oppression. As Wood (1995: p. 6) points out,

> By the 1930s, Bay Street was under the control of White-minority merchants. Because the Black majority did not hold economic or political power . . . Bay Street became the symbol of White economic and political repression. At Christmas, people would stream onto Bay Street from the Black residential areas known as *over-the-hill* . . . Separated from Bay Street by a low hill, the over-the-hill area became the heart and soul of pre-Independence Black Bahamian culture. Consequently, the presence of Black Bahamians on Bay Street for the Junkanoo parades signified the taking over by Blacks of the White domain.

REFERENCES

Berger, B. (1991), 'The Culture of Modern Entrepreneurship,' in B. Berger (ed.), *The Culture of Entrepreneurship*, San Francisco: ICS Press, pp. 13–32.

Bird-David, N. (1990), 'The Giving Environment: Another Perspective on the Economic System of Gatherer-Hunters,' *Current Anthropology*, 31(2), 189–96.

Boettke, Peter J. and Virgil Henry Storr (2002), 'Post-Classical Political Economy: Polity, Society and Economy in Weber, Mises and Hayek,' *American Journal of Economics and Sociology*, 61(1), 161–91.

Chow, Rey (2002), *The Protestant Ethnic and the Spirit of Capitalism*, New York: Columbia University Press.

Craton, M. and G. Saunders (1992), *Islanders in the Stream: A History of the Bahamian People*, Vol. 1: *From Aboriginal Times to the End of Slavery*, Athens: University of Georgia Press.

Craton, M. and G. Saunders (1998), *Islanders in the Stream: A History of the Bahamian People*, Vol. 2: *From the Ending of Slavery to the Twenty-First Century*, Athens: University of Georgia Press.

Ferguson, A. (2000), *I Come to Get Me! An Inside Look at the Junkanoo Festival*, Nassau, Bahamas: Doongalik Studios.

Geertz, C. (1973), *The Interpretation of Cultures: Selected Essays*, New York: Basic Books.

Giddens, A. (1992), 'Introduction,' in M. Weber, *The Protestant Ethic and the Spirit of Capitalism*, T. Parsons (trans.), London: Routledge.

Glinton, P. (1993), *An Evening in Guanima: A Treasury of Folktales from the Bahamas*, Nassau, Bahamas: Guanima Press.

Glinton-Meicholas, P. (1994), *How to Be a True-True Bahamian: A Hilarious Look at Life in the Bahamas*, Nassau, Bahamas: Guanima Press.

Glinton-Meicholas, P. (1998), *The 99¢ Breakfast*, Nassau, Bahamas: Guanima Press.

Greenfeld, Liah (2001), *The Spirit of Capitalism: Nationalism and Economic Growth*, Cambridge, MA: Harvard University Press.

Hamilton, Richard (1996), *The Social Misconstruction of Reality: Validity and Verification in the Scholarly Community*, New Haven, CT: Yale University Press.

Johnson, H. (1996), *The Bahamas from Slavery to Servitude: 1783–1933*, Gainesville: University Press of Florida.

Knowles, K. (1998), *Straw! A Short Account of the Straw Industry in the Bahamas*, Nassau, Bahamas: Media Publishing.

Kulii, E.A. and B.T. Kulii (2001), 'Brer Rabbit,' in W.L. Andrews, F.S. Foster and T. Harris (eds.), *The Concise Oxford Companion to African American Literature*, New York: Oxford University Press, pp. 46–7.

Lavoie, D. and E. Chamlee-Wright (2000), *Culture and Enterprise*, New York: Routledge.

MacKinnon, M. (1988), 'Part I: Calvinism and the Infallible Assurance of Grace: The Weber Thesis Reconsidered,' *British Journal of Sociology*, **39**(2), 143–77.

Marshall, G. (1982), *In Search of the Spirit of Capitalism: An Essay on Max Weber's Protestant Ethic Thesis*, New York: Columbia University Press.

Marx, K. (1994), *Selected Writings*, Indianapolis, IN: Hackett Publishing.

Marx, K. and F. Engels (1998), *The Communist Manifesto*, London: Verso.

McCloskey, D.N. (1985), *The Rhetoric of Economics*, Madison: University of Wisconsin Press.

North, D.C. (1994), 'Economic Performance through Time,' *American Economic Review*, **84**(3), 359–68.

Ryle, G. (2009), 'The Thinking of Thoughts: What Is 'Le Penseur' Doing?,' in *Collected Essays 1929–1968*, Vol. 2, New York: Routledge.

Samuelsson, Kurt (1964), *Religion and Economic Action: A Critique of Max Weber*, New York: Harper & Row.

Schütz, A. (1976), *Collected Papers: Studies in Social Theory*, A. Brodersen (ed.), The Hague: Martinus Nijhoff.

Storr, Virgil Henry (2004), *Enterprising Slaves and Master Pirates: Understanding Economic Life in the Bahamas*, New York: Peter Lang.

Storr, Virgil Henry (2009), ''B' Rabby as a True-True Bahamian: Rabbyism as Bahamian Ethos and Worldview in the Bahamas' Folk Tradition and the Works of Strachan and Glinton-Meicholas,' *Journal of Caribbean Literatures*, **6**(1), 125–46.

Tawney, R.H. ([1937] 1953), 'A Note on Christianity and the Social Order,' in *The Attack and Other Papers*, London: George Allen & Unwin.

Turner, T. (1998), *Once below a Time: Bahamian Stories*, London: Macmillan Education.

Viner, J. (1978), *Religious Thought and Economic Society: Four Chapters of an Unfinished Work*, J. Melitz and D. Winch (eds.), Durham, NC: Duke University Press.

Weber, M. (1947), *The Theory of Social and Economic Organization*, New York: Free Press.

Weber, M. (1949), *The Methodology of the Social Sciences*, New York: Free Press.

Weber, M. ([1921] 1978), *Economy and Society: An Outline of Interpretive Sociology*, 2 volumes, Berkeley: University of California Press.

Weber, M. ([1930] 1992), *The Protestant Ethic and the Spirit of Capitalism*, London: Routledge.

Wood, V.N.M. (1995), 'Rushin' Hard and Runnin' Hot: Experiencing the Music of the Junkanoo Parade in Nassau, Bahamas,' unpublished dissertation.

PART II

Understanding economic life by using culture

12. Pastor response in post-Katrina New Orleans: navigating the cultural economic landscape

Emily Chamlee-Wright

12.1 INTRODUCTION

The chapters presented early on in this volume sketch out what I have elsewhere described as a program of study on 'cultural economy' (Chamlee-Wright 2006, 2010).[1] Whereas political economy of development seeks to reveal the systemic connections between economic change and the political-institutional environment, a cultural economy of development seeks to reveal the systemic connections between economic change and the socio-cultural environment. Cultural economy recognizes that entrepreneurs—whether economic, political or social entrepreneurs—are situated within a particular cultural context and are therefore enabled and constrained by it (Chamlee-Wright 1997; Lavoie, this volume, Chapter 3; Lavoie and Chamlee-Wright, this volume, Chapter 7). Cultural economy also recognizes that entrepreneurs see the world and identify opportunities through a culturally defined lens and draw upon cultural narratives to make sense of the world and carve out strategies for effective action (Storr 2004). Further, how economic, political and social entrepreneurs navigate and deploy resources embedded within networks of family, neighborhood, civic, religious and professional life is a key element of cultural economic inquiry (Chamlee-Wright 2010; Chamlee-Wright and Storr 2015). What strategies are likely to be seen as possible has a great deal to do with the shared mental paradigms (or collective narratives) prevalent within the social context. Which strategies are selected, and which are likely to meet with success, has a great deal to do with the resources—including socially embedded resources—an individual can draw upon.

These insights apply to a variety of development contexts. Economic life in the urban Ghanaian context, for example, is fundamentally shaped by gender dynamics and, correspondingly, by the resources that are available and unavailable to the typical female entrepreneur operating in the informal sector (Chamlee-Wright 1997, this volume, Chapter 16). Yet culture shapes post-industrialized economic life just as it shapes economic life in the developing world. Gender dynamics, for example, while playing out in vastly different ways, are just as important in shaping contemporary western market environments as they are in informal markets in sub-Saharan Africa.

Further, the insights that emerge from a research program on cultural economy are also essential to understanding redevelopment in the aftermath of catastrophic disaster. Though the standard economic development literature does not see it as such, a post-disaster environment, even one situated in the industrialized world, is in many ways similar to and presents many of the same challenges we identify in developing world contexts. A catastrophic disaster has devastating wealth effects, to be sure. Even more significantly, the social systems that make up what Hayek described as the 'extended order' are swept away, at least in the immediate aftermath and location of disaster. Businesses that provided access to goods and services one requires—in both ordinary times and the extraordinary circumstances a post-disaster setting creates—are no longer functioning. Schools and daycare facilities that help parents cope with childcare needs are closed. Workplaces that provide families with income are no longer functioning. While it is true that, unlike the case in a developing world context, individuals caught in the throes of disaster in the developed world can expect these social systems to return eventually, catastrophic disaster presents overwhelming logistical hurdles at the same time that it removes the common mechanisms for leading functional lives in a complex social context. Further, post-disaster policy can wreak havoc on the rules and institutions usually considered the cornerstone of smooth social coordination and robust economic development. In the aftermath of disaster, for example, policymakers find it tempting to suspend or undermine the integrity of basic rules such as contract enforcement and property rights (Chamlee-Wright 2007). Thus, many of the institutional problems that plague developing world contexts can be present (even if in more isolated form) in a post-disaster context.

Most important for the present discussion, the entrepreneurial role is just as critical to the post-disaster context as it is in the context of the developing world. Always alert to profit opportunities that radical change can create, market entrepreneurs identify shifting needs and efficient ways of meeting those needs. By making basic existence in a post-disaster environment possible, for example by providing access to clean water, food, tools and construction materials, such responses can make the pivotal difference as to whether the early stages of rebuilding can commence. Similarly, social entrepreneurs survey the post-disaster context for opportunities to meet the radically changed needs of people impacted by disaster. As Storr and I argue elsewhere, social entrepreneurs have a particularly important developmental role to play in meeting the immediate needs of disaster victims that the market and government agencies cannot easily or quickly address, overcoming the collective action problem a post-disaster setting presents by smoothing the path for residents and business owners to return early on and advocating for communities in the policy arena (Chamlee-Wright and Storr 2010a). We argue further that the political economy context in which social entrepreneurs operate can have significant influence on their success in fostering robust recovery and redevelopment.

In the present chapter, I argue that the cultural economy context also shapes the role social entrepreneurs play in the post-disaster redevelopment effort. Below, I examine the role that New Orleans church pastors played as social entrepreneurs following Hurricane Katrina. The analysis presented here is part of a multi-year study of the political, economic and social factors affecting disaster preparedness, response and long-term recovery (see Boettke et al. 2007). A principal theme of this project is how residents and other stakeholders leverage socially embedded resources in their redevelopment efforts (Chamlee-Wright and Storr 2009a, 2009b, 2010b; Chamlee-Wright 2010). Much of the empirical work conducted for the project took the form of in-depth qualitative interviews. The research team conducted 301 qualitative interviews in the greater New Orleans area and in Hancock and Harrison counties, Mississippi, and interviews and/or surveys of 103 New Orleans evacuees who were still living in Houston, Texas three years after the storm. The New Orleans field data collected between February 2006 and August 2008 include interviews with 22 church pastors from Central City, Gentilly, the Upper and Lower Ninth Wards, New Orleans East, Broadmoor and Lakeview neighborhoods and St. Bernard Parish, a community that lies to the east of the Lower Ninth Ward.

Building from these data, I argue that New Orleans pastors were both enabled and constrained by the cultural context in which they operated and that the narratives from which they drew shaped their strategies for action. Further, I describe how New Orleans pastors navigated, deployed and in some cases manipulated socially embedded resources in order to devise and carry out strategies for post-disaster recovery. This description of entrepreneurial action illustrates the ways in which cultural context, and one's position within it, both enables and constrains creative response to a development challenge. Further, the cases described below illustrate the ways in which social entrepreneurs understand and respond to complex development challenges by calling upon narratives that reflect the socio-cultural context in which they operate. Finally, by examining pastor response in the wake of Hurricane Katrina, this chapter examines the role that social entrepreneurs can play in reconfiguring socially embedded resources as they pursue their development strategies.

12.2 CULTURAL ECONOMY IN DEVELOPMENT AND REDEVELOPMENT

In Chapter 3 of this volume Lavoie emphasizes the importance entrepreneurial discovery and action have for understanding the process of economic development. But, he argues, even the best theories of entrepreneurship—and here he was speaking primarily of Israel Kirzner's work on entrepreneurial discovery as the driving force of the market—have tended to ignore the role that cultural context and cultural perspective have in shaping the entrepreneurial process. Culture, in the sense in which Lavoie is using the term, is the 'complex of meanings that allows us to comprehend human action; it is the background context that renders purposeful action intelligible. Culture is the language in which past events are interpreted, future circumstances are anticipated, and plans of action are formulated' (Lavoie, this volume, Chapter 3: p.49). Thus, entrepreneurial discovery is not just a matter of 'finding' a profit opportunity, but a matter of interpreting the context in which the entrepreneur is operating and creatively responding to it. As Lavoie argues, identifying and seizing entrepreneurial opportunities is not like noticing $20 bills on the beach that others have missed. Rather, entrepreneurial discovery is more akin to reading and interpreting a complex text.

The interpretive dimension of entrepreneurial discovery is a principal source of the non-deterministic and ceaseless nature of the entrepreneurial process. Once an entrepreneurial discovery has been made, the discoverer will forever see the world differently (Kirzner 1979; Lavoie, this volume, Chapter 3). And, once the world is seen differently, this new perspective readies the entrepreneur's mind—directs the entrepreneur's alertness—toward certain kinds of profit opportunities (and away from others). A complex social order, then, will necessarily generate multiple and competing interpretive lenses, minds readied in various ways, alertness pointed in various directions and perspectives shaped by diverse experience and nuanced learning. All are seeing the same world, but the diversity of perspectives and the various directions in which the entrepreneurial gaze is focused lead to diverse and often path-dependent discovery.

Not only does the interpretive process generate multiple, sometimes overlapping, often competing entrepreneurial perspectives, but a complex and extended social order means that the 'text' the entrepreneur must 'read' is by necessity a complicated one. In such a complex environment the relevant meanings to be drawn out will not, for the most part, be obvious. Successful discovery requires the entrepreneur to develop a particularly directed gaze that allows the entrepreneur to 'read the minds' of unknown others far removed from the entrepreneur's immediate context. The best interpretive readings draw upon shared cultural meanings that bridge the distance between the entrepreneur and the multitude of others the entrepreneur seeks to reach.

In my work on urban female entrepreneurship in sub-Saharan Africa, I develop the theme of cultural embeddedness of entrepreneurial discovery further (Chamlee-Wright 1997, 2002). Cultural knowledge, I point out, is not singular within any given cultural context, but is instead dispersed across individuals in overlapping webs of significance. Social actors occupy a particular space within a given cultural context in which their networks, sphere of influence and cultural lenses intersect. One's position within a culture pre-directs the gaze of the entrepreneur and positions him or her in ways that both enable and constrain opportunities for particular kinds of discovery.

Storr (2004) develops the themes sketched out by Lavoie still further by placing particular emphasis on collective narratives. Storr argues that collective narratives shape entrepreneurial behavior and the course of economic development. He argues, for example, that Bahamian narratives that relate to the country's particular histories of slavery and piracy have shaped entrepreneurial patterns manifest in the contemporary context.

Much of the emphasis in this period of cultural economy work was placed on how the particular perspectives that economic, political and social entrepreneurs held shape their strategies and decisions. Given the difficulty of overcoming the economics discipline's bias favoring the notion of the 'perspective-less perspective,' this emphasis was necessary. But cultural embeddedness affects more than just the interior life of entrepreneurs and the opportunities they notice. As Storr's (2004) work emphasizes, cultural embeddedness also shapes the very world in which entrepreneurs operate and the resources they have (and do not have) available to them to deploy. This is true of financial and physical resources, and it is true of resources that are embedded within the social context. The complex and heterogeneous nature of socially embedded resources provides a context in which entrepreneurs emerge and operate (Chamlee-Wright 2008a). And frequently it is socially embedded resources that the entrepreneur must navigate, deploy and manipulate if his or her entrepreneurial plans are to succeed (Chamlee-Wright and Myers 2008).

Below, I examine the cultural context in which New Orleans pastors operated, in particular the ways in which their location within the cultural

context both constrained and enabled their ability to maneuver in the wake
of disaster. Further, I describe two sets of narratives upon which pastors
drew that framed their work as social entrepreneurs in the redevelopment
process, namely narratives of history and place that connected church
with 'home,' and narratives that recast Hurricane Katrina as a 'blessing.'
Finally, I examine the ways in which pastors navigated, deployed and in
some cases manipulated socially embedded resources within their local
networks in their redevelopment efforts.

12.3   THE CULTURAL POSITION OF NEW ORLEANS
CHURCHES AND PASTORS

The cultural space that New Orleans church pastors hold affords opportunity and imposes limitation in their role as social entrepreneurs. Church
life, particularly church life within the African American community, has
been central to the social and political history of New Orleans and therefore represents an important source of legitimacy and authority (Nelson
and Nelson 1971; Lincoln and Mamiya 1990; Pinn 2002). Further, church-
based social networks represent an important source of social capital in
what is one of the poorest cities in the United States (Brown and Brown
2003; Barnes 2005; McKenzie 2008). Church networks can strengthen
bonds within extended families by regularly drawing them back together,
and facilitate connections beyond family by placing individuals who are
otherwise socially and geographically distanced from one another into
closer proximity. These bonds can be critical sources of support preparing
for and in the aftermath of disaster (Beggs et al. 1996a, 1996b; Hurlbert
et al. 2001; Aldrich 2012). Pastors enjoy high status and can carry a good
deal of authority among congregants and residents in neighborhoods
that surround the church. And, following Hurricane Katrina, research
confirms that church-based social capital has been a source of individual
and community resilience and recovery (Jackson 2006). As Storr and I
argue elsewhere, the authority members of the Mary Queen of Vietnam
(MQVN) Catholic Church community ascribed to their pastor, Father
Vien, meant that his calls to return and begin the rebuilding process were
heeded, in most cases, without question (Chamlee-Wright and Storr
2009a; Chamlee-Wright 2010).

The centrality of church life in the New Orleans context clearly has
an enabling role to play as pastors have engaged in the redevelopment
effort. The social space that pastors occupy allows them a particular kind
of access to resources important to redevelopment. For example, pastors
have particular and up-close knowledge of their congregants, which allows

them to prioritize their own effort and resources. Knowing that he could not help every member of his congregation, one Desire area pastor and building contractor chose carefully the people to whom he offered his contracting services pro bono. He selected residents he considered to be solid citizens who would serve as nodal points of support for other members of their extended family and help to tip the balance towards functional families returning rather than people involved in various criminal activities (Chamlee-Wright 2010). Such refined choices require a degree of local knowledge that is both intimate (similar to the knowledge that circulates within families) and social in that the local knowledge to which pastors have access extends across families within the congregation and the neighborhood in which the church is situated.

Similarly, Pastor Henry Ballard of the Christian Fellowship Family Worship Center in St. Bernard Parish leveraged the network of local knowledge available to him as a clergyman so that he and his congregants could tap resources available through various relief organizations. Pastor Ballard explains:

> On any given Sunday or during the week, I'll let the congregation know, 'If you hear or have heard of anything that's gonna benefit somebody else, please tell me, because I'm only in so many places at so many times. But if you're there—if you hear about a program that [is] helping low-income families . . . let us know that so that we can get that information out to as many people as we can get it out to.' And so that's what's been working right now . . . It's just a matter of connecting with people.

Pastor Randy Millet of the Adullam Christian Fellowship, also in St. Bernard Parish, observed that the success churches have demonstrated in facilitating the delivery of relief services and the longer-term redevelopment effort has a great deal to do with the fact that 'Nobody knows the people like the pastors.' He observes that the local knowledge the pastor already possesses pre-disaster enables the church to function more effectively post-disaster, relative to more socially distant relief agencies. Further, Millet observes that because churches—a critical source of emotional and material support—are already established within a community pre-disaster, they have a particular advantage in providing relief and recovery assistance post-disaster.

> I think this has been the church's finest hour . . . I do missionary work all the time, and the very first thing that I do [when] I go into Africa, or I go into Haiti, or I go into Mexico [is] I look for somebody that's already doing the work. I'm not looking for somebody to say, 'Hey, would you like me to pastor, and help, and feed these people?' No, I'm going to search until I find somebody that's already doing it. If they're doing it with nothing, then I can get behind them

because their heart is already in it. And knowing this I knew that I needed to get back home and just start doing what I can, and the church would find me. I knew that [the government] would never be able to duplicate what the church can do, and there's reasons for it. And what I'm going to say is not an indictment on any other organization. It's just that the church is set up to handle it, and this is why. Nobody knows where the next disaster's going to take place. Could be California. Could be New York. Could be anywhere. But it doesn't matter, because the church is already there. We're already there. There's three places where people run when they're desperate. The first place is family, the second place is friends, and the third place is the church.

While the prominence of the church affords many advantages in general, particular redevelopment strategies and records of redevelopment success varied widely across churches. As with all property owners, churches that had flood insurance were far better equipped to begin repairs early than those that had to find financial support elsewhere. And, just as with residential property owners, the confusion surrounding flood risk meant that many churches had falsely assumed that their neighborhood was not particularly prone to flooding (Chamlee-Wright 2007). Further, what role pastors and the church's organizational structure could play for the surrounding neighborhood depended upon whether the congregants were largely drawn from the neighborhood in which it was situated or dispersed across the city. For example, parishioners from the MQVN Church were concentrated within a one-mile radius of the church. This meant that the church's substantial relief efforts enabled the recovery of a specific neighborhood, as well as members of a specific congregation (Chamlee-Wright and Storr 2009a). On the other hand, relatively few members of, for example, the Jerusalem Missionary Baptist Church in Central City lived in the community. The church's pastor, Allen Cotton, observed:

Most of the members when I became a pastor were not living in the community. At one point they did—growing up they did, but, because of the blight, because of the crime, because of the fact that a lot of [the properties were] rental property, they moved out when they were able to purchase their own homes but still had their connection to the church.

Thus the church's recovery assistance to parishioners and recovery efforts aimed at local residents were entirely separate enterprises.

Large churches that had a financial base to support a full-time pastor fared better than small churches in which the pastor drew no salary from the church. Full-time (paid) pastors were able to become, in essence, full-time redevelopment strategists and case managers for their congregants. Unpaid pastors who relied upon outside employment for their support, on the other hand, more often than not lost their paid job as a consequence of the storm. Many could not return to New Orleans without a means of providing for themselves and their families.

When asked about the importance of pastors returning and the role that a paid ministry plays in post-disaster recovery, full-time pastor James Willis of the Carver Desire Baptist Church in the Upper Ninth Ward observes:

> I came back and so my church came back and many of my members came back. We started having worship last February [of 2006]. We were the first church opened in the Ninth Ward. As a result of that, a lot of my membership has come back. People are tied to their churches. That's something very, very important to bear in mind that people are tied to their churches. If given the chance, they'll come back to their churches. And, when our church reopened, I have members right now that commute from as far away as Mobile, Alabama to come to church here on Sundays. I have at least 20 or 25 people that commute on Sunday from Baton Rouge and places in between to come to church here on Sundays. As a result, our church is able to maintain its presence in the community, to be a light in the community to help instill hope . . . But none of that would have happened if I had not come back.

Though some of Pastor Willis's congregants were still commuting back to New Orleans from other locales in early 2007, their connection to the church helped to maintain a connection to their property and the city, making an eventual return more likely. Many churches, however, were too small and the congregations too poor to support a full-time pastor before Katrina, and after the storm the full-time commitment to the recovery process or even a return to New Orleans was often impossible.

Thus the cultural place that churches and their pastors held within their communities pre-Katrina both enabled and constrained their redevelopment efforts post-Katrina. The authority vested in the local pastors and the local knowledge they possessed benefited churches and the communities they served. If the pastor was able to return early on, the resumption of religious services, and the provision of relief and rebuilding assistance helped to coax residents back to the city and begin the rebuilding process. On the other hand, smaller and financially vulnerable churches tended to lack the means and the scale to leverage widespread recovery. While access to financial resources was critical to whether pastors could return to New Orleans, those pastors who did return were able to draw upon and deploy socially embedded resources as well. As I discuss in the next section, narratives of history and place, and religious/spiritual re-interpretations of Katrina as a blessing were among these resources.

12.4   NARRATIVES OF HISTORY AND PLACE

As Storr (2004) argues, stories—particularly the stories we tell about ourselves—help to shape our understanding of what is desirable, what is possible, and what the best course is to realize what we aim to achieve. Elsewhere, Storr and I identify the critical role that community narratives have played in drawing residents back to New Orleans and shaping their recovery efforts. That residents within the MQVN community thought of their New Orleans neighborhood as a 'second homeland' served as an important draw for residents to return and begin the rebuilding process (Chamlee-Wright and Storr 2009a). Further, the commonly shared narrative that this immigrant community had been through far worse in its migration out of Vietnam and to New Orleans—that, by comparison, Katrina was a 'mere inconvenience'—established a benchmark of expectation that the community could and would rebuild (Chamlee-Wright and Storr 2010b). Similarly, residents in the badly damaged Ninth Ward expressed a pronounced sense of place that New Orleans in general, and their Ninth Ward neighborhoods in particular, offered a unique array of qualities that made a distinct form of the good life possible and their return following Katrina all but inevitable (Chamlee-Wright and Storr 2009b).

Church pastors tapped into these narratives of history and place in their attempts to connect to congregants scattered across multiple and disconnected evacuation sites, to call them home, and to inspire them to play a role in the recovery effort. Father Vien and Father Luke of the MQVN Catholic Church, for example, told and retold the community's migration story in the media, from the pulpit and at community events, and always as backdrop to how special their particular neighborhood was and how resilient members of the community were (Chamlee-Wright and Storr 2009a, 2010b).

If neighborhoods offered a distinct sense of place, churches provided a sense of 'home' within that place, and residents and pastors alike frequently described their congregations as 'family.' Commenting on the swiftness of pastors who had returned early to rebuild their churches, Pastor Ballard observed: 'This is home. So I think that that made all the difference in the world in terms of who came back as quick as they came back because this is all we have.' Further, the metaphor of church as home and congregation as family helped connect outside volunteers into the recovery effort by conveying to them what was distinctive and special about their church community. Speaking of volunteers from Rick Warren's Saddleback Church in California who had come to help renovate his church, Broadmoor pastor Allen Cotton remarked:

You're coming to our home . . . We were brought up to keep food, extra food, just in case somebody spontaneously stopped by. That is the New Orleans way, and so when we found out that [volunteers] were coming to help rebuild, certainly, we got red beans and rice, and chicken, and all kinds of stuff . . . They just had a field day, and then they learned to eat the New Orleans way, and what I mean by that [is] they overate [laughter] . . . Now you got the bug . . . It's just a fun filled atmosphere with love here. We share with one another, we cry with one another, and that's what church, I find, is all about.

The narrative of 'church as home' means that the restoration of a church can play an essential role in restoring a sense of place in a context that otherwise has lost much of its appealing character, at least for the present and more than likely for many years following the disaster. One's house may still be wrecked by the storm, but if the church is restored, the narrative asserts, one can still 'come home.'

An element that is particular to New Orleans is the importance specific neighborhoods assume in New Orleanians' sense of place. As Pastor Willis observed, 'Sense of neighborhood is very, very strong in New Orleans. People love their neighborhoods. People will be born, raised and die in the same neighborhood.' And a neighborhood's history can feature prominently in that sense of place. Residents from the Upper Ninth Ward, for example, recall the pivotal role Ruby Bridges and the William Frantz Elementary School played in school desegregation in 1960. Residents and community leaders in Broadmoor and Central City will frequently recall the fact that, in the early part of the twentieth century, their neighborhoods were the site of racial tolerance in which African Americans, Jews, and Irish and Italian immigrants lived side by side and conducted business with one another. St. Bernardians frequently recall with pride the fact that Spanish expatriates from the Canary Islands, who established themselves as trappers, farmers and fishermen, originally settled the parish. To be sure, when recounted by contemporary residents these stories are often retold in idealized and sanitized form. Nonetheless, the stories, even if retold imperfectly, carry weight.

Community leaders, including pastors, in the Pontchartrain Park–Gentilly Woods neighborhood within the Gentilly[2] area drew upon this community's history, and its relevance for the African American community as both explanation and inspiration for the redevelopment of the neighborhood. Though it was once a shallow swamp, levees and a modern drainage system allowed developers to reclaim the area. Originally, Gentilly Woods was an exclusively white neighborhood, developed in the 1950s with access to public transportation, parks, schools and other amenities. Adjacent to Gentilly Woods, Pontchartrain Park was among the first residential neighborhoods expressly planned and designed to

attract middle-class and professional African American residents. While
the provision of amenities, such as a professionally designed golf course,
was an outgrowth of segregationist policies that barred blacks from other
municipal recreational facilities, such amenities also represented a rare
and valued resource to the growing class of middle- and upper-income
African Americans (Storr, Chamlee-Wright and Storr 2015; Colten 2006).
The architectural style of the Gentilly area, which assumed automobile
ownership and the availability of central air conditioning, broke with
the shotgun style homes that characterized poor black neighborhoods
of the old New Orleans and instead represented an aesthetic and life-
style usually associated with white residential communities. Following
desegregation, Gentilly Woods shifted from an exclusively white to a predominantly African American community. In the 1980s, Gentilly Woods
and Pontchartrain Park merged into what colloquially became known as
'Pontilly,' sharing the recreational spaces.[3]

The distinctive history of the Gentilly area has shaped the sense of place
residents attribute to it. As one Gentilly Woods resident recalls,

> When we first moved back here, it was mostly whites back here. You see, this
> is considered Gentilly Woods. You go down about two miles, it's a little canal,
> that's Pontchartrain Park. That's where I came up. That was the first historical
> black district where 90 percent of the people that lived [in Pontchartrain Park]
> were either working for the post office, or they were educators. These was [*sic*]
> brand new houses, and the average mortgage was less than $215 month. This
> [was] 57 years ago. And that's why a lot of people are not leaving here. They're
> coming back because this is a historical district.

Another resident explains, 'Gentilly Woods was first. But Pontchartrain
Park was still predominantly where black people, professionals started
to migrate and build houses, so it's a historic [neighborhood].' She goes
on to explain that, up to that point, property ownership for African
Americans had only been possible in the Ninth Ward. 'It just wasn't that
feasible for black people to own property all over, but the Ninth Ward
was all property owned by black people, and that's historical. That's
why you see generations of people down there, and it's their people, it's
black people' (Storr, Chamlee-Wright and Storr 2015). Pontchartrain
Park, then, represented an entirely new frontier in black ownership
that would once again establish a context in which generations of black
families, this time middle- and upper-income black families, would call
it home.

Reverend Hadley Edwards of the Bethany United Methodist Church
recited this history as he explained the church's role in the redevelopment
effort.

I don't know how much you know about Pontchartrain Park becoming an all-black subdivision away from the inner city in the 50s when housing was a divided issue where there were actual rules that did not allow black and white people to live in the same neighborhoods, and you had black professionals who had come home from World War II who had served this country, who had what is called the GI Bill and had all of those other opportunities that they could make life better. You had persons who were now school teachers. You had police officers. You had postal persons—persons working at the postal service, mail carriers in particular. And this subdivision was developed and created by that clientele of people—a more professional black community. And that's who lived here [and] raised their children here. Their children became if not the first, the second generation of [black] college graduates . . . Those are the roots of the people who are living here now . . . Some of the rebuilding that you see are . . . land exchanges from one generation to the next, and so they're coming to live on the spot that they were raised.

Though at the time of these interviews Gentilly was still struggling to regain its population, it was nonetheless further along in the recovery effort compared to some communities. Pastor Edwards attributes this recovery to Gentilly's place in the history of New Orleans and to middle-class professional African Americans in particular.

We have come a long way . . . The initial spirit of this community and its original inception has everything to do with it . . . This community was founded when there was a system afoot in America that held you down. And against all of those odds these people built a community where they can be family, where they can have a life of normalcy as black people living the American dream in Pontchartrain Park. History has said it is the first all-black subdivision in the south, significant in that it wasn't a segregated place . . . but it was a subdivision that was selected by black people.

Into this narrative of history and place, Pastor Edwards weaves the importance of the church and the church pastor—that if the community was to survive, the church and its leader would be playing a central role. When asked why he chose to return, Pastor Edwards responds:

Oh, I'm a pastor. I'm pastor of this church. I had to come back because I had responsibilities of, number one, making sure that if it was nothing but ruins I had to make sure that the ruins were handled properly. I had to come back because I knew that this was really my job and that the people needed—whatever people that would come back—would need a leader, and I've never abandoned anything in my life. I felt that that was an important piece. I was key to the recovery of New Orleans.

Pastor Edwards observed that simply by returning and resuming services, church leaders played a vital role in the recovery of the city as a whole.

For the longest [time], we were the only church within a ten-mile radius that was open for worship. We were the only church in a ten-mile radius [where] people could gather. The only place. Yes, we gathered between the rafters when the place was fully gutted out and there was nothing but two-by-fours and studs all around us, but we were gathering. And we were to this community the hope saying, 'Yeah, this community will live again.'[4]

Though the church itself required extensive repairs, Pastor Edwards began by attending to the exterior landscaping as a way to reconstruct the sense of place people attributed to the church and, by extension, to the community as a whole.

The first thing we had was landscaping, because everything was dead out here. When a church called from California that partnered with us and wanted to know how [they] could help . . . guess what I told them I wanted? I said I need some landscaping. That's the most important thing. And the reason that we needed that is because everywhere else you looked in this neighborhood you saw death. Everywhere else you looked in this neighborhood, no life. Not coming ever. But I knew that it was going to be different at our church. I knew we were coming back. But if you are in real estate and you're trying to sell someone a house, how can you sell them a house in the middle of a wilderness? . . . We didn't even have walls. [We] didn't have lights. But we had landscaping because as people came to their [homes], as people looked at the mammoth job that needed to be done, if they saw a green spot—if they saw a place for a bird and a live tree for that bird to sing—it was gonna sing at Bethany. And that would give them hope.

To Pastor Edwards, the church can play a pivotal role in the recreation of the sense of place and, in particular, a sense of home. When asked why people return to New Orleans, Pastor Edwards says that it is the 'love for New Orleans. Love for the community. [When they were away] they have tried to go to these other people's churches and they can't find a church like Bethany.' But, once they return, people need social spaces to gather and reconnect to their community.

It's not hard to get people to come out of a FEMA trailer into a spacious place that you can sit, you can be cool, you can be comfortable, you can be with your friends. It's a social gathering place . . . Did you notice the sign out there that says 'Welcome Home to Bethany United Methodist Church'? Well, I just had the sign lady this morning . . . She said do you want to keep 'Welcome Home'? I said yes. I said because this for a long time is going to be home for somebody who's homeless, and I want you to come in here and feel at home. A FEMA trailer can't make you feel at home. A junked up apartment can't make you feel at home. But I want you to feel at home in this space.

The challenge facing Pastor Edwards and other pastors was to draw people back into their communities and persuade them to take on the significant challenges associated with the rebuilding process. This persuasive effort required pastors and other social entrepreneurs to interpret the post-disaster context in a way that would make the journey back to a restored community somewhat smoother than it might otherwise have been and, most importantly, worthwhile. By providing a hospitable social space, particularly one that recreates a sense of home, in a city that has suffered catastrophic loss in residential, commercial and public properties, pastors were well situated to play a critical role in calling people back and calling them together. Once people had been called together, pastors were in a particularly good position to draw upon and reinforce narratives of neighborhood history and place—the narratives that made people want to return, reinvest and rebuild.

12.5 REDEFINING KATRINA AS A BLESSING

Within the interview data collected for the larger study another common narrative emerges: that, despite all the destruction it wrought, Hurricane Katrina was a blessing in disguise. Two groups in particular tended to assert the importance of this narrative. Many of the interview subjects who had evacuated from New Orleans following the storm and were still living in Houston three years later described Katrina 'as a blessing' in that it had allowed them to improve their situation in a way that would not have been possible in New Orleans, such as gaining access to better schools for their children. The other respondents who tended to frame Katrina in positive terms were those who ascribed divine intent to the events that followed in the wake of the storm. Some of the purported blessings were grand; for example, a Broadmoor resident observed that never before had there been such a profound sense of community and shared vision at work in her neighborhood (Chamlee-Wright and Storr 2009c). Some of the purported blessings were modest; for example, a Gentilly resident felt blessed by the fact that the storm had brought her into the company of many kind-hearted volunteers and into possession of a newly renovated home—made particularly beautiful by her new hardwood floors (Storr, Chamlee-Wright and Storr 2015).

Pastors also took up this theme of 'Katrina as blessing' in that it was Katrina that 'reconnected people to what was really important' and provided an 'opportunity for [the pastor] to serve his people' and gain 'clarity of purpose' for what the mission of the pastoral ministry was to be, which was rebuilding the church community and, as a consequence, playing a role in the redevelopment of New Orleans.

For example, Allen Cotton, pastor of Broadmoor's Ora-Vista Baptist

Church, believes that Katrina brought spiritual growth to the members of
his community.

> So tragedy has a way of bringing a change, and so when Katrina came it was
> a growth. Spiritually . . . one thing Katrina did was it caused people to believe
> and trust in God again, and to value and to change their priorities, and revalue
> things in life, because the carpet [and other material possessions were] no longer
> valuable . . . In an era that I grew up in, you can visit an elderly person's house.
> Their furniture is all covered with plastic because they want their sofa to last to
> eternity, and I grew in an era where you could *look* in someone's living room,
> but you weren't permitted in there, because it was like a museum. There was
> china that they would buy [but] they were just for decoration. You can't eat
> off the china. And after the storm, Katrina came, who's eating off the china
> now? Katrina drank out of your glasses that nobody else could touch. And
> people's value changed. [Now] nothing is too good in my house for people to
> use. [Before Katrina] we get out of our cars, and 'beep' [lock the car], and we go
> straight into our houses . . . And after Katrina, no. You get out of the car, you
> look for somebody [and say], 'Hey, how are you doing?' Now, your car parked,
> but you standing in your door an hour, two hours, talking to your neighbor,
> getting to know people . . . One of the benefits that Katrina taught [was to] get
> to know people again.

In terms of the redevelopment challenge, this sense of connection or
reconnection to one's neighbors can have tangible impact. Social interactions among neighbors following disaster can play an important role
in overcoming the collective action problem catastrophic disasters pose
(Chamlee-Wright 2008b). In the aftermath of disaster, people may be
willing to return to and reinvest in a community if they are relatively
certain that the community will be viable in the long run. If residents
and other stakeholders remain disconnected from one another, however,
it is difficult to know whether others are committing to the long-term
redevelopment process. Engagement with members of one's community,
either through formal recovery efforts or through informal chats in the
driveway, helps individuals send and receive signals regarding the level of
commitment to the redevelopment effort, thereby mitigating the collective
action problem (ibid.).

Another variation of the 'Katrina as blessing' narrative was that
Katrina and the redevelopment challenge offered an opportunity for
redemption and a place in history that was part of a divine plan. Pastor
Millet of the Adullam Christian Fellowship likened the St. Bernard Parish
community, its temporary need for help from others, and its redevelopment to the biblical story of Naomi in the Book of Ruth. The story
holds that Elimelech, his wife Naomi and their sons Mahlon and Chilion
migrated from Bethlehem to Moab, whereupon Elimelech dies. The sons
marry Moabite women: Chilion marries Orpah and Mahlon marries

Ruth, after which the sons also die. Naomi, whose name means 'my gracious one' or 'my delight,' changes her name to Mara, which means 'the bitter one.' Despondent, Naomi decides to return to Bethlehem and entreats Orpah and Ruth to return to their families and remarry. Orpah does return to her family, but Ruth, in an act of courage, pledges her loyalty to Naomi, taking Naomi's home, family, people and God as her own. Naomi and Ruth return to Bethlehem together. With no other way to support herself and her mother-in-law, Ruth gleans the fields belonging to Boaz, a close relative to Elimelech's family. Impressed by Ruth's loyalty to her mother-in-law, Boaz allows Ruth to continue to collect food for the remainder of the harvest season. In keeping with Levirate law, the nearest kinsman to Elimelech would be obliged to repurchase land that had been sold for the family's maintenance, and to marry Ruth in order to carry on Elimelech's family line. After negotiating away another man's claim as nearest kinsman, Boaz becomes the 'kinsman redeemer' in which he redeems the family land by repurchasing it, Ruth by marrying her, and Elimelech's family line by having with Ruth a son, Obed. In choosing to remain with Naomi, Ruth's loyalty and courage place her at the center of biblical history and within Jesus's lineage, as Obed becomes the grandfather to King David. Pastor Millet connects this story to the post-Katrina context of St. Bernard Parish.

> Boaz basically went to the nearest kinsman redeemer and said, 'Are you going to redeem this woman, because she needs help? She lost her husband. Are you going to take her in? Because if you're not I will.' The man said, 'No, you take her.' So Boaz went back and he took Ruth to be his wife, and Ruth found herself in the lineage of Jesus Christ, a Moabite woman who found favor with God. And what the Lord has shown me is [that] St. Bernard is like Naomi. [The people of St. Bernard] are devastated, they're bitter, they're down and they're hurting, and [I tell them] 'You have a choice, son. It's just a choice. You can leave and go live your life. Nobody will blame you.' And every one of these people have these choices. But if you choose to, if you will do as Ruth, you will glean in the fields of others for a while, but make no mistake about it, I'm your kinsman redeemer, and you will be in the palace again . . . And it's not even about getting in the palace like Ruth did, and it's not even about becoming rich, or becoming famous, or . . . having a vibrant ministry. Naomi's countenance changed, and Naomi was provided for. So that means that, if we'll glean the fields with just the other ministries and the help from others for a season, St. Bernard will come back in Spring again, and it will live again, and that's what I want to see . . . [M]ake no mistake about it, these people are coming back, and strong, and better, the best of the best. They will not be denied. They're living in FEMA trailers. Some of them are living in tents, but they're coming home. They want to be home . . . I can tell you it's a closely knit community, and for me, if this is what God's chosen for me to do, then so be it, because I want to see our community returned. Now, I'm one pastor doing one small part, but whatever I'm called to do I want to be faithful to do my part. And I believe

that if, in the end, this is what we do know, Orpah walked out of the Bible and Ruth walked right into her destiny. And I believe it like this: great men are put in circumstances, and they have to make choices.

This passage illustrates the importance narrative plays in bolstering the resolve of pastors themselves to return and rebuild. When Pastor Millet describes the courage and loyalty that are required to take one's place in history, he is describing his own deliberations about returning as much as he is describing the people of St. Bernard. Thus, even if the narratives were simply personal, they have an important impact if they help to bring key stakeholders back to the community who tend to foster wider recovery efforts. But again, given the position pastors hold within their communities, that they regularly share these narratives in their sermons and private counsel of parishioners, these narratives are likely to be shared widely. If the decision to return and rebuild in the aftermath of catastrophic disaster is framed in terms of practicality and tangible costs and benefits, the case favoring such a commitment is relatively weak, and the prospects for community-wide redevelopment are therefore less bright. By reframing the recovery effort as an opportunity for spiritual growth, redemption and taking one's place within a divinely inspired history, however, the calculus changes. By telling the Katrina story differently, loss of material possessions becomes a lesson learned, setbacks become tests of one's mettle, and victims become heroes.

12.6   NAVIGATING AND RECONFIGURING SOCIALLY EMBEDDED RESOURCES

Churches have played another critical role in the redevelopment process by identifying and tapping resources embedded within various social networks. Many of these networks extend beyond the local context. For example, following Katrina, 36 New Orleans-based African American churches partnered with 360 churches around the country under the name Churches Supporting Churches (CSC). With the explicit intent of fostering community redevelopment by rebuilding churches first, CSC offered support to pastors trying to reconnect to their congregants, paid the salaries of local pastors for the early months following their return and provided financial and volunteer support for the physical rebuilding of church facilities. Churches that were well connected to their national networks found support through special appeals for funds and volunteers. Churches also tapped the resources of national non-profit organizations. For example, local churches partnered with Operation Blessing International

(OBI) to organize disaster relief in the months following the storm. Partnerships with national non-profit organizations also fueled efforts toward longer-term redevelopment. The First Baptist Church of New Orleans in Lakeview, for example, partnered with Habitat for Humanity to construct Musicians Village, a project that built 72 single family homes in the Upper Ninth Ward through volunteer labor and support.

But, as important as these outside resources have been to the redevelopment of New Orleans, the pastor's ability to identify, tap and in some cases reconfigure resources embedded within the community, including personal assets, resources within the local networks of support and resources within the congregation, was also vital.

When asked what made it possible for him to come back, Pastor Willis of Carver Desire Baptist Church replied that it was a combination of the fact that he had extended family he could rely upon early on and the fact that he was able to reconnect to his congregants while they were still scattered across various cities in the South. The support from his extended family allowed him to survive the early months away from New Orleans. The contact with his congregants while they were still figuring out their next steps allowed him to orchestrate a return relatively quickly.

> Our church had the means, meager means, but still had means to if necessary support me. They didn't have to do it early on. I was fortunate that I had family that we stayed with in Dallas. And we didn't have great expenses . . . I think one of the key things for me anyway was that, immediately after the storm, the first thing I did was search for my members to find out how they were, where they were, what kind of shape they were in, what's their situation. My wife and I spent weeks locating our members. And then, when we found a substantial number of them, we actually got in the car, and we drove around Texas and Louisiana to go and visit with them to see for ourselves what their condition was, offer them whatever help we could. That helped a lot. It keeps people tied together as a community, as a family, as a body. That's the way we've always viewed ourselves. The pastor is always the pivotal point in something like that. And I believe pastors showing concern for his people endears the people not only to him, but to the church and the idea of church and family. And so that being the case and seeing that I was still on my job, the members began to send their tithes, their offerings—not to me, but to the church so that the work can go on.

Pastor Willis observed further that because the people continued to contribute to the church, even from their evacuation sites in other cities, he could devote all of his time to helping members of his congregation return. He and his wife also leveraged their own assets to facilitate the return of their congregants. Because they had a two-story home, they were able to move in to the second floor relatively quickly, allowing them to lend their trailer—which they affectionately called 'Motel 6'—to people who had returned to take stock of their situation in New Orleans or to begin the rebuilding process.

Because of their connection to their congregants, their local knowledge of their situations, and the trust that they enjoyed among the church membership, pastors were in a particularly strong position to identify sources of support. Further, this close connection to and local knowledge of the membership also meant that the pastors were well positioned to leverage that support toward a broader redevelopment effort. By providing direct assistance to returning congregants, serving as a hub for finding other forms of relief and longer-term support, and rebuilding the church and resuming services, pastors helped to restore the sense of place so critical to drawing people back to their communities. While identifying and tapping resources embedded within the local community is critical, some pastors found the configuration of those resources wanting for the particular challenges post-disaster redevelopment presented. Father Jerry Kramer, pastor of the Church of the Annunciation in Broadmoor, determined that the church could be an effective player in the community's redevelopment, but it would have to reconfigure the assets it had and develop new partnerships, particularly with the Broadmoor Improvement Association (BIA), which was spearheading the redevelopment planning process. As soon as he was able to return to the city in late 2005, he put what physical facilities they had available (in this case, a double-wide trailer) toward providing services to the people living in the residential community that surrounded the church. It was his interactions with the residential community that led him to consider how he could leverage the church's assets in a way that would help the redevelopment effort being orchestrated through the BIA.

> Everybody who came out of the double-wide hugged my neck and said thank you so much. This was the first chance we have had to like sit, relax, connect, you know, be a human being since the storm. Just sit around with people we knew or share some common things and share . . . But the other thing they told me, I heard this from every single person who came through was, 'We have lived in this neighborhood for whatever [length of time], and we did not know what those buildings were.' [They were] talking about the church. [M]y relevancy test for [the] church is [to ask] 'If you were to go away, would anybody miss you?' And we failed [that test] miserably. I said, 'This has to change.' So that's how we began. I told the Broadmoor [Improvement Association] people, 'All right, you can have everything we have. I don't want to date. I don't want to horde. I don't want to live together. I want to get married. We have to get married.' So, we gave them half of our office trailer, and we gave them money for everything.

But space and the modest financial support the church provided to BIA would not be enough if the community was to effectively address the fact that the vast majority of residents in the neighborhood had still not returned, and the homes were in danger of becoming permanently unin-habitable. Father Kramer reports that Hal Rourke, the president of the Broadmoor Development Corporation (BDC), called Kramer to ask for a far more significant level of support. In order to give the BIA and the BDC the space and resources they would need to advance the redevelop-ment effort, Father Kramer eventually persuaded the diocese to take out a mortgage on properties the church owned in downtown New Orleans. Prior to Katrina, the $10 000 per month the properties generated in rental income had kept the church solvent.

> [Hal said] 'We need for you to basically move off your campus for about ten years, fix it up . . . bring volunteers in 100 at a time, for about ten years, and then run [the organization] . . . Would you do that for us?' And I said that's a pretty stupid idea . . . so we'll do it. And so we did. And that's how that mission was born. So what we did was we took out a $1.1 million loan we can't pay back. We used the [downtown] property as collateral. The diocese just fought us tooth and nail. They saw us committing suicide, and the only advocate we had was a bishop and he stood with us. And we got it through because we just basically said let us die with our boots on. Let us die with some dignity.

The $1.1 million loan went to purchase three properties adjacent to the church that would house the BIA and the BDC. The rental income from the church now went toward the interest payments on the loan and could no longer be used for operating funds.

> [I told the congregation] 'We might just be in this trailer for like 10, 20 years and that's what we're gonna do because the church [should be] out on the street. God cares about people, not buildings, and God still needs to hit the streets. And that's the way it's going to be, and I know you didn't sign up for this when you came to this church, but that's what we're gonna have. So, if you don't like that, if you just want to like look at stained glass and read from the prayer book and be comfortable, we got four Episcopal churches on St. Charles where you would like it better . . . But you need to go now if this is not gonna work for you. And we're not changing course. This is what we're doing.' And so about half of them left. And, you know, there was really serious [resistance from] the old guard, but they're all gone now . . . When I got here, the median age was like 114. We've gotten a lot younger now.

The joint efforts of the Church of the Annunciation, other churches in the Broadmoor community, the BIA and the BDC resulted in what is widely considered one of the most successful cases of post-Katrina neighborhood planning and redevelopment (Chamlee-Wright and Storr 2009c). Though early on the city's redevelopment planning process placed the future of the Broadmoor community in doubt, the collaborations described above all but eliminated this threat. Collaborative efforts within the community led to a partnership with Harvard University's Kennedy School of Government, which enabled the BIA to carry out a comprehensive community assessment, craft a redevelopment plan that met professional standards within the urban planning industry, attract resources from private foundations and government redevelopment funds, and attract Broadmoor residents back to the community.

In one sense, Father Kramer's efforts are remarkable in that the reconfiguration of the social and financial assets was so radical. Not only did he shift the entire financial structure of support for the church, by making the congregation financially responsible for its internal and outreach operations, but he orchestrated a cultural shift within the church membership. Some congregants bought into Father Kramer's vision of what the church would be doing, others left, and new members attracted by the role the church was playing in the community joined. In another sense, however, Father Kramer's efforts were not altogether unusual. Particularly when faced with the overwhelming challenges catastrophic disaster presents, entrepreneurs of all kinds—whether social entrepreneurs or market entrepreneurs—may reconfigure the socially embedded resources they have available. A cooking school that had opened shortly before Katrina became a principal source of meals for relief workers after Katrina (Runst 2010). Neighborhood associations that had focused on neighborhood beautification before Katrina became hubs for information about recovery assistance and case management after Katrina. Performance venues connected their network of musicians with relief support immediately after the storm, and helped to redevelop the New Orleans music scenes in the months and years that followed (D'Amico 2010). Consortia of churches focused on evangelism pre-Katrina shifted their efforts toward managing scores of volunteer groups post-Katrina. While the degree of reconfiguration may be modest or radical, this creative response ought to be considered a normal dimension of the entrepreneurial process.

12.7   CONCLUSION

The challenge that Lavoie sketches out in Chapter 3 of this volume is to incorporate both discovery and interpretation as part of our understanding of entrepreneurship. Like Kirzner, he recognizes that the entrepreneurial discovery process is the driving force behind development. But genuine discovery, particularly discovery in a complex and extended social order, is not simply a matter of opening one's eyes when others have theirs closed. Genuine discovery is a matter of complex interpretation. And it is culture, Lavoie argues, that gives us the framework of understanding we need to make sense of the world around us and perceive entrepreneurial opportunities.

The post-disaster context is one that presents daunting social coordination and development challenges but few obvious solutions. Instead, discovery unfolds as social entrepreneurs piece together their response out of the material and socially embedded resources available to them. Church pastors occupy a particular place within the cultural economy landscape in general, and the cultural context of New Orleans in particular. This place has the potential to constrain as well as enable robust development, but making the most of the socially embedded resources available to them has been part of the creative response pastors have demonstrated post-Katrina.

In the months and years following Katrina, pastors deployed the local knowledge that had been made available to them by virtue of their relationship to families within their congregation and the neighborhoods in which their churches were situated. This local knowledge enabled pastors to prioritize which forms of support (within their means to provide) would be most helpful for advancing individual and collective redevelopment efforts. This local knowledge also enabled them to decide to whom such support would be best directed. Pastors depended upon the trust and authority they enjoyed within their communities to attract continued financial support for church operations, to coax congregants home, and in many cases coax congregants to play a role in the recovery effort beyond making repairs on their own homes.

The interpretive lens pastors possess by virtue of the place they hold within the cultural context also provided narratives that sealed their commitment to returning, to rebuilding their churches and to taking part in the broader redevelopment effort. Further, such narratives served to draw others back to New Orleans. By reasserting neighborhood-based narratives of history and place, pastors connected personal efforts toward rebuilding a home to the broader effort of restoring a community—a community with a sense of place and history worthy of restoring. By weaving the church into this narrative, particularly with metaphors that equate church with home and congregation with family, the resumption of services and the restoration of the church facilities created an essential bridge by which residents could feel 'at home' even if their own residential property was still in need of significant repair. Recasting Katrina as a blessing placed the costs of rebuilding and the sacrifices one might be willing to endure in a new light. Instead of a purely financial and logistical decision, the decision to return and rebuild became tied to something greater than the individual. By tapping into values of community, spiritual growth, redemption and honor, the 'Katrina as blessing' narrative made a more persuasive case for committing to the redevelopment effort, even if the personal costs one would face were significant.

Though the entrepreneurial discovery process is indeed one that requires creative interpretation of complex circumstances, the discovery process can also involve the deliberate manipulation and reconfiguration of socially embedded resources. As some pastors discovered, the structure of the socially embedded resources they had available to them were not a good match for the redevelopment challenge. Though any particular structure of socially embedded resources may serve some purposes well, in the face of dramatically changed circumstances, the pre-existing structure may not be well suited to address the most pressing concerns. Social as well as market entrepreneurs may in some circumstances be in a position to reconfigure socially embedded resources in such a way that the challenges presented in the new circumstances can be addressed more effectively. This possibility for entrepreneurial reconfiguration of socially embedded resources suggests a potentially fruitful avenue for future research in cultural economy.

NOTES

1. Elsewhere, Chamlee-Wright and Storr (2015) refer to this program of study as 'social economy.'
2. The area known as 'Gentilly' includes the Pontchartrain Park, Gentilly Terrace, Gentilly Woods, Dillard, St. Anthony, Fillmore, Lake Terrace/Lake Oaks and Milneburg neighborhoods.
3. By the time Katrina hit, Pontchartrain Park was characterized as predominantly African American (97 percent), with a 92 percent home-ownership rate. Poverty rates were low relative to other neighborhoods in New Orleans. Only 10 percent of the population in Pontchartrain Park fell below the poverty line. Though more diverse, Gentilly Woods was also predominantly African American (68 percent), with whites making up 25 percent of the population. And again, at 14 percent, poverty rates in Gentilly Woods were well below the Orleans Parish average. See http://www.gnocdc.org/orleans/6/29/income.html.
4. Like Pastor Willis, Pastor Edwards credited the fact that he could move back into his own home as a critical asset for the congregation as a whole, as it gave him a base of operations.

> My home was spared. That's an important piece you need to know. I lived on the West Bank pre-storm, so my home was spared from floodwaters. I just had the wind damage. I had a livable house, and so as a person with a livable house it made sense for me to be here. It made sense for me to get—I'd worked in Dallas. I'd worked in a relief center there that took in lots and lots of New Orleans people and people that I knew and was helping them, so that was good for me to be on that end helping and getting people settled, and it was a comfort. I made people comfortable when they identified, oh, from home, and then helping the situation. Some of those same folks, when they came back home, they followed me home to Bethany.

REFERENCES

Aldrich, D. (2012), *Building Resilience: Social Capital in Post-Disaster Recovery*, Chicago: University of Chicago Press.

Barnes, Sandra (2005), 'Black Church Culture and Community Action,' *Social Forces*, **84**(2), 967–94.

Beggs, J., V. Haines and J. Hurlbert (1996a), 'Situational Contingencies Surrounding the Receipt of Social Support,' *Social Forces*, **75**, 201–22.

Beggs, J., V. Haines and J. Hurlbert (1996b), 'The Effects of Personal Network and Local Community Contexts on the Receipt of Formal Aid during Disaster Recovery,' *International Journal of Mass Emergencies and Disasters*, **14**, 57–78.

Boettke, Peter, Emily Chamlee-Wright, Peter Gordon, Sanford Ikeda, Peter Leeson and Russell Sobel (2007), 'The Political, Economic, and Social Aspects of Katrina,' *Southern Economic Journal*, **74**(2), 363–76.

Brown, R. Khari and Ronald Brown (2003), 'Faith and Works: Church Based Social Capital Resources and African American Political Activism,' *Social Forces*, **82**(2), 617 41.

Chamlee-Wright, Emily (1997), *The Cultural Foundations of Economic Development: Urban Female Entrepreneurship in Ghana*, London: Routledge.

Chamlee-Wright, Emily (2002), 'Savings and Accumulation Strategies of Urban Market Women in Harare, Zimbabwe,' *Economic Development and Cultural Change*, **50**(4), 979–1005.

Chamlee-Wright, Emily (2006), 'The Development of a Cultural Economy: Foundational Questions and Future Direction,' in J. High (ed.), *Humane Economics: Essays in Honor of Don Lavoie*, Cheltenham, UK and Northampton, MA, USA: Edward Elgar Publishing, pp. 181–98.

Chamlee-Wright, Emily (2007), 'The Long Road Back: Signal Noise in the Post-Katrina Context,' *Independent Review*, **12**(2), 235–59.

Chamlee-Wright, Emily (2008a), 'The Structure of Social Capital: An Austrian Perspective on Its Nature and Development,' *Review of Political Economy*, **20**(1), 41–58.

Chamlee-Wright, Emily (2008b), 'Signaling Effects of Commercial and Civil Society,' *International Journal of Social Economics*, **35**(7–8), 615–26.

Chamlee-Wright, Emily (2010), *The Cultural and Political Economy of Recovery: Social Learning in a Post-Disaster Environment*, London: Routledge.

Chamlee-Wright, E. and J. Myers (2008), 'Discovery and Social Learning in Non-Priced Environments: An Austrian View of Social Network Theory,' *Review of Austrian Economics*, **21**(2–3), 151–66.

Chamlee-Wright, E. and Virgil Henry Storr (2009a), 'Club Goods and Post-Disaster Community Return,' *Rationality and Society*, **21**(4), 429–58.

Chamlee-Wright, E. and V.H. Storr (2009b), '"There's No Place like New Orleans": Sense of Place and Community Recovery in the Ninth Ward after Hurricane Katrina,' *Journal of Urban Affairs*, **31**(5), 615–34.

Chamlee-Wright, E. and V.H. Storr (2009c), *Filling the Civil Society Vacuum: Post-Disaster Policy and Community Response*, Mercatus Policy Series, Policy Comment 22, Arlington, VA: Mercatus Center, George Mason University.

Chamlee-Wright, E. and Virgil Henry Storr (2010a), 'The Role of Social Entrepreneurship in Post-Katrina Community Recovery,' *International Journal of Innovation and Regional Development*, **2**(1–2), 149–64.

Chamlee-Wright, E. and Virgil Henry Storr (2010b), 'Community Resilience in New Orleans East: Deploying the Cultural Toolkit within a Vietnamese-American Community,' in J. Rivera and D. Miller (eds.), *Community Disaster Recovery and Resiliency: Exploring Global Opportunities and Challenges*, London: Taylor & Francis, pp. 99–122.

Chamlee-Wright, E. and Virgil Henry Storr (2015) 'Social Economy as an Extension of the Austrian Research Program,' in P.J. Boettke and C. Coyne, (eds.) *Oxford Handbook of Austrian Economics*, Oxford: *Oxford University Press*.

Colten, Craig E. (2006), *The Unnatural Metropolis: Wresting New Orleans from Nature*, New Orleans: Louisiana State University Press.

D'Amico, Daniel (2010), 'Rock Me like a Hurricane! How Music Communities Promote Social Capital Adept for Recovery,' in Emily Chamlee-Wright and Virgil Storr (eds.), *The Political Economy of Hurricane Katrina and Community Rebound*, Cheltenham, UK and Northampton, MA, USA: Edward Elgar Publishing, pp. 126–42.

Hurlbert, J., J. Beggs and V. Haines (2001), 'Social Capital in Extreme Environments,' in N. Lin, K. Cook and R. Burt (eds.), *Social Capital: Theory and Research*, New York: Aldine de Gruyter, pp. 209–31.

Jackson, Joyce Marie (2006), 'Declaration of Taking Twice: The Fazendeville Community of the Lower Ninth Ward,' *American Anthropologist*, **108**(4), 765–80.

Kirzner, Israel (1979), *Perception, Opportunity and Profit*, Chicago: University of Chicago Press.

Lincoln, Charles Eric and Lawrence H. Mamiya (1990), *The Black Church and the African-American Experience*, Durham, NC: Duke University Press.

McKenzie, Brian D. (2008), 'Reconsidering the Effects of Bonding Social Capital: A Closer Look at Black Civil Society Institutions in America,' *Political Behavior*, **30**(1), 25–45.

Nelson, Hart M. and Anne Kusener Nelson (1971), *The Black Church in America*, New York: Basic Books.

Pinn, Anthony (2002), *The Black Church in the Post-Civil Rights Era*, Maryknoll, NY: Orbis Books.

Runst, Petrik (2010), 'Entrepreneurship and Social Networks in Post-Disaster Environments,' in Emily Chamlee-Wright and Virgil Storr (eds.), *The Political Economy of Hurricane Katrina and Community Rebound*, Cheltenham, UK and Northampton, MA, USA: Edward Elgar Publishing, pp. 107–25.

Storr, Virgil Henry (2004), *Enterprising Slaves and Master Pirates: Understanding Economic Life in the Bahamas*, New York: Peter Lang.

Storr, Nona, Emily Chamlee-Wright, and Virgil Henry Storr (2015) *How We Came Back: Voices from Post-Katrina New Orleans*, Arlington: Mercatus Press.

13. National cultures, economic action and the homogeneity problem: insights from the case of Romania

Paul Dragos Aligica and Aura Matei

13.1 INTRODUCTION

The influential thesis that 'culture matters' is in many cases investigated using research designs predicated on the assumption of aggregated entities called 'national cultures.' The existence of a nationally identifiable and relatively homogeneous political, civic and economic culture is a basic building block of an important part of the literature studying how culture shapes and is shaped by economic activity. Examples abound, from comparative politics research originating in the well-known work of Gabriel Almond and Sidney Verba (1963) and illustrated today by authors such as Ronald Inglehart (1990, 1997), to economics and management studies such as in Charles Hampden-Turner and Alfons Trompenaars's book tellingly entitled *The Seven Cultures of Capitalism: Value Systems for Creating Wealth in the United States, Japan, Germany, France, Britain, Sweden and the Netherlands* (1993). The underlying assumption of this approach (now associated with an entire family of research programs) is that, for descriptive and analytical reasons, one may use as units of observation and units of analysis a series of 'social facts' called 'cultures' sufficiently homogeneous at the national level to be described as cohesive aggregate-level variables. These phenomena or 'social facts' called 'national cultures' are shaping and are being shaped by other social, economic and institutional factors.

Using the 'homogeneity-central tendency' perspective is both legitimate and fruitful in many cases. Relevant insights have been gained using the theoretical-methodological lenses provided that way. However, even without questioning the ontological and causal nature of 'national cultures,' one may easily think of an alternative approach. What if one is approaching the problem of 'national cultures' using a 'heterogeneity-variance' perspective? It may be very interesting to see how values are distributed around the central value taken as a national average, be it a mode, mean or median. Also, the problem may be approached using various degrees of disaggregation. It may be interesting to see the various clusters emerging on different parameters within 'national systems.' Further, it may be interesting to see in what measure certain values and certain aspects have more relevance than others in the broader scheme of things in a national economy. And it may be interesting to see how different ways of conceptualizing and estimating such non-modal, non-average cultural profiles and values reveal various forms and intensities of impact on the institutional and economic system. The idea is simple, and it does not require more than the adoption of a certain mindset of a methodological nature. It may be the case that homogeneity prevails in a given case. Yet approaching the case by trying to press the heterogeneity angle may help in identifying facets and patterns that otherwise would have remained either uncovered or unexplored. In the end, it is about a heuristic strategy. It is not even a claim about the essential heterogeneous nature of 'national cultures'; it is simply a way to avoid the trap of essentialism hidden in the aggregated–homogeneity perspective.

Such an approach seems rather promising in many respects. First, its contribution is descriptive. With existing characterizations of 'national cultures,' it is interesting and tempting to go beyond the aggregated and average-modal level and explore the diversity and heterogeneity in place (also see Lavoie and Chamlee-Wright, this volume, Chapter 7 for a discussion of 'national culture'). Second, it is plausible that variance matters, and especially the specific texture and composition of the variance matter a lot. Even if they are a minority, the bearers of a specific set of cultural values may have an important impact on the economy and institutional structure of a country (also see Storr and Colon, this volume, Chapter 15). Small socio-cultural enclaves may be able to induce change beyond their small socio-demographic size. In fact, there is a robust corpus of literature from David McClelland (1961) to Richard Florida (2002) on entrepreneurship, creativity and social change that emphasizes the role of outliers in generating innovation and determining the general evolution of social systems including (especially) local and national economies. It is thus not too far-fetched to think that, in at least some circumstances, national economic and institutional systems are shaped more by the outlier, minority cultural forces than by the mainstream, modal ones.

Nothing in this argument is revolutionary. In a sense, this approach is what happens in practice when a researcher wants to understand a cultural phenomenon and its impact in a country or society—dehomogenization and disaggregation. Despite the talk of 'national cultures,' one could notice how many times, once a causal and explanatory challenge is on the

table, the analysis dispenses rapidly with the national-level generalizations and clichés and moves rapidly to different, more relevant, levels of
analysis. In this chapter we make the argument explicit: aggregated-level,
homogeneity-based analysis and description of a national (economic)
culture are incomplete and limited, and more often than not require
several levels of disaggregation and dehomogenization in order to reach
meaningful data and insights.

Moreover, in the process we come to make an additional, related point
that has been lingering in the literature since Oskar Morgenstern's classical study *On Accuracy of Economic Observations* (1950: p.4) formulated
it explicitly in the context of economics: 'the value of an observation
depends not only on its immediate level of accuracy but also the particular way the observation has been combined with others (many of them
non-numerical).' In a sense, our chapter is an extension of Morgenstern's
argument. To make sense of a culture and its impact on economic action,
we need many observations, at many levels, from many angles and with
many textures, forms and contents. Morgenstern's book is built around
the idea that there are many reasons why one should be deeply concerned
with 'accuracy' of quantitative economic data and observations and
explores the problem of errors. In our argument we go beyond this point.
We acknowledge the problem of errors and the fact that in examining the
problem of accuracy and relevance of data we are forced to use in most
cases 'only a common sense approach—or what we believe to be common
sense' (Morgenstern 1950: p.7). We focus on a deeper problem, which is
the limits of the homogenization–aggregation approach even in circumstances in which errors are a minor problem.

This specific theoretical and methodological problem has been an
increasingly important theme in the neo-Austrian school, more specifically in the research program that follows the line of arguments that
link human action to belief systems, cognition and interpretations. The
research program elaborates a nuanced view of the role of 'culture' both
as a component of the social and economic reality and as an explanatory
variable in the theories and approaches aimed at analyzing and interpreting that reality. This program, first fully articulated by Don Lavoie, has
been further developed by Peter Boettke, who has repeatedly discussed the
role of culture in the traditional Austrian political economy framework,
and has been given a more radical thrust in the line of research advanced
by two other students of Don Lavoie, Emily Chamlee-Wright and Virgil
Storr. Their work pursues consistently the logical and methodological
implications of the interpretive and cultural turn articulated by Lavoie;
'culture is not an immutable given with which a society must learn to
love. Nor is it homogenous within nations, or even within families. It is a

complex of diverse tensions, ever evolving, always open to new manifestations and permutations' (Lavoie and Chamlee-Wright 2000: p. 18).

In taking the cultural-interpretive turn to a new level—and especially in
Storr's *Understanding the Culture of Markets* (2013: p. 3)—the notion of
culture is to be dehomogenized and disaggregated in a programmatic way,
based on a methodology of interpretation. Because, 'rather than homogenous and static, cultures are both heterogeneous and dynamic,' they
are hence to be approached through a rather discriminating conceptual
filter, a strategy that opens the way for further advances in an applied and
empirical direction of this line of investigations.

> If economics is a science which recognizes people's thoughts and beliefs as the
> essential data and is concerned with the culture of markets, then the privileging
> qualitative over quantitative methods of apprehending history is more appro-
> priate. Stated another way, any empirical approach that hopes to illustrate and
> complement a social science that aims at recovering the meanings that individu-
> als attach to their actions and environments would necessarily emphasize thick
> descriptions. (Storr 2013: p. 92)

In this respect, this chapter is also a contribution to this direction of
research and builds on this revealed existence of an underlying logic in
the approaches inspired by the Austrian tradition. Oskar Morgenstern's
Austrian roots and the neo-Austrian economics and culture research
program spearheaded today by Storr both reveal the existence of this
dehomogenizing logic. Finally, we explore the issue without rehash-
ing standard epistemological arguments, but by illustrating the basic
parameters of the theme using as a vehicle a concrete example. The
Romanian case is a good vehicle for basic explorations in many relevant
directions of interest, while having a significant potential for interesting
generalizations.

13.2 THE AGGREGATIVE, HOMOGENEITY, NATIONAL LEVEL IN COMPARATIVE PERSPECTIVE

The 'national culture' aggregative approach consolidates the diversity of
cultures, attitudes and values coexisting in a given social space, and it does
it at the level of geopolitical units known as 'national states' or 'nations.'
This strategy allows, first, a broad picture of the 'culture' in case and,
second, its relative positioning in relationship to other similar entities (or,
more precisely, operational constructs). Concentrating a diversity of features into several data points facilitates inter-cultural comparability. Yet

a question remains—how useful are the insights obtained for our understanding economic action in the specific cases of the nations portrayed? How relevant the information thus conveyed, and how descriptively appropriate it may be, remains a matter of circumstance and debate. It depends on the research questions being asked. The limits become clearer and clearer the more one delves into the data. We look at how Romanian economic, political and civic cultural values are situated in the context of other European countries in order to illustrate this point. We use as a vehicle the data of the European Social Survey (Norwegian Social Science Data Services 2008), the most recent round which provides all the relevant data.

We start with economic values per se. Two types of attitudes regarding economic and social action are of particular interest in the context of this discussion: attitudes towards inequality and the necessity of public intervention to reduce it, and attitudes towards the role of the state in the economy. Most European respondents agree that 'Large differences in people's incomes are acceptable to properly reward differences in talents and efforts,' and Romanians do not take a different stance than the rest. The only clear outlier, with a reduced tolerance towards inequality, is Hungary. The other group is composed of respondents who neither agree nor disagree with the statement. This group brings together Finland, Croatia, Portugal, the Russian Federation, Sweden, Slovenia and Slovakia. However, even though differences in income based on talent and effort are generally acceptable, government intervention is called for to 'reduce differences in income levels.' In most European countries, respondents agree with this intervention (2 on a scale of 1 to 5, where 1 indicates strongly agree and 5 strongly disagree). Hungary stands out as the country with strong agreement (the median is 1), and the median among respondents from Denmark is 3, neither agreement nor disagreement. As an intermediary conclusion, we find that Romania stays close to the European median of apparent acceptance of income inequality based on inequality in talent and efforts, accompanied by a desired government intervention to reduce differences in income levels.

At this juncture let us note as a parenthesis that the approach we employ in this chapter will follow the practice of using various estimations of 'attitudes' as a proxy for 'culture.' However, we are fully aware that culture is not reducible to 'attitudes' but something much more complex and multifaceted. Our reductionist strategy will not however undermine the robustness of our argument, because that additional complexity would operate, by its very nature, exactly in the direction of increasing the heterogeneity. Hence if one may make the argument for heterogeneity based on a discussion of 'attitudes,' by implication that argument will be even stronger when projected on the background of a more nuanced approach to the definition and operationalization of 'culture.'

Further, in order to get a better sense of the Romanian views on the role of the state, especially in the area of social protection in comparison with the rest of the Europeans, we consider the following items from the European Social Survey:

> Should or should not be the government's responsibility to: a) ensure a job for everyone who wants one?; b) ensure adequate health care for the sick?; c) ensure a reasonable standard of living for the old?; d) ensure a reasonable standard of living for the unemployed?; e) ensure sufficient child care services for working parents?; f) provide paid leave from work for people who temporarily have to care for sick family members?

Again, a broad comparative setting is emerging. The most non-interventionist attitudes are to be found among Swiss respondents, followed at a considerable distance by the Dutch. France, Belgium and the United Kingdom share moderately non-interventionist attitudes, followed by the group closer to the average, but still non-interventionist, made up of Germany, Ireland and Slovakia. Middle-of-the-road, neither interventionist nor non-interventionist attitudes come from Denmark, Sweden, Poland, Finland, Norway and Slovenia. The next group, of mild interventionists, consists of Romania and Estonia, followed by a Mediterranean-dominated group of Turkey, Portugal, Cyprus, Spain and Croatia plus Hungary. High interventionism is displayed by Israel, Bulgaria, Russia and Greece, with the highest scores for Latvia and Ukraine. Again, Romanian respondents are close to the European median, with a slightly more pronounced preference towards interventionism. How important and relevant this insight is when it comes to more specific economic policies and actions taking place in Romania, however, it is difficult to say. Note that Romania shares the cluster with the acclaimed economic-policy libertarian Estonia and also with Hungary, a country whose erratic-interventionist economic policies are a recurrent headache for the EU and IMF. The face value explanatory capacity of this data set seems rather feeble.

The overall picture regarding the state as an economic actor can be better grasped if complemented with information on the attitudes towards entrepreneurship. The *Amway European Entrepreneurship Report 2012* provides a comparative perspective across 16 European countries (Amway GmbH and GfK Nuremberg, Germany 2012). The Romanian respondents' attitudes towards self-employment are mostly positive (66 percent), but lower than the 16-country average (69 percent). Romanian attitudes are in the close vicinity of Portugal and Spain, surpassing Austria,

Turkey and Germany. The most positive towards self-employment are the Dutch (85 percent), followed by the French, the British and the Italians. Somewhat surprisingly, the negative attitudes among Romanians are at a significantly lower level than the average: 16 percent of Romanian respondents view self-employment negatively compared with the overall average of 25 percent. This places Romanian respondents in company with the French and the British. Most pessimistic about entrepreneurship are Hungarians (47 percent view it negatively), followed by the Austrians and the Germans (35 percent). Again, we get some perhaps interesting information about Romania, but how relevant and operational is it? What could one make of all these data? It seems that whatever sense we get from the data comes more from our intuitive corroboration of the data with other data, insights and images than from these data in themselves. We are not suggesting that the exercise is not useful, but rather that the answer regarding the epistemic value added at stake is neither simple nor obvious. We are reminded of Morgenstern's point that the value of such observations is dependent on how they are combined with other, 'non-numerical,' observations. Lavoie and Chamlee-Wright (2000) have also warned about approaches to the issue of culture that see it as a phenomenon that could be represented as a list of formalizable traits and operationally reducible to a set of quantitative indices. In a similar vein Storr (2013) has offered a critique of the statistical homogenization of culture and specifically of relying on national surveys seen as a quantitative rendering of cultural phenomena.

We can see now why a case like Romania illustrates our point. As it is a relatively small, not particularly well-known culture, most readers have limited basic ideas, data and views about what Romanian 'culture' is or should look like. Thus by simply going through this mental exercise we can get a sense of what happens when we interpret statistics like those above—how little is left for us to hang on to when we are not able to mobilize all kinds of additional knowledge, information and data based in personal and tacit knowledge about the case. Usually, our next best option is to use similar or related cases to help us by extension and analogy.

For example, to offset the limits, one may say that we have to extend the range of values and attitudes surveyed. As economic attitudes and values are always intertwined with political ones, we need to take a look at those, too. This is in a sense a quantitative solution. But extending the coverage of the aggregated–national level does not take us very far. We will look at two relevant sets of political values: trust in political institutions and self-positioning on the right–left political spectrum. General trust in the main political institutions aggregates the answers given by respondents with regard to trust in a country's parliament, in the legal system, in the police, in politicians, in political parties, in the European Parliament and in the United Nations. A comparison of the median scores across countries reveals a cluster made up of Ukraine and Bulgaria, which have extremely low trust in politics, followed by another one, bringing together Latvia, Croatia and Hungary. Moderate levels of low trust are found in the Czech Republic, Greece, Poland and the Russian Federation. A cluster of low trust countries, but near the average, is made up of Portugal, Israel, Romania and Turkey. Extremely high trust is found in Denmark and Finland, followed by Norway, the Netherlands and Sweden. Cyprus and Switzerland come next, and closer to the average are Estonia, Spain and France. The group comprising Slovakia, Slovenia, Ireland and the United Kingdom captures the average. Asking respondents to self-position on the political spectrum generates two clusters: Bulgaria, Cyprus, France, Germany, Italy, the Netherlands, Slovenia and Spain display more leftist attitudes, while more right-oriented countries include Finland, Moldova, Norway, Poland, Romania, Sweden, Turkey and Serbia. In brief, these findings reveal Romanian respondents to be close to the European average in both regards, but with an inclination towards distrust in political institutions and a slight preference for center-right political attitudes. What does this mean? Corroboration with data, insights and assessments outside of this data set may help, and even then the result may be confusing.

Finally, one of the fundamental determinants of social and economic action is mutual trust among individuals, which describes, in part, social capital in a community (Putnam et al. 1994; Knack and Keefer 1997; Tabellini 2005, 2008; Sapienza et al. 2007; Guiso et al. 2008). The European Social Survey helps to place Romania in context. Turkey is the country where people have least trust in their fellow citizens, followed by a cluster made up of Romania, Bulgaria and Greece. Croatia, Slovakia, Poland, Hungary and the Russian Federation share a moderate lack of trust. At the other end of the continuum, with high mutual trust, we find Denmark, Norway, Sweden, Finland and the Netherlands. Moderately high trust is to be found in Switzerland and Ireland. Average trust levels, neither very high nor very low, are found in a cluster consisting of Slovenia, the Czech Republic, Latvia, Spain and France. This is an interesting result. In fact, the clustering makes some immediate intuitive sense, and the result seems to have direct explanatory traction. But was that the outcome of the data set or the outcome of a confirmatory corroboration with already existing views we have about European countries and their cultures?

In summary, we can get a certain sense of the Romanian economic culture by looking at national-level central tendencies in a comparative context. One may extend that context from a European to a global one. Some marginal value will definitely be added by this move. Yet no substantial, major qualitative jump will take place. When that happens, it seems to be the result of an implicit corroborative cognitive process in which the main carry capacity is coming from implicit triangulation and intuitive residuals. For somebody willing to study the relationship between national culture, economic activity and various facets of economic institutions and performance, the aggregative approach offers a limited space for interpretative and analytical maneuvers if one factors out corroboration and triangulation.

13.3 BEYOND THE NATIONAL AGGREGATES AND HOMOGENIZATION: THE PROBLEM OF DUALISM

The very concept of a 'national culture' as operationalized in the data sets above is legitimate yet problematic. There are three basic elements that go into the construct. The first and most important is the strong parameter created by the existing political boundaries of the state. We may be talking about national culture, but we do it in the terms defined and enforced by a political entity, the Modern State. In our understanding of 'national culture' there are also (second) certain implicit notions of ethnicity and (third) an emphasis on a common language. Somehow, one of these three (or a combination of them) is presumed to ensure the unifying vector. They are in one way or another presetting the very concept of 'national culture,' as used in the mainstream operationalization.

It goes without saying that, to reach a concept like 'Romanian national economic culture,' one has to engage in an entire set of particular simplifications, assumptions and stylized facts regarding the phenomenon. The question is, in what measure do those simplifications and stylizations undermine the very purpose of identifying the relevant cultural forces at work in a social system? Are the strong parameters created by the state sufficient to generate a satisfying basis for the kind of simplifications and homogenization we practice? Once the variety of linguistic, ethnic, religious and other differences have been lumped into an aggregated construct, driven by national state–induced parameters, how much explanatory power is left?

Returning to the Romania case study, the country appears to be relatively homogeneous. According to the most recent population census (National Institute of Statistics 2011a), the ethnic structure is composed of 88.6 percent self-declared Romanians, 6.5 percent Hungarians, 3.2 percent Roma, and other ethnic groups with less than 0.3 percent of the population, such as Ukrainians, Germans, Turks, Lipovan Russians, and Tatars. Linguistically, 90.65 percent of the population speak Romanian as their native language, 6.66 percent Hungarian, 1.3 percent Romani, 0.26 percent Ukrainian, 0.14 percent German, 0.13 percent Turkish, and less than 0.1 percent Russian or Tatar. Religion has a similarly homogeneous pattern: 85.95 percent of Romanian permanent residents are Orthodox, 4.56 percent are Roman Catholic, 3.16 percent are members of the Reformed Church, 1.93 percent are Pentecostals, 0.84 percent are Greek Catholic, 0.62 percent are Baptists, 0.45 percent are Seventh-Day Adventists, and other denominations have less than 0.45 percent each. Only 0.11 percent of the population declare they are atheists.

Yet, taking a closer look, things are not so simple. There are strong reasons to probe the homogeneity perspective with heterogeneity conjectures. For example, a key feature of the societies of the Southeastern European region is their dualism. Once we place the Romanian case in the narrower context of the Balkans and consider the country through the conceptual lenses of dualism, the limits of the homogeneity and national-level aggregated approach to the study of its culture become clearer. Social and economic dualism is a feature that has its origins in the modernization process, which has shaped in a distinctive way both the structure and the dynamics of the polities and societies of these countries.

The concept and theory of dualism originate in the study of European-owned plantations in Southeast Asia (Boeke 1953). Although the European-owned plantations reflected capitalist lines, they coexisted with an indigenous economy in which people worked and lived along the traditional lines. The South Asian example was extreme, but telling. The 'advanced' and 'backward' sectors coexisted—capitalism coexisted with a traditional economy based on pre-capitalist values and culture. In a dual economy, the capitalist economy (with its values and culture) has to accommodate and/or overcome traditional ones. The two, while in contact with each other, are not fully integrated.

It is obvious that a traditional, an agricultural and a modern industrial sector have different values and cultural patterns. Dualism may be described at three levels: economic, social and cultural. Any description of the economic system would be incomplete without references to the social and cultural element that encapsulates it. Modernization itself may be conceptualized as a dualist story, a transition that may be described in both a social-economic way, following an economic and institutional perspective, and cultural-spiritual ways, following the Max Weber–Reinhard Bendix perspective. Irrespective of the approach, the dualist perspective has a strong analytical and descriptive potential and could be and in fact has been extended to a variety of societies and cultures. In fact, the neo-Austrian approach has made important steps in this respect not only in developing a dehomogenized empirical approach to specific cases, but also in exploring a multifaceted approach that goes beyond the dual model. For instance, Storr (2004) explores a certain form of dualism in Bahamian economic culture. In addition, he argues that cultural dualism is, in part, a form of a broader phenomenon, a reflection of the 'multiple spirits that animate the market' (Storr 2013: p.69). Any economy or social system that has several distinctive sectors may be approached using a pluralist mode, irrespective of their nature. The levels and dimensions of the approach may be multiplied, in the function of the empirical realities on the ground. Returning to the initial concept of dualism, the notion is today applied even to more developed economies, where there are for instance core regions and less developed peripheries. It is also obvious that economic development involves the transfer of resources, capital accumulation and productivity growth in the modern sector and a displacement of the traditional sector. In brief, understanding the dynamics of such dual systems requires three things: first, understanding the traditional sector; second, understanding the modern sector; and, third, understanding the interrelationship—interaction and symbiosis—between the traditional sector and the modern one.

The dualist model is relevant to all countries in analyzing their modernization. The Southeast European ones, including Romania, are no exception (also see Runst, this volume, Chapter 14, on East and West Germany). But, as extensively explained in Aligica (2003), while the majority of other European countries went through a transition period of economic dualism, they overcame it and then entered the mature phase of an industrial economy. The Balkan countries' development and modernization trajectory was diverted by dualism in a specific direction; specifically, what was supposed to be a stage of economic development became a structural feature. The dualism of the region is evident to foreigners, and in fact it became a trademark of the region. The typical description of these countries was epitomized by a British diplomat: 'In analyzing their national character you have two distinct classes to deal with—the governmental and commercial which wear coats, trousers and boots and the peasant which affect jackets, petticoats and sandals' (Hulme Beaman, quoted in Mazover 2000). In other words, the cultural and social dualism was so blatant that it was reducible to pure anthropological typologies.

For the Balkan countries, including Romania, dualism was a constant and active deterring factor on the development path. Pioneers of development theory (Love 1996) used the Balkans and Southeastern Europe as their basic source of inspiration and case study before and immediately after World War II (Rosenstein-Rodan 1959). The statistics

on the population employed in agriculture and the traditional sector
before World War II are revealing: the percentage of the population
employed in the traditional sector was 80 percent in Bulgaria, 75 percent
in Greece, 77 percent in Romania, 80 percent in Turkey and 78 percent in
Yugoslavia. The percentage of national product from agriculture (usually
including forestry and fisheries) was 40 percent in Bulgaria, 40 percent in
Greece, 45 percent in Romania, 50 percent in Turkey and 40 percent in
Yugoslavia.

The numbers were slightly smaller at the beginning of the Cold War.
Then the countries of the region went on different paths. Turkey and
Greece benefited from the NATO shield and the European integration
process. The rest of the region went through forced industrialization
imposed by the communist regimes. Yet, interestingly enough, industrialization apparently did not solve the problem. Thus, after the collapse
of communism, it is tempting to consider that the economies and societies
of the region were challenged by a 'double dualism': on the one hand, a
modern sector versus a traditional sector (or at least surviving fragments
of it) and, on the other hand, a (post)communist sector versus a market
sector. Old dualism seemed to have survived. Employment in agriculture,
as well as the rural population, remains very high in each country of the
region for the 1990–2000 decade: Albania (58 percent, 61 percent); Bosnia
and Herzegovina (32 percent, 59 percent); Bulgaria (35 percent, 32 percent);
Croatia (17 percent, 44 percent); Greece (34 percent, 41 percent); Republic
of Moldova (43 percent, 54 percent); Romania (38 percent, 45 percent);
Slovenia (17 percent, 50 percent); the former Yugoslavian Republic of
Macedonia (40 percent, 40 percent); Turkey (65 percent, 31 percent); and
Yugoslavia (Serbia/Montenegro) with agricultural employment unavail-
able and the rural population at about 50 percent.

What does that mean in the context of our discussion? It means that
there are strong reasons to be careful when we are working with perspectives that assume homogeneity and in which methodological aggregation
is taken for granted. There are a lot of possible implications that should be
at least explored. We outline a few possibilities below.

For instance, dualism has strong implications for the political culture
of a society (Aligica 2003: pp. 307–8). From a cultural standpoint, the
existence of dualism implies the existence of an important segment of the
population with a specific traditional, cultural and behavioral pattern. It is
expected that, in the region, the values associated with traditional societies
and cultures are much more present, and will continue to be, and that this
reality will imply a tacit, but significant, resistance to change in the political culture of the countries of the region. That, as has been extensively
documented in the literature, could take specific political culture forms,

including collectivism, authoritarianism, and animosity toward individual rights and toward ethnic and religious diversity and differences (Jelavich and Jelavich 1974; Mazover 2000). Moreover, there is a strong correlation between those cultural traits and a nationalist political culture (Aligica 2003).

There are additional considerations that should be taken into account. Culture in itself and by itself may not be so powerful. Yet, when it is anchored in a specific economic and institutional structure that reinforces it, it may be resilient. Economic dualism is one of the deepest and most important structural forces. Its economic structure may shape the attitudes and values of the people and contribute to the lock-in. The key issue in this respect is that traditional societies are social exchange societies. As explained in Aligica (2003: p. 309), strong interpersonal social networks are one key feature of traditional societies, and their strength might explain the resilience of dualism. In a dualist system social exchange networks penetrate the entire society, including the modern sector. If market relations do not connect the traditional sector to the modern one, social networks do. But they do more than that—they penetrate deeply the modern sector and affect its structure and functioning. The stronger the traditional sector, the stronger the penetration. That is the reason why the ratios of urban to rural and agricultural to industrial used above are not an entirely accurate statistic of the strengths of the traditional sector. Political society has its share of such penetration too. Moreover, the system of patronage and clientelism, as mechanisms of linking the sectors, may become a defining feature of the political society in dualist countries. Therefore, in the measure in which the culture has been a problem for the development of the region, it is important to note that culture is part of an entire system that combines various social and economic elements in surprising ways. The impact of culture on political and economic dynamics is thus a complex phenomenon that cannot be side-stepped easily.

When approaching a case like Romania, it is important never to neglect the fact that structural heterogeneity caused by dualism may still play a role and that economic dualism represents an anchor for social and cultural dualism. Together the three generate a reinforcing system that has significant direct and spillover effects on the political economy system and on the policies of the state. The Romanian case, seen in the narrower comparative context of the Balkan states through dualism theory conceptual lenses, reveals thus the possibility of a pattern of heterogeneity that otherwise is missed in the national-level aggregation of cultural economic indicators. That being said, it may be the case that all these presumed dualist features do not play a significant role today or are in the process of remission. The argument about the assumptions and methods of our approaches to the study of economic culture is nonetheless valid. Heterogeneity matters and, when we have reasons to explore it, we should go without hesitation beyond the heterogeneity perspective in the direction indicated by the guiding conjecture in point.

13.3.1   The Minorities: A Constant Source of Heterogeneity

The Romanian case offers a second way to illuminate the limits of the aggregative, national-level approach. The role certain ethnic, religious and cultural minorities had in the economic history of Romania could not be captured in the aggregative and homogenized approaches discussed in section 13.2. It is important to emphasize this fact, because the minority outlier factor is one of the key sources of economic performance that may get lost in the aggregative strategy (McClelland 1961; McClelland and Winter 1971). In the case of Romania, as the great economist and economic historian Nicolas Spulber explained, 'The fluctuations in the positions of the Jewish population in the Romanian economy directly reflect the ebb and flow of Romanian entrepreneurship over the century considered' (1966: p. 271).

One could hardly understand economic modernization in Romania without taking into account this minority, which has never been larger than 4.5 percent of the entire population (or at some point 5 percent by some accounts). As Spulber explained, 'The overwhelming majority of the population—the peasantry—manifested little inclination for trading, at least until the beginning of the twentieth century.' In fact, the peasant household 'was self-contained, independent of the market; the peasant was mason and carpenter, while his wife was spinner and seamstress' (ibid.: p. 271). Thus, on the eve of World War I, 'the occupational pattern of the Jewish workforce reflected clearly its position in the economy.' That position was due to the Jewish enterprising spirit as well as various discriminatory restrictions in place.

> While the Jewish workforce represented only 2.3 per cent of the total workforce, it accounted for 12.2 per cent of the total manpower in industry and for 31.3 per cent of the total manpower in trade. In contrast to the pattern of total manpower in which 76 per cent engaged in agriculture and only 9.6 and 4.1 per cent respectively were employed in industry and trade, 79.1 per cent of the Jewish workforce was engaged in industry and trade (41.8 and 37.3 per cent respectively). The Jewish minority had acquired thus unmistakable urban and industrial-commercial characteristics. It may be noted that the Jewish population included a relatively high percentage not only of owners big and small in industry and trades, but also a high percentage of the workers: 32.1 per cent

of industry's owners were Jews—but so were 81.2 per cent of the industrial workers and artisans. No significant numbers of Jews were employed in mining or in public institutions. (ibid.: p. 105)

The Jewish minority continued to play a key role for the entire period of pre-communist Romanian modernization. A Royal Superior Economic Council inventory of the economic positions of the Romanians, Jews and other minorities published by the end of the 1930s and quoted by Spulber, 'shows that at the time, the councils of administration of the industrial societies were staffed one-third each by Romanians, Jews, and "others,"' while 'out of the individual industrial and commercial firms 48.6 percent were Romanian, 31.1 percent Jewish, 20.3 percent "others"' (ibid.: p. 115). This was for a minority of less than 5 percent.

To conclude, the evidence of the role of minorities in the overall economic development at the national level is overwhelming. And, in general, the relevance of a perspective that clearly identifies the role of such minority outliers is well established. At the same time, the limits of an approach that tries to gain explanatory power by aggregating data under the homogeneity assumption at the national level is clear too. This presents another question: where do we go from here?

In answering this question, the idea is not that an aggregated perspective is meaningless or useless or that disaggregated approaches are the unique key to understanding culture and its economic implications. After all, what is a disaggregated approach? What may be seen as aggregated from one angle may be seen as disaggregated from another angle or level. There are degrees of aggregation and disaggregation. The 'national' level is just one among others. The idea is that in our approaches we need to combine different angles and different strategies, at different levels, some of them focusing on aggregation and homogeneity, others focused on disaggregation and heterogeneity. We need a combined, multifaceted approach that captures different levels and facets of the phenomenon of interest. Being fixated on the 'national culture' level and its correlation with various macro and national economic indicators misses the point.

13.3.2 Regional Differences

In the case of Romania, one may follow several directions of disaggregation that are embedded in the very way the data are collected. For instance, one may unpack the aggregated data and, using the relevant national surveys, explore the dimensions and aspects of heterogeneity of the Romanian economic, political and civic cultural values. One may look for instance at differences across historical regions, across the rural–urban divide, across education and occupational profiles and across the generational divide. While the rest of the set contains rather familiar themes that in one way or another are present in each culture, the first, the regional divide, deserves attention.

There are nine 'historical regions' in Romania: Transylvania (19.97 percent of the entire population and 23.93 percent of the country's area), Muntenia (21.53 percent of the population and 19.68 percent of the total area), Moldavia (20.89 percent of the population and 19.37 percent of the total area), Oltenia (10.39 percent of the population and 12.25 percent of the total area), Dobrogea (4.42 percent of the population and 6.53 percent of the total area), Banat (4.86 percent of the population and 7.22 percent of the total area), Crisana (5.03 percent of the population and 6.42 percent of the total area), Maramures (4.15 percent of the population and 4.50 percent of the total area) and Bucharest (8.81 percent of the population and 0.10 percent of the total area), the capital city, which, although traditionally part of Muntenia, is typically analyzed as an entity of its own, given its specific economic and social features (the most socially and economically developed region in Romania).

These regions have a long history during which they received rather diverse cultural influences. Transylvania and its adjacent regions (Banat, Crisana and Maramures) and Bucovina (the northern part of Moldavia) have been mostly influenced by the Habsburg Empire and the Kingdom of Hungary, of which they were part until 1918. During the 1530s, Moldavia became a tributary to the Ottoman Empire, with internal and partial external autonomy. After 1812, its eastern part, now forming the Republic of Moldova, was ceded by the Ottoman Empire to the Russian Empire. The western part of Moldavia remained autonomous, and united in 1859 with Wallachia to form the Kingdom of Romania. Wallachia refers to the southern regions of Muntenia (including Bucharest) and Oltenia. This region was under Ottoman suzerainty almost from its original founding in the fourteenth century, with brief periods of Russian protection during the seventeenth and eighteenth centuries. Dobrogea was under Ottoman rule until 1878, when its northern part joined Romania and its southern part Bulgaria. There are strong reasons to suspect that there are some elements of heterogeneity in place when we talk about the Romanian national economic culture.

What does all that mean more precisely? The comparative analysis of the 'historical regions' reveals statistically significant patterns of both heterogeneity and homogeneity. Let us illustrate our case using as a starting point a Romanian Value Study, conducted by the Research Institute for the Quality of Life (2008). When it comes to social capital and trust in others, respondents in Transylvania display the highest levels of trust in their fellow citizens, and those in Bucharest the smallest. Respondents in Moldavia and those in Southern Romania closely approximate the median. Trust in national political institutions reveals statistically significant differences across regions. Transylvanian and Moldavian respondents report slightly higher levels of trust in national institutions, while respondents in Bucharest have little trust in them. Some results are intriguing: when it comes to the perceived freedom and control over their own lives, the Transylvanian respondents seem to think less than others that they are in control of their lives (60 percent compared to the 66 percent national average), while those in Moldavia seem to believe in a higher proportion than the average that they are in control of their lives (71 percent). This goes against conventional wisdom, as people in Transylvania are considered to be more entrepreneurial and active, quite the opposite to those in Moldavia.

Attitudes towards economic action have been the focus of a research project conducted by the Center for Institutional Analysis and Development Bucharest (Aligica and Matei 2011). A significant difference emerged when the preference for stability over financial gain was estimated using the following survey question: 'A small but stable wage is preferable to a large but uncertain one.' The respondents from Maramures, Dobrogea, Oltenia and Muntenia tend to be more risk averse, while uncertainty is better dealt with by respondents in Banat, followed by those from Bucharest, Transylvania and Crisana. Similarly, in the case of resistance to change and traditionalism, the differences across historical regions are statistically significant. Respondents from Muntenia are the most resistant to change, followed by those in Oltenia. Respondents in Dobrogea have the highest preference for change, followed by those from Transylvania, Bucharest, Moldavia and Banat. When it comes to perceptions on the role of the state, some variation at a regional level emerges again. The most distrustful are respondents from Oltenia, followed by those from Moldavia. State actions are viewed slightly more favorably by respondents in Bucharest, followed by those in Maramures. Yet there are no statistically significant regional differences with regard to self-positioning on the right–left political scale (Comsa 2008). This finding is also confirmed by data from the Public Opinion Barometer (Soros Foundation, Romania 2007).

A very interesting insight comes from a set of two additional questions. Of the respondents, 79 percent agree that, during the time of Ceausescu (the communist dictator 1964–89), communism was a good idea improperly applied. Most favorable of communism are respondents from Oltenia (94 percent of respondents from the region agree with the statement), Banat (88 percent), Muntenia (86 percent) and Dobrogea (85 percent). Least favorable of communism are respondents from Transylvania (71 percent of respondents from the region agree with the statement), Moldavia (72 percent) and Bucharest (73 percent). Although these approval ratings of communism are high, the ratings for capitalism are slightly higher: 83 percent of respondents agree that 'capitalism is a good idea improperly applied.' Respondents in Dobrogea, Oltenia and Maramures are more frequent supporters of capitalism than respondents in Transylvania (the smallest share of supporters—75 percent), Crisana and Banat.

In brief, the data show that when it comes to economic, political and civic culture there are several reasons to think that telling a 'national culture' story may miss some important aspects of the phenomena of interest. As one may expect, the other potential cleavages (generational, educational and rural–urban) reinforce this conclusion. We have in such cases patterns of heterogeneity and homogeneity that deserve to be identified as such, for both analytical and disciplinary reasons.

13.3.3 A Multitude of Cleavages

Let us start with the rural–urban divide. The respondents from rural areas display significantly lower levels of trust in others than those in urban areas. In fact, the smaller a rural community is, the lower the trust in others. Urban respondents are slightly more liberal than their rural counterparts. Respondents from rural areas prefer a larger degree of stability and wage predictability over higher but unpredictable revenues. Communism is viewed more favorably by rural respondents than by urban ones, but there are no statistically significant differences with regard to how capitalism is viewed. However, and it is very important to note this, the heterogeneity is less evident in opinion surveys than in other statistics. Other data show a much larger cleavage. For example, entrepreneurs are three times more frequent in urban than in rural areas (National Institute of Statistics 2011b). While objective economic and social conditions are considerably different in the two types of areas, opinions frequently converge. The same convergence may be seen when it comes to the perceived control over one's own life, self-positioning on the right–left political scale, and trust in national political institutions. An unexpected finding is that when it comes to resistance to change there are no significant differences between rural and urban areas. Distrust of state action is another line of homogeneity between the two.

In brief, the data show us that, despite the economic and social discrepancies revealed by other data sets, there is convergence among rural and urban areas with regard to culture and values. The rural–urban divide seems to be shrinking. Cultural dualism defined on the basis of that cleavage is not dead yet, and the differences have not yet been blurred. The analysis reveals sufficient divergence to give ground for further relevance of the notion, yet it seems that Romania has passed, historically speaking, the stage where the traditional rural–urban cultural dualism is paramount. New forms of cultural heterogeneity may be now on the rise. One possible explanation for the trend towards urban–rural homogenization may have to do with the widespread access to similar communication technologies by the people in rural areas. Another may have to do with large urban–rural migration movements during the 1990s transition. Not only did people migrate, but their ideas and values were disseminated across the new communities they became part of. Alternatively, it may be the case that apparent convergence is mainly a function of the questions asked in the survey and the survey design. A more refined approach would reconfirm the cultural dualism hypothesis. Also, a differently structured survey might identify the emergence of new cleavages and heterogeneities. In the context of our discussion the bottom line is that, again, we have come to a point where the limits of the 'national culture' aggregative perspective are becoming evident. To understand the cultural phenomenon and its implications one has to go beyond that perspective.

Needless to say, an exploration of the contours of the Romanian economically relevant culture via the patterns of education and occupational profiles leads to a similar conclusion. At least in the light of our analysis (Aligica and Matei 2011), the emerging results are neither surprising nor very illuminating. But it is nonetheless worth noting observations such as these: The occupational status does not produce statistically significant differences in the perceived fairness of state action. Approval of communism is higher among housewives and domestic workers, peasants, the self-employed and pensioners. The least favorable to communism are students. Approval of capitalism is homogeneous across occupational statuses. The educational status does produce significant differences in attitudes and values when it comes to preference for stability over financial gain. Respondents with tertiary and post-tertiary education are less risk averse than the average. That is to say, the more educated a respondent is, the less risk averse that person is with regard to his/her job. Resistance to change and traditionalism follow the same pattern. Education however is irrelevant when it comes to attitudes towards capitalism. But education produces differences in attitudes towards communism: respondents with tertiary education display a significantly lower approval of communism than respondents without, among which graduates of vocational training and of post-secondary education display a more pronounced approval of this political and economic regime (Aligica and Matei 2011).

Last but not least, one may look at age groups. Again, we don't need to go into details to make the point, as again we are talking about a domain where heterogeneity is normally expected. It is interesting to note though that the group most skeptical regarding the fairness of state intervention is the 25- to 34-year-old group. At the other extreme are respondents aged 55 and older. Approval of communism is the highest in the age group 45–54. This is especially relevant since these are the individuals most economically active in established business, as shown by other survey data (Petru et al. 2011: pp. 17–18). Although age groups have different opinions about communism, they seem to share the same attitude towards capitalism, as there is no significant difference across age groups in support for capitalism. The trust in others varies across age groups, but not very markedly. Trust in national political institutions has no statistically significant differences across age groups.

To conclude, the discussion has focused only on a small set of issues and facets that spring naturally from the very structure of the basic categories and coding used in the data collection for national surveys. Yet, out of it, one may see emerging a complex and interesting pattern of homogeneity and heterogeneity. Some of the features thus illuminated may be politically and economically relevant. But the specific relevance is something to be decided as a function of specific research questions and specific research agendas. There are questions that could be dealt with only in terms of national-level aggregated data, but their number is rather small. For the rest, one simply needs to go beyond that, and adopt a question- and problem-driven mode.

13.4 CONCLUSION

We have seen how the conceptualization and operationalization of 'national economic culture' via statistical aggregation under the assumption of national homogeneity have limits that require a complementary approach. Without denying the usefulness of the homogeneity-focused, aggregated perspective, we have shown, using as a vehicle the Romanian case, the need to have it bolstered by a heterogeneity-focused approach, even if the heterogeneity hypotheses may have a mere heuristic and methodological role to play. One way or another, the national-level aggregated approach—a popular approach to the study of the relationship between national economic cultures and economic and institutional performance—could gain substantial explanatory and descriptive potential if seen as part of a broader approach that is foundationally based on the perspective that raises the issue of heterogeneity as a key investigative theme.

In brief, even a small step forward in the direction of dehomogenization and disaggregation means a lot in terms of value added when it comes to cultural analysis and investigation in a systematic and constructive manner of the role of culture in economic action. Are the analysis and interpretation of such data still dependent on tacit knowledge and implicit corroboration? Absolutely. The Austrian theorists' insights in this respect and O. Morgenstern's observation about the role of the 'non-numerical' and the 'common sense approach' are as valid as ever (Morgenstern 1950: pp. 5–6). And this is precisely the key point. Instead of pretending that this is not the case and that we could reduce culture to aggregated data points that are fully meaningful independently of any additional corroboration and tacit or implicit knowledge and insights, it may be more effective if we simply accept this epistemic reality as a fact and try to get the most out of it by exploring systematically its methodological and theoretical implications.

REFERENCES

Aligica, P.D. (2003), 'Structural Constraints: Implications of Economic Dualism for the Development and International Integration of South Eastern Europe,' *Journal of Southern Europe and the Balkans*, **5**(3), 299–314.

Aligica, P.D. and Matei, A. (2011), *Forta de munca in mediul rural: Contributii exploratorii* [Rural labor force: exploratory contributions], Bucharest: Center for Institutional Analysis and Development Eleutheria.

Almond, G.A. and S. Verba (1963), *The Civic Culture: Political Attitudes and Democracy in Five Nations*, Princeton, NJ: Princeton University Press.

Amway Gmbh and GfK Nuremberg, Germany (2012), *Amway European Entrepreneurship Report 2012*, Puchheim, Germany: Amway Gmbh, Corporate Affairs Europe.

Boeke, J.H. (1953), *Economics and Economic Policy of Dual Societies, as Exemplified by Indonesia*, New York: International Secretariat, Institute of Pacific Relations.

Comsa, M. (2008), 'Ideological Self-Placement: Identification, Sophistication, Bases,' in B. Voicu and M. Voicu, *The Values of Romanians: 1993–2006: A Sociological Perspective*, Iasi, Romania: Institutul European, pp. 63–114.

European Commission (2001), *Eurostat Yearbook*, Luxembourg: European Commission.

Florida, R.L. (2002), *The Rise of the Creative Class: And How It's Transforming Work, Leisure, Community and Everyday Life*, New York: Basic Books.

Guiso, L., L. Zingales and P. Sapienza (2008), 'Social Capital as Good Culture,' *Journal of the European Economic Association*, **6**(2–3), 295–320.

Hampden-Turner, C. and A. Trompenaars (1993), *The Seven Cultures of Capitalism: Value Systems for Creating Wealth in the United States, Japan, Germany, France, Britain, Sweden and the Netherlands*, New York: Currency Doubleday.

Inglehart, R. (1990), *Culture Shift in Advanced Industrial Society*, Princeton, NJ: Princeton University Press.

Inglehart, R. (1997), *Modernization and Postmodernization*, Princeton, NJ: Princeton University Press.

Jelavich, C. and B. Jelavich (1974), *The Balkans in Transition: Essays on the Development of Balkan Life and Politics since the Eighteenth Century*, Hamden, CT: Archon Books.

Knack, S. and P. Keefer (1997), 'Does Social Capital Have an Economic Payoff? A Cross-Country Investigation,' *Quarterly Journal of Economics*, **112**(4), 1251–88.

Lampe, J.R. and M.R. Jackson (1982), *Balkan Economic History, 1550–1950: From Imperial Borderlands to Developing Nations*, Bloomington: Indiana University Press.

Lavoie, D. and E. Chamlee-Wright (2000), *Culture and Enterprise*, New York: Routledge.

Love, J.L. (1996), *Crafting the Third World: Theorizing Underdevelopment in Romania and Brazil*, Stanford, CA: Stanford University Press.

Mazover, M. (2000), *The Balkans: A Short History*, New York: Modern Library.

McClelland, D.C. (1961), *The Achieving Society*, New York: Van Nostrand.

McClelland, D.C. and D.G. Winter (1971), *Motivating Economic Achievement: Accelerating Economic Development through Psychological Training*, New York: Free Press.

Mitchell, B.R. (1998), *International Historical Statistics: Europe 1750–1993*, New York: Stockton Press.

Morgenstern, O. (1950), *On Accuracy of Economic Observations*, Princeton, NJ: Princeton University Press.

National Institute of Statistics (2011a), *Population and Household Census*, Bucharest: National Institute of Statistics.

National Institute of Statistics (2011b), *Statistical Yearbook*, Bucharest: National Institute of Statistics.

Norwegian Social Science Data Services, Norway—Data Archive and Distributor of ESS Data (2008), ESS Round 4: European Social Survey Round 4 Data, data file ed. 4.1.

Petru, T.-P., A. Benyovszki, L.-Z. Gyorfy, A. Nagy, D. Matis and S. Pete (2011), *Entrepreneurship in Romania 2011: Country Report*, London: Global Entrepreneurship Monitor.

Putnam, R.D., R. Leonardi and R.Y. Nanetti (1994), *Making Democracy Work: Civic Traditions in Modern Italy*, Princeton, NJ: Princeton University Press.

Research Institute for the Quality of Life (2000), *Report*, Bucharest: Research Institute for the Quality of Life, Romanian Academy.

Rosenstein-Rodan, P.N. (1959), *How to Industrialize an Underdeveloped Area*, Cambridge, MA: Center for International Studies, Massachusetts Institute of Technology.

Sapienza, P., A. Toldra and L. Zingales (2007), *Understanding Trust*, NBER Working Paper No. 13387, September, Cambridge, MA: National Bureau of Economic Research.

Soros Foundation, Romania (2007), *Public Opinion Barometer*, May, Bucharest: Soros Foundation, Romania.

Spulber, N. (1966), *The State and Economic Development in Eastern Europe*, New York: Random House.

Storr, V.H. (2004), *Enterprising Slaves and Master Pirates: Understanding Economic Life in the Bahamas*, New York: Peter Lang.
Storr, V.H. (2013), *Understanding the Culture of Markets*, New York: Routledge.
Tabellini, G. (2005), 'The Role of the State in Economic Development,' *Kyklos*, **58**(2), 283–303.
Tabellini, G. (2008), 'Presidential Address: Institutions and Culture,' *Journal of the European Economic Association*, **6**, 255–94.
United Nations (1997), *UN Statistical Yearbook*, New York: United Nations.

14. Between community and society: political attitudes in transition countries

Petrik Runst

14.1 INTRODUCTION

The puzzle of how open, market societies came about is deserving of additional research. My research focuses on the beliefs and values among citizens of former Soviet-controlled countries. These former Soviet countries transitioned away from a centrally planned economy toward market economic institutions at the same time that they developed their democratic institutions.

As North (2005) has stated, simply replacing one institutional structure by another does not guarantee its survival as long as there is not also a transformation of values. Several Austrian scholars have highlighted the importance of culture in explaining economic and political processes (Boettke 1998; Lavoie and Chamlee-Wright 2000; Storr 2010; Chamlee-Wright 2011b; Runst 2013, 2014; Boettke et al., this volume, Chapter 6). Both Lavoie and Chamlee-Wright (2000) and Boettke (1998; Boettke et al., this volume, Chapter 6) stress that successful development depends on a transformation of value and belief systems, and without such a transformation the political reforms will be incomplete at best, or they are subject to policy reversals. Runst (2013, 2014) shows empirically that certain cultural aspects affect the decision to become self-employed and how to vote in post-socialist countries.

In this chapter, I will relate Hayek's (1988, [1982] 2013; also see Runst and Gick 2013) hypotheses concerning our instinctual hostility toward market principles to the context of transitional economies. I connect Hayek's theory with the distinction between community (*Gemeinschaft*) and society (*Gesellschaft*), famously made by Tönnies (1887), where community incorporates small-group norms and society includes an extended, more anonymous group. Specifically, I argue that the prolonged absence of a market economy led to attitudes closer to small-group norms.[1] During the

1990s, individuals in former socialist countries were not in favor of market principles, when compared to individuals with non-socialist backgrounds.

In section 14.2, I will provide some theoretical background. In section 14.3, World Value Survey (WVS) data are presented. The results show that attitudes in formerly socialist countries are less in favor of market economic principles than in other countries. However, the exploration of WVS data, as well as most of the previous empirical literature, is confined to a set of necessarily narrowly defined variables, as discussed in section 14.2. Storr (2010) and Chamlee-Wright (2011b) explain how a more qualitative empirical tool kit can be more successful in understanding cultural narratives. Therefore, I present the results of 26 interviews from East and West Germany in section 14.4. The interviews show that the statements in the East German sample are closer to the theme of 'community' than 'society,' or small-group ethics rather than extended-order ethics. Germany was split into two parts for a timespan of 40 years. It can be treated as an illustrative natural experiment that allows us to understand the effects of living in a totalitarian command economy on the political and economic beliefs and values. Furthermore, living standards in the Eastern part have almost reached Western levels. The dislike for the principles of a market economy, and the similarity to small-group ethics, is therefore not merely a result of lower living standards. Section 14.5 concludes.

14.2 BETWEEN COMMUNITY AND SOCIETY

Social scientists have established the institutional prerequisites of economic growth, including secure property rights, sound money, free trade, and others (Bengoa and Sanchez-Robles 2003; Acemoglu and Johnson 2005; Acemoglu et al. 2005; Boettke and Fink 2011; also see Shirley 2008). It is, however, less clear why some countries adopt these institutional foundations more successfully than others.

In *Culture and Enterprise* (2000), Lavoie and Chamlee-Wright take on this question of 'What cultural influences are at play in fostering such an institutional setting?' The authors posit that, 'If there is a spirit of enterprise, a set of stories or images in the culture that celebrate some form of entrepreneurial creativity, then economic prosperity is more likely' (also see Lavoie and Chamlee-Wright, this volume, Chapter 7). Similarly, Boettke (1998) asks whether economics may shed light on why 'some rules can "stick" in one particularity, yet possess no meaning in another' (ibid.: p. 12). Customary rules that emerge from within a particular history cannot be ignored if we seek to understand the process of institutional change.

North (2005) highlights the importance of informal institutions. Following decolonization, Latin American countries attempted to adopt political rules modeled after the US constitution, but failed to achieve political stability and economic development (ibid.: p. 113). On the other hand, the development of a belief system compatible with market economic principles emerged in Britain during the eighteenth century (ibid.: pp. 143–5). North suggests that, while formal political institutions can change overnight, belief systems or informal institutions evolve slowly but affect the viability of the more formal rules of the game in the long run (ibid.: pp. 49–52).

Boettke et al. (this volume, Chapter 6) develop this idea further. The larger the distance between the informal institutions, or *mētis* (such as local norms, customs, and practices), and the formal political rules, the more difficult it will be to adopt the political rules. If the underlying culture in a country is not supportive of the formal institutional reform process, institutional changes will not be forthcoming. Similarly, Inglehart (1997), who studied value change across 43 countries between 1970 and 1990, states that all stable economic and political systems have both a compatible and a supportive cultural system that legitimates the formal institutions (ibid.: p. 15). Boettke et al. (this volume, Chapter 6) deduce that transition countries that display lower support for market economic principles are less likely to implement institutional reforms.

One way in which these cultural elements can affect formal political institutions is through the process of democracy—voting. If economic transition and democratization occur simultaneously, as was the case in Eastern Europe, the extent to which the culture supports market economic principles affects long run economic development. If voters do not embrace free markets and liberal democracy, or are even hostile towards these institutions, they will vote for policies that increase government intervention and centralize political power. McCloskey argues that, around the years 1600 to 1700, the elite in Holland and Britain began to reevaluate the innovation and creativity of commercial town life. She suggests that the emerging commercial values were the prerequisite for the subsequent economic and institutional development (2010: pp. 10, 449–50).

Historically, merchants and financiers often stood at the bottom of social hierarchies, as they exemplified the impersonal market forces that permeate modern lives. McCloskey illustrates the widespread skepticism around commercial exchanges by presenting literary sources (ibid.: Chapter 3). For instance, McCloskey notes that Cicero believed the merchant lived by making the worse product seem better (ibid.: p. 21). Further, she claims that a shift in rhetoric was a necessary precondition for the development of a modern market economy and sustained innovation. Since around the year 1700, British, Dutch, and later Northern European and Japanese writings testify to this change. McCloskey cites Adam Smith, who praised the honest pursuit of profit, John Stuart Mill, who wrote about the positive sum game of exchanges, and John Locke, who moved to a more commutative concept of justice that honored everyone, irrespective of birth. In addition, she makes note that Jane Austen's use of the word 'honest' no longer has noble connotations but stands for being 'upright' (ibid.).[2]

Runst (2014) provides empirical support for the hypothesis that the more successful Eastern European post-socialist transition countries were more in favor of market economic principles than their less successful counterparts. He shows that differing attitudes at the beginning of the 1990s translated into different voting behavior, which affected the transition process.

While it is difficult to untangle the particular sources of anti-market sentiments, the empirical literature identifies 'time spent under socialism' as one important factor (Mason 1995; Schwartz and Bardi 1997; Hayo 2004; Alesina and Fuchs-Schündeln 2007; Rovelli and Zaiceva 2009; Runst 2014). Admittedly, time spent under socialism is still somewhat ambiguous, in that it does not identify the particular factors or characteristics about this time spent under socialism which then lead to anti-market bias. It is possible that individuals develop different attitudes because of indoctrination under socialism. However, it is quite difficult to test such a hypothesis. Psychologists Schwartz and Bardi (1997) suggest how beliefs in hierarchy, propriety, and constraint are adopted in order to reduce the discrepancy between what is desired and what can be done. Runst (2013) points to a lack of experience concerning market economies and interactions therein. In the absence of this experience, the task of navigating a competitive environment is, indeed, daunting. In line with this view, Runst (2014) shows that Eastern European countries with more positive attitudes towards markets (Hungary, Poland, the Czech Republic, Slovakia, Slovenia, and Estonia) share certain historical characteristics, such as attempted reform movements, some market exposure, less time spent under socialism, and more religiosity.

I propose that a helpful way in which to understand the differences in these attitudes is described by the distinction between community (*Gemeinschaft*) and society (*Gesellschaft*), famously articulated by Tönnies (1887) and, much more recently, discussed in the social capital literature (Coleman 1988; Putnam 2001). Similar to the case today, Tönnies regards the family, the neighborhood, and friendship as the primary examples of the communal form of social organization. The morality of community is characterized by altruism, in the dignified act of help, voluntarily given, by the stronger member of the group. There is only a certain level of inequality within community, and the group is bound together by strong social ties and a common purpose. Community is often compared to the conditions in which humankind lived for the greatest part of their existence, in the pre-agricultural foraging band of only a few individuals.

In contrast, society is based on self-interest, exchange, economic competition, and creative destruction. Society corresponds to the extended society based on often anonymous market relationships between geographically and socially distant individuals which has only emerged relatively recently in human history. The group, whether kin or not, no longer possesses the cohesive power of an economic production unit. A summary of the dichotomy between community and society, discussed in this section, can be found in Table 14.1.

Admittedly, the stylized dichotomy between community and society is somewhat exaggerated. Artifacts and metals were traded at least 30 000 years ago, illustrating that, in fact, elements of community and

Table 14.1   Community–society dichotomy

	Community and small-group ethics	Society and extended-order ethics
Archetype	Family, tribe	Network of strangers
Size	Small	Large
Networks	Tight-knit groups, based on economic necessity	Less tight-knit groups, broader, more far-reaching networks
Economic coordination	Cooperation amongst individuals, mutual help and support, political allocation	Competition amongst firms and individuals seen as driver of prosperity
Radius of altruism	Solidarity with the in-group	In-group exists, but self-interest regarded as acceptable motivator for action
Material inequality	Seen as problematic and oppressive	Acceptable, as long as it reflects differential commercial success
Market exchanges	Often regarded as exploitative, anonymous and chaotic	Seen as a positive sum game
Governance preference	Active political life, government intervention, or economic planning	Minimal government beyond the rule of law
Popular villain	Greedy merchants or businessmen	–

Table 14.2   Attitudes and wealth—World Value Survey, all countries, Wave 3

	Government responsibility	Left/right
Variable name	E037	E033
Scale	1–10	1–10
GNI < 10 000	6.58	5.72
GNI 10 000–20 000	6.47	5.3
GNI 20 000–30 000	4.7	5.52
SD	3.0	2.3

elements of society may be present simultaneously. Likewise, modern society is not devoid of personal human interaction and communal encounters (Langrill and Storr 2012). Even though the community–society dichotomy does not reflect history perfectly, the interviews I conducted show that the community–society dichotomy is arguably real in the minds of people. I argue that the community versus society dichotomy is closely related to studies on 'anti-market bias' in post-Soviet countries, with 'anti-market bias' representing the characteristics of community (see Table 14.1). Anti-market bias can be analyzed using World Value Survey data.

The WVS is a repeated cross-section survey, undertaken in more than 50 countries, at five-year intervals, and contains many variables concerning attitudes and opinions. Table 14.2 illustrates that it is important to control for income when making attitude comparisons between countries. It displays the progression from a GNI of less than 10 000, to between 10 000 and 20 000, and more than 20 000 dollars. Attitude variables are measured on a Likert scale from 1 to 10. An individual who strongly dislikes market economic principles will score 10 (governments are fully responsible, as opposed to individuals), and at the other end a score of 1 indicates a belief that individuals are fully responsible, as opposed to governments. Table 14.2 shows that there is less support for government intervention in more prosperous countries.

Figure 14.1 displays the scatterplot for government responsibility and GNI per capita for all available countries in the WVS. Formerly socialist countries (denoted by the number 1) lie consistently above the trend line; they are more in favor of government intervention, after controlling for income. Using alternative functional forms (polynomials or logs) does not affect this result. The ball-shaped data points are East and West Germany. A scatterplot for left–right ideology and GNI per capita gives almost identical results.[3]

A number of studies have emphasized the tendency of formerly socialist

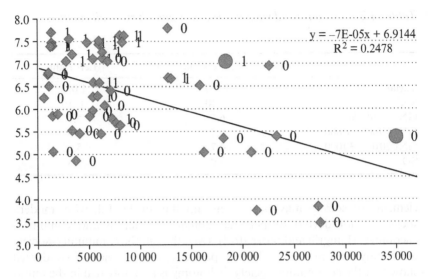

Note: 1 denotes formerly socialist; 0 denotes not socialist.

*Figure 14.1   Government responsibility and GNI—World Value Survey,
all countries, Wave 3, 1995*

countries to display lower support for market economic principles, even
at the beginning of the transition period (Mason 1995; Schwartz and
Bardi 1997; Hayo 2004; Alesina and Fuchs-Schündeln 2007; Rovelli and
Zaiceva 2009; Runst 2014). Schwartz and Bardi (1997) describe differences in political attitudes based on student and teacher samples from
Western and Eastern European countries. They conclude that individuals
from formerly socialist countries emphasize hierarchical values. Hayo
(2004) shows how support for market reform is generally low, based on
the Central and Eastern Eurobarometer database from 1990 and 1996
(CEEB). On a scale from −1 to 1, the mean support for free market reform
across countries was 0.12 (Hayo 2004). Mason (1995) reaches the same
conclusion by using data from the International Social Justice Project.
Although the authors find that many people somewhat agree or strongly
agree with the ideologically-charged notion of a market economy (average
of 31.5 percent and 45 percent respectively), once specific policy questions
are asked the respondents in formerly socialist economies show strong
support for alleviating income equality, secure jobs, and a strong role for
the government in the economy. 'On all three orientations, equality, need,
and role of the state, East Central Europeans lean toward a more egalitarian and statist system than do those in West Europe, Japan or the US'

(Mason 1995). Rovelli and Zaiceva (2009) report a low and heterogeneous support for transition and a slow increase between 1991 and 2004, based on the New Barometer surveys. Alesina and Fuchs-Schündeln (2007) show that East Germans were more in favor of state intervention than West Germans in 1997 and 2002, and they believe more strongly that life outcomes are determined by social conditions.

In the following section I describe the methods and data that I use in my study.

14.3 METHODOLOGY

Large scale survey analysis shows that attitudes in post-socialist countries are considerably more in favor of government intervention than others. The disadvantage of these types of surveys, however, is their non-interactive nature. The researcher has very little room to expand his/her understanding beyond the prior hypotheses he/she brings to bear on the data. As a result, the current description of attitudes in formerly socialist countries is thin; that is, while we know that differences in attitudes exist, we do not understand the specific narratives that sustain the preferences for higher government intervention in formerly socialist countries. In contrast, semi-structured interviews provide a consistent structure and allow the interviewer to ask follow-up questions that deviate from the prepared line of questioning (Chamlee-Wright 2011a: p. 323). Interviews facilitate an iterative learning process as the investigator, the investigator's theoretical lens, and the subjects under investigation are in close proximity to each other (Chamlee-Wright 2011b: p. 159; also see Storr 2010).

Lavoie and Chamlee-Wright (2000) state that a research agenda that seeks to describe and understand such cultural underpinnings of markets must focus on stories, heroes, myths, and metaphors, and requires qualitative methods. In order to generate a thicker description of attitudes about market transition and related political and moral attitudes I conducted 26 in-depth interviews with mostly East German participants. East German living standards improved between 1871 and the 1930s (only interrupted by World War I and the Great Depression), after which a fascist and a communist political system was put into place (ending in 1989). It will therefore be insightful to compare the main themes of the interview with East and West German participants, referring to the distinction of 'community' and 'society.' This natural experiment allows a comparison between two similar populations that have experienced two distinct political and economic systems. My interest is to describe the impact of socialist institutions on cultural narratives.

The interviews were conducted in June and July 2009. I talked to neighbors of acquaintances; I recruited in inner city pedestrian precincts, called people randomly on the phone, and used hub-and-spoke methods. Most Eastern interviewees (19) live in a cluster of five cities in the state of Saxony and were interviewed in their homes. Although the main emphasis lies in East German narratives, I also created a West German sample, which proved to be useful for a subset of topics (for example, perceived psychological differences, and evaluation of reunification). Western individuals (9) were recruited in the city of Heilbronn (in the state of Baden-Württemberg) and the surrounding area. The interviews of the Western sample were conducted either in their homes (5) or in a small public park near a shopping area (4). I have included different age and socioeconomic groups with two restrictions: there are no unemployed individuals in the sample and no individuals above age 65 or below age 20. Thus, the analysis concentrates on individuals of working age who materially benefited from the reunification.

Each interview lasted between 20 minutes and two hours. owing to the low sample size, it is not a representative data set but seeks to identify typical narratives, or recurring stories that people tell. These interviews are meant to generate knowledge not about economic or political facts, but about how people think about them.

The questions were semi-structured. Participants could therefore steer the conversation toward issues which they thought important, and the questions were consciously left open-ended. The overall subject of the interviews was participants' experiences during the 20 years since reunification, and questions were asked concerning a variety of topics such as changes in their work and personal life, psychological well-being, political assessments, and general comparisons between pre- and post-1989/90. A few key questions are listed below:

- How would you describe your life before 1989?
- Is there anything that sticks out in your memory?
- How would you describe the work life in the German Democratic Republic (GDR)?
- What impressions did you have of West/East Germany when the wall fell?
- What expectations did you have in 1990? Have they turned out to be true?
- How did life change for East Germans after reunification? How would you describe positive, as well as negative, changes?
- How would you characterize the development in East and West Germany over the next 10 to 20 years?

The three key themes that emerged from the interviews are presented in section 14.4. Section 14.4.1 discusses the low level of satisfaction interviewees expressed in regard to the material improvements and, to a lesser extent, improvements in freedom. It also presents quotes that illustrate the role of psychological and social stresses as a potential reason for the low levels of satisfaction. Section 14.4.2 discusses interviewees' dissatisfaction with the reunification process and their pessimism concerning future development. Finally, section 14.4.3 presents quotes that speak to the perceived immorality of markets stemming from their tendency to create inequality, and an underlying concern about the relationship between individual effort (as measured by labor hours) and payments.

14.4 INTERVIEW RESULTS

These themes relate to Tönnies's (1887) community versus society dichotomy. The first theme, perception of freedom and changes in living standards, is decidedly negative for East Germans asked about conditions after 1989. Concerns such as 'increased economic uncertainty' and 'deterioration of the social safety net' can be understood as relating to market exchanges and governance preference (see Table 14.2). The concerns express a violation of small-group ethics. Similar connections are clear in Part B, dissatisfaction and pessimism concerning reunification, and in Part C, morality of markets.

All interview responses are from East Germans except when noted otherwise.

14.4.1 Perception of Freedom and Changes in Living Standards

One of the most striking results exists in the form of an omission. There was a general reluctance to positively evaluate the significant improvements in economic freedom and its effect on living standards, even though initial differences between the socialist East and market-based West were quite visible and are empirically well established (Komlos and Kriwy 2003). Further, East German wages had converged to about 78 or 80 percent of Western levels by 2008 (Fuchs-Schündeln 2009; Goebel et al. 2009). Similarly, advances in personal freedom did not receive much attention, although they were emphasized by two interviewees. None of the participants talked about a relationship between economic freedom and increases in living standards. In fact, even though the sample is skewed by not incorporating unemployed individuals, there was a strong tendency to either omit or de-emphasize material improvements.

Economic freedoms were likely de-emphasized as they are seen as a double-edged sword: they deliver prosperity on the one hand but are also regarded as being related to a number of social and psychological problems. Although the perceived problems are diverse, two narratives are dominating. First, there is a sense of increased economic uncertainty, an increased work related psychological pressure, and an elevated burden of responsibility. As a socialist economy, the German Democratic Republic displayed low income inequality, and skill related income premiums were negligible. In addition, the unemployment rate was zero. The marginal worker was assigned a task, even when productivity was below wage. In the absence of markets, interpersonal competition and accountability are relatively unimportant. In comparison, the newly developing market economy is perceived to be competitive and more hierarchical.

Although many individuals in the Eastern sample mentioned material improvements, they de-emphasized the importance. For example, in response to the question 'How did life change for the East Germans?' Mr. Schmidt[4] states: 'The relief from this economy of scarcity could be felt all right. One cannot deny that.' Likewise, Jürgen says: 'Life has become better, as one can buy the things that one really needs.' Some directly stated that they do not care much about material improvements. Schweigert says: 'Product diversity . . . that is actually not that important to me.' Similarly, Nestinger states: 'Walking through C&A [a clothing store] hasn't impressed me down to the present day, all that colorful stuff.'

A number of Eastern participants de-emphasized the material improvements after 1990 by portraying the material living standards in the planned economy as quite acceptable. Mr. Berger explains: 'We didn't do badly . . . Nobody was hungry.' Mrs. Ahrens states: 'I didn't do badly during GDR times. I was a worker's child. I was allowed to study. I already had secured a job before reunification, which was then gone. You also have to look at it from this perspective . . . As a worker's child one did well.' Others tended to underestimate the improvements, as this conversation between Mr. Dengler and the interviewer shows: 'They have not converged the last 10, 20 years.' When asked 'What aspects weigh more heavily in your opinion, the positive or the negative ones?' Mr. Dengler responds with: 'I can hardly say.' More strongly, Müller says: 'For many, I do not count us among them, it cannot go down any further.'

Most frequently, however, interviewees from East Germany suggested that the benefits of the market economy are outweighed by negative factors. The first factor is psychological. Mr. Schweigert summarizes: 'Considerable improvements, I consciously say, in a predominantly material sphere . . . on the other hand, significant deterioration of a perceived social safety [net].' Additionally, Mrs. Jürgen says: 'And also the fear . . .

in the past I was not afraid about losing my job.' Similarly, Mr. Heinert states: 'Nobody tells you to do it like this or like that. In principle, you can do anything, but you are also responsible. This is also not quite easy.'

The following conversation with a married couple also speaks to the same theme: '(*Husband*) Everything was arranged in that sense. In the framework of that country, your work was arranged, it was arranged how you get to work, what you have to do and what you cannot do. Nobody was hungry. There was a certain safety in the framework of that regime. (*Wife*) It was social. (*Husband*) Yes, social.' Finally, Schmidt states, 'I am of the opinion that we have changed from the dictatorship of the proletariat into the dictatorship of money, and this is quite noticeable. The one who does not have money in this society will be pushed aside. That is a terrible phenomenon really. The humanistic . . . has been lost.'

The statements above demonstrate an increased material prosperity but also an economic uncertainty. A more stressful work life was another source of psychological distress for Eastern interviewees, which is not surprising in the presence of high unemployment rates. Schweigert states: 'Otherwise many things have converged, also in quite a negative sense, things such as competitiveness, also in the work life, etc. . . . that things like mobbing[5] are also becoming more frequent.' And Schmidt says: 'In contrast to the GDR, work life is very performance oriented. You are only evaluated on the basis of how much revenue you produce.'

The second factor was social in nature: Many participants from the East complained about a loss in solidarity. Cooperation and equality are perceived to be replaced by more pronounced status hierarchies. Mrs. Schmidt describes: 'Our generation has a different sense of togetherness. We had acquaintances in the old states [West Germany] . . . It is less common there to have good relationship with your neighbors.' Mr. Berger says: 'Work life has changed negatively. At work everybody is doing his own thing now, and everybody wants to brag about his own achievements in front of the management. Back then, it was different. The idea of collectivism was more pronounced.' And his wife adds: 'A firm can only be successful as a community, just like a family.' A similar sentiment is expressed by Mr. and Mrs. Müller: '(*Wife*) The relationships that existed [amongst individuals] back then are broken. (*Husband*) Because everybody . . . just for himself. (*Wife*) What was happening in the residential communities has crumbled.' And, finally, Mr. Schweigert states: 'Today, everybody drives his own car and is careful to only be in contact with people who are on his social level . . . This cements the social stratification.'

In contrast to the gains in economic freedom, advances in personal liberties are regarded as slightly more important. Again, however, given the transition from an authoritarian police state to a rights based constitutional democracy, Eastern interviewees did not emphasize this point either. As Jürgen states, 'What stayed the same . . . you couldn't say anything then, and you cannot say anything now . . . We were Christians, we had a harder time . . . I received my apprenticeship last . . . and had to take what was assigned to me . . . and, now, you also have to do what your boss wants.'

The GDR was a centralized command economy and a totalitarian police state. Within a society of about 16 million, comprehensive files were kept on 6 million citizens, the majority of the adult work force. An intricate network of spies tapped into every societal network.[6] It included ordinary people who spied on their neighbors and 'friends.' Thus, a 'climate of fear and suspicion' was created that made deviant behavior costly (Fullbrook 1995: p.54) and significantly restricted individual behavior, such as freedom of speech or possible career trajectories. Surprisingly, only three Eastern individuals talked about increases in personal freedom. Mr. Berger for example states: 'Before, no freedom to travel, in general, many restrictions in many spheres . . . Expression of opinion was not possible without further ado.' And Nestinger says: 'It was, of course, a doctrinaire system. I could not study although I had very good grades. That is the most beautiful part for me. Not necessarily that I can choose between 14 different brands of beer.' And, finally, Mr. Schweigert mentions 'significant improvements in regard to freedom of speech, diversity, press, media, literature.'

In contrast to the Eastern sample, all seven Western individuals emphasized both material improvements and increased personal freedoms. They used emotional language and expressed feelings of happiness when talking about the fall of the Berlin Wall. All but one Western interviewee, who was uncertain, portrayed the economic convergence as completed or on the way to completion.

14.4.2 Dissatisfaction and Pessimism Concerning Reunification

On July 1, 1990 East Germany started using the common German currency, removed all inner German tariffs, and operated under some West German business laws. On October 3 of the same year East Germany was integrated into the Federal Republic. Treuhand, a public agency, took over all companies. It then privatized them rapidly through direct sales, as opposed to vouchers, which was more common in Poland, the Czech Republic, Slovakia, and others. The factors which led to recommendations by Treuhand negotiating teams to the board were sale price, employment, and investment guarantees. An alternative privatization plan was unsuccessfully proposed by the Social Democratic Party. It sought to keep companies under state control and restructure later, when they would be more competitive (Dyck 1997).

The interview responses highlight a general dissatisfaction concerning the developments of the last 20 years and a pessimistic future outlook. Given the increases in living standards in East Germany, one might have expected this to be less severe in this sample. To the contrary, however, dissatisfaction and pessimism are strong, sometimes contradicting the facts about living standards (Komlos and Kriwy 2003). Nestinger summarizes: 'I actually think it [the reunification] went quite wrong. The free market economists thought . . . they opened the borders and let the people [firms] come across. One should have thought about how to structure the country anew.' Similarly, as Jürgen says, 'I think that now, just like 20 years ago, when the people took to the streets, I think that this will come again . . . For many it is . . . they live worse than in GDR times . . . Everybody had a job, an apartment, a daycare spot.' Concerning future prospects Dengler says: 'They have not converged in the last ten years. Honestly, I doubt whether they will have converged in the next ten years.' Likewise, Schweigert states: 'And that the biggest part of the East [East Germany] lags behind in the development process.' Finally, as Berger explains, 'One had hoped to be adjusted [to the same income level as the West]. But, at the moment, I do not look into the future too optimistically.'

Given that the wage gap has considerably decreased, in addition to other benefits, such as infrastructural improvements and reductions in pollution, it is surprising that interviewees tell narratives expressing dissatisfaction concerning reunification and pessimism regarding the future. It is probable that this is not so much due to the real material changes, but rather it might be a result of the social and psychological stresses described above. It is well established (Brickman and Campbell 1971; Myers 1992; for an overview see Diener et al. 2006) that expectations adjust rapidly in the face of changing living conditions, also known as the hedonic treadmill hypothesis. Thus, in the wake of increasing material living standards, expectations rise, too. Increases in prosperity, therefore, do not lead to higher levels of satisfaction. There is strong evidence that individuals care about their relative income position instead (McBride 2001; Ferrer-i-Carbonell 2005; Clarke et al. 2008; Easterlin and Plagnol 2008; Mentzakis and Moro 2009).

14.4.3   The Morality of Markets

The mixed perception of freedom and the dissatisfaction with the reunification process is mirrored in the narratives concerning the market economy. The interview responses show that the market economy itself is regarded as problematic. More specifically, there is a consistent narrative shared by East German interviewees which portrays markets as unjust because of their perceived tendency to generate inequality. Rudolf says: 'On the one hand everything (is) more free . . . self-determined. On the other hand . . . the divide between rich and poor has become wider, all the disadvantages of capitalism.' Mr. Berger states: 'One must let the people have a greater share in profits. But, if politics does not keep the economy in check, and if it lets it run freely, such as in recent times . . . and this creates dissatisfaction, of course . . . and then the idea of collectivism plays a big role again.' Nestinger states that 'Only unions can put a lid on the excesses [of capitalism]' and 'The conservative government back then, the market economists have said we're opening the borders, we let the money come across, they will get it right. Of course they got it right, but [only] as far as their own wallets are concerned.'

Underneath this concern about inequality seems to be a deeper, implicit theory of morality. The interviewees express their unease with the perceived injustice of wide income disparities and lament a general disconnect between labor hours and pay. It appears as if a labor theory of value is endorsed. Seen through this moral lens, it is, of course, unjust to pay higher wages to bankers than hairdressers, as the amount of labor effort will only marginally differ between the two. Contrast this with the neoclassical theory of value and price, in which productivity differences and market conditions will lead to different incomes. However, the narratives that are told by the participants do not accept this mechanism on a moral basis. Instead, they seem to regard a deviation from the labor theory of value as unjust. Hours worked ought to be rewarded, not the market value that is actually created. As Schweigert states, 'One does not need to talk about current salaries of managers and bankers, and then to contrast this with the salary of a hairdresser, but these are of course things that cannot be justified by performance . . . and Europe is then in danger of social rifts, which, in the end, can only lead to political instability.' Similarly, Müller says: 'There is no proportionality between what is performed and what comes in [in terms of salary].' Likewise, Ahrens opines: 'Back then, everybody had to work, regardless of what they did. They had to work, although the work wasn't really required. They were somehow employed, he had a task, and that was important in that sense.' Finally, Jürgen states: 'Everybody had a job [before reunification] . . . even though many of these jobs did not benefit anybody . . . Today . . . the ones who have a job are very busy . . . If the money were available one could distribute the work more evenly . . . There is enough work to be done, if you look around. What's missing is somebody who pays for it.'

14.5 CONCLUSION

Interviewees in East Germany clearly emphasize their discontent with the increased inequality and greater uncertainty (for example, of becoming unemployed) that have followed reunification. They express their increased stress levels in an environment of competition (for example, rivalries and missing solidarity at work as opposed to camaraderie). The new freedom and individualism are taken with a grain of salt, as they come with the burden of responsibility and are perceived to undermine humanism, sharing, solidarity, and community.

One has to be careful to avoid misunderstanding. Individuals certainly have reasons for the beliefs that they hold. The difficult years of transition were characterized by high unemployment and uncertainty. The new society is more competitive and less secure than the old one. The purpose of this chapter is not to say that the interviewees' statements are completely wrong. I have simply pointed out that a dislike of markets and a sense of missing community exist among East Germans. These attitudes can also be plausibly regarded as a result of a missing life experience within the market society. Given the high unemployment rate and job uncertainty at the time of the interviews, some negativity may be coming through that would otherwise be less severe.

There is an important takeaway to the study. There may be reason for gradual transition from socialist policies to free market policies if this might reduce short run hardship and reduce negative attitudes around free markets. The consequences of the dislike of the market society are real and problematic. Anti-market parties were elected in many formerly socialist countries (and received strong support from East German voters), which affected the pace of development negatively.

NOTES

1. Admittedly, trying to illustrate that the community versus society views are a result of isolation and come from 'instinctual man' is a difficult hypothesis for which to provide evidence. I present evidence for a somewhat weaker claim, which is that East versus West German views can be compared to the community versus society dichotomy.
2. Similarly, Greif (1994) illustrates how culture shapes institutional rules. Around the year 1400, the emphasis on collectivist values among Maghrebi traders, on the one hand, and the city of Genoa, on the other, which was known one for its individualist traditions, led to development of distinct institutions in the two societies.
3. Where 'left' corresponds to a more social democratic and socialist world view, 'right' stands for conservative and nationalistic views, and a centrist position is taken up by classic liberal positions.
4. Pseudonyms are used throughout the text in order to protect the anonymity of the interview subjects.

5. Work place harassment by an individual or a group of colleagues.
6. According to Fullbrook, the State Security Service (*Staatssicherheit*) had at least 85 000 official employees and more than 100 000 unofficial ones in a country of 16 million people. (Fullbrook 1995: pp. 46–50)

REFERENCES

Acemoglu, Daron and Simon Johnson (2005), 'Unbundling Institutions,' *Journal of Political Economy*, **113**(5), 949–95.
Acemoglu, Daron, Simon Johnson and James Robinson (2005), 'Institutions as Fundamental Cause for Long Run Growth,' *Handbook of Economic Growth*, **1**(A), 385–472.
Alesina, Alberto and Nicola Fuchs-Schündeln (2007), 'Good Bye Lenin (Or Not?): The Effect of Communism on People's Preferences,' *American Economic Review*, **97**(4), 1507–18.
Bengoa, Marta and Blanca Sanchez-Robles (2003), 'Foreign Direct Investment, Economic Freedom and Growth: New Evidence from Latin America,' *European Journal of Political Economy*, **19**, 529–45.
Boettke, Peter J. (1998), 'Why Culture Matters: Economics, Politics, and the Imprint of History,' *Journal of the LSE Hayek Society*, **2**(1), 9–16.
Boettke, P.J. and Alexander Fink (2011), 'Institutions First,' *Journal of Institutional Economics*, **7**(4), 499–504.
Brickman, P. and D.T. Campbell (1971), 'Hedonic Relativism and Planning the Good Society,' in M.H. Apley (ed.), *Adaptation-Level Theory: A Symposium*, New York: Academic Press, pp. 287–302.
Chamlee-Wright, Emily (2011a), 'Qualitative Methods and the Pursuit of Economic Understanding,' *Review of Austrian Economics*, **23**(4), 321–31.
Chamlee-Wright, Emily (2011b), 'Operationalizing the Interpretive Turn: Deploying Qualitative Methods towards an Economics of Meaning,' *Review of Austrian Economics*, **24**(2), 157–70.
Clarke, Andrew E., Paul Frijters and Michael A. Shields (2008), 'Relative Income, Happiness, and Utility: An Explanation for the Easterlin Paradox and Other Puzzles,' *Journal of Economic Literature*, **46**(1), 95–144.
Coleman, James (1988), 'Social Capital in the Creation of Human Capital,' *American Journal of Sociology*, **94**, S95–S110.
Diener, Ed, Richard Lucas and Christie Napa Scollon (2006), 'Beyond the Hedonic Treadmill: Revising the Adaptation Theory of Well-Being,' *American Psychologist*, **61**(4), 305–14.
Dyck, Alexander (1997), 'Privatization in Eastern Germany: Management Selection and Economic Transition,' *American Economic Review*, **87**(4), 565–97.
Easterlin, Richard A. and Anke C. Plagnol (2008), 'Life Satisfaction and Economic Conditions in East and West Germany Pre- and Post-Unification,' *Journal of Economic Behavior and Organization*, **68**, 433–44.
Ferrer-i-Carbonell, Ada (2005), 'Income and Well-Being: An Empirical Analysis of the Comparison Income Effect,' *Journal of Public Economics*, **89**, 997–1019.
Fuchs-Schündeln, Nicola (2009), 'Introduction: A Symposium on the East German Labor Market,' *Economics of Transition*, **17**(4), 625–802.

Fullbrook, Mary (1995), *Anatomy of a Dictatorship: Inside the GDR 1949–1989*, Oxford: Oxford University Press.

Goebel, Jan, Roland Habich and Peter Krause (2009), 'Zur Angleichung von Einkommen und Lebensqualität im vereinigten Deutschland,' *Vierteljahreshefte zur Wirtschaftsforschung*, **78**(2), 122–45.

Greif, A. (1994), 'Cultural Beliefs and the Organization of Society: A Historical and Theoretical Reflection on Collectivist and Individualist Societies,' *Journal of Political Economy*, **102**(5), 912–50.

Hayek, Friedrich von (1988), *The Fatal Conceit*, Chicago: University of Chicago Press.

Hayek, Friedrich von ([1982] 1996), 'Die überschätzte Vernunft in *Die Anmaßung von Wissen*,' W. Kerber (ed.), Tübingen: Mohr Siebeck, translation (2013) by Petrik Runst and Evelyn Gick, *Journal of the History of Economic Thought*, **35**(2), 239–56.

Hayo, Bernd (2004), 'Public Support for Creating a Market Economy in Eastern Europe,' *Journal of Comparative Economics*, **32**, 720–44.

Inglehart, Ronald (1997), *Modernization and Postmodernization*, Princeton, NJ: Princeton University Press.

Komlos, John and Peter Kriwy (2003), 'The Biological Standard of Living in the Two Germanies,' *German Economic Review*, **4**(4), 359–473.

Langrill, Ryan and Virgil Henry Storr (2012), 'The Moral Meaning of Markets,' *Journal of Markets and Morality*, **15**(2), 347–62.

Lavoie, Don and Emily Chamlee-Wright (2000), *Culture and Enterprise*, London: Routledge.

Mason, S. David (1995), 'Attitudes toward the Market and Political Participation in the Postcommunist States,' *Slavic Review*, **54**(2), 385–406.

McBride, Michael (2001), 'Relative-Income Effects on Subjective Well-Being in the Cross-Section,' *Journal of Economic Behavior and Organization*, **45**, 251–78.

McCloskey, Deirdre (2010), *Bourgeois Dignity: Why Economics Can't Explain the Modern World*, Chicago: University of Chicago Press.

Mentzakis, Emmanouil and Miro Moro (2009), 'The Poor, The Rich and the Happy: Exploring the Link between Income and Subjective Well-being,' *Journal of Socio-Economics*, **38**, 147–58.

Myers, D. (1992), *The Pursuit of Happiness*, New York: Morrow.

North, Douglass (2005), *Understanding the Process of Economic Change*, Princeton, NJ: Princeton University Press.

Putnam, Robert (2001), *The Collapse and Revival of American Community*, New York: Simon & Schuster.

Rovelli, Riccardo and Anzelika Zaiceva (2009), *Transition Fatigue? Cross-Country Evidence from Micro Data*, IZA Working Paper No. 4224, Bonn: IZA.

Runst, Petrik (2013), 'Post-Socialist Culture and Entrepreneurship,' *American Journal of Economics and Sociology*, **72**(3), 593–626.

Runst, Petrik (2014), 'Popular Attitudes towards Markets and Institutional Reform,' *Review of Social Economy*, **72**(1), 83–115.

Runst, Petrik and Evelyn Gick (2013), 'Introduction and Commentary to Hayek's "The Overrated Reason,"' *Journal of the History of Economic Thought*, **35**(2), 233–7.

Schwartz, Shalom and Anat Bardi (1997), 'Influences of Adaptation to Communist Rule on Value Priorities in Eastern Europe,' *Political Psychology*, **18**(2), 385–410.

Shirley, Mary M. (2008), 'Institutions and Development,' *Handbook of New Institutional Economics*, **VII**, 611–38.
Storr, Virgil Henry (2010), 'Schütz on Meaning and Culture,' *Review of Austrian Economics*, **23**, 147–63.
Tönnies, Ferdinand (1887), *Gemeinschaft und Gesellschaft*, Leipzig: Fues's Verlag, translated in 1957 as *Community and Society*.

15. Subalternity and entrepreneurship: tales of marginalized but enterprising characters, oppressive settings and haunting plots*

Virgil Henry Storr and Bridget Colon

15.1 INTRODUCTION

There is a wealth of conceptual literature examining the relationship between culture (shared values and beliefs) and enterprise. Since Weber's ([1930] 1992) discussion of how the spirit of modern capitalism in the West led to economic prosperity, economists, sociologists, anthropologists and entrepreneurship scholars have focused on how culture impacts on economic activity (see Gudeman 1986; Berger 1991; Bird-David 1992a, 1992b; Chamlee-Wright 1997, this volume, Chapter 16; Harrison and Huntington 2000; Lavoie and Chamlee-Wright 2000; Boettke and Storr 2002; Granovetter 2004). Much of the empirical work within the entrepreneurship literature has concentrated on how differences in national cultures affect either rates of entrepreneurship or the characteristics of entrepreneurs in that context. It does not concern itself with voices from the margins.

Following Hofstede (1980), entrepreneurship scholars have argued that cultures that are more individualistic, more comfortable with uncertainty and more masculine, and that have low power distance are likely to have higher levels of entrepreneurship. Thus collectivist, risk-averse, feminine and high power distance cultures are likely to have lower levels of entrepreneurship. As Hayton et al. (2002: p. 34) argue, Hofstede's taxonomy of cultural values and their effects on entrepreneurship has inspired much of the behavioral research that exists on the relationship between national culture and enterprise. Using either Hofstede's results or other surveys that attempt to measure national or regional culture, studies such as Shane's (1992, 1993) and Davidsson's (1995) have discussed the impact of culture on national rates of innovation and firm-formation rates respectively.

These studies corroborate Hofstede's contention that a certain set of national and regional cultural characteristics is related to the national and regional levels of entrepreneurship (Hayton et al. 2002: p. 35).

The other major strand of empirical work on culture and entrepreneurship has relied on surveys of entrepreneurs in various cultures, focusing on how entrepreneurs differ across countries or regions (Hayton et al. 2002: p. 37). Scheinberg and MacMillan (1988) and Shane et al. (1991) discuss how the motives of entrepreneurs differ across cultures. McGrath et al. (1992) and Mueller and Thomas (2000), on the other hand, focus on the similarities between entrepreneurs across contexts. Similarly, A. Morrison (1999: p. 68) concludes that the ideal typical entrepreneur, regardless of culture, 'is intelligent and analytical; is an effective risk manager and networker; possesses a strong set of moral, social and business ethics; exhibits a basic trader's instinct; and is dedicated to life-long learning in its many forms.' Entrepreneurs, regardless of context, appear to have higher masculinity and individualism scores and lower uncertainty avoidance scores than non-entrepreneurs in their respective countries.

Regional and country-specific studies have, however, taught us a great deal about the relationship between culture and entrepreneurship in certain contexts. Entrepreneurs in the former Soviet bloc and Britain's black colonies, for instance, have relatively high levels of distrust and low levels of perceived internal locus of control (John, this volume, Chapter 10; Storr, this volume, Chapter 11). Using fiction from the former Soviet Union and Eastern Europe and literature from anglophone Africa and the West Indies, this chapter considers the position of the subaltern in relation to entrepreneurship in these contexts. Our aim is to *get at* the cultural frames that guide subaltern entrepreneurs and to explain the origins of some of the cultural attitudes and factors that impact on entrepreneurship in these regions. A narrative-based approach, we contend, is particularly suited to recovering subaltern voices and understanding the tales of marginalized peoples.

Section 15.2 describes the methodology employed in this chapter and outlines the case for using literature to understand the relationship between culture and enterprise, especially in marginalized contexts. This follows Nummela and Welch's (2006) charge that, in order to understand international entrepreneurship better, 'there is a need to broaden our viewpoint, look outside our own research traditions, and offer fresh perspectives.' Although perhaps relatively new to entrepreneurship studies, the approach is not a novel one. Storr (2004) applied this method to a single context using literature and folklore from the Bahamas to discuss the models of entrepreneurship that competed for cultural dominance. Moreover, the use of literature and other cultural productions to make sense of economic life is not without precedent within the field of economics. Similarly, reading cultural works such as novels to understand a given culture better is common in cultural studies and anthropology.

Section 15.3 focuses on the kinds of cultural practices that became common under the Soviet-style systems that prevailed in twentieth-century Central and Eastern Europe. Next, Section 15.4 discusses how colonialism and neocolonialism 'distorted' entrepreneurial lenses in anglophone Africa and the British West Indies. Section 15.5 offers a concluding discussion.

15.2 METHOD

This chapter argues for an alternative approach to the study of the relationship between culture and entrepreneurship to those typically found in the entrepreneurship literature. We contend that an important but little pursued method for getting closer to the culture of entrepreneurship in a particular context is to focus on the tales of entrepreneurship that prevail in that context. To get a sense of the economic culture in a particular place, we argue, it is important to focus on the stories that exist about success and failure and the myths that people believe about how to get ahead (Chamlee-Wright, this volume, Chapter 16). Why focus on stories? First, efforts to score cultural traits must necessarily reduce cultures, which are inherently rich, dynamic and complex, to collections of measurable characteristics (for example, indices of individualism and masculinity). The color, the verve, the flavor of the different varieties of entrepreneurship that exist get lost in this move to come up with quantitative measures of culture (see Storr, this volume, Chapter 11). Second, culture affects not only levels of entrepreneurial activity but also the kinds of activities perceived as entrepreneurial. As Rehn and Taalas (2004) discuss, what counts as entrepreneurship is not easy to determine and varies across (and is contested within) different cultures. Third, and most important for our purposes here, these studies have tended to ignore marginalized voices. Entrepreneurship, however, is the engine of economic development (Harper 2003), so understanding the challenges facing subaltern entrepreneurs is critical to understanding the prospects of the world's poorest.

Spivak ([1988] 1995) famously articulated that subalterns could not speak. By this, she did not mean that they were mute, that they were unable to tell us their stories, that they could not complain about their conditions or that they could not protest. They can and do cry out when they are wronged. Rather, she meant that no one listened to their cries, their tales, their complaints or their protestations. According to Spivak, the subaltern is the perpetual, voiceless and unrecoverable 'Other' in the hegemonic discourse that is taking place in the centre and that continues to impact (negatively) on subaltern lives at the periphery. The subaltern, simply, does not have a seat at the boardroom tables where discussions take place, for instance on development strategies, which have a tremendous impact on subaltern lives (Escobar 1995).

Our task, Spivak insists, is not to protect the subaltern; nor should we attempt to speak on his or her behalf. Spivak views this as a dubious project, since it perpetuates rather than helps to end subalternity. Instead, we must create spaces from which subalterns can speak for themselves and be heard. Spivak writes, 'who the hell wants to protect subalternity?—Only extremely reactionary, dubious anthropologistic museumizers. No activist wants to keep the subaltern in the space of difference . . . You don't give the subaltern voice. You work for the bloody subaltern, you work against subalternity.'

Yet how do we work against subalternity? How do we recover and recognize subaltern voices? How do we as entrepreneurship scholars ensure that we are listening to the subaltern? Embracing qualitative approaches to our empirical work, especially ethnographic methods, can ensure that we open ourselves up to marginalized voices. As Geertz (1983: p.57) explains, ethnography (correctly done) can: 'produce an interpretation of the way a people lives which is neither imprisoned within their mental horizons, an ethnography of witchcraft as written by the witch, nor systematically deaf to the distinctive tonalities of their existence, an ethnography of witchcraft as written by a geometer.' Economic anthropologists (and some economists) have profitably employed these methods, teaching us much about how economic practices differ across cultures. Bird-David (1992b), for instance, has argued that different communities organize their economic lives on the basis of different 'primary metaphors,' which color how people think about their opportunities, their situations and their relationships. Bird-David discovered that the metaphor of 'forest as parent' informed economic life amongst the Nayaka. This metaphor, which deprecates land ownership, as everyone is considered a child of the forest with rights to its bounty, differs significantly from the metaphor that underpins economic life throughout the West, where private property is key.

Lavoie and Chamlee-Wright (2000: p.22) similarly argue that we get at culture 'by way of intimate, detailed, qualitative research, immersed in the complex context of one particular situation.' We get at culture by *reading* cultural texts. To get a sense of a people's world views and values, watch the films and television shows that they watch, read the books and poems that they read and write, listen to their folktales, and examine the photographs they take and the art (paintings, sketches and sculptures) they produce. For Lavoie and Chamlee-Wright (this volume, Chapter 7: p. 147), 'If you want to get a sense of whether a community is apt to grow wealthier, we are suggesting you find out what stories they tell, what myths they believe, what heroes they admire and what metaphors they use.' Lavoie and Chamlee-Wright focused on how the culture industries in the USA portrayed businessmen. Although there were cases in which wealthy business characters used their fortunes for good, Lavoie and Chamlee-Wright (2000: p. 87) found that most businessmen were portrayed as being morally bankrupt. The US cultural industry, they argue, both reflects and transmits American attitudes towards successful businesses and businessmen.

A people's literature, similarly, teaches us much about their lives, beliefs and values. As novelist Toni Morrison (1993: p. 372) observed, 'narrative remains the best way to learn anything' and, as Preston (1995: p. 943) remarked, 'the imaginative reach of personal narrative and other forms of more literary writing allows us important access into the lives of particular people in particular places.' Economists have long recognized the value of literature as a pedagogical tool and as a source of data for their research efforts. As Watts (2002: p. 378) discovered, 'there are a surprising number of economists who have used literary sources.' Economic historians, Watts notes, have cited passages from authors such as Swift and Defoe, game theorists have analyzed characters and situations from works of fiction, and economists have also analyzed economic arguments and ideas that have appeared in fictional passages. Watts highlighted several ways in which economists of a 'literary bent' used literature as a way of '(a) describing human behavior and motivations more eloquently, powerfully, or humorously than economists typically do, and thereby make economists' writing more interesting and effective; [and] (b) using literary descriptions as basic evidence of individual behavior or of economic conditions and institutions in a particular time and place.'

Using literary descriptions as basic evidence of economic conditions and institutions can be employed profitably in trying to understand the circumstances of marginalized populations. Members of the subaltern group can and do speak through their imaginative productions. As Schiff (1979: p. 73) writes, 'ethnic voices, when they speak of oppression, state their theme with authority.' Literature can bring the tales of the subaltern to life by providing eloquent accounts of subaltern lives, and, when the accounts are written by members of these groups, they can give us tremendous insight into the lifestyles and mental models of the subaltern. 'The Novel,' as Lamming (1983: p. xxxvii) writes, had a peculiar function in the Caribbean. The writer's preoccupation has been mainly with the poor; and fiction has served as a way of restoring these lives—this world of men and women from down below—to a proper order of attention; to make their reality the supreme concern of the total society.

The 'novel' has undoubtedly played a similarly restorative function amongst other marginalized peoples. Novelists such as Gogol and Havel in Central and Eastern Europe, and Ngugi, Armah and Achebe in Africa, have spoken quite eloquently about subaltern lives from a subaltern perspective and have done much to teach us about politics, economics and culture in those contexts. Indeed, as Preston (1995: p.949) writes, 'literary writing has far more potential than generic, rigorous analytical prose to reach into the deep and often unsavory . . . forces that divide or join people.' Critical to understanding the economic lives of marginalized peoples, our chief concern here, literature from the margins can show how culture has impacted on entrepreneurship in these communities. Consequently, our discussion of the relationship between culture and economy in the former communist and colonized countries will rely on this literature.

This chapter deploys the literary descriptions of the subaltern in several contexts in order to illuminate the cultural circumstances of subaltern entrepreneurs and to speak to the origins of those circumstances. This approach offers a way to overcome the challenge of incorporating marginalized voices into the discourse about entrepreneurship. Although there are obviously great differences between these regions, the former Soviet bloc and Britain's black colonies were selected because of (a) the undeniable presence of subaltern peoples and (b) the wealth of literary descriptions of the subaltern in those contexts. These criteria would obviously apply to other regions as well, but we attempted to balance the trade-off between breadth and depth in the hope of showing the value of a narrative-based approach in multiple settings, but realizing that looking at even two regions would mean that we would at times have to paint with broad strokes—broader than we would prefer. Additionally, the body of literature of a people can be overwhelmingly vast, can touch on a variety of themes and is often impossible to master. This is certainly true of the literatures that we engage with below. Here again, we attempted to strike a balance between depth over breadth because our aim was primarily illustrative. A number of the novels from these regions deal with subjects that are simply irrelevant for our purposes here, and so they are not touched on in this study. The novels and stories that we do focus on below were selected because they offered rich fodder for considering the relationship between subalternity and entrepreneurship in the selected regions. Decisions about which themes to focus on and which to ignore in the presentation below were guided, where possible, by the entrepreneurship studies that looked at culture in the selected regions. The novels selected offer rich illustrations of some of the cultural challenges facing subaltern entrepreneurs, and they offer clues to the source of some of the cultural attitudes that color entrepreneurship in these regions. Thus the examples presented below both illustrate points that were made elsewhere in entrepreneurship studies and offer narratives that present the cultural circumstances of subaltern entrepreneurs in a way that is impossible without employing a narrative-based approach, as we do here.

15.3 CULTURE AND ENTREPRENEURSHIP IN RUSSIA AND THE FORMER SOVIET BLOC

Entrepreneurship studies have stressed the importance of personal networks for entrepreneurs in pre- and post-Soviet Central and Eastern Europe. As Batjargal (2006: p.309) has described, for instance, 'Personalizing any relationship is a key cultural feature of the Russians for many centuries.' The inability of the Soviet economy consistently to deliver the goods necessary for survival meant that Russians had 'to mobilize resources from informal sources such as family and friends.' *Blat*—the value of a person's connections or, more specifically, the amount of pull that an individual has with suppliers, government clerks or any other actor who trades in relational capital, all important before the collapse of communism—remains an important part of economic life in Russia. For discussions of the economic implications of *blat*, see Hewett (1988), Ledeneva (1998) and Boettke (2001). Indeed, this 'economy of favors,' which emerged as a means of overcoming the persistent shortages and inherent weaknesses of the Soviet system, continues to play a considerable role in the distribution of resources in post-Soviet Russia. As Gaddy and Ickes (2001) demonstrated, relationships in Russia have been transformed into relational capital. Because this relational capital cannot be easily cashed out or transferred, however, the personalized nature of the Soviet economy has lingered in the post-Soviet Russian economy. Personal ties are not only valuable, but also self-protective and quite robust, since those who would lose relational capital if the ties were broken are the only ones in a position to break them.

The flip side of this reliance on relations is that Russians have tended to maintain a narrow radius of trust. Arguably, this tendency (distrustfulness) pre-dates the Soviet Union and has a long history in Russia. Nevertheless, the Soviet experience contributed to the prevalence and depth of this feeling. Batjargal (2006: p.317) has suggested that Russian entrepreneurs typically 'search for partners within limited spatial and temporal boundaries' and describes them as being 'relationally inert.' Batjargal writes, 'past investments in contacts tie them up tightly with old contacts and prevent them from going actively [after] new contacts who are potential clients, suppliers, investors.' Russian entrepreneurs' networks have not expanded since the Soviet system collapsed, he found, because of 'widespread distrust, suspicion and attitudinal ambivalence among the Russians' (ibid.).

Not surprisingly, it is possible to find tales in Russian literature that speak to this tendency of Russian entrepreneurs to rely on relational capital and maintain a narrow radius of trust. More than speaking to the existence or prevalence of these cultural traits and how they impact on entrepreneurs, these tales add another dimension. They offer insights into how and why these attitudes towards strangers developed and how these characteristics enter into and affect enterprise in this context. Indeed, the Russian entrepreneur's 'distrust, suspicion and attitudinal ambivalence' are understandable, given the characters that emerge as the heroes in these tales and the way that strangers and entrepreneurship are portrayed.

Consider, for instance, Gogol's ([1842] 1996) *Dead Souls*, a tale of economic life in Russia under serfdom, in which both the Russian conception of entrepreneurship as an act of deception and Russians' suspicion of strangers receive eloquent treatment. *Dead Souls* tells the tale of Chichikov, a dismissed civil servant and would-be feudal lord, who prospers not by producing something of value, but through trickery and guile. In his Russia, feudal lords were forced to pay taxes on their slave holdings. Strangely, landowners remained liable for their serfs who had died since the last census, that is, until a new census was taken. Sensing an opportunity to outwit the system, Chichikov plans to buy the souls of these dead serfs and to use them as collateral in order to borrow the funds he needs to finance his own estate. Although he is challenged in the courts, his scheme succeeds. Gogol portrays Chichikov as an economic hero, and his narrative suggests that the quickest way to succeed is to manipulate the system and to direct your entrepreneurial attention towards 'get-rich-quick' schemes and extra- and quasi-legal opportunities to attain wealth. Additionally, Gogol's tale highlights the Russian tendency towards wariness when dealing with strangers, which Batjargal (2006) emphasizes. Another lesson relates to getting ahead by using connections (and the names of dead serfs), although, as Gogol shows, this advancement comes at a high cost. Gogol understands but does not like this aspect of his hero. As Gogol ([1842] 1996: pp. 392–3) charges his readers, 'the dishonest practice of accepting bribes has become a necessity . . . [but a good Russian] must rise up against falsity.' Gogol's book formed the basis of another novel, *The Heart of a Dog* (Bulgakov [1925] 2005), in which the same story was transplanted from the era of serfdom to 1920s Soviet Russia when the New Economic Policy was in force.

Another possible explanation for the 'distrust' that Batjargal (2006) claims has a long history in Russia and is simply a part of the Russian culture is that communism was a system that corrupted almost everyone and that it was the lessons learned during communism that continued to color entrepreneurship in post-Soviet Russia and the rest of the former Soviet bloc (Kuran 1995). Several tales that describe life under communism illustrate this point. In *The Beggar's Opera* ([1975] 2001), Havel's 'translation' of John Gay's eighteenth-century play of the same name as in the original, every man is either a thief or a pimp and every woman is either a prostitute or a madam. Czech writer Milan Kundera explores a similar theme, noting that communism corrupted everyone and pleased few. His novel *The Joke* (Kundera 1992) explains how one simple joke mailed to a girl as a flirtatious enticement by the hero Ludvig destroyed his political career. The lesson is a stark one, that is, that any form of honesty might wind up destroying one's future. In learning to conform, Ludvig felt forced into false friendships; he lost his ability to have any real relationships, since he 'lost . . . any chance of resurrecting [his] trust in men' (ibid.: p. 115). The moral is clear—honesty is dangerous in a society based upon lies.

Bulgakov's (1996) novel *The Master and Margarita* also highlights the theme of corruption under communism and the resulting 'distrust' of others it engenders. This novel was banned in the Soviet Union, with only a heavily censored version appearing in state-authorized outlets. The full novel, however, was available through *samizdat* (clandestine distribution channels). The novel deals with the lives of ordinary Muscovites as a people who, because of the structure of Soviet society and its failings, are wary of strangers, are haunted by the secret police, and are forced into petty corruptions in order to survive. Bulgakov presents them as a people who love money but have become corrupted by it.

Similarly, in the story of 'Milan' in Simecka's (1993) *The Year of the Frog*, the nameless hero has to pretend to be someone else to overcome his father's legacy as a dissident who wound up in the prison camps. The hero is pitied by some for his plight, and shunned by others, but is in no way a contented and willing participant in the life he is forced to live, whilst feeling like 'vomiting' (ibid.: p. 7). The hero goes from one job to another, all of which he is overqualified for and none of which are able to make up for all of the opportunities that he lost because of his father's position. In addition to being a novel about having to 'live a lie,' this is a novel about the frustration of living under a system that blames you for your place in society, whether or not it was one you chose, and that gives you little in the place of all that it takes away. In the novel, there was no way that an individual could find out what his natural abilities were, since he lived under another's plan, never his own. Stated another way, in addition to speaking to the distrust that communism engenders, Simecka describes this society as one that breeds a perception of an external locus of control.

As Rupke (1978) showed, levels of perceived internal locus of control are positively correlated with entrepreneurship across cultures. Kaufman et al. (1995) discovered, however, that even Russian entrepreneurs had significantly lower levels of perceived internal control than US entrepreneurs. Zamyatin's (2006) *We*, which was banned in the USSR because it is a critique of the dystopian aspirations of Sovietism, focuses on why people who have lived under communism possess lower levels of perceived internal locus of control than others. The novel set in the fictional 'One State' parodies Soviet Russia with its lack of individuality. The hero, D-503, is perfectly content until he falls in love with I-330 and develops an imagination, which is prohibited because it breeds discontent and breaks the rules. To find happiness, D-503 submits to an operation to remove his imagination and soul. The Soviet system, Zamyatin's novel suggests, stripped men of their individuality, imagination, humanity and essence. The Soviet system, as portrayed in *We*, is a deeply alienating social system in which the locus of control rests with the state.

Rehn and Taalas (2004: p.237) have argued that '*the Union of Soviet Socialist Republics might be seen as the most entrepreneurial society ever. In fact, one can, with a specific notion of entrepreneurship in mind,*' they contend, 'claim that the system forced all citizens to become microentrepreneurs, to enact entrepreneurship in even the most mundane facets of everyday life.' According to Ledeneva (1998), for the subaltern under Soviet rule, securing the basic goods needed for survival meant relying on connections, calling in favors and operating in the black market. As she argues, the subaltern correctly perceived that in order to enjoy greater material comforts you had to be a member of the *nomenklatura* (the political elite) or be willing to use trickery to get ahead. Under communism, Ledeneva found, the successful entrepreneurs (as economic heroes) were individuals who used deception, were corrupt, and enjoyed political patronage. The novels discussed above confirm the findings by Kaufman et al. (1995), Batjargal (2006) and others about entrepreneurship in the former Soviet bloc, and suggest that the effects of communism still color entrepreneurship in that region. Entrepreneurship was pervasive under communism, but it was entrepreneurship of a type directed at achieving what was possible in a system in which shortages and inefficiencies abounded—an entrepreneurship distorted by 'widespread distrust, suspicion and attitudinal ambivalence among the Russians' (Batjargal 2006: p. 317)—not the absence of entre-preneurs, but the existence of a world view that celebrated confident men as economic heroes (as in Gogol's novel), viewed everyone with some suspicion (as in Kundera's work) and was characterized by an external locus of control (as in Zamyatin's *We*).

15.4 CULTURE AND ENTREPRENEURSHIP IN BRITAIN'S BLACK COLONIES

The relationship between colonialism, neocolonialism and entrepreneur-ship has received little attention in the entrepreneurship literature. No arti-cles that deal substantively with this nexus were published between 2000 and 2006 in ten key entrepreneurship journals that the authors consulted. Elsewhere, however, we have argued that colonialism leads to lower levels of entrepreneurship and higher levels of corruption (Storr 2002). Colonialism was a system in which only those who had innate privilege (in other words, the colonizers), those who received political patronage, or those who employed deception in their business practices could succeed. As a result, the colonized either convinced themselves that success was impossible and so did not try or began to equate success in business with connections, bribery, kickbacks and so on.

Although they do not deal specifically with colonialism, the profile of black entrepreneurship as being hampered and distorted in post-independence Africa and the West Indies because of their colonial and neocolonial experiences is confirmed by the few studies that do exist on entrepreneurship in these regions. Corruption and perceptions of exter-nal locus of control, these studies conclude, have dulled entrepreneurial success among the subaltern in Africa and the anglophone Caribbean. Ryan (1995), for instance, concluded that levels of entrepreneurship amongst blacks in the Caribbean were relatively low because of a number of factors, including cultural ones. Ramachandran and Shah (1999) similarly found that European- and Indian-owned firms outperformed black-owned firms in Sub-Saharan Africa, and that black entrepreneurs had less education and lacked the critical networks that their white coun-terparts enjoyed. Additionally, as Kiggundu (2002: p. 250) summarizes, *Kalabule* (Ghana) and *Magendo* (Uganda) are two societal practices that illustrate the challenges of African entrepreneurship. These practices both refer to illicit, improper or illegal business conduct used to criminalize entrepreneurial activities in order to allow those in positions of control and influence to make quick and illegal money. These practices, which Kiggundu asserts are unfortunately quite commonplace across the African continent, affect entrepreneurs in a variety of sectors (from taxi drivers to store owners) and undermine 'trust and confidence among entrepreneurs.'

Anglophone African and Caribbean novelists have explored these very themes. Nigerian novelist Chinua Achebe's (1960) *No Longer at Ease* draws our attention to a common attitude in Nigeria (and elsewhere) regarding *blat*. Reasoning on the difficulty of keeping one's hands clean in a context where corruption is rampant, Obi, Achebe's (1960: p. 100) leading character, laments that refusing a bribe can create more problems than accepting one. Although Obi, a mid-level bureaucrat in the Nigerian government, finds his society's permissive attitude towards corruption abhorrent, and so struggles to stay clean, his tale is, in the end, a tragic one. He is simply unable to resist the temptation. Achebe's Nigeria in *No Longer at Ease* is a corrupt society that corrupts everyone, where entrepreneurs deal in bribes and public officials expect kickbacks.

Ghanaian author Ayi Kwei Armah (1968) tells a similar tale in his novel *The Beautiful Ones Are Not Yet Born*, albeit with a more hopeful ending. This is the story of a man who tries to resist the insidious system of bribes and corruption that exists in his country, only to face ridicule from his compatriots and the disappointed looks of his family members. Set in post-independence Ghana, where the 'national game' of theft and bribery is so common 'that the point of holding out against it escapes the unsettled mind' (Armah 1968: p. 109), Armah's novel not only is an extraordinary exegesis of the deleterious effects of corruption, but demonstrates vividly how difficult it is to overcome the cultural and institutional pressures that exist in that system. Indeed, to the man's compatriots he is either a fool or a coward for taking 'refuge in honesty' (ibid.: p. 51). Even his wife ridicules him, likening him to the confused chichidodo bird, who 'hates excrement with all its soul. But the chichidodo only feeds on maggots, and you know the maggots grow best inside the lavatory' (ibid.: p. 45). He wants to eat but does not like how and where the food grows. After all, in Ghana 'everybody prospers from the job he does' (ibid.: p. 32); and 'the foolish ones are those who cannot live life the way it is lived by all around them, those who will stand by the flowing river and disapprove of the current. There is no other way, and the refusal to take the leap will help absolutely no one at any time' (ibid.: p. 108).

Ngugi wa Thiongo's (1982) mythical novel *Devil on the Cross* explores the perceptions of entrepreneurs that can develop in a context where corruption is prevalent. In his tale, entrepreneurs are not seen as producers but as parasites. As Gitutu, a character in the novel asks,

How do you think Grogan and Delamere became rich? I would sleep with my mother before I believed that it was their own sweat that made them so wealthy

... Who has ever become rich by his own sweat? Who has ever become rich through his salary alone? (Ngugi 1982: p. 102)

In Ngugi's original tale, the devil ('Satan, the King of Hell') hosts a competition between Kenyan entrepreneurs to see which one is the biggest thief and robber. Entrepreneur after entrepreneur mounts the stage to brag about their wealth (their cars, their homes, their women), to tell of their conquests and to share their philosophies on business; 'he will tell us how he first came to steal and rob and where he has stolen and robbed,' the master of ceremonies announced, 'and then he will tell us briefly his thoughts on how to perfect our skills in theft and robbery' (ibid.: p. 87). Ngugi's characters consistently link entrepreneurship and theft.

Several Anglo-Caribbean cultural texts, similarly, link entrepreneurship to theft, corruption and shady dealings. In Lamming's (1970) *In the Castle of My Skin*, for instance, the local businessman is named Mr. Slime. Antiguan novelist Jamaica Kincaid's (1988) *A Small Place* also recounts how commonplace it is for politicians and bureaucrats in Antigua to become successful entrepreneurs by using and misusing their public offices. She describes how even the wives, girlfriends and associates of politicians are able to become successful entrepreneurs because they benefit from government contracts and are granted exclusive distribution rights over certain imports. Colonialism, Kincaid asserts, is to blame for all of this corruption. She (ibid.: p. 34) asks of her former colonizers,

> Have you ever wondered to yourself why it is that all people like me seem to have learned from you is . . . how to take the wealth of our country and place it in Swiss bank accounts? . . . how to corrupt our societies. . . ? You will have to accept that this is mostly your fault.

The studies that deal with entrepreneurship in Britain's black colonies have described black entrepreneurship in these regions as lagging behind entrepreneurship amongst other ethnic groups in these countries. As Boxill (2003) explains, these differences between entrepreneurs in the same political and economic environments have led entrepreneurship scholars to look to cultural factors to explain relatively low levels of black entrepreneurship. The novels discussed above confirm the findings of Ryan (1995) and Kiggundu (2002) that entrepreneurship in Britain's black colonies is colored by perceptions of entrepreneurship as corruption (as in *Devil on the Cross*) and link those perceptions with colonialism (as in *A Small Place*). The novels also offer weighty expositions of the cultural milieu that can constrain black entrepreneurship in these regions.

15.5   DISCUSSION

Why should we listen to subaltern voices? What can they teach us about
how culture affects entrepreneurship, about how corruption affects entrepreneurship and about how totalitarian, oppressive social systems affect
entrepreneurship, even after those systems have begun to wither away?
What can we learn about the challenges that those oppressed peoples who
have lived through and survived communism and colonialism face by
paying attention to their stories? Can novels written by members of these
oppressed groups and set in these oppressive contexts help us to understand subalternity and entrepreneurship?

Previous studies on the relationship between culture and entrepreneurship have primarily relied on survey data to get at cultural traits. This
approach has proved to be quite fruitful. There are, however, some gaps
in that literature. Extant studies have tended to ignore marginalized voices
and typically reduce culture to a collection of indices. Using subaltern
literature, however, fills in both gaps. In particular, the approach allows
us to focus readily on (a) the psychic toll that communism and colonialism exacted on their victims and (b) the challenges that subalterns must
contend with and overcome as they engage in entrepreneurship.

The novels discussed are meant to be illustrative and were chosen
because they contained subaltern voices and described in vivid detail
subaltern attitudes towards business dealings and subalterns' perceptions
of their prospects for economic success. As is clear from the discussion
above, however, colonialism and communism were corrupting systems
that forced people to live a lie, that encouraged them to be suspicious
of strangers and that led several of them to equate business success with
bribes, kickbacks and *blat*. Kundera's Ludvig learns the hard way to be
distrustful of others. Gogol's Chichikov, who trades in the dead souls
of serfs, and Ngugi's Kihaahu, who leaves no crumbs when he eats, are
representative models of successful entrepreneurs, if not economic heroes.

How next to proceed? Further research is needed along several paths.
First, there is a dearth of studies on the relationship between entrepreneurship and corruption. The various ways that corruption can distort, redirect
and dampen entrepreneurial energies are an important and understudied
line of research. Second, many marginalized people are engaged in the
informal economy. Reports have suggested that more than half of the economic activity in poor countries occurs within the informal economy (see
Abedian and Desmidt 1990). The above study suggests that using subaltern literature can give us insights into subaltern attitudes and beliefs and
helps us understand why much of the subaltern's economic activity occurs
within the informal sector (unlicensed, untaxed, underground enterprises).

We do not, however, spend much time in this study applying this method to the informal economy *per se*. Finally, and perhaps most importantly, this discussion of subalternity and entrepreneurship stressed the cultural barriers to subaltern entrepreneurship and not the cultural tools that might spur their success. There must, however, be more optimistic tales or more opportunistic readings of the above tales that can be utilized. There are no such things as progress-prone and progress-resistant cultures—all cultures are diverse and can draw on (perhaps muted) tales that encourage entrepreneurship.

We can learn much from the legacies of entrepreneurship within these contexts (Boxill 2003). We can tell new tales and underline old ones. Writers from subaltern cultures can write: (a) novels in which the conceptual link between piracy and business, a link that makes sense given their experiences with colonialism and communism, is challenged and broken; (b) plays in which the permissive attitude towards political patronage and corruption is called into question; and (c) songs in which the heroes are successful business people who prospered by knowing the right things and not by knowing the right people. The work of development, this study suggests, needs to be done by local poets, singers, novelists, playwrights and artisans. To repeat a previous quotation, 'if you want to get a sense of whether a community is apt to grow wealthier, we are suggesting you find out what stories they tell, what myths they believe, what heroes they admire and what metaphors they use' (Lavoie and Chamlee-Wright, this volume, Chapter 7: p. 147). Poets can stir our progress, but as students of subalternity and entrepreneurship we have the job of paying attention to their verses.

NOTE

* This chapter previously appeared in the *International Journal of Entrepreneurship and Innovation*, Vol. **8**, No. 4 (2007). It is reprinted here (with minor edits) with the permission of the publisher.

REFERENCES

Abedian, I. and M. Desmidt (1990), 'The Informal Economy in South Africa,' *South African Journal of Economics*, **58**(4), 258–68.
Achebe, C. (1960), *No Longer at Ease*, New York: Anchor Books, Doubleday.
Armah, A.K. (1968), *The Beautiful Ones Are Not Yet Born*, Portsmouth, NH: Heinemann.
Batjargal, B. (2006), 'The Dynamics of Entrepreneurs' Networks in a Transitioning

Economy: The Case of Russia,' *Entrepreneurship and Regional Development*, **18**(4), 305–20.

Berger, B. (1991), *The Culture of Entrepreneurship*, San Francisco: ICS Press.

Bird-David, N. (1992a), 'Beyond the Original Affluent Society: A Culturalist Reformation,' *Current Anthropology*, **33**, 25–34.

Bird-David, N. (1992b), 'Beyond "the Hunting and Gathering" Mode of Subsistence: Culture-Sensitive Observations on the Nayaka and Other Modern Hunter-Gatherers,' *Man*, **27**, 19–44.

Boettke, P.J. (2001), *Calculation and Coordination: Essays on Socialism and Transitional Political Economy*, New York: Routledge.

Boettke, P.J. and V. Storr (2002), 'Post-Classical Political Economy,' *American Journal of Economics and Sociology*, **61**(1), 161–91.

Boxill, I. (2003), 'Unearthing Black Entrepreneurship in the Caribbean: Exploring the Culture and MSE Sectors,' *Equal Opportunities International*, **22**(1), 32–45.

Bulgakov, M. (1996), *The Master and Margarita*, London: Vintage.

Bulgakov, M. ([1925] 2005), *The Heart of a Dog*, London: Vintage.

Chamlee-Wright, E. (1997), *The Cultural Foundations of Economic Development: Urban Female Entrepreneurship in Ghana*, New York: Routledge.

Davidsson, P. (1995), 'Culture, Structure and Regional Levels of Entrepreneurship,' *Entrepreneurship and Regional Development*, **7**(1), 41–62.

Escobar, A. (1995), *Encountering Development: The Making and Unmaking of the Third World*, Princeton, NJ: Princeton University Press.

Gaddy, C. and B. Ickes (2001), *Russia's Virtual Economy*, Washington, DC: Brookings.

Geertz, C. (1983), *Local Knowledge: Further Essays in Interpretive Anthropology*, New York: Basic Books.

Gogol, N.V. ([1842] 1996), *Dead Souls*, New York: W.W. Norton & Company.

Granovetter, M. (2004), 'Economic Action and Social Structure: The Problem of Embeddedness,' in F. Dobbin (ed.), *The New Economic Sociology: A Reader*, Princeton, NJ: Princeton University Press, pp. 245–73.

Gudeman, S. (1986), *Economics as Culture: Models and Metaphors of Livelihood*, London: Routledge.

Harper, D.A. (2003), *Foundations of Entrepreneurship and Economic Development*, New York: Routledge.

Harrison, L.E. and S.P. Huntington (2000), *Culture Matters: How Values Shape Human Progress*, New York: Basic Books.

Havel, V. ([1975] 2001), *The Beggar's Opera*, Ithaca, NY: Cornell University Press.

Hayton, J., G. George and S. Zahra (2002), 'National Culture and Entrepreneurship: A Review of Behavioral Research,' *Entrepreneurship Theory and Practice*, **26**(4), (Summer), 33–52.

Hewett, E.A. (1988), *Reforming the Soviet Economy: Equality versus Efficiency*, Washington, DC: Brookings.

Hofstede, G. (1980), *Culture's Consequence: International Differences in Work Related Values*, Beverly Hills, CA: Sage.

Kaufman, P., D. Welsh and N. Bushmarin (1995), 'Locus of Control and Entrepreneurship in the Russian Republic,' *Entrepreneurship Theory and Practice*, **20**(1), 43–56.

Kiggundu, M.N. (2002), 'Entrepreneurs and Entrepreneurship in Africa: What Is Known and What Needs to Be Done,' *Journal of Developmental Entrepreneurship*, **7**(3), 239–58.

Kincaid, J. (1988), *A Small Place*, New York: Plume.

Kundera, M. (1992), *The Joke*, New York: HarperCollins.

Kuran, T. (1995), *Private Truths, Public Lies: The Social Consequences of Preference Falsification*, Cambridge, MA: Harvard University Press.

Lamming, G. (1970), *In the Castle of My Skin*, Ann Arbor: University of Michigan Press.

Lamming, G. (1983), 'Introduction,' in *In the Castle of My Skin*, Ann Arbor: University of Michigan Press.

Lavoie, D. and E. Chamlee-Wright (2000), *Culture and Enterprise*, New York: Routledge.

Ledeneva, A.C. (1998), *Russia's Economy of Favours: Blat, Networking and Informal Exchanges*, Cambridge: Cambridge University Press.

McGrath, R.G., I.C. MacMillan, E.A. Yang and W. Tsai (1992), 'Does Culture Endure, or Is It Malleable? Issues for Entrepreneurial Economic Development,' *Journal of Business Venturing*, 7(6), 441–58.

Morrison, A. (1999), 'Entrepreneurship: What Triggers It?,' *International Journal of Entrepreneurial Behavior and Research*, 6(2), 59–71.

Morrison, T. (1993), 'Interviews,' in H.L. Gates and K.A. Appiah (eds.), *Toni Morrison*, New York: Amistad.

Mueller, S.L. and A.S. Thomas (2000), 'Culture and Entrepreneurial Potential: A Nine Country Study of Locus of Control and Innovativeness,' *Journal of Business Venturing*, 16(1), 51–75.

Ngugi, T. (1982), *Devil on the Cross*, Portsmouth, NH: Heinemann.

Nummela, N. and C. Welch (2006), 'Qualitative Research Methods in International Entrepreneurship: Introduction to the Special Issue,' *Journal of International Entrepreneurship*, 4(4), 133–6.

Preston, L.M. (1995), 'Theorizing Difference: Voices from the Margins,' *American Political Science Review*, 89(4), 941–53.

Ramachandran, V. and M.J. Shah (1999), *Minority Entrepreneurs and Private Sector Growth in Sub-Saharan Africa*, Discussion Paper RPED No. 086, Washington, DC: World Bank.

Rehn, A. and S. Taalas (2004), '"Znakomstva I Svyazi" (Acquaintances and Connections)—*Blat*, the Soviet Union, and Mundane Entrepreneurship,' *Entrepreneurship and Regional Development*, 16(3), 235–50.

Rupke, R.H. (1978), 'Entrepreneurial Potential and Assessments,' unpublished master's thesis, Pepperdine University, Malibu, CA.

Ryan, S. (1995), 'Blacks as Entrepreneurs in the Caribbean and the Caribbean Diaspora,' in S. Ryan and T. Stewart (eds.), *Entrepreneurship in the Caribbean: Culture, Structure, Conjuncture*, St. Augustine, Trinidad and Tobago: University of the West Indies, ISER.

Scheinberg, S. and I.C. MacMillan (1988), 'An 11 Country Study of Motivations to Start a Business,' in B. Kirchhoff, W. Long, W. McMullan, K. Vesper and W. Wetzel, Jr. (eds.), *Frontiers of Entrepreneurship Research*, Wellesley, MA: Babson College.

Schiff, E. (1979), 'To Be Young, Gifted and Oppressed: The Plight of the Ethnic Artist,' *MELUS*, 6(1), 73–80.

Shane, S. (1992), 'Why Do Some Societies Invent More than Others?,' *Journal of Business Venturing*, 7(1), 29–46.

Shane, S. (1993), 'Cultural Influences on National Rates of Innovation,' *Journal of Business Venturing*, 8(1), 59–73.

Shane, S., I. Kolvereid and P. Westhead (1991), 'An Exploratory Examination of the Reasons Leading to New Firm Formation across Country and Gender,' *Journal of Business Venturing*, **6**(6), 431–46.

Simecka, M. (1993), *The Year of the Frog: A Novel*, Baton Rouge: Louisiana State University Press.

Spivak, G.C. ([1988] 1995), 'Can the Subaltern Speak?,' in B. Ashcroft, G. Griffiths and H. Tiffin (eds.), *The Post-Colonial Reader*, New York: Routledge, pp. 28–37.

Storr, Virgil Henry (2002), 'All We've Learnt: Colonial Teachings and Caribbean Underdevelopment,' *Le Journal des Economistes et des Etudes Humaines*, **12**(4), 589–615.

Storr, Virgil Henry (2004), *Enterprising Slaves and Master Pirates: Understanding Economic Life in the Bahamas*, New York: Peter Lang.

Watts, M. (2002), 'How Economists Use Literature and Drama,' *Journal of Economic Education*, **33**(4), 377–86.

Weber, M. ([1930] 1992), *The Protestant Ethic and the Spirit of Capitalism*, London: Routledge.

Zamyatin, Y. (2006), *We*, New York: Modern Library.

16. Indigenous African institutions and economic development*

Emily Chamlee-Wright

16.1 INTRODUCTION

In the attempt to establish institutions which foster economic development in the third world, economists often look to the West as a model. This indeed has been the case in Ghana, West Africa. In Ghana's urban centers, the large buildings which house Barclays Bank, Standard Chartered Bank, and Ghana Commercial Bank loom over the traditional market stalls and street traders. This sight might be heartening to those who recognize third world entrepreneurs' limited access to capital as the primary constraint in advancing economic development. Indeed, these institutions play an important role in financing large scale industry and high volume import and export exchange. But this is only a small proportion of market activity in Ghana. The majority of business people never enter the doors of such institutions.

The most striking feature of West African markets is the overwhelming proportion of female traders. While a few items will traditionally be sold by men, most of the trading activity is conducted by women. For example, the United Nations Development Fund estimates that 80 percent of all food production, processing, and marketing in West Africa is carried out by women. While limited access to capital is of general concern to development theorists, the limits facing female entrepreneurs are considered to be particularly severe (Simms 1981). The presence of formal Western-style credit institutions has done little to alter the situation.

The observations presented here are three-fold. First, the reasons why Western-type credit institutions have not reached the average West African entrepreneur will be explored. It will be argued that formal banking procedures have evolved to fit a Western cultural context and cannot be expected to fill the same role in the West African context. Second, indigenous credit and mutual assistance institutions which could potentially fulfill this role will be identified. Such institutions will be shown to reflect the cultural context in which they emerged, and how they in turn can accommodate specific credit needs. Third, the obstacles facing such indigenous institutions will be identified, with the purpose of suggesting shifts in policy. The analysis presented here is primarily based on findings from interviews of 49 market women conducted in the central markets of Accra and Kumasi, two prominent trading centers in Ghana, and the smaller market Madina, which is outside of Accra.[1]

16.2 WESTERN CREDIT INSTITUTIONS AND THE LOCAL ENTREPRENEUR

Recognizing the inability of Western credit institutions to reach the small entrepreneur is not to suggest a case of market failure or that such institutions were not as important a part of Western economic development as we had thought. Rather, these institutions are quite successful when operating within a specific cultural context. While it is easy to recognize the impact a certain cultural context has in general, the fact that formal Western institutions also emerge out of and reflect a particular culture is often lost, when analyzing third world institutions.

Western or Western-type financial institutions have emerged in a setting where the entrepreneurs are for the most part educated, literate, and male (so entrepreneurs are not at risk of being locked out of the process simply for the reason of gender). Entrepreneurs demonstrate their creditworthiness with a documented credit history, and the cultural setting they live in supports this method of accountability with rules of record keeping and documentation. Thus, it is not surprising that institutions which have emerged in this context are not successful in providing financial services to the bulk of the population in the West African context, given that small entrepreneurs are for the most part illiterate women, the least educated members of society. It is a matter both of the small business person not accepting the practices of the formal banking institutions and of the formal banking institutions not having much interest in reaching out to this section of the market. In short, it is simply too costly for the formal institutions to offer lending services to the small entrepreneur.

Market women are not likely to be familiar with complicated bank procedures, particularly the written forms. Many women, even in the urban markets, speak only their local language and not the official language, English. For the banks' part, the only gauge of creditworthiness of potential borrowers is to require a long term savings account. The majority of market women could scarcely dream of acquiring the sum needed for an initial deposit (Lycette 1985). This is not to say that a credit history does not exist, but rather that the formal institutions have no way of acquiring this information, as it is embedded within the kinship and 'sororal' alliances. Even if they are able to establish a savings account, any loan amount for which they would be eligible would not be worth the bank's time to process and administer. Having evolved in a Western context, formal banking institutions have developed a corporate culture and a system of rules into which Ghanaian market women simply do not fit.

16.3   INDIGENOUS SOLUTIONS TO ACQUIRING CREDIT

Indigenous financial arrangements provide an alternative to the formal banking system. The potential of these alternative arrangements is not widely considered to be promising, however, given that the amount of credit most often extended is no more than a few dollars (Robertson 1984). Yet there are still reasons not to dismiss the indigenous arrangements out of hand. First, we must recognize that the bulk of investment activity is financed through indigenous arrangements and not the formal banking institutions. Thus, even if the indigenous sector faces strict constraints, it is nevertheless serving a valued function in the market that is not met elsewhere. Secondly, it is not necessarily the case that larger loans are needed. The relative success of development programs such as the micro-loans project in Bangladesh and other areas indicates that small loans of just a few dollars can make a substantial difference. Thirdly, to the extent that the indigenous arrangements are stunted, it is often the result of state regulation and restrictions on trade. Thus, an investigation into the operations of indigenous financial solutions will help us identify which regulatory practices cause the most disruption to their ability to function.

The size, scope, and function of indigenous credit and mutual assistance societies will first be detailed, indicating the essential features for their proper functioning. Then the major obstacles attenuating the progress such societies might deliver will be discussed. Lastly, the relevant institutional and policy shifts which ought to be considered if the indigenous solutions are to provide the maximum possible benefits will be addressed.

Women's associations vary in size, scope, and function. Such societies are traditionally based in kinship and tribal structures. It might be said that migration both into the city by those from the rural areas and out of the city to the suburban areas has caused irreparable damage to the kinship and tribal systems such that they can no longer perform the advisory and credit functions to the degree that they once did. But, to the extent that these structures provide less support for those in the urban environment, other culturally based support systems are evolving to fill the void.

Christian churches, particularly in Accra, provide another layer of community involvement. Almost all the Christian church organizations provide some form of mutual aid on a regular basis. Many also play an advisory role for traders looking to expand their business.[2] Some even provide an opportunity to acquire credit through church programs specifically designed to start people in business. Thus, to the extent that the ability for kinship and tribal structures to provide these services is faltering in the urban areas, the religious institutions are stepping in with similar services of their own. As Western religious institutions replace traditional forms, they have had to adapt and expand their role in the new context. Specifically, they have had to take on at least some of the functions previously performed by traditional structures.

The second important support system that is filling the void left by the decline of tribal and kinship structures in the urban areas is the formation of female societies which cut across tribal and kinship lines. These can range from small clusters of three to five women who trade near one another on the street to the elaborate trade organizations of several hundred women in the established markets. Inclusion in the clusters or organizations is not solely determined by tribal affiliation or kinship ties (though these are still important when they exist). Successful face-to-face interaction which is repeated daily engenders the trust necessary for the formation of close bonds. Physical proximity allows traders in a specific area to observe one another's behavior, as well as establish a reputation for themselves. The question arises: can we not then speak of these clusters or organizations of women as a *culturally* based phenomenon? In other words, does gender constitute a cultural structure as, for instance, tribal affiliation does?

The answer is 'yes' when we recognize that, in the West African context, gender itself provides the basis for cultural specificity. West African women indeed have a culture distinct from that of West African men. The same is the case for children in the West. Deborah Tannen's (1990) work demonstrates that same-sex play groups during childhood lead boys and girls to develop distinct cultures from one another, and this explains many of the systematic differences between the ways in which adult men and women relate to one another. Tannen's argument is that, as children establish same-sex peer groups, boys and girls develop separate language patterns. Besides communication, male peer groups use language to establish status, or hierarchical relationships. Female peer groups, on the other hand, use language to establish connection, or more lateral relationships. As these different language patterns develop, so do distinct cultures. As Western children enter into adulthood, the male–female relationship tends to replace the same-sex peer group as the primary relationship. Yet each sex retains the behavioral and linguistic patterns learned as children. Thus communication between men and women is essentially cross-cultural communication.

Given that this is the case in the West, consider the importance a female specific culture is likely to play in the traditional West African context. The conjugal unit, while not incidental, rarely replaces gender specific groupings as the primary relationship. The mother–daughter relationship, for instance, plays a primary role throughout a woman's life, even as the daughter marries. The strict division of labor across gender perpetuates the importance of same-sex peer groups into adulthood as women work side by side with one another. The traditional role female cooperation plays in production, child rearing, and the enforcement of social norms (Sudarkasa 1981; Wipper 1984) also perpetuates the influence of a gender specific culture into adulthood. The most dramatic instance lies in the traditional compound system which separates living quarters for men and women (Robertson 1984).

Most of the market women, particularly those at the more marginal levels of operation, exhibit a strong sense of camaraderie with the women who trade in their immediate area. The traders form themselves into close-knit groupings, or clusters, sometimes as small as three to five women. These connections serve a vital economic function of mutual support. Even direct competitors will sell for one another in the case of sickness. Most traders are socially as well as financially linked with other traders.

Anthony Kronman (1985) describes this method of reciprocal behavior as 'union,' whereby individuals seek to 'reduce divergence [of interests] by promoting a spirit of identification or fellow-feeling between the parties' (ibid.: p. 21). As opposed to other arrangements designed to combat opportunism, 'union' does not assume opposition of interests. Rather '[union] seeks to eliminate the condition of separateness that makes the opposition of interests possible in the first place' (ibid.: p. 22). Thus, casual chat, gossip, and in-depth discussions which involve traders in one another's lives serve more than just a social function, but are also an important prerequisite for securing mutually supportive financial relationships.

Robert Axelrod (1981) describes how a high probability of repeated interaction generates cooperation under conditions where (1) there is no sanction for breaking the rules of cooperation, (2) there is no way to gauge the behavior of other players outside of the game, and (3) there is no way to change the other players' utility function. While Axelrod's analysis is internally consistent, it is not as applicable to the specific case of West African market women as Kronman's 'union.' First, West African market women do indeed have sanctions for breaking the rules of a credit society. Indigenous arbitration methods (discussed below) and the threat of ostracization are time honored methods of minimizing such opportunistic behavior when it does occur.

Second, the ability of traders to gauge one another's behavior in their day to day trading activities is a vitally important source of information. Simply bumping into another trader day after day is not enough to ensure a successful cooperative link. Trust, of which repeated interaction is only a part, must also be established. Trust involves careful assessment of another's character, not simply calculating the probability of seeing the same person again. A trader may faithfully return to the market day after day, but, if she is frequently rude to her customers, is a spendthrift, or is drunk on a regular basis, other traders are not likely to see her as a good risk. The repeated interaction enables this assessment, but by no means constitutes trust in and of itself. Third, Axelrod's condition that the players cannot interact outside of the game, or in other words cannot influence the feelings one has for the other, is clearly not applicable in this case. The bonds of friendship are paramount in establishing the financial support networks.[3]

Women at the upper end of the scale who have been financed by their husbands, however, often do not show as much interest in joining together with other women. One relatively prosperous batik trader refused to take part in any of the trade or credit associations. In fact, she reported that she did not gossip or go out of her way to be sociable with the neighboring traders. She resented the thought that illiterate women would try to tell her how to run a business. She thought that the associations were more for the illiterate traders, not for someone as well educated as she. This woman's business was financed, however, by her husband, who held a prominent civil service position. Further, the fact that her husband was able to buy a large house gave her the opportunity to produce the batik herself, as the process requires a large protected space. This gives further indication that the female camaraderie plays more than just a social role, but serves a financial function, which relatively wealthy women need less.[4]

16.3.1 Hawkers (Street Vendors)

The smallest forms of indigenous credit and mutual assistance occur among clusters of women who sell in the same area. Such clusters will gather to engage in group 'susu.' Members of a group susu association make either daily or weekly contributions to a common pot. The pot is then distributed to members in turn, usually on a monthly basis.[5] These arrangements can be on-going or for specific purposes. Engaging in group susu has the advantage over saving with a 'susu man,' as he charges a commission of one day's savings per month. Further, depending on the rules the group wishes to follow, the women who receive the pot first have a source of free credit.

While the susu arrangement offers a financial resource, credit can also come in the form of goods. Women who have lost their capital will often rely on friends to advance them produce or other goods, for which they will pay at the end of the day or the week. One woman who lost her capital through fines levied by the city council helps her friend sell rice in return for a small sum at the end of the day. This amounts to a transfer, as there is no benefit to the rice seller for 'hiring' her friend, yet the ethic of mutual support is reinforced so that the rice seller could rely upon similar support if such a situation were to befall her. Besides financial support, this arrangement also affords the opportunity for the woman who has lost her capital to maintain her position in the peer group, so that when she is able to secure her own goods for sale she will be able to ease back into the market culture.

Generally, among street vendors, there is little opportunity to belong to an on-going mutual assistance society,[6] as they do not have the financial capital necessary to make regular contributions, but the 'hat will be passed' as needed to aid friends who have given birth, are getting married, or must provide funeral arrangements for a family member.

Since trading on the street is officially illegal, a system of de facto property rights has emerged on the sidewalk. As the city council guards make their way down the street, the hawkers pass an audible signal to alert each other to the guards' presence. As if choreographed by Busby Berkeley himself, the traders hoist large trays of fruit, vegetables, fish, utensils, and other goods atop their heads. Women who sell goods too heavy to place on their heads need to secure a position close to the entrance of the established market. Once the signal is heard, they can quickly move their goods inside the market and lose the city guards in the maze of the market (a maze far more familiar to the women than the male guards). Many women 'inherit' these positions in the market from their mother, an aunt, or a sister. When a position is well established, any woman who attempts to encroach upon this space will be harassed out of the spot by the surrounding women with a barrage of insults. This de facto property rights system enables larger groupings, as women can count on their peers returning to the same spot in the market.

Let me point out, however, that de facto property rights are not as efficient as full rights of ownership. Following Armen Alchian and Harold Demsetz's (1973) identification of the essential elements of private ownership, de facto property rights fall short of the mark. Specifically, while de facto private property rights provide some level of stability and excludability, the element of transferability is significantly stunted. Stability is maintained as long as a trader consistently returns to the same location. Further, neighbors will often exclude would-be interlopers from taking over a selling position in the case of the limited absence of another trader. But the efficient allocation of the resource depends on the ability of a trader to smoothly transfer it to another. While selling positions can be 'handed down' from mother to daughter,[7] for example, generally traders cannot sell the space to the highest bidder. Among her neighbors, a trader's legitimate claim to a selling position holds only as long as she maintains that position. Thus, while the de facto property rights system works remarkably well, it cannot guarantee the efficient allocation of resources.

Many women are fortunate enough to have established a contact with a store-front shop owner, with the agreement that the owner will allow the street vendor to hide in the shop when the city guards pass by. While there is an opportunity for side payments here, most women who have such a position acquired the favor through personal contacts. The lack of payment, however, should not be seen as a sign that such permission does not represent a valuable resource to the street vendors, as it enables them to engage in more substantial credit relationships, again, because of the decreased flight risk. Further, the stable position enhances profits, as the trader is able to establish a regular clientele.

Among the hawkers who secure stable trading positions at the entrance of a store, the group susu societies grow from about four to about 12 members. The monthly pot for a four-member group where each contributes C200 per week is C3200 ($7.53), while the monthly pot of a 12-member group with the same contribution is C9600 ($22.59). The annual return per member does not change as the size of the group grows, but the larger monthly pot will be more helpful in acquiring costly pieces of equipment or a move into selling a more lucrative product. Further, because of the combined effect of the reduced flight risk and the benefits of building a regular clientele, the contributions tend to increase among traders who have established trading positions. Thus, we see that a well-established trading position translates into substantial financial gain when we consider the difference between a C9600 ($22.59) *per capita* annual return for a susu association with contributions of C200 per week, and a C28 800 ($67.76) per capita annual return where the contributions increase to C600 per week. Below I will discuss some of the particular obstacles hawkers face in acquiring even more stable trading positions.

16.3.2 Market Stalls

Credit and savings associations and mutual assistance societies take on a different character once inside the established market stalls. Though the market stalls officially belong to the city council, the de facto property right in the market stall allows for more complex credit and mutual assistance associations to develop. The number of participants in even the informal arrangements often increase to 20 or 30. The amount of contributions also increases, partly because these women have more money to save, but also because a woman is very unlikely to abandon a stall to avoid contributing to a group susu organization. Trust still plays an extremely important role here, as newcomers are not quickly included in such arrangements. A trader's behavior is carefully observed and her character closely assessed before she is given a chance to prove her trustworthiness. If she drinks too much or comes to the market late, her neighboring traders are likely to conclude that she will not last long in the market, and thus she would be a risk to the rest of them if she were to be included in any financial arrangements.

Within the established markets, a separate trade association exists for almost every type of good sold. The functions performed generally do not include credit, though informal side arrangements are facilitated by the frequent contact made between members in the associations. They also serve a quasi-political function, as grievances to the city council will be made through these organizations. They serve a regulatory function by reinforcing behavioral norms. Consistently rude or dishonest behavior can be met with termination from the association. In turn, the association provides financial security in the form of mutual assistance benefits for funerals, marriages, and births. Health benefits are also often provided out of the fund of regular contributions. Membership within the association is not required, though it is particularly advantageous for those far from their home villages and separated from the family support system.

Though sometimes there are attempts made by a particular association to restrict the number of sellers and enforce cartel prices, these efforts have been largely unsuccessful. The general feeling in the market is that such anti-competitive behavior is not a legitimate role of the associations.[8] The hair stylists' association tried to prohibit any non-member from practicing inside Makola market in central Accra. The issue was brought before the market queen, who ruled in favor of the hairstylists who wished not to be a part of the association.

The other major functions these associations fill are giving business advice to those having financial difficulty and providing arbitration services. Disputes between members of the same association can usually be handled internally. If the dispute involves traders of two different associations, the case can then be brought to the market queen.[9] Each major market chooses a market queen. Traditionally, the market queen is chosen by consensus. Through sustained face-to-face interaction in the market, the most trustworthy and experienced traders were easily identifiable. In the larger urban markets, there is the possibility for more than one choice; thus an election process is implemented. The results are essentially the same, however. As long as a leader maintains the respect of the traders, a market queen is likely to serve many terms.[10]

16.3.3 Lock-Up Shops

The next level of market activity is the lock-up shops, concrete structures in which traders can leave their goods overnight. These women have all the options open to them for acquiring credit that the stall traders do, but will frequently have further opportunities for acquiring credit. Some cloth manufacturers, for example, put high volume traders in contact with one another, the hope being that by pooling their resources they will be able to purchase even larger quantities. This is also a way for the manufacturer to share the risk, and thereby grant more cloth on credit. If a member of the cluster is short on her share of a payment, the other members will cover it knowing that they may need the favor returned at some future time. These clusters often form the basis for expanded business ventures, and are a trusted source of business advice.

The capital needed by a trader to secure a lock-up shop is considerable. To be assigned use of the space, she must pay the city council C26 000 ($61.18). She is also responsible for the construction of the structure itself (a structure which still officially belongs to the city council even though she pays for its construction). A simple 8-feet by 12-feet concrete structure costs about C550 000 ($1294). In addition to this, she pays an annual rent to the city council of C20 000 ($47).[11] If she has this kind of working capital, she is far more likely to be able to secure a loan through one of the official banking institutions. Once she is operating at this level, it is generally not a problem acquiring credit in this way. The problem is in reaching that level. The minimum savings and deposit requirements for starting and maintaining a savings account (the only way to prove one's creditworthiness to the official banking establishment) are a distant possibility for most traders in the market.[12]

16.4 IMPEDIMENTS TO INDIGENOUS INSTITUTIONS FOSTERING ECONOMIC DEVELOPMENT

What is stopping the evolved indigenous institutions from fostering more economic development? In her study of Ivorian market women,

Barbara Lewis (1976) cites the erosion of tight kinship ties and particularly the individualist character of the market as the reasons for the decline of the rotating credit associations and indigenous mutual assistance societies. It seems unlikely however that, after centuries of competitive markets, individualism is the cause of these relatively recent problems. She does not seriously consider the role government policies have played in stunting the effectiveness of indigenous arrangements of credit and mutual assistance, a line of inquiry essential to understanding the Ghanaian context. More than any other influence, state and municipal control of resources and market mechanisms has inhibited indigenous institutions from providing credit and mutual assistance and thus has retarded the development of the local economy.

16.4.1 Criminalizing Market Activity

In 1979, Flight Lieutenant J.J. Rawlings staged a military coup to oust the corrupt head of state Acheampong. Rawlings promoted his regime with an anti-corruption campaign, ordering the incarceration (and sometimes death) of bureaucratic elites who hoarded consumer goods and dealt in political favors. The rhetoric of the military regime struck a popular chord with the average citizen, who had been locked out of the system of privilege yet was spending more and more for basic requirements. Rather than being seen as a reflection of perverse incentives introduced by the marketing board structure, the relatively high prices of corn, cassava, yam, and other basic items were unfortunately seen as part of the general graft and corruption.

In retaliation for selling above the state-controlled prices, the major markets of Accra were destroyed. In central Accra, government soldiers flattened Makola Market Number One with dynamite. Many women were beaten and publicly flogged, their heads shaven, and often imprisoned. This contributed considerably to the general decay of indigenous markets in the early 1980s, where even produce which grows abundantly in the Ghanaian climate could not be found for sale in the urban areas.[13]

For a short period, government control was turned over to civilian rule, but conditions did not improve, as the president, Dr. Hilla Limann, retained the policy of stringent price controls. On December 31, 1981 Rawlings staged another coup, this time stepping up his anti-capitalist rhetoric. Drawing on a mixture of dependency theory, anti-Westernism, and Nkrumah's neo-colonialism, Rawlings favored at least a partial withdrawal from the global economic system (Haynes 1989: p. 109). Never did Rawlings blame his own interventionist policies for the continued economic decline. Only in 1983, when he was in considerable danger of losing political control, did he grudgingly release the price controls as a condition of an IMF Economic Recovery Program (ERP). Since the controls were lifted, the local economy has slowly improved, but the experience has left deep scars.

Currently, the illegality of trading on the street is still a major barrier to the most marginal of all traders against accumulating the capital necessary to secure a market stall, cooking equipment, or any other means of expanding a business. While officially trading on the street is illegal, unofficially it is tolerated. This does not mean, however, that the city council simply turns a blind eye. Rather, the ambiguous status of hawkers places them in the precarious position of being hit from both sides.[14]

The most cautious strategy a street vendor can take is to always keep moving, as the general rule is that city guards will not fine a trader as long as she does not loiter in one spot. This however means that she cannot establish a predictable trading position and therefore cannot build a regular clientele. On the other hand, hawkers who establish a consistent trading position run a greater risk of being fined or at least pressured for a bribe. Evidently, the guards are keen enough to price-discriminate. The bribes can be a token C200 (about $0.50) or a bag of rice or tomatoes every couple of weeks, or can be a more substantial amount of C1000 to C2000 ($2.35 to $4.71) a week if the city council guard chooses to target a trader he knows is running a profitable enterprise.

While these kinds of costs are imposed upon hawkers because of their officially illegal status, the fact that trading is unofficially tolerated means that the city expects a daily tax from each trader. Thus, the ambiguous status of the street vendor is as much a curse as it is a blessing. The daily tax[15] paid to the city council guards, the fines levied when a trader is caught setting her wares down on the sidewalk,[16] the loss taken when supplies are confiscated by the city council, and the regular tributes paid to the city council guards to avoid citation, when added together, represent a substantial burden upon street vendors.

In Accra, about 1500 traders per month have their goods confiscated and must pay at least C5000 to the city. A single C5000 citation can mean the difference between being able to feed a family and economic ruin. Besides the taxes and fines, there are implicit costs. Even if the fine is paid and the goods are returned, perishable supplies are often spoiled, as it may take several days to borrow the money from friends and family. Further, once confiscated, the goods are in considerable danger of disappearing into the pockets of city council employees. In turn, the trader is likely to lose a valuable source of credit if, because of the financial burden of the fines and the loss of her goods, she is unable to pay or late in paying her suppliers.

Monthly incomes of street vendors have a wide variance, anywhere from C7000 ($16) to C28000 ($66). Thus, the daily tax and two small tributes of C250 translate into 23 percent of a C7000 monthly income. Nearly 95 percent of a C7000 monthly income is lost to the city council if the trader is unfortunate enough to be issued a single C5000 fine. As the city guards tend to extract more from successful traders, those at the upper end of the income scale also lose a considerable amount of their income to the city council and the pockets of the city guards. The daily taxes, regular tributes of C3000 per month, and one C5000 fine translate into 33 percent of a C28000 monthly income. This percentage increases if the trader's goods are spoiled or stolen while in the custody of the city council. For instance, if a trader also loses half of a C10000 stock of goods, the effective rate rises to just over 50 percent. A trader is not likely to be fined every month, yet two to three fines a year can devastate any savings a trader may have accumulated, dashing chances of establishing a stationary selling position, a prerequisite for substantial levels of both formal and indigenous credit.

Fortunately, the city council no longer controls prices. However, a considerable amount of waste and inefficiency is still introduced by other restrictions on market activity. As valuable resources are diverted from the productive market sector to the unproductive bureaucratic sector, the potential of the local economy to enhance the financial prospects of the most marginal entrepreneurs is mitigated.

16.4.2 Unintended Consequences of Bureaucratic Intervention

While legal sanctions against street vending have the obvious and intended consequence of frustrating this sort of market activity, bureaucratic maneuvering often erects systematic, though unintended, barriers to successful market interaction. Finally recognizing the deleterious effects of price controls, all was to be remedied as the city council began to rebuild the markets after 1983 when the ERP was under way. Yet all was not remedied. The market traders were compensated with new stalls, but the city council could not rebuild the trust relationships which had developed over decades of face-to-face interaction among neighboring traders. Market women were given new stalls, but not the same neighbors. The potential benefits from forging new relationships have been dampened given the general atmosphere of uncertainty. No trader is sure when another similar occurrence will happen.

Since the inception of the ERP, other reasons have been found to relocate traders, either to make room for a parking lot (the result of a successful lobbying campaign by the taxi companies) or to thin out the market to help the flow of traffic. No matter what the motivation, the result is the same: the destruction of the credit and mutual assistance societies that had emerged over years of interaction with the same people. Further, such disruptions particularly frustrate elderly traders, such that they do not return to the new locations. This is a devastating blow to the indigenous credit institutions, as a vacuum of experience and trust is left, rather than a gradual transition of authority.[17]

Currently, the Accra city council is planning to spread the markets out to alleviate traffic problems in the most central part of the city. The criterion by which the city council decides who gets moved to the new location will be according to the size of the delivery trucks involved. For example, yams are delivered in large vehicles which block traffic; thus yam sellers will be removed to the new more distant location. Tomatoes, on the other hand, are delivered in smaller vehicles, so tomato vendors will be allowed to remain in the central markets. This proposal demonstrates the inherent danger of allowing market decisions to he made solely on the basis of bureaucratic concerns.

This is not to say that traffic congestion is not a problem in central Accra, but overriding market considerations is not the solution. If the campaign is successful, the move will once again wrench traders from their network of trust and support, and thereby undermine the evolved system of indigenous credit. If entrepreneurs anticipate the move and shift their behavior in response to such a policy measure (for example, yam sellers may switch to selling tomatoes), this will in turn increase the costs and risks associated with buying and selling yam, an important dietary staple.[18] The solution lies not in overriding the market process, but rather in allowing it to work. The congestion problem will be best addressed by a system of market, not state set, prices for selling space. Below, I will return to the issue of privatization.

16.5 LACK OF SCARCITY-INDICATING PRICES FOR SELLING SPACE

On any given day, a market trader could walk into the city council offices and acquire selling space within the market. According to the city council, many spaces are currently vacant. For C25 000 ($59), a trader can secure an assignment to a market stall. Yet many street vendors will tell you that there are no available spaces in the market. Others will say that there are spaces available, but the prices are too high. When asked how much they would have to pay to acquire space in the market, they quote prices two to sometimes three times higher than the price quoted by the city council. This is particularly puzzling given that during the previous year the city council provided new market stalls at no cost to which street traders could move. However, the women stubbornly refused to stay and returned to trading on the street.

Was this a case of the hawkers acting irrationally or at the very least belligerently? Are city council officials simply lying when they say that spaces are available? Or are the market traders simply confused, not realizing that the stalls are available and less expensive than they think? The answer is 'none of the above.' The fact is that spaces are available in the market. Further, the city council did (unsuccessfully) attempt to move traders from the street by providing free selling space. Yet the traders are not confused, nor was their response to the offer of free selling space irrational or simply belligerent. The confusion stems solely from the fact that the stall prices do not reflect relative scarcity or desirability.

As the state officially owns the market stalls, it is incapable of reflecting their true value in the price structure. The fact that some spaces are available at the prevailing rate should not lead to the conclusion that the rent charged by the city council comes close to reflecting scarcity conditions. In charging a single rate, the city council assumes that a homogeneous good, 'market stall space,' is being offered. But not all market stalls are created equally. The market stalls span a wide heterogeneous array in terms of location, access to facilities, sanitary conditions, and customer appeal.

Some stalls are near the openings of the market and attract a significant amount of traffic. Yet the same price will be charged for a stall which is tucked away in an obscure part of the market which sees little traffic. Some stalls are on a dirt surface, yet it will cost as much as another stall on concrete, which will attract customers even during the rainy season and will not ruin a trader's goods with mud stains. The case mentioned above, when hawkers were offered stall space at no cost only to return to the street, was again a situation where the selling space was inappropriately priced. In fact, the 'free' selling space was placed in an obscure corner of the city and attracted little traffic. Thus the zero price charged was simply too high, as the opportunities for profit were more abundant on the street.

Likewise, the differences between the accounts as to the prices and availability of selling space reflect, not confusion on the part of the traders, but the city council's inability to appropriately price heterogeneous resources. Most street traders know that some stalls are available at the set price of C25 000. But they are quick to point out that the only stalls available at this price are in a poor location and will not attract customers. The prices that they quote, which are two to three times higher than the official price, are the prices in the secondary market. As a trader leaves the market, she will pass on the stall space at a price which reflects the true value of the resource.[19] However, the secondary market is officially illegal, and therefore ownership cannot be guaranteed if a stall is acquired through a black market transaction.

It is not being argued that the city council officials are simply too simple-minded to see the obvious. In fact, on the surface, the market stalls do seem all to look alike. If we only look at their structure and design, they are more alike than different. Their heterogeneity is only manifest as the market process unfolds. In other words, it is only through market activity that one can discover what the true value of such resources are. Thus, merely encouraging greater attentiveness on the part of the city council will not produce a price structure which appropriately reflects relative scarcity. As it is absent a mechanism for discovering what the value of these resources is, the bureaucratic process has no means of acquiring this sort of particularized knowledge. Prices which reflect the relative scarcity and desirability of a resource can be discovered only through a market process.

16.6   POLICY IMPLICATIONS

Full scale privatization of the marketplace stalls and shops would solve or at least mitigate the most debilitating obstacles facing indigenous trade. By affording the occupants of market stalls private ownership rights, the pricing and allocation of stall space would fully reflect market conditions rather than arbitrary state set prices. Private ownership would also afford the opportunity to un-bundle the resource by allowing owners of stalls to rent to more than one occupant. Traders could then either divide the space, split the selling day or week, or invoke a combination of the two. This would reduce the per person cost of acquiring space in the market and thus reduce the crowding on the street.

Privatization would also open the way for private developers to erect new structures, which would likewise reduce the level of crowding. A private developer would price the spaces in a new structure according to market conditions and not need to rely on a rigid set price structure as is the case under municipal management. Further, if private developers have the opportunity to erect new markets, they will have to compete for occupants, not only by pricing the stall space according to market conditions, but through services as well. Once entrepreneurs have a choice as to whom they rent or buy from, as opposed to having to rent from the state, the market will reward those developers who provide services seen as essential to the marketplace, such as toilet and locker facilities, security, or shelter from the rain, all cited as serious drawbacks to the current marketplace environment.

This is not to say that all developments will necessarily provide these services. Some may offer only the barest elements of a marketplace structure. But the prices of such stalls would then reflect the lack of services and would allow the opportunity for those on the lower end of the income scale to establish a fixed location in order to trade. This is an essential move for the most marginal of the traders, as this is a clear indication of a person's creditworthiness to a potential lender (either to a formal banking institution or to indigenous sources of credit). Thus an array of quality will allow for an array of prices, such that the move from street vending to a fixed location is not such a cataclysmic jump.

Private rather than municipal management of the marketplace is likely to result in fewer cases of full scale upheaval, and the resulting loss of valuable credit and mutual support networks. The allocation of stall space and location will be based on market conditions, not political or bureaucratic considerations. If a marketplace is the most profitable venture, political maneuvering will not override market conditions as it does in the case of municipal management. If market conditions were to shift dramatically, however, at least in the private context, the traders would have the option of establishing themselves in a new space as a block, by renting a row of stalls, for instance. This option is a virtual impossibility under current municipal management. Further, in the private context, there is the opportunity for long term leasing and purchasing arrangements to emerge, such that traders would have to be compensated if they were to be enticed to move, again an option which is clearly not available under municipal management.

Thus privatization efforts will have the expected benefits of both rational market pricing and allocation of resources, but they will have some not so obvious benefits as well. Private development would supply new market space at prices which reflect scarcity conditions. The array of rental rates or prices likely to emerge would provide opportunities for the most marginal traders to establish a fixed location and therefore access to greater sources of credit. The private context would allow the un-bundling of resources, providing even further opportunities for the small scale entrepreneur. Perhaps most importantly, by fostering stable property rights, privatization efforts would support and enhance the performance of indigenous credit and mutual assistance networks.

Clearly the economics profession is aware of the advantages market coordination affords over bureaucratic control, yet sound policy conclusions seem to consistently elude us in third world contexts. The arguments made here suggest that we have missed opportunities for promoting economic development because we have ignored the cultural specificity in which institutions emerge. Specifically, we have tended to assume that one model, the Western model, of credit is the only path towards development. Rather than forcing West African culture into the mould of Western institutions, we are likely to meet with more success if we advocate policies which allow indigenous institutions to work to their full potential.

NOTES

*   This chapter previously appeared in the *Cato Journal*, Vol. **13**, No. 1 (1993) and as a contributed chapter to J. Dorn, S. Hanke and A. Walters (eds.), *The Revolution in Development Economics* (Cato, 1998). It is reprinted here (with minor edits) with the permission of the publisher.

1.   In Accra, interviews consisted of 15 street vendors, 12 stall traders, and 9 lock-up shop traders. In Kumasi, interviews consisted of 4 street vendors, 3 stall traders, and 8 lock-up shop traders. In Madina, 3 stall traders were interviewed.

2.   Of the 25 women who were asked about their religious affiliation, four were Muslim, two were agnostic, and the rest were Christian. Among the Christians, 14 different churches were represented. Of those, only the Assemblies of God, Central Gospel Church, and Deeper Life Ministries did not offer mutual assistance for funerals, births, and marriages. All but the Anglican Church and the Central Gospel Church offered regular opportunities to receive business advice.

3.   Klein and Leffler's (1981) discussion concerning the role advertising (or investment in one's reputation) plays in the success of contractual performance is also illuminating here. According to Klein and Leffler, such investment is like posting a bond, signaling a credible commitment to fulfilling the contract. Kronman's 'union' still seems more applicable, however, in the case of West African market women, given the emphasis placed on shared interests in the 'sororal' order.

4.   Of the stall traders interviewed, 15 out of the 18 (about 83 percent) belonged to trading associations, whereas only 5 out of 12 (about 42 percent) of the more prosperous lock-up shop operators belonged.

5.   Hawkers who have no fixed trading position tend to save anywhere from C200 to C500 ($0.47–$1.18) per week. Thus, if there are four members in the group, each will receive C800–C2000 ($1.88–$4.71) once a month. See Little (1965, 1973) for details of rotating credit associations in other areas.

6.   Some women will still have such support within their home village. But access to such support will most likely require returning to the village, as much of the assistance is given in kind rather than in cash. Women are reluctant to take advantage of this source of support if it means they must give up the independence and financial prospects the urban setting offers.

7.   This process happens over time. The mother, for instance, will begin by bringing her daughter to the market. The daughter will circulate goods on the street, returning to her mother's position for more supplies when needed. Eventually, the daughter may sit with her mother, establishing a rapport with the other traders. By the time the mother quits the market, the daughter has already established her legitimate claim to her mother's selling space.

8.   Of the 30 women interviewed inside the established markets, 20 were members of a trading association. The traders who did belong were asked if their association regulated the prices they charged. Virtually all said that their association (16 represented in all) did not. Most traders indicated that they would quit the association if it attempted to put such controls on their business.

9.   Officially, the case could ultimately be appealed to the city council. According to

Francis Eshun, the public relations officer of the Accra city council, these disputes are often simply 'petty female squabbles' and the council is reluctant to become involved. If the city council must pass down a judgment, it generally supports the decision of the market leaders so as to discourage future requests for intervention by the council. Though it is a misconception that these disputes and their resolution have no real economic consequences, it is on the other hand a fortunate one. Endorsement of the policy of staying out of 'petty female squabbles' ensures that the integrity of the system of conflict resolution is not undermined by bureaucratic tinkering.

10. There is also a market queen who presides over the collection of all the smaller markets in the urban areas. In Accra, this position had been held by a woman named Manan Lokko since the early 1950s. Since she was too old to come to the market every day, her role was primarily symbolic. However, she was an extremely important symbol, as was demonstrated by her ability to mobilize opposition to city policies. When the city council announced they were moving the market women away from the Rex Cinema, a central location in Accra, in order to start construction of new office space, the market queen was able to summon thousands of women to the steps of the city council. The administrators inside the city council reported many staff problems during this time, because all the workers in the office had some tie, either a sister, a mother, an aunt, or a wife, in the market, who was pressuring them to use their influence in the city council to stop the policy from being implemented.

11. Note that these figures do not include taxes, the magnitudes of which will depend on the particular good sold and the volume of trade. The operating taxes range from C40 per day (about $0.10) for small scale street vendors to C100000 per year ($235) for larger scale cloth sellers in lock-up shops.

12. Both Standard Chartered and Ghana Commercial Bank require an initial deposit of C10000 ($28.58) to open a saving account. They will not consider a loan for less than C100000 ($235). For a first time loan, they require cash collateral of half the amount of the loan, plus property or a guarantor. In addition, the borrower must insure the shop and goods such that the loan will be paid off in the event of extensive accidental damage or theft. Barclays Bank requires a minimum initial deposit of C50000 ($113) to open a savings account and will not consider lending less than C1000000 ($2353). Again, the first time borrower must provide cash collateral of half the amount of the loan, plus property or a guarantor. Barclays Bank requires the borrower to purchase life insurance in order to secure the loan. A policy for a healthy 30-year-old will cost around C150000 ($353). Barclays Bank also requires potential borrowers to carry out the bulk of their transactions in the form of checks. Small entrepreneurs deal only in cash both when purchasing supplies and in accepting payments.

13. Many women abandoned the urban areas to return to their rural villages, as subsistence farming was more lucrative than urban trade under such circumstances.

14. The ambiguous status of these women is demonstrated by the attitudes of the city council guards. At midday, guards can be seen carrying on polite conversation with and purchasing *kenkey* or small meat pies from the same women to whom they are meant to be issuing a citation. Yet, once or twice a week, guards can also be seen making their way up a street violently smashing the stools and tables upon which women sit or set their wares. During these demonstrations, no fines are issued and no bribes are solicited. There is no purpose here other than to send a clear message that the street traders are in fact criminals.

15. The daily tax is C40 or about $0.10. The irony that trading on the street is illegal, yet taxable, is not lost on the street vendors. One such woman proclaimed that, if the city guards were all fired, hawkers would then be able to save enough of their money to build their own market stalls and not have to trade on the sidewalk.

16. Usually the fine is C5000 (about $12), but, if the trader is a repeat offender or if the volume of goods she trades is unusually large, the fine can be doubled or even tripled.

17. The effects of these policies can be seen in the differences between the markets in Accra and Kumasi and other areas more distant from such political upheaval. The described

indigenous institutions in Kumasi are more stable and offer more substantial opportunities for support than in Accra, where most of the political and bureaucratic maneuvering has taken place.

18. This proposed 'solution' also reflects the male bias at the bureaucratic level. Only someone who has never done the shopping for the family at the end of a long day of selling in the market would see separating the items needed for the traditional daily meals across distant ends of the city as a solution.

19. Note that stall space in a good location is a valuable resource which is often passed from one generation to the next. A well-placed market stall acts as both a source of venture capital for a daughter or niece expanding a business (or perhaps a granddaughter starting out) and a source of social security for the retiring trader. As an older woman makes a gift of the space to a daughter, niece, or granddaughter, she can expect some form of support (either financial or in kind) from the recipient.

REFERENCES

Alchian, A. and H. Demsetz (1973), 'The Property Rights Paradigm,' *Journal of Economic History*, **33**(1), 17–25.

Axelrod, R. (1981), 'The Emergence of Cooperation among Egoists,' *American Political Science Review*, **75**(2), 306–18.

Haynes, J. (1989), 'Ghana: Indebtedness, Recovery, and the IMF, 1977–87,' in T. Parfitt and S. Riley (eds.), *The African Debt Crisis*, New York: Routledge, pp. 99–125.

Klein, B. and K. Leffler (1981), 'The Role of Market Forces in Assuring Contractual Performance,' *Journal of Political Economy*, **89**(4), 615–41.

Kronman, A. (1985), 'Contract Law and the State of Nature,' *Journal of Law, Economics, and Organization*, **1**(1), 5–32.

Lewis, B. (1976), 'The Limitations of Group Action among Entrepreneurs: The Market Women of Abidjan, Ivory Coast,' in N. Hafkin and E. Bay (eds.), *Women in Africa: Studies in Social and Economic Change*, Stanford, CA: Stanford University Press, pp. 135–56.

Little, K. (1965), *West African Urbanization: A Study of Voluntary Associations in Social Change*, Cambridge: Cambridge University Press.

Little, K. (1973), *African Women in Towns*, Cambridge: Cambridge University Press.

Lycette, M. (1985), *Financing Women in the Third World*, ICRW Occasional Paper No. 1, Washington, DC: International Center for Research on Women.

Robertson, C. (1984), *Sharing the Same Bowl: A Socioeconomic History of Women and Class in Accra, Ghana*, Bloomington: Indiana University Press.

Simms, R. (1981), 'The African Woman as Entrepreneur,' in C. Steady (ed.), *The Black Woman Cross-Culturally*, Cambridge, MA: Schenkman, pp. 141–68.

Sudarkasa, N. (1981), 'Female Employment and Family Organization in West Africa,' in C. Steady (ed.), *The Black Woman Cross-Culturally*, Cambridge, MA: Schenkman, pp. 49–63.

Tannen, D. (1990), *You Just Don't Understand*, New York: Ballantine Books.

Wipper, A. (1984), 'Women's Voluntary Associations,' in J. Hay and S. Stichter (eds.), *African Women South of the Sahara*, New York: Longman, pp. 69–86.

17. The role of culture in the persistence of traditional leadership: evidence from KwaZulu Natal, South Africa

Laura E. Grube

17.1 INTRODUCTION

In May 1996, President Nelson Mandela and the nation of South Africa celebrated the adoption of the South African constitution. There was a sense of optimism surrounding the new democracy. But it was clear that if the young democracy was to succeed it would have to deal with issues of land tenure and poverty in rural communities. The African National Congress (ANC) created the Reconstruction and Development Programme (RDP), which outlined development goals for urban and rural areas and described a land reform program aimed to provide secure tenure to all South Africans. There was a plan for land redistribution in order to address remaining disparities: apartheid had left 87 percent of land in the hands of whites and 13 percent of land to the majority black population. In order to address rural poverty, municipal governments were created in all urban and rural areas.

Almost 20 years later, however, many communities are still organized under traditional leadership and/or traditional councils.[1] Similarly, communal land tenure continues in many rural areas.[2] The puzzle, then, is how have these institutions persisted despite government efforts to overturn or weaken them?

The number of South Africans who live in areas with traditional leaders is significant. Koelble and LiPuma (2011: p.8) estimate that 15 million South Africans (total population in 2010 approximately 50 million) are part of a community overseen by traditional leadership. Others estimate that the figure is closer to 18 million, or 40 percent of the rural population (Vawda 2011: p.281). According to Williams (2010: p.6), there are 774 traditional communities in South Africa.[3] These traditional communities each have their own set of community rules, traditional leadership may be more or less active, and the communities show different levels of support for the traditional leadership.

Although there are differences among traditional communities, chiefs are typically appointed by birthright. Chiefs select headmen to carry out various responsibilities in the community, including land allocation. Chiefs are understood to be the custodians of land, but do not have the right to sell land (according to custom) and cannot allocate land without the input of the community. In communities where there are traditional councils, which consist of elected and non-elected members, these councils manage and allocate land. Land rights within traditional communities are communal. Each family has land that, within the community, is understood to be for their use only; however, they do not have individual freehold title.

The literature on traditional leadership offers several explanations for the persistence of traditional leadership and communal land tenure. Ntsebeza (2005) presents traditional leadership today as the result of rent-seeking by traditional leaders and emphasizes that legislation preserves the status of traditional leadership.[4] He describes negotiations between the ANC and traditional leaders—the Inkatha Freedom Party (IFP) and the Congress of Traditional Leaders of South Africa (CONTRALESA)—that led to political compromises leading up to 1994 and afterward (also see Waetjen and Mare 2009: p. 355). Oomen (1996: p. 56) has referred to traditional leaders as 'important vote brokers' in the 1994 election, encouraging support for the ANC in rural areas. Indeed, many scholars argue that the Traditional Leadership and Governance Framework Act (TLGFA) and the Communal Land Rights Act (CLARA) both sustain traditional leadership as an institution in South Africa. Other scholars, including Vawda (2011: p. 295), have taken a more complex view, explaining that traditional leaders can draw their authority only from their followers and that their continued existence is closely tied to the king (for cultural legitimacy) and local, provincial, and national government.[5]

The purpose of this chapter is not to argue the legitimacy or illegitimacy of traditional leadership in South Africa. There are communities in which individuals support traditional leaders. I explore evidence from one community in KwaZulu, Natal (for other case studies see Alcock and Hornby 2004; Mashele 2004; B. Cousins 2008). According to the 2005 South African Social Attitudes Survey, 64 percent of people in rural KwaZulu Natal reported a level of trust in their traditional leaders.[6]

Instead, the goal of this chapter is to better understand why the institution of traditional leadership persists. I argue that, while vested interests and lack of political competition provide some explanation, this explanation is incomplete. Cultural beliefs that underlie traditional leadership help the institution 'stick.' The remainder of the chapter is organized as follows. In section 17.2, I consider some of the relevant literature on the relationship between culture and economic activity. Section 17.3 offers a brief description of research methods, including information about qualitative data and the community where interviews were conducted. In section 17.4, I explain the structure of traditional leadership, notions of property, and rule of law provided under traditional leadership. I illustrate how *mētis* (in other words, history and identity and the belief systems) undergird traditional leadership and reduce the cost of the institution in section 17.5. Section 17.6 offers concluding remarks.

17.2 THEORETICAL FRAMEWORK

Austrian economists have argued that in order to understand an individual's behavior it is important to look to the meanings that individuals attach to their actions. As Mises explains (1963: p.26), 'We cannot approach our subject if we disregard the meaning which acting man attaches to the situation, in other words, the given state of affairs, and to his behavior with regard to this situation.' Similarly, Hayek has said that meaning is at the center of understanding human action. As Hayek writes (1952: p.44), 'so far as human actions are concerned . . . things are what the acting people think they are . . . [and] unless we can understand what the acting people mean by their actions any attempt to explain them . . . is bound to fail.'

Lavoie, following the intellectual line of Mises and Hayek, criticized economists for an 'objectivist bias.' Relying on the works of Gadamer, Schütz, and others, Lavoie (2011) argued that economic action could not be studied in the same way as the natural sciences. The objects in the social sciences have particular, already interpreted meanings, whereas in the natural sciences the objects of study are external objects. As Gadamer (1976: p.15) explains, within the social sciences 'There is always a world already interpreted, already organized in its basic relations, into which experience steps.' As economists, we are tasked with uncovering these already interpreted meanings and focusing on the individual plans of economic actors.[7]

Storr (2010) has written on the connection between meaning and culture. Storr refers to Schütz's 'social stock of knowledge' (or culture) as providing individuals with an interpretive scheme through which they make sense of the world, formulate plans, and make decisions (ibid.: pp.157–8). As he writes,

> An individual's 'subjective stock of knowledge' contains everything that he has 'learned' over the course of his life; how to walk, talk, read, ride a bicycle, drive a car, relate to his friends and colleagues, program a computer, reason like an economist; what his capabilities are and his limitations; what is appropriate and inappropriate in a variety of the circumstances; what is typically relevant and what is usually irrelevant in various situations; which phenomena he should view as common and which uncommon; his own life history, the stories he was told as a child, what he gained through interacting with his fellows; the customs and folklore of his community. (Ibid.: p. 158)

These pieces of individual and collective history help to frame a given decision and guide economic action. Storr (2013) has similarly relied on Geertz's (1973: p. 5) conception of culture as 'webs of significance' in which man is suspended and which 'he himself has spun.' Geertz's visualization implies that snapshots of experience are stitched together and combined to form a framework. This is not to say that all action is determined based on an individual's culture, but that culture may direct focus to a particular set of opportunities or choices—the knowledge of past experience acts upon man while at the same time man maintains his agency to choose his own history.

Austrian economists have undertaken case studies to explore how culture impacts economic action. Examining microlending in Zimbabwe, Chamlee-Wright (2005) illustrates an incompatibility between group microlending institutions and existing attitudes about lending among certain groups in the country (also see Chamlee-Wright, this volume, Chapter 16). Chamlee-Wright interviews entrepreneurs and discovers that there is an individualistic attitude related to concerns over shirking (in other words, the moral hazard problem) and worries that fellow-borrowers may become ill. This seemingly simple example illustrates the point that these social stocks of knowledge, or culture, inform interpretation and decision-making. Within the context of an office in the United States, group lending may seem uncomfortable because of established norms; however, it seems unlikely that someone would worry that illness might prevent a colleague from repaying. In Zimbabwe, a country where tuberculosis and HIV/AIDS affect many, individuals recognize and avoid situations in which the health of another could affect their own financial well-being.

Storr (2002) has raised the question of whether or not countries can get 'stuck' with institutional arrangements that are ill suited to their current economic challenges. Seeking to understand the poverty in the anglophone Caribbean by examining the region's history and the impact that experience has on the current economy, Storr (ibid.) argues that beliefs which developed during colonialism about race and economic success have caused many residents in Caribbean countries to associate economic success with political favoritism rather than hard work and perseverance.[8] Storr (ibid.) utilizes North to explain how or why certain countries remain chained to the past. As North has described, a society can get 'stuck' in a particular institutional matrix. 'Societies that get "stuck" embody belief systems and institutions that fail to confront and solve new problems of societal complexity' (1994: p. 364). North explains that this can happen because of imperfect feedback in the learning process. North (ibid.) indicates that the learning process is a function of '(1) the way in which a given belief structure filters the information derived from experiences and (2) the different experiences confronting individuals and societies at different times.'

Experiences and institutions are culturally filtered. In fact, culture—beliefs and values—shapes society's pay-off structure (North 2005: p. 33). For instance, the perceived rate of return to military technology in medieval Europe may have been high and, as society moved into the fifteenth century, individuals had to perceive that the costs and benefits had shifted (North 1994: p. 364). In other societies, piracy may remain the predominant form of wealth acquisition as long as individual actors do not perceive a better alternative. Similarly, scholars have shown that some post-Soviet reform programs failed not because they were bad policies, but in part because individuals associated 'private property' and 'capitalism' with corruption and greed. Such associations make acceptance of market reform difficult (Levin and Satarov 2000; Aslund 2007).

Likewise, development programs that have sought to introduce new institutions and policies in an effort to push countries out of poverty have sometimes failed because those institutions have failed to stick. Chamlee-Wright's (2005) exploration of group microlending programs sheds light on how culture can explain the persistence of certain institutions as well as why others do not stick. In Zimbabwe, she explains, individual lending is the norm, and the efforts to implement group lending have been less than successful. Similarly, Boettke et al. (this volume, Chapter 6) explain that market reforms in the early 1990s were extremely difficult in Russia because the people had lived without market institutions for 70 years. In these examples, institutional change is in effect *constrained* by culture.

Boettke et al. (ibid.) present a theory of why institutions 'stick' based on the regression theorem. The authors emphasize the link between formal institutions and the underlying *mētis* in order to create a taxonomy of institutions, distinguishing between foreign or indigenously introduced and exogenous or endogenous institutions. *Mētis*, according to the authors, 'includes skills, culture, norms, and conventions, which are shaped by the experiences of the individual' (ibid.: p. 129). As they explain, indigenously introduced, endogenous institutions (IEN) are most likely to contribute to sustainable development, as these institutions often are spontaneous orders based on local knowledge and come forth as the result of efforts by local actors. These institutions are consistent with the underlying *mētis*, or culture.

The answer to how history or culture matters for development, then, is the relationship between culture and the institutions in society. Efforts to institute the 'right' institutions will fail if these institutions are not under-pinned by the culture.

There is a long and complicated history surrounding land and land rights in South Africa. For many blacks in rural areas, oral histories tell of ancestors who fought early settlers and then more recent ancestors who were forcibly removed from land under the apartheid system. The beliefs around traditional leadership and communal land in many rural black areas, including KwaZulu Natal, I argue, are inconsistent with post-1994 policies regarding land and governance structures. Despite legislation that established municipal governments throughout all urban and rural areas and efforts to bring individual property rights to land, traditional leader-ship and communal land persist. Further, historical experience colors how individuals view new policies. As my case study illustrates, some individu-als do not want to make decisions about land without the input and help of traditional leaders. Walker (2008) suggests that this is part of an existing suspicion of national government from the apartheid and post-apartheid years.

In exploring the question of why communal land and traditional leader-ship persist in South Africa, the role of vested interests and lack of political competition can explain part of the story. In KwaZulu Natal, there is a set of political actors that have a strong interest in maintaining tradi-tional leadership. Municipalities are in fact not a substitute for traditional leadership, but have been created to act as a complement to the existing systems. Still, as the Austrian economics literature argues, culture can also constrain the movement from one institutional structure to another. The history of South Africa and firsthand accounts of the significance of communal land and traditional leadership suggest that culture does in fact play a role.

The remainder of this chapter explores the relationship between culture and traditional leadership and communal land. Specifically, I discuss culture as meaning, incorporating ideas about history and tribal identity, and beliefs around property rights. Within the Gumbi community, elders tell stories of the history of the clan, tracing the Gumbi back to the time of King Shaka.[9] Community members express a desire for the chief to be involved in important community decisions. Traditional leadership and communal property are closely related. The idea of formally demarcating properties within a traditional community makes many worry that the traditional leadership would be effectively destroyed, as the traditional leader is thought to be the custodian of the land. Added to these tensions are beliefs that ancestors reside on family plots in communal lands and that communication with ancestors can take place only from the grave site. Further, there is a sense of belonging to rural communal land and a desire to be able to return to the land to engage in ceremonies, including weddings and funerals.

17.3   RESEARCH METHODS

The analysis presented here is a combination of research obtained through primary sources as well as secondary sources. Primary source information was collected through interviews conducted in South Africa in April 2007 and March 2009. The first series of interviews were conducted in the Gumbi community outside of Mkuze, KwaZulu Natal. The aim of the research was to better understand the land restitution process and the role of traditional leadership in the decision to place a claim, and then the role of traditional leadership in the management of the Gumbi Trust. A total of 13 interviews were conducted with the aid of a translator. The chief, headmen, community members, and consultants to the community (including the attorney for the community) were interviewed.

KwaZulu Natal is unique in that it is home to the Inkatha Freedom Party, the leading black opposition party to the ANC. In addition, the province has a monarch, King Zwelithini. Because of these two institutions, the perception of traditional leadership differs from that in other provinces. As Ntsebeza (2005) points out, traditional leadership is highly contested in South Africa, and there are numerous examples of traditional leaders who sustained their position based on support from the apartheid government rather than the support of the local community. My research focuses on traditional leadership in KwaZulu Natal.

The areas selected for research were chosen because the author had access to someone who could act as an intermediary. Without someone to negotiate contact with a traditional community, it is extremely difficult to speak to leaders and community members. I recognize that the communities where interview data were collected are not illustrative of all the situations in South Africa. Rather, I seek to illustrate the diversity of experiences in traditional communities, while locating areas of similarity.

Recognizing the variations in experience with traditional leadership across South Africa, in the next section I present a general description of traditional leadership, focusing on the province of KwaZulu Natal.

17.4   THE ZULU AND TRADITIONAL LEADERSHIP

The Zulu and the institution of traditional leadership have evolved through time. As Hall (1984: p.65) has observed, 'the Zulu appear not as an "ethnic group" with fixed and timeless patterns of behavior, but as a people with a rich history of change and response to differing economic, social, and political circumstances.' Prior to 1879 and the destruction of the Zulu kingdom, the 'Zulu' were those who lived under the Zulu king, and Cetshwayo was the last king to rule the Zulu without significant colonial interference. They occupied the areas between the Phongolo and Thukela rivers, in today's KwaZulu Natal (the distance between these rivers is over 200 kilometers, or 124 miles, in places).

The Zulu king still operates as the most important figure in traditional leadership, although his role today is much more limited, and the term 'Zulu' is applied to describe a much broader group of people than it did historically (many of those who live in KwaZulu Natal province). Traditional leadership in KwaZulu Natal has the largest constituency of the provinces and consists of a king, 280 chiefs, and approximately 10000 headmen (Vawda 2011: p.294). For the purposes of this analysis, I will focus on traditional leadership at the *regional level* and describe some key characteristics of traditional leadership as it exists today, relying primarily on the work of Martin Hall (1984), Jeff Guy (1994), Benedict Carton (2000), Ben Cousins (2008), and H.W.O. Okoth-Ogendo (2008).

17.4.1   The Homestead and Traditional Leadership

At the base of the traditional leadership structure are the homesteads (*imizi*), which represent individual clans (Guy 1994: p.21). These clans are led by an adult male (homestead-head), who, in many cases, has several wives and children. The homesteads consist of a circle of huts around a cattle kraal, with each hut belonging to a wife and her children (ibid.: p.10). Cattle are placed at the center, in part as protection against theft. Cattle are valuable not only for their milk and meat, but also for exchange purposes. Today not all homesteads follow this pattern. Along the periphery of a homestead may be other family members, such as aunts and uncles, cousins, or even individuals who are not related to the family, though offer services to the maintenance of the homestead.

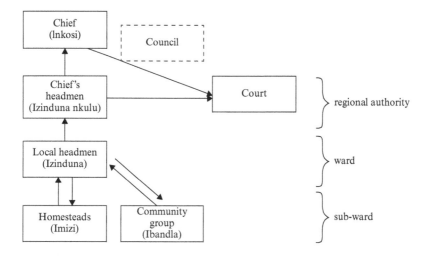

Source: Adapted from Alcock and Hornby (2004).

Figure 17.1 Traditional leadership structure, regional level

The homesteads, with the exception of grazing lands, act independently. Grazing land, however, is shared by all community members.

King Zwelithini is considered to be the leader of all traditional leaders, and the king has his own advisors and councils. Although traditional leadership is organized as a hierarchy, most decisions are made at a local level and rely on devolution of power. Figure 17.1 illustrates the governance structure with the chief (*inkosi*), regional headmen (*izinduna nkulu*), and local (ward) headmen (*izinduna*).

The chief is selected according to birthright, as the first-born son of the previous chief. He is advised by a council, which consists of members of the royal family, respected men in the community, and the chief's headmen and local headmen. The chief's headmen assist the chief in the administration of law and can act as the prosecutors in the tribal court. If there is disagreement between the local headmen, the chief's headmen may mediate and help to resolve the dispute. The local headmen operate at the ward, or most local level, and handle issues around land allocation, disputes among neighbors, or any other issues that may occur in the community. As Alcock and Hornby (2004) show, the selection of local headmen varies from community to community, but in general the chief has a greater say in the selection of the chief's headmen, and the community has greater influence over the selection of the local headmen (ibid.).

Many of the responsibilities of local headmen and traditional leadership relate to land allocation. The chief is the custodian of the land, although he makes decisions regarding land in consultation with the community. Males maintain use rights to specific land from family members, and if the land is not adequate they may be granted additional land. This happens through the local headmen, who in turn discuss the allocation with community members. T. Cousins and Hornby (2000) have studied Ekuthuleni, a traditional community in KwaZulu Natal. In Ekuthuleni, allocations are made to relatives of existing community members who demonstrate a need for land. Allocations may also be made to single mothers and widows.

There are costs related to traditional leadership. Households pay an annual levy for land and the services provided through the chief and headmen (Alcock and Hornby 2004: p. 13). Additionally, limited economic opportunity as a result of retaining traditional land tenure arrangements is a cost to traditional communities. The land arrangement, namely the lack of freehold title, inevitably deters businesses in rural areas (de Soto 1989). Therefore, people must seek employment outside the communities and in nearby cities. Poverty estimates for rural areas are as high as 70.9 percent, with unemployment near 70 percent (Andrews and Jacobs 2009: pp. 2–3).[10] These figures inevitably do not include informal activities—small farming, 'tuck shops' (small corner stores), or other side businesses—but these informal activities are also limited in terms of growth opportunities and employment.[11]

Despite these costs, in numerous case studies scholars find that communities value traditional leaders and would like them to maintain their roles (Alcock and Hornby 2004; Mashele 2004; B. Cousins 2008). In some communities, people strongly value their history and identity, and this is one reason that they choose to live in traditional communities.

17.4.2 New Legislation and Traditional Leadership

The most significant change to traditional leadership since 1994 has been the 1998 Municipal Structures Act and the 2003 Traditional Leadership and Governance Framework Act (TLGFA). The Municipal Structures Act created local governments in all urban and rural areas and assigned these local municipal councils responsibility for development. Traditional leaders may have up to 20 percent representation on the council; however, they are not allowed voting rights.

Vawda (2011) captures the response of chiefs to the Act and the demarcation process. Chief Gwala supported the arrangement and was pleased to be included as part of the Durban municipality. He stated, 'we are hoping that now [that] we will be under Metro they will consider assisting us with electricity. Perhaps the Durban municipality will see that it is not good for some areas to lack basic services while others have everything' (quoted in ibid.: p. 298). Another chief was more critical of the Act:

> I am not calling for an alternative state, but I am saying we should work with one another, but under the same conditions as we did during those days of the KwaZulu government. We need to work together but we don't want to have a situation where the mayor undermines us. (Ibid.: p. 301)

This second chief is clearly calling for more decision-making power and autonomy for traditional leadership.

The TLGFA sought to reform the structure of traditional leadership by creating traditional councils which contain elected members in addition to people appointed by the chief. The council represented in Figure 17.1 has a dotted outline to indicate that this is sometimes, as I have explained, members of the royal family, respected men in the community, and the chief's headmen and local headmen and, in other cases, communities have transitioned to elected members. Once registered, a traditional community is recognized by the provincial government, and the council becomes a new governing body within traditional leadership which supersedes traditional authorities. The council may have 'traditional leaders and members of the traditional community selected by the senior traditional leader,' and at least 40 percent of members must be elected, and those members should serve five-year terms.

Section 4(1) of the Act lists the functions of traditional councils, including among others: '(a) administering the affairs of the traditional community in accordance with customs and traditions . . . (c) supporting municipalities in the identification of community needs . . . (h) promoting the ideals of co-operative governance, integrated development planning, sustainable development and service delivery.'

The functions of traditional leadership are given in one sentence, section 19: 'A traditional leader performs the functions provided for in terms of customary law and customs of the traditional community concerned, and in applicable legislation.'

Rules around land administration and allocation were established a year later, through the Communal Land Rights Act (CLARA). CLARA defined the role of traditional leadership in land allocation and provided for the transfer of state land (which is beneficially occupied by individuals) to a person, a traditional leader, or a communal property association. In 2010, this Act was repealed because of a procedural error when it was adopted in Parliament. As of February 2015, a new law has not been introduced. Instead, the government has been extending the Interim Protection of Informal Land Rights Act (1996). This Act similarly protects the rights of an individual or a community, but does not allow for freehold title. Because CLARA was repealed, there has been less of an incentive for communities to change their structure.

Although the TLGFA has been law since 2003, as Alcock and Hornby (2004) and Smith (2008: p. 35) describe, traditional councils have not been implemented in all communities (figures could not be located in the literature or provincial government resources). Further, as B. Cousins (2008: p. 109) and others recognize, the *de jure* rules are often not consistent with the *de facto* rules; in other words, even if a traditional council is registered, it may not in actuality replace traditional leadership in the administration and allocation of land. Both of these considerations illustrate that traditional leadership is resistant to change.

17.5 THE PERSISTENCE OF TRADITIONAL LEADERSHIP

The persistence of traditional leadership in KwaZulu Natal can be explained by (1) the vested interests of and the lack of competition faced by traditional leaders, (2) the saliency of the Zulu's history and tribal identity, and (3) their beliefs around property rights.

17.5.1 Vested Interests and Lack of Competition

During apartheid, Zulu leadership also relied on ideas surrounding identity, sometimes referred to as 'Zulu Nationalism,' to promote traditional leadership and the IFP. In 1970 the state created the Zulu Territorial Authority, and Mangosuthu Buthelezi called for 'self-determination and self-realisation' for 'the Zulu Nation' (Waetjen and Mare 2009: p. 356). As Waetjen and Mare explain, he did not want to be simply a puppet of the state. Instead, he had much larger ambitions to promote the sovereignty of the Zulu kingdom and uphold Zulu ethnic politics, including the leadership of King Goodwill Zwelithini. Buthelezi worked to create Zulu pride and nationalism, and King Zwelithini became his leading symbol of Zulu identity: 'the King presented himself as the father of Zuluness, declaring that "history has put me where I am and all Zulu history demand that I make the unity of my people my first priority"' (ibid.: p. 358).

Vested interests may also contribute to institutional path dependence. In South Africa, chiefs want to remain in leadership and may try to affect the relative benefits of traditional leadership in different ways. King Zwelithini's actions may be interpreted as trying to increase the perceived benefits of 'Zuluness' (and traditional leadership). The unity of the Zulu is important for King Zwelithini, as he, like a chief, is a king only if he has people to lead.

While traditional leaders seek the preservation of traditional leadership, the national government would prefer to have the support of traditional leaders in order to gain votes in rural areas. Violent conflict between the IFP and the ANC during the late 1980s and early 1990s is still in memory. The 2009 National House of Traditional Leaders Act (previously the 1994 Council of Traditional Leaders Act) illustrates a compromise between groups. Supported by CONTRALESA, the legislation provides resources for the National House and outlines powers and duties: nation building, peace, stability, cohesiveness of communities, preservation of the culture and traditions of communities, socio-economic development, and service delivery. Each province then adopted a separate law to create its own provincial House of Traditional Leaders. These laws also provide the financial resources for the buildings, maintaining the buildings, and money for employees, including traditional leaders. The South African government spends R48 million per month (or about $8 000 000) supporting royal houses, chiefs, and headmen (Koelble and LiPuma 2011: p. 25). Even with this new arrangement, however, vested interest does not explain why people choose to live under traditional leadership. This may explain why traditional leaders supply their services, but it does not explain why individuals demand the services.

There is also no competition for traditional leadership. Legislation and policies encourage cooperation between traditional leadership and municipal government (see Municipal Structures Act 1998; Municipal Structures Second Amendment Act 2000). Thus there has been an effort to characterize the two institutions as complementary rather than substitutes. If people live in a traditional community, they can receive benefits from both traditional leadership and municipal government. For example, within a traditional community, individuals are under a rule of law and enforcement of law through the local court. And, as members of a traditional community, they do not forgo benefits from the municipality. The municipality still provides basic services such as water and electricity, as well as police services and enforcement of law. These benefits contribute to the incentive structure and help to explain how traditional leadership continues to operate side by side with municipal systems. Vested interests and lack of political competition offer a compelling but incomplete explanation for why traditional leadership has persisted. In some communities, there is a demand for traditional leadership. Theory suggests that long lasting institutions are supported by culture (North 1994, 2005; Boettke et al., this volume, Chapter 6). Evidence both from case studies and from survey data demonstrates that individuals do in fact value traditional leadership, and that the relationship between individuals and the institution of traditional leadership is complex. This chapter focuses on how culture can help to explain the persistence of traditional leadership and communal land.

17.5.2   History and Tribal Identity

The importance of history and specifically tribal identity is evident today. KwaZulu Natal, more than any other province, claims an identity (Zulu). Although all provinces can create their own constitutions, only the Western Cape and KwaZulu Natal have exercised the right. The drafted constitution of KwaZulu Natal was denied by the national government because it asserted 'the autonomy of KZN as the homeland of the Zulu people' (Simeon and Murray 2004: p. 285).

Prior to colonial intervention, identification within a clan or tribe was a person's primary source of protection against violence from other clans or tribes and forms of economic hardship. The Zulu army was a formidable force, and under the leadership of King Shaka (1816–28) the Zulu consolidated power to control what became Zululand—the area between the Phongolo and Thukela rivers. As historian Jeff Guy describes, the spread of unpalatable grasses in Zululand caused different groups to seek additional grazing land (1994: p. 9). The Mthethwa, the Ndwandwe, and the Zulu were competing for the same lands. Both King Zwelithini (1968–present) and Buthelezi (leader of the Inkatha Freedom Party since 1975) have promoted the story of Shaka in an effort to unite the Zulu people.

Evidence suggests that other communities also have histories and a sense of identity that ties them to traditional leadership. Within the Gumbi community, for instance, elders share stories which have been passed down through oral history. Chief Mbhekiseni Zeblon Gumbi, brothers of the deceased Inkosi Myekeni Gumbi, and other elders of the community are able to trace their history back to the era of Shaka.[12] During Shaka's conflicts with Zwide (*inkosi* of the Ndwandwe), Zwengendaba (*inkosi* of the Jele, later known as Gumbi), and his brother, Somkhanda, supported Zwide. Zwide was defeated, and, as a result, Zwengendaba and Somkhanda headed for protection in Swazi territory. In order to disguise their identity, the new group under Somkhanda took the surname Gumbi. Gumbi was the first name of a respected young woman within the clan.[13] Somkhanda eventually died near Golela and was succeeded by Ntini. Community members view themselves as being part of a line that extends back through the generations.

With the arrival of the Voortrekkers to the area in 1837 and the British

soon after (the Colony of Natal was established in 1845), the social structure and livelihood of the Zulu and other indigenous groups was severely
tested. There was increased competition for land. Before the National
Party and the apartheid system, colonialists created the Glen Grey Act
(1894), which limited the amount of land that could be controlled by an
indigenous person. In 1905, a poll tax to be paid by all males over the
age of 18 was instituted. This forced more laborers into jobs on farms
and in the mines. The Natives Land Act was then passed in 1913 which
prohibited blacks from owning or renting land in the majority of the
country.[14] Although the exact year is not known, the Gumbi lost their
land to white farmers even before 1913 and then worked on white farm-
land. Commissioned by the British government following the annexation
of Zululand to Natal in 1897, the Final Report of the Zululand Lands
Delimitation Commission estimates that there were 448 heads of household in the Gumbi clan. Although the Gumbi are recognized, they were
not allocated any land within reserve territory. Instead, they found themselves on crown land or land reserved for white farmers.

Apartheid and pre-apartheid legislation continues to color the perception toward new policies and contributes to suspicion surrounding
new (national government) policies. Community member and headman
Sakhile explains how the Gumbi worked for the white farmers: '[We]
worked a long time, suffered a lot, working on farms for six months and
get[ing almost] nothing.' The benefits for six months' work, explains
Sakhile, were the ability to inhabit the land and a few bags of meali meal,
but no money. White farmers dictated how the Gumbi lived on the land. A
limit of five cattle per household was imposed. As one Gumbi community
member explained, 'the farmers sa[id], "reduce cows," [they are] overgraz-
ing the land.'[15] The limit of five per household significantly affected a family's wealth as well as its cultural identity. Cattle serve as a store of wealth
for barter and are required to pay lobola, a tradition in which a groom
honors his bride's family by offering them cattle.[16] In addition to land
confiscations, the apartheid government also sought to engineer cultural
boundaries between ethnic groups and governance structures.

Apartheid policies led to more forced removals, both in urban and
in rural areas, as well as changes to traditional leadership structures.
The Bantu Authorities Act (1951) gave increased authority to Africans
by establishing Bantu tribal, regional, and territorial authorities, and
the Promotion of Bantu Self-Government Act (1959) created eight
commissioners-general to represent the government in each homeland.
Ten years later, the Bantu Homelands Citizenship Act was adopted,
requiring that all blacks be citizens of a homeland and effectively cancel-
ling citizenship rights to the Republic. Ntsebeza (2005) has emphasized

how traditional leadership was compromised during this time period, as the national government sought to promote indigenous leaders who were more cooperative towards the national government. While his presentation cannot be dismissed, it is also important to recognize that many traditional leaders and the institution of traditional leadership are still respected in many communities (B. Cousins 2008: p. 126).

In the Gumbi community, there is sadness as the elders describe how the chief was expected to perform hard labor on white farms. Many years later, the community continues to show respect for the chief. See, for instance, the Gumbi community's claim to the Land Claims Commission. Although the chief did not initiate the Gumbi land claim, those involved were eager to have his approval, recognizing that his support would help to bring other community members on board. Nathi explains:

> We wanted him [Inkosi Zeblon] to be involved. He is a leader. People go to him and ask questions, and we wanted him to know [about the operations of the Gumbi Trust] so he can answer questions. [Also] Inkosi brings respect [to the project]. If there is a new idea, people will accept more easily if Inkosi is involved.

The community was awarded 18 500 hectares in land and R30 million in equitable redress. The Gumbi officially received the land on June 24, 2006. The land is held by the Gumbi Trust.

Although land legislation granting freehold title exists, many people have concerns regarding the meaning of freehold title and have a general uneasiness over new kinds of property rights. There is a general fear of government involvement in rural areas. Land nationalization schemes proposed by the ANC government were met with the greatest resistance in rural areas. Walker notes that, in rural communities, people 'harboured deep suspicions of "government" as an unaccountable, untrustworthy force' (2008: p. 53). This suspicion comes from a long history of intervention and land confiscation.

Clan history is an important element to individuals in the Gumbi community. Community members are eager to share the struggles that their ancestors and they themselves have endured. In other societies, individuals might emphasize history as the distance between the past and future, with an eye to changes and differences. Another way to consider history (perhaps closer to the view of community members in the Gumbi clan) is as an explanation for today. When an elder is telling the history of the Gumbi, it is almost as if he is providing a detailed story of how it is that you are encountering him at that spot at that moment. In the explanation, clan history and identity cannot be disentangled from traditional leadership. The traditional leader is the name of the clan, he has moved the community to safe territory, he has labored side by side with the community members, and he must be consulted today regarding a land claim. Traditional leadership persists then, in part, because of the way in which history and identity provide meaning for the present.

17.5.3 Beliefs around Property Rights

Traditional property rights within the Zulu regions of South Africa do not permit property to be sold, nor do they offer a title which may be leveraged as a financial resource. Consequently, few businesses exist in traditional communities, and job opportunities are limited. As noted in section 17.4.1, poverty estimates for rural areas are as high as 70.9 percent, with unemployment near 70 percent (Andrews and Jacobs 2009: pp. 2–3). The persistence of traditional leadership and the traditional land tenure system that traditional leadership controls would seem to be costly. Beliefs around property rights, specifically the understanding of how land is important to living family members and holds a tie to ancestors, provide insight into how traditional leadership and communal property are perceived to be largely beneficial.

Communal land is part of the institution of traditional leadership. A chief is a chief only if he has people and land to identify as part of the clan (Mashele 2004: p. 352). Further, there is recognition that, if land were sold, this would result in the chief 'not having land, which will be the end of ubukhosi' (traditional leadership) (Alcock and Hornby 2004: p. 17). Chiefs are the custodians of land, and families have use rights to homesteads and other land within the community. Neither the chief nor family members have a right to sell land. Sons retain use rights to land. There are several reasons that the prohibition against land sales continues.

Being able to communicate with ancestors is a major reason that individuals remain on family land and are resistant to being able to sell land. Ancestors are buried on the family plot.[17] Although Christian missionaries were active in Zululand as early as the 1830s and many Zulus consider themselves Christian, the Christian beliefs have been adopted in addition to existing religious beliefs (Carton 2009: p. 133). Berglund (1976) and others have identified the difficulty in separating 'traditional' (pre-Christian) beliefs and Christian influences. As Monteiro-Ferreira (2005: p. 357) explains, 'rather than conceiving of an all-governing God, the Zulu peoples, following ancestral African religious systems, believe in the existence of over-present ancestral spirits who watch over daily activities, promote social harmony, and create a sense of accountability among its members.' Similarly, as Alcock and Hornby (2004: p. 14) note, all rightful heirs of a homestead have the same surname as the former homestead-head and have the ability to communicate with ancestors. Further, 'ancestors are only able to recognize communication that takes place from a specific, ritualized place on the homestead plot' (ibid.). This ability to access the guidance of ancestors is important for the future success of the clan.

In her account of the Bhangazi restitution claim on the eastern shores of Lake St. Lucia in KwaZulu Natal, Walker interviews Phineas Mbuyazi, who brought the land restitution claim. Mbuyazi gives three reasons for wanting to return to the shore of Lake St. Lucia: (1) *isiko* (local clan-based customs); (2) *ulwandle* (the sea); and (3) the lake with its hippos (2008: p. 115). Mbuyazi believes that the hippos are his ancestors and performs rituals to ask the hippos for forgiveness. After years of negotiations, a review panel decided that the Greater St. Lucia Wetland Park should remain a nature conservancy. Rather than receive title deed to the St. Lucia land, community members were awarded a portion of eco-tourism revenues and alternative land. Mbuyazi thanked the decision-makers, and noted that, 'when the authorities began to agree that we could visit our graves, that's when I began to see that there was a dawn, a light at the end of the tunnel' (ibid.: p. 140).

Although family members may leave to work in the city, they return to the rural areas throughout the year for holidays, weddings, and funerals. Koelble and LiPuma (2011) point out that city populations throughout South Africa (and especially Johannesburg) are ethnically diverse, and that city officials have sought to highlight that these centers are integrated spaces. There is evidence, however, that at least some of those who live and work in the city do not actually view themselves as fully a part of an integrated city population. Instead, the authors explain, many blacks still view themselves as belonging to a rural area. Government workers and university students alike 'circulate narratives of returning home' (ibid.: p. 15). The rural homesteads are the sites of important ceremonies; they also provide a safe place for family members to stay if they find themselves down on their luck. Further, many black South Africans plan to retire in rural areas.

Identifying some of the shared beliefs, however, does not mean that every individual in a traditional community holds those beliefs or is the same. And, although 'youth' are certainly not a homogeneous population, there is evidence that younger people generally seem to see less of a role for traditional leadership (Oomen 2005: p. 187; Waetjen and Mare 2009). There could be several reasons for this. Young people may be more likely to resist things that they consider to be of the past, or 'old-fashioned.' Young people also express a desire to live in urban areas (where they are more likely to find jobs and have access to more goods and services), where traditional leadership is not practiced. This trend highlights that not only is culture not uniform, but it is also not static.

Still, many individuals who live in rural areas or have family plots in rural areas are hesitant about the idea of upgrading tenure. The family plot is one of the most important ties to ancestors, a place to celebrate life events, and it represents some economic stability. The family plot belongs to many different people, of both past and present, making it difficult to determine who the relevant decision-makers are, and how, if the land were sold, all parties would be compensated. In addition to these complexities, the ability to parcel out plots from the community would change the role of traditional leadership. If the traditional leader is no longer considered the custodian of the land, he is also not considered a leader to those who reside on the land.

17.6 CONCLUSION

The persistence of traditional leadership presents a puzzle: why does the institution remain despite government efforts to weaken it? Some scholars have argued that traditional leadership continues because of vested interests and lack of competition. This explanation, however, not only is oversimplified, but also does not adequately address the demand side. Why do individuals demand the institution? Even if municipalities and traditional leadership act as complements, aspects of the institution still appear costly (for example, communal land).

Culture, or patterns of meanings that some South Africans attach to traditional leadership and communal land, can help to explain why these institutions have persisted. In the Gumbi community, for example, there are individuals who view their clan and tribal history and identity as essential to who they are. Similarly, there are individuals who feel that it is important to have the chief's support regarding current issues that affect the community. Recognizing this has a few key implications. Perhaps the most significant is that these institutions do not change overnight. Histories and beliefs cannot be washed away in order to make room for new political structures. Twenty years after the new national government, traditional leadership remains a governance structure in many rural areas.

Finally, as long as traditional leaders do have support, policies should acknowledge that the traditional leadership structures exist. A better understanding of why individuals value traditional leadership could also present opportunities to learn how these structures can collaborate with municipalities. There is some evidence, for example, that traditional leaders could play a role in crime reporting and prevention (Tshehla 2005).

NOTES

1. Although some individuals may object to the use of the term 'traditional leadership,' I use the term because it is recognized in literature and by persons in South Africa. I do not claim that traditional leadership should be considered 'traditional' in the sense that it has not changed since the pre-colonial period.
2. 'Communal land' does not imply that an individual does not have the right to exclude others. As I explain in section 17.4.1, within a traditional community a family has access to land that is understood to be for its use only, and there is land which is used 'in common.' Throughout the chapter I use the term 'communal land' to refer to land in which individuals do not have title deed and the land is allocated and used according to community rules.
3. I use the term 'community' to mean a group of individuals whose rights in land are derived from shared rules determining access to land held in common by the group.
4. Ntsebeza is one of the strongest critics of traditional leadership. In *Democracy Compromised* (2005), he presents a case study of the Xhalanga District in the Eastern Cape and describes how traditional leaders did not have popular support in the area, but were backed by the apartheid government. Ntsebeza also makes note in the Foreword of his book that traditional leaders did not agree to meet with him, and therefore he does not have their input on the history he presents. Mahmood Mamdani is another critic of traditional leadership. His book *Citizen and Subject* (1996) describes the bifurcated legacy of the colonial state, and he argues that the rural population remain 'subjects' to decentralized despots (traditional leaders).
5. Mpilo Pearl Sithole (2005) and Patekile Holomisa (president of CONTRALESA) also argue that traditional leadership persists for reasons aside from vested interests.
6. The 2005 South African Social Attitudes Survey results are available online at http://www.datafirst.uct.ac.za/dataportal/index.php/catalog/327.
7. In his theory of institutions, North similarly draws attention to the mental frameworks that individuals engage in decision-making. '[W]e find that people decipher the environment by processing information through preexisting mental constructs through which they understand the environment and solve the problems they confront' (1990: p. 20).
8. Interestingly, Storr (2004) writes on Junkanoo, a semi-annual festival in the Bahamas, as helping to cultivate the belief that enterprise can in fact lead to economic success (ibid.: p. 93). These examples illustrate that the culture of people in various geographic regions, countries, and cities varies by location but also varies within location.
9. A clan is a group of individuals who share a common ancestor. A tribe consists of multiple clans.
10. In 2009, the Human Sciences Research Council (HSRC) defined poverty as a family of four with R1290 of income per month. With an exchange rate of 0.12 rand per US dollar in May 2009, this would be approximately $155 per month, or about $5 a day. According to a 2010 Statistics South Africa report, the bottom 5 percent of South Africans earners reported R570 per month in income, the bottom 10 percent R845 per month, and the bottom 25 percent R1500 per month. The median is reported at R2800. For more information, see http://www.statssa.gov.za/publications2/P02112/P021122010.pdf.
11. De Soto's 1989 work provides insight into informal markets in Peru (especially see Chapter 2, 'Informal Trade'). As de Soto explains, extra-legal status and the uncertainty associated with carrying out informal businesses are one reason that businesses remain small. Another reason is limited access to credit.
12. Interview with Nathi Gumbi, April 28, 2007.
13. Interview with Nathi Gumbi, April 28, 2007.
14. Another key law was the Native Administration Act No. 38 of 1927, which gave the governor-general power to appoint and remove traditional leaders. Scholars critical of traditional leadership point to this Act as evidence that the remaining traditional leaders were complacent.

15. Interview with UMama (pseudonym), April 29, 2007.
16. This tradition is not practiced as often because of the limited number of cattle. Instead, a bride price in rand may be offered. Today, there is some debate about whether the practice should be eliminated altogether, as it presents a significant financial burden and therefore may discourage marriage.
17. In land claims, grave sites are one way that individuals and communities established land as once belonging to a particular family and community.

REFERENCES

Alcock, Rauri and Donna Hornby (2004), *Traditional Land Matters: A Look into Land Administration in Tribal Areas in KwaZulu Natal*, Pietermaritzburg: Leap Project.

Andrews, N. and P. Jacobs (2009), *Nourishing Rural Poverty: South Africa's Unchanging Land Relations*, Pretoria: Human Sciences Research Council.

Aslund, Anders (2007), *Russia's Capitalist Revolution: Why Market Reform Succeeded and Democracy Failed*, Washington, DC: Peterson Institute for International Economics.

Berglund, A.-I. (1976), *Zulu Thought-Patterns and Symbolism*, Bloomington: Indiana University Press.

Carton, Benedict (2000), *Blood from Your Children: The Colonial Origins of Generational Conflict in South Africa*, Charlottesville: University of Virginia Press.

Carton, Benedict (2009), 'Awaken Nkulunkulu, Zulu God of the Old Testament: Pioneering Missionaries during the Early Stage of Racial Spectacle,' in Benedict Carton, John Laband and Jabulani Sithole (eds.), *Zulu Identities: Being Zulu, Past and Present*, New York: Columbia University Press, pp. 133–52.

Chamlee-Wright, Emily (2005), 'Entrepreneurial Response to Bottom-Up Development Strategies in Zimbabwe,' *Review of Austrian Economics*, **18**(1), 5–28.

Cousins, Ben (2008), 'Characterising "Communal" Tenure: Nested Systems and Flexible Boundaries,' in Aninka Claassens and Ben Cousins (eds.), *Land, Power, and Custom*, Cape Town: UCT Press, pp. 109–37.

Cousins, T. and D. Hornby (2000), *Leaping the Fissures*, Cape Town: Programme for Land and Agrarian Studies (PLAAS), University of the Western Cape.

de Soto, Hernando (1989), *The Other Path*, New York: Harper & Row.

Gadamer, Hans-Georg (1976), *Philosophical Hermeneutics*, D.E. Linge (trans.), Berkeley: University of California Press.

Geertz, Clifford (1973), *The Interpretation of Cultures*, New York: Basic Books.

Guy, Jeff (1994), *The Destruction of the Zulu Kingdom*, Pietermaritzburg: University of Natal Press.

Hall, Martin (1984), 'The Myth of the Zulu Homestead: Archaeology and Ethnography,' *Africa: Journal of the International African Institute*, **54**(1), 65–79.

Hayek, F.A. (1952), *The Counter-Revolution of Science*, Indianapolis, IN: Liberty Press.

Koelble, Thomas and Edward LiPuma (2011), 'Traditional Leaders and the Culture of Governance in South Africa,' *Governance: An International Journal of Policy, Administration, and Institutions*, **24**(1), 5–29.

Lavoie, Don (2011), 'The Interpretive Dimension of Economics: Science, Hermeneutics, and Praxeology,' *Review of Austrian Economics*, **24**(2), 213–33.

Levin, M. and G. Satarov (2000), 'Corruption and Institutions in Russia,' *European Journal of Political Economy*, **16**, 113–32.

Mamdani, Mahmood (1996), *Citizen and Subject: Contemporary Africa and the Legacy of Late Colonialism*, Princeton, NJ: Princeton University Press.

Mashele, Prince (2004), 'Traditional Leadership in South Africa's New Democracy,' *Review of African Political Economy*, **31**(100), 349–54.

Mises, Ludwig von (1963), *Human Action: A Treatise on Economics*, 3rd rev. ed., San Francisco: Fox & Wilkes.

Monteiro-Ferreira, Ana Maria (2005), 'Reevaluating Zulu Religion: An Afrocentric Analysis,' *Journal of Black Studies*, **35**(3), 347–63.

North, Douglass (1990), *Institutions, Institutional Change, and Economic Performance*, Cambridge: Cambridge University Press.

North, Douglass (1994), 'Economic Performance through Time,' *American Economic Review*, **843**, 359–68.

North, Douglass (2005), *Understanding the Process of Economic Change*, Princeton, NJ: Princeton University Press.

Ntsebeza, Lungisile (2005), *Democracy Compromised: Chiefs and the Politics of the Land in South Africa*, Leiden: Brill.

Okoth-Ogendo, H.W.O. (2008), 'The Nature of Land Rights under Indigenous Law in Africa,' in Aninka Claassens and Ben Cousins (eds.), *Land, Power, and Custom*, Cape Town: UCT Press, pp. 95–108.

Oomen, Barbara (1996), 'Talking Tradition: The Position and Portrayal of Traditional Leaders in Present-Day South Africa,' thesis, University of Amsterdam.

Oomen, Barbara (2005), *Chiefs in South Africa: Law, Culture, and Power in the Post-Apartheid Era*, New York: Palgrave Macmillan.

Simeon, Richard and Christina Murray (2004), 'Quasi-Federalism in South Africa: Democracy, Good Governance, and the Management of Conflict,' in Bruce Berman, Dickson Eyoh and Will Kymlicka (eds.), *Ethnicity and Democratic Development in Africa*, Oxford: James Currey.

Sithole, Mpilo Pearl (2005), 'The Secular Basis of Traditional Leadership in KwaZulu-Natal,' *Alternation*, Special Edition 2, 102–22.

Smith, Henk (2008), 'An Overview of the Communal Land Rights Act 11 of 2004,' in Aninka Claassens and Ben Cousins (eds.), *Land, Power, and Custom*, Cape Town: UCT Press, pp. 35–71.

Storr, Virgil Henry (2002), 'All We've Learnt: Colonial Teachings and Caribbean Underdevelopment,' *Journal des Economistes et des Etudes Humaines*, **12**(4), 589–615.

Storr, Virgil Henry (2004), *Enterprising Slaves and Master Pirates: Understanding Economic Life in the Bahamas*, New York: Peter Lang.

Storr, Virgil Henry (2010), 'Schütz on Meaning and Culture,' *Review of Austrian Economics*, **23**(2), 147–63.

Storr, Virgil Henry (2013), *Understanding the Culture of Markets*, New York: Routledge.

Tshehla, Boyane (2005), 'Here to Stay: Traditional Leaders' Role in Justice and Crime Prevention,' Institute for Security Studies, *SA Crime Quarterly*, **11**, 15–20.

Vawda, Shahid (2011), 'Governance Policy and Democracy: Reconstituting

Traditional Authorities in the eThekwini Municipality (Durban): 1994–2003,' in Donald I. Ray, Tim Quinlan, Keshav Sharma and Tacita A.O. Clarke (eds.), *Reinventing African Chieftaincy in the Age of AIDS, Gender, Governance, and Development*, Calgary, AB: University of Calgary Press, pp. 267–324.

Waetjen, Thembisa and Gerhard Mare (2009), 'Shaka's Aeroplane: The Take-Off and Landing of Inkatha, Modern Zulu Nationalism and Royal Politics,' in Benedict Carton, John Laband and Jabulani Sithole (eds.), *Zulu Identities: Being Zulu, Past and Present*, New York: Columbia University Press, pp. 352–62.

Walker, Cherryl (2008), *Landmarked: Land Claims and Land Restitution in South Africa*, Athens: Ohio University Press.

Williams, Michael (2010), *Chieftaincy, the State and Democracy: Political Legitimacy in Post-Apartheid South Africa*, Bloomington: Indiana University Press.

APPENDIX

Abbreviations

ANC	African National Congress
CLARA	Communal Land Rights Act
CONTRALESA	Congress of Traditional Leaders of South Africa
IFP	Inkatha Freedom Party
RDP	Reconstruction and Development Programme
TLGFA	Traditional Leadership and Governance Framework Act

18. Network closure, group identity and attitudes toward merchants

Ryan Langrill and Virgil Henry Storr

18.1 INTRODUCTION

The nature and evolution of the spirits animating commercial activity are best understood by a cultural approach to economics which focuses on the meanings that individuals attach to their circumstances and actions. This approach can illustrate how the values and ambitions of people in different times and places shape commercial activity as well as how the changes in resource availability and external institutions shape people's values and ambitions.

This chapter discusses two 'spirits of capitalism' in Tokugawa Japan: Osaka's merchant spirit and Edo's warrior spirit. The two cities had vastly different demographics, which sparked in merchants different values and ambitions. Those values and ambitions, in turn, generated a peculiar 'spirit,' which governed commercial activity and shaped the city's economic landscape. The chapter will continue as follows: section 18.2 examines how 'closure' can initiate cultural change. Section 18.3 provides a brief history of Tokugawa Japan. Section 18.4 discusses the divergence of Osaka's and Edo's cultures and economies, and how those two relate. Finally, section 18.5 concludes by discussing the chapter's implications.

18.2 THEORETICAL CONSIDERATIONS

Max Weber's *The Protestant Ethic and the Spirit of Capitalism* argues that a unique 'spirit,' rooted in Calvinism and characterized by 'worldly asceticism,' animates capitalism in the West. As Weber (2002: p. 12) explains, modern capitalism in Western Europe and America was animated by a spirit of capitalism that combined the penchant for the 'making of money and yet more money, coupled with a strict avoidance of all uninhibited enjoyment.' This spirit was different than the traditionalist spirit, which thrived in the West prior to modern capitalism, where economic decisions were made on the basis of tradition or superstition. Instead, the spirit of modern capitalism describes a 'particular frame of mind that . . . strives systematically and rationally in a calling for legitimate profit' (Weber 2002: p. 88). The values and ambitions in modern capitalism were hard work and capital accumulation, without attendant desires to consume more. These factors shape the economy's outcomes and, according to Weber, this spirit explains (in part) modern capitalism's successes.

Weber's analysis provides a foundation for doing cultural economics. As Storr (2013: p. 69) explains, 'though Weber may have gone down the wrong path (the Protestant ethic may not have given birth to the spirit of modern capitalism), the manner in which he drove, arguably, still exists as a model for conducting culturally aware economic analysis.' Additionally, as Storr (ibid.: pp. 69–70) continues, 'a (modified) Weberian approach . . . would seem to call for identifying the economic spirits that animate a society's markets, examining their cultural and historical roots and describing how they impact economic life.' In short, to identify the spirit that animates an economic life, you have to pay attention to a community's collective narratives (also see Storr, this volume, Chapter 11; Chamlee-Wright, this volume, Chapter 12; Storr and Colon, this volume, Chapter 15). This echoes Lavoie and Chamlee-Wright (2000: p. 53), who argue that, 'if you want to get a sense of whether a community is apt to grow wealthier, we are suggesting you find out what stories they tell, what myths they believe, what heroes they admire, what metaphors they use.'

The spirits that animate economic activity are expressed through collective narratives. Collective narratives express the interpretive frames that people use to make sense of their circumstances and decide how to act. As Gerteis (2002: p. 609) explains, 'collective narratives are . . . the sites where [interpretive] schemas take concrete empirical form.' These narratives celebrate some activities. This encourages people to pour into them their resources and creative energies—to become praiseworthy. These narratives demean certain other activities. This discourages people from them and pushes them to punish those who do—to punish the blameworthy. Storr (2004) argues that a community's folklore is a paradigmatic transmitter of its collective narratives. Several factors influence the nature and content of the collective narratives that evolve and so the economic spirits that come to animate economic life within particular contexts. The degree to which the social networks exhibit closure, for instance, can have a profound effect on the kind of collective narratives that develop within a particular context.

Social network closure plays a role in Chamlee-Wright and Storr's (2009, 2011) investigations of how a community's collective narratives shape its response to disaster and its likelihood of successfully recovering from that disaster. For instance, they find that people in New Orleans's St. Bernard Parish shared a narrative of the community as a 'close-knit, family oriented community comprised of hard workers' that celebrated the blue-collar worker (Chamlee-Wright and Storr 2011: p.266). The parish was a closed network: it was composed of multi-generational families of blue-collar workers who had little interaction with neighboring parishes. When official disaster relief proved insufficient after Hurricane Katrina, they knew because of the collective narratives they shared that they could expect the support of others in their community and that others would work to rebuild even without outside help (Chamlee-Wright, this volume, Chapter 12). The 'go it alone' attitude that their closed network encouraged allowed them to rebuild more successfully than communities whose networks exhibited less closure.

The simple model below describes how network closure affects collective narratives and so economic spirits. Where upward mobility is impossible, low-status actors tend to develop networks that exhibit closure (also see Storr and Colon, this volume, Chapter 15, p. 343). Closure encourages collective narratives that celebrate in-group successes and their shared identifying characteristics. Where upward mobility is possible, low-status actors will invest in relationships with high-status actors; these low-status networks will exhibit less closure, and subsequent collective narratives will mirror those of the high-status groups.

Imagine, for instance, that individuals are either members of low-status group L or members of high-status group H. Ls invest in relationships with other Ls or with Hs based on their relative costs. In situation A, Hs are plenty (Figure 18.1A), as such L–H relationships are cheaper. In Situation B, Hs are scarce (Figure 18.1B). The scarcity of Hs in situation B makes relationships with them costly, encouraging Ls to invest more in L–L relationships. The collective narratives expressed by Ls in the two

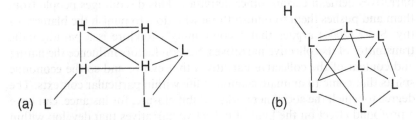

Note: H represents individuals with a high-status identity; L represents those with low-status identity; lines represent relationships between individuals.

Figure 18.1   Differing social structures

situations will follow their relationships. In Situation A, *L*s' investments in relationships with *H*s shift *L*s' collective narratives towards *H*s'. In situation B, *L*s' investments in relationships with one another will shift collective narratives towards the celebration of their shared identity. This thought experiment, we argue, mirrors the diverging collective narratives expressed by merchant classes in Tokugawa Japan's Osaka and Edo.

When commerce and innovation are low-status, this model predicts that a closed network will be more likely to celebrate them, whereas they are less likely to have an enthusiastic subculture if there is social mobility. Stated another way, countries with a fluid aristocracy (in other words, social mobility is possible) will be less likely to produce a subculture that admires commerce, since the people engaged in commerce have a potential payoff from adopting aristocratic values. Paradoxically, a rigid (or non-existent) aristocracy that excludes the commercial class will cause the commercial class to celebrate their shared identity. Out of this shared identity may come the emergence of pro-commercial attitudes and with these attitudes a productive economy. This story mirrors the Netherlands' rise: the first modern economy lost its aristocracy in the revolt against Spain, and subsequently experienced modern economic growth. We use this model to explain the differences in merchants' collective narratives in Tokugawa Japan's Osaka and Edo. Osaka's merchants celebrated commercial society, while Edo's merchants tried to do business by the way of the warrior.

18.3   STATUS GROUPS IN TOKUGAWA JAPAN

The Tokugawa era (1603–1868) followed the end of over a hundred years of civil war and Japan's unification under Oda Nobunaga and Toyotomi Hideyoshi. Tokugawa Ieyasu established a hereditary line of shoguns, who in Edo (present day Tokyo) headed the central government and ruled jointly with over 200 domain lords (*daimyo*). In 1636, the Tokugawa closed Japan. Only a few Dutch and Chinese traders could visit, and only on an artificial island in Nagasaki. Neither could Japanese travel abroad. The ban on foreign contact lasted until American commodore Matthew Perry's expeditions to Japan in 1853 and 1854, which signaled the end of a closed nation and precipitated the end of Tokugawa rule. The imperial Meiji government, which took over in 1868, embarked on a massive modernization campaign. Arguably, the commercial culture and informal institutions of Japanese merchants, especially those in Osaka, enabled the industrialization and modernization.

Hideyoshi introduced (and Ieyasu formalized) a four-tier hereditary status system inspired by Chinese Neo-Confucianism. Hideyoshi believed that social mobility was dangerous: if any poor child could rise to lead armies—as he had done—the chaos of the Warring States period would continue (Sheldon 1983: p. 477; Howland 2001: p. 355).[1] The system assigned everyone a status based on their role in the social order. At the top were *samurai*, whose duty was to govern those below them. Samurai were approximately 7 percent of Japan's population; they lived in towns and cities (country life was proscribed), and, though their role was largely bureaucratic rather than military, only samurai could wear swords. Below the samurai were peasant farmers, who made up about 80 percent of the population and paid a vast majority of the taxes. Artisans were lower still, and merchants were the lowest. Together these two lowest groups were known as *chōnin* (townsmen). The Tokugawa restricted chōnin, like samurai, to town or city life. Unlike the samurai, chōnin had a legal right to engage in commerce.

The Tokugawa legal system operated on the principle of 'rule by status,' a middle ground between the rule of law and the rule of arbitrary authority. As Hall (1974: p. 45) notes, the system 'assured an equality of treatment under law appropriate to the status of each individual.' While the four-status system was in theory fully inclusive, the shogun recognized eight levels in legal dealings. In descending order these were: daimyo, court nobles in Kyoto, samurai, Buddhist and Shinto priests, peasants, chōnin, 'outcastes,' and finally 'non-persons' (Howland 2001: p. 358). Movement between (non-commoner) groups was rare, especially after the first few decades of the system.[2] Hall (1974: p. 48) suggests that the status system worked fairly well because it reflected a division of labor that would have existed without legal authority. The status system, however, entrenched specific families as samurai and established impersonal governance.

Each status carried with it obligations to the other statuses. Samurai, for instance, had an obligation to keep order. The peasants, likewise, had an obligation to support the samurai. Neo-Confucian orthodoxy believed that the chōnin did little of importance. As Tokugawa era philosopher Ogyu Sorai explained,

> the samurai and peasants have no means of subsistence besides their land. They are constant factors in government and it is the duty and basic principle of government to see always to their well-being. Merchants, on the other hand, carry on an insignificant occupation . . . It should be no concern of government if they ruin themselves. (Sheldon 1983: p. 478)

Consequently, chōnin owed little to samurai but had little formal recourse against a samurai who broke a contract or defaulted on his debts. For instance, a merchant who wanted to bring a case against a samurai had to disgrace himself by crawling on his hands and knees to the magistrate.

18.4 THE DIVERGENCE OF MERCHANT NARRATIVES AND IDENTITIES

Osaka and Edo were two of Japan's three major cities. The third, Kyoto, was home to the emperor and his court. Sixteenth-century Edo was a small fishing village; Ieyasu's capital held over 1 million people, perhaps the largest city in the world (Chandler 1987). In contrast to Japan's 7 percent samurai population, Edo's was around 50 percent samurai (Cullen 2006: p. 152). Edo was thus the samurai's city, a result of Ieyasu's alternate-attendance policy (*sankin kōtai*). The policy required a daimyo's family to live permanently in Edo, and allowed the daimyo himself to return only every other year to the province he ruled. The *sankin kōtai* was a brilliant way of consolidating power. Local rulers spent half their time away from their people, and their heirs would come to power having lived only in Edo. Each year, the daimyo paraded to or from Edo, spending extravagant resources. The parades drained a daimyo's material resources. The mandated absence drained the immaterial trust between the daimyo and his people.

Osaka began the Tokugawa era as a military center and rival to Edo's power. Tokugawa Ieyasu's predecessor, Toyotomi Hideyoshi, had a young son, Hideyori. Ieyasu pledged to protect Hideyori until he was old enough to rule, at which time Hideyori would rise to shogun. Hideyori was the catalyst for two rebellions against Edo: the second, in 1615, left Hideyori dead and the impressive Osaka castle dismantled. Osaka's status composition after this incident was as extreme as Edo's but with an absence of samurai. The Tokugawa removed any resource that could contribute to rebellion: he built an indefensible castle to replace Hideyori's formidable one, he barred from settling in the city any who could bear or use weapons, he banned daimyo from even entering the city, and he demolished all bridges between Edo and Osaka. Ieyasu pacified Osaka as well as he did the daimyo: Osaka would fight no rebellion—at least on a battlefield.

While Edo and Osaka began with similar identities, rivals for political power, this similarity vanished. Ieyasu's pacification of Osaka changed the direction of its culture. The entertainers in Osaka, Deal (2007: p. 78) writes, produced 'new literary and theatrical forms that especially appealed to the interests and tastes of the new urban class.' Nishiyama (1997: p. 11) finds 'Two clearly differentiated types of culture ... One was the culture of Kamigata [including Osaka and Kyoto] . . . the other was the culture of the city of Edo.' Osaka's thinkers diverged as well from the Neo-Confucian orthodoxy. And, as Árnason (1997: p. 317) writes, 'a distinctive and sophisticated merchant ideology did emerge in the course of the eighteenth-century transformation of Tokugawa thought . . . in Osaka.' Below, we will discuss how each city's social networks influenced its merchants' interests, tastes and ideologies.

18.4.1   Edo

Edo's network structure did not exhibit closure. Chōnin and samurai lived in separate quarters of the city but interacted daily. The daimyo and samurai dominated the city's social and economic life: the daimyo's tax collections were the city's primary source of income, so a merchant needed to cater to the daimyo; the shogun and daimyo controlled all administrative appointments, so nepotism was the road to political and social power (Nakamura and Miyamoto 1982: p. 238). In the service of the shogunate or daimyo, even merchants could earn the right to wear two swords and use surnames (Crawcour 1963: p. 394; Howland 2001: p. 356). Chōnin and lower samurai, whose peak professional success was in becoming part of a powerful household, intermingled constantly in Edo's theater district and Edo's famous 'pleasure quarter,' Yoshiwara. In Edo, Nishiyama (1997: p. 38) writes, 'close relations existed among members of the warrior class, between warriors and chōnin.' These relations included both daily interactions and patron–client relationships between merchant houses and powerful samurai houses.

The above model predicts that, when the networks of the low-status group intermingle with those of the high-status group, low-status individuals will adopt the high-status identity. Ieyasu's alternate-attendance policy forced geographically and linguistically diverse people together, and the daimyo and their cohorts generated a distinct dialect of Japanese. Chōnin of all strata competed to place themselves and their daughters in the service of aristocratic households just to learn the dialect (Nishiyama 1997: p. 35). The dialect gave chōnin men better access to business dealings and chōnin women better marriage prospects (Nishiyama 1997: pp. 35–6). The samurai had good reason to select business partners who had learned the dialect: the merchant's investment had value only in business with the samurai, so a merchant who betrayed a samurai would have a useless asset. This dialect, because of the intense competition to learn it, would spread and eventually become modern Japanese.

The samurai aristocracy borrowed heavily from the customs and lifestyles of the imperial court nobles, which provided legitimacy for the new aristocracy by associating them with Japan's historic, and spiritual, rulers. While adopting the visage of the imperial court, the samurai romanticized their own status: the Tokugawa and samurai invented the 'way of the warrior' or *bushido* (Callahan and Ihara 1979; Ikegami 2005). Playwrights and historians retroactively imputed bushido, a combination of traditional and Confucian values, to the samurai of the past. 'Eventually,' Nishiyama (1997: p. 35) writes, 'the customs and lifestyles of the top warrior stratum came to represent Edo as a whole.'

Edo chōnin, nicknamed *Edokko*, embraced the samurai's constructed identity. The Edokko adopted the 'manly spirit' of bushido and abandoned prudence to match the profligacy of the daimyo during their extravagant alternate attendance (Takenaka 1969: pp. 142–3; see also Vaporis 2005). Wealthy merchants, in imitation of this profligacy, would even throw money into the streets to watch a mob collect it (Sheldon 1983: p. 483). Edokko sought to signal a carefree attitude towards money, in order to match the low value of making money in Confucian society. The Edo commoners even embraced the violence that the samurai valorized, settling conflicts—from love rivalries in the pleasure quarters to business disputes—with force. Edo's streets were Japan's most violent (Nishiyama 1997: p. 38).

In a witty novelette, late-eighteenth-century Edo writer Santō Kyōden wrote a list of five qualities that typify the Edokko:

1. He receives his first bath in the water of the city's aqueduct; he grows up in sight of the gargoyles on the roof of Edo castle.
2. He is not attached to money; he is not stingy. His funds do not cover the night's lodging.
3. He is raised in a high-class, protected manner. He is quite unlike either warriors or country bumpkins.
4. He is a man of Nihonbashi (the downtown area) to the bone.
5. He has *iki* (refinement) and *hari* (strength of character). (Nishiyama 1997: p. 42)

Nishiyama (1997: p. 42) notes that, while specific details were wrong, Santō's 'points of pride' accurately characterize the Edokko in Edo period literature. Jōkanbō Kōa, a near contemporary of Santō, contrasts Edo's pride with Osaka's: he rebukes the great Osaka playwright Chikamatsu Monzaemon for featuring flawed commoners as heroes. Instead, Jōkanbō (in Shirane 2002: p. 460) writes, 'please show me the ways of a loyal retainer, a filial son, a benevolent aunt, and a chaste wife.'

Edo's plays, scholarship and literature demonstrate a convergence to near-universal admiration for the high-status samurai. Scholars who supported the Tokugawa regime saw the arts as explicitly a vehicle for 'encouraging good and chastising evil' (in Shirane 2002: p. 360). The regime interfered in the arts when they violated Tokugawa values or lampooned embarrassing events, but little interference was needed; the arts in Edo thus came to reflect samurai values. In Edo, the *aragoto*, or 'rough' style, of kabuki dominated, which Shirane (2002: p. 236) writes 'featured courageous heroes, bold, masculine characters who displayed superhuman powers in overcoming evildoers.' For examples of this 'rough' kabuki, see Ichikawa (2002a: pp. 29–40, 2002b: pp. 45–65) and Oan (Shirane 2002: p. 41). The plots followed a similar pattern: some wrong is done, and the protagonist—sometimes a loyal retainer, sometimes a brother—punishes the evildoer; sometimes the revenge is explicit, and sometimes the avenger conceals his intentions until later in the play. The art reached its pinnacle in Chūshingura, an entire genre devoted to the tale of the '47 rōnin.' An incident at Edo castle in 1701 inspires the story: The Akō domain's daimyo drew his sword and attacked a high-ranking official, purportedly after the official insulted him. As punishment, the shogun confiscated the daimyo's lands and forced the daimyo to kill himself, leaving his retainers masterless (hence, rōnin). The official escaped unpunished. Two years later, 47 of the daimyo's former retainers broke into the official's house and beheaded him. Afterwards, the rōnin turned themselves in and the shogun ordered all but one to commit suicide. Almost immediately, puppet plays, literature and kabuki adaptations of the event began to appear in Edo, and the story has become 'Japan's national legend' (H. Smith 2003: p. 37). The rōnin's graves continue to attract people who come to worship.

The Edo merchant shared the samurai devotion to glory. Santō Kyōden's merchant characters reflect Edokko values: one story features a wealthy merchant's son, Enjirō, who achieves the glory he cannot get with physical prowess through a series of publicity stunts (Santō [1785] 2002). In another story the protagonist merchant, Rihei, is 'the owner of the Quick and Easy Shop and dedicate[s] himself to turning a fast profit' (Santō [1790] 2002: p. 713). Edo writer Hiraga Gennai lampooned merchants in his description of hell: speculative merchants bought up the scarce land, while

> One entrepreneur asked to be granted a monopoly on handling clothes taken from the newly dead before they crossed the River Between Worlds. In return, he guaranteed, whenever hell guards lost at dice, he would give them very low interest rates on the tiger-skin loincloths they pawned with him. 'If implemented,' said petition after petition, 'your benevolence will spread downward for the betterment of all hell'—as if the profits were for others. Even in hell, they say, money talks. It's a very canny place. (Hiraga, in Shirane 2002: pp. 464–6)

The network structure and the collective narratives that emerged in Osaka were quite different.

18.4.2 Osaka

Osaka was nearly devoid of 'high-status' samurai and had no imperial court. Merchant social networks, then, exhibited a greater degree of closure than those in Edo. Consequently, according to the above model, merchants would adopt those values and ambitions that facilitated commerce. Early in the Tokugawa era, most successful merchant families made money through favorable contacts with the authorities (Sakudō 1991: p. 147) or through dealings with incompetent daimyo (Takekoshi 1930: p. 247). These privileged merchant families had disappeared by the end of the seventeenth century. In fact, the Yodoya, the greatest of the first wave of merchant families and founders of the great rice market of Dojima, were exiled and had their wealth confiscated by the shogun in 1705 (N. Smith [1937] 1979: p. 123; Sheldon 1983: p. 483). While many early merchant families were former samurai who had become merchants, their replacements were born merchants. The Tokugawa's unpopularity among Osaka chōnin can be seen in the chōnin's reaction to being selected for an administrative appointment: while Edo chōnin highly sought these positions, Osaka chōnin did 'not particularly welcome' them (Sheldon 1973: p. 35).

A lack of formal contract enforcement required trust in buyer–seller relationships within Osaka. Moreover, the lack of aristocracy encouraged a generalized trust. Formal contracts were secondary to oral agreements concluded with a simple clap of the hands (N. Smith [1937] 1979: p. 85). If a merchant violated a contract, he lost all credit with other Osaka merchants; of course, this system of informal enforcement could not keep the daimyo from repudiating debts. Contracts represented personal, rather than legal, relationships. As a temple magistrate wrote, 'a contract of money loan is made with mutual trust and friendship on the part of creditor and debtor, so that it seems hardly proper to treat strictly according to the rules of law an action brought to enforce such a claim' (Wigmore 1892: p. 129; see also ibid.: p. 452). While there were exceptions, merchants generally developed long-term relationships with one another, and Osaka was these relationships' nexus.

Osaka merchants married ethics to commerce, which drove Osaka's success as a business center in the absence of formal contract enforcement as well as the success of long-term multi-generational families and business relationships. Osaka's art, literature and scholarship display the chōnin commitment to frugality, honesty and calculation. During the eighteenth century, Osaka had more book publishers than either Kyoto or Edo (Moriya 1991: p. 115). Among the books were guides for common merchants authored by common merchants. These instructional handbooks taught practical information and moral considerations. The handbooks contained business advice and personal savings charts, one of which advocated saving starting at age 11 (Najita 2009: 40). An itinerant teacher-preacher, Wakizaka Gidō, emphasized prudence in his didactic 'story of a wise old man in Holland who told about a drug of well-being that was bitter and a drug of poverty that was sweet, and about vagrant people in the streets buying the sweet pill for immediate gratification' (Najita 2009: p. 34).

The 'floating world' (*ukiyo-e*) is the Tokugawa era's best-known genre of art and literature. The floating world first emerged in Osaka and then spread to Edo and Kyoto, where it flourished (Akai 1991: p. 183). It is distinguished by 'maximum expression with minimum resources,' reflecting Osaka's frugal ethic rather than Edo's profligate ethic (Nakane 1991: p. 229).

Ihara Saikaku, son of an Osaka merchant, is probably this period's greatest novelist in Japan, and many of his writings feature an explicit merchant ethic. Frugal and prudent merchants do well for themselves; extravagant and vain merchants end up ruined and poor (Ihara 1989). According to Ihara, successful merchants demonstrated 'frugality, persistence, a ready mind for figures, mastery of the abacus, a pleasant manner, honesty, and imagination ... while in contrast the warrior class [was] useless, misguided, and worthy of sympathy rather than admiration' (de Bary 1989: p. 31).

Ihara, like Wakizaka, used a medicine metaphor in his *The Japanese Family Storehouse: or The Millionaire's Gospel* (written in 1688) to discuss the value of frugality and hard work. According to Ihara (1969: p. 59),

> For each of the four hundred and four bodily ailments celebrated physicians have produced infallible remedies, but the malady which brings us the greatest distress to mankind—to even the wisest and cleverest of us—is the plague of poverty.
>   'Is there a treatment to cure this?' a poor man asked a gentleman of great wealth.
>   'My dear fellow,' the rich man replied, 'if you have lived till now without knowing such things, you have wasted precious years. In matters of health the best time to take preventative measures is before you reach the wrong side of forty, and you have left this consultation until rather late ... I have, it so happens, an excellent nostrum called "The Millionaire Pill."'

This 'Millionaire Pill,' Ihara's character goes on to tell, should be taken twice daily and is a mixture of early rising, the family trade, work after hours, economy and sound health. The rich man goes on to warn that 'it is [also] imperative to abstain from certain noxious things,' which include expensive clothing and other luxuries, involvement in the tea ceremony, sword drawing and other aristocratic activities, and excessive participation in religion. Older men who established fortunes could indulge in these enjoyments, and then only in moderation. Ihara emphasized, according to Shirane (2002: p.47), that 'money ... cannot, in the end, buy love,' and instead that a chōnin's personal success comes from 'individual talent ... intense training, and emotional integrity rather than, as in medieval aristocratic society, through family connections and inheritance.' Ihara shows Osaka chōnin's rejection of Confucian hierarchy in *Tales to Various Provinces*, where he writes (in Shirane 2002: p. 57), 'In my opinion, humans are spooks. There's nothing you won't find somewhere in the world.' Shirane (2002: p.57) comments that 'The half-humorous term "spooks" suggests a transformation, as if humans were capable of being or turning into an infinite number of shapes'—a rejection of the Confucian hereditary system. Ihara is not alone in throwing off convention: Osaka's style of haiku, Danrin hakai, such as that written by Nishiyama Sōin, stressed 'spontaneity and freedom of form,' Shirane (2002: p. 175) writes, in explicit contrast to Kyoto's Teitoku style, which 'tried to impose order on linked verse.'

Chikamatsu Monzaemon's plays similarly celebrated the values of Osaka merchants. Along with Ihara Saikaku, Chikamatsu Monzaemon was among the Tokugawa era's greatest dramatists. Chikamatsu was prominent in the early eighteenth century, and his medium was primarily *bunraku*, or puppet theater; he wrote many plays involving samurai and other great men. His greatest contribution, however, was pioneering a genre of plays about common people facing their daily problems, presented with the same level of seriousness as great men's problems were (Keene 1998: p.6).

Consider, for instance, Chikamatsu's *The Uprooted Pine* (written in 1718). In *The Uprooted Pine*, Yojibei, a merchant, was falsely arrested in Osaka's pleasure quarters for assault. His father, though a wealthy merchant, refused to pay to release Yojibei. 'If a man's life is in danger because he has broken the law,' his father explains, 'he can be saved by money. This trouble would never have arisen if only Yojibei had realized that money is so precious a treasure that it can save human lives ... the more affectionately I think of him, the harder I find it to give him the money' (Chikamatsu 1961: pp.151–2). Yojibei's father condemns him for 'wicked extravagance,' spending too much time with expensive prostitutes. Yojibei's wife, similarly, condemns Yojibei's prostitute for causing him to neglect 'the family business' (ibid.: p.154). These attitudes could

410 *Culture and economic action*

have been taken right out of Ihara's *Millionaire's Gospel*; the commitment to hard work and frugality is a key value, not just a means to wealth. Chikamatsu reiterates this throughout his plays: his most famous play, *The Love Suicides at Amijima* (written in 1721), has a protagonist doomed to commit suicide 'for neglect of his trade' (ibid.: p. 201).

When Chikamatsu wrote kabuki instead of puppet plays, he pioneered the 'soft' style in contrast to Edo's 'rough' style. One of his plays, *Summer Festival*, Brandon and Leiter (2002: p. 12) write, 'is based on a domestic "world" in which commoners . . . are the major figures,' not great heroes. The protagonist in *Matahei the Stutterer*, though a samurai, has a weakness the audience values him for overcoming. Matahei does not avenge a mentor, or win a great battle, but instead learns to overcome his stutter to make the most out of his life (Chikamatsu [1708] 2002: pp. 68–92).

The Kaitokudō merchant academy, which was Osaka's center of scholarship and learning, similarly celebrated hard work and frugality. Above the school's entrance were ideographs that indicate the school is a place 'to reflect deeply into the meaning of virtue'; Kaitokudō scholars did just that (Najita 1987: p. 2). Chōnin academics, everyday merchants and their children learned practical commercial skills, such as how to use the abacus, and that commerce was inseparable from virtue. The Osaka merchants' honesty and trustworthiness became points of pride, and the Kaitokudō studied and propagated these values. It will be useful to discuss the school's philosophy in greater depth, as the topics covered show the width of the gap between Osaka's values and Edo's.

Miyake Sekian, who founded the school in 1726, defended the universality of virtue. In his opening lecture he opposed the status-contingent virtue favored by orthodox Neo-Confucians. According to Miyake (2005: p. 274), 'with ceaseless effort, ordinary humans can rise to become sages.' Miyake was a disciple of a major Neo-Confucian scholar, Ito Jinsai. Ito emphasized the teachings of *Mencius*, a Confucian text that supported Ito's claim that all people possess virtue, not just those endowed with special wisdom or social status. Ito's philosophy made his Neo-Confucian foundation appealing to Osaka's chōnin and 'infused . . . humanistic "compassion" for the inevitable "passion" that informs the daily lives of human beings, as in the activities of the new commerce so readily evident in the world he taught' (Najita 1987: p. 43). Miyake spoke also to the importance of ethically engaging in commerce. He defended profit only if it was in accordance with righteousness and contractual trust (ibid.: p. 197). According to Najita (ibid.: p. 91), 'merchants should not even think of their occupation as being profit-seeking but as the ethical acting out of the moral principle of "righteousness."'

Chōnin scholars also engaged with the subject of change, which samurai scholars largely ignored. Tokugawa's institutional structure guaranteed samurai and peasants their livelihood—even when it was a poor livelihood. Samurai received stipends and could not supplement their income with commerce. Peasants, as long as they were first sons, were likewise guaranteed family land and a predetermined position in the town's governance based on their family's tenure. Merchants and artisans had nothing guaranteed to them. Consequently, their fortunes were in flux, some rising to wealth from poverty and others descending from wealth into poverty.

Kaitokudō's golden age produced the Nakai brothers, Chikuzan (1730–1804) and Riken (1732–1817). Chikuzan was a Kaitokudō administrator and wrote on merchants' place in the social order. He criticized the Tokugawa regime for the absence of merchants in the realm's governance. Samurai, he explained, never made a living in the market and never managed the finances of anything other than their own household; it was a recipe for disaster to let samurai manage the entire realm's finances. Merchants, based on their success marrying ethics and commerce, could bring invaluable practical experience to the realm. Chikuzan's brother Riken lived much of his life in isolation, and he wrote defending the Kaitokudō's central concept that every person had access to virtue. Riken thought the Tokugawa regime irredeemable and attacked his brother's desire to reform the regime; he, thus, retreated into a 'dream world,' where he imagined a society consistent with his worldview. In Riken's dream world, 'the people are happy and adorn themselves with colorful pins and ribbons designating the kind of work they do,' which would give merchants something comparable to the samurai's sword-wearing privilege (ibid.: p. 213). Riken was the last Kaitokudō scholar interested in preserving a Confucian foundation of morality. While Ito's disciples used *Mencius* to show the universal capacity for moral knowledge, Riken turned to the *Doctrine of the Mean*. While the orthodoxy 'denied the subjective dimension of moral virtue, claiming the self to be passionate and that, this being the case, human beings had as their only recourse . . . the reliance on totally external norms that must be identified with the social intent of the ancient kings when they first created history' (ibid.: pp. 198–9), Riken dissented. If the 'mean' was the golden point for moral action, finding that mean required individuals' active, subjective interpretation. As Najita (ibid.: p. 200) summarizes, 'for the concept of the "mean" to be philosophically viable, the individual self must be an active, cognizing agent and not merely a passive recipient of "external norm."'

The Kaitokudō closed in 1868, a victim of the turmoil surrounding the Tokugawa's fall, but the school's final generation produced two notable political economists, who were also immensely successful financiers: Yamagata Bantō and Kusama Naokata. Kusama's masterwork was an

illustrated history of money in Japan, the *Sanka zu'I*. The work chroni-
cled Japan's evolution from a barter economy to a precious-metal money
economy. Much of this story involves a great deal of Tokugawa misman-
agement. He wrote, 'if money as . . . [a] fixed item of value could be relied
on as a norm of constancy, then goods, however voluminous could be
traded in ways that were righteous and fair' (ibid.: p. 236). The period's
unreliability of money, combined with trade barriers between provinces,
caused localized famines even though rice's price had steadily declined
over the previous century.[3] Even in this unstable monetary environment,
merchants had been able to flourish. As Najita (ibid.: p. 244) explains,
'merchants, and especially those in Osaka, had developed a system of large-
scale trade based on contractual trust . . . The marketplace, in other words,
was a moral arena at the ground level of human existence, and "profit" was
calculated in terms of [the] contractual relationship of "trust."'

While Kusama attacked the Tokugawa regime on practical matters,
Yamagata attacked the regime's epistemic foundation. Yamagata's mas-
terpiece, *Yume no shiro* or *In Place of Dreams*, rejects the validity of a
society based on dreams or superstition, in which he includes Confucian
texts and the supernatural aspects of Buddhism and Shinto. According to
Yamagata (Najita, 1987: p. 256), 'the universe precedes human morality
. . . knowledge of that universe . . . cannot be derived through the analysis
of moral historical texts.' Texts had didactic value, but they were not a
substitute for evidence. Yamagata admired Western scientists and their
scientific method, which 'built their studies on a theory of knowledge
that tested and validated new findings and discarded the errors and false
assumptions of the past' (quoted in ibid.: p. 256). These false assumptions included the foundation of the Tokugawa regime's power: the belief
that ancient kings preceded the people. Instead, Najita writes, Yamagata
argued that 'in Japan the system of noncentralized rule came to be erected
over some one thousand years as its way of organizing society, which, as
he put it, "ought to be thought of as beautiful"' (ibid.: p. 256). With *Yume*,
Yamagata built a secular humanism with the people as the central virtuous
actors and commerce as both a legitimate road to virtue and the source of
a resourcefulness necessary for the governance of the realm. Yamagata, in
a (perhaps) apocryphal story,

> requested that the lord of Sendai pay him for his services not with cash but with
> the spillage of the handful of rice caused by a bamboo shaft at each checkpoint
> enroute to the marketplace in Edo. Known as *sashigome*, this spillage was put
> to speculative use by Yamagata in the rice market and an impressive profit was
> said to have been reaped for [house] Masuya. This anecdote coincided with
> Yamagata's view of the aristocracy as being inattentive to the mathematical cal-
> culation of the 'margin' that determined the well-being of the whole. (Ibid.: p. 250)

Yamagata's story shows that, by the end of the Tokugawa period, Osaka merchants had their own narrative for themselves and for Japan.

18.5 DISCUSSION

Osaka and Edo demonstrate the simple model developed above and show the emergence of different spirits of capitalism. Edo merchants' virtues and ambitions mirrored the aristocracy as a result of their entangled social networks; commerce was valued only as a path to extravagance. In contrast, Osaka's egalitarian social structure meant that merchant networks exhibited closure; thus, Osaka merchants' collective narratives celebrated commerce and the common people. McCloskey's (2010) challenge to economists, that material factors or technology alone cannot explain the modern world and that positive attitudes towards commerce and innovation are necessary—if not sufficient—for modern economic growth, opens the door to this cultural economic approach. Indeed, economics' central question may not have a full answer without it.

The Moriya house's head wrote in 1987:

> We must realize, however, that the force that has driven Japan rapidly forward since the Meiji era to the position it holds today among the advanced industrial nations, despite centuries of pre-Meiji isolation, was powered by the skills and abilities that created the society, economy, and culture during those centuries of isolation in the Tokugawa era ... it is exceedingly important to recognize that the dynamic energy generated by the rapid interactions with the advanced industrial nations was rooted in the qualitative intelligence of the people who created the socioeconomic culture of that Tokugawa era. (Quoted in Najita 2009: pp. 21–2)

Admittedly, only a subculture in Tokugawa Japan embraced commerce, and even smaller subcultures embraced innovation. However, Osaka's collective narratives celebrated commerce, and Osaka prospered. Only when Japan's rulers finally embraced commerce did Japan experience modern economic growth. Japan's rapid industrialization following Tokugawa's fall may indicate that latent potential existed. The Tokugawa's perennial confiscations, forced loans, price controls, restrictions on speculation, and policies such as regulating such minutiae as the times of the year vegetables could be sold do not build a successful economy (Takizawa [1927] 1968: p. 68).

As harmful as the Tokugawa regime's barriers to commerce were, they were not all that kept Japan from modern economic growth. While, at least in Osaka, people admired commerce, people did not similarly admire innovation. Merchants who happened upon innovations, such as the use of rapeseed oil in lighting or the 'accidental' discovery of clear sake, exploited the innovations deftly: rapeseed oil allowed many new people to afford lighting, and clear sake, which can be enjoyed warm, usurped cloudy sake's popularity. Though people would exploit any accidental discoveries, active discovery carried a stigma. The house laws of some of the great merchant houses, like Mitsui and Kōnoike, expressly forbade innovation and encouraged their members to preserve traditional sources of wealth. Only a few, such as those who engaged in Dutch learning, or *Rangaku*, actively tried to innovate.

Consequently, collective narratives matter. They shape how people perceive commerce and so shape whether they will succeed economically. Where successful merchants can graduate into the aristocracy, collective narratives will tend to support those who mimic the aristocracy. When successful merchants get their values and ambitions from other merchants, collective narratives will tend to celebrate commerce.

NOTES

1. The Warring States (or Sengoku) period lasted from about 1467 to 1573, if the rise of Oda Nobunaga is taken to be the end of the period. Hane (1991: pp. 91–130) provides an overview of this period.
2. Sheldon (1983: p. 482) writes that there must have been some rare cases of merchants buying samurai status 'by allying with impecunious samurai families, because [Tokugawa] Yoshimune issued a law specifically illegalizing it.'
3. Taxes were paid in rice. Most daimyo and samurai had fixed income in rice. When taxes were collected, there was political pressure for inflation, in order to increase the money incomes of the samurai who were holding rice. The Dojima rice exchange at Osaka is a response to the difficulties that resulted from this transacting in rice. The exchange, which has been labeled the 'world's first organized futures market,' thrived outside of, and sometimes against, formal law (West 2000: p. 2576). Yamagata Bantō writes of the market that 'the system of rice speculation in Osaka is the essence of wisdom which controls the blood circulation [of the economic system] . . . For rice is sent from almost all districts to Osaka.' He then goes on to explain the importance of the price nexus in Osaka. 'Damage done by locusts to rice plants in western provinces,' he explains, 'will lead to a rise in price, while a rich harvest in the north means a fall . . . These have as reliable an effect as the edicts of a god or the commands of a general. However, they are not decrees of heaven nor the result of secret consultations.' Merchants in Osaka, he claims, could trade rice certificates and deal in futures, whereas in Edo rice transactions involved hauling rice to and from different warehouses.

REFERENCES

Akai, Tatsurō (1991), 'The Common People and Painting,' in Chie Nakane and Shinzaburō Ōishi (eds.), *Tokugawa Japan: The Social and Economic Antecedents of Modern Japan*, Conrad Totman (trans.), Tokyo: University of Tokyo Press, pp. 167–91.

Árnason, Jóhann Páll (1997), *Social Theory and Japanese Experience: The Dual Civilization*, London: Kegan Paul International.

Brandon, James and Samuel Leiter (2002), *Kabuki Plays on Stage: Brilliance and Bravado, 1697–1766*, Honolulu: University of Hawai'i Press.

Callahan, Caryl and Ihara Saikaku (1979), 'Tales of Samurai Honor: Saikaku's Buke Giri Monogatari,' *Monumenta Nipponica*, **34**(1), 1–20.

Chamlee-Wright, Emily and Virgil Storr (2009), 'Club Goods and Post-Disaster Community Return,' *Rationality and Society*, **21**(4), 429–58.

Chamlee-Wright, Emily and Virgil Storr (2011), 'Social Capital as Collective Narratives and Post-Disaster Community Recovery,' *Sociological Review*, **59**(2), 266–82.

Chandler, Tertius (1987), *Four Thousand Years of Urban Growth: An Historic Census*, New York: Edwin Mellon Press.

Chikamatsu, Monzaemon (1961), *Four Major Plays of Chikamatsu*, Donald Keene (trans.), New York: Columbia University Press.

Chikamatsu, Monzaemon ([1708] 2002), 'Matahei the Stutterer,' in J.R. Brandon and S.L. Leiter (eds.), *Kabuki Plays on Stage*, Vol. 1: *Brilliance and Bravado, 1697–1766*, Holly Blumner (trans.), Honolulu: University of Hawai'i Press, pp. 68–92.

Crawcour, E.S. (1963), 'Changes in Japanese Commerce in the Tokugawa Period,' *Journal of Asian Studies*, **22**(4), 387–400.

Cullen, Louis (2006), 'Tokugawa Population: The Archival Issues,' *Japan Review*, **18**, 129–80.

Deal, William E. (2007), *Handbook to Life in Medieval and Early Modern Japan*, New York: Oxford University Press USA.

de Bary, Wm. Theodore (1989), 'Introduction,' in Ihara Saikaku, *Five Women Who Loved Love*, Wm. Theodore de Bary (trans.), North Clarendon, VT: Tuttle Publishing, pp. 13–58.

Gerteis, Joseph (2002), 'The Possession of Civic Virtue: Movement Narratives of Race and Class in the Knights of Labor,' *American Journal of Sociology*, **108**(3), 580–615.

Hall, John W. (1974), 'Rule by Status in Tokugawa Japan,' *Journal of Japanese Studies*, **1**(1), 39–49.

Hane, Mikiso (1991), *Premodern Japan: A Historical Survey*, 2nd ed., Boulder, CO: Westview Press.

Howland, Douglas R. (2001), 'Samurai Status, Class, and Bureaucracy: A Historiographical Essay,' *Journal of Asian Studies*, **60**(2), 353–80.

Ichikawa Danjūrō (2002a), 'The Felicitous Soga Encounter,' Laurence R. Kominz (trans.), in J.R. Brandon and S.L. Leiter (eds.), *Kabuki Plays on Stage*, Vol. 1: *Brilliance and Bravado, 1697–1766*, Honolulu: University of Hawai'i Press, pp. 29–40.

Ichikawa Danjūrō (2002b), 'Just a Minute!,' Katherine Salzman-Li (trans.), in J.R. Brandon and S.L. Leiter (eds.), *Kabuki Plays on Stage*, Vol. 1: *Brilliance and Bravado, 1697–1766*, Honolulu: University of Hawai'i Press, pp. 45–65.

Ihara, Saikaku (1969), *The Japanese Family Storehouse: or The Millionaire's Gospel Modernised*, G.W. Sargent (trans.), Cambridge: Cambridge University Press.

Ihara, Saikaku (1989), *Five Women Who Loved Love*, Wm. Theodore de Bary (trans.), North Clarendon, VT: Tuttle Publishing.

Ikegami, Eiko (2005), *Bonds of Civility: Aesthetic Networks and the Political Origins of Japanese Culture*, Cambridge: Cambridge University Press.

Keene, Donald (1998), 'Introduction,' in Chikamatsu Monzaemon, *Four Major Plays of Chikamatsu*, Donald Keene (ed.), New York: Columbia University Press.

Lavoie, Don and Emily Chamlee-Wright (2000), *Culture and Enterprise*, London: Routledge.

McCloskey, Deirdre N. (2010), *Bourgeois Dignity: Why Economics Can't Explain the Modern World*, Chicago: University of Chicago Press.

Miyake, Sekian (2005), 'Kaitokudo Inaugural Address,' in William Theodore de Bary, D. Keene, G. Tanabe and P. Varley (eds.), *Sources of Japanese Tradition*, Vol. 1, New York: Columbia University Press.

Moriya, Katsuhisa (1991), 'Urban Networks and Information Networks,' in Chie Nakane and Shinzaburō Ōishi (eds.), *Tokugawa Japan: The Social and Economic Antecedents of Modern Japan*, Conrad Totman (trans., ed.), Tokyo: University of Tokyo Press, pp. 97–123.

Najita, Tetsuo (1987), *Visions of Virtue in Tokugawa Japan: The Kaitokudō Merchant Academy*, Chicago: University of Chicago Press.

Najita, Tetsuo (2009), *Ordinary Economies in Japan: A Historical Perspective, 1750–1950*, Berkeley: University of California Press.

Nakamura, James I. and Matao Miyamoto (1982), 'Social Structure and Population Change: A Comparative Study of Tokugawa Japan and Ch'ing China,' *Economic Development and Cultural Change*, **30**(2), 229–69.

Nakane, Chie (1991), 'Tokugawa Society,' in Chie Nakane and Shinzaburō Ōishi (eds.), *Tokugawa Japan: The Social and Economic Antecedents of Modern Japan*, Conrad Totman (trans., ed.), Tokyo: University of Tokyo Press, pp. 213–31.

Nishiyama, Matsunosuke (1997), *Edo Culture, Daily Life and Diversions in Urban Japan, 1600–1868*, Honolulu: University of Hawai'i Press.

Sakudō, Yōtarō (1991), 'The Management Practices of Family Business,' in Chie Nakane and Shinzaburō Ōishi (eds.), *Tokugawa Japan: The Social and Economic Antecedents of Modern Japan*, Conrad Totman (trans., ed.), Tokyo: University of Tokyo Press, pp. 147–66.

Santō Kyōden ([1785] 2002), 'Grilled and Basted Edo-Born Playboy,' in Haruo Shirane (ed.), *Early Modern Japanese Literature: An Anthology, 1600–1900*, Translations from the Asian Classics, New York: Columbia University Press, pp. 687–710.

Santō Kyōden ([1790] 2002), 'Fast-Dyeing Mind Study,' in Haruo Shirane (ed.), *Early Modern Japanese Literature: An Anthology, 1600–1900*, Translations from the Asian Classics, New York: Columbia University Press, pp. 711–29.

Sheldon, Charles D. (1973), *The Rise of the Merchant Class in Tokugawa Japan, 1600–1868: An Introductory Survey*, New York: Russell & Russell.

Sheldon, Charles D. (1983), 'Merchants and Society in Tokugawa Japan,' *Modern Asian Studies*, **17**, 477–88.

Shirane, Haruo (ed.) (2002), *Early Modern Japanese Literature: An Anthology, 1600–1900*, Translations from the Asian Classics, New York: Columbia University Press.

Smith, Henry D., II (2003), 'The Capacity of Chūshingura: Three Hundred Years of Chūshingura,' *Monumenta Nipponica*, **58**(1), 1–42.

Smith, Neil Skene (ed.) ([1937] 1979), *Materials on Japanese Social and Economic History: Tokugawa Japan*, Washington, DC: University Publications of America.

Storr, Virgil (2004), *Enterprising Slaves and Master Pirates: Understanding Economic Life in the Bahamas*, New York: Peter Lang.

Storr, Virgil (2013), *Understanding the Culture of Markets*, New York: Routledge.

Takekoshi, Yosaburō (1930), *The Economic Aspects of the History of the Civilization of Japan*, 3 volumes, London: George Allen & Unwin.

Takenaka, Yasukazu (1969), 'Endogenous Formation and Development of Capitalism in Japan,' *Journal of Economic History*, **29**(1), 141–62.

Takizawa, Matsuyo ([1927] 1968), *The Penetration of Money Economy in Japan and Its Effects upon Social and Political Institutions*, New York: AMS Press.

Vaporis, Constantine (2005), 'Lordly Pageantry: The Daimyo Procession and Political Authority,' *Japan Review*, **17**, 3–54.

Weber, Max (2002), *The Protestant Ethic and the Spirit of Capitalism*, New York: Penguin Classics.

West, Mark D. (2000), 'Private Ordering at the World's First Futures Exchange,' *Michigan Law Review*, **98**(8), 2574–615.

Wigmore, John Henry (1892), *Materials for the Study of Private Law in Old Japan*, Vol. III, Tokyo: Asiatic Society of Japan.

19. The cultural and political economy of drug prohibition

Kyle W. O'Donnell

19.1 INTRODUCTION

For political economy—a discipline that has long reveled in illuminating the unintended consequences of government interventionism—drug prohibition has been one of the most fruitful subjects of analysis. Indeed, through their work on the economics of prohibition, economists have made many significant contributions to scientific knowledge, as well as public policy discourse. This includes analyses of the effects of prohibition on illicit drug prices (DiNardo 1993; Freeborn 2009), potency (Thornton 1991: pp. 89–110), and consumption (Saffer and Chaloupka 1999; DeSimone and Farrelly 2003; Burrus 2006); the structure and organization of black markets (Coomber 2003; Poret and Téjédo 2006); and the welfare implications of drug policy (Erickson 1969; Miron and Zwiebel 1995; Poret 2002; Miron 2004: pp. 43–74; Conlin et al. 2005; Becker et al. 2006).[1]

While this research has greatly expanded our understanding of the economics of prohibition, there are a number of important social, cultural, and institutional aspects of this subject that remain relatively unexplored. As D'Amico (2012: p. 70) explains, 'while many have noticed prohibition's effect on physical capital, less attend to its influence upon knowledge, social-learning processes, institutional development, and the accumulation of social capital.' Indeed, the relationship between prohibition and non-market phenomena—especially the norms, social rules, informal institutions, and culture surrounding drug use—remains an underdeveloped area of study. However, the interaction between culture and government intervention would appear to raise numerous problems and questions of potential interest to political economists (for example, see Carilli et al. 2008).

The literature on drug prohibition in the United States seeks to explain how drug culture—norms, beliefs, attitudes, and other informal institutions pertaining to drugs—has changed from the late nineteenth century to the present day, linking these changes to government intervention *qua* drug prohibition (Brecher 1972: pp. 6–7, 17–20; Morgan 1981; Zinberg 1984: pp. 192–217; Musto 1999; DeGrandpre 2002, 2006: pp. 208–42; Parsons 2009: pp. 91–2). Before the advent of national drug control legislation in the early twentieth century, the US had an essentially free market for psychoactive drugs—including cocaine, cannabis, morphine, and heroin—which were inexpensive and widely available, and could be easily purchased from pharmacies, department stores, and even mail order catalogs (Brecher 1972: pp. 3–7). Nevertheless, and despite what may appear to modern readers as a remarkably laissez-faire environment, the US was not crippled by 'epidemic' drug addiction, nor did such drug use present the 'social problem' that it does today.[2] 'The vast majority of nineteenth-century opiate use was, like alcohol today, in fact "moderate use" . . . Just as most of the circumstantial and casual use of opiates in the nineteenth-century did not escalate into opiate dependence, most cases of dependence did not lead to compulsive, out-of-control addiction' (DeGrandpre 2006: p. 129).

In fact, narcotic dependence was often seen as a relatively benign habit, especially compared to alcoholism, and many individuals led long, fulfilling professional and personal lives while simultaneously maintaining life-long drug habits; indeed, some health and temperance advocates even encouraged alcoholics and heavy drinkers to switch to narcotics consumption (Brecher 1972: pp. 8–10, 33–9; Parssinen and Kerner 1980; Morgan 1981: pp. 34, 89–90; DeGrandpre 2006: p. 131; Vrecko 2010). Moreover, prior to drug prohibition, a significant portion of regular narcotics users and addicts were middle-class women, professionals, lawyers, and doctors. The 'average' opiate *habitué* was a middle-class, middle-age female with drug use typically being just one aspect of her life, rather than the driving force behind it (Ball and Chambers 1970; Brecher 1972: pp. 5–7, 17–20, 33–9; Parssinen and Kerner 1980; Morgan 1981: pp. 38–43; DeGrandpre 2006: pp. 103–37; Heyman 2009: pp. 3–7).

In sum, there is a strong sense in which the nature of the perceived 'drug problem' was altogether different from that which would likely be conceived of at present. Brecher (1972: pp. 6–7) captures the essence of this sociocultural transformation in the following passage, which serves as a synoptic elegy to this laissez-faire era of drugs in the US:

> Opiate use was also frowned upon in some circles as *immoral*—a vice akin to dancing, smoking, theater-going, gambling, or sexual promiscuity. But while deemed immoral, it is important to note that opiate use in the nineteenth century was not subject to the moral sanctions current today. Employees were not fired for addiction. Wives did not divorce their addicted husbands, or husbands their addicted wives. Children were not taken from their homes and lodged in foster homes or institutions because one or both parents were addicted. Addicts

continued to participate fully in the life of the community. Addicted children and young people continued to go to school, Sunday school, and college. Thus, the nineteenth century avoided one of the most disastrous effects of current narcotics laws and attitudes—the rise of a deviant addict subculture, cut off from respectable society and without a 'road back' to respectability.

There are significant, even fundamental, qualitative differences between the above image of the nineteenth-century 'drug problem' in the US and today's perspective after nearly a century of prohibitionist drug policies. Yet the economics of prohibition has thus far offered little insight into the nature of these phenomena (assuming such phenomena are even recognized). Hence, this chapter begins to address some of the gaps in the political economy of prohibition by bringing economic analysis to bear upon these sociocultural problems.

In order to better grasp the problems and unique issues that the cultural and political economy of drug prohibition attempts to address, it is crucial that we examine some of the qualitative, cultural, and institutional aspects of psychoactive drug use—that is, *why culture matters for drugs, the drug problem, and drug prohibition.* Rather than being objectively defined by chemistry and pharmacology alone, the effects and uses of psychoactive drugs are also a function of the drug user's social context and the subjective meaning the drug user attaches to the drug (Blum 1970; Zinberg 1984; Knipe 1995; DeGrandpre 2002, 2006; Nutt 2012: pp. 51–71). The *drug effect* is the product of a complex relationship between the variables that Zinberg (1984) calls *drug, set*, and *setting*. The *drug* is the chemical substance itself that creates a particular pharmacological effect in the individual. The *set* is the individual's internal comportment and includes personality, emotional state, and subjective beliefs and expectations about the drug. The *setting* comprises the external factors affecting drug use, and includes the physical environment, as well as culture, social norms and informal rules, the law, and other institutions (Zinberg 1984; also see Kleiman et al. 2011: p. 12). The perceived effects and behavioral outcomes of drug use are produced by the interaction of these factors together, which cannot be separated from one another (Goldberg 1999: pp. 22–40).[3]

This idea that the effects and uses of drugs are a function of drug, set, and setting (Zinberg 1984) is consistent with Austrian economists' emphasis on economic action within a particular context (or culture). Early Austrians such as Carl Menger pointed out that decision-making does not involve objective facts, but subjective valuations. F.A. Hayek and, more recently, Don Lavoie (this volume, Chapter 3) and Richard Ebeling have stressed that *interpretation* always takes place within a cultural context in which individuals assign meaning to action and the effects of action. As Ebeling explains, 'meaning and significance can be attached to . . . activities only in terms of an understanding and interpretation of the knowledge, intentions, and expectations of the actors themselves' ([1986] 1990: p.367). Further, Chamlee-Wright (this volume, Chapter 5) and Boettke (2001) have provided some insight into the interaction between culture and government intervention. Chamlee-Wright explores the relationship between government intervention and the cultural economy of Ghanian market women, while Boettke describes how incompatibilities between cultural beliefs and government policy result in policy failure. This chapter is an effort to expand on the growing literature connecting culture and economic action.

Specifically, the goals of this chapter are: (1) to establish *why culture matters* for understanding drugs, drug use, and drug policy—or the *drug problem*; (2) to develop a basic framework for the economic analysis of drug prohibition and culture; and (3) to sketch the outline of a potential research agenda on the cultural and political economy of prohibition and interventionism more generally. Section 19.2 outlines an economic approach to drug-using behavior and drug culture and discusses its application to comparative institutional analysis of culture and interventionism. Section 19.3 introduces drug prohibition to the analysis and examines several channels and mechanisms through which intervention can affect drug culture and informal institutions. I offer several pattern predictions with some preliminary empirical evidence as part of a potential research agenda on this subject. Section 19.4 concludes the chapter and discusses a few possible implications of these ideas.

19.2   THE ECONOMIC APPROACH TO DRUG-USING BEHAVIOR AND DRUG CULTURE

It is vital to recognize that psychoactive drug use is an adaptive, instrumental behavior reflecting the purposiveness and rationality of the drug user (cf. Müller and Schumann 2011). When framed in this manner, it becomes much clearer how drug use can be apprehended and interpreted with the tools of economic theory, perhaps the simplest approach being the direct analogy to consumer theory.[4] An individual seeks to maximize her utility function, which includes the desired end Z, subject to her income constraint. There are a variety of drugs that may help the individual achieve her desired end, Z. We can imagine that the optimal choice, with a given income and set of market prices, includes the drug z whose effects are most well suited for achieving Z. The selection of drug z, however, is less straightforward and involves a few considerations. The individual has to decide not only what drug to use, but also the quantity of the drug and *how to use* the drug (for example, smoking, snorting, or injecting via syringe). Because the drug effect is influenced by so many variables—including a number of dynamic, subjective factors, for example drug, set, and setting—and because there are multiple uses for any given drug, the set of all possible drug actions is quite large.[5] What is needed for actors to make plans, choose a course of action, and achieve their goals successfully is additional constraints upon choice and behavior, or guides that direct human action.

Drug culture and institutions serve this vital function by restricting the range of desired and expected drug effects, acceptable drug uses, and thus the set of possible drug actions. *Institutions* are rules and constraints on behavior that serve a number of vital functions. They coordinate expectations, plans, and action, increase the predictability and stability of society, and enable cooperation and exchange between individuals. *Culture* can be seen here as a web of shared meanings, mores, understandings, and tacit knowledge. Culture is a 'window' through which actors observe, interpret, and give meaning to their world. Culture, as Lavoie (this volume, Chapter 3: p.49) describes, is the 'complex of meanings that allows us to comprehend human action; it is the background context that renders purposeful action intelligible. Culture is the language in which past events are interpreted, future circumstances are anticipated, and plans of action are formulated.'

For our purposes, I propose that we conceptualize the role and relationship between culture and institutions as complementary (though not always) to each other in shaping human action. Institutions shape outcomes by setting constraints upon the choices and opportunities of actors, while culture (as the actor's interpretative framework) influences behavior by directing, or focusing, the actor's attention upon certain means and ends. As Storr (this volume, Chapter 8: p.189) states, 'culture directs (but does not determine) his [the human actor's] actions and acts as the prism through which he views his problem situation; it "suggests to him both means and ends."' To briefly illustrate by way of popular analogy to driving, we can think of institutions as the rules of the road, the traffic lights, the guardrails on highways, and even the road system itself, which both determine possible courses of action and set limits on acceptable actions. Culture, then, is closer to a travel guide that suggests certain situations, as well as a map, or GPS directions, that suggests appropriate means to ends. Thus culture focuses the actor's choice set to a feasible decision problem. Together, culture and institutions shape human action and the emergent patterns and outcomes that result from many individual actions.

Returning to drug use behavior within the presentation above, we might think of C as the culture or context of drug use, which frames the actor's decision problem, for example, entering the production function for Z, where $Z = (f(z)|C)$ or $f(z|C)$. C restricts (or focuses) the possible effects of a drug z, as well as the set of ends to which it might be put, such that, relative to the unconstrained (noncultural) drug use function $[f(z) \rightarrow (x_1, \ldots, x_j) \rightarrow (Z_1, \ldots, Z_m)]$, the actor's drug use function within the cultural context is constrained to a set of feasible alternatives, where $f(z|C) \rightarrow (x_1, x_2, x_3|C) \rightarrow (Z_1, Z_2|C)$.[6] Thus agents are able to make plans, choose appropriate means, and act within the context of the drug culture and institutions. However, it is important to note that the drug culture is not simply another input to an actor's objective function, nor is it directly subject to choice, but is in some sense inseparable from the function itself, framing the choices, opportunities, and means–ends relationships in the actor's mind—including for what ends drugs can be used and when it is appropriate to do so, how to use them, and what are their likely drug effects. Although there is space for individuals to choose, or perhaps merely modify, their cultural framework at the margin, the capacity to do so is limited, and most individuals simply accept their culture 'as is,' given to them through tradition and social learning (Lavoie and Chamlee-Wright, this volume, Chapter 7: p. 168).

There are further problems for analysis, which are raised in the above discussion, especially concerning the formation and development of C, as well as its relevant inputs and determinants. One obvious approach would model C as a result of social interaction, that is, a function of the plans and actions of many individuals as pertaining to drug use. C would operate therefore as an underlying variable that acts as a constraint on individual behavior while also being determined by individual decisions. We could thus expect C to reflect the purposes, plans, and preferences of the individuals who use drugs. If the members of a particular community all highly value sociality and openness, for example, then we might expect their C to shape the set of drug actions for drug z around relatively more sociable effects and uses, such as increased joviality or specifying use at parties.

However, the above treatment is not to say that drug users necessarily create rules and sanctions controlling drug use in a conscious, intentional manner, that is, that they consciously choose the particular elements of C. Rather, the drug culture emerges as the unintended result of a multitude of individuals pursuing their goals through the use of psychoactive drugs: an ongoing process characterized both by unconscious rule-following behavior and also by moments of deliberate reasoning, as when a drug user adopts personal rules dictating what is appropriate, such as when, where, and how to use. The above is consistent with Zinberg's (1984: pp. 152–71) work showing that controlled opiate users develop rules, rituals, and sanctions to reduce the risk of possible harms from drug use—including rules and rituals for avoiding addiction and overdose—doing so unconsciously at times and deliberately at others.

In addition, Chamlee-Wright (2008) offers several valuable insights for my framework through her 'Austrian' perspective on social capital, which theorizes about social capital in terms of its structure and social learning processes embodying the heterogeneous plans, actions, norms, relationships, and knowledge of purposive individuals. In particular, Chamlee-Wright (ibid.: p. 47) argues that 'societies advance by embedding accumulated knowledge in forms that are "ready at hand." Social norms and institutions, cultural practices, and law, are bundles of accumulated knowledge that allow us to solve complex coordination problems without directly possessing detailed knowledge of how they function.' So too, I would argue, does the drug culture encompass what society 'knows' about drugs, although what the content of that knowledge is, how it is aggregated or assembled, and other qualitative questions remain open to investigation.

19.3   PROHIBITION AND THE DRUG CULTURE

This section introduces prohibition, and analyzes several key mechanisms through which prohibition can affect drug culture: (1) the selection process for illicit drug users; (2) the transmission and use of knowledge in drug culture; and (3) the combined impact on the 'path' of cultural evolution and social change.

19.3.1   Prohibition as a Selection Mechanism

The basic goal of interventionist drug policy is to reduce drug use deemed 'abusive' or problematic. The argument for prohibition is based upon a seemingly straightforward economic argument: reducing the supply of a drug will cause the price to rise and the quantity demanded to fall, thus lowering both overall drug use and abuse. However, as Zinberg (1984: p. 194) argues, the idea that raising the price of a drug would 'automatically' reduce drug abuse is dubious and 'ignores the strong probability that only the less committed moderate users who propound the social sanctions would be the ones discouraged.' In other words, there is little inherent reason to suspect that a price increase would have an equiproportional effect on all 'types' of drug users. Indeed, we might reasonably expect moderate, controlled drug users to have a relatively more price-elastic demand for drugs compared to heavier, compulsive or 'hard-core' users.[7]

Furthermore, in addition to simply raising the price of illicit drugs, prohibition is enforced through legal sanctions that add to the price of illicit drug use. Again, however, different people will perceive the subjective cost of potential legal punishment differently, with legal sanctions being more likely to discourage drug use by those who would suffer the most from legal punishments as well as those who simply value conforming to the law as a moral or ethical issue. Although we cannot say *a priori* whether or not the individuals who would be less discouraged by legal punishment are also likely to be similar 'types' of drug users, it does not seem unreasonable to suppose that they would tend to be the more problematic, heavier drug users. Hence, prohibition is more likely to discourage moderate and controlled drug users than the heavier, problematic users.

Prohibition can be understood as a selection mechanism insofar as it weeds out some group N' from the initial set of drug users N, with the separation being a result of the set of constraints imposed by prohibition (Hodgson and Knudsen 2006). The value to viewing prohibition as a selection mechanism becomes much more apparent when we recall the role for social and cultural context in determining drug use patterns and outcomes. Owing to the culturally embedded nature of drug use, and because the drug culture is shaped by the preferences, beliefs, and purposes of the individuals who use drugs, the composition of the drug-using population can impact various social phenomena and outcomes relating to drugs, for example drug use patterns, consequences of abuse and addiction, perceived costs and benefits from drug use, and even the nature of the drug problem itself. Thus drug prohibition can be meaningfully analyzed as a selection mechanism for the set of individuals who become or remain illicit drug users—discouraging moderate, occasional drug users relatively more effectively than heavy, 'hard-core' drug users—which then influences the drug culture and institutions that will tend to emerge under prohibition.

This analysis of selection mechanisms within institutional evolution and social change comports well with the institutional 'stickiness' framework of Boettke et al. (this volume, Chapter 6), which explains the persistence of institutions in terms of how closely they align with the *mētis* of society— that is, underlying beliefs, skills, practices, and local knowledge. The *mētis* varies among different groups of people, reflecting their diverse backgrounds, cultures, and knowledge, and thus the 'stickiness' of particular institutions will vary between groups and across time and place. If new institutions are put into place (for example, new laws as part of prohibition) that are inconsistent with the underlying *mētis*, then such institutions are unlikely to be effective. Further, and I would argue more importantly, if a society's *informal* institutions are shaped or influenced by the *mētis*, then interventions (for example, prohibition) that affect the *mētis* of a community or population might thereby indirectly affect the informal institutions that evolve and persist (or not).[8]

For example, imagine N were the set of all people who drink alcohol in a population, where the overwhelming majority of drinking behavior is moderate, controlled use. Now imagine a selection process is imposed on N that filters out multiple moderate drinkers for each compulsive drinker or alcoholic, resulting in N' having a much larger proportion of heavy drinkers and alcoholics. A representative sample of the purposes, beliefs, values, and attitudes held by the members in each set is likely to have shifted in accordance with the transformation from N to N'. As a result, the drinking cultures of N and N' will likely diverge as norms, cultural attitudes, and informal rules evolve within each that tend to reflect their particular beliefs, purposes, and values.

19.3.2 The Use of Knowledge in Illicit Drug Culture

The ability of individuals to make use of knowledge that is widely dispersed throughout society is essential to the coordination of the complex array of plans and activities that individuals pursue through cooperation and exchange under the division of labor. Outside of the market process, where the price system is the primary institution serving this need, information and knowledge are transmitted and utilized through social learning processes embedded within culture, norms, and institutions. Undergirding these processes of social learning and cultural transmission is a complex web of social networks, composed of diverse individuals, relationships, and information flows (Chamlee-Wright 2008; Chamlee-Wright and Myers 2008).

So too is psychoactive drug use embedded within drug culture, a system of social networks, and a structure of social capital. To be sure, drug-using behavior is an evolved social phenomenon that exists, and is sustained, through social learning and cultural transmission of an extensive body of dispersed tacit knowledge pertaining to every aspect of such activities. For example, one must first know where, when, and from whom to acquire the drug. One must then know how to use that particular drug, including techniques for preparing it and ingesting it, as well as what to expect from its consumption. One must know what dangers to avoid and how to reduce the risk of potential harm from drug use. It is clear to scholars who have performed field research that illicit drug use is deeply embedded within a multitude of rituals, norms, customs, and practices, each with its own instrumental purpose (Zinberg 1984; Sharp 1991).

Injection drug use, for example, is one of the most intricate forms of illicit drug use. Rather than being a wild, out-of-control behavior, as many might imagine, injection drug use is often a highly structured and orderly activity, regulated by numerous rules and practices that define and guide participants through the intricacies of preparing the drug and the tools for using it (needles, syringes, and so on), the proper techniques for injecting it, and other rules governing the etiquette of this social activity (Zinberg 1984: pp. 119, 127–31, 153–6, 162–3; Sharp 1991). Furthermore, as so much of these rituals, intricate practices, and informal controls is contained in inarticulate bits of tacit knowledge, processes of social learning and cultural transmission are essential for sustaining this requisite knowledge base.

Owing to the criminal sanctions imposed by prohibition, individuals will tend to place a higher value on trust, secrecy, and privacy around their illicit drug use than for licit activities. This can impact the structure of social networks and social capital among drug users, thereby affecting patterns of information transmission and knowledge accumulation within the drug culture. In order to reduce their risk of legal punishment, illicit drug users will tend to shift a larger proportion of their illicit exchanges, relationships, and interactions to individuals with whom they share a closer, more trusting relationship, relative to their licit dealings. At the macro-level, illicit drug users will therefore tend to form close-knit and exclusive social networks characterized by a higher proportion of *strong ties* to *weak ties* relative to other ordinary licit networks. The primary benefit to illicit drug users of dense, strong-tied networks is the support they provide to 'bonding social capital'—which can effectively align incentives, promote cooperation, and limit defection in potential prisoners' dilemma situations: a significant risk under prohibition (Carilli et al. 2008).

While illicit drug users tend to choose strong over weak ties on the margin, many (especially moderate and occasional users) go even further, deliberately severing connections between their drug use and the non-drug-using aspects of their lives. Often, such actions are intended to enhance informal drug controls or minimize the harms from drug use. For example, Zinberg (1984: pp. 119, 130–31, 152–5) explains that many controlled opiate users exert significant effort both to hide their drug use from non-drug-using relations, in order to avoid social condemnation, *and* to maintain a precarious relationship with addicts that is close enough to reliably obtain opiates, but distant enough to avoid being pulled into the 'junkie subculture.'

While this behavior can be an effective means of drug control at the individual level, the combined effect at the meso- or macro-level may actually be to reduce the effectiveness of informal social controls on drug use. The absence of links between illicit drug subcultures and mainstream society limits the flow of knowledge about illicit drugs—especially relating to alternative norms for controlled use—which can stifle social learning and the discovery of beneficial social capital combinations through 'social entrepreneurship' (Chamlee-Wright 2008). This implies that, when controlled drug users are more effective at concealing their behavior and, thus, are more successful in pursuing their goal of private drug control, it is more likely that their private, tacit knowledge about controlled drug use including that such behavior is even possible will remain undiscovered by social entrepreneurs who could promote informal drug controls. Indeed, it seems highly likely that this pattern of secrecy around controlled drug use is a significant contributing factor behind popular beliefs that grossly overestimate the ratio of abusive to moderate drug users, or that harbor serious doubt about the notion of controlled drug use itself (Zinberg 1984: p. 155).

19.3.3 Evolution of the Drug Culture under Prohibition

Among the various possible implications of the above pattern predictions, I am especially concerned with how the combination of prohibition as selection mechanism and the use of knowledge in illicit social networks affects the drug culture—especially the beliefs, norms, and informal rules of drug use among drug users—and related processes of social learning and cultural evolution.

Prohibition tends to discourage primarily occasional or moderate drug users, increasing the ratio of compulsive users (addicts) to controlled users. This effect alone might even seem to be enough to cause the drug culture to change in a predictable pattern, namely that illicit drug culture will be driven much more by hard-core drug users, and reflect their *mētis*. Thus, as Zinberg (1984: p. 195) postulates, 'since it is the moderate, occasional users who develop controlling sanctions and rituals, the policy whose goal it is to minimize the number of dysfunctional users may actually be leading to a relative increase in the number of such users.' Furthermore, even if compulsive drug users do develop their own culture, rules, sanctions, and institutions, as they indeed do, they 'are likely to adhere to and articulate rules that operate to support compulsivity rather than control it' (Zinberg 1984: p. 156).

My analysis offers some support for Zinberg's argument and to extend it. In particular, it is somewhat unclear why—even if we accept that the ratio of compulsive to controlled users has increased—the remaining moderate and occasional users could not just develop their own distinct subculture and institutions that support controlled use, separate from the hard-core subculture. This problem is also magnified by the fact that, even under prohibition, the majority of illicit drug users are in fact occasional or controlled users.[9]

It is important to recognize the significant instrumental role for social networks and social capital under prohibition. Such social structures are necessary for almost every aspect of illicit drug use, for example obtaining illicit drugs, learning how to use them, and avoiding unnecessary harm (see Zinberg 1984: pp. 153–6, 162–3). In fact, social networks and social capital almost certainly become *more* important under prohibition, since government intervention forces various activities and exchanges underground, bypassing many established market institutions, and channeling them instead through non-market institutions and social processes, which rely much more heavily on personal connections and relationships. Therefore, illicit drug users are likely to generate dense, strong-tied social networks and close-knit, exclusive social capital structures, which restrict the flow of information. They also bypass the immense body of knowledge embodied within licit market processes by diverting their interactions and exchanges through non-market or underground market substitutes.

Moderate and occasional drug users enjoy increased privacy and security but at the cost of forgone discovery and utilization of much knowledge, and the array of potential benefits it might offer. This includes knowledge that could be beneficial, both directly to drug users themselves (for example, more accurate, accessible information about drugs, their potential uses, and how to use them; knowledge about substitutes with fewer side effects or more desirable effects; and knowledge of how to minimize the risks and potential harms of drug use) and indirectly to the non-drug users of a community or society, especially by reducing the external costs associated with drug use (such as knowledge about how to reduce the risk of overdosing; practices that limit the spread of infectious diseases; and norms that encourage socially acceptable behavior and punish violations). This brings us closer to a potential resolution to Zinberg's argument.

Under prohibition, controlled drug users rely extensively on illicit social capital to achieve their drug-related ends—for example obtaining supplies and learning how to use—and often turn to hard-core users and the 'junkie subculture' out of perceived necessity (Zinberg 1984: pp. 119, 127–31, 153–6). These latter interactions place controlled users in a precarious situation, where they strain themselves to simultaneously maintain control over their drug use, conceal this activity from non-drug users, and avoid getting drawn into the junkie subculture. Yet, owing to the constraints that controlled users face (for example, legal punishment, social ostracism, and isolation), they are unlikely to establish a viable subculture that effectively fosters controlled drug use (and supports its own survival), and hence may lack a feasible alternative to the junkie subculture. Thus, 'in the absence of a highly visible, communicative population of controlled users with its own discrete rituals the addict subculture is the only readily available source of expertise about the drug' (Zinberg 1984: p. 153). As a result, the controlled users often adopt many of their rituals and norms from the compulsive, hard-core users.

19.4 CONCLUSION

Prohibition tries to reduce consumption of a particular drug and the total number of its users, both by raising the price of the illicit drug and by criminalizing its distribution and possession. Yet prohibition is unlikely to have a uniform effect on all types of drug users but will tend to discourage moderate, controlled users more effectively than compulsive, hard-core users. In effect, prohibition will reduce total use but will also raise the ratio of hard-core to moderate users.[10] Total drug abuse will still be lower under prohibition, but only insofar as policy does not affect the patterns and quality of drug use or drug users' type (changing moderate users into problematic abusers)—that is, if these facts are determined exogenously or remain constant across changes in policy regimes or institutional constraints. Yet my analysis and empirical evidence suggest, in fact, that this condition does not hold. The facts of drug use—patterns, likely outcomes, and even the propensity for abuse and addiction—are not objectively defined parameters 'given' by exogenous forces. Rather, they are a function of dynamic (even subjective) factors, including users' beliefs, expectations, and sociocultural context. Thus, through its effects on the social learning processes and cultural context of drug use, prohibition can affect the patterns and qualities of illicit drug use, and possibly even exacerbate drug abuse problems.

Prohibition tends to increase the ratio of hard-core to moderate drug users. This also increases the relative influence of the hard-core users over the drug culture to more closely reflect their values and goals, which may vary dramatically from those of moderate users and non-users. This effect is amplified by the constraints on moderate users that give hard-core users the comparative advantage over illicit-drug-related social learning and cultural transmission, since they have lower opportunity costs of participating in illicit activity than moderate users. Furthermore, criminalization pushes social networks and drug culture underground, where the discovery, transmission, and use of knowledge are distorted and stifled. Since moderate users lack a culture of controlled drug use, they largely adopt rituals and practices from hard-core users and junkie subculture, which leads moderate drug users to fall into the drug abuse problems of hard-core users as well. Ultimately, it is possible for prohibition to reduce the total number of drug users (or total use), while simultaneously increasing the actual number of hard-core, problematic users and addicts (or total abuse).

Additional research is needed to study the relationship between prohibition, culture, and drug use. First, further analysis of social selection processes, especially under varying circumstances, could yield valuable insights for the cultural and political economy of prohibition, as well as for institutional economics more generally (cf. Hodgson and Knudsen 2006, 2010). Similar mechanisms are certainly at work within a multitude of cultural, political, and institutional processes, and a better understanding of their operation would go a long way towards enhancing our grasp of many other phenomena.

Second, the dynamics of interventionism (cf. Ikeda 1997), with a focus on the relationships between culture, the market process, and politics, could be explored as well through this framework. One research project might examine the feedback mechanisms that connect politics, intervention, and culture. For example, suppose that prohibition affects popular knowledge, beliefs, and attitudes towards drug use, as discussed in this chapter, such that knowledge of controlled drug use fades or is otherwise obscured. For non-illicit-drug-using members of 'mainstream' society, it is likely the case that the most prominent examples of illicit drug users are also the most problematic, for example street addicts and compulsive drug users. But what if non-illicit-drug users instead imagined a moderate user whose use causes little if any damage to himself or others? These easily accessible mental images may help explain why voters might support or might not support further government intervention related to drug use.

NOTES

1. The literature on the economics of prohibition has become rather large in recent years, so a concise review may be impractical, though Thornton (1991), Miron and Zwiebel (1995), and Miron (2004) provide excellent overviews of the economic literature, as well as original contributions of their own. It is also notable for a topic as controversial as drug policy that there is a significant core of positive economic analysis shared both by scholars who tend to support government intervention as a means for achieving the ends of drug control—for example, Kleiman (1992: pp. 67–163), Kleiman et al. (2011)— and by those who are much more skeptical of interventionism—for example, Thornton (1991), Miron (2004), and Benavie (2009).
2. On the complex history of the emergence of a 'drug problem' in the USA, see Musto 1999; also Hickman 2004; Cohen 2006.
3. This is well summarized by Blum (1970: p.230):

    > Because we are . . . dealing here . . . only with those [drugs] having direct effects on consciousness (the 'mind'), it is necessary to make explicit that there are no uniform, consistent effects, and, thus, none of the mind-altering substances is inherently harmless, vicious, or magical in its properties. What we often attribute solely to the

drug's physical or physiological properties and loosely refer to as the drug effect is a complex interaction among these varied factors: its pharmacological properties; the personality, character structure, expectations, and attitudes of the individual taking the drug; and the sociocultural setting or context, including not only the broader social values but the subcultural ones, as well as the immediate environment.

Similarly, Knipe (1995: p.67) describes the relationship as one in which the drug is an antecedent variable, that is, a constant, whose physiological effect is filtered through culture as the independent variable, causing a change in the dependent variable, the behavioral outcome.

4. In particular, see the broad approach to economics in Mises (1949) as well as Becker (1976).
5. The range of effects attributed to a specific drug, like cocaine or heroin, across time is enormous, and if listed explicitly would reveal numerous internal contradictions and reversals across time and place (see Goldberg 1999: pp.22–59; DeGrandpre 2006: pp.103–37; also see the cross-cultural studies in Blum 1970; Knipe 1995).
6. For my purposes, I do not find it necessary to strictly distinguish between drug culture (as interpretative framework) and drug institutions (as constraints) in this basic formal presentation, though future work might construct a more complete treatment; for example, *C* might *frame* the actor's *perceived* decision problem, while institutions constrain her opportunity set and payoffs to different actions.
7. 'Hard-core drug users' and similar phrases refer to drug users with certain distinctive characteristics, and largely follow common usage in the scholarly literature on illicit drugs and drug policy. Drug users could be considered 'hard-core' if, for example, they devote a significant fraction of their time, energy, and resources to drug use (relative to some range of social acceptability), or their drug use significantly interferes with other areas of their life outside drugs.
8. To the extent that a society's *informal* institutions matter for economic performance and social outcomes (for example, net results of drug use) relative to other factors, this transmission mechanism could significantly expand the range and weight of unintended consequences from interventionism. Indeed, there is a growing body of empirical research on the relative importance of informal institutions for economic development and other outcomes, with notable results in support of the proposition that *informal institutions rule* (cf. Williamson 2009).
9. The proportion of people who become problematic users, or abusers, varies between drugs and method of use; this rate ranges as high as around 30 percent for smoked cocaine and injecting heroin, with the majority only ever using these drugs on one or a few occasions (Kleiman et al. 2011: pp.5–6). While this figure is still considerable, it nevertheless debunks the idea that occasional, moderate drug use is a rarity or impossible.
10. Therefore, if the policy goal is to reduce drug abuse and addiction, simply measuring the decrease in *total* use under prohibition will overstate its actual efficacy.

REFERENCES

Ball, John C. and Carl D. Chambers (1970), *The Epidemiology of Opiate Addiction in the United States*, Springfield, IL: Thomas.

Becker, Gary S. (1976), *The Economic Approach to Human Behavior*, Chicago: University of Chicago Press.

Becker, Gary S., Kevin M. Murphy and Michael Grossman (2006), 'The Market for Illegal Goods: The Case of Drugs,' *Journal of Political Economy*, **114**(1), 38–60.

Benavie, Arthur (2009), *Drugs: America's Holy War*, New York: Routledge.

Blum, Richard H. (1970), *Society and Drugs: Social and Cultural Observations*, San Francisco: Jossey-Bass.

Boettke, Peter J. (2001), 'Why Culture Matters: Economics, Politics, and the Imprint of History,' in *Calculation and Coordination: Essays on Socialism and Transitional Political Economy*, New York: Routledge, pp. 248–65.

Brecher, Edward M. (1972), *Licit and Illicit Drugs: The Consumers Union Report on Narcotics, Stimulants, Depressants, Inhalants, Hallucinogens, and Marijuana— Including Caffeine, Nicotine, and Alcohol*, New York: Little, Brown.

Burrus, Robert T., Jr. (2006), 'The Impact of Weight-Based Penalties on Drug Purity and Consumption: A Theoretical Analysis,' *Eastern Economic Journal*, **32**(4), 629–46.

Carilli, Anthony M., Christopher J. Coyne and Peter T. Leeson (2008), 'Government Intervention and the Structure of Social Capital,' *Review of Austrian Economics*, **21**, 209–18.

Chamlee-Wright, Emily (2008), 'The Structure of Social Capital: An Austrian Perspective on Its Nature and Development,' *Review of Political Economy*, **20**(1), 41–58.

Chamlee-Wright, Emily and Justus A. Myers (2008), 'Discovery and Social Learning in Non-Priced Environments: An Austrian View of Social Network Theory,' *Review of Austrian Economics*, **21**, 151–66.

Cohen, Michael M. (2006), 'Jim Crow's Drug War: Race, Coca-Cola, and the Southern Origins of Drug Prohibition,' *Southern Cultures*, **12**(3), 55–79.

Conlin, Michael, Stacy Dickert-Conlin and John Pepper (2005), 'The Effect of Alcohol Prohibition on Illicit-Drug-Related Crimes,' *Journal of Law and Economics*, **48**(1), 215–34.

Coomber, Ross (2003), 'There's No Such Thing as a Free Lunch: How "Freebies" and "Credit" Operate as Part of Rational Drug Market Activity,' *Journal of Drug Issues*, **33**(4), 939–62.

D'Amico, Daniel J. (2012), 'Comparative Political Economy When Anarchism Is on the Table,' *Review of Austrian Economics*, **25**(1), 63–73.

DeGrandpre, Richard (2002), 'Constructing the Pharmacological: A Century in Review,' *Capitalism, Nature, Socialism*, **13**(1), 75–104.

DeGrandpre, Richard (2006), *The Cult of Pharmacology: How America Became the World's Most Troubled Drug Culture*, Durham, NC: Duke University Press.

DeSimone, Jeff and Matthew C. Farrelly (2003), 'Price and Enforcement Effects on Cocaine and Marijuana Demand,' *Economic Inquiry*, **41**(1), 98–115.

DiNardo, John (1993), 'Law Enforcement, the Price of Cocaine and Cocaine Use,' *Mathematical and Computer Modelling*, **17**(2), 53–64.

Ebeling, Richard ([1986] 1990), 'Austrian Economics—An Annotated Bibliography [on] Methodology of the Austrian School,' in Stephen Littlechild (ed.), *Austrian Economics*, Vol. 1: *Schools of Thought in Economics*, Aldershot, UK and Brookfield, VT, USA: Edward Elgar Publishing, pp. 367–70.

Erickson, Edward (1969), 'The Social Costs of the Discovery and Suppression of the Clandestine Distribution of Heroin,' *Journal of Political Economy*, **77**(4), 484–6.

Freeborn, Beth A. (2009), 'Arrest Avoidance: Law Enforcement and the Price of Cocaine,' *Journal of Law and Economics*, **52**(1), 19–40.

Goldberg, Ted (1999), *Demystifying Drugs: A Psychosocial Perspective*, New York: St. Martin's Press.

Heyman, Gene M. (2009), *Addiction: A Disorder of Choice*, Cambridge, MA: Harvard University Press.

Hickman, Timothy A. (2004), '"Mania Americana": Narcotic Addiction and Modernity in the United States, 1870–1920,' *Journal of American History*, **90**(4), 1269–94.

Hodgson, Geoffrey M. and Thorbjørn Knudsen (2006), 'The Nature and Units of Social Selection,' *Journal of Evolutionary Economics*, **16**(5), 477–89.

Hodgson, Geoffrey M. and Thorbjørn Knudsen (2010), *Darwin's Conjecture: The Search for General Principles of Social and Economic Evolution*, Chicago: University of Chicago Press.

Ikeda, Sanford (1997), *Dynamics of the Mixed Economy: Toward a Theory of Interventionism*, London: Routledge.

Kleiman, Mark A. (1992), *Against Excess: Drug Policy for Results*, New York: Basic Books.

Kleiman, Mark A., Jonathan P. Caulkins and Angela Hawken (2011), *Drugs and Drug Policy: What Everyone Needs to Know*, New York: Oxford University Press.

Knipe, Ed (1995), *Culture, Society, and Drugs: The Social Science Approach to Drug Use*, Prospect Heights, IL: Waveland Press.

Miron, Jeffrey A. (2004), *Drug War Crimes: The Consequences of Prohibition*, Oakland, CA: Independent Institute.

Miron, Jeffrey A. and Jeffrey Zwiebel (1995), 'The Economic Case against Drug Prohibition,' *Journal of Economic Perspectives*, **9**(4), 175–92.

Mises, Ludwig von (1949), *Human Action: A Treatise on Economics*, Auburn, AL: Ludwig von Mises Institute.

Morgan, H. Wayne (1981), *Drugs in America: A Social History, 1800–1980*, Syracuse, NY: Syracuse University Press.

Müller, Christian P. and Gunter Schumann (2011), 'Drugs as Instruments: A New Framework for Non-Addictive Psychoactive Drug Use,' *Behavioral and Brain Sciences*, **34**(6), 293–310.

Musto, David F. (1999), *The American Disease: Origins of Narcotic Control*, Oxford: Oxford University Press.

Nutt, David (2012), *Drugs—Without the Hot Air: Minimising the Harms of Legal and Illegal Drugs*, Cambridge: UIT Cambridge.

Parsons, Nicholas Lawrence (2009), 'Methedrine, Ice, Crank, and Crystal: An Historical and Cultural Examination of Methamphetamine in the United States,' Ph.D. thesis, Washington State University.

Parssinen, Terry M. and Karen Kerner (1980), 'Development of the Disease Model of Drug Addiction in Britain, 1870–1926,' *Medical History*, **24**, 275–96.

Poret, Sylvaine (2002), 'Paradoxical Effects of Law Enforcement Policies: The Case of the Illicit Drug Market,' *International Review of Law and Economics*, **22**(4), 465–93.

Poret, Sylvaine and Cyril Téjédo (2006), 'Law Enforcement and Concentration in Illicit Drug Markets,' *European Journal of Political Economy*, **22**(1), 99–114.

Saffer, Henry and Frank Chaloupka (1999), 'The Demand for Illicit Drugs,' *Economic Inquiry*, **37**(3), 401–11.

Sharp, Rachel (1991), *Ways of Using: Functional Injecting Drug Users Project*, Sydney, NSW: Macquarie University Centre for Applied Social Research.

Thornton, Mark (1991), *The Economics of Prohibition*, Salt Lake City: University of Utah Press.

Vrecko, Scott (2010), 'Birth of a Brain Disease: Science, the State and Addiction Neuropolitics,' *History of the Human Sciences*, **23**(4), 52–67.

Williamson, Claudia R. (2009), 'Informal Institutions Rule: Institutional Arrangements and Economic Performance,' *Public Choice*, **139**, 371–87.

Zinberg, Norman E. (1984), *Drug, Set, and Setting: The Basis for Controlled Intoxicant Use*, New Haven, CT: Yale University Press.

20. Cultural and institutional co-determination: the case of legitimacy in exchange in *Diablo II*

Solomon Stein

20.1 INTRODUCTION

When Austrian economists look at the role culture plays in economic action, it is primarily seen as operating in the background, giving shape to the observed structure of institutions and individual behavior that is the subject of economic analysis. Often, given the historical reality confronted in trying to give meaning to human affairs, this treatment is entirely acceptable: economists never observe action situations in which, out of some *ur*-environment, a society emerges. However, when considering how to understand the role of culture in theory, decisions that are entirely justified in these historical cases may not be giving us the whole story. In particular, while the current theoretical treatments of the role of culture in economic action tend to treat cultural factors as being logically antecedent to institutional forms, the actual relationship could be more akin to co-determination: that a certain culture develops in a particular area may be causally linked to the institutional forms chosen before the distinctive elements of that culture emerge. These causal linkages may dissipate or be severed, but there is no reason to think this is logically necessary: the culture and institutions of a society could continue to coevolve, just as their interplay shaped the initial formation of the cultural/institutional system.

Situations in which there is comparatively little historical distance may give us as social scientists a chance to examine these questions without having by necessity to treat culture as a prior constraint. The dramatic rise of the Internet as a social phenomenon, and the parallel increase in popularity of online, multiplayer video gaming, presents us with such a situation. From simple text-based games stored on bulletin board systems and mainframes, online games have evolved to be persistent online worlds such as *World of Warcraft*. While an individual who plays these games does not enter as a *tabula rasa*, free from a cultural framework, the players of each game do confront a novel choice situation, providing an excellent historical case to examine the possible role institutional differences have in fostering cultural differentiation.

Of the many possible online games (and thus possible cultures) to study, the case of *Diablo II*[1] is particularly interesting because of the distinctly economic character of some of the major communities to emerge surrounding the game. These communities, despite being established for the same purpose (to facilitate in-game exchange), with respect to the same environment, adopted different initial institutional structures to further this end. As this chapter will argue, this initial institutional choice led to the development of directly opposed cultures regarding certain kinds of in-game behavior. It may be argued that, insofar as these communities were oriented towards exchange in the artificial environment of a video game, inferences from behavior in this context to the 'real world' may be suspect.[2] The response to this possible methodological objection is twofold: first, despite the seeming triviality of this environment, this is nevertheless a case of purposive human actors attempting to achieve their goals, and as such illustrates the operations of universal phenomena of action; second, contrary to the expectations this critique would create in terms of observed outcomes, these communities did in fact concern themselves with solving the coordination problems they confronted and, as this chapter will show, did so in ways consistent with how these problems are successfully confronted in 'real-world' situations.[3]

This chapter proceeds as follows: Section 20.2 explores the relationship within the Austrian literature between culture and economic activity, with a particular focus on the ways the current theories handle institutions. Section 20.3 presents an overview of *Diablo II* as an economic environment. Section 20.4 discusses in detail one particular community that emerged from *Diablo II*, and explores the complementary role of culture and institutions in the governance of the community. Section 20.5 concludes.

20.2 THE ROLE OF CULTURE IN ECONOMIC ACTION

20.2.1 Culture as an Interpretive Lens

Within Austrian economics, the study of the role of culture is a natural outgrowth of the emphasis on subjectivism. If, as Hayek argues, 'in the social sciences the things are what people think they are' (Hayek 1943:

p. 3), then understanding how individuals form the meanings that structure their understanding of the world must be an important part of the scientific process. Drawing upon a tradition in economic sociology and anthropology that can be traced back to Max Weber, the cultural approach within Austrian economics sees culture as a primary input into meaning formation: culture is 'a historically transmitted pattern of meanings that is shared by a group of people and learned by new members as they become part of the group' (Storr 2013: p. 3).

Much as concern for the role of culture is an outgrowth of Austrian subjectivism, the adoption of the interpretive understanding of culture is part of a movement by some scholars within Austrian economics towards adoption of the continental hermeneutic tradition as the basis for understanding human action.[4] Of particular importance for this chapter is the importance of culture in determining the impact of various institutions on action, as Emily Chamlee-Wright (this volume, Chapter 16) does in the context of financial institutions in Ghana.[5] In this case, despite the presence of established Western financial institutions such as large commercial banks, access to credit remained significantly restricted for most members of society. Why had the presence of conventional financial and credit institutions not had the results we would expect from observing their role in Western society? The answer, for Chamlee-Wright, is the cultural context in which these institutions were developed. In a culture where economic activity is associated with 'educated, literate, and male' (Chamlee-Wright ibid.: p. 356) entrepreneurs, the emphasis on written documentation and formal record-keeping is well suited. When instead the sort of economic activities that require small-scale credit access are considered the province of illiterate women[6] then these same institutions are no longer going to be serving the same function.

This approach sees the prevailing culture of a group as serving a role vis-à-vis institutions analogous to the role institutions play with regard to individual behavior: much as institutions shape the choices individuals make within their institutional context, culture alters the impact of institutions that take place within a cultural context. This contextual role can serve to explain the failures of certain kinds of development, as before, and also inform discussions of transition economies (Boettke 2001). As Chamlee-Wright explains, 'In a post-communist world, we finally seem to have resolved the question as to whether private property rights or government ownership is superior in terms of generating economic success. The more critical question now is how societies can adapt the right institutions to their particular [cultural] context' (Chamlee-Wright 2006: p. 186).

20.2.2 Culture as a Prior Constraint on Institutions: *Mētis*

One of the most influential (and most explicitly formulated) statements of this constraining role is Boettke et al.'s chapter on 'Institutional Stickiness and the New Development Economics' (this volume, Chapter 6). In this work, Boettke et al. detail the role that past events play in constraining present efforts at economic development through the use of a taxonomy of institutions that distinguishes between institutions by origin: foreign-introduced exogenous (FEX), indigenously introduced exogenous (IEX), and indigenously introduced endogenous (IEN). These categories emphasize that all observed institutions are not alike: reforms and policies introduced by international financial agencies or as a result of postwar reconstruction (foreign and exogenous) are of a different sort than national constitutions (indigenous exogenous), which in turn are of a different sort than language (indigenous endogenous).

In particular, these sorts of institutions differ by how grounded they are in 'the practices, customs, values, and beliefs of indigenous people,' which are in turn partially formative of *mētis*, defined as 'local knowledge resulting from practical experience' (ibid.: p. 129) This *mētis* serves the same role as, and may be identical to,[7] the interpretive concept of culture employed in Chamlee-Wright's work. Indigenous, endogenous institutions are, of all the institutional forms, most closely aligned (owing to their origins) with this *mētis*, and thus tend to be the most sticky. As an institution deviates from this underlying form, it (like the Western financial institutions with respect to urban female entrepreneurs in Ghana) is less likely to persist over time.[8] The 'New Development Economics' thus has at its core a claim regarding the constraining role of culture on institutions: 'In circumscribing what shape FEX and IEX institutions may take, IEN institutions point to an important result for development economics. Successful institutional changes in developing parts of the world must have IEN institutions at their core' (ibid.: p. 133–4). IEN institutions, and thus *mētis*, constrain other viable institutional forms. Ultimately, this is reflected in a 'regression theorem' wherein the current durability of an institution is tied to its past durability (and thus ultimately, again, the underlying *mētis* or cultural constraints).[9]

20.2.3 Beyond Culture as a Constraint

The *mētis* approach has tremendous appeal, and the institutional 'regression theorem' makes sense in confronting the constraints on institutional change in development contexts. However, we might wonder if, just as *mētis* constrains institutions, the current or past institutions have a role in determining the character of *mētis*. As Storr (2013: p. 87) points out, often the analysis of institutions constrained by culture morphs slightly to *exclude* culture, on the grounds that this idea of institutions as 'culturally derived and culturally mediated' (ibid.: p. 81) constitutes the exhaustive role of culture in economic activity: Culture constrains institutions, which in turn constrain economic behavior. Against this view and in favor of a more expansive analysis of the role of culture, Storr adds one more feature of institutions, that they are 'culturally filtered' (ibid.: p. 89).

Culture thus not only grants or withholds legitimacy from institutions, but also fundamentally shapes the role that the institution is seen as having in each actor's interpretation of the world. Taking this idea seriously means not only asking what elements of a culture give stability or legitimacy to certain institutions and not others (or why a culture might adopt certain foreign-introduced innovations and reject others), but also trying to understand what role an institution plays in the structure of reality as experienced by members of that culture. Differences in outcomes within seemingly similar institutional settings may be explained by understanding the very different meanings ascribed to the same institutional forms. For example, imperfect enforcement of a formal rule appears much different when understood to be intentional *de facto* changes in the regulatory environment rather than the result of incompetence or corruption. (Just consider the difference between attitudes towards imperfect enforcement of the speed limit compared to most other crimes!)

This is not the only direction in which we can extend our analysis beyond viewing culture as 'merely' a constraint on institutional choice, which is to note the reciprocal relationship between institutional conditions and subsequent cultural development. In particular, institutions which are *not* IEN (and thus maximally representative of the underlying cultural meanings) that nevertheless play a role in the structure of action are in important ways engaged in a dialectical relationship with the currently existing pattern of meanings. Especially if outright rejection of the 'invading' institution is impossible (as it often is), individual actors confronting it need to choose how best to integrate the very real existence of this institution into their view of the structure of reality. Institutions, especially to the extent they persist while not matching completely the underlying *mētis*, shape the directions of cultural change. Thus a more complete description of the relationship between culture and institutions might view institutions as culturally (1) derived, (2) mediated, (3) filtered, and (4) *determining*. This determining role attempts to capture the way institutions alter the process of cultural replication between a society and new entrants to that society. It is this fourth role that gives rise to the co-determination (and subsequent coevolution) between the institutions and culture of a given society, by influencing the actions of those who give rise to the new society under consideration.

20.3 *DIABLO II*: ECONOMIC CULTURE AND ENVIRONMENT

20.3.1 *Diablo II* as an Economic Space[10]

This section examines the economic environment within *Diablo II*, with a focus on the in-game institutions for exchange and the role assigned to them by players in structuring economic conduct. Gameplay in *Diablo II* began with a player's choice of character type (known as classes). Each of the seven classes had different strengths and weaknesses at overcoming the computer-controlled monsters that populated the game environment. Players ventured into the game world and defeated these monsters, becoming gradually stronger and acquiring items and equipment from slain monsters: improved character ability and improved quality of equipment allowed a player to defeat stronger monsters, earning rewards of a higher quality. Difficulty and reward continued to scale until an 'end-game' was reached, with the most difficult monsters and correspondingly powerful equipment.

As the algorithm that governed what rewards were obtained from any particular monster did not take into account at all what would be most beneficial to the player who actually defeated it, the large majority of acquired items and equipment, even those considered widely to be powerful, would be of no use to the character that obtained them. The benefits of trade were significant, and finding an exchange partner with whom to solve the mutual coincidence of wants thus became a paramount element of participation in the economic environment of the game's multiplayer community.[11]

That there would be these significant gains to finding exchange partners during online gameplay was not an accident, but rather an element built into the design of *Diablo II*, and the game developers did include some elements of the game's interface to facilitate player-to-player exchange. At the most elementary level, a major improvement was a system for trading: two characters while in the same game instance in an area where monsters did not spawn could open the trade interface. This interface then covered the game screen and allowed each player to display items they currently held in their inventory: after any negotiations[12] both parties could indicate that they wanted to conduct a trade by clicking a check mark. When both sides had indicated their consent in this way, the contents of each player's display would be transferred to the other's inventory. In contrast to more modern game environments which often have sophisticated exchange institutions programmed in to allow for global exchange among all members of a given game server, this trade interface was the only method of conducting transactions within the game interface that allowed for exchange with institutional protections against reneging.[13] While property rights over one's own inventory were protected by the rules of the game environment (that is, no in-game circumstance could cause you to involuntarily relinquish objects from your own storage), no other property rights between players existed or were enforced. Notably, this included any form of fraud, ranging from simple attempts at deception[14] to complicated confidence schemes,[15] which were commonly encountered alongside all of the normal exchange activity.

Of course, before any of these mechanisms for exchange could be used, players needed to engage in significant amounts of search in order to find potential exchange partners. While one could join random publicly visible games and search for exchange partners, a few elements of the game deterred this behavior. First, monster difficulty in any given game instance was proportional to the number of players, meaning that joining a game only to search for trade partners functionally taxed other players in that game who were clearing monsters. Second, restrictions on the amount of equipment that could be stored in the inventory of any single character meant that most players had a set of characters used purely for their ability to store additional items (known as 'mules') who were unlikely to be in public games. Finally, playing the game required consistent use of mouse and keyboard inputs, and attempting to type while in the middle of combat could be anywhere from annoying to fatal. Players quickly developed a distinction between elements of gameplay: search for exchanges ('trading') became a distinct activity.[16]

To facilitate finding players interested in trading, a few different institutions existed or emerged to coordinate which games to join and to communicate potential terms of exchange. Within the in-game interface, the two primary institutions were (1) naming conventions for game sessions[17] and (2) public chat channels for trading.[18] Since these institutions were present in the in-game client, taking advantage of them was part of the active search for exchange opportunities while a player was logged in, and limited in scope by the size restrictions: joining a game session for trading one could simultaneously interact with up to seven other characters, and a full trade channel would have a few dozen individuals. Even with frequent movement between games and channels, this severely limited the scope of search possible within the game interface.[19] In addition, any players whose play schedules did not overlap with one's own, despite their participation in the realm's economy, were foreclosed as trading partners because one could never communicate or exchange with these players.

20.3.1.1   Trade games

As mentioned above, one method used to communicate the desire to trade was by setting the name of one's public game session to indicate that the purpose of that game was exchange behavior. Often, if no current trade game sessions were in existence, a game session with the simple name 'trade' would be created. If 'trade' were full, or trade possibilities in that game were exhausted, more complicated names for game sessions would be used, in a rough hierarchy by how much they deviated from 'trade.'[20] Once in a game, players were expected to have in their inventory any items they desired to trade, and would run between other players in town to open the trade interface and check to see if there were any possible exchange opportunities. Informal norms regarding behavior in these games were brusque:[21] upon the trade interface being opened, conversation was often limited to both players attempting to ask 'wug?' (short for 'what you got?'). Whoever was slower to type in this query was expected to display the items for trade: once all the items were displayed, the initial player was expected to indicate what items he desired or to terminate the trade session.

If a player was interested not in general exchange behavior but had one specific exchange in mind, another method of signaling that interest was by creating a new game session with a title reflecting this desire. This way, when players opened the join game interface, they would observe the desired exchange among the various game sessions they could join.[22] Often, these game session names would read 'X for Y,' and tended to decline in use as the desired exchange became more complicated.[23] Etiquette here was mostly modeled after the way exchange was conducted in trade games, but with (ideally) less bargaining, as players had in some sense agreed to the exchange in question before entering the trade interface.

20.3.1.2   Public trade channels

Instead of joining games, players could also join public chat channels while they were not in any particular game session. The chat features hosted by the server were built into the online interface, and among the default public channels a player could elect to join were those designated by the developers for trading. These public channels had a very thin implementation: just a chat terminal inside the game client with a character limit on each sent message. No moderation or other restriction on sending messages existed, while the number of lines of text displayed in the channel was fixed.[24] Visibility in the chat channels was thus purely a function of having repeated one's desired message more recently than enough other players to keep it within the visible text area in the game client. With no restrictions on how fast characters could post messages, the visible space in a trade channel was an economic commons, and, as we might expect given the absence of any effective governance, the results of the individual interest in message visibility led to an aggregate outcome that was less desirable. Strategies to maximize the time one's message spent visible ranged from just mass copying and pasting, to adding in lines of additional ASCII characters to maximize the screen real estate taken up by one's message, to using automated chat programs to send messages faster than could be done by an individual.

20.3.2 Cheating as the Default: Rule Enforcement and Cultural Interpretation

Another area where the developers of *Diablo II* hoped to improve upon the original was the ability to maintain an online environment where the multiplayer servers would enforce the default rules of the game world.[25] In this regard, one of the notable experiences for players of online *Diablo II* was the market failure to keep various modifications created by players in order to bypass or alter certain elements of the game from being used: hacking of various forms was rampant.[26] Many players who had hoped for an online realm experience where the game environment was not abused found themselves disappointed, especially when attempts by the developers to curtail various exploits were inconsistent and often far slower than the innovations of those developing the hacks.

Players confronting the reality that these various hacks and cheats existed and (notwithstanding periodic enforcement on particular margins[27]) that playing online and interacting with the rest of the population meant encountering these hacks had to determine how to fit these behaviors into the meaning of game activity. Especially since many of these exploits fundamentally altered exchange behaviors,[28] players' interpretation of the presence of these hacks strongly influenced their views on exchange. For players who perceived the lack of enforcement as an implicit sanction on the gameplay that arose from the presence of exploits, the in-game economic situation often seemed unproblematic, if somewhat inconvenient as a result of the inherent limits of exchange inside the game client. For those players whose interpretation of the rampant hacking was not to accept it into the sphere of 'normal' game behavior but instead to view it as a sizeable defect, the in-game exchange environment was constantly tainted with behaviors that ought to have been outlawed.[29] This latter view then cared not only about the instrumental value of a behavior within the game, but also about that activity's *legitimacy*: whether it was something supported in the game itself.

Often, attitudes concerning legitimacy combined with a distaste for the strongly impolite informal norms surrounding in-game exchange behavior: articles decrying the state of online economic behavior often conflate the two. One such guest article on *Diablo II* fansite Diabloii.net titled 'The Complete Waste of Time Known as Trading on B.net'[30] argues that the 'wug' etiquette 'has come to represent everything that is wrong in the trade scene.' Along with the writer's disdain for the norms that governed exchange and advertising in the trade channels, in both this article and a follow-up published a few months later[31] the association is made between supporting the current system of exchange norms and using counterfeit or hacked items. These articles were written at a time (January–June 2003) when the level of enforcement of anti-hack provisions by Blizzard was at a nadir, and the increasing ubiquity of hacked items was a topic of significant community discussion, as evidenced by the frequency of guest articles dealing with the consequences, sources, and ethics of hacking in the *Diablo II* community.[32]

Legitimate players during this period certainly perceived themselves as being in a minority position. Arguments regarding the ethics of cheating often hinged on exactly how much cheating constituted *cheating*, and many discussions of item duplication also took on an instrumentalist character.[33] The pervasiveness of cheating also left many legitimate players feeling as though they were forced either to exit the online economy and play in a state of autarky or to accept to some extent the use or exchange of illegitimate items.[34]

The failures to enforce restrictions on exploits in the online environment of *Diablo II* revealed that at least two ideal-typical forms of player existed for the game: one group for whom the experience of a maximally powerful character was seen as the fun element of the game environment, and for whom all means that were instrumentally viable were seen as acceptable ways to reach that goal,[35] and another group who valued instead using the intended in-game means (which included participation in a system of exchange behavior) to overcome the challenges set out by the developers.[36] Especially for legitimate players, finding effective ways to create spaces where they could operate with some expectation of mainly interacting with other legitimate players was of paramount importance, particularly as they perceived the community as a whole to be increasingly difficult to interact with. The in-game exchange institutions (including the institutional reality of little to no penalty for game exploits) as discussed above thus took on very different roles in the structure of gameplay for members of the (dominant) instrumentalist cultural system than they did for legitimate players. Trade game sessions, while a shared institution, came to have norms that were seen by legitimate players to be determined by a view of the game they did not share.[37] As discussed above, the two separate cultural systems each incorporated the reality of an absence of certain kinds of rule enforcement regarding game behavior very differently: the institutional rules-in-use governing game behavior were subject to seriously divergent cultural filtration.[38]

20.3.3 Trade Forum Institutions as Culturally Determined

Despite these differences, the fundamental constraints on in-game search for exchange partners remained the same for both groups. Many players discovered that these constraints could be largely ameliorated by conducting the search for exchange partners outside of the limits of the game environment. As referenced above, given the sizeable demand to obtain the 'best' items regardless of method, one such search involved the purchase of items in a vibrant online secondary market of real-money exchanges. For players interested in making exchanges instead of outright purchases, message boards proved to be one of the most well-suited institutions available for conducting a search for exchange partners, since many of the shortcomings of the in-game exchange environment were overcome because of the nature of the message board medium.[39] In contrast to the very narrow set of possible exchange partners present during an in-game search (and the costliness of expanding the set by hopping between game sessions and channels repeating one's trade proposals), desired trades posted on forums could be viewed by every visitor (even individuals who, because of play timing, would never have been encountered in-game), and the details of exactly what items were offered for exchange and at what terms could be typed out once, and at more length than could normally be possible during in-game exchanges. In addition, trade negotiations could be conducted over several days at each player's leisure, could involve more than bilateral haggling, and provided publicly available information regarding current prices.

In addition, many of the tools on a message board are ideal for crafting a durable reputation for each member, and consequently allowing an environment with greater trust between individuals participating in the exchange community. In most cases, message boards require a registration, which involves creating a unique and durable identity, and keeping statistics on message board activity, which were publicly available (such as duration of a message board user's account, and the number of posts made). The rules of the forum were also determined and enforced by the creators of the forum, rather than being dictated and enforced by the game developers. In the case of Diabloii.net, the opportunity to create and enforce a new set of rules to govern their forum community allowed them to structure the rules governing exchange in a way that ensured legitimate players could create an exchange community they could be a part of. Crucially, compared to the case with other trading forums, the rules governing exchange on the Diabloii.net forums did not have incentive-compatibility issues with a cultural lens that saw a large portion of the in-game community as anathema. Diabloii.net's trade forums[40] retained the use of in-game items as the acceptable objects to be exchanged, while simultaneously instituting a Do Not Trade list which precluded many of the commonly counterfeit or hacked items from being offered. In contrast, the other major player-run trade forum, d2jsp, has its origins in coding the d2jsp 'bot' to automate gameplay, and even when converted to only handle trades, it chose to do so through the implementation of a scrip currency, 'forum gold,' obtained by donations to the forum administrators. Since the administrator of d2jsp obtained a form of seignorage, he had a direct pecuniary incentive to accommodate the maximal amount of exchange on the forum possible, and thus to be far more permissive.[41]

20.4 THE GOVERNANCE OF A LEGITIMATE COMMUNITY: THE DIABLOII.NET TRADE FORUM

The particular institutional rules of the Diabloii.net forum would not alone have created the environment needed for legitimate players to feel as though they could have a market space in which exchange could be actually conducted. However, the general enforcement of rules of conduct, including restrictions on exchanges of hacked and duplicate items, led to an environment where, even though fraud and cheating were considered by members of the Diabloii.net forums the norm amongst the *Diablo II* community as a whole, especially when dealing with anonymous individuals in-game, the trade forum had a reputation *as a whole* that was strong enough to ensure that merely having an account in good standing regardless of one's individual reputation was often sufficient for other members interested in legitimate play to be willing to make exchanges. The high levels of trust extended between forum members allowed coordination on two levels: players could both trust that the items they were acquiring would for the most part have been acquired through legitimate means, and also conduct exchanges in a way that reflected trust, rather than the ruthless opportunism of the broader in-game exchange community. Examples of high-trust behavior included changes in the form of exchange such as drop trading[42] and mule trading.[43] These levels of trust were even more important when gameplay patches introduced items that were precluded from being traded using the trade interface, meaning that a return to the 'Trade Dance' was inevitable if players wished to exchange those items.

Even when members reported instances of failures of that trust, most forum members felt that the general level of trust internal to the forum (particularly for individuals with sufficient longevity, measured by number of posts) was high enough to warrant forgoing the in-game protection of the trade interface. As one forum member, GIR, expressed it, 'Usually there's a certain degree of trust between people here on the forums during trades.' Others expressed more caution with respect to new users, such as Atticus: 'Would you trust someone with 38 posts? I'd only do drop trades with people with 500+ >.>'. Yet still the forum's reputation outweighed the role of longevity for Rius666: 'Most time I don't even care to look at the number of posts that people have. I've come to rely on and trust these forums as they have some very reliable, honest, and just good people around.'[44]

Forum members not only counted on their exchange partners to honor their word, but often would go out of their way to spread reputational information that might influence traders not to associate with players who were not legitimate, regardless of their trustworthiness. One example of this was the foray of a member, ecaftermath, into the trade forums. After having admitted in another subforum on Diabloii.net that he used an automation program to farm for items ('botting'), both of his posts[45] looking for exchange opportunities had trade forum members reply to inform others that he had admitted to this illegitimate activity. The culture of legitimate play and the exchange community centered around it rarely encountered cases such as ecaftermath, not because traders chose to over-look rules violations 'just this once' in order to conduct individual trades, but on account of the sheer rarity of illegitimate players in the exchange community. While the community was far from purely insular, legitimate players expected and very nearly always received an honest and legitimate deal, and when that expectation was disappointed there was the possibility of recourse, at the very least by reputational mechanisms.

A key institutional feature in shaping these expectations (aside from those native to all message boards, such as access controls) was the Do Not Trade list. This list established a class of objects (ranging from one's account, to real money, to items on an established list of known counterfeits) that could not be offered for trade on the forum. The Do Not Trade list is perhaps the most crucial institutional innovation which allowed the Diabloii.net forums to distinguish themselves as forums for legitimate players. Joining a forum where these items were not for sale represented a clear selection into a framework inside of which certain commonplace behaviors in the broader game community were frowned upon and, if discovered, grounds for expulsion from the trading network.

This reputation for legitimacy was already well established by the start of 2004, where the archive begins, as evidenced by the following exchange from March of 2004 discussing trade values:

> Xarxov: I had a question. Haven't the values of some of those stuff gone down yet, especially the runes? i am just curious. thx.[46]
>
> IDupedInMyPants: I think that depends heavily upon what forum you go to. I know on at least two other forums [likely referring to the official Battle. net forums and d2jsp] runes have been devalued heavily, mainly because these forums aren't as legit and have other forms of higher-value currency, in a manner of speaking, and don't have much need for runes after they finish the words they want. This seems also to be the case in the channels as well.
>
> But as far as legit players go, I don't see rune demand really dropping off, since that is going to be their main form of high currency even as more and more players complete their runewords. What we have to keep in mind is that these values reflect trends for this forum only.[47]

Maintaining the distinctiveness of the Diabloii.net exchange environment even required adoption of alternative units of currency from the broader economic system when the primary media of exchange were banned duplicate items. Of course, for players choosing this trade forum precisely for the legitimacy, this was a benefit, rather than a cost, of participation.[48] Ignorance of the particular culture of the diabloii.net trade forum sometimes led individuals entering the community from the broader game culture to take actions that, while considered unproblematic outside of the forum, are sources of considerable controversy when publicly revealed. Consider the following exchange involving GEiST, who posted a list of items he wished to trade that presented visual evidence that he used a maphack.[49] Confronting him was a trade forum regular, superdave, with some advice regarding his choice to maphack:[50]

> superdave: dude most people on this site play legit . . . maphack is definitely frowned upon
> GEiST: ok, and your point is?
> are they duped items? no
> are they items found with a bot? no
> are those items legit? yes
> are you making an offer? No
> i appreciate the help but it is not really needed, the new maphack helps to make a list of a character with a press of a button.

Obviously the differing idea of what constitutes a 'legit' item is telling in and of itself: that an item obtained while using hacks is legitimate by virtue of it not being hacked or duplicated or found via directly using a bot. Additionally, the justification for use of a significant hack[51] here is both purely instrumental and also trivial, merely being an aid to record-keeping. At least initially, GEiST presents this argument with a lightness that suggests he does not understand the cultural understanding of the forum. The discussion continues:

> superdave: my point is . . . you would get more people to trade for your items if you did what others on this site do and hide that fact that you use a hack . . . It was a heads up that many people here who will not trade with you
> GEiST: do you have kids?
> do you/will you tell them that babies are from that stupid-looking bird?
> come on . . . everybody uses the maphack, why hide the obvious?
> superdave: you won't make too many friends here with a comment like that . . . on other sites people do use maphack. The vast majority here DO NOT. . . thats why they choose to come here . . . personally i don't give a ratz azz if you find that the game is too hard and you need to use a cheat program like maphack . . . i simply was informing you that . . . maphack is frowned upon by many of the forum users here and as a result you wouldn't be able to do as many trades as you would have hoped for . . . so to answer your question 'why hide the obvious?' you came here to trade . . . if people didn't know that you were using 'the maphack' i am sure that more people would have expressed interest in some of your stuff

The clash of cultures here is made even more evident: one obvious area where the overall picture of reality into which this exchange is taking place differs between members of the forum is the perceived incidence of illegitimate gameplay: while even forum regulars certainly cannot claim that the forum is completely free of those sorts of behaviors, GEiST seems sure that (much like the broader community) the forum is a place of pervasive exploits. Other community members are quick to corroborate superdave's view of the forum:

> Nolomite: Not everyone does [use maphack], Geist—just the people that aren't able to beat the game without it.
> Two_Rivers: [Regarding GEiST's claim that everyone uses maphack] That's possible the worst thing you could say on this forum. I don't use maphack, just as many people here don't. While some people do, they have the decency to not flaunt it.

Nolomite's response (echoing the sentiment in superdave's statement) that use of hacks is a signal of inability to complete the game legitimately is a perspective echoed in many pro-legitimate articles and statements to the effect that the use of hacks or other exploits must be the result of a lack of skill: often these statements were accompanied by exhortations for those currently playing using exploits to attempt to play through the game legitimately, implicitly suggesting they would not be able to. GEiST then presents his own view on the point of playing the game, and subsequently responds to more suggestions that his use of maphack will marginalize him in the forum community with some indignation:

> GEiST: i dont play to beat the game, i play for fun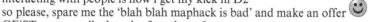
> interacting with people is how i get my kick in D2
> so please, spare me the 'blah blah maphack is bad' and make an offer
> GEiST: are you all a bunch of stuck-ups?
> quit acting like ostrichs, everybody uses the maphack, get over it, you dont know me, nor do i know you
> i am not here to make friends or to hear your pro-legit BULL****, i am here to trade
> 'oh hacks are bad but 99% of players are using it, we dont want to admit it because all we do is hanging on the forums, we have no clue whatsoever what happens in the game right now but hey, we have authority, might as well use it!' what the hell, have you been living under a rock for the past 7 years?
> welcome the 21st century, where people play games for fun, not to make a pseudo-community . . . i mean . . . wow life goes on . . .
> i use maphack, so what? Mephisto is going to complain about it? [Mephisto was a boss commonly farmed for item drops]
> no hard-feelings, my $0.02
> do i have offers on those items or do i close/delete/whatever the thread?
> Xircon: [While closing the thread] No, But I will. lol, everyone uses mh [maphack]? No, that is very much not true.

The role of the forum and the purpose of gameplay are quite divergent between GEiST and the members of the forum community he interacts with here. Most noteworthy are his consistent view of the forum as a purely economic space (mirroring the culture of exchange in the in-game environment): in each response, his closing argument is oriented towards the exchange aspect ('do I have offers?') and tries to set aside the fact that community members here not only have moral evaluations of that kind of conduct but also would be willing to divert energy from making exchanges in order to make known their disapproval. The juxtaposition of his claims (made 15 minutes apart!) to play for the personal interaction but to disapprove of the creation of a community meant to play in a way that deviates from his conception of 'fun' is also an interesting, if ineffective, rhetorical technique. Occasionally, as this exchange illustrates, the boundaries of access to the legitimate trade network were clearly defined, but on cultural rather than formal grounds.

The relationship between the Diabloii.net economy and the exchange interactions that took place on other, less legitimate sites such as d2jsp and (ironically) the official Battle.net forums was a result of the (accurate) perception of the cultural difference between attitudes towards legitimate play on those other forums. In particular, because of the differences in relative scarcity, Diabloii.net banned listing a single item in multiple venues, particularly d2jsp. This simultaneously restricted the ability of sellers to claim illusory outsider offers from in-game sources and prevented cross-listing.

Overall the formal institutions, informal norms, and cultural perspective of the Diabloii.net forum worked to create a mutually reinforcing system of practices that could resist erosion by outside forces over time, and create an environment where players could simultaneously benefit from gains from trade and still remain confident that they were not doing so at an (unacceptable) level of compromise of their idea of how the game ought to be played.

20.5 CONCLUSION

The economic history of *Diablo II*'s online community is primarily one of rule-breaking. Item duplication, gray-market downstream item sales on eBay, hacking, and fraud constitute many of the memorable aspects of participation in an economic environment with limited property protection and intermittent and unpredictable enforcement of stated game rules. For a significant number of the players in this community, the resulting game was subjectively better off for these economic shortcomings: high-power items were cheap and plentiful, the pace of character development was accelerated, and the presence of only minimal protections against fraud meant the possibility of an enjoyable (and relatively harmless) career as a con artist in a world without significant penalties.[52]

For a small subset of the players, however, the appeal of *Diablo II* came from an altogether different source, a view that forsook those elements in favor of the game 'as it was meant to be played.' Developing a market space where these ideals could be reinforced that still remained economically functional meant moving outside of the game environment and onto the trade forum, as a new economic and social space. This space was shaped by the co-determination between ideas of the culture of legitimate play and institutions of governance chosen to structure economic conduct. That institutions such as the Do Not Trade list stuck is certainly the result of the underlying *mētis* of the constituent members of the economic community, but that that *mētis* was able to stick (and, indeed, continues to do so) to the institutional forms of the forum was also a product of the construction of those institutional rules.

NOTES

1. *Diablo II* and its expansion, *Diablo II: Lord of Destruction*, were released by Blizzard Entertainment in 2000 and 2001 respectively. Both games received tremendous critical acclaim and still have an active playing community to this day.
2. Essentially this objection captures the intuitive idea that 'it is only a game' and thus not commensurate with decision-making with more at stake.
3. Another potential objection, that these successes are on account of the simplicity or comparatively low stakes of the environment relative to the real world, might be valid. I attempt to address this objection by giving a complete description of the problem situation faced by actors in this environment. Further, the issue at stake in this chapter is not primarily the level of success achieved by the institutions under examination. Rather, I want to examine the origins of those institutions as rooted in the cultural beliefs regarding economic activity held by those implementing them.
4. This move was partially seen as 'updating' the epistemological foundations of praxeology to match the developments in continental philosophy on those margins between when Mises had developed his Neo-Kantian formulation and the present. For a more extensive treatment of the implications of hermeneutics for economics, see Ebeling (1986), Lavoie (this volume, Chapter 3), or the special issue dedicated to Lavoie's work in the *Review of Austrian Economics* (Vol. **24**, No. 2).
5. Another area (closely related to development) where culture plays a significant role is the understanding of entrepreneurial action, especially as an immanent critique of Kirzner's (1973) theory, such as Chamlee-Wright (1997: pp. 49–50), Lavoie (this volume, Chapter 3), or Storr and John (this volume, Chapter 4).
6. This is presumably the result of the patterns of meanings assigned to gender in this culture.
7. *Mētis* 'includes skills, culture, norms, and conventions, which are shaped by the experiences of the individual' (Boettke et al., this volume, Chapter 6: p. 129). While this definition includes culture, it is unclear if this meaning of culture is exactly identical to the one employed in this chapter. Even if *mētis* is more expansive, the argument regarding the relationship of culture and institutions presented here holds: to the extent that culture is constitutive of *mētis*, and *mētis* is what constrains institutional stickiness, culture is serving as a prior constraint on institutions.
8. Or, at least, to persist in the disruptive form, or less likely to yield the benefits often hoped for when development agencies or foreign states transplant institutions between contexts.
9. This is not to say that the *mētis* concept is a story of cultural determinism, as *mētis* can change. As Coyne (2007: p. 24) puts it, 'Instead [of cultural determinism], culture can be seen as a short-term constraint.'
10. Elements of this section are adapted from Salter and Stein (2013), which also has a more extensive discussion of the technical parameters of the exchange environment. Since the focus here is on the exchange institutions, rather than understanding the factors influencing the emergent medium of exchange, these details have been omitted.
11. *Diablo II* had both a single-player mode and a multiplayer, online mode. Players of the online mode would choose a 'realm' by geographic locations (players were segregated into geographic regions for latency purposes) and then create an account and a character as detailed before. The online interface, which players would enter upon logging in and choosing a character, was a series of online chat rooms, from which players could create an instance of the game environment itself, which up to seven other characters could join. Instances could be public or private, and players could join either by finding an open public game from a list of them or by typing in the name of the game instance they were interested in joining (and, in the case of a private game, the appropriate password).
12. While in the trade interface, any typed chat (which normally was sent to anyone in the same game instance) would be seen only by one's trade partner.

13. Players were of course still able to transfer items between characters by throwing them onto the ground and having anyone who could reach them pick them up. In contrast to the case in *Diablo*, where the Trade Dance had been viable partially because all characters' movement speed was constant and equal, character mobility was much higher and more variable in *Diablo II*, making this sort of 'drop trading' even more risky.

14. One common simple fraud included negotiating a trade (often one where the scamming side was significantly overpaying), then having the trade fail to complete (commonly by not leaving enough space in inventory), and then returning after having 'made room' and re-trading, but this time offering an item that appeared superficially to be identical but was in fact of little to no value, hoping the other party wouldn't re-inspect the item and rely on the (misleading) visual cues in the game interface.

15. Schemes could range from using two players in the same trade game as confederates to set up a fake arbitrage profit, claiming to be able to create duplicate items and then hoping other players would give items in hopes of receiving duplicates back, and the creation of (fake) in-game player associations (known as clans) with elaborate membership tests that often included 'trust checks' of throwing items of moderate to high value on the ground in areas where they were supposedly secure, and then using various unexpected behaviors to grab the items off the ground. (Most commonly, this last scam was run using a character able to teleport from place to place on-screen, who could appear next to the item much faster than anticipated or ignore supposedly obstructing terrain features.)

16. That is, trading was seen as distinct from farming, rushing, leveling, engaging in player-versus-player combat, and so on.

17. Which can be viewed as an indigenous, endogenous institution.

18. Which, having been planned by the developers of the online interface, can be viewed as an indigenous but exogenous institution.

19. While definitive information regarding the size of the player base on any particular realm during the time period in question for this chapter is unavailable, *Diablo II* today still sees over 10 000 characters logged in concurrently throughout each day on the USEast realm. As the game was more widely played during the 2000s than it is now, this can be considered a lower bound on activity during that era. These limitations on the scope of search thus drastically curtailed the population over which search could take place relative to the population of potential trade partners.

20. Common trade game sessions names included: trading, tradin, trades, tradez, trade here, trade post. In general, the more likely a player would be to join the game by typing the name into the join game interface (as opposed to seeing it listed as open), the more popular the name selection.

21. Likely reflecting the underlying constraints: spots in an active trade game session were limited, and inefficient trade practices increased the costs in terms of time not spent engaged in other game activities while logged in to the server.

22. At least, some subset of the population would observe it. The server filtered the list of open games to restrict it to games on the highest difficulty level that character could join, so deciding which difficulty to make trade games was often a bit of an art: most mule characters likely to actually be holding the item you'd like to trade for would be on the minimum difficulty, but almost all end-game activity was on the highest difficulty.

23. Games did allow a longer area for a description (maximum of 255 characters instead of about 25 for game session names), and so sometimes game session names would reference information contained in these descriptions.

24. Messages were displayed sequentially, with older messages scrolling up out of the window (players could then scroll up to them if they desired).

25. While this seems like a strange feature when considering modern games where this is not only an expected feature but also increasingly the requirement (online-only play), this was a significant improvement to the purely locally hosted multiplayer of the original *Diablo*.

26. A rough taxonomy of exploits might go as follows: there were various ways to 'hack'

and directly alter elements of the gameplay (such as having revealed all hidden information regarding the state of the game session, 'maphack'), 'hacked items' which were items created via some sort of direct alteration of item properties, and then 'dupes' (short for duplication) where items that already existed (items either actually found or hacked into the game) had duplicate copies created.

27. Most commonly, methods of item duplication often involved intentionally generating a large amount of lag on the online servers, something that disrupted play across entire realms: these exploits when discovered would often be patched relatively quickly. Causing latency to render entire populations unable to play any form of the game was apparently a point where Blizzard made serious efforts to correct the exploits quickly. Other sorts of hacking often persisted for months or years.

28. Either by drastically changing the relative scarcity of items via counterfeiting or by the introduction of hacked items into the exchange environment.

29. Players in this camp fell all along the typology of expectations outlined in Storr and Chamlee-Wright (2010), seeing Blizzard's failure to enforce formal rules against hacking as apathy, inability, or even some sort of collusion with the individuals operating the downstream secondary market in in-game items (who had significant real-world economic interest in keeping various game exploits from being patched).

30. B.net is an abbreviation for Battle.net, the online server architecture that hosted the online play; https://web.archive.org/web/20070118113454/http://www.diabloii.net/columnists/a-bnet-trade.shtml (originally posted February 21, 2003).

31. https://web.archive.org/web/20060301111503/http://diabloii.net/columnists/a-bnet-trade2.shtml (originally posted April 3, 2003).

32. A list of guest articles on Diabloii.net in this period is available at https://web.archive.org/web/20030810223105/http://diabloii.net/columnists/index.shtml.

33. For instance, one such article, 'Duping Helps the D2 Economy!' (https://web.archive.org/web/20030618201249/http://diabloii.net/columnists/a-dupes-pro-con.shtml), argues that having trivial access to the rarest items in the game levels relative differences between players by allowing players who would otherwise never have time or inclination to farm them themselves. Of course, to someone for whom the legitimate acquisition of those items was the point of gameplay, this would be a difficult argument to comprehend.

34. One guest article recounting 'My Life as a Legit Player' discusses duping as follows: 'I personally don't, seeing as how I'm always busy doing something like playing the game. However, I have almost no doubt in my mind that I use duped gear. At this point, there is probably no way to find legit gear in the trade . . . channels' (https://web.archive.org/web/20030623165553/http://www.diabloii.net/columnists/a-legit-player.shtml).

35. Purchasing hacked gear from online retailers of in-game items, for instance.

36. To some extent the demographics of online games played a role in this difference: legitimate players tended to see use of hacks or purchasing in-game items as characteristic behavior from the immature, entitled, AOL-using young teenage demographic, while those defending hacking often stereotyped legitimate players as envious, no-life have-nots.

37. As well as being full of goods to be exchanged that were anathema to the whole point of gameplay!

38. The complete absence of any enforcement or protection from fraud is another area where many players saw inaction by Blizzard as sanction to engage in scams, as discussed above.

39. For those unfamiliar with the operation of online message boards, any given board (or forum) tends to have sub-boards divided by topic. Within each forum, members can both open new threads or reply to existing open threads opened by others: threads have a title that functions like the subject line of an email, followed by a text body. These threads are then listed to someone navigating the forum, traditionally with the thread containing the most recent reply at the top, followed by the second most recent, and so on. Since characters in-game could interact only with other characters on the same

realm, the natural division for *Diablo II* trade forums was for each realm to have a separate subforum.

40. Specifically, the USEast trade forum, the archives of which from January 2004 to December 31, 2008 make up the data from which the examples in this chapter are drawn. Changes to the forum structure of the host website have made the original site no longer available. The author's record of the contents, archived in 2010, is available upon request.

41. The institutions on the d2jsp forum were thus both culturally determined (the initial permissiveness with respect to game exploits was part of the *mētis* of the forum) and culturally determining (in that the institutional setup that was created supported the perpetuation of the permissive attitudes). These institutional forms gave something which the previous culture could 'stick' to.

42. That is, exchanges conducted merely by throwing the items to be exchanged on the ground and then picking up one's side of the deal. This could be preferable for a variety of reasons: most common was pure convenience in not having to use the official trade interface, but also common was a situation in which one's exchange of item A for item B involved storing item A on a character different from the one item B was intended to be used by. Trading by dropping allowed both parties to extend the courtesy of allowing the other to leave the game and pick up the item on the intended character (allowing a transfer, or 'trans'). Holding games for transfers was considered excellent practice, and normally the sort of information reported positively in the eBay-style trade feedback system implemented on the forum.

43. The basic operation of a mule trade is as follows: one player creates a new account, places the items from his end of the exchange on a character on that account, and sends a private message to the other with the password. That player then logs in, takes his items, and replaces them with his side of the exchange. Sometime later the original owner can log in and obtain his items. This method obviously presents significant risk of confiscation for the individual going first. This has clear advantages in that it circumvents the normal requirement of both parties to the exchange being online simultaneously.

44. Posts excerpted from Thread #269172.

45. Threads #559525 and #559019.

46. Following the release of patch 1.10 in October 2003, Blizzard had tried to solve the problems of the early 2003 economy and the rampant hacked and duplicate items by creating a system known as the Ladder, a new economy segregated from all the old characters. Following the total reset of the wealth level of the economy, Xarxov's expectation that trade values would be falling is reasonable: for any given item over the course of a Ladder 'season' (the period between wealth resets) both the quantity of any given item that existed and the rate at which new items entered the economy would be increasing (since, as players completed items and became more powerful, the speed at which they farmed items increased). Of course, as the reply indicates, the demand side of the rune market depended heavily upon the legitimacy of one's play style: if one could reasonably expect to acquire the rewards of illegitimate play then runes were an intermediate good to the acquisition of duplicate versions of the very best items that could be created. Of course, for a legitimate player who eschewed use or exchange of duplicates, often runes represented inputs to the best items one could use, and there would be no substitution out of runes as wealth increased.

47. Excerpted from Thread #126925.

48. This also served to raise the costs of benefiting from the governance of exchange behavior on the forum while nevertheless engaging in illegitimate in-game activity: doing so often meant having to maintain an inventory of items entirely to exchange within the legitimate network.

49. While the original images are long gone from the Internet, a few different things could make maphack use obvious, including the presence of visual information on the game screen that is not available in the native game client, or the presence of details that are

normally only stored server-side regarding items (such as database ID numbers, or other properties which have implications in the game engine but are generally hidden from players, such as item level).

50. Quotes from this exchange are excerpted from Thread #310982, with some irrelevant posts removed.

51. As GEiST suggests here, maphacks (which revealed the hidden information of the map of the game upon entering any particular instance) were often bundled with other hacks and features.

52. Of course, compared to some other online environments (notably space-themed role-playing game EVE Online), theft in *Diablo II* is relatively small-time: transactions in EVE are sufficiently high-stakes for there to exist a significant private market for assurance to cover areas where the in-game property protections are unable to do so.

REFERENCES

Boettke, P. (2001), *Calculation and Coordination: Essays on Socialism and Transitional Political Economy*, New York: Routledge.

Chamlee-Wright, Emily (1997), *The Cultural Foundations of Economic Development: Urban Female Entrepreneurship in Ghana*, New York: Routledge.

Chamlee-Wright, Emily (2006), 'The Development of a Cultural Economy: Foundational Questions and Future Direction,' in J. High (ed.), *Humane Economics: Essays in Honor of Don Lavoie*, Cheltenham, UK and Northampton, MA, USA: Edward Elgar Publishing, pp. 181–98.

Coyne, Christopher J. (2007), *After War: The Political Economy of Exporting Democracy*, Stanford, CA: Stanford University Press.

Ebeling, Richard (1986), 'Toward a Hermeneutical Economics: Expectations, Prices, and the Role of Interpretation in a Theory of the Market Process,' in I. Kirzner (ed.), *Subjectivism, Intelligibility and Economic Understanding*, New York: New York University Press, pp. 39–55.

Hayek, F.A. (1943), 'The Facts of the Social Sciences,' *Ethics*, **54**(1), 1–13.

Kirzner, Israel (1973), *Competition and Entrepreneurship*, Chicago: University of Chicago Press.

Salter, Alexander W. and S. Stein (2013), 'Endogenous Currency Formation in an Online Environment: The Case of Diablo II,' *Review of Austrian Economics*, forthcoming.

Storr, Virgil H. (2013), *Understanding the Culture of Markets*, New York: Routledge.

Storr, Virgil H. and E. Chamlee-Wright (2010), 'Expectations of Government's Response to Disaster,' *Public Choice*, **144**(1–2), 253–74.

Index